DICTIONARY

OF

ARCHITECTURAL

AND

BUILDING

TECHNOLOGY

Fourth edition

cowan, Henry M. Peter

The Dictionary of Architectural and Building Technology is a comprehensive summary of vocabulary used across the building industry, from the preparation of the brief through architectural and technical design and documentation, to construction technology and facilities management.

This fourth edition has added 1750 new or substantially revised entries, and over 330 of the existing entries have been updated. There are 70 additional illustrations. The terms have been assembled and cross-referenced by specialists from a range of disciplines with considerable international experience. SI metric and Imperial units are included, and line drawings enhance the explanations.

This impressively comprehensive work will enable students and professionals coming from technical, management and professional fields to grasp vocabulary from outside their areas as they contribute towards the built environment.

Henry J. Cowan is Professor Emeritus of Architectural Science in the University of Sydney. He is a Past-President of the Building Science Forum of Australia, an Honorary Fellow of the Royal Australian Institute of Architects, a Corresponding Member of the Accademia Pontaniana, and an Officer of the Order of Australia. He is the author of 23 other books and numerous articles.

Peter R. Smith is a member of the Faculty of Architecture at the University of Sydney and a Fellow of the Royal Australian Institute of Architects. He has contributed as co-author or chapter author to a dozen books on building science subjects.

To Gary T. Moore,
Professor of Environment-
Behaviour Studies
and Dean of the
Faculty of Architecture
of the University of Sydney

Dictionary

of

Architectural

and

Building

Technology

Fourth edition

Henry J. Cowan
and
Peter R. Smith

With contributions by

W. K. Chow,
Fergus R. Fricke,
Graham E. Holland,
Warren G. Julian,
David Leifer,
Cedric Marsh,
Douglas Noble,
David Rowe,
Steven Szokolay and
Ayca Tuzmen

Routledge
Taylor & Francis Group

LONDON AND NEW YORK

First published 1973
by Chapman and Hall
Second edition published 1986
by Chapman and Hall
Third edition published 1998
by Routledge

This edition published 2004
by Routledge
2 Park Square, Milton Park, Abingdon,
Oxon, OX14 4RN

Simultaneously published in the USA
and Canada
by Routledge
270 Madison Ave, New York NY 10016

*Routledge is an imprint of the Taylor &
Francis Group*

Transferred to Digital Printing 2010

© 2004 Henry J. Cowan and Peter R. Smith

Typeset in Times New Roman and
Helvetica
by Keystroke, Jacaranda Lodge,
Wolverhampton

*British Library Cataloguing in Publication
Data*
A catalogue record for this book is
available from the British Library

*Library of Congress Cataloging in
Publication Data*
Cowan, Henry J.
    Dictionary of architectural and building
    technology/Henry J. Cowan and Peter
    R. Smith; with contributions by W. K.
    Chow . . . [et al.]. — 4th ed.
        p. cm.
    ISBN 0–415–31233–7 (hb) —
    ISBN 0–415–31234–5 (pb)
    1. Architecture—Dictionaries.
    2. Building—Dictionaries. I. Smith,
    Peter R. II. Chow, W. K. III. Title.
    NA31 .C63 2004
    720'.3—dc22
                                2003023444

ISBN 0–415–31234–5 pb
    0–415–31233–7 hb

Contents

Contributors

Henry J. Cowan, the sole author of the first edition of this dictionary, is Professor Emeritus of Architectural Science in the University of Sydney. He has a PhD and a Doctorate of Engineering by examination from the University of Sheffield, and an Honorary Doctorate of Architecture from the University of Sydney. The Institution of Engineers, Australia, awarded him the Chapman Medal and the Monash Medal, and the Institution of Structural Engineers, London, a Special Service Award. He is a Past-President of the Building Science Forum of Australia, an Honorary Fellow of the Royal Australian Institute of Architects, a Corresponding Member of the Accademia Pontaniana, and an Officer of the Order of Australia. He is the author of 23 other books and numerous articles.

Peter R. Smith, co-author of the second and third editions, has BArch, MArch and PhD degrees from the University of Sydney, and is a Fellow of the Royal Australian Institute of Architects. Following some years in architectural practice, he joined the Faculty of Architecture at the University of Sydney, where he has served as Department Head and Associate Dean, as well as teaching a wide range of technical subjects. He has served on professional, standards and industry committees dealing with concrete, timber, energy conservation, solar energy and general building industry matters. He has contributed as co-author or chapter author to a dozen books on building science subjects.

W.K. Chow joined The Hong Kong Polytechnic (now The Hong Kong Polytechnic University) in 1981, and is now a Chair Professor of Architectural Science and Fire Engineering in the Department of Building Services Engineering, teaching and developing courses up to master degree level; and has supervised PhD research projects on architectural science, fire and safety engineering for over 20 years. He has BSc, MST and PhD degrees. He is a Fellow of the Chartered Institution of Building Services Engineers and the Hong Kong Institution of Engineers; and the Founding President of the Society of Fire Protection Engineers (Hong Kong Chapter) set up in October 2002. He has served on government department committees dealing with building requirements and fire safety matters. Over three hundred of his papers have been published in journal and conference proceedings in fire engineering, indoor air quality and building energy.

Fergus Fricke, BE (Melbourne) and PhD (Monash), is an Honorary Associate Professor at the University of Sydney. He has taught acoustics to architecture, engineering and music students, published over 200 papers in architectural, building and environmental acoustics and established the postgraduate audio programme at the University of Sydney. He has held positions at Monash, Southampton, Sheffield, Purdue and Sydney Universities and has served on Australian and international standards committees on acoustics as well as the editorial boards of several acoustics journals. He was a contributor to the second and third editions.

Graham E. Holland, BArch and PhD (Sydney), is an Honorary Associate in the Faculty of Architecture at the University of Sydney. His special interest is in building construction, and he is co-author, with Dr Peter Smith, of a web-based teaching text *Design in Brickwork* (www.brickbydesign. com). He is the author of a book on owner building, a number of articles, and a book on polychromatic brickwork also on the World Wide Web. He was a contributor to the second and third editions.

Warren Julian, BSc, BE, MSc(Arch) and PhD (Sydney), originally an electrical engineer, is Associate Professor of Architectural and Design Science at the University of Sydney. He is the author of about 200 books and papers on lighting and related subjects, Life Fellow of IES(ANZ), Editor of *Lighting*, and Vice-President (Technical) of the *Commission Internationale de l'Éclairage* (*CIE*). He was a contributor to the second and third editions.

David Leifer is a registered architect and an incorporated engineer. He is a Past Chairman of the NZ Chapter of the Chartered Institution of Building Services Engineers, a past board member of the International Facility Management Association of Australia, and a director of the facility

management company – FM Solutions Pty Ltd. He has taught at the Mackintosh School of Architecture, Glasgow (1984–86), the Schools of Architecture at the Universities of Queensland (1986–93) and Auckland (1993–2000), and is the present co-ordinator of the graduate programme in facilities management at the University of Sydney.

Cedric Marsh, MA(Cantab), MIStructE, FCSCE, graduated from Cambridge in 1944 and spent the rest of the war at the Royal Aircraft Establishment, Farnborough. He designed aluminium structures with SMD Ltd in Slough, with Aluminium Laboratories Ltd in Geneva, and with the Aluminum Company of Canada in Montreal, followed by a period of private consulting and academic positions at the University of Waterloo and Concordia University, Montreal, where he shared in the creation of the Centre for Building Studies, that offers courses leading to Bachelor and Master of Building Engineering. He is the author of *Strength of Aluminum*, now in its fifth edition. He chairs or participates in structural code writing committees in Canada, the USA and Europe. Areas of research include elastic stability, seismic action and general behaviour under load of various materials. Retired in 1997 as a Distinguished Professor Emeritus.

Douglas E. Noble has BSArch and BArch degrees from California State Polytechnic University, and MArch and PhD degrees from the University of California, Berkeley. He is a Fellow of the American Institute of Architects. He teaches design and design computing at the University of Southern California in Los

Angeles. He is a practising architect and has served as a consultant to a number of firms, is chair of the Los Angeles AIA CAD Committee and the former president of the Association for Computer-Aided Design In Architecture (ACADIA), and the Director of the Graduate Building Science programme at USC. His interests are in the areas of computer-supported design and the science of design, and he is the author of several books in this area.

David Rowe, ASTC (mechanical engineering), FIEAust, CPEng, has enjoyed a career which included some 30 years' involvement with design and construction of building services for public buildings in NSW. He joined the staff of the University of Sydney in 1991 to establish the building services postgraduate programme. In 2002, he was awarded the degree of Master of Design Science (Honoris Causa). He was a contributor to the third edition.

Steven V. Szokolay, DipArch, MArch, PhD, had some years of architectural practice in Sydney and London, then he taught in Liverpool, Nairobi and Brisbane, where he was Director of the Architectural Science Unit and later the Head of Department of Architecture. Now retired, he still supervises the work of several PhD candidates. He was twice Chairman of the ANZ Solar Energy Society, foundation editor of its journal: *Solar Progress*, President of the ANZ Architectural Science Association and of PLEA (Passive and Low Energy Architecture) International. He served (and serves) on numerous (State and Commonwealth) government and standards committees and

has a modest consulting practice. He is the author of a dozen books, co-author and chapter author in many others and a contributor to the *Encyclopaedia of Science and Technology*.

Ayca Tuzmen has degrees of BArch from Middle East Technical University, MArch (New Jersey Institute of Technology), and MCS and PhD (Arizona State University). After a career as an architect, urban planner, research associate and software designer, she joined the University of Sydney as a lecturer in the Design Computing program, teaching courses at both undergraduate and postgraduate levels. She is a member of ACADIA, member of eCAADe, and a registered architect of the Turkish Institute of Architects. She is author of a dozen refereed journal and conference papers related to the role of computing in collaborative design, and has been organiser, moderator and referee for a number of conferences.

Contributors to the Third Edition

José Carlos Damski has more than 20 years' experience in computer science. Following an MSc in computer science and electrical engineering in Brazil, he obtained his PhD from the University of Sydney. He has been a postdoctoral fellow, with research interests in computational models of design using AI techniques, in areas such as creativity, visual reasoning and design presentation.

Hilaire Graham, BArch (Sydney) and MArch (London), has worked as an architect on major urban and building projects, and as an FM consultant. She currently lectures on facility management, and was the 1997 NSW Chairman of the Facility Management Association.

Gerard A. O'Dwyer has BDesSc and BArch degrees from the University of Queensland, and an MDesSc from the University of Sydney. He is an Associate of the Royal Australian Institute of Architects, and worked for seven years as an architect before joining the Sydney University staff.

Craig Pearce, DipEE (Caulfield) and MDesSc (Sydney), after 30 years in the building industry, coordinated and taught several courses in the building services postgraduate programme. He is now acting in a senior capacity with Ove Arup and Partners.

Michael A. Rosenman, BArch, MBdgSc and PhD (Sydney), is an architect of 31 years' experience, concerned with design theory and method related to computer-aided design, in the fields of optimisation, knowledge-based systems, expert systems, and evolutionary design. He is a Senior Research Fellow, and the co-author of a book and some 80 book chapters, papers and reports.

Preface to the fourth edition

The first edition of this dictionary was published in 1973 and reprinted in 1976. The second edition, published in 1986, had about 1500 additional entries, and the third edition, published 1998, had a further 2000 new entries, many of those taken over from the previous editions being updated. This fourth edition has added 1750 new or substantially revised entries, and over 330 of the existing entries have been updated. There are 70 additional illustrations.

National differences in terminology and spelling, and in the units of measurement, present some problems. This volume is published in England, and while many of the contributors are located in Australia, some are in various countries around the world, and most have varied international experience. In most cases we have used the current SI units, with the old British/American units in brackets. In some fields, such as illumination and acoustics, SI units are also in general use in the USA. Following British practice, pressures are given in Pa and stresses in N/mm^2; but Australian and other SI-oriented readers need merely substitute MPa for N/mm^2 for stresses. There are additional entries with cross-references where American terminology or spelling differ notably from the British and Australian. Following Australian and British practice, we have used mm for most dimensions, rather than cm which is more usual in Europe.

We have endeavoured to provide for the likely interest of readers by allowing the subject matter, as in the previous editions, to range somewhat beyond the field of building technology. Many information technology terms are included, largely in the fields of document transmission, document management and communications, which are likely to be encountered in the building industry. For the same reason we have given data on the chemical elements in building materials, and quoted some basic laws of physics relevant to environmental design. For the benefit of readers new to practical building, we have explained some elementary terms of building construction.

A substantial number of obsolete terms of measurement are included, such as *apostilb* and *Petersburg standard*, which were still in use in the mid-twentieth century. These are rarely explained in books published at the time they were current, but may already have become obsolete by the time many of our readers were educated. For the same reason some obsolete designations of materials are given. A few people are still familiar with the composition of *aqua regia*, but not many would know today what was meant by *oil of vitriol*; however, these terms were used without explanation as recently as the beginning of the twentieth century.

We have added explanations for a few more recent terms such as *subscriber trunk dialling*, which were once self-explanatory, but have fallen

out of use with the advance of technology; and included descriptions
of some of the machinery and tools
which are in everyday use by their
particular trades, but would not necessarily be known by all members of
the professional team. We have
tried to include the context in which
words are used, where necessary; and
to organise words like *bond*, which
have many meanings, in different
contexts.

We have included some terminology of traditional masonry construction and carpentry, which has
acquired a new importance because of
the current interest in heritage buildings; geometric terms for structures
which are no longer employed for
economic reasons, and terms used
in analytical methods of engineering
design which became obsolete with
the advent of computers, but are still
in reference books on library shelves.
We have also explained a few terms of
Ancient Roman building construction
which are untranslatable, like *opus
reticulatum.*

On the other hand, we have endeavoured to include many new terms
that have come into use since the
publication of the previous edition by
assembling a team of specialists in the
various branches of building science
and technology, and we have reviewed
all the third-edition entries in the
light of current knowledge. The fourth
edition includes additional terms used
in the field of fire engineering, as well
as the increasingly important fields
of facility management and building
services engineering.

Many of the entries have cross-
references to other entries, indicated
by the use of SMALL CAPITALS. These
give further information, particularly
on technical terms used in the entry,

or on materials or equipment of a
similar type.

The dictionary is fairly comprehensive on metals, stone, concrete,
ceramics and plastics, but names only
a few widely used timbers, such as
Douglas fir. The range of timbers used
worldwide is too great for a complete
listing in a general dictionary of building technology, and some names, such
as oak, maple, and mahogany, denote
different species in different parts
of the world. May we refer readers
to the glossaries that local timber
industry organisations usually supply
with their compliments.

We have included a substantial
number of abbreviations, such as
DAR and PTFE, and the initials of
organisations such as ASHRAE and
HMSO. These are quite clear to people familiar, respectively, with timber,
plastics, air conditioning and British
publications, but can be puzzling for
other readers. Generally, we considered that it was sufficient to write out
the words represented by the initials,
but where appropriate there is a cross-
reference to an entry under the full
name.

In the case of organisations, we
have, where possible, checked their
current names and locations from
their web pages. Given the rate of
change we have observed, particularly
in the names and organisational structure of government-sponsored organisations, it is inevitable that some
of these details will be overtaken
by the time readers look them up.
On the other hand, we have generally
kept references to former names and
abbreviations, to assist in identifying
publications under the organisations'
former names.

Finally we hope that readers who
find mistakes, omissions or missing

cross-references, which undoubtedly
remain, will be so kind as to let us
know about them, so that they can be
corrected in a future edition or reprint.

H.J.C & P.R.S.
Sydney, October 2003

Abbreviations

Some abbreviations explained in the entry in which they occur are not included in this list. Additional explanations of abbreviations are given in the following Dictionary entries.

°	degree	K	kelvin, degree kelvin, potassium
AC	alternating current		
Al	aluminium	kg	kilogram
Ba	barium	kJ	kilojoule
Btu	British thermal unit	kN	kilonewton
C	carbon, Celsius	kVA	kilovolt-ampere
Ca	calcium	kW	kilowatt
cal	calorie	kWh	kilowatt-hour
cd	candela	l, L	litre
CIE	*Commission Internationale de l'Éclairage*	lb	pound
		lm	lumen
Cl	chlorine	ln	natural logarithm
cm	centimetre	log	logarithm
cos	cosine	lx	lux
cosh	hyperbolic cosine	m	metre, prefix milli
Cu	copper	m^2	square metre
dB	decibel	m^3	cubic metre
dB(A)	decibel (A-scale)	Mg	magnesium
DC	direct current	min	minute
e	base of the natural logarithm (= 2.718...)	MJ	megajoule (= 1 000 000 J)
		mm	millimetre
e.g.	for example	mm^2	square millimetre
etc.	... and so on	µm	micrometre (= 0.000 001 m)
F	Fahrenheit, fluorine	MPa	megapascal
Fe	iron	N	newton, nitrogen
ft	foot	Na	sodium
ft^2	square foot	nm	nanometre (= 0.000 000 001 m)
ft^3	cubic foot		
h	hour	O	oxygen
H	hydrogen	Pa	pascal
Hz	hertz (= cycles per second)	Pb	lead
I	second moment of area	psf	pounds per square foot
i.e.	that is	psi	pounds per square inch
in.	inch	S	sulphur
in^2	square inch	s, sec	second
J	joule	Si	silicon

SI	SI metric system (*Système International d'Unités*)	WC	water closet
		Zn	zinc
sin	sine	λ	thermal conductivity
tan	tangent	π	circular constant
V	volt		$(= 3.1416\ldots)$
W	watt	Ω	ohms

Note on typography

Cross-references to other entries are printed in SMALL CAPITALS. *Italics* are used for emphasis, not as a cross-reference.

A

AAC *Abbreviation for* Autoclaved Aerated Concrete, a type of CELLULAR CONCRETE, with a density around 650 kg/m³ and a thermal conductivity of some 0.08 W/m.K; usually available in the form of blocks or planks, possibly reinforced. Often laid with a thin adhesive bed in place of mortar. Can be cut with a saw; can be used for load-bearing walls (up to two storeys) and the planks also for floors and roofs.

abacus The ancient Greek calculating frame consisting of beads sliding on thin rods, still widely used in Asia. The name was given to the uppermost member of the classical column head, which is a plate of varying thickness, because of its similar appearance.

abatement The reduction of a health hazard to an acceptable level by encapsulation, removal or demolition.

Abney level *Same as* CLINOMETER.

Abrams' law Experimental rule enunciated by D. A. Abrams in 1919: 'With given concrete materials and conditions of tests, the quantity of mixing water determines the strength of concrete, as long as the mix is of workable plasticity.' *See figure.*

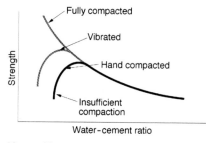

Abrams' law

abrasion The wearing away of the surface of a material by the cutting action of solids. There are numerous abrasion resistance tests. Comparing similar materials by the same test gives satisfactory results; however, the correlation between different tests is difficult, and the method of testing must always be specified. Abrasion tests may be rolling or sliding in nature, with or without abrasive. Usually the test is run for a definite number of strokes with a definite pressure, and the loss of weight is measured.

abrasion resistance The capacity of a surface to resist deliberate ABRASION or ordinary wear.

ABS plastic Acrylonitrile-butadiene-styrene, a thermoplastic material of good chemical resistance.

abscissa The *x*-axis, or horizontal axis, of a CARTESIAN COORDINATE system.

absolute humidity (AH) Generally, the moisture content of air, in gram of water vapour per kg of dry air, although in specialist terms it would mean the mass of water per unit volume of the air/vapour mixture (g/m³). See also HUMIDITY RATIO.

absolute temperature Temperature measured from ABSOLUTE ZERO. When measured in CELSIUS (centigrade), it is called the *Kelvin* scale (K). Measured in FAHRENHEIT, it is called the *Rankine* scale, but this is rarely used.

absolute value The magnitude of a quantity irrespective of whether its sign is positive or negative.

absolute volume The actual volume of the particles of sand, concrete aggregate, etc. It is determined by immersing the aggregate in water, and measuring the volume displaced.

absolute zero The lowest temperature which can be reached in theory, when the molecules of a perfect gas would possess no kinetic energy, and its volume would become zero. This occurs at −273.16°C (−459.67°F). The *absolute temperature* scale is measured from absolute zero. *See* KELVIN.

absorber plate A component of the

solar flat plate collector that absorbs solar radiation and converts it into heat.

absorber, porous *See* POROUS ABSORBER.

absorber, resonant *See* RESONANT ABSORBER.

absorber, suspended *See* SUSPENDED ABSORBER.

absorptance *(a)* In lighting, the ratio of the LUMINOUS FLUX absorbed by a body to the flux which it received. *(b)* In radiation, a surface property of bodies, either (i) the ratio of radiant heat absorbed by a surface to the incident irradiance, or (ii) the ratio of radiant heat absorbed by a surface to the heat that would be absorbed by a perfect absorber BLACK BODY (which, by definition, is numerically the same). It is wavelength-dependent, but can be used referring to a given broad range of wavelengths, (*e.g.* solar) or for a specified narrow band of wavelengths. It can be measured for a beam radiation of specified angle of incidence, or as a total hemispherical absorptance. (*See also* SELECTIVE SURFACE.)

absorption *(a)* The process whereby a liquid is drawn into the permeable pores of a porous solid. *(b)* Transformation of radiant energy to a different form of energy by the intervention of matter, as opposed to *transmission* which is the passage of radiation through matter without change of its frequency. *(c)* Absorption of sound. *See* SOUND ABSORPTION.

absorption coefficient *See* SOUND ABSORPTION COEFFICIENT.

absorption cycle A refrigeration cycle. It utilises two phenomena: *(a)* the absorption solution (absorbent plus refrigerant) can absorb refrigerant vapour; and *(b)* the refrigerant boils (flash cools itself) when subjected to a lower pressure. These two phenomena are used to obtain refrigeration. In the *lithium bromide* absorption machine, the bromide is used as an absorbent, and the water as a refrigerant. *See also* COMPRESSION CYCLE.

absorption factor *Same as* ABSORPTANCE.

absorption pit or trench A hollow excavation (maintained with perforated walls and a top covering, or by filling with coarse rubble) to receive waste water or STORMWATER and allow it to be

slowly absorbed into the surrounding soil.

absorption rate The amount of water absorbed by a brick in one minute. *Also called suction rate.*

absorptivity In precise terms, refers to absorption by a transparent or translucent medium, per unit thickness. Often used erroneously, intended to mean ABSORPTANCE.

abutment A massive masonry or concrete structure which resists a THRUST.

AC *Abbreviation for* ALTERNATING CURRENT.

ACADIA The Association for Computer-Aided Design in Architecture.

acanthus Leaf of a Mediterranean plant used as decoration in Corinthian and composite order capitals and in scrolls, friezes, etc.

accelerated weathering Determination of the weather-resisting properties of materials (such as paints and plastics) by cycles imitating as closely as possible natural weathering conditions. Machines designed for this purpose are called WEATHEROMETERS.

acceleration The rate of change of velocity. The *acceleration due to the Earth's gravity* has a mean value of 9.807m/s^2 (32.2ft/s^2).

accelerator A substance which speeds up a chemical reaction, as opposed to a RETARDER. *(a)* In concrete, an additive which increases the rate of hydration of the cement, and thus shortens the time of setting, or increases the rate of hardening or of strength development. *(b)* In synthetic resins or glues, a CATALYST which increases the hardening rate. The accelerator is mixed with the resin immediately before use.

accelerometer, accelerograph An instrument for measuring, recording the acceleration of the body to which it is attached. The recorded time history of acceleration is an *accelerogram.*

accent lighting Lighting used to emphasise a particular part of the visual field. *See also* DIRECTIONAL LIGHTING.

acceptable indoor air quality Indoor air that contains no contaminants in concentrations known to be harmful to human occupants and that is not offensive to a majority of people on initial entry to a space.

access In computing, the process of obtaining data from storage or an instruction from memory.

access for the disabled (handicapped) See BARRIER-FREE DESIGN.

access control system System for control and monitoring of access to and within a building.

access floor See RAISED FLOOR.

access provider A company or organisation that provides Internet access, and in some cases an online account on their computer system, to their subscribers.

access stair A stair which is not needed as a required, or fire, stair.

accidental error An error due to an accidental cause, which may be either positive or negative; it is therefore likely to be *self-compensating* if sufficient data are taken as opposed to a SYSTEMATIC ERROR.

acclimatisation The process of ADAPTATION by persons accustomed to a different climate, whereby the strain resulting from exposure to environmental stress is diminished. It is thought to have a physiological component (endocrine adjustments, changing blood circulation), but also a psychological and behavioural component ('getting used to').

accommodation (visual) The process of focusing the eyes on objects at different distances.

accordion door A door consisting of more than two leaves, or of narrow vertical panels hung from an overhead track. The panels interlock or butt against each other to form a flat surface when the door is closed, but fold back like the bellows of an accordion when the door is opened.

ACD *Abbreviation for* Automatic Closing Device.

acetone A quickly evaporating solvent (CH_3COCH_3) used in paint removers and thinners, and also for lacquers.

acetylene A highly flammable gas (C_2H_2) which is colourless and highly poisonous. It can be generated by the action of water on calcium carbide; however, it is more commonly used in bottled form. It is occasionally employed for heating and lighting. Combined with bottled oxygen *(oxy-acetylene)* it is used for cutting and FUSION WELDING of steel.

ACH *Abbreviation for* Air Changes per Hour.

achromatic lens A lens designed to minimise CHROMATIC ABERRATION. See FLINT GLASS.

ACI American Concrete Institute, Detroit.

acid A chemical compound containing hydrogen which can be replaced by metallic elements, and which produces hydrogen ions in solution. It neutralises *bases* to form *salts,* has a PH VALUE of less than 7, and turns blue LITMUS red.

acid etched A finish to in situ and precast concrete made by washing with dilute acid to remove some of the surface mortar, giving a lightly textured finish. Hydrochloric acid has been used, but this contributed to corrosion and has been replaced by phosphoric acid.

acid rain Rain that is significantly more acidic than normal rain, especially with a PH VALUE below 5.0.

acid rock An igneous rock with a preponderant silica content, *e.g. granite.*

acid soil A soil which produces an acidic reaction; a soil which has a PH VALUE below 6.5.

acid steel A steel made in a furnace lined with an acid refractory, such as silica, and under an acid slag.

ACID system *Abbreviation for* Access Control and Intruder Detection, a computer-based building security system.

ACM Association for Computing Machinery, New York.

acoustic board A low density FIBRE-BOARD with good SOUND ABSORPTION. It is often perforated to provide improved absorption.

acoustic definition In acoustics, the degree to which individual notes (or parts of a note) in a musical performance stand apart from the sounds which have already been played. It depends on the ratio of the intensity of the direct and reflected sound as well as the delay in the reflected sound. *Also called clarity.*

acoustic impedance The application of a periodic force or pressure at some point in a medium or dynamic system results in a periodic velocity of fixed phase. The acoustic impedance of a medium or system is the complex ratio of the SOUND PRESSURE to the particle velocity (due to the sound). The greater the change in acoustic impedance, from one part of a medium or system to another, the smaller the amount of acoustic energy transmitted. *See also* IMPEDANCE TUBE.

acoustic insulation *See* SOUND INSULATION *and* DISCONTINUOUS CONSTRUCTION.

acoustic model analysis Analysis of the behaviour of sound, especially in auditoria, by means of physical models. As the scale is reduced the WAVELENGTH of the sound has to be decreased (frequency increased) in accordance with DIMENSIONAL ANALYSIS.

acoustic perfume *See* MASKING SOUND.

acoustic plaster Plaster with high sound absorption. It normally contains pores which may be provided by gas bubbles resulting from aluminium powder or detergent (*see* CELLULAR CONCRETE) or by the use of VERMICULITE aggregate.

acoustic quality The acoustic quality of a room (for music especially) depends on many factors, including the size, shape and surface finishes. In order to describe and predict the acoustic quality of spaces many terms and criteria have been developed (*see also* BACKGROUND NOISE, DEFINITION, DYNAMIC RANGE, ECHO, ENSEMBLE, LIVENESS, LOUDNESS, REVERBERATION TIME, TIMBRE *and* WARMTH) but the combinations of these to attain acoustic quality is still poorly understood.

acoustic ray tracing *See* RAY TRACING.

acoustic reflector A panel installed above or alongside the position of a musician or speaker, in order to reflect additional sound toward an audience (*see figure*).

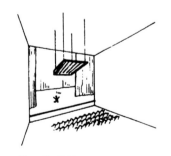

Acoustic reflector

acoustic seal A seal around a door or window to minimise sound transmission through the air gaps.

acoustic strain gauge A STRAIN GAUGE for measuring surface strains by vibrating a stretched wire which is matched against a note from a similar wire vibrating in a reference gauge. The tension in the wire changes with the strain, and the note changes accordingly.

acoustic tile Rectangular sound-absorbing tile normally used as a ceiling where it is either glued to a *substrate* or used in a grid as a SUSPENDED CEILING. The tile is usually lightweight, sometimes perforated, and it may have a fibreboard, fibreglass, cellulose or similar base.

acoustical cloud A reflecting surface suspended from the ceiling of an auditorium which provides early reflections or prevents ECHOES whilst still maintaining the reverberant qualities of the auditorium.

acoustical louvre A louvre incorporating sound-absorbing material which acts as a MUFFLER. The effectiveness of such louvres is limited.

acoustics The science of sound. *See also under* NOISE *and* SOUND.

ACPH *Abbreviation for* Air Changes Per Hour.

acre A British/American unit for area, equal to 10 square CHAINS, and to 0.4047 HECTARES, or $4047 \, m^2$.

acronym An artificial word derived from the initial letters or syllables of a name or phrase, in a form that can be pronounced.

acrylic paint Paint made with ACRYLIC RESIN as the principal binding agent.

acrylic resins Thermoplastic materials produced by the polymerisation of the monomeric derivates of acrylic acid to form *polymethyl methacrylate*. They are obtainable in transparent and also in opaque form, and they have good resistance to outdoor weathering; however, they are attacked by many organic solvents. Being thermoplastic, they are not fire-resistant. They are known by the trade names *Plexiglas*, *Perspex* and *Lucite*. *See also* POLYCARBONATE.

ACS American Ceramic Society.

ACSA Association of Collegiate Schools

of Architecture, Washington, DC, which has members in the USA and Canada.

actinic light The photochemically active wavelengths of natural and artificial light (from green to ultraviolet), which damage fabrics and some building finishes. They can be screened by GLASS (, ACTINIC).

actinometer *See* PYRHELIOMETER.

activated carbon filter A filter employed in ventilating and air conditioning systems for the removal of odours and toxins.

activation energy Energy required to initiate a chemical reaction.

active earth pressure *See* EARTH PRESSURE.

active filter Any of a number of sophisticated power electronic devices for eliminating HARMONIC DISTORTION.

active noise control The reduction of a noise by the production of another (using a microphone, signal processor, amplifier and loudspeakers), which is out of phase with the first, at a position where the noise is to be reduced. Active noise control systems are now commonly used in ducted air conditioning systems where low-frequency noise needs to be controlled.

active solar energy An incorrect term often used for ACTIVE SYSTEMS of solar energy utilisation.

active systems (of solar energy utilisation) Systems employing solar collectors, using electricity (parasitic energy) for pumps or fans to circulate the heat transfer fluid (water or air); as opposed to PASSIVE SYSTEMS.

activity The term used in NETWORK programming to denote a basic component of the work required for a building project. *Critical activities* are those which lie on the critical path. *Non-critical activities* are those which do not lie on the critical path. *Near-critical activities* are those which come to lie on the critical path if circumstances alter, *e.g.* if CRASHED TIME is used.

activity settings Varied workplaces which provide for particular functional individual and group requirements.

actuator An element of an automatic control system which translates a signal from the controller into an action by a controlled element such as a flow control device.

acuity *See* VISUAL ACUITY.

acute angle An angle of less than 90°.

acute arch Same as LANCET ARCH.

AD *Abbreviation for:* *(a)* Air Dried; *(b)* Anno Domini; *(c)* Area Drain; *(d)* As Drawn.

A–D converter (or ADC) *Abbreviation for* ANALOG TO DIGITAL CONVERTER.

ADA The Americans with Disabilities Act, which gives civil rights protection to individuals with disabilities similar to those provided to individuals on the basis of race, colour, sex, national origin, age and religion.

adaptability model A model of thermal comfort recognising the process of ACCLIMATISATION, whereby thermal preferences and NEUTRALITY TEMPERATURE depend on the given local climate and are liable to change after moving to a different climate, but can also change within the annual cycle.

adaptation *(a)* (in vision) The process taking place as the eye becomes accustomed to the luminance or the colour of the field in view, or to its darkness. *(b)* The final state of the process. *(c)* (in thermal comfort) The variation of thermal preference of individuals, depending on recent (*e.g.* 30 days') experience: becoming accustomed to changed temperature conditions (*see also* ADAPTABILITY MODEL).

adaptive learning algorithm An algorithm inserted into a computer-based building services control and monitoring system designed to adjust behaviour of a controlled function in the light of past experience.

addendum Written information adding to, clarifying or modifying the bidding documents. An addendum is generally issued by the owner to the contractor during the bidding process and, as such, addenda are intended to become part of the contract documents when the construction contract is executed.

additions to a contract Further work added: a VARIATION to a contract.

additive *See* CONCRETE ADMIXTURE.

address *(a)* In computing, the location of an instruction or data in computer memory. *(b)* In telecommunications, the location of some hardware component where data can be sent from or to, *e.g.* EMAIL address.

adhesion The property of matter by which close contact is established between two or more surfaces when they are brought intimately together. Force is required to separate the interfacial surfaces.

adhesive Glue for joining two pieces of material.

adiabatic A change in the condition of a body without any exchange of heat with the surroundings. An adiabatic change cannot normally be ISOTHERMAL.

adiabatic process A process in which no heat flows in or out of a system.

adjacency The locational requirement between planning units, which are ranked according to strength of adjacency as important, desirable, unimportant, undesirable.

admittance (Y) A measure of the ability of building elements to exchange heat with the room air (to admit or release heat); dimensionally the same as the U-value (W/m^2K), but it takes into account also the THERMAL CAPACITY of the material.

admittance procedure A calculation routine to convert calculated values of heat flow rates into and out of a space (and the deviation of these from the day's average) into temperatures, usually carried out for hourly intervals. The term may be used to include the calculation of these heat flows (the dynamic response) by using the concepts of TIME LAG and DECREMENT FACTOR.

admixture *See* CONCRETE ADMIXTURE.

adobe Construction with large sunbaked, unburnt bricks. *See also* COB WALLING *and* PISÉ DE TERRE.

ADPI *Abbreviation for* Air Distribution Performance Index.

adsorption Condensation of a gas on the surface of a solid. For example, SILICA GEL has the ability to collect water vapour by adsorption, and thus keeps dry the cases of instruments sensitive to moisture.

advanced natural ventilation Ventilation of buildings by means of natural flows of energy and air, which are controlled automatically or manually by occupants to improve thermal performance. Techniques may include, for example, thermal

chimneys to assist buoyancy as a driver of air flows; adjustment of air flow control devices to improve removal of heat during hot weather and retention of it in cold periods; night-time cooling of massive thermal elements.

adz US spelling of ADZE.

adze One of the oldest traditional tools for working timber, now rarely used. It has a cutting blade mounted at right angles to a wooden shaft.

AEC *Abbreviation for* Architecture, Engineering and Construction.

aelotropic Having physical properties which vary according to the direction in which they are measured, as opposed to ISOTROPIC. *See also* ORTHOTROPIC.

aeolian Wind-blown, *e.g.* aeolian soil (*loess*).

aeolian tone Sound produced by wind or airflow over a wire.

aerate To introduce air (for example into a building material during manufacture).

aerated concrete A form of CELLULAR CONCRETE.

aerator Device which adds air to water by injecting bubbles into flowing water, or into the aerobic chamber of a WASTE WATER TREATMENT plant.

aerial *(a)* Above ground installation for power lines or telephone lines or cables installed on a pole or overhead structure. *(b)* An antenna for radio or television transmission or reception.

aerobic A state where free oxygen is present (opposite of *anaerobic*).

aerodynamics That part of the mechanics of fluids which deals with the dynamics of gases, particularly the study of forces acting on bodies in moving air. *See also* BOUNDARY LAYER, MACH NUMBER *and* WIND TUNNEL.

aerofoil blade A fan blade with aerofoil cross-section intended to improve strength of the blade and mechanical efficiency of the fan.

aerogel An experimental material made from a silica dioxide gel. It has very low density and high insulating properties. Currently in use by NASA, studies are underway to transfer this technology to architecture and construction.

aerogenerator A WIND TURBINE coupled with an electricity generator.

aerosol paints Paints packaged for spray application in a container pressurised by compressed liquefied gas or air.

affinity analysis Analysis of adjacency requirements of particular functional spaces to produce a hierarchy of relationships used in space planning.

AFNOR *Association Française de Normalisation*, Paris.

aftershock Shock which follows a primary EARTHQUAKE.

AG *Abbreviation for* Above Grade, *see also* AGL.

Ag Chemical symbol for *silver* (argentum).

agate A natural aggregate of crystalline and colloidal silica (SiO_2), coloured by metallic oxide. It is sometimes translucent or attractively banded; these varieties are classed as semi-precious stones, and they have been used in sculpture and architecture. It is also extremely hard, and for this reason used for the bearings of scientific instruments.

age hardening The hardening of an ALLOY which results from the formation of tiny particles of a new PHASE within the existing solid solution. *Also called precipitation hardening* or *ageing.*

age of air Once air enters an enclosure, it is assumed to 'age'. The *local mean age* is the average time it takes for air, once entering an enclosure (time = 0), to reach a given point. The *room mean age* is the average age of the local mean ages for all points.

ageing of concrete The final stage in the chemical reaction between cement and water during which the concrete continues to gain strength slowly. It continues for many years. *See also* SETTING *and* HARDENING.

ageing of metals The process of AGE HARDENING.

agglomerate Small particles bonded together into an integrated mass.

aggregate *See* CONCRETE AGGREGATE.

aging *Same as* AGEING.

agitator *(a)* A device for mixing or stirring liquid. *(b)* A rotating drum on a truck used to retain the plasticity of mixed concrete during transit.

AGL *Abbreviation for* Above Ground Level.

agreed energy targets Targets for annual energy consumption in a building as agreed between the owner and/or occupier and a performance rating authority.

agricultural drain, agricultural pipe drain An assembly of pipes for draining subsoil. The pipes may be porous or perforated.

AH *Abbreviation for* Absolute Humidity.

AHU *Abbreviation for* Air Handling Unit: mechanical fan in ductwork for propelling ventilation air.

AI *Abbreviation for* ARTIFICIAL INTELLIGENCE.

AIA American Institute of Architects, Washington, DC.

AIEE American Institute of Electrical Engineers, now incorporated into the IEEE.

AIMA Acoustical and Insulating Materials Association.

air absorption The absorption of sound by air can be a significant factor in the propagation of sound at higher frequencies. The rate of absorption is proportional to the distance travelled by the sound and increases with the relative humidity and, to a lesser extent, depends on the temperature of the air.

air balance The condition achieved in an air distribution system when the maximum quantity of air that can be delivered to each point of use is just sufficient to meet heat load requirements at full load.

air barrier The position within a facade system where the outside air pressure is separated from the inside air pressure. In a FACE-SEALED system the air barrier is the outside face, while in a RAIN SCREEN system it is to the inside of the drained cavity.

air brick A brick perforated for ventilation purposes.

air change rate A unit of ventilation, defined as the volume of air passed through the ventilation system, per hour, divided by the volume of the room ventilated. The number of air changes required varies from 60 for laundries to 1 per hour for store rooms. The range for normal occupancies lies between 2 and 6. A more accurate method is to estimate the supply of air on the basis of persons occupying the space.

air changes per hour The number of changes per hour that will be induced by a supply of air for ventilation.

air compressor A machine which takes in air at atmospheric pressure, and compresses it to a much higher pressure, generally for the purpose of operating *pneumatic tools*.

air conditioning Artificial ventilation with air at a controlled temperature and humidity. Heating air, and moistening it if necessary, are relatively inexpensive. However, air conditioning normally implies cooling and DEHUMIDIFICATION of the air, which require appreciable expenditure of energy. *Also written* air-conditioning. *See also* EVAPORATIVE COOLING *and* NATURAL VENTILATION.

air conditioning duct *See* DUCT *(b) and* DUCT LINING.

air cooled chiller A refrigeration machine designed to reject heat to atmosphere by way of an air-cooled CONDENSER *(a)*. Because it uses SENSIBLE HEAT exchange rather than latent heat as in a COOLING TOWER, it is slightly less efficient but also much simpler to maintain.

air curtain A stream of temperature-controlled high-velocity air, projected downwards across an external opening.

air diffuser *See* DIFFUSER *(d)*.

air diffusion (distribution) performance index (ADPI) The percentage of locations in a room where measurements of effective draft temperature and air velocity meet specified standards. A high percentage of people are comfortable in sedentary (office) situations where the effective draft temperature θ as defined below, is between -1.5 and $+1$ K and the air velocity is less than 0.35 m/s.

$$\theta = (t_x - t_c) - 8(V_x - 0.15)$$

where t_x = local air steam dry-bulb temperature, °C; t_c = average (control) room dry-bulb temperature, °C; and V_x = local airsteam centreline velocity, m/s.

air door *Same as* AIR CURTAIN.

air drying Drying a material, such as timber, in the air instead of seasoning it in a kiln. *Air dry timber* has a moisture content which is approximately in equilibrium with that in the surrounding atmosphere.

air duct *See* DUCT *(b)*.

air entrainment The process of air or gases being drawn into a fire, plume or jet.

air felting Forming a mat from an air suspension of fibres. It is used for certain types of particle board to prevent the absorption of moisture which necessarily occurs in *wet felting*.

air filter A device inserted in an air stream to trap entrained particulate matter.

air gap (plumbing) A vertical separation between the bottom of a tap or other water outlet, and the highest level of water in a basin or cistern below it. This prevents contaminated water being drawn back into the water supply in the case of failure of the water supply pressure *(see figure)*.

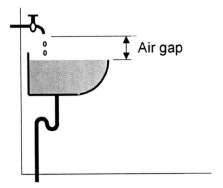

Air gap

air heating system A solar heating system using air as the heat transfer medium.

air inlet (or anti-siphon) valve Used in solar water heating systems at the highest point, the valve is closed when the system is operating (internally pressurised), but opens when the system is being drained, to let in air and prevent negative pressure which could cause a collapse of pipes. It avoids leaving water in the pipes where it could freeze. Some water supply authorities require such a valve to be fitted where there is a risk of sucking back stored water (*e.g.* from a cistern or a pool) into the mains (when being emptied).

air lock (between rooms) A lobby or small room, with self-closing doors, to allow access between two other spaces while restricting the amount of air exchanged between them. Used between habitable spaces and contaminated areas, and also at the entrance to a building to restrict the ingress of outside air. Often pressurised to prevent the ingress of contaminated air, or ventilated to extract it.

air lock (in hyperbaric applications) Device that permits passage between regions of differing air pressures, most often used for passage between atmospheric pressure and chambers in which the air is compressed, such as CAISSON work. A typical modern air lock consists of a cylinder of steel plate with airtight doors located at both ends, together with valves to admit or to exhaust compressed air. One of the doors must always be closed; before the other is opened, the pressure within the air lock must be equalised with that on the opposite side.

air lock (in pipework) A condition in a piped service in which air has been 'trapped' or 'locked' within the circuit. This can create noise and restrict the circulation of fluid.

air outlet See CEILING DIFFUSER, PUNKAH LOUVRE and REGISTER.

air quality See FILTER and VENTILATION.

air seasoning Same as AIR DRYING.

air slaking The process of exposing QUICKLIME to the air. It gradually absorbs moisture and breaks down into HYDRATED LIME powder.

air sterilisation A process of killing micro-organisms in ventilation air by means of exposure to ultra-violet light.

air termination In a LIGHTNING PROTECTION SYSTEM, a conductor or rod positioned to intercept a lightning discharge and to create a ZONE OF PROTECTION. The *rod* is sometimes termed a *finial*.

air washer Component of an AIR CONDITIONING plant which removes suspended dirt by spraying or washing.

AIRAH Australian Institute of Refrigeration, Air Conditioning and Heating, Melbourne.

air-bag loading A load applied in a model test or a full-scale test by pumping up a bag, pressing against a firm foundation, with an air compressor. *Also called pneumatic loading.*

airborne sound Sound transmitted from one part of a building to another in which the initial transmission path is within air,

e.g. speech, as opposed to STRUCTURE-BORNE SOUND or IMPACT SOUND where there is direct excitation of the structure of the building, *e.g.* by out of balance forces from machinery in a plant room, hammer blows or footsteps. Airborne sound transmission through a masonry wall or floor will approximately conform to the MASS LAW.

airconditioning See AIR CONDITIONING.

air-entraining agent An additive to cement or an admixture to concrete which causes minute air bubbles to be incorporated in concrete or mortar during mixing. It is claimed that this increases workability and frost resistance. *See also* ENTRAPPED AIR.

air-inflated structure Same as PNEUMATIC STRUCTURE.

air-supported structure *(a)* See PNEUMATIC STRUCTURE. *(b)* A more expensive and less common type is a closed membrane structure, consisting of two layers of membrane, inflated with air at a pressure sufficient to support the loads acting on it. This avoids the need for the continual operation of an air compressor.

air-to-air heat transmission coefficient *Same as* THERMAL TRANSMITTANCE.

AISC American Institute of Steel Construction, Chicago. The former Australian Institute of Steel Construction is now merged with SIA to form The Australian Steel Institute (North Sydney).

aisle *(a)* A wing (Latin, *ala*) attached to the nave of a church, usually separated from it by a line of columns. *(b)* Hence, any division in a church, such as a passage between pews. *(c)* Hence, a passage between seats in any building, such as a theatre or concert hall.

AITC American Institute of Timber Construction, Englewood, Colorado.

Al Chemical symbol for *aluminium.*

alabaster Pure GYPSUM in densely crystalline form. Due to its softness it is easily carved and polished.

alarm gong A device in a sprinkler system to sound the alarm when a sprinkler head activates. It is activated by water flow in the pipework.

albedo The ratio of the amount of light reflected by a surface to the light falling onto it.

alclad Steel sheet, or any other metal product, which has been coated with aluminium or aluminium alloy as a protection against corrosion.

algebraic mean An obsolete term for the average of all values (*i.e.* their sum, divided by the number of values), considering their positive or negative sign. Usually simply called *mean*. *See also* ARITHMETIC MEAN, GEOMETRIC MEAN, MEDIAN *and* MODE.

algorithm Corruption of al-Khowarazmi (a ninth-century Arab mathematician); the term originally used to denote arithmetic using the Indian–Arabic (*i.e.* decimal) numerals. It now generally implies a sequence of logical processing rules, set up to solve a problem.

aliasing An inaccuracy which occurs when a smooth ANALOG signal is converted to a DIGITAL signal: *(a)* In acoustics, when a signal is sampled at a rate less than twice the component maximum frequency, phantom low frequencies can be generated. *(b)* In digital graphics, the rough edge effect caused by converting a smooth diagonal line into rectangular pixels.

alidade *See* PLANE TABLE.

alite *See* TRICALCIUM SILICATE.

alkali *(a)* A synonym for BASE. *(b)* More correctly, and in a more limited sense, a generic term for the hydroxides of sodium, potassium, lithium, rubidium and caesium, which are called the *alkali metals*.

alkali–aggregate reaction Chemical reaction between certain aggregates and the sodium and potassium compounds contained in Portland cement. Aggregates liable to this type of reaction may cause deleterious expansion in mortar or concrete.

alkaline soil A soil which produces an alkaline reaction; a soil with a PH VALUE above 7.3.

alkyd paints Paints using ALKYD RESIN as the VEHICLE for the pigment. There are interior, exterior and fire-retardant types.

alkyd resin A THERMOPLASTIC synthetic resin, derived from an alcohol, such as glycerol, and an organic acid, such as phthalic acid.

Allen head A hexagonally recessed head of a BOLT or SCREW. A hexagonal key of the appropriate size is used to drive or tighten it. *See also* CROSS-HEADED SCREW.

alligatoring Cracking of the surface bitumen of a BUILT-UP ROOF due to shrinkage. Also called *crocodiling*.

allotropy The ability to exist in more than one state, *e.g.* carbon has three allotropic varieties which are diamond, graphite and amorphous carbon.

allowable stress *Same as* MAXIMUM PERMISSIBLE STRESS.

alloy A substance with metallic properties, composed of two or more elements, which after mixing in the molten state do not separate into distinct layers on solidifying. Normally alloys are mixtures of metals. Structural steel (which is a mixture of iron and carbon) is a notable exception. Alloys may be composed of chemical compounds, solid solutions, EUTECTICS, EUTECTOIDS or of aggregations of these with each other and with pure metal.

alloy diagram *Same as* PHASE DIAGRAM.

alloy steel A steel to which one or more elements, other than carbon, have been added, as opposed to CARBON STEEL (although, strictly speaking, carbon steel is an alloy).

alluvial soil Soil deposited by flowing water (generally during a flood) in recent times (geologically speaking) on land which is not permanently submerged.

alpha brass A copper–zinc alloy which contains more than 64 per cent copper. It has good tensile strength and considerable ductility.

alpha iron Unalloyed iron below 910 °C (1670 °F). It has a body-centred cubic space lattice, and it is magnetic below the magnetic change point which, in pure iron, is 767 °C (1414 °F). *See also* GAMMA IRON *and* PHASE DIAGRAM.

alpha particle A helium nucleus, *i.e.* a helium atom which has lost two electrons and consequently has a double positive charge. It contains two protons and two neutrons. The *alpha radiation* emitted by radium, etc. consists of a stream of alpha particles.

alpha testing A stage of software development where the software is first tested for bugs by real users, rather than the developers themselves. In contrast to BETA TESTING, software at the alpha testing stage is usually assumed to have some significant BUGS or unimplemented portions.

alphameric character *Same as* ALPHANUMERIC CHARACTER.

alphanumeric character Any one of the letters of the alphabet (in upper or lower case), the ten numerical digits, punctuation marks and other printable characters. It requires at least seven BITS to express a character in binary notation.

alternating current An electric current which reverses its direction of flow at regular intervals (commonly at 50 or 60 cycles per second (50 or 60 Hz)), as opposed to a *direct current*.

alternative officing Accommodation strategy seeking to change an existing workplace, including concepts such as HOTELLING, HOT DESKING and HOME WORKING.

alternator An alternating current generator. It is usually driven by a heat engine or a water turbine. *See also* DYNAMO.

altitude The angle between a point on the surface of a sphere and its *horizon*. It is the vertical coordinate for locating the point; the horizontal coordinate is the AZIMUTH (*see figure*). *See also* DECLINATION.

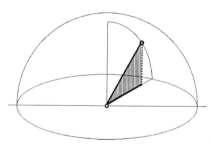

Altitude

alum A double sulphate of aluminium and a univalent metal, such as potassium. It is used to make GYPSUM plaster harden faster. Alum was the raw material for the first production of metallic aluminium; this is now generally made from BAUXITE.

alumina Aluminium oxide (Al_2O_3). Hydrous alumina is BAUXITE.

aluminium A white metal of atomic weight 26.98. Its chemical symbol is Al, its atomic number is 13, it has a valency of 3, a specific gravity of 2.70, a melting point of 660.1 °C, and a coefficient of thermal expansion of 23.5×10^{-6} per K. Most aluminium is produced from BAUXITE by an electrolytic process, which depends on a cheap source of electric power for its economy. Aluminium metal is silvery-white in colour. It oxidises very readily, but the oxide skin formed provides a protective coating which inhibits further oxidation. Aluminium is readily alloyed with copper, silicon, nickel, manganese, magnesium and other metals, and a very wide range of alloys are available for casting, forging, stamping, rolling and extruding. *Also called aluminum* (US).

aluminium bronze A copper–aluminium alloy, containing 3–11 per cent of aluminium.

aluminium foil A thin sheet of aluminium, about 0.15 mm thick. It is commonly used for REFLECTIVE INSULATION.

aluminous cement *See* HIGH-ALUMINA CEMENT.

aluminum US spelling of ALUMINIUM.

AM *Abbreviation for* AMPLITUDE MODULATION.

amalgam An alloy of mercury and some other metal.

ambient The conditions (temperature, humidity, sound field or lighting) existing in the general surroundings, but excluding any local effects being studied.

ambient lighting The general background lighting, excluding the effects of TASK LIGHTING.

ambient sound The resultant sound, at a point of interest, from all sources near and far.

ambisonics A technique for recording sound using four unidirectional microphones and reproducing 'surround' sound using four loudspeakers.

amenities Activities provided in association with a facility, which provide comfort and convenience.

American bond *Same as* COMMON BOND.

American Ephemeris Since 1960 published in the same form as the British NAUTICAL ALMANAC.

amino-plastics A generic term for urea FORMALDEHYDE and melamine formaldehyde resin.

ammeter An instrument for measuring electric current, graduated in *amperes*. *See also* GALVANOMETER.

ammonia A colourless, alkaline, toxic gas of composition NH_3, with a pungent odour. It has a boiling point of $-33\,°C$. It is used as a refrigerant in large VAPOUR COMPRESSION refrigeration plants. Not favoured in air conditioning applications due to its toxicity.

ammonium chloride Generally known as sal ammoniac.

amorphous Not crystalline.

amorphous silicon An alloy of silica and hydrogen, in a non-crystalline arrangement, used to produce PHOTOVOLTAIC CELLS.

amortisation A method of liquidating a debt by making annual payments to a sinking fund.

amp *Abbreviation for* AMPERE.

amperage The flow of electric current, measured in *amperes*, in a circuit.

ampere (A) The unit of electrical current, named after the nineteenth-century French physicist A. M. Ampère. One ampere is the constant current which, if maintained in two straight parallel conductors of infinite length, of negligible circular cross-section, and placed at a distance of 1 metre apart in a vacuum, produces between them a force equal to 2×10^7 NEWTON per metre length. It is also equivalent to a current flow of 1 coulomb per second.

amphitheatre An oval, circular or semicircular building with seats rising in ascending rows around an ARENA.

amplifier A device for increasing the power level of a signal.

amplitude A measure of the extreme range of a fluctuating quantity which is usually taken as the difference between the maximum (or minimum) value and the mean value.

amplitude modulation A method of encoding a signal on a carrier wave (for the purpose of recording or transmitting it) by varying the amplitude of the wave at a constant frequency. *See also* FREQUENCY MODULATION.

anabatic Flow occurring when air at a lower level is heated (*e.g.* by solar radiation) thus becoming lighter (but not light enough to break through the cooler upper layers) and flowing upwards along a slope. The opposite of KATABATIC.

anaerobic A state where free oxygen is absent (opposite of *aerobic*).

anaerobic digestion A bacterial digestion process which removes the offensive odour of many organic wastes.

analemma A distorted 'figure 8' shaped graph, representing the EQUATION OF TIME.

analog, analogue Continuously varying, and therefore capable of being represented numerically only by REAL NUMBERS, or physically by objects capable of infinitely small movements (such as the hands of a clock). Compare with DIGITAL. (Usually spelled *analogue* when used as a noun.)

analog computer A computer which accepts time-varying inputs. Analog computers are generally designed to solve a specific problem, and they are therefore less versatile than DIGITAL COMPUTERS.

analog to digital converter (ADC) A unit for translating output signals from an analog device (such as a sound level meter or temperature probe) into digital form for input into a digital computer system.

analogy Similarity or correspondence between different phenomena or concepts, usually through properties other than physical features; as in the analogy between a door and a tap through the function of controlling flow.

analysis The process of resolving or separating a problem into its component parts and determining the relationships between them. The result of that process. Contrasted to *synthesis*. *See also* SYSTEM ANALYSIS.

anatase *See* TITANIUM WHITE.

anchor (or rock anchor) A cable or bar, held in a hole drilled into rock or preexisting concrete by a fixed anchorage, and with provision for tensioning at the free end. Used to prevent the uplift of foundations, to tie back retaining walls, or to stabilise a rock face. *See also* GROUND ANCHOR.

anchor bolt A bolt usually embedded in a structure, *e.g.* in concrete, with a protruding threaded section. *Also called holding-down bolt.*

anchorage Device, frequently patented, for permanently anchoring the tendons at the ends of a POST-TENSIONED member, or for temporarily anchoring the tendons of PRE-TENSIONED members during hardening of the concrete.

anchorage zone In POST-TENSIONED concrete, the region adjacent to the anchorage of the tendon, which is subjected to secondary stresses resulting from the distribution of the prestressing force (*see figure*). Unless suitably reinforced, the concrete may split due to secondary tension. In PRE-TENSIONED concrete, the region in which the transfer bond stresses are developed.

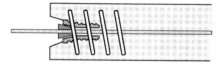

Anchorage zone

ancient lights In historical English law, windows which existed for so long a time as to constitute immemorial usage in law (20 years or more), became an 'ancient light' which the law protected from disturbance.

anechoic chamber A room for acoustic testing in which a FREE FIELD exists because all the surfaces are highly absorbent. Also called a *free-field* room. Anechoic chambers are used for measuring the SOUND POWER and DIRECTIVITY of sound sources amongst many other things. *See also* REVERBERATION CHAMBER.

anemometer Instrument for measuring wind speed. High air velocities can be measured with the *deflecting vane anemometer* which gives a direct reading, and the *rotating vane anemometer* (*see figure*) which counts the rotations. Instruments suitable for lower air speeds are the KATA

Anemometer

THERMOMETER (now largely obsolete), the HOT-WIRE ANEMOMETER, and the IONISATION ANEMOMETER.

aneroid barometer *See* BAROMETER.

angiosperm One of the two main divisions of seed plants; it includes most of the world's flowering plants, and all hardwoods; the other main division is the GYMNOSPERMS.

angle cleat A small bracket formed of ANGLE IRON, which is used to locate or support a member of a structural framework.

angle factor or shape factor A factor used in calculating radiant energy exchange between surfaces. It expresses the geometrical relationship between the two surfaces.

angle grinder A hand-held powered grinder, in which the axis of the grinding wheel is at right angles to the machine. Used for cleaning up welds, and general small cutting and grinding tasks.

angle iron A steel section, either hot-rolled or cold-formed, consisting of two legs at an angle (which is almost invariably a right angle). An angle iron may be *equal* (both legs the same width) or *unequal.*

angle of friction The angle ϕ between the force due to the weight of a body resting on a surface, and the resultant force when the body begins to slide. The coefficient of friction $\mu = \tan \phi$. *See also* FRICTION.

angle of illumination *Same as* ANGLE OF INCIDENCE.

angle of incidence The angle which an arriving ray or wave makes with the normal to the surface on which it falls. *See also* ANGLE OF REFLECTION.

angle of internal friction The ANGLE OF FRICTION (ϕ) in granular soils. It is defined by the equation: shearing resistance = normal force on surface of sliding $\times \tan \phi$. For perfectly dry or fully submerged granular soil (clean sand or gravel) it equals the ANGLE OF REPOSE. *See also* RANKINE THEORY *and* BULKING.

angle of reflection The angle which a reflected ray or wave makes with the normal to the surface which is reflecting it. *Same as specular angle.*

angle of repose The steepest angle at which a heap of dry soil will stand.

angle of shearing resistance *See* COULOMB'S EQUATION.

angle section *See* ANGLE IRON.

anglepoise A LUMINAIRE, mounted on a table, floor, wall or equipment, whose position and angle can be changed by pulling or pushing. The new position is usually held by means of links and strings or, rarely, by a GOOSENECK.

ångström Obsolescent unit of measurement for very small lengths, equal to 1×10^{-10} metre or 0.1 nanometre; abbreviated as Å.

anhydride An oxide which produces an acid when combined with water.

anhydrite Anhydrous calcium sulphate ($CaSO_4$). It is found naturally as a mineral or it may be made from GYPSUM by removing the water of crystallisation, usually by heating above 163 °C (325 °F). Anhydrite produced from gypsum is more reactive than the naturally occurring mineral.

anhydrous A term applied to minerals which do not contain water of crystallisation.

anhydrous lime *Same as* QUICKLIME.

animal glue GLUE made from animal waste products.

animation In computer graphics, the display of a series of frames in quick succession so as to achieve a computer-produced animated movie. Can be used for the study of the behaviour of physical phenomena where time-variance is important, such as airflow, bending of beams, etc.

animation program Program designed for creating ANIMATION sequences.

anion A negative ion, the opposite of a *cation* which is positive.

anisotropic Having different physical properties in different directions, as opposed to *isotropic*.

annealing *(a)* Heating glass uniformly to its annealing temperature to remove residual stresses, and then cooling it slowly at a controlled rate. *(b)* Heating a metal alloy (such as steel) to a temperature about 50 K above the upper limit of the TRANSFORMATION TEMPERATURE range. By contrast, TEMPERING is carried out below this range. The object is to remove stresses induced by previous treatment and improve ductility. The annealing temperature is held for at least an hour (more for thick pieces), and cooling is slow.

annual cost (of a building) The total annual operating costs of a building, as opposed to capital costs. The annual operating costs of a multi-tenanted building are borne by the owner, and subsequently split between the tenants in the ratio of the area of their tenancies to the total, or by some other such formula stipulated in the lease agreement.

annual mean daily insolation The average solar energy per square metre available per day over the whole year.

annual rings *Same as* GROWTH RINGS.

annual solar savings The annual savings due to the use of a solar energy device.

annular Ringlike.

annulus A figure bounded by two concentric circles, *i.e.* a thick ring.

annunciator A panel which provides information to lift passengers by means of display and/or sound.

anobium borer A wood borer of the family *Anobiidae*, which attacks many species of seasoned timber, both HEARTWOOD and SAPWOOD. Also known as the *furniture borer*, because it has a long lifecycle and may remain active in old timber items for a long time before being noticed. Its FRASS has a gritty feel. *See also* LYCTUS BORER.

anode The positive electrode of an electrolytic cell or battery. The *cathode* is the negative electrode.

anodising A process for producing a film of aluminium oxide on aluminium or aluminium alloys, to protect the surface from corrosion. The film is slightly porous, and it is usually sealed, *e.g.* with lanoline dissolved in spirit. Colours can be introduced before sealing. Aniline dyes are liable to fade if used externally. Mineral pigments are used externally.

ANSI American National Standards Institute, New York.

ant capping A TERMITE SHIELD made of galvanised iron or similar material.

ant, white *See* TERMITE.

anteroom A small room adjacent to a larger room, often used as a waiting room.

ante-solarium A balcony which faces the sun.

anthropometry The comparative study of the sizes and proportions of the human body with a view to determining its average dimensions.

anti-aliasing The process of smoothing of the image or sound roughness caused by ALIASING. With images, approaches include adjusting pixel positions or setting pixel intensities so that there is a more gradual transition between the colour of a line and the background colour. With sound, aliases are removed by eliminating frequencies above half the sampling frequencies.

anti-bandit glazing Glazing designed to resist violent attack, often consisting of thick LAMINATED GLASS or polycarbonate, set into suitably robust frames.

anticlastic A surface with a negative GAUSSIAN CURVATURE.

anticlockwise The opposite to CLOCKWISE. *Also called counterclockwise.*

anti-corrosive paint Paint which delays corrosion, particularly of steel. It is used as a *primer*, rarely as a finishing coat. Although paints, especially those containing zinc, are effective at reducing corrosion, the preparation of the surface is an essential part of the paint *system.*

anticyclone In meteorology, a high-pressure area with winds rotating CLOCKWISE in the northern hemisphere, and ANTICLOCKWISE in the southern hemisphere.

antifreeze Substance added to water to lower its freezing point. Solar water heaters usually use a mixture of water and propylene glycol to prevent freezing.

anti-friction metal A white metal based on ANTIMONY, LEAD or TIN, used to reduce friction.

antilogarithm If b is the LOGARITHM of a, i.e. log $a = b$, then a is the antilogarithm of b, i.e. $a = \log^{-1} b$.

antimony A bluish white metal. Its chemical symbol is Sb (Stibium), its atomic number is 51, its valency is 3 or 5, its atomic weight is 121.76, its specific gravity is 6.62, and its melting point is 630.5 °C. Antimony and its alloys expand on solidification, thus reproducing the fine details of the mould.

antimony oxide A white pigment, which has flame-retardant properties. It has better OPACITY than whiting, but not as much as TITANIUM WHITE.

antinode A point, line or surface of an interference pattern at which the amplitude of the variable of interest (*e.g.* pressure or velocity) is a maximum.

antisiphon trap An air TRAP which contains an additional volume of water in an enlarged pipe, to increase the resealing quality of the trap.

anti-vibration mounts Flexible elements inserted between the base of a machine and its supporting structure to prevent transmission of vibration.

antivirus software A class of program that searches a HARD DRIVE, FLOPPY DISKS and incoming data for any known or potential VIRUSES.

apartment A dwelling, usually one of many in a building. *See also* CONDOMINIUM, DUPLEX, FLAT, HOME UNIT, MAISONETTE *and* OYO.

apex The highest point of any structure.

apex stone Same as SADDLE STONE.

aphelion Point in the orbit of a planet or comet that is farthest from the sun, the opposite of *perihelion.*

apogee Point in the orbit of the moon, planet or satellite farthest from the earth, the opposite of *perigee.*

apostilb (asb) An obsolete unit of LUMINANCE. For matt surfaces, 1 apostilb = 1 blondel = $1/\pi$ candela per square metre = 0.318 cd/m^2.

apparent brightness The subjective response to the relationship between all the LUMINANCES in the visual field. *Also called luminosity* or SUBJECTIVE BRIGHTNESS.

apparent power In alternating current systems, the product of voltage and current (volt-amps or kVA). *See also* POWER.

apparent solar time *Also called true solar time.* The time according to the position of the sun in the sky. It differs from MEAN SOLAR TIME, because the sun's motion is not entirely uniform. *See also* EQUATION OF TIME.

apparent volume (of a porous substance) The BULK VOLUME minus the open pores, or the true volume plus the closed pores. The *apparent density* is the mass divided by the apparent volume.

applet A small PROGRAM that can be sent along with a WEB PAGE to a user. Applets are written using JAVA programming language and can perform interactive animations, immediate calculations, or other simple tasks without having to send a user request back to the SERVER.

applications software, programs Programs designed to solve problems in a specific problem domain, as opposed to systems software which is designed to perform a variety of general tasks for its user. For example, word processing software is designed for a very specific collection of tasks.

appliqué One material applied to another, generally as a decoration.

apron *(a)* A relatively wide flashing, or a flashing that surrounds or partly surrounds a projecting construction. *(b)* A concrete slab on grade, in front of or around a building. *(c)* A guard installed on the underside of a lift car to prevent the trapping of objects or limbs of people whilst a car, which uses advance opening LIFT DOORS, is levelling at a landing.

AQL *Abbreviation for* Acceptable Quality Level, the average quality at which the producer should work to satisfy the customer.

aqua fortis Concentrated nitric acid.

aqua regia A mixture of nitric acid and hydrochloric acid in the proportion of 1:3, so called by alchemists because it dissolves gold.

aqueduct An artificial channel for the conveyance of water, usually an ancient structure carried on masonry arches.

aquifer A layer of rock or soil which conducts water.

arc *(a)* Sparking that results when undesirable current flows between two points of differing potential. This may be due to leakage through the intermediate insulation or a leakage path due to contamination. *(b)* The ionised current path between a welding electrode and the work. *(c) See* ARC OF A CIRCLE.

arc lamp A luminaire with an ARC LIGHT.

arc light A high-intensity electric-discharge lamp employing an ARC discharge between two electrodes in air.

Modern DISCHARGE LAMPS use an arc within a glass or quartz vessel, containing a gas or a metal vapour.

arc of a circle A portion of its circumference. The length of an arc which subtends an angle θ degrees at the centre, is $\theta \pi D/360$, where D is the diameter *(see figure)*.

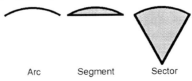

Arc   Segment   Sector

Arc of a circle

arc welding FUSION WELDING in which the heat is derived from an electric arc formed either between two electrodes, or between the parent metal and one electrode. Air must be excluded from the arc, either by the use of a flux coating on the electrode, or by a shielding gas or powdered flux. *See also* ACETYLENE, ARGON-ARC, HELIARC, SHIELDED-ARC *and* SUBMERGED-ARC WELDING.

arcade *(a)* A number of arches arranged in a line, so that their horizontal thrusts are absorbed by the adjacent arches. *(b)* Hence, a covered walk with an arcade on one side or arcades on both sides. *(c)* Hence, a covered walk with shops or other buildings on one side, which may or may not have arches on the other side. *(d)* Hence, a covered walk lined by shops or other buildings on both sides, and lit from the top, originally by daylight, but now generally by electric light. This latter use is also called a GALLERIA.

arch A structure designed to carry a load across a gap mainly by compression. *See* CATENARY ARCH, CIRCULAR ARCH, CORBELLED ARCH, CROWN, FLAT ARCH, HORSESHOE ARCH, JACK ARCH, PARABOLIC ARCH *and* SPRINGINGS.

arch bar A support for a FLAT ARCH, or for brickwork with normal bond (not an arch) carried above an opening.

arch brick, stone A brick, stone VOUSSOIR.

arched girder Same as BOWSTRING GIRDER.

Archimedes' number (Ar) The ratio of

the buoyancy forces to the incoming momentum of an air inlet.

Archimedes' principle *See* PRINCIPLE OF ARCHIMEDES *and* LEVER PRINCIPLE.

arching *(a)* A system of arches. *(b)* The arched part of a structure. *(c)* The transmission of load in a horizontal structure of masonry or brickwork through arch action, instead of bending, due to the horizontal restraint exercised by the supports, as shown in the figure. *(d)* Transfer of stress in foundation soil from a highly to a less-highly stressed part due to arch action.

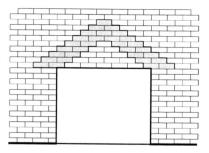

Arching (c)

architectural concrete US usage to describe exposed or non-structural concrete.

architrave *(a)* The lowest of the three parts of the ENTABLATURE of the classical orders. It is beneath the frieze and rests on the capital of the column. *(b)* Hence the moulded frame surrounding a door or window. *(c)* Hence the trim which covers the joint between an opening in a wall and the wall finish, particularly for a wooden door or window in a plastered wall.

archival storage Long-term storage of artefacts or documents, with the emphasis on keeping them secure and preventing deterioration, rather than on easy access. In computing, a means of storing information as files on a backup medium such as magnetic disk or tape, CD-ROM, DVD, etc.

archiving The process of creating and maintaining files on an ARCHIVAL STORAGE medium. The periodic process of sorting through a library or filing system, culling superseded or infrequently used material and transferring it to remote, condensed storage.

arcuated Spanning with arches as opposed to TRABEATED.

are A metric unit of area, equal to $100 \, \text{m}^2$. It is customary to use the HECTARE, which equals $10\,000 \, \text{m}^2$.

area *See* CROSS-SECTIONAL AREA *and* DUBOIS AREA.

area per person The net available area divided by the number of FULL-TIME EQUIVALENT employees.

arena *(a)* The sandy area forming the stage of an *amphitheatre*. *(b)* Any public place where contests are held.

arenaceous Sandy. Composed largely of sand, as opposed to *argillaceous*.

Argand lamp An oil lamp, invented by François Pierre Argand in the 1790s. Air passes both inside and outside of a hollow tubular wick, surrounded by a glass chimney, which is fed oil from an elevated oil reservoir.

argenite Black silver sulphide, resulting from the corrosion of silver.

argillaceous Clayey. Composed largely of clay or shale, as opposed to *arenaceous*.

argon-arc welding A form of SHIELDED-ARC WELDING in which the arc is protected by the inert gas *argon*, or a mixed gas containing argon and carbon dioxide. *See also* HELIARC WELDING.

arithmetic mean Normally taken to be the *average* of a set of values, *i.e.* their sum divided by the number of items. Occasionally also defined as the sum of their ABSOLUTE VALUES divided by the number of items, although examples of this definition are usually given by counting numbers of objects, so that all the values are positive integers anyway. *See also* GEOMETRIC MEAN, MEDIAN *and* MODE.

arm *See* LEVER ARM.

armature *(a)* In a relay, the moving part that is attracted to the electromagnet. *(b)* In a generator, the windings in which a voltage is induced. *(c)* In a motor, the rotating part or rotor.

armoured cable An insulated electric cable wrapped with a flexible steel covering.

armoured concrete An obsolete term for reinforced concrete.

armoured wood Wood covered with metal.

armour-plate glass *See* BULLET-RESISTING *and* TEMPERED GLASS.

array A table of related numbers or values.

arrester A non-linear device to limit the amplitude of voltage on a power line. The term implies that the device stops over-voltage problems (*e.g.* lightning). In actuality, the amount of voltage that can be removed by the operation of an arrester is limited by other factors in the installation.

arrestor An apparatus designed to intercept and retain silt, sand, oil, grease, sludge and other substances in a waste discharge.

arris A sharp edge formed by the meeting of two surfaces, particularly two mouldings.

arris gutter A V-shaped gutter.

arrival rate The number of passengers arriving for service at a lift system during a five-minute peak period.

arrow The graphic representation of an ACTIVITY in a CPM NETWORK. One arrow represents one activity; however, it is not a vector quantity, and not normally drawn to scale. The intersection of two arrows marks an EVENT.

Art Moderne The style popularised by the *Exposition Internationale des Arts Décoratifs et Industriels Modernes*, held in Paris in 1925. It influenced design, including architectural design, in Europe, the USA and Australia until the Second World War. The term *Art Deco* has a slightly different meaning, but is often used synonymously.

Art Nouveau An artistic style of the late nineteenth century, characterised by sinuous organic forms.

articulated detail A detail in which the joints between materials, or the salient edges, are recessed to emphasise their location, but to hide any crack.

articulated structure A structure constructed with PIN JOINTS.

articulation (acoustics) A measure of the probability of understanding a spoken message in a particular environment such as a noisy or reverberant room. *See also* ARTICULATION LOSS *and* SPEECH INTELLIGIBILITY.

articulation index A calculated prediction of ARTICULATION or SPEECH INTELLIGIBILITY.

articulation loss A measure of the probability of not understanding a spoken message in a particular environment.

artificial intelligence The endowing of machines with some of the characteristics of intelligence, such as learning, recognition and reasoning, normally associated with humans.

artificial light Light produced by electrical processes or the burning of fuel. The preferred term is *electric light* or, as appropriate, gaslight or oil-light. *See* FILAMENT LAMP, FLUORESCENT LAMP, LUMINAIRE, MAINTENANCE FACTOR *and* PSALI.

artificial seasoning Seasoning timber by some means other than NATURAL SEASONING.

artificial sky A hemisphere, usually 6–7 m (20–25 ft) in diameter, lit inside to imitate the natural sky. A model, scaled in accordance with the principles of dimensional analysis, is placed at the centre of the hemisphere, and measurement of internal lighting conditions are made with PHOTOVOLTAIC CELLS. Most artificial skies are calibrated for the overcast condition represented by the CIE STANDARD OVERCAST SKY. A simpler type of artificial sky, which can only be used to investigate windows in a wall, consists of a mirror-lined box lit from above; this creates lighting through the windows similar to that from an infinitely distant source.

artificial stone PRECAST CONCRETE made with careful attention to appearance, frequently in imitation of natural stone.

AS *Abbreviation for* Australian Standard.

asbestos A mineral occurring in fibrous form, consisting of various silicates. It is highly resistant to high temperatures, and was widely used as a fire-resisting material. The fibres are flexible enough to be woven like textiles, or used as reinforcement in cement to form building boards, or sprayed onto surfaces with a cement binder. However, it has been found that the fine fibres can be inhaled, causing a hazard to the health of the miners and manufacturers, and possibly to the occupants of buildings with free asbestos. In most countries it has been replaced by other fibres.

asbestos cement sheet Building sheet made from cement with an admixture of ASBESTOS fibres. Although highly resistant to both fire and weathering, its use has been discontinued because of the hazard associated with asbestos fibres. *See* FIBRE CEMENT *and* FIBRO.

as-built drawings Obsolete term referring to contract drawings marked up to reflect changes made during the construction process. Now better known as RECORD DRAWINGS or *record documents*.

A-scale on a sound level meter A filtering system that has characteristics approximately matching the response of the human ear at low sound levels.

ASCE American Society of Civil Engineers, Reston, Virginia.

ASCII *Abbreviation for* American Standard Code for Information Interchange. This is the standard association of a pattern of seven bits with an ALPHA-NUMERIC or control character so that components of a computer system can recognise input or output.

ASEE American Society for Engineering Education, Washington.

ashlar Squared stonework as opposed to rubble. *Coursed ashlar* is laid in regular horizontal courses. *Random ashlar* consists of rectangular blocks whose horizontal and vertical joints do not line up. *Ashlar brick* is brick which has been rough-hacked on the face to make it resemble stone.

ASHRAE American Society of Heating, Refrigerating and Air Conditioning Engineers, Atlanta.

ASHRAE scale A seven-point scale of thermal comfort used for voting in thermal comfort studies, rating the thermal condition: 3 is 'hot', 0 is 'neutral' and −3 is 'cold'. (In earlier versions the scale ran from 7 to 1.) It is said to be more objective than the BEDFORD SCALE.

ASHVE American Society of Heating and Ventilating Engineers, now ASHRAE.

ASI Australian Steel Institute, North Sydney.

ASME American Society of Mechanical Engineers, New York.

ASP *Abbreviation for* Active Server Pages. An ASP is an HTML page that includes one or more scripts (small embedded programs) that are processed on a Microsoft web server before the page is sent to the user. An ASP is similar to a *common gateway interface* (CGI) application in that both involve programs that run on the SERVER, usually tailoring a page for the user.

aspect The direction in which a building faces. *Also* the view beyond a workplace, generally to the exterior.

aspect ratio The ratio of the longer to the shorter side of a rectangle.

asphalt A black sticky mixture of hydrocarbons used for waterproofing basements and flat roofs. In the USA the term is used both for the naturally occurring product and that obtained from the distillation of petroleum. Elsewhere the artificial asphalt is usually called *bitumen*.

asphalt mastic A thick adhesive, consisting of asphalt, bitumen or pitch, and a filler, such as sand. It is used for bedding woodblock floors, bedding and pointing window frames, and for laying and repairing flat roofs.

asphalt roofing Waterproof roof laid either with bituminous felt or with mastic asphalt.

asphalt shingles Roof shingles, widely used in the USA, made of felt saturated with asphalt or tar, and surfaced with mineral granules.

assay Estimation of metal content in an ore by chemical analysis or heat treatment.

assembly language Language employing mnemonic codes instead of the binary codes used in MACHINE LANGUAGES. An assembly language for a particular machine language will generally be in one-to-one correspondence with the MACHINE LANGUAGE. The primary advantage of assembly languages over machine languages is the ease with which humans can write, read and debug programs written in them.

asset management The management of building elements, systems, equipment, fixtures and fittings from procurement, operation and maintenance to renewal.

Assman psychrometer A pair of WET-AND-DRY BULB THERMOMETERS mounted in a nickel-plated cover to shield them from radiation. To achieve uniform ventilation, the air is drawn mechanically over the thermometers with a small fan.

association matrix A matrix produced in the briefing stage of a project to define the desirability for different functional spaces to be near to, or separated from one another, and the importance of their relationships in the overall design.

ASTM American Society for Testing and Materials, Philadelphia.

astragal (a) A small semicircular moulding, often decorated with a bead. (b) A moulding covering a joint around a door or window, and for glazing bars. (c) A small metal strap for fixing a pipe to a wall. (d) A moulding, attached to one of a pair of swinging doors, against which the other door strikes.

atm *Atmosphere*, an obsolescent unit of pressure. The standard PRESSURE exerted by the weight of the air at the surface of the Earth is 101.325 kPa (14.7 psi), and this equals 1 atmosphere.

atmospheric layers The Earth's atmosphere is divided into four layers: the troposphere (nearest Earth), the stratosphere, the ionosphere and the exosphere. Atmospheric conditions change with time and latitude; the layers are thicker at the equator and thinner at the poles.

atmospheric pressure *See* PRESSURE, ATMOSPHERIC.

atomic heat The quantity of heat required to raise the temperature of one MOLE of an element through 1 K.

atomic number The number of a chemical element when arranged with the others in increasing order of ATOMIC WEIGHT, as in the PERIODIC TABLE. It is equal to the total number of positive charges in the nucleus, or the number of orbital electrons in a neutral atom of the element.

atomic weight The relative weight of an atom of an element, taking the weight of an atom of carbon as 12. The classification was originally based on hydrogen as unity; hydrogen has now an atomic weight of 1.008. *See also* ISOTOPES.

atomise To break up a liquid into very fine drops.

atrium (a) The inner hall of a Roman house, with an opening in the roof and a rectangular basin to receive the rainwater. (b) The forecourt of an early Christian basilica. (c) An enclosed courtyard or sky-lighted space in a modern multi-storey building, surrounded by arcades or balconies. (d) A space within a building that provides an open vertical link between several floors.

attenuation Diminution or weakening, particularly of sound.

Atterberg limits *See* LIQUID LIMIT *and* PLASTIC LIMIT.

attic Roof space between the top-storey ceiling and the roof.

attic fan or ventilator (a) A mechanical fan in the attic of a house, which removes hot air from the roof space in hot weather. (b) A large diameter fan usually located centrally in a house, built into the ceiling, to draw air from the rooms (thus inducing fresh air intake through vents) and push it into the attic, to force out the hot air from the attic space through a ridge vent or other ventilator openings.

attribute Information describing a property of an object. Attributes are assigned VALUES.

Au Chemical symbol for *gold* (aurum).

AUC *Ab urbe condita* (from the founding of the city), the system of dates used in ancient Rome. 0 AUC is about 753 BCE.

audible sound Acoustic oscillation of such character as to be capable of exciting the sensation of hearing. *See also* AUDIO FREQUENCY.

audience absorption The absorption of sound by audiences in an auditorium. In most auditoria it is the major contributor to the total absorption in the room. Audience absorption is specified in one of two ways: absorption per person or absorption per square metre of audience area.

audio frequency Any frequency in the range 16 Hz to 16 kHz, the conventional limits of human audition. The frequency range of 20 Hz to 20 kHz is also in common usage.

auditorium (a) Room especially designed to have satisfactory acoustics for speech, music or both. (b) In a theatre, the space assigned to the audience, as opposed to the stage. Fire regulations frequently require that the two spaces be capable of separation by means of a fire-resistant curtain.

auger *(a)* A tool for boring holes in wood. Its shaft has a helical flute which serves to remove the material from the hole after it has been cut. *(b)* A tool for boring holes in soil. The *post-hole auger* is a hand-operated tool which can be used to obtain BOREHOLE SAMPLES. Larger holes must be made with a powered *earth auger*, or by conventional excavation methods.

auralisation The technique, based on numerical simulation and using *binaural* sound recordings, which allows listeners to experience music or speech as it would sound in a room being designed, or in a virtual room.

Austen steel *See* CORTEN STEEL.

austenite An allotropic form of GAMMA IRON, which has a face-centred lattice. It is not stable in carbon steels at room temperature. However, it exists in stable form in certain alloy steels containing nickel and chromium. *See also* FERRITE.

autoclave A pressure vessel in which materials are exposed to high pressure steam. In the building industry, auto-claving is used for the rapid curing of pre-cast concrete products, sand–lime bricks, fibre cement products and hydrous calcium silicate insulation products.

autogenous healing The closing of fine cracks in concrete and mortar through chemical action. It occurs naturally if the concrete or mortar is kept damp and undisturbed.

automated speech recognition Hardware/software systems capable of translating the spoken word or conversation into another useable representation, such as text. Automated speech recognition systems are either speaker-dependent (trained to a single user's speech) or speaker-independent (capable of interpreting different speakers). An area of research in ARTIFICIAL INTELLIGENCE.

automatic control valve A valve controlling the flow of fluids in response to signals from a sensor or controller.

automatic door A power-operated door which opens automatically at the approach of a person or vehicle and closes automatically.

automatic fire alarm A FIRE DETECTOR which automatically initiates a signal notifying the existence of a fire.

automatic gain control Circuitry in sound recording and broadcasting systems which maximises the recorded/broadcast signal level automatically, whilst preventing CLIPPING.

automatic interference checking An automated process whereby a computer program checks whether two objects interfere with each other in space, *e.g.* ducts and beams.

automatic lift A lift which starts and stops in response to the pushing of a button; this is now the normal procedure.

automatic tracking A device that permits solar collectors to 'track' or to follow the sun during the day without manual adjustment. Usually for concentrating collectors.

automation Automatic handling of work during production and in transit between machines. The word was coined by the Ford Motor Company.

autoplumb An optical device which acts like a plumb bob, but without the problems of bob swing and wind effects on the line.

autotransformer A transformer used to step voltage up or down. The primary and secondary windings share common turns, and it provides no ISOLATION *(c)*.

auxiliary source A power source dedicated to providing emergency power to a critical load when the normal supply is interrupted.

auxiliary storage Storage external to a computer.

average recurrence interval (ARI) The average time between recurrences of a storm event of a certain severity at a particular location.

Avogadro's hypothesis 'Equal volumes of different gases at the same pressure and temperature contain the same number of molecules'. Named after the Italian physicist who enunciated it in 1811. *Avogadro's number* is the number of molecules contained in the MOLE of any gas; it is about 6.1×10^{23}.

avoirdupois weight From the Old French for *goods of weight*. The normal system of weights used in FPS UNITS.

A-weighting *See* SOUND PRESSURE LEVEL *and* A-SCALE ON A SOUND-LEVEL METER.

AWG *Abbreviation for* American Wire Gauge.

awning An exterior lightweight shade, either of rigid construction or canvas, providing a roof over a door or window.

awning window A push-out type window SASH, either top-hinged or mounted on FRICTION STAYS, either a single pane or multiple sashes from floor to ceiling.

axial load *See* CONCENTRIC COLUMN LOAD.

axial-flow fan A propeller fan with the blades mounted on the axis, as opposed to a CENTRIFUGAL FAN.

axiom A simple proposition of a self-evident nature, which requires no proof, and generally cannot be proved. *Also called postulate.*

axis, major and minor The greatest and the smallest diameter of an ELLIPSE.

axis, neutral *See* NEUTRAL AXIS.

axisymmetric plume A smoke plume such as occurs in an atrium, where air is entrained from all sides and along the entire height of the plume until the plume becomes submerged in the smoke layer (*see figure*).

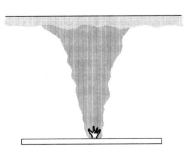

Axisymmetric plume

axonometric projection A pictorial PROJECTION which overcomes some of the limitations of the ISOMETRIC PROJECTION. The plan is drawn in true shape but rotated at an angle, usually 45°. Vertical lines are drawn to true length, projected up from the plan. (*Axonometric projection* is sometimes used to describe a projection, similar to ISOMETRIC, in which the plan axes are inclined at an angle other than 30°.)

azimuth The horizontal angle subtended by an object, such as the sun, with the standard MERIDIAN OF LONGITUDE. The vertical angle is the ALTITUDE (*see figure*).

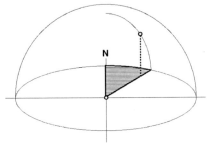

Azimuth

B

back arch Same as DISCHARGING ARCH.

back hoe A tractor-mounted shovel capable of digging below grade; it digs towards itself, and the digging mechanism rotates on a vertical axis to dump the material (*see figure*). *Also spelled* backhoe. *Also called back-acter in the UK. See figure.*

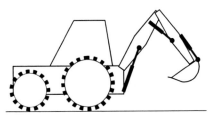

Back hoe

back pressure In plumbing, air pressure in a pipe that is above atmospheric pressure.

back prop *(a)* A strut placed at an angle to the vertical used to support timbering in deep trenches. *(b)* (verb) To replace props after stripping formwork to provide support during full curing.

back putty, bed putty Putty behind glazing to bed it into a frame.

back sawing Sawing a log into rect-angular sections so that the longer dimen-sion of the cross-section is roughly *tangential* to the growth rings (as opposed to QUARTER SAWING) (*see figure*). Back sawing provides a more interesting FIGURE on the broad face of a board, but the board is liable to cup during drying.

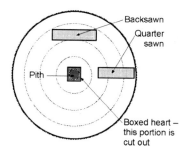

Back sawing

back siphonage The flowing back of polluted or contaminated water from a plumbing fixture into the pipe which feeds it.

backdraft A phenomenon that occurs when a fire takes place in a confined area such as a sealed aircraft fuselage and burns undetected until most of the oxygen within is consumed. The heat continues to produce flammable gases, mostly in the form of carbon monoxide. These gases are heated above their ignition temperature and when a supply of oxygen is introduced, as when normal entry points are opened, the gases could ignite with explosive force.

backfill *(a)* Crushed stone or coarse soil placed around foundation walls to provide drainage for water. *(b)* Rough masonry or brickwork built behind a face or between two faces. *(c)* Brickwork in the spaces between studs of timber frames; also called NOGGING. *(d)* Filling over the EXTRADOS of an arch.

backflow *(a)* Flow in the direction contrary to the normal intended flow. *(b)* The unintended flow of water from a potentially polluted source into a *potable water* supply. *See also* BACK SIPHONAGE.

background In computing: *(a)* used in multi-task processing systems for low-priority tasks carried out when the computer is not executing high-priority jobs (the *foreground*); *(b)* the plane on the computer screen used for the placing of windows, etc.

background noise The AMBIENT SOUND (*e.g.* from air conditioning, traffic, wind or birds or a combination of these) in the absence of the sound of interest or under investigation (*e.g.* speech, music or aircraft).

backhand welding Welding with the blowpipe directed towards the completed weld.

backing brick Low-cost brick used behind face brick or masonry.

backing coat A coat other than the finishing coat, particularly of plaster.

backlighting Lighting of an object from the rear.

backset The distance from the edge of a door to the centre of the keyhole or knob.

backup A copy of data kept as a means of security.

backup material A material placed at the back of a curtain wall, particularly for fire protection.

BACNET A software protocol developed by the American Society of Heating, Ventilating and Airconditioning Engineers (ASHRAE) to enable conforming digital elements of a building monitoring and control system to communicate with each other and with a central microprocessor.

baffle A reflecting surface used to reduce the distribution of sound in an acoustical system.

bag of cement The bag of cement is frequently used as the unit for batching the aggregates and the water. In the USA the standard bag weighs 94 lb (*i.e.* 24 bags to the LONG TON), while in most SI countries it is 40 or 50 kg.

bagasse Waste fibrous product from the crushing of sugar cane. It is used as raw material for both HARDBOARD and PARTICLE BOARD. Also a source of BIOMASS for combustion for renewable energy production.

bain marie A fitting used in cafeterias and the like, consisting of a bath of heated water into which open containers of food are placed to keep them hot while awaiting serving.

baked enamel *See* VITREOUS ENAMEL.

baked finish A durable and tough paint or varnish finish obtained by baking, generally at a temperature above 65 °C.

bakelite One of the earliest synthetic resins, named after its inventor L. H. Baekeland. It is produced by the condensation of phenol with FORMALDEHYDE. Many other plastics of different compositions are now marketed by the Bakelite Company.

balanced cuts Cuts of tile at the edge of a floor or surface that will not take full-sized tiles; the cuts on opposite sides of such an area shall be the same size.

balanced design In reinforced concrete, a design which produces simultaneous overstressing of the steel in tension and the concrete in compression, *i.e.* neither material reaches its limit before the other. It occurs only when a *balanced percentage of reinforcement* is used. A beam which has more steel is *over-reinforced*, and one which has less steel is *under-reinforced*.

balanced load An alternating current power system consisting of more than two current-carrying conductors, in which these conductors all carry an equal current.

balanced sash A vertically sliding sash in a SASH WINDOW.

balance-point temperature A characteristic of the building: the outdoor temperature at which the heat loss of a building is the same as the sum of internal and solar heat gains, so there is no heating or cooling requirement.

balcony A platform projecting either from an inside or an outside wall of a building.

balcony beam A beam that supports a balcony. It usually has a horizontal projection, and is therefore subject to combined bending and torsion. A BOW GIRDER is a curved balcony beam.

balcony spill plume A smoke plume that flows under and around a balcony before rising, giving the impression of spilling from the balcony, from an inverted perspective (*see figure*). Characteristics of the resulting balcony spill plume depend on characteristics of the fire, width of the spill plume and height of the ceiling above the fire. In addition, the path of horizontal travel from the plume centreline to the balcony edge is significant.

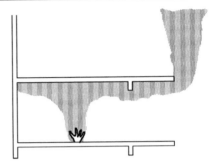

Balcony spill plume

balk A large squared timber, usually of softwood. Also spelled *baulk.*

ball breaker A heavy steel ball used for demolition. *Also called wrecking ball.*

ball catch A type of door fastening in which a spring-controlled metal ball in the door engages a hole in the door frame.

ball cock or ball valve An automatic *float valve* for controlling the level of water in a cistern or storage tank (*see figure*). An empty ball of copper or plastic floats up as the level of water in the cistern rises, and shuts the valve when a predetermined level is reached. (*Also written ballcock.*)

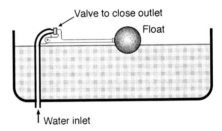

Ball cock

ball mill A mill in which material is finely ground by rotation in a steel drum with steel balls or pebbles. It is used for grinding cement.

ball test A test for determining the WORKABILITY of freshly mixed concrete. A cylindrical metal weight with a hemispherical bottom is dropped from a standard height, and the depth of penetration is measured. *See also* COMPACTING FACTOR TEST *and* SLUMP TEST.

ball valve *Same as* BALL COCK.

ballast *(a)* An electrical inductance device used to control DISCHARGE LAMPS. *(b)* Heavy material to prevent uplift of part of a scaffolding or structure.

ballast factor The ratio of lamp lumen output on a particular ballast as compared to that lamp's rated lumen output on a reference ballast under standard test conditions (free, unmoving air at $25\,^\circ$C).

balloon frame Timber frame in which the studs run in one piece to the roof plate. The floor joists are nailed to the studs. The development of the balloon frame in the USA in the 1830s led to a great reduction in the labour content of timber houses, by replacing the complex timber joints (such as *mortice and tenon, tongue and fork, dovetailing*) with simple nailed joints. It became possible only after suitable nails were mass produced. The timber frame has become progressively lighter through efficient interconnection of members.

ball-peen hammer The engineer's hammer, used for metalwork and stone masonry. It has a hemispherical peen (or small end) and a flat face.

balsa wood A very soft wood (although technically a hardwood) weighing only $110\,\text{kg/m}^3$ ($7\,\text{lb/ft}^3$). It is widely used for models, and it can also be used as insulation in coreboard.

baluster Wooden post (in the past often elaborately carved or turned) holding up the handrail of a staircase, balcony, etc. *Also called banister.* The entire assembly of balusters is a *balustrade.*

bamboo A giant tropical grass with a hollow jointed stem, which is relatively strong and stiff. It is widely used in southern Asia for SCAFFOLDS, and to a lesser extent as a building material for houses in place of timber. A major problem is that joints cannot be formed by nailing.

band gap The difference in energy between the state of the highest valence band and the lowest conduction band of a SEMICONDUCTOR.

band saw A saw consisting of an endless belt, one edge being cut to form the teeth, as opposed to a CIRCULAR SAW.

band shell A curved sounding board placed over a bandstand.

bandpass filter A device which transmits energy at all frequencies within a defined band/range of frequencies and greatly attenuates the energy at all other frequencies. *See also* CENTRE FREQUENCY.

bandwidth *(a)* In acoustics, the range of FREQUENCIES which can pass through a system. *See also* CENTRE FREQUENCY *and* OCTAVE-BAND. *(b)* In communications, a measure of the capacity of a transmission line or channel. Large bandwidth means a line is capable of transferring large amounts of information simultaneously.

banister *(a) Same as* BALUSTER. *(b)* A handrail for a staircase.

bank guarantee The security offered by financial institutions to contract signatories supporting contractual obligations.

bank of lifts A number of GROUPS of lift cars located together physically. Each group serves a particular ZONE of the building.

banker A bench on which stonemasons or bricklayers prepare material.

banquette A long upholstered bench seat.

bar An obsolescent unit of pressure, equal to 100 000 Pa (approximately atmospheric pressure).

bar chair A rigid device, usually of steel or plastic, which supports the reinforcement in its proper position and prevents its displacement both before and during concreting.

bar chart A chart that shows a magnitude by the length of a bar *(see figure)*. See GANTT CHART *and* HISTOGRAM.

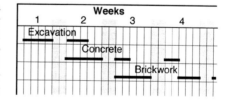

Bar chart

bar joist An open web steel joist formed with a bent bar as the web.

bar mat Steel reinforcing bars assembled as a mat by welding or by ties. The bars are generally placed in two layers at right angles to one another.

bar schedule A listing of the reinforcement required for a concrete structure or structural member. It gives the size, length, and shape of each bar type, together with the dimensions of any bar bends needed, and the number of each type required.

bar support *Same as* BAR CHAIR.

bar, deformed *See* DEFORMED BAR.

bar-code A type of code based on bands of lines of differing widths to be read by a BAR-CODE SCANNER to provide information to a computer.

bar-code scanner An optical device for reading data coded as BAR-CODES.

bare conductor An electrical conductor without insulation or other covering.

bare lamp An electric lamp, typically a GLS incandescent or tubular fluorescent, without shielding or other light control device. *See also* BATTEN *(d).*

barge board A sloping board covering the projecting portion of the timbers of a gable roof. In the nineteenth century it was often elaborately decorated. *Also called verge board.*

barite Barium sulphate (BaSO$_4$). It is used as aggregate for high density concrete, *e.g.* for concrete used in radiation shields for atomic reactors. Also spelled *baryte.*

barium A heavy alkaline earth metal. Its specific gravity is 3.59.

barium plaster A gypsum plaster containing barium salts, used to plaster X-ray rooms.

barium sulphate *See* BARITE.

bark pocket A patch of bark, partially or wholly enclosed in a wooden board. It is a source of weakness.

barometer An instrument used for the measurement of *atmospheric* pressure. The *mercury barometer* consists of a vertical tube, about 800 mm long, closed at the end, which is filled with mercury and placed in a pool of mercury. The atmospheric pressure on the pool of mercury balances the mercury column in the tube, and a vacuum forms above it. The *aneroid barometer* consists of a hermetically sealed metal box, exhausted of air so that the ends of the box approach or recede from one another with change in air pressure. The movement is magnified by levers.

barrel The normal measure of capacity used in the oil industry. It equals 42 US gallons, or 0.159 m^3 (159 litres).

barrel bolt A round bolt for locking a door or a window. It slides in a cylindrical barrel, usually formed from sheet metal.

barrel of a pipe The portion of a SPIGOT and SOCKET-jointed pipe away from the joint. These pipes are normally bedded on the barrel to avoid the stresses that would be set up if all the weight of the backfill were taken on the (protruding) sockets. *See figure* under SOCKET.

barrel tile Clay roofing tile with a single curvature, similar to a MISSION TILE.

barrel vault A semi-cylindrical or partly cylindrical roof structure of constant cross-section. It was widely used in masonry construction, particularly in Romanesque architecture. A much thinner form is today built in reinforced or prestressed concrete as a *shell roof.*

barrier-free design Design of buildings to facilitate full access to all parts of the building for persons confined to wheelchairs, or with other ambulatory or sensory disabilities.

baryte *Same as* BARITE.

bas relief Sculpture carved in low relief, *i.e.* the figures project slightly from the face of the background.

basal metabolic rate The continuous and unconscious heat production associated with the life-supporting processes of the human body.

basalt A fine-grained, dark coloured IGNEOUS ROCK of basic composition.

base *(a)* A substance which neutralises acids, producing salt and water. It has a PH VALUE greater than 7 and turns red LITMUS blue. *(b)* The lowest part of a monument, column, wall or pier. *(c) See* LAMP BASE.

base building services Building services systems in an investment building, owned and operated by the building owner for treatment of common areas used by tenants.

base coat *(a)* The first coat of paint applied to a surface, *i.e.* the PRIMER COAT. *(b)* The first coat of PLASTER.

base line *(a)* In PERSPECTIVE PROJECTIONS, the intersection between the ground plane and the picture plane. *(b)* In construction work, a definitely established line from which other measurements for laying out a building are taken.

base load Electrical energy usage that is more or less continuous, as opposed to PEAK POWER. The generating capacity that supplies base load operates continuously, and is therefore more attractive to the supplier.

base metal In a welded or soldered joint, the metal to be joined, as distinct from the *filler metal*, which is deposited during the welding or soldering process.

base moulding A wooden moulding used to trim the upper edge of an interior baseboard or SKIRTING.

base year The year used as the basis for relating past and future calculations in life-cycle costing and net present value analysis.

baseboard *Same as* SKIRTING.

baseboard heater *Same as* SKIRTING HEATER.

baseplate A plate distributing the load at the base of a column. It also accommodates the HOLDING-DOWN BOLTS.

basket weave bond A checkerboard pattern composed of squares of bricks laid alternately at right angles to one another (*see figure*).

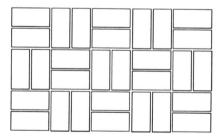

Basket weave bond

bass ratio The ratio of the reverberation time at low frequencies (125 and 250 Hz) to that at mid-frequencies (500 and 1000 Hz).

bat *(a)* A piece of brick used for closing a gap. One end is whole, and the other is cut or broken. A HALF BAT is obtained by halving a brick across its length. *(b)* Short for BATTEN. *(c)* Alternative spelling for batt in BATT INSULATION.

batch box A container used to measure by volume the components of a batch of concrete, mortar or plaster. *See also* MIX PROPORTIONS.

batch mixer A machine which mixes one batch of concrete or mortar at a time, as opposed to a *continuous mixer*.

batch of concrete Quantity mixed at one time.

batch processing A method of processing data by computers as a single unit rather than as they arise, as opposed to REAL TIME PROCESSING.

batch splitting The division of a batch into two or more sub-batches.

batswing burner For gaslight, also called *fishtail burner*. An early gas lamp which spreads the flame in a single plane. It was superseded by the *Argand gas lamp*, developed from the ARGAND oil LAMP, and eventually by the WELSBACH MANTLE.

batt insulation Flexible insulation, usually made from glass, rock or slag fibres, and packaged into rectangular *batts*. These are frequently placed between the studs or joists of a timber frame. The batts generally have a VAPOUR BARRIER on one side.

batten *(a)* A narrow strip of wood used either as a support for light construction, or as a cover over a joint. *(b)* A wooden board fastened at an angle across several parallel boards to hold them together; *also called* a *cross batten*. *(c)* An incandescent lampholder attached directly to the surface. *(d)* A simple LUMINAIRE containing one or more tubular fluorescent lamps.

batten seam A seam in metal roofing formed around a batten. *See also* STANDING SEAM, where there is an illustration.

batter Inclination from the vertical or horizontal.

batter board US term for a horizontal board set near ground level, used for setting out footings and/or walls, called a *profile* in the UK and Australia, and sometimes a *hurdle*.

batter piles PILES driven at an angle to the vertical to provide lateral support to the structure.

battery A combination of BATTERY CELLS connected to increase the voltage (a *series connection*) or current (a *parallel connection*). The term is commonly used, incorrectly, to refer to a single cell.

battery cell *(also called cell)* A device that converts chemical energy contained in its active materials directly into electrical energy by means of a electrochemical reaction. Most batteries used in building services are *rechargeable*.

battery disconnect switch Master switch that disconnects a battery reservoir from a UPS. Provides personnel protection when batteries or UPS require service.

battery reservoir A combination of cells or batteries used to power a UPS system's inverter when it is in the emergency mode.

baud rate The measure of signalling speed in telecommunications. The number of discrete signal events per second. Named after J. M. E. Baudot.

Bauhaus A design school established in Weimar, Germany in 1919, very influential on aesthetics and teaching methods.

baulk *Same as* BALK.

bauxite Hydrous aluminium oxide, named after Les Baux in France. It is the principal raw material for the manufacture of aluminium metal. It is also used in the manufacture of HIGH-ALUMINA CEMENT. Also spelled *beauxite*.

bay window Same as BOW WINDOW, although a bay window is usually polygonal rather than curved on plan.

Bayesian problem Bayesian formulation is a statistical approach which provides an integrated framework under which *(a)* predictive analysis can be carried out in a routine manner, *(b)* the inference results (albeit numerical) can be based on finite sample sizes, and *(c)* knowledge of available information, *e.g.* expert's judgement about the failure pattern of a component, can be incorporated in the current analysis in a standard way. In the context of analysing competing risks data, Bayesian methods may also provide a means for introducing dependence among the component lifetimes.

bayonet cap A LAMP BASE used on electric lamps to provide positive anchoring into the lampholder: sometimes it is also used to ensure correct polarity or geometrical position. A common base, particularly in the UK and Australia, for general lighting service lamps: it has two projecting studs that fit into grooves in the lampholder. *See also* EDISON CAP.

BC *See* BCE.

BCA British Cement Association, Crowthorne, Berks (formerly Cement and Concrete Association).

BCD *Abbreviation for* Binary-Coded Decimal.

BCE Before the Common Era *(same as* before the Christian era, BC). BCE is becoming more usual in secular writing.

BCR *Abbreviation for* Benefit/Cost Ratio.

BCS British Computer Society, Swindon, Wilts.

bead *See* GLAZING BEAD.

beam A structural member which supports loads across a horizontal opening by flexure (*see* NAVIER'S THEOREM). JOIST *and* GIRDER are synonyms for beam.

beam ceiling A ceiling formed by the underside of the floor, showing the beams supporting it. The term is also used for a false ceiling imitating exposed floor beams.

beam column A beam which transmits a direct axial load, as well as bending. The term is also used for a column subject to bending.

beam compass An instrument for drawing large circles. It consists of a long horizontal beam and two movable heads.

beam component That component of flux received directly (or by specular reflection or transmission) from a point source (such as the sun or small lamp). It is a DIRECT COMPONENT.

beam irradiance (or irradiation) Parallel 'rays' of radiation arriving from a source (*e.g.* the sun) directly to the surface considered, previously referred to as *direct radiation*.

beam test A test of a specimen in bending. If not further defined, it means a bending test of an unreinforced concrete beam to determine the MODULUS OF RUPTURE of the concrete.

beam-and-slab floor A floor system, particularly in reinforced concrete, whose floor slab is supported by beams, as opposed to a FLAT PLATE and FLAT SLAB.

bearer A horizontal structural member, generally of timber, which supports a load. Generally refers to a larger beam which supports a number of smaller JOISTS.

bearing *(a)* Support for a rotating shaft. *(b)* Support for a beam or column.

bearing capacity The load which a PILE or a foundation can safely support.

bearing pile A PILE which carries a vertical load, as compared with a SHEET PILE which resists earth pressure. The load may be carried on a load-bearing layer, such as rock *(end-bearing pile)* or by friction between the surface of the pile and the surrounding soil *(friction pile)*.

bearing plate A plate placed under a heavily loaded support of a beam, column, frame, etc. to distribute the load over a wider area. Called a *baseplate* when used under a column.

bearing pressure The load on a bearing, BEARING PLATE or FOUNDATION, divided by its area.

bearing span The length of a beam between its bearings.

bearing wall or load-bearing wall A wall or partition which supports the portion of the building above it in addition to its own weight, as opposed to a CURTAIN WALL or partition which supports only its own weight.

Beaufort scale A scale for wind speed, which ranges from 0 for complete calm to 12 for a cyclone. The wind speed (in km/h) equals $3B^{1.5}$, where B is the Beaufort number of the wind.

beauxite *Same as* BAUXITE.

bed A strip of mortar on which bricks or (ridge, hip, verge and valley) tiles are laid.

bedding plane The surface between two beds or strata in a stratified SEDIMENTARY ROCK.

Bedford scale A seven-point scale used for voting in comfort studies, expressing thermal satisfaction, where 3 is 'much too warm', 0 is 'comfortable' and −3 is 'much too cool'. Whilst the ASHRAE SCALE is said to express the thermal sensation at the discriminatory level, this is expressing comfort at the affective level.

bedrock Solid rock underlying superficial formations.

beeswax The natural secretion of bees, from which the honeycomb is formed. It is soluble in turpentine and used in WAX polishes and stains.

Beggs' deformeter The original device for indirect model analysis, developed by G. E. Beggs at Princeton University in 1922. It applies vertical, horizontal or rotational deformation at one end of a scale model of the structure, and the corresponding thrust, shear or bending moment along the structure is then deduced from its deflected shape by the RECIPROCAL THEOREM.

bel A scale unit used in the comparison of powers, named after A. G. Bell, the inventor of the telephone. The practical unit is the DECIBEL = 0.1 bel.

Belfast truss A wooden BOWSTRING GIRDER for spans up to 15 m (50 ft).

belfry A tower in which a bell is hung.

Belgian truss *Same as* FINK TRUSS.

belite *See* DICALCIUM SILICATE.

bell curve *See* FREQUENCY DISTRIBUTION CURVE.

bell push A button which rings a bell when pushed.

bell transformer A small transformer which changes the mains voltage to that used by a bell or chime, usually 12 V.

bell-and-spigot joint *Same as* SPIGOT-and-socket joint.

bellcast An outward tilt at the bottom edge of a boarded or shingled wall. It helps to shed water clear of the (usually masonry) wall below, but its use is mainly decorative.

belt sander A powered SANDER in which a continuous belt of abrasive material is driven over rollers at both ends across a face plate.

belvedere A building, upper storey or turret, especially built because it commands a fine view.

BEMS *Abbreviation for* computer-based Building Energy Monitoring System.

bench photometer A rail with a reference light source and an accurate scale used to calibrate photometers.

benchmark A permanent reference mark, fixed to a building or to the ground, whose height above a standard DATUM LEVEL has been accurately determined by a survey.

benchmarking *(a)* The process of identifying optimum performance characteristics. *(b)* Performing a task to measure the performance of systems. In computing, it is usually standardised so that the efficiency of different SOFTWARE and/or HARDWARE can be evaluated.

bend A turn in a pipe whose radius of curvature is larger than that of an ELBOW. *See figure under* PIPE FITTINGS (water and gas).

bending formula *See* NAVIER'S THEOREM.

bending moment (M) The moment at any section of a beam of all the forces that act on the beam on one side of that section *(see figure)*. If the equilibrium at any section is considered, the bending moment resisted by the beam must balance the loads acting on it. There are two opposite sign conventions. The one normally employed in architectural text books and in building codes states that a bending moment is positive when the beam is bent concave or downwards *(sagging)* and negative when it is bent convex or upwards *(hogging)*. Thus the bending moment in a simply supported beam is positive, and that in a cantilever is negative. *See figure under* NEGATIVE BENDING MOMENT.

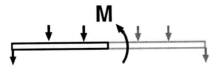

Bending moment

bending moment diagram Diagram showing the variation along the span of a member of the moment that is tending to bend that member. It indicates whether the bending moment is *positive* or *negative* and where the maximum bending moment occurs.

bending schedule *See* BAR SCHEDULE.

beneficial occupancy A point in time when the owner of a project can begin to make beneficial use of the facility, although there may still be work to be completed.

bent A two-dimensional frame which is capable of supporting horizontal as well as vertical loads.

bentonite A clay composed principally of MONTMORILLONITE. Its expansion and contraction on wetting and drying are exceptionally high.

benzene A highly flammable hydrocarbon of the aromatic series (C_6H_6), obtained from the distillation of coal tar. It is used as a solvent and a paint remover.

benzine A highly flammable mixture of hydrocarbons obtained from the fractional distillation of petroleum. Apart from its use as a motor fuel, it is employed as a solvent in quick-drying finishes.

Berlin blue *Same as* PRUSSIAN BLUE.

berm An embankment of earth, either built against the wall of a building (in EARTH-INTEGRATED CONSTRUCTION), or to surround a fuel tank or the like, to contain possible spillage.

Bernoulli's theorem 'Along any one streamline in a moving liquid, the total energy per unit mass is constant.' It consists of the pressure energy, the kinetic energy and the potential energy:

$$\frac{P}{\rho} + \frac{1}{2}v^2 + z = \text{constant}$$

where p is the pressure, ρ is the density, v the velocity and z the head of the liquid.

Berry strain gauge A demountable strain gauge. It consists of a long bar with one fixed and one movable point, which operates a DIAL GAUGE through a lever.

bespoke Manufacture of building components to the requirements of a specific building, rather than for a standard range. This increases the cost of manufacture, but it may reduce the cost of construction. The term is used in the UK more frequently than in the USA or Australia.

bespoke building A term coined by P. A. Stone to contrast industrialised or 'off-the-peg' building with traditional, tailor-made building.

Bessemer process A method, developed by H. Bessemer in 1856, of producing steel. Air was blown through molten pig iron contained in a refractory-lined, pear-shaped cylindrical vessel, open at the upper end for the escape of gases, called the *Bessemer converter.*

best practice Management practice that delivers optimum performance.

beta brass A copper–zinc alloy whose zinc content is between 46 and 50 per cent.

beta particle An electron. The *beta radiation* emitted by the atomic nuclei of radioactive substances during their spontaneous disintegration consists of a stream of electrons.

beta testing Testing a nearly-finished version of a piece of software, with the goal of finding BUGS missed by the developers. Usually beta testing is carried out by people outside the developer's organisation.

béton The French word for concrete; the same word is used in German and Russian.

béton translucide GLASS–CONCRETE CONSTRUCTION with clear glass inserts.

bevel A junction between two surfaces which is not a right angle (*see figure*). A CHAMFER is made by bevelling a square edge symmetrically.

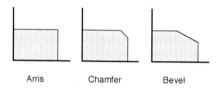

   Arris   Chamfer   Bevel

Bevel

bevel square An L-shaped tool used by carpenters for setting out, with one adjustable blade which can be set to any angle.

bevelled siding, clapboard US terms for WEATHERBOARD.

bevelled washer A washer made from a tapered piece of steel plate, so that it is thinner on one edge than on the other. It was originally made for steel sections with tapered flanges.

BFRL Building and Fire Research Laboratory, a testing laboratory in the National Institute of Standards and Technology (NIST), USA.

bhp *Abbreviation for* BRAKE HORSEPOWER.

bid Term used in the USA for tender (hence bidding = tendering).

bid bond (tender bond) A written form of security for the purpose of guaranteeing that the bidder will accept the contract, if the bid is successful.

bidet A low basin-like plumbing fixture on which the user sits. It is intended especially for bathing the genital/anal region.

BIFSA Building Industries Federation South Africa.

bill of materials A list of information about the parts of an object including such ATTRIBUTES as identification, quantity, material, size, weight and cost.

bill of quantities A list of numbered items, which describe the work to be done on a building contract. Each item shows the quantity of work involved. When the contract is sent out to tender with a bill of quantities, the contractor is expected to submit a priced bill. Payments to the contractor are based on these prices and the measured work actually done, which usually varies at least in part from the work originally envisaged. Bills of quantities are normally drawn up by a QUANTITY SURVEYOR. They are not used in the USA.

billet of steel An intermediate product in the hot-working of steel. It has been rolled or forged down from the ingot, and will be further worked into sections or forgings. A large billet is known as a *bloom.*

billion Formerly in Europe, 1×10^{12} *i.e.* a million million. In the USA, and generally worldwide, 1×10^9, *i.e.* a thousand million.

bimetallic corrosion *See* ELECTRO-CHEMICAL CORROSION.

bimetallic strip A strip fused together from two metals with widely differing coefficients of thermal expansion. It consequently deflects with a change in temperature. It is used as a control element in THERMOSTATS, and in FIRE DETECTORS.

binary alloy An alloy containing two principal elements.

binary arithmetic An arithmetic system based on the two digits 0 and 1. It is generally used by electronic computers, because the digits correspond to the two possible conditions of an electrical circuit (go or no go). The binary digits, or BITS, are converted by the computer to decimal arithmetic, so that it can be operated by the conventional decimal system.

Binary system	Decimal system	
0	0	
1	1	
10	2	
11	3	
100	4	
101	5	etc.

See also BOOLEAN ALGEBRA.

binary digit A digit in BINARY ARITH-METIC, *i.e.* either 0 or 1. It is commonly abbreviated to BIT.

binary image A DIGITAL IMAGE composed of PIXELs with a single BIT value of 0 (dark) or 1 (bright).

binaural recording Binaural recordings are made using a manikin head, or with microphones located close to the ear canals on a live head so that the sound can be experienced as modified by the head and PINNAE. This type of recording gives a more realistic reproduction of sound fields when played through headphones than the usual stereophonic recording techniques.

binder *(a)* An adhesive or cementing material. *(b)* A soil consisting mainly of fine particles for binding a non-cohesive soil. *(c)* A masonry unit used to bind an inner and an outer wall. *(d)* A structural member, particularly of timber, which binds together components of a structure.

binding wire US term for TIE WIRE.

binomial function Any function containing two, and only two, parameters, of which one is generally variable.

biochemical oxygen demand (BOD) The measure of the consumption of oxygen by biodegradable matter in an effluent over a specified period of time.

biocide A substance used in a water treatment programme intended to eradicate microbiological organisms that may constitute a risk to health, *e.g. Legionella pneumophila.*

bioclimatic chart A graphical method of depicting the human comfort zone, as developed by Olgyay (1953). It shows the interaction of four environmental variables (DRY-BULB TEMPERATURE, RELATIVE HUMIDITY, air velocity and thermal radiation) for a person engaged in a specific activity and wearing a specified amount of clothing; with relative humidity on the abscissa and dry-bulb temperature on the ordinate. The comfort zone is an aerofoil-shaped area at the centre of the chart, for still air and no radiation, extended upwards for increasing air movement and downwards for increasing thermal radiation.

biodegradable Capable of being reduced to substances harmless to the environ-ment, by natural biochemical processes such as oxidation and the action of bacteria, insects, etc.

biofuel A fuel of biological origin, such as BIOGAS or methane. Its use contributes to the sustainability of natural resources, but it may require modification of the engine in which it is used, and it may cause an unpleasant smell.

biogas A gas produced by the anaerobic digestion of organic materials, notably sewage sludge. It can be used as a BIOFUEL.

biomass Organic material of a non-fossil origin (living or recently dead plant and animal tissue) including plants, animal wastes and portions of municipal wastes. When converted to energy by combustion or other means, it constitutes a renewable fuel.

biparting door A two-leaved sliding door that meets at the centre of an opening.

birdseye Dimpling of the tangential surface of some hardwoods, notably maple, which forms small circular features which are decorative.

birdsmouth A notch cut on the lower face of a sloping piece of material in order to join a horizontal piece.

BIS Bureau of Indian Standards, New Delhi. Formerly ISI.

biscuit Tiles, earthenware products, etc. in the intermediate stage of manufacture after the first firing, but before glazing.

biscuit brick A thin piece of brick, used to disguise the edge of a concrete slab which bears on part of the thickness of a brick wall. *Also called brick slip.* Its use is generally avoided because it can be dislodged.

bit *(a)* An interchangeable cutting tool used in a CARPENTER'S BRACE, in a rock drill, etc. *(b)* The tip of a soldering iron, which is heated and tinned. *(c)* An abbreviation for BINARY DIGIT, *i.e.* the smallest unit of information recognised by a DIGITAL COMPUTER.

bit string A sequence of related BITs.

bitmap A mapping between each PIXEL on a screen and a set of BITs in the memory.

bit-mapped graphics (raster graphics) The method of storing graphics objects (or images) by associating one or more BITS of data with each PIXEL in the object's area.

bitplanes The number of BITS dedicated to storing information about each pixel of a graphics object or scene. Sometimes referred to as the colour depth of the storage scheme. *See also* DIGITAL IMAGES.

bitumen A black sticky mixture of hydrocarbons used for waterproofing basements and flat roofs, and for damp-proof courses. It is obtained from natural deposits (*asphalt*) and from the distillation of petroleum.

bituminous felt Waterproof felt soaked in bitumen used in BUILT-UP ROOFING.

bituminous paint A thick black coating material containing mainly BITUMEN, used for dampproofing and for waterproofing, particularly on roofs.

black body The designation of a theoretical surface that absorbs all the radiation falling on it, irrespective of frequency; so called by analogy to the absorption of all light, making a surface appear black. Such a surface is said to be *non-selective*. Its nearest practical approximation is the inside of a hollow sphere with a matt black surface at a uniform temperature, viewed through a small hole.

black bolt A hot-formed bolt for making site connections in steel structures. Because of imperfections in the surface, the holes in the pieces to be connected must be made a little larger than the bolt diameter, and perfect contact between the bolt and the sides of the holes is not possible; consequently the permissible loads are lower than for HIGH-TENSILE BOLTS or BRIGHT BOLTS.

black lead *Same as* GRAPHITE.

black light Invisible ultraviolet radiation within the range of wavelengths that excite FLUORESCENT PAINTS and dyes, so that they become visible.

black mortar Mortar with the addition of ash, either because a black colour is required for pointing, or to reduce cost.

black-body radiation The quality and quantity of radiation emitted by an ideal BLACK BODY. It conforms to the STEFAN–BOLTZMANN LAW.

black-body radiator *See* FULL RADIATOR.

black-body temperature The tempera-ture of a body whose emissivity is unity, *i.e.* an ideal BLACK BODY.

blackout A total loss of commercial power.

blanc fixe A white pigment, consisting of BARITE.

blank door A false door, finished only on one side. *Also called* a *blind door*.

blank wall A wall without openings.

blank window A walled-up window.

blanket insulation THERMAL INSULATION with a flexible lightweight blanket of MINERAL WOOL or a similar material.

blast furnace A tall, cylindrical, refractory-lined furnace used for the production of iron from iron ore.

blast-furnace slag A by-product of steel manufacture which is sometimes used as a substitute for Portland cement. It consists mainly of the silicates and alumino-silicates of calcium, which are formed in the blast furnace in molten form simultaneously with the metallic iron. Blast-furnace slag is blended with Portland cement clinker to form PORTLAND BLAST-FURNACE SLAG CEMENT. It is also used for topping on built-up roofing, as lightweight aggregate, and for making MINERAL WOOL.

bleaching The removal of colour from a surface by chemical or photochemical means.

bleeder valve A small valve used to drain fluid from a pipe or container, such as a radiator.

bleeding (a) Accumulation of water and cement on the top of concrete due to settlement of the heavier particles. Bleeding may be caused by too high a water content, by overworking of the concrete near the surface, by excessive traffic on the wet concrete, or by improper finishing of the surface. The result is the formation of LAITANCE. (b) Exudation of gum, resin or sap from the surface of timber.

blended cement A blend of PORTLAND CEMENT and another material, such as POZZOLANA, BLAST-FURNACE SLAG or HYDRATED LIME.

blind door *Same as* BLANK DOOR.

blind nailing *Same as* SECRET NAILING.

blind rivet A RIVET for use where access is only possible from one side. A mandrel is drawn through the hollow rivet shank, snapping off after spreading its end against the blind side of the materials to be joined. Originally developed for the aircraft industry. *Also called pop rivet* or *cherry rivet. See also* EXPLOSIVE RIVET.

blind wall *Same as* BLANK WALL.

blind window *Same as* BLANK WINDOW.

blinding glare GLARE so intense that, for an appreciable length of time after it has been removed, the visual system remains impaired. *See also* DISABILITY GLARE.

blistering An enclosed pocket of air between plies of roofing felt, or between layers of paint and substrate.

bloated clay Expanded clay, used as LIGHTWEIGHT AGGREGATE.

block *(a)* A device with one or more pulleys for rope or chain to increase mechanical advantage (usually called *block and tackle*). *(b)* A large quarried stone for further working. *(c)* A solid piece of timber or other material. *See also* BUILDING BLOCK.

block house A LOG CABIN constructed of squared timbers.

block insulation A slab of insulation which is rigid or semi-rigid.

blockboard A board built up from glued strips of timber typically 25 mm wide and surfaced with veneer.

blocking The process of arranging areas (blocks) horizontally to maximise the space occupancy in accordance with the required functional adjacencies, within a given physical envelope.

blockwork Walls built of concrete blocks (*see* BUILDING BLOCK).

blondel (*also spelled blandel*) An obsolete unit of LUMINANCE. 1 blondel = 1 apostilb = $1/\pi$ candela per square metre = 0.318 cd/m^2.

bloom *(a)* A large BILLET. *(b)* An efflorescence or coating (which can be removed by rubbing or brushing) on a masonry wall, a painted or varnished surface, etc.

blow holes Holes in the surface of concrete caused by imperfect compaction.

blowlamp (blowtorch in USA) A lamp with a strong flame fuelled by kerosene, petrol or propane gas used for melting solder and lead and for paint removal. *Blowtorch* is occasionally used for an oxy-acetylene torch, which produces much higher temperatures.

blue brick A high-strength brick whose blue colour results from firing in a kiln with a flame that has a low oxygen content.

blue metal Broken stone used as a COARSE AGGREGATE for concrete, tarmacadam, etc., crushed from any hard igneous or sedimentary rock of a bluish colour, *e.g.* dolerite.

blue sky *See* CLEAR SKY.

blueberry Small blisters or bubbles in the flood coat of a gravel-surfaced roofing membrane.

blueprint *(a)* A contact print on ferro-prussiate paper made from a drawing on transparent material; it can be printed in daylight, and developed in water. At one time this was the most common method for copying drawings. *(b)* Hence, a master plan for a project, irrespective of the form in which it is presented.

bluestone A natural stone of dark blue colour; however, the term is also used for dark-coloured stones ranging from dark green to grey. The geological type of the rock varies from place to place, and the term 'bluestone' has been used for stones as diverse as basalt, dolerite, slate and sandstone.

bluing Increasing the apparent whiteness of a white pigment by adding a small amount of blue.

blushing White or milky appearance in high gloss paint caused by moisture or chemical incompatability.

BM *Abbreviation for* BENCHMARK *and* BENDING MOMENT.

BMCS *Abbreviation for* computer-based Building Monitoring and Control System.

BMS *Abbreviation for* computer-based Building Monitoring System.

BMT *Abbreviation for* Base Metal Thickness. In galvanised or coated metal products, the thickness of the base metal before application of any coating. *See also* TCT.

BMU *Abbreviation for* Building Maintenance Unit. A mechanical roof-mounted device for suspending a cradle over the side of a tall building, providing access for window cleaning and maintenance.

board and batten Vertical timber cladding of wide boards with battens covering the joints.

board foot An obsolete measure for timber, 1 in. thick by 12 in. square.

board insulation *Same as* INSULATING BOARD.

board-marked The finish to in-situ and precast concrete made by sawn timber boards used as formwork.

bob Same as PLUMB BOB.

BOD *Abbreviation for* BIOCHEMICAL OXYGEN DEMAND.

body coat The final coat of paint.

body-centred cubic lattice A crystal structure which has an atom at each corner of a cube, and one in the centre. It may be imitated by packing spheres in horizontal layers.

body-tinted glass HEAT-ABSORBING GLASS containing small amounts of metallic or other colouring additives, as opposed to REFLECTIVE GLASS, which is surface-coated.

boiled oil Linseed oil used in quick-drying paint. It is heated for a short period to about 260°C (500°F), *not* boiled, and a small quantity of drier (*e.g.* manganese dioxide or LITHARGE) is added.

boiler A device for raising the temperature of a fluid, usually water, by transfer of heat from the combustion of a fossil fuel or a derivative such as electricity.

boiling water unit A small appliance, connected to the water supply, designed to maintain its contents of water close to boiling point. The water is used to make a number of cups of tea or coffee in quick succession, and it is automatically reheated.

bole The main stem of a tree.

bollard A short post installed in a public street or footpath, to help define the boundary of various uses and prevent vehicular access to pedestrian or otherwise sensitive areas. It may incorporate a low-powered LUMINAIRE, and may be removable by use of a key.

bolster (*a*) A short horizontal member capping a column to provide a greater bearing area or to reduce beam span. (*b*) A wide bricklayer's chisel.

bolt (*a*) A sliding pin or rod for locking an opening, such as a door or a window. (*b*) A pin or rod, SCREW-THREADED in whole or in part, used to connect two pieces. It usually has a nut at one end and a fixed enlarged head. *See also* ALLEN HEAD, BLACK BOLT, BRIGHT BOLT, COACH BOLT *and* HIGH-TENSILE BOLT.

Boltzmann constant A constant, equal to 1.3805×10^{-23} J/K, used in statistical formulae relating to the behaviour of gases. *See also* STEFAN–BOLTZMANN LAW, which refers to thermal radiation.

BOM *Abbreviation for* BILL OF MATERIALS.

bond (*a*) The system in which bricks, blocks and stones are laid in overlapping courses in a wall in such a way that vertical joints in any one course are not immediately above the vertical joints in an adjacent course. The basic distinction is between ENGLISH BOND, DOUBLE FLEMISH BOND and STRETCHER BOND. *See also* ENGLISH CROSS BOND, SINGLE FLEMISH BOND, DIAGONAL FLEMISH BOND *and* COMMON BOND. Most bonds require a QUEEN CLOSER to line up the joints at the corners. (*b*) The adhesion or grip exercised by concrete or mortar on surfaces to which it is required to adhere. The most important bond is between concrete and reinforcing bars. This is largely produced by the SHRINKAGE of the concrete, which creates a normal pressure between the concrete and the steel, and this produces a frictional force resisting pull-out of the steel. (*c*) The strength and durability of the connection of pieces by an ADHESIVE layer. (*d*) Adherence of the plaster to the wall, and between the various coats of plaster. (*e*) Attraction between atoms which causes them to aggregate into larger units. (*f*) A sum of money held as security against the performance of some contractual duty.

bond beam A beam formed from reinforced and grouted channel-shaped blocks usually on top of a concrete block wall.

bond breaker A material used to prevent adhesion between surfaces such as layers of concrete and joint sealants.

bond stone A long stone, used as a HEADER, running through the thickness of the wall to give additional transverse bond.

bond timber Horizontal timbers once used as a bond for a brick wall. The battens were sometimes secured to them. Bond timbers were liable to rot unless suitably protected.

bonded tendon A prestressing TENDON which is bonded to the concrete. In pre-tensioned members this is achieved directly by casting the concrete around them. In post-tensioned members the annular spaces around the tendons are grouted after stressing.

bonding (electrical) Deliberate connection of two or more points to reduce any difference of potential (voltage) between them.

bonding conductor In a LIGHTNING PROTECTION SYSTEM, a conductor intended to provide a connection between the lightning protection system and other metal parts and/or the structure.

book matching Alternating wood VENEERS face up and face down as cut, or laying side by side to get a mirror image.

Boolean algebra An algebra of logic, where a proposition may be either true or false, and therefore suited to BINARY ARITHMETIC.

Boolean operation In solid geometry, the process of adding (*union*), subtracting (*difference*) or finding the overlapping volume (*intersection*) of two solid objects.

boom The member of a crane from which the load is suspended providing positioning of the load which can both SLEW and LUFF. *See also* JIB.

booster fan A fan used to step up the static pressure in an air distribution system in order to serve a remote area, used only intermittently (*e.g. in* a conference room).

booster pump An auxiliary pump used to maintain the water pressure of a domestic water or a sprinkler system, if need be, or to increase it to meet a demand.

booting *Short for* BOOTSTRAPPING.

bootstrapping The loading of an operating system into a computer's working memory.

borax Sodium metaborate.

bore The internal diameter (ID) of a hole, pipe, etc.

bored pile A pile formed by pouring concrete, usually containing some reinforcement, into a hole bored in the ground, as opposed to a PRECAST PILE driven into the ground with a pile driver.

borehole (or core) samples Samples obtained by boring or drilling for the purpose of determining the nature of the foundation material. In the case of *clay*, it is necessary to obtain *undisturbed samples*, since the properties of clay are greatly affected by working. PENETRATION TESTS may be carried out in addition.

borrow pit A pit from which soil is taken for use as fill elsewhere.

borrowed light A window in an internal wall that allows the admission of daylight from the adjacent space.

bottle trap (or waste) A form of TRAP for waste pipes from a sink or basin. It has a central tube for the flow down and an annular space for the flow up and out sideways to the drain; the 100–150 mm long outer tube (the bottle) can be screwed out for cleaning.

bottom chord The bottom horizontal member of a truss.

bottom plate The bottom, horizontal structural member of a stud-framed wall. *Also called* a *sill plate* in North America.

bottom terminal lift landing The lowest landing in a building, served by a lift, where passengers are able to enter or leave the car.

boulder A naturally rounded rock larger than GRAVEL.

boundary conditions for structural problems The known conditions of displacement, slope, force or moment at the edges of a structural member. The stresses in shell structures cannot normally be determined, unless the restraints at their edges are known.

boundary layer The layer of a fluid, such as air, adjacent to its boundary with a solid, for example a building. Inside this layer the velocity of the fluid falls to zero at the boundary.

boundary layer wind tunnel In studying the effect of wind *around* buildings it is necessary to model the buildings in the path of the wind. The large buildings need to be represented with some accuracy; but the effect of small buildings can be included in a roughening of the surface which models the boundary layer.

boundary microphone A microphone designed to pick up sound when placed on a reflective surface such as a table top whilst maintaining a flat frequency response and avoiding COMB FILTERing effects. Also known as a 'pressure zone microphone'.

boundary representation (B-rep) A solid geometry representation describing an object in terms of its surface boundaries: vertices, edges and faces.

boundary trap A TRAP in sewerage piping from a building, located near the property boundary to prevent sewer gases from the public sewer system travelling into the individual property.

Bourdon gauge A pressure gauge consisting of a tube bent into an arc, which tends to straighten out under internal pressure. It actuates a pointer which moves over a scale.

Boussinecq pressure bulb A bulb formed by the ISOSTATIC LINES in a semi-infinite elastic solid carrying a single concentrated load. The analysis, primarily used for determining the stresses in the soil beneath a heavy foundation, was published by the French mathematician J. Boussinecq in 1885.

bow Curvature of a piece of timber, in the plane of the shorter side of the cross-section (*see figure*).

Bow

bow girder A girder curved horizontally in plan, *i.e.* an arch turned through a right angle. It serves as a SPANDREL on a curved facade, to support *balconies*, etc. (*see figure*). A bow girder is subject to combined bending and torsion.

Bow girder

bow window A curved projecting window, usually on the ground floor. An ORIEL WINDOW usually projects from an

upper storey. A *bay window* is similar but polygonal on plan, rather than curved.

Bow's notation Notation for the RECIPROCAL DIAGRAM, proposed by Robert Bow in 1873. It numbers the spaces in and around a truss, instead of the joints.

bowstring girder (or truss) A tied arch, which can be used like a girder, since the horizontal reactions are internally absorbed by a tie (the bowstring). The curved top chord is stiffened by light diagonal members. A *Belfast truss* is a wooden bowstring girder for spans up to 15 m (50 ft).

box beam *Same as* BOX GIRDER.

box frame *(a)* A rigid frame formed by load-bearing walls and floor slabs (*see figure*). It is suitable for buildings which are permanently divided into small repetitive units. *(b)* The frame of a DOUBLE-HUNG WINDOW.

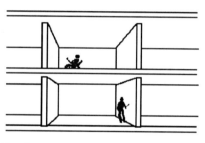

Box frame

box girder A hollow beam whose cross-section is shaped like a box. It uses material where it is most highly stressed both by bending moments and by twisting moments. Consequently it is used for large spans and for locations where eccentric loading, etc. causes torsion.

box gutter A gutter of rectangular cross-section, built behind a parapet or in a roof valley (*see figure*).

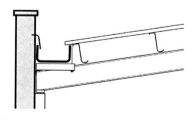

Box gutter

boxed heart A piece of squaresawn timber, cut so that the pith, or central part, is cut out, *e.g.* by *back sawing*. This is done in most Australian and some other hardwoods in which the HEART is unsound. *See figure under* BACK SAWING.

Boyle's law 'The volume V occupied by a given mass of any gas at constant temperature varies, within moderate ranges of pressure, inversely as the pressure P to which it is subjected, *i.e.* PV = constant'. It was proposed by the seventeenth-century English natural philosopher, Robert Boyle. *See also* CHARLES' LAW.

bps *Abbreviation for* Bits Per Second.

BRAB Building Research Advisory Board, Washington, DC.

braccia *See* CUBIT.

brace *See* CARPENTER'S BRACE.

bracing The ties and struts used for supporting and strengthening a frame, *e.g.* to resist horizontal loads.

bracket (a) A *synonym for* KNEEBRACE. (b) An overhanging member projecting from a wall to support a weight. (c) A projecting gas or electrical wall fitting. (d) A piece of timber attached to the carrying member of a staircase supporting the TREAD.

brackish water Water containing between 100 and 10 000 parts per million of salt. *See also* BRINE.

brad A small, thin nail, usually 25 mm or less in length, with a fine head.

bradawl A small awl pushed into timber to make a starting hole for nails or screws.

bradder A small NAIL GUN for driving machine nails equivalent to BRADS.

brake horsepower The useful mechanical power supplied by an engine. It can be measured with an absorption dynamometer or a friction brake applied to the flywheel of the engine.

brake shoes The moving parts of a brake, *lined* with a material with a high coefficient of friction material, so that a vehicle can be brought to rest or a lift can be held in a stationary position, when applied to the brake drum.

branch circuit A division of a load circuit with current limited by a fuse or circuit breaker.

brass A copper–zinc alloy. *See* ALPHA BRASS *and* BETA BRASS.

Brazilian test *Same as* SPLITTING TENSILE TEST.

brazing A process for joining two pieces of metal by means of *brazing solder.* Copper–zinc (brass), copper–zinc–silver, and nickel–silver alloys are used as brazing solders, and their melting point is generally above 500 °C, but well below the melting point of the metal to be brazed. This is above the temperature used for SOLDERING, but below that used for WELDING.

BRE Building Research Establishment, Garston, England, and East Kilbride, Scotland.

break-before-make Operational sequence of a switch or relay where the existing connection is opened prior to making the new connection.

breakdown (a) A term used for the separation of an EMULSION into its constituents. (b) The failure of an electrical insulating material, thereby allowing the flow of current.

breakdown repairs Reactionary maintenance work carried out in response to a failure or wilful damage.

break-in noise The transfer of noise, from the surrounding environment, through the walls of a duct, into the duct.

breaking ground First excavation indicating the start of construction.

breaking load The ULTIMATE LOAD of a structural member that fails by FRACTURE.

break-out noise The transfer of noise in a duct, through the duct walls, into the surrounding environment.

breast beam *Same as* BREASTSUMMER.

breastsummer Originally a long and heavy timber beam (or *summer*) carrying the frontage of a building (or *breast*). It is a very large lintel supporting a masonry or brick wall. *Also called bressumer.* The term is still used for steel or concrete girders which provide an opening in a load-bearing wall, *e.g.* over a shop window.

breathing zone Occupied space in a building where human breathing normally occurs, usually considered as being between 100 and 1800 mm above the floor and 600 mm from walls. *Also called occupied zone.*

breccia A stone CONGLOMERATE composed of angular fragments.

breeze block Building block made of coke breeze. Largely superseded by CELLULAR CONCRETE or LIGHTWEIGHT AGGREGATE concrete blocks.

B-rep *Abbreviation for* BOUNDARY REPRESENTATION.

bressumer or brestsummer *Same as* BREASTSUMMER.

BRI *Abbreviation for* Building Related Illness; diagnosable symptoms brought on by the internal environment that endure after the sufferer has left the building; as opposed to SICK BUILDING SYNDROME.

brick A building block, generally small enough to be lifted comfortably with one hand, and useable in a BONDED wall. The biblical brick was made of ADOBE reinforced with straw; but burnt bricks have been found which appear to be even older. The modern CLAY brick is hard-burnt, and sometimes glazed. Bricks are also made of CONCRETE and of CALCIUM SILICATE. *See also* EXTRUDED BRICK, FACE BRICK, BOND, HEADER, PRESTRESSED BRICK, STRETCHER *and* SUCTION RATE.

brick construction Construction in load-bearing brick, as opposed to BRICK VENEER or BRICK NOGGING.

brick earth A sandy clay suitable for making bricks.

brick elevator A powered continuous belt or chain for the inclined movement of materials, *e.g.* bricks. *Also called tile elevator*, etc.

brick facing *Same as* BRICK VENEER.

brick nogging Brickwork infilling between the studs of a wooden frame or a framed partition. *Also called brick-and-stud work.*

brick on edge A STRETCHER on its edge. This makes more economical use of bricks, but produces a thinner and weaker wall. *Also called rowlock.*

brick veneer A veneer of bricks (stretchers) built outside a timber or steel frame, used mainly in houses, but also in commercial construction; the frame supports the load. A brick veneer building looks like a brick building, but is essentially a framed structure. *Also called brick facing.*

brick-and-stud work *See* BRICK NOGGING.

brickwork movement joint A joint between two adjoining brick walls, or between a brick wall and an adjacent structure, to permit temperature and moisture movement without impairing structural integrity.

bridge (computing) A hardware device used for connecting two computer networks of the same topology and the same media access control (MAC) protocol. *See also* ROUTER.

bridging *See* COLD BRIDGING *and* SOLID BRIDGING.

brief The detailed instructions, given by a client to a design professional to describe the client's requirements for a project. In practice, the brief is usually developed during a series of discussions between the two parties.

bright bolt A steel bolt which has been turned to fit exactly into the holes of the steel pieces to be joined, as opposed to a BLACK BOLT.

brightness The visual sensation that results from the luminance of an object, surface or light source. *See* APPARENT BRIGHTNESS.

brilliance In acoustics, a bright, clear, ringing sound, rich in harmonics. It comes from the relative prominence of the treble and the slowness of its decay.

brimstone Same as SULPHUR.

brine Water containing more than 100 000 parts per million of salt. *See also* BRACKISH WATER.

Brinell hardness test A test for hardness, named after its originator, the nineteenth-century Swedish engineer J. A. Brinell, using a hard 10 mm ball. The *Brinell hardness number* is the ratio of the load to the surface area of the indentation.

brise soleil A sun break or sunshading device, particularly of the type used by Le Corbusier.

British system of measurement The traditional units based on the foot and the pound, as opposed to the METRIC SYSTEM.

British thermal unit (BTU) The amount of heat required to raise the temperature of 1 lb of water through 1 °F. In SI UNITS the JOULE is used. 1 BTU = 1055J.

brittle coating A technique used in experimental stress analysis, coating a model of the structure with a brittle lacquer (*Stresscoat*), which cracks at a definite strain. The direction and magnitude of the principal tensile stresses are thereby determined. Brittle lacquers can also be used to analyse residual stresses due to heat treatment.

brittle failure Sudden failure which is typical of concrete, brick and other CERAMICS. It also occurs in metals, particularly in high carbon steels and in cast iron. Low temperature increases the tendency to brittle failure, as does rapid application of the load (shock). *See also* CRUSHING FAILURE *and* FRACTURE.

brittle lacquer *See* BRITTLE COATING.

brittle–ductile range The range of temperature over which a material (particularly steel) may change from brittle to ductile, or vice versa. Above that range it is entirely ductile, and below it is entirely brittle.

brittleness Lacking ductility. A brittle material ruptures with little or no PLASTIC DEFORMATION. Brittle failure occurs by the rupture of interatomic bonds, and this occurs more readily in tension than in shear (or diagonal shear resulting from compression). Hence brittle materials have a much lower strength in tension than in compression. However, since plastic failure does not occur, their compressive strength is often high.

broach The profile of the opening in a lock into which the key fits. *Also called keyway.*

broadband transmission Transmission carrying multiple SIGNALS on a single transmission line or channel. The BANDWIDTH of the channel is divided into separate subchannels or frequency bands each capable of carrying a signal. Contrast with BASEBAND TRANSMISSION.

broadcast The sending of information to several receivers at once.

broken joints Joints arranged, as in a BOND, so that they do not fall in a straight line and weaken the structure.

broken pediment A PEDIMENT with a gap at its apex.

broken white Off-white, generally with a touch of cream.

bronze An alloy of copper and tin, in varying proportions. Small quantities of zinc, nickel, phosphorus, aluminium and lead are sometimes added.

brownout *(a)* A low voltage condition lasting longer than a few cycles. Brownouts differ from SAGS only in duration. *(b)* An intentional reduction of voltage by a utility in response to a power demand in excess of its generation capability. Nominal reductions are 3, 5, or 8 per cent.

brownstone A reddish-brown or brown sandstone, used extensively in the eastern USA during the middle and late nineteenth century. Hence a building faced with brownstone.

browser (browser client) Software residing on a CLIENT machine attached to the WORLD WIDE WEB. The browser is responsible for interpreting for display on the local machine information transferred in HTTP (HyperText Transfer Protocol) format from a web server machine over the network.

BRS Building Research Station, Garston, England. Now incorporated in the Building Research Establishment (BRE).

BSI British Standards Institution, London.

BThU or BTU *See* BRITISH THERMAL UNIT.

bubble diagram A diagram of the schematic layout of spaces in a design represented by circles of areas to scale, linked by lines indicating the desired adjacencies. Manipulations, such as the sum of the distances between the circles multiplied by numerical 'strength' of the desired association, produce a value indicating the efficiency of the layout as specified by an ASSOCIATION MATRIX. This method allows various layouts to be compared.

bubble model A demonstration model devised in the 1930s by the English physicist W. L. Bragg to illustrate crystal structure. Uniform soap bubbles, about 1.5 mm in diameter, are blown on to a water surface. These are then disturbed to form grain boundaries and DISLOCATIONS IN [the] CRYSTALS.

Buckingham's theorem *See* PI-THEOREM.

buckle To load a structural member, notably a column or strut, until it bends suddenly sideways (*see figure*). The material is not necessarily damaged by buckling, but it loses its *elastic stability*. *See* EULER FORMULA, LATERAL BUCKLING, LOCAL BUCKLING *and* TORSION BUCKLING.

Buckle

budgetary control The process of comparing actual expenditure with budgeted amounts and the subsequent adjustment of expenditure in order to keep within total budgeted amounts.

buffer (computing) A temporary, dynamic storage to allow incoming or outgoing data to be exchanged with the computer's memory and with a remote device at different rates.

buffer (mechanical) A device comprising a means of braking using fluids or springs, capable of absorbing the kinetic energy of motion of a descending lift CAR or COUNTERWEIGHT, when either has passed a normal limit of travel, by providing a resilient stop. An *oil buffer* dissipates energy; a *spring buffer* accumulates energy.

bug An error or malfunction in a computer program or system. *See* DEBUGGING.

bugle-head screw A screw with the head smoothly curved to the shank, designed to embed itself into the paper covering of plasterboard without tearing it.

buildability Building costs are greatly reduced if the entire building process of a complex design is considered before construction commences. This is facilitated by making use of the CRITICAL PATH METHOD, working out both the critical time path and the critical resources path.

building block A masonry unit, usually larger than a brick. It is often hollow, and may be made of concrete, burnt clay or terra cotta.

building board Board used for ceilings and for the interior lining of walls generally less than 15 mm (½ in.) thick and more than 0.6 m (2 ft) wide. The term is not precisely defined and includes boards made from a wide range of materials.

building code (US)/regulation (Australia) /by-law (UK) A set of laws governing the design and construction of buildings, likely to include references to other regulatory or advisory documents such as Codes of Practice and national or international standards.

building efficiency A ratio of the rentable or net lettable area to the gross area, expressed as a percentage.

building envelope A generic term for all outer elements of a building (walls, roof, floor) that separate the inside from the outside.

building environmental assessment method A method for assessing building environment, such as the GBTool.

building model A representation of a building. In a computer this takes the form of a computer building model incorporating both graphic and non-graphic information.

building paper Heavy paper, sometimes reinforced with fibres and waterproofed with bitumen. It is intended to allow some vapour permeability, unlike a VAPOUR BARRIER.

building service entry The point where commercial power enters the building.

building services A collective term for the services and utilities required to maintain the interior environment and functioning of a building.

building services engineering The professional discipline dealing with heating, ventilation and air-conditioning, including acoustics and sound control, fire safety engineering, plumbing and draining, lifts and escalators and electrical installation.

built-in (or fixed-ended) beam or slab A condition of support which prevents the ends from rotating in the plane of bending. It does not imply longitudinal constraint. Built-in beams and slabs are STATICALLY INDETERMINATE.

built-up roofing Flat roof built with multiple layers of ROOFING FELT, as distinct from a roof built with a single layer. *Also called composition roofing* or *roll roofing.*

bulb The glass outer envelope component of a LAMP.

bulb angle A steel or aluminium angle section enlarged at one end, *i.e.* a section intermediate between an angle and a channel (*see figure*).

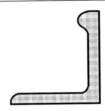

Bulb angle

bulb of pressure *See* BOUSSINECQ PRESSURE BULB.

bulb tee A strengthened steel or aluminium T-section, used particularly as a sub-purlin. *See also* BULB ANGLE.

bulk density The weight of a porous material per unit volume, including the voids. *See also* SPECIFIC GRAVITY *and* APPARENT VOLUME.

bulk insulation Thermal insulation that relies on its resistance to conduction heat flow, usually a fibrous or porous material, such as glass wool or polystyrene foam slabs.

bulk modulus of elasticity The ratio of the triaxial (tensile or compressive) stress, equal in all directions, to the corresponding change in volume. The most common example is that of hydrostatic pressure and the corresponding volumetric strain.

bulk replacement (of lamps) The replacement of ELECTRIC LAMPS as part of a planned maintenance programme before they fail, compared with SPOT REPLACEMENT.

bulk volume of a porous substance The total volume, including closed and open pores. *See also* APPARENT VOLUME *and* TRUE VOLUME.

bulking Increase in the volume of sand when it is in a damp condition, as compared with its volume when dry. It must be allowed for when measuring sand by volume, instead of by weight. Bulking increases appreciably with increasing moisture content, and then declines again. Completely inundated sand occupies practically the same volume as dry sand.

bull float A tool for finishing newly placed concrete.

bull header A brick made with one long corner, or arris, rounded. It is used for rounded sills and corners.

bullet-resisting glass An armoured glass consisting of a laminated assembly of four or more sheets of glass alternating with sheets of transparent plastic resin, bonded under pressure and heat.

bullnose The rounding of an ARRIS to a radius so as to occupy a considerable proportion of the available face (*see figure*). *See also* PENCIL ROUND.

Bullnose

bull's eye *(a)* A small circular or oval opening or window. *(b)* The centre of a disc of CROWN GLASS.

bundled reinforcement A group of up to four parallel reinforcing bars in contact with each other, enclosed in stirrups or ties, and used as a reinforcing element in a concrete structural member.

bundled tube structure A structural system which consists of several TUBE STRUCTURES bundled together, *e.g.* in the Sears Tower in Chicago.

Bunsen burner A type of burner, widely used in laboratories, in which the amount of air to be mixed with gas can be adjusted before burning. The idea is attributed to R. W. Bunsen, a nineteenth-century German chemistry professor. The concept was used in gas lighting.

buoyancy The reduction in the weight of a body immersed in a liquid, particularly in water, due to the upward pressure exerted by the liquid. If the body floats in the liquid, its weight is equal to the weight of the liquid displaced. This is known as the PRINCIPLE OF ARCHIMEDES, after the Greek philosopher who discovered it in Sicily in the third century BCE.

buoyant foundation A reinforced concrete raft foundation so designed that the weight of the load carried by it (generally its own weight and that of the building) equals the weight of the soil and water displaced. It is particularly useful in fine-grained soils whose WATER TABLE is near the surface.

burette A cylindrical graduated glass tube fitted with a ground glass stop cock, used for the measurement and delivery of small volumes of liquid in a laboratory.

burl A FIGURE in wood caused by an adjacent knot, enlarged rootstock or other large excrescence. It is decorative on veneers, but may be a source of weakness in boards. *See also* CROTCHWOOD.

burlap A coarse fabric of hemp or jute. It is frequently used to cover concrete during curing to reduce evaporation. *Also called hessian.*

burnt sienna SIENNA which has been CALCINEd, and consequently turned brown.

burnt umber UMBER which has been CALCINEd, and consequently turned reddish-brown or red.

burr The rough or sharp edge left on metal by a drill, saw or other cutting tool.

bus bar A bare, *i.e.* uninsulated, electrical conductor, from which circuits can be tapped. *Also spelled busbar.*

bush (plumbing) An adaptor to connect two pipes of different diameters. One end has a female thread or bore to suit the smaller pipe diameter, and the other a male thread or surface of the larger diameter. Because of the different diameters, the two portions overlap. *See figure under* PIPE FITTINGS (water and gas).

bush hammered A finish to in-situ and precast concrete made by hammering with a knurled-headed tool to remove the mortar surface and expose the aggregate.

bushel A unit of capacity, used particularly for grain. It equals 32 US quarts (= 0.0352 m³), or 32 British quarts (= 0.0364 m³).

butment *Same as* ABUTMENT.

butt joint A joint between two pieces of material which are in line *butting* against each other (*see figure*), with or without cover plates, as opposed to a *lap joint. See also* FISHPLATES.

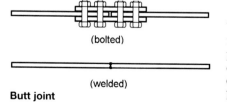
(bolted)

(welded)

Butt joint

butt strap A cover plate used in a BUTT JOINT.

butterfly roof A roof consisting of two sloping surfaces, connected at the *lower* edges.

button punching Punch-like crimping at regular intervals of adjoining metal roofing sheets to lock them together.

buttress A projecting structure built against a wall to resist a THRUST (*see figure*) (a) for retaining wall, (b) for Gothic church). A *flying buttress* is suspended in the air for the same purpose.

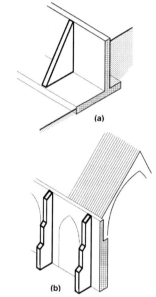
Buttress

byte A set of BITs operating as a unit, usually eight bits, corresponding to a single character.

Byzantine arch *Same as* HORSESHOE ARCH.

C

°C Degree CELSIUS. °C is used for readings on a thermometer, but K (Kelvin) is preferred for temperature differences.

c *Abbreviation for centi*, one hundredth.

C *(a)* Chemical symbol for *carbon. (b)* A high level programming language.

C&CAA Cement and Concrete Association of Australia (previously CACA), Sydney.

c/s *Abbreviation for* cycles per second. Since the introduction of SI units, this is called *Hertz*, abbreviated Hz.

C++ An extension of the C programming language.

ca About (Latin *circa*), generally used to indicate approximate dates of historical events or buildings.

Ca Chemical symbol for *calcium.*

CAAD *Abbreviation for* Computer-Aided Architectural Design.

CAADRIA Computer-Aided Architecture Design Research In Asia (Association).

CAB plastic *Abbreviation for* CELLULOSE ACETATE BUTYRATE plastic.

cabin hook A hooked rod or bar that engages in an eye on a door or window to hold it open.

cabinet scraper A flat steel blade for drawing across planed timber to prepare for sandpapering.

cable *(a)* A structural member that is flexible and can therefore resist only tension, and not compression or flexure. *See also* ARCH. *(b)* One or more electrical conductors enclosed in an insulating sheath.

cable duct Rigid duct to enclose insulated electric conductors, with removable covers, used mainly above ground. Concrete or plastic pipes are generally used for this purpose below ground.

cable lay *See* LAY.

cable management The physical arrangement and management of reticulation required for electrical, data and telecommunications cables.

cable stays Straight cables connected directly to a roof or floor structure without suspenders, and anchored to a mast. They transfer the load from the structure to the top of the mast, whence it is transmitted to the ground, and thus allow substantial increases in the clear span of the structure (*see figure*).

Cable stay

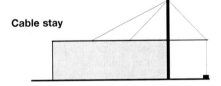

cable structure *See* SUSPENSION ROOF.

cable tray An open rectangular tray, in which cables travel through a building.

cable, electric The conductor through which an electric appliance or lamp receives its power.

cable, prestressing *See* TENDON.

cable, suspension *See* SUSPENSION CABLE.

CACA Cement and Concrete Association. For Britain see BCA, for Australia see C&CAA, for United States see PCA.

CAD *Abbreviation for (a)* Computer-Aided Design; *(b)* Computer-Aided Drafting.

CAD/CAM *Abbreviation for* Computer-Aided Design / Computer-Aided Manufacturing.

CADD *Abbreviation for* Computer-Aided Drafting and Design.

cadmium plating Plating with metallic cadmium, applied to steel bolts used in conjunction with aluminium to prevent ELECTROCHEMICAL CORROSION.

cadmium yellow Cadmium sulphide, a permanent pigment ranging in colour from pale yellow to orange.

CAE *Abbreviation for* Computer-Aided Engineering.

CAFM *Abbreviation for* Computer-Aided Facility Management.

caisson A watertight chamber used for construction in waterlogged ground, or below water, usually sealed and pressurised, as opposed to a COFFERDAM.

caisson pile A cast-in-place concrete pile, made by driving a tube, excavating it, and filling the hole with concrete.

calcareous Containing calcium, or more commonly calcium carbonate ($CaCO_3$).

calcimine *Same as* KALSOMINE.

calcine An old-fashioned term, dating from the days of alchemy and early chemistry, for altering the composition of a substance by heating it below the temperature of fusion.

calcite The crystalline form of calcium carbonate, $CaCO_3$. It is a common constituent of limestone, marble and some igneous rocks.

calcium A silvery-white metal. Its chemical symbol is Ca, its atomic number is 20, its atomic weight is 40.08, its specific gravity is 1.55, its valency is 2, and its melting point is 851 °C. Its oxide is QUICKLIME.

calcium carbonate One of the abundant minerals in the Earth's crust ($CaCO_3$). It is the material of which limestone, chalk and marble are composed, and a principal raw material for cement and mortar.

calcium chloride An ACCELERATOR used for concrete.

calcium hydroxide Slaked lime ($Ca(OH)_2$).

calcium oxide Quicklime (CaO).

calcium sulphate Anhydrite ($CaSO_4$).

calcium sulphate hemihydrate *Same as* PLASTER OF PARIS.

calcium-aluminate cement *Same as* HIGH-ALUMINA CEMENT.

calcium-silicate brick A light-coloured brick made principally from sand and lime. It is usually hardened by AUTO-CLAVING. *Also called a sand-lime brick.*

caldarium The hot room in an Ancient Roman bath.

calibre Originally the diameter of a cannon-ball or bullet. Hence the bore of the gun, or of any pipe.

California bearing ratio (CBR) A standard test for determining the bearing capacity of a foundation. It is defined as the ratio of the force per unit area required to penetrate the foundation soil with a circular piston (area $3\,in^2 = 1935\,mm^2$) at a rate of $0.05\,in$. ($1.27\,mm$) per minute, to the force required for penetration of a standard material (usually crushed rock). The measurement is commonly made after 2 mins penetration.

calipers US spelling of CALLIPERS.

calking US spelling of CAULKING.

callipers A pair of steel legs, joined by a pivot. They may be *external* (curved convex for measuring the outside diameter) or *internal* (curved concave for measuring the inside diameter of a tube). *Also spelled calipers.*

callow brick An underburnt brick.

calorie (cal) The quantity of heat required to raise 1 g of water through 1 K. The term is, however, commonly used (incorrectly) without prefix for the large or kilocalorie, which equals 1000 cal. In SI UNITS the calorie has been replaced by the JOULE; $1\,cal = 4.187\,J$. For conversion to FPS units, 1 kilocalorie = 3.968 BTU.

calorific value The amount of heat liberated by the complete burning of a unit mass of a fuel.

calorifier A closed tank in which water is heated by submerged hot pipes.

calorimeter *(a)* An instrument for measuring the heat exchange during a chemical reaction. It is particularly used for measuring the heat produced by the combustion of a material. *(b)* A vessel containing the liquid used in CALORIMETRY.

calorimetry The measurement of thermal constants, such as specific heat, latent heat or calorific value. This is generally done by observing the rise of temperature which a heat exchange causes in a liquid (commonly water) contained in a calorimeter.

cam A mechanism for converting circular into regular or irregular linear motion. It consists of a wheel, of a carefully designed non-circular form, attached to a shaft. For example, cams are used to open and close the valves in an internal-combustion engine.

CAM *Abbreviation for* Computer-Aided Manufacturing. *See* CAD/CAM.

camber A slight upward curvature of a structure to compensate for its anticipated deflection.

cambium The cellular layer of wood tissue between the bark and the sapwood of a tree.

cameo A striated precious stone (such as ONYX) or a shell carved in relief to exhibit the various colours in the layers. Hence, any modelled relief exhibiting different colours.

cames Lead strips of H-section, used to assemble small pieces of glass, often diamond-shaped, into a LEADED LIGHT.

campanile A bell tower, particularly one which is tall and detached from the building.

Canada balsam A yellowish liquid of pine-like odour, soluble in ether, chloroform and benzene. It is used for lacquers and varnishes, and also as an adhesive for lenses, because its refractive index is almost identical with that of most optical glasses.

candela (cd) The SI unit of luminous intensity, or luminous flux per unit solid angle (formerly called the candle). It is a fundamental unit defined in terms of the luminance of a standard radiator.

candle power An obsolete unit of luminous intensity whose place has been taken by the CANDELA.

canopy A roof-like covering, usually projecting, over an entrance or window, or along the side of a wall.

cant brick A special shaped brick formed with one splayed short edge (*see figure*).

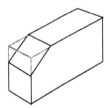

Cant brick

cantilever A projecting beam, truss or slab supported only at one end.

cantilever bridge A bridge continuous over several spans which is made STATICALLY DETERMINATE by the insertion of hinges, using the GERBER BEAM principle. It is particularly useful where bridges have to be supported on poor foundations which may settle, since the bridge can take up small foundation movements without statically indeterminate stresses.

cantilever retaining wall A wall retaining soil by cantilever action, as distinct from a retaining wall which spans between COUNTERFORTS or BUTTRESSES as a continuous slab. The wall normally consists of three cantilevers (*see figure*): the wall which resists the horizontal EARTH PRESSURE, the HEEL and the TOE, both of which resist vertical earth pressures.

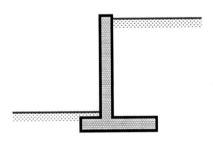

Cantilever retaining wall

cantilever steps *See* GEOMETRICAL STAIR.

cantilever, propped *See* PROPPED CANTILEVER.

canvas A strong, unbleached, closely woven cloth of flax, hemp or cotton.

cap *(a)* The topmost member or part of a structure or a building element. *(b)* A fitting used to close the end of a tube or pipe. *(c)* A PILE CAP. *(d)* Synonym for a *detonator*. *(e)* An alternative term for a LAMP BASE.

cap cables *Same as* CAPPING CABLES.

capacitance In electricity, the property of a system that allows it to store an electric charge. It is measured in FARADS.

capacitance strain gauge A strain gauge that utilises the principle that the capacitance of a parallel plate condenser is changed by varying the separation of the plates.

capacitive reactance The behaviour of alternating current as it interacts with CAPACITANCE encountered in a circuit.

capacitor A device consisting of two conducting surfaces separated by an insulating material or DIELECTRIC. A capacitor stores electrical energy, blocks the flow of direct current, and permits the flow of alternating current to a degree dependent essentially on the capacitance and frequency.

capacity reduction factor A factor used in the ULTIMATE STRENGTH DESIGN of structures to provide a margin of safety against collapse or serious structural damage. It allows primarily for deficiencies in the structural materials, and it is additional to the LOAD FACTOR. *Also called strength reduction factor.*

capillary action The action of a CAPILLARY TUBE, when dipped into a container of water, to cause the level in the tube to rise above that of the container. It is caused by SURFACE TENSION.

capillary fitting A PIPE FITTING for copper pipes, in which the inside diameter of the fitting is very slightly larger than the outside diameter of the pipe. When SOFT SOLDER or HARD SOLDER is introduced to the joint, the molten solder fills the gap by CAPILLARY ACTION.

capillary groove A groove formed between two pieces of building material to increase the narrow space and thus prevent CAPILLARY ACTION.

capillary tube A tube with a very fine bore.

capillary water Water held by CAPILLARY ACTION in the soil *above* the water table.

capital *See* COLUMN CAPITAL.

capital cost (of a building) The prime cost of construction, including acquisition of the land, design, materials, equipment and erection. *See also* ANNUAL COST *and* LIFE-CYCLE COST.

capping cables Short TENDONS introduced into *statically indeterminate prestressed structures* in the zone of negative bending moment (*see figure*).

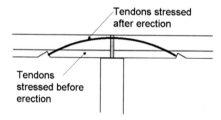

Tendons stressed after erection

Tendons stressed before erection

Capping cables

capture Video is captured (or digitised) by sampling over time selected frames in a continuous full-motion sequence. Each of these frames is then captured as any still image would be (see DIGITAL IMAGES). The frames are played back in rapid succession to simulate the original full motion.

capture card When video sequences are captured, the storage requirements are very high. On most computers this is accomplished by special hardware (video or capture cards). The card converts an incoming analog video signal (from a video camera, VCR, or other similar device) to digital form, and usually compresses the data as well, before sending it to the computer's RAM or an attached hard drive.

car The load-carrying unit of a LIFT (elevator) system, comprising the enclosure, or cab, the car frame, platform and doors.

car door closer A device attached to a LIFT DOOR which ensures that the car doors and landing doors close automatically,

using the stored energy of a spring or weights.

car top inspection station Control panel located on the top of a lift car which allows the lift to be removed from normal service, and controlled from the car top.

carat *(a)* For weighing precious stones, 1 carat = 0 2 g. *(b)* For measuring the gold content of an alloy, pure gold = 24 carat, so that 22-carat gold contains 2 parts of alloying metal.

carbon A non-metallic element. Its chemical symbol is C, its atomic number is 6, its valency is 4, its atomic weight is 12, and its melting point is above 3500 °C. It occurs in several allotropic forms: in crystalline form as diamond and as graphite, and in amorphous form as charcoal, coke, etc. Its specific gravity depends on its form.

carbon arc lamp A high-intensity electric-discharge lamp employing an arc discharge between two carbon electrodes.

carbon black Finely divided amorphous carbon, used as a mineral pigment in plastics, concrete, paint, etc. It is produced by burning petroleum or natural gas in a supply of air insufficient for complete combustion.

carbon copy *See* CC.

carbon dioxide A colourless gas normally found in the atmosphere at concentrations between 300 and 350 ppm. It is absorbed by plants, and produced by the decomposition and/or combustion of fossil fuels and by animal metabolism. It is a contributor to global warming. It is sometimes used as a marker for the adequacy of ventilation in enclosed spaces.

carbon fibre An extremely strong thin fibre used to make high-strength composite materials.

carbon filament lamp The first successful electric FILAMENT LAMP invented independently by Edison and by Swan in 1879. The carbon was replaced in quick succession by thorium oxide, by tantalum, and then by tungsten, in each case because it could operate at a higher temperature and therefore gave a better light.

carbon monoxide A colourless and odourless gas, toxic in very low concentrations. It is the product of incomplete combustion of fossil fuels.

carbon steel A STEEL containing up to 1.7 per cent of carbon, but generally less than 1.0 per cent. *See also* PHASE DIAGRAM.

carbon trading Sale of rights to emit to atmosphere defined quantities of carbon dioxide, by organisations operating with below-average emissions, to parties who are above-average emitters.

carbonation Chemical reaction between calcium compounds and carbon dioxide; calcium carbonate is produced. The reaction occurs slowly when carbon dioxide is absorbed from the atmosphere.

carbonisation The heat-treatment of coal (or other solid fuels) in a closed container. It produces COKE and coal gas, as well as coal tar and a variety of compounds used by the chemical industry. CHARCOAL is produced similarly from wood.

carborundum Silicon carbide (SiC), an abrasive, not to be confused with CORUNDUM.

carburising The introduction of carbon into the surface of steel by holding it at a suitable temperature in contact with carbon and nitrogen, for example by CASE HARDENING.

carcass In building construction, the load-bearing part of the building without the finishes. *Also spelled carcase.*

cardioid microphone A microphone containing two sensitive elements arranged so as to give a polar response which is substantially unidirectional. When drawn as a polar diagram, the response is approximately heart-shaped.

Carnot cycle An ideal cycle for a heat engine, described by S. Carnot in France in 1824. It gives the maximum theoretical efficiency for a heat engine which cannot, however, be attained by any practical engine.

carpenter's brace A cranked hand tool used for turning the drilling BIT to make holes in timber. It has been largely superseded by electrical drills.

carpenter's level A straight bar of wood or metal with horizontal and vertical SPIRIT LEVEL tubes, used by carpenters and others to set out vertical and horizontal lines.

carpet A knitted, woven or needle-tufted heavy fabric used as a floor covering. *See also* WARP *and* WEFT.

carpet pile The tufts of yarn that stand erect from a carpet. The height of the pile is measured from the top of the backing material to the surface of the carpet.

carpet underlay or underlayment Material laid directly on the floor to act as padding for the carpet laid over it.

carport A shelter for a car, attached to or near a house, which contains a roof, but no door. It usually does not have walls on all sides.

Carrara marble Marble from the Carrara quarry in Northern Italy, opened in the first century AD and in almost continuous production since then. It produces a white marble of uniform texture and strength.

carrel A small enclosure in the stack of a library, designed for individual study.

carriage In stair construction, a supporting beam similar to a STRINGER *(b)*. Stringers are located at each end of the treads, and carriages are placed below the middle of the treads.

carriage bolt A bolt which is threaded at one end to receive a nut, and has a circular head at the other end. The circular head is prevented from rotating by a square or ribbed neck. *Also called coach bolt.*

Cartesian coordinates The coordinates conventionally used for plotting a curve; a system of coordinates that defines the location of a point in terms of its perpendicular distances from each of a set of mutually perpendicular axes. They are named after the seventeenth-century mathematician René Descartes. In two dimensions, the horizontal axis is called the *abscissa* and the vertical axis the *ordinate* (*see figure*). In three dimensions, Cartesian coordinates are usually called the x-, y- and z-axes.

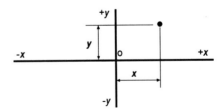

Cartesian coordinates

case hardening CARBURISING the exterior of a low-carbon steel, so as to increase its surface hardness without impairing its overall DUCTILITY. For example, the carbon may be absorbed from a molten bath of sodium cyanide, and the steel is then QUENCHed to produce a hard case.

CASE tools *Abbreviation for* Computer-Aided Software Engineering tools.

casein glue Adhesive manufactured from milk powder.

casement window A window contained in case frames which is hinged and opens outwards; as opposed to a SASH WINDOW. The opening SASH is side-hinged or mounted on FRICTION STAYS opening sideways.

cash flow Receipts and expenditure of money by an organisation or individual during a time period. *See also* DISCOUNTED CASH FLOW METHOD.

casino Originally a small country house or summer house. Later a public room or building for social occasions, and more recently for gambling.

cast in place Cast liquid in its permanent location, where it hardens as part of the building, as opposed to PRECAST. Monolithic concrete must be cast in place.

cast in situ Same as CAST IN PLACE, as opposed to PRECAST.

cast iron Iron with a total carbon content between 1.8 and 4.5 per cent. It is one of the two traditional forms of iron, the other being WROUGHT IRON. Steel is intermediate between the two in carbon content, but prior to the invention of the *Bessemer* process it could only be produced at great expense. Cast iron was used extensively in the nineteenth century for structural members and for railings. It is hard, brittle, and easy to cast into moulds. *Grey cast iron* contains some free carbon in the form of GRAPHITE; in *white cast iron* all the carbon is present as IRON CARBIDE.

cast stone *Same as* ARTIFICIAL STONE.

castellated Having turrets and battlements on a building in the style of a castle.

castellated beam A steel beam formed by cutting a ROLLED STEEL JOIST along the web in a zigzag shape. The two halves are then welded together at the crests of the cuts (*see figure*). The resulting beam is deeper, but it has a series of holes in the web. The SECTION MODULUS can be

doubled by this technique, but the shear strength is reduced.

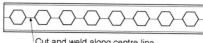
Cut and weld along centre line

Castellated beam

caster A wheel set in a swivel frame, attached to a piece of furniture or to a mobile machine.

Castigliano's method *See* STRAIN ENERGY METHOD.

casting resins PLASTICS which can be cast. They may be THERMOSETTING RESINS or COLD-SETTING RESINS.

catalyst A substance which causes or ACCELERATES a chemical reaction without being itself transformed in the process.

catenary The curve assumed by a freely hanging cable of uniform section, due to its own weight. The stresses in it are purely tensile. Its mathematical equation is

$$y = a \cosh(x/a),$$

where *a* is a constant.

catenary arch An arch shaped like an inverted catenary, so that the stresses due to its own weight are purely compressive. *See also* PARABOLIC ARCH.

cathode The negative electrode of an electrolytic cell or battery. The *anode* is the positive electrode.

cathode-ray tube An evacuated glass tube, in which a narrow beam of electrons, emitted from an electron gun, impinges on a fluorescent screen. The beam is subjected to transverse magnetic and electrostatic fields, whose intensities control the position of the luminous spot. It can thus be used for the graphic display of measurements, or in VISUAL DISPLAY UNITS.

cathodic protection A method of applying a small electric current to metal structures to counteract the corrosive effects of contact between dissimilar metals in the presence of an electrolyte.

cation A positive ion, the opposite of an *anion* which is negative.

catwalk An elevated narrow walkway.

caulking The process of making a joint

watertight. The term originally implied stopping up the joints with OAKUM and melted pitch. It is now also applied to stopping with mastics, rubber, silicone and other flexible sealants. *Also spelled calking* (USA).

caustic potash Potassium hydroxide (KOH).

caustic soda Sodium hydroxide (NaOH).

cavetto A round concave moulding containing a QUADRANT of a circle, used in a CORNICE or at the base of a classical column, where it also known as a TORUS.

cavitation A problem occurring when a pump impeller tends to create a vacuum on one side. The 'vacuum' fills with low-pressure vapour, which eventually collapses, and the impact of the incoming liquid may cause erosion of the impeller.

cavity batten A timber strip placed temporarily in the cavity of a brick wall to catch mortar droppings. It is removed as each row of *cavity ties* are placed, and replaced above them.

cavity insulation *(a)* The thermal insulating effect of a cavity or air space between two material layers. In very thin wall cavities air conduction may reduce the insulating effect. In very wide cavities convection currents may develop, also reducing its resistance. The optimum effect is obtained by cavities of 25–90 mm. *(b)* Insulating material placed in a floor, wall or ceiling cavity.

cavity resistance (R_c) The resistance to heat flow by virtue of having a gap within a wall, etc. It depends on the surfaces facing the cavity. It is much increased if one or both of these surfaces have a low emittance, *e.g.* if lined with a reflective foil, as this would reduce radiant heat transfer. In some instances the cavity may be filled with a foam (possibly in situ foaming), but in this case the cavity resistance is lost (the foam is in contact with both faces); the foam will act as BULK INSULATION.

cavity shell *See* DOUBLE-WALLED SHELL.

cavity wall A wall built of an inner and outer leaf, or *wythe* (*see figure*). It usually consists of two leaves of STRETCHER brickwork (110 mm or 4½ in. nominal thickness) with a cavity of about 50 mm,

to make the wall 275 mm or 11 in. thick overall. It is usually used as an external wall, where the cavity drains any water penetrating the outer leaf. The cavity provides good acoustic insulation, and is of some assistance in insulating against solar heat loads. The wall has poor thermal resistance against heat loss. The two leaves are tied by metal wall ties at intervals. The inner leaf carries the floor joists and the roof framing. Cavity walls are not used in very cold climates, such as the North-East of the USA, because the cavity would fill with ice. A BRICK VENEER wall is also a cavity wall, with only the outer leaf being of brickwork.

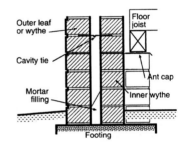

Cavity wall

CBD *Abbreviation for* Central Business District.

CBEMA curve A set of curves representing the capabilities of computers to withstand voltage disturbance of various magnitude and duration. Developed by the Computer Business Equipment Manufacturers Association (CBEMA), it has become a de facto standard for measuring the performance of all types of equipment and power systems, and is commonly referred to by this name.

CBR *Abbreviation for (a)* California Bearing Ratio; *(b)* Case-Based Reasoning.

cc *(a)* Cubic Centimetre; *(b)* Centre to Centre; *(c)* Carbon Copy, originally a copy of a typewritten document sent to a third party. Now used in email with an analogous meaning.

CCA Copper-chrome-arsenate, a timber PRESERVATIVE. At the time of writing there is debate about the toxicity of the arsenic content.

CCT *Abbreviation for* CORRELATED COLOUR TEMPERATURE.

CCTV *Abbreviation for* Closed-Circuit Television.

CD *Abbreviation for* COMPACT DISK.

cd/m² CANDELA per square metre, the unit of LUMINANCE.

CD-ROM *Abbreviation for* Compact Disk Read-Only Memory.

CE In the Common Era (*same as* in the Christian era, AD), the system of dates used in most countries. CE is becoming more usual than AD in secular writing.

CEBS Commonwealth Experimental Building Station, Sydney. Later renamed Experimental Building Station (EBS), the National Building Technology Centre, and now part of the Commonwealth Scientific and Industrial Research Organisation (CSIRO) Division of Manufacturing and Infrastructure Technology.

CEBTP *Centre Expérimental de Recherches et d'Études du Bâtiment et des Travaux Publics*, Paris.

CEI Council of Engineering Institutions, London, now succeeded by Engineering Council — EC(UK).

ceiling The upper surface of an interior space. It is usually *suspended* from the structure of the floor or the roof above, and covers it.

ceiling cavity In lighting design, the part of the room above the luminaire plane. The *ceiling cavity ratio* is a number calculated from its proportions, used in lumen- or flux-method calculations.

ceiling diffuser An air outlet from an air conditioning duct, which diffuses the air over a larger area to produce an even distribution and avoid draught (*see figure*): *(a)* shows a rectangular or circular outlet, and *(b)* shows a linear outlet combined with a luminaire.

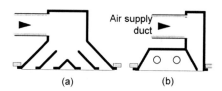

(a)   (b)

Ceiling diffuser

ceiling fan A slowly rotating overhead fan with a wide sweep. It moves large volumes of air at a low speed, and it is widely used in hot-humid climates to improve thermal comfort.

ceiling jet (fire engineering) A flow of smoke under the ceiling, extending radially from the point where the fire plume strikes the ceiling.

ceiling joist A JOIST which carries the ceiling below it, but not the floor or roof over the ceiling.

ceiling plenum *See* PLENUM.

ceiling tile *See* ACOUSTIC TILE.

celerity Swiftness of movement, specifically the velocity of the surge wave travelling within a pipeline during a WATER HAMMER analysis.

cell *See* BATTERY CELL.

cell (spreadsheet) A spreadsheet is organised as a rectangular grid of elements called cells. Each cell has a unique address consisting of the row and column containing it. Various information such as text, numbers and formulas can be entered into spreadsheet cells.

cellular concrete Lightweight concrete containing a substantial proportion of air or gas bubbles. It is produced either by adding a foaming agent (such as detergent) or a gas-forming agent (such as aluminium powder) to the mix. Cellular concrete, which contains sand, is lighter than LIGHTWEIGHT AGGREGATE concrete, but heavier than water. Cellular concrete which floats on water can be made from cement, water and a foaming or gas-forming agent; this material has insufficient strength for structural purposes, and is used mainly as a thermal insulator and as a stiffener for a light-gauge steel or aluminium structure. *Also called aerated concrete*, or *foamed concrete*.

cellular plastic *Same as* EXPANDED PLASTIC.

celluloid One of the first THERMOPLASTIC materials to be made artificially, but now rarely used. It is made from plasticised NITROCELLULOSE with camphor.

cellulose acetate butyrate More commonly known as CAB plastic, it is used for pipes and injection mouldings. The cellulose is made from bleached wood pulp or cotton linters, and is esterised with butyric acid and acetic anhydride.

cellulose insulation Thermal insulation created from a cellulosic fibre (such as recycled newspaper) treated with a fire-retardant.

cellulose nitrate *Same as* NITRO-CELLULOSE.

Celsius scale The temperature scale fixed by the boiling point of water (100 °C) and its freezing point (0 °C), suggested by the Swedish physicist Celsius in 1740. *Also called centigrade scale.* To convert to the Fahrenheit scale (°F), multiply by 1.8 and add 32.

cement *See* PORTLAND CEMENT, *see also* COLOURED CEMENT, EXPANSIVE CEMENT, HIGH-ALUMINA CEMENT, HYDRAULIC CEMENT, LOW-HEAT CEMENT, NATURAL CEMENT, PORTLAND BLAST-FURNACE SLAG CEMENT, PORTLAND–POZZOLAN CEMENT *and* WHITE CEMENT.

cement clinker The product of burning the raw cement mix. Cement is made by finely grinding the clinker. PORTLAND CEMENT mix is normally burnt at a temperature of approximately 1400 °C (2600 °F) in a rotary KILN.

cement grout A cement slurry which is sufficiently fluid to penetrate into rock fissures, masonry joints or prestressing ducts without segregation.

cement gun A machine for placing mortar or concrete through a nozzle under pressure. The mixture of cement and small aggregate is forced by compressed air through a hose to the nozzle, where water is added from a separate pipe. The resulting material is known as *gunite, pneumatically applied mortar*, or *shot-crete*.

cement mortar A mixture of sand and cement.

cement paint A paint which can be used over cement. It is either a mixture of cement and pigment, or a paint based on alkali-resistant vehicles such as *casein* or *tung oil*.

cement slurry A liquid mixture of water and cement.

cementation Injecting cement grout under pressure, *e.g.* into fissured rock.

cementite The iron carbide (Fe_3C) constituent of cast iron and steel. It is crystalline, hard and brittle.

cement-stabilised soil Soil, usually natural but sometimes imported, formed into a pavement by the addition of cement and water, mixed in situ, and compacted with a roller. If the natural soil is suitable, it can constitute a cheap and effective light-duty pavement.

CEN *Comité Européen de Normalisation*, Brussels.

CENELEC *Comité Européen de Normalisation Electrotechnique*, Brussels.

centering A temporary structure on which the masonry of a vault or arch is supported until the structure becomes self-supporting.

centi- The Latin prefix for hundred, used now for one hundredth, *e.g.* 1 centimetre = 0.01 m.

centigrade scale An obsolescent term for CELSIUS SCALE.

centimetre One hundredth of a METRE, = 0.394 in.

central heating Heating a building using a centrally located heat-raising plant (often in the basement or on a SERVICE FLOOR), distributing heat using water or air as the heat transport medium, through pipes or ducts to heat emitters in all rooms of the building or group of buildings.

central processing unit (CPU) The component of a computer system responsible for the processing of all data. Employing specialised memory cells called REGISTERS, the CPU fetches data from memory, performs operations on it while it resides in the registers, and returns the results to RAM. Often called simply *processor*. *See also* MICRO-PROCESSOR.

central receiver power plant Solar thermal power plant using a large array of tracking mirrors (heliostats) to reflect the sun's rays to a receiver on top of a tower to produce steam used to generate electricity.

centre frequency This term is used to define a bandpass filter. The centre frequency is the geometric mean of the upper and lower cut-off frequencies of the filter, *e.g.* an octave-band filter with an upper cut-off frequency of 1414 Hz and a lower cut-off frequency of 707 Hz would have a centre frequency of 1000 Hz and would be known as a 1000 Hz octave-band filter.

centre of gravity *Same as* CENTROID.

centre of mass *Same as* CENTROID.

centre of pressure The point of action of the resultant force acting on an area subjected to liquid pressure. Since liquid pressure increases with depth, its location is below the centroid.

centre punch A small bar of hard steel with a blunt point. It is used to mark the centre of a hole to be drilled, so that the drill starts in the correct place. There is an illustration under PUNCH.

centrifugal chiller A packaged CHILLER to produce chilled water based on a CENTRIFUGAL refrigerant COMPRESSOR.

centrifugal compressor, fan, pump A compressor, fan (*see figure*), pump with an impeller of *paddle-wheel* form, in which the fluid enters axially at the centre and is discharged tangentially by centrifugal force. By contrast, an AXIAL-FLOW

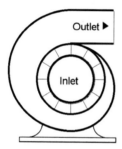

Centrifugal fan

FAN is a propeller fan, with the blades mounted on the axis.

centring *Same as* CENTERING.

centroid The point of any plane figure through which all CENTROIDAL AXES pass. It is often referred to as the *centre of gravity* or *centre of mass* of the figure, since a piece of cardboard or sheet metal of this shape balances if hung freely from the centroid.

centroidal axis An axis of any plane figure about which the moment of the area is zero. *See* MOMENT OF AN AREA.

ceramic disc tap Tap in which the water is controlled by a disc made of ceramic material, the mating surfaces being sufficiently hard-wearing and accurately formed that a compressible rubber washer is not required.

ceramic mosaic Ceramic tiles, arranged in patterns on a paper backing, and sold in sheet units ready for placing.

ceramic tile Clay tile for wall, floor or roof.

ceramic veneer Large units of thin TERRA COTTA, generally moulded by EXTRUSION.

ceramics *(a)* In building, any component made from burned clay, such as brick, terra cotta, ceramic tile (glazed or unglazed), stoneware pipe and other pottery. *(b)* In solid-state physics, compounds of metallic and non-metallic elements; these include clay, cement and natural stone.

certification Documentation of the compliance with statutory requirements by an accredited third party.

CF *Abbreviation for* CONFIGURATION FACTOR.

CFC *Abbreviation for* Chlorinated Fluorocarbons, also known as *fluorinated hydrocarbons* or as *halocarbons*. Most are known under the trade name of *freons*. Synthetic non-toxic, non-flammable, non-corrosive and non-irritant refrigerants. They were widely used as refrigerants for COMPRESSION CYCLE refrigeration machines until it was found that they have an OZONE DEPLETION potential. They are now being replaced by the HCFCS and the HFCS.

CFD *Abbreviation for* COMPUTATIONAL FLUID DYNAMICS.

CG *Abbreviation for* CENTRE OF GRAVITY.

CGI *Abbreviation for* COMPUTER GRAPHICS INTERFACE.

cgs units The units of the traditional metric system, based on centimetre, gram and second. Another system is *MKS units*, based on the metre, kilogram and second. They have been superseded by SI UNITS.

chain An obsolete measure of length, equal to the surveyor's chain of 66 ft = 20.12 m.

chair insulation The thermal insulation provided to a sedentary worker by the upholstery of the chair at his or her workplace, additional to the intrinsic insulation provided by clothing.

chair rail A rail, usually of timber, fixed to an internal wall at a suitable height to prevent the backs of chairs from damaging the wall finish. Sometimes also fixed across windows to prevent the chairs from striking the glass.

chair, bar *See* BAR CHAIR.

chalet Originally a herdsman's hut in the

Swiss mountains; hence a house built in the style of an Alpine cottage.

chalk A soft LIMESTONE.

chalk line A length of string which has been thoroughly coated with chalk dust. It is pulled tight across a piece of timber or other material, and plucked, thus producing a straight chalky line which serves as a guide during cutting.

chalking Disintegration of paint and other coatings, which produces loose powder at, or just beneath, the surface.

chamfer A right-angled corner cut symmetrically, *i.e.* at 45°. *See also* BEVEL *and* SPLAY.

chamfer strip An insert placed into an inside corner of concrete formwork to produce a chamfer.

chandelier A LUMINAIRE consisting of multiple arms, hung from the ceiling. It was originally designed to support a large number of candles, but was later made with multiple gas jets (GASOLIER) and with electric lights. See also CRYSTAL CHANDELIER.

channel section A metal section shaped [.

chaos A branch of mathematical physics that combines mathematics and numerical (computer) techniques to provide a new way to analyse certain problems. It involves the behaviours of non-linear dynamical systems and their response to initial and boundary conditions, particularly in regions of mathematical instability. It may provide insight into the complex nature of turbulence.

character *See* ALPHANUMERIC CHARACTER.

character printer Printing device whose technology is based on producing a single character or symbol at a time, similarly to a typewriter, as opposed to a LINE PRINTER.

character set The set of numbers, letters, graphics and symbols accepted as legal by a computer.

character string A sequence of ALPHANUMERIC CHARACTERS, which are interpreted as text rather than as numbers or formulas.

characteristic curve A graph showing a relationship, for example between the fluid flow rate and the increase in pressure in a CENTRIFUGAL FAN.

characteristic impedance The ratio of the sound pressure at a point in a medium transmitting the sound to the particle velocity at the same position. It is equal to the product of the density of the medium and the speed of sound in the medium.

charcoal A fuel consisting of almost pure carbon produced from wood by CARBON-ISATION. Also used as an adsorbent.

charger An AC-to-DC rectifier used to restore and maintain the charge in a storage BATTERY, for example in a UPS system or an emergency power system.

Charles' law 'The volume of a given mass of gas, kept at a constant pressure, increases by $\frac{1}{273}$ of its volume at 0°C for each degree rise of temperature.' *Also known as Gay-Lussac's law. See also* BOYLE'S LAW.

Charpy test An impact test carried out on a notched specimen fixed at both ends. The energy absorbed during fracture is measured by a pendulum.

chase A groove cut into a wall or floor to receive a small pipe, conduit, cable or flashing. A very large chase is a DUCT.

check *See* SEASONING CHECK.

check valve A valve used in pipework to allow the fluid to flow in one direction only.

chemical anchor A masonry anchor in which a high-strength adhesive is introduced into the hole to bond the bolt to the masonry.

chemical symbol Abbreviation of the English or Latin names of the chemical elements, particularly for use in chemical formulas; for example C for carbon and Fe for iron *(ferrum)*.

cherry picker A platform at the end of an extendable boom, usually mounted on a wheeled vehicle for mobility. It is used for hoisting people, mainly to perform work in places difficult to access. *Also called hydraulic platform.*

chert A very fine-grained, hard siliceous rock, which sometimes includes the remains of siliceous organisms. It tends to splinter when it is fractured. *See also* FLINT.

chevron *(a)* The meeting of two rafters at an angle at the ridge of a roof. *(b)* Hence a decoration consisting of two lines meeting at an angle, or a zigzag pattern of lines.

chiaroscuro The disposition of light and shade in the pictorial composition of a painting. The term is also used in sculpture and photography.

chicken wire A netting of lightweight galvanised wire, usually with a hexagonal mesh.

chilled beam A device, usually long and narrow, installed at ceiling level of an air conditioned space and chilled below room temperature to provide a sink for mainly radiant heat.

chilled ceiling A ceiling that is cooled by circulation of CHILLED WATER which produces a cooling effect by acting as a sink for radiant and convected heat.

chilled water Water at a temperature substantially below ambient temperature, used as a heat transfer medium for the cooling and dehumidification cycle in some air conditioning systems.

chiller A self-contained machine comprising a refrigerant compressor, an EVAPORATOR and a CONDENSER designed to produce chilled water.

chimney cowl A revolving metal ventilator over a chimney.

china clay *Same as* KAOLIN.

China wood oil *Same as* TUNG OIL.

Chinese white Zinc oxide (ZnO). A permanent, non-poisonous white pigment.

chip An INTEGRATED CIRCUIT etched on SEMICONDUCTOR material and hermetically sealed, usually plugged into a printed circuit board. Chips may contain processing, memory, input-output or other circuits.

chipboard *Same as* PARTICLE BOARD.

chips Small broken fragments. The term is commonly employed for small-size aggregates used for decorative concrete surface finishes (*e.g.* marble chips).

chirp A sound consisting of a single tone whose frequency is rapidly and continuously oscillated between two audible limits. It is often used as an emergency signal, because it can be easily heard.

chisel A metal hand tool with a cutting edge at one end. Different chisels are used for working metal, wood and stone. A *cold chisel* is used for cutting metal which has not been softened by heating, and it has a hardened and tempered steel

edge. A *wood chisel* is usually mounted in a wooden handle.

chi-square test In STATISTICS, a test of compatibility of observed and expected frequencies, based on the function

$$\chi^2 = \sum_{i=1}^{k} \frac{(n_i - e_i)^2}{e_i}$$

where n_i and e_i are the ith pair of the observed and expected frequencies, and k is the number of frequencies.

chloride *See* CALCIUM CHLORIDE *and* POLYVINYL CHLORIDE.

chlorinated rubber A white powder formed when natural rubber is treated with chlorine under heat and pressure. It is soluble in coaltar solvents, and produces paint films of exceptionally good chemical resistance.

chlorination Disinfectant treatment of drinking water, and sometimes sewage, with a source of chlorine, such as bleaching powder (*calcium chloride*).

chlorine A highly reactive gas, and a powerful oxidising agent frequently used in the form of bleaching powder (*calcium chloride*). Its chemical symbol is Cl, its atomic number is 17, its atomic weight is 35.5, and its boiling point is −34.6°C.

chlorofluorocarbons *Same as* chlorinated fluorocarbons, *see* CFC.

chooser On Macintosh operating system, the facility that controls the selecting of PRINTERS, FILE SERVERS, and other networked devices.

chopped strand mat Fibreglass mat used in FRP, produced by mechanically chopping fibreglass strand into short lengths, laid in random directions and lightly bonded together.

chord (*a*) A principal member of a truss, usually on its top or its bottom. (*b*) A term sometimes used for the CLEAR SPAN of an arch. (*c*) A straight line connecting two points on a curve. (*d*) The sound of two or more notes from a musical scale played simultaneously.

CHP *Abbreviation for* Combined Heat and Power generation, a type of COGENERATION, where the residual heat in electricity generation is utilised for CENTRAL or DISTRICT HEATING. Also referred to as a *total energy system.* This can increase the overall efficiency to almost 80 per cent (*e.g.* 35 per cent of the fuel energy is utilised as electricity and 45 per cent as heat).

chroma The attribute of a colour that allows the observer to judge how much colour it contains; in the Munsell colour system (*see* MUNSELL BOOK OF COLOR), the chroma scale correlates the saturation of the colour, and it ranges from /1 in arbitrary steps to express departure from the equivalent grey.

chromatic aberration A lens defect which results in coloured fringes on images due to the variation of the refractive index with the colour (or wavelength) of light.

chromatic scale Musical scale consisting of 12 equal semitones per OCTAVE, so that the ratio of the frequencies of any two successive semitones is $2^{1/12}$. *See also* DIATONIC SCALE.

chromaticity Of, pertaining to or characterised by a colour or colours.

chromaticity diagram *See* CIE CHROMATICITY SYSTEM.

chromium A bright, silvery metallic element, used in STAINLESS STEEL and other alloys. Its chemical symbol is Cr, its atomic number is 24, its atomic weight is 52.0, its specific gravity is 7.14, and its melting point is 1830 °C.

chromium plating Electroplated surface of chromium applied as a decorative and protective finish, which is extremely hard. Chromium plating for steel is usually done over a coating of nickel; this in turn is electro-deposited on a coating of copper, which is the first coat on the steel. (None of these metals provides GALVANIC PROTECTION to the steel.)

CHU Centigrade Heat Unit, now obsolete. The heat required to raise 1 lb of water through 1 °C.

churn To change the location of people and furniture to suit new organisational requirements.

churn rate The total number of employee workspace moves per annum, expressed as a percentage of the total number of employees in the facility.

CI *Abbreviation for* CAST IRON.

CIA Concrete Institute of Australia, Sydney.

CIAM *Congrès Internationaux d'Architecture Moderne.* The first Congress was organised in 1928 by a group led by Le Corbusier and the art historian Siegfried Giedion. Altogether ten congresses were held, and the organisation was formally dissolved after disagreement over its objectives in 1959.

CIB *Conseil International du Bâtiment pour la Recherche, l'Étude et la Documentation,* Rotterdam; the international coordinating body for building research.

CIBS Chartered Institute of Building Services, London; *now called* CIBSE.

CIBSE Chartered Institution of Building Services Engineers, London.

CIC *Abbreviation for* Computer-Integrated Construction.

CIDB *Centre d'Information et de Documentation sur le Bruit,* Paris.

CIE *Commission Internationale de l'Éclairage,* Vienna. The international coordinating body for standardisation and research into light (visible and non-visible) and its applications.

CIE chromaticity system A method of specifying colour using a coordinate system, *Yxy.* Other derived, transformed systems have been developed, such as *Lab* and *Luv.* The colorimetric specification of the CIE chromaticity diagrams describes colours by reference to two coordinates, *x* and *y* (or *a* and *b* or *u* and *v*). This is in addition to the luminance (*Y* or *L*) of each colour which must be determined (with a PHOTOMETER) in order to describe fully a light source (or surface).

CIE contrast rendering factor (CRF) A measure of the revealing power of a lighting system compared with a reference system, usually the lighting within a uniformly illuminated sphere.

CIE general colour rendering index (CRI) This gives a measure of the colour-rendering properties of a light source compared with that of a full radiator at the same correlated colour temperature as the source. It uses a set of eight test colours to assess the properties of lamps used for general lighting applications. The scale is 0 to 100, with higher numbers indicating superior colour rendering. Most incandescent lamps have general CRIs of 100.

CIE standard clear sky An idealised sky whose luminance varies in accordance with a complex formula devised by Richard Kittler. The luminance is a maximum in the very bright aura around the sun (the circumsolar region) and a minimum at an angle of 90° to the aura. *See also* INDIAN STANDARD CLEAR SKY.

CIE standard overcast sky An idealised fully overcast sky whose luminance at any point of ALTITUDE θ is

$$L_\theta = \frac{1}{3} L_z (1 + 2 \sin \theta)$$

where L_z is the luminance at the ZENITH. *Also called a Moon–Spencer sky.*

CIFM *Abbreviation for* Computer-Integrated Facility Management.

cill *Same as* SILL.

CIM *Abbreviation for* Computer-Integrated Manufacturing.

cinder concrete A concrete made with cinders as LIGHTWEIGHT AGGREGATE.

CINVA *Centro Interamericano de Vivienda y Planeamiento*, Bogotá, Colombia.

circadian rhythm Physiological responses due to the DIURNAL (day–night) cycle.

circle The curve generated by a point equidistant from another point. It has a constant radius and constant curvature. It can consequently be drawn with a compass or even a piece of string.

circle, great, small *See* GREAT CIRCLE *and* SMALL CIRCLE.

circuit A system of conductors (*i.e.* wires and appliances) capable of providing a closed path for electric current.

circuit breaker A device for opening an electric circuit automatically in case of an overload, usually by thermal means (heating a bimetallic strip) and/or magnetic means (creating an electromagnet) operating a spring-loaded latch. It is a more elaborate device than a FUSE.

circuit switching A method of organising the transmission of messages across a NETWORK. In circuit switching networks a dedicated circuit is allocated for the entire duration of a transmission (telephone switching networks use this method). Contrast with PACKET SWITCHING.

circular arch or shell An arch or shell with a constant radius of curvature, *i.e.* forming part of the circumference of a circle, as opposed to an ELLIPTICAL, PARABOLIC or CATENARY arch. A *semicircular* arch is one forming a complete semicircle.

circular functions The functions obtained from the radius of a circle and its horizontal and vertical projections (*see figure*). *Also called trigonometric functions.*

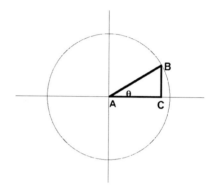

Circular functions

$\sin \theta = BC/AB$; $\cos \theta = AC/AB$; $\tan \theta = BC/AC$; $\sec \theta = AB/AC$; $\csc \theta = AB/BC$; $\cot \theta = AC/BC$.

circular measure The measurement of an angle in *radians*. A radian is the angle subtended by an ARC equal in length to the radius of the circle. 1 radian = 57.296 degrees. 1 degree = 0.017 453 radians.

circular saw A saw in the form of a circular steel blade with teeth along its rim. *See also* BAND SAW.

circulation space The space within a facility that provides access between functional areas for people, goods and vehicles.

circumference The curve that forms an encompassing boundary, especially of anything rounded.

circus *(a)* In Ancient Rome, a large, *oval* arena surrounded by rising tiers of seats, for the performance of public spectacles. *(b)* In modern architecture, a circular arena surrounded by tiers of seats and covered by a tent or permanent roof, particularly for the performance of acrobatic or equestrian acts. *(c)* A circle placed at the junction of two or more streets.

cistern *(a)* A small tank containing water, for example for flushing a WATER CLOSET. *See also* BALL COCK. *(b)* A reservoir for storing rainwater.

CITC Canadian Institute of Timber Construction, Ottawa.

Cl Chemical symbol for *chlorine*.

cladding *(a)* A synonym for CURTAIN WALL. *(b)* Covering a structural material with a protective surfacing material, *e.g. alclad* which is aluminium alloy (for strength) covered with pure aluminium (for corrosion resistance). *(c)* Weatherproof material applied to the exterior of a building.

clamp-on CT A CURRENT TRANSFORMER which clamps around a current-carrying conductor, so the conductor does not have to be opened for insertion of the transformer primary. Particularly suited for monitoring where current must be sensed at many points for relatively short periods.

clapboard A long, thin board, graduating in thickness from one edge to the other, used for WOOD SIDING. The thick edge overlaps the thin portion of the board. Called *weatherboard* in the UK and in Australia.

clarity The degree that discrete sounds in a musical performance stand apart from one another. *See also* DEFINITION.

class A group of objects or concepts with common characteristics.

classification of soils Soils in which gravel and sand predominate are classified by PARTICLE-SIZE ANALYSIS. For engineering purposes, clays are classified by their PLASTICITY INDEX, since it is not practicable to analyse them either by sieving or by sedimentation.

claw hammer A hammer with a split, claw-shaped peen, used by carpenters for drawing nails. *See also* BALL-PEEN HAMMER.

clay A fine-grained COHESIVE soil produced either by the decomposition of rock, or as a sedimentary deposit. It generally consists of hydrated silicates of aluminium with various impurities, and is in part COLLOIDal. When clay is mixed with coarser grained soils, the clay fraction is usually considered the part which is finer than 2 µm (0.002 mm) diameter. Its

UNCONFINED COMPRESSIVE STRENGTH depends greatly on the water content. Soils containing clay may cause *settlement* of the foundation. Clay is the principal raw material for the manufacture of *brick. See also* CHINA CLAY.

clay puddle A mixture of clay, water and sometimes sand worked while wet into a water-impervious layer of foundation material. It is used as a cut-off wall to prevent the ingress or egress of water.

clay tile *(a)* Roof tile made from clay. *(b)* QUARRY TILE for flooring or wall surfacing. *(c)* Glazed clay tile for flooring or wall surfacing.

clean agent Electrically non-conducting, volatile or gaseous fire extinguishant that does not leave a residue upon evaporation.

clean power An electrical power supply to sensitive electrical equipment, fed via a conditioner to eliminate irregularities in phase and voltage.

clean room A room with air filters and air precipitators to keep lint, dust and airborne pathogens below a level that is normally specified for that particular room, and with smooth surfaces that prevent dust collection. Clean rooms are required for certain biological and medical experiments, and for the assembly of precision products.

cleanout Inspection opening in drainage pipework. *Also called rodding eye.*

clear height The unobstructed vertical height of a space.

clear sky *(a)* A sky with less than three-tenths cloud cover. *(b) See* CIE STANDARD CLEAR SKY *and* INDIAN STANDARD CLEAR SKY.

clear span The distance between the inside faces of the supports.

clear timber Timber practically free from defects.

clearance The space by which an object avoids contact with another. In the case of LIFTS: *(a) bottom car clearance* is the clear vertical distance from the pit floor to the lowest part, (with the exception of guide shoes, rollers, safety jaw assemblies, platform aprons and guards), when a lift car is resting on its fully compressed BUFFERS; *(b) top car clearance* is the shortest vertical distance between the top of the car crosshead and the nearest part of the overhead structure, or any other obstruction, when a lift car floor is level with the top landing floor; *(c) running clearance* is the distance between the lift car sill and the lift well entrance sill.

clearstorey The portion of a high room extending above the single storey height of an adjacent portion of the building, and containing *high-light windows* for admitting daylight and sunlight. *Also spelled clearstory, clerestorey and clerestory.*

cleat, angle *See* ANGLE CLEAT.

cleavage fracture A fracture along the cleavage planes, characteristic of a BRITTLE fracture, and showing little plastic deformation. It usually occurs abruptly, without warning.

cleavage plane In natural stone, the plane along which natural stone can be split most easily, due to either bedding or metamorphic action. *See* SLATE.

clepsydra Water clock used by the ancient Greeks, which measures time by the discharge of water.

clerestory or clerestorey *See* CLEAR-STOREY.

client A computer using services or resources provided by a remote machine, called a SERVER.

climate If *weather* is the momentary state of atmospheric conditions, then *climate* is the integration in time of weather conditions, temperature, dryness, wind, etc., characteristic of a geographical location. (Or, as Michael Glantz of the US Center for Atmospheric Research once put it: 'Climate is what you expect, weather is what you get.') *See also* COMFORT ZONE.

climate change Warming of the surface of the earth, attributed to GREENHOUSE EFFECT due to accumulation of greenhouse gases, mainly carbon dioxide, in the atmosphere.

climbing crane A crane that is moved up as the structure rises. It is eventually dismantled, and taken down in pieces.

climbing formwork Formwork which is raised or pulled in stages to speed the placement of concrete. *See also* SLIPFORM.

clinker brick An over-burnt, and often deformed, brick.

clinker, cement *See* CEMENT CLINKER.

clinometer A hand-held instrument for measuring vertical angles on a sloping site, *also called* an *Abney level* or an *inclinometer.*

clip assembling Assembling short video clips into a sequence comprising a finished video product.

clipboard An area in computer memory (RAM) where data can be temporarily stored for later access. The clipboard resides in VOLATILE memory and can only store one item at a time. A *scrapbook* can be used to store multiple items on disk.

clip-fastening A system of INVISIBLE FIXING using clips attached to the substrate to engage with brackets or mouldings on the back of the item being fixed, so that installation can be completed usually without tools.

clipping *(a)* In acoustics, the distortion of a signal at the limit of the DYNAMIC RANGE of an amplifier or other electronic component. *(b)* In computer graphics, the process of cutting objects or a view by another object. For example, a view or a drawing can be clipped by using a clipping plane to hide those portions of the view behind the clipping plane, or a line may be used to clip or trim another line or several lines.

clo The unit for the insulating effect of clothing. It is an arbitrary measure ranging from 0.05 clo for a brief swimsuit to 4.0 clo for heavy outdoor clothing used in the Antarctic.

clock time *See* LOCAL TIME, REFERENCE LONGITUDE and TIME ZONE.

clockwise The direction in which the hands of a clock move. The movement of a screwdriver driving a right-handed screw into its hole is clockwise.

close grain Wood with narrow growth or annual rings. The opposite is *coarse grain.*

closed cell (of foamed plastic and similar materials) Formed with hollow cells which are closed and do not interconnect, so that the material does not absorb liquids.

closed circuit cooling tower A COOLING TOWER where the condenser water is circulated through a closed coil which is cooled by water sprayed on the outside of the coil.

closed system A system in which all components for an INDUSTRIALISED BUILD-ING are made by one manufacturer, and are generally designed only for one type of building.

close-packed hexagonal lattice An arrangement of atoms in crystals which may be imitated by close-packing spheres of identical diameter on a hexagonal grid.

closer *See* CAR DOOR CLOSER, KING CLOSER *and* QUEEN CLOSER.

cloud *See* ACOUSTICAL CLOUD.

cloudy sky *(a)* A sky with majority cloud cover, usually more than seven-tenths. *(b) See* CIE STANDARD OVERCAST SKY.

clout nail A nail with a large flat head, used for fastening sheet metal.

CLTD *Abbreviation for* Cooling Load Temperature Difference, coefficients presented in tabulated form in ASHRAE literature, calculated for specified constructions, which would need to be multiplied by the U-value of the actual construction, said to be a 'simplified' method of cooling load calculation.

CMIT CSIRO Manufacturing and Infra-structure Technology (Melbourne and other sites), which includes the former CEBS, EBS and DBCE.

CMYK *Abbreviation for* Cyan, Magenta, Yellow (the primary subtractive colours), and blacK; used in subtractive colour mixing, as with dyes, paints and pigments. On colour display terminals, a CMYK option displays colours less saturated than RGB, to represent the appearance of the colours when printed.

CNC *Abbreviation for* Computer Numeric Control.

coach bolt Bolt having a CUP HEAD, used for fixing timber. Since the cup head cannot be held with a spanner, there is a square portion of shank below the head, which forces its way into the timber to prevent the bolt from turning (*see figure*). *Also called carriage bolt.*

Coach bolt

coach screw A large wood SCREW, hav-ing a square or hexagonal head intended to be turned by a spanner, instead of a slotted head (*see figure*).

Coach screw

coanda effect A surface tension effect by means of which an air stream blown horizontally in contact with a horizontal flat surface such as a ceiling will travel for a considerable distance in contact with it.

coarse aggregate The larger size of CONCRETE AGGREGATE used for mixing concrete, as opposed to *fine aggregate.*

coarse grain Wood with coarse growth or annual rings. The opposite is *close grain.*

coarse stuff A blend of sand, hair and LIME PUTTY used as a BASE COAT for PLASTER.

coarse-grained soil A soil in which sand and gravel predominate.

coat A single layer of a liquid or paste, such as paint or plaster. See also BASE COAT and PRIMER COAT.

coaxial cable A cable used for com-munication consisting of a central core conductor surrounded by an outer conductor.

cob walling A term synonymous in some places with ADOBE and in others with PISÉ DE TERRE.

cochlea The inner part of the ear that undertakes frequency analysis and trans-forms the sound to neural impulses for transmission to the brain.

cocktail party effect The ability to hear one sound or conversation whilst in the presence of other sounds or conversations.

code of practice A document describing good practice for a trade or activity. Usually it does not have legal authority by itself, but it may be called up by an enforceable regulation.

coding The process of translating an algorithm into a set of computer instruc-tions in a computer language.

coefficient of elasticity *Same as* MODULUS OF ELASTICITY.

coefficient of expansion The THERMAL EXPANSION of a material per unit length per degree temperature change; it has different values for Celsius and Fahrenheit degrees, but is otherwise the same for metric and FPS units.

coefficient of friction The *coefficient of static friction* is defined as W/P, where W is the *limiting* FRICTION, or force at which the body just starts to move, and P is the contact force. The coefficient of *kinetic friction* (which is lower) is the W/P required to maintain motion against frictional resistance. ROLLING FRICTION is the resistance offered when a body rolls over a surface. The *coefficient of rolling friction* is Wr/P, where r is the radius of the rolling body. *See also* ANGLE OF FRICTION.

coefficient of performance (of a heat engine or heat pump) A measure of the efficiency of conversion of mechanical work to cooling or heating effect in a refrigeration system. Because of the thermal balance of a heat pump, it may be greater than unity.

coefficient of utilisation In the USA and Canada, the term used in lighting for UTILISATION FACTOR.

coefficient of variation (CV) The ratio of the STANDARD DEVIATION of a series of results to their *mean*. In the manufacture of materials it may be taken as a measure of quality control.

coffer A recessed panel in a ceiling.

cofferdam A watertight enclosure built of piles or clay, for the purpose of providing dry ground for excavating foundations.

cog A HOOKED BAR with a 90° bend.

cogeneration On-site generation of electricity in parallel with mains supply. Electrical supply is drawn from the mains at times of peak site demand and is supplied to the mains when site demand is low. Waste heat from the internal combustion prime mover is often recovered for use in the facility.

cogged joint A joint formed by structural timbers crossing at right angles. Each timber is notched over the area where they cross.

cohesion The property of a fine granular material, such as CLAY, whereby the particles cling together, especially when wet, but without the addition of an adhesive.

cohesionless soil A granular soil which consists of clean sand and/or gravel. From COULOMB'S EQUATION, its shear strength depends entirely on the normal pressure, and it is zero on a free surface.

cohesive soil A sticky soil which contains an appreciable proportion of fine-grained particles (CLAY).

coign, coin *Same as* QUOIN.

coincidence dip *See* COINCIDENCE EFFECT.

coincidence effect A decrease in the SOUND TRANSMISSION LOSS or ATTENUATION of a partition, floor or wall over a range of frequencies where bending waves are the dominant method of transfer of energy in the partition. The part of the transmission characteristic over which this occurs is known as the *coincidence dip*, and the lowest frequency at which the coincidence effect occurs is the COINCIDENCE FREQUENCY.

coincidence frequency The lowest frequency at which the COINCIDENCE EFFECT occurs for a given partition. The coincidence frequency is often erroneously referred to as the frequency at which the greatest reduction in the transmission loss occurs due to bending waves.

coke A fuel consisting of almost pure carbon produced from coal by CARBONISATION.

cold bridging In a well-insulated construction, cold bridging occurs when elements (usually structural members or door and window frames), which have greater thermal conductivity than the rest of the construction, bridge across between its faces. This reduces the effectiveness of the insulation, and may give rise to a pattern of surface condensation and staining.

cold chisel A chisel made sufficiently hard for cutting cold metal.

cold draw *(a)* A method of relieving stresses anticipated as a result of expansion or contraction due to heating or cooling by deformation of a long pipe at a change of direction. *(b) See* COLD-DRAWN WIRE.

cold riveting Closing the head of a RIVET by pressure without heating it. It is much simpler than hot riveting, but in building practice it is restricted to aluminium rivets.

cold soldering SOLDERING without the application of heat, for example with copper AMALGAM. Some glues containing metal powder are marketed, incorrectly, as cold solders.

cold working The shaping of a metal while at room (or at a slightly elevated) temperature which is below the temperature of recrystallisation, as opposed to *hot working*. It includes cold forging, cold rolling and wire drawing. Cold working may be used to produce a desired shape with a better surface finish than can be obtained by hot working, and it always increases the strength. *See also* WORK HARDENING.

cold-cathode lamp An electric DIS-CHARGE LAMP using a high voltage glow discharge between unheated electrodes, *also called*, generically, *neon lighting*.

cold-drawn wire Wire made from rods which have been hot rolled from steel billets, and then cold drawn through a die. This increases the strength, but also lowers the ductility of the steel. Cold-drawn wire is extensively used for reinforced and for prestressed concrete; for the latter, diameters range generally from 2 mm (0.080 in.) to 7 mm (0.276 in.).

cold-setting resin A resin which becomes rigid due to chemical reaction with a *hardener* at room temperature. Cold-setting resins usually set more quickly when heated.

cold-worked steel reinforcement Steel bars, wires or sections which, subsequent to hot rolling, have been subjected to rolling, twisting or drawing at room temperature.

Colebrook equation An empirical relationship between the properties of a fluid and a pipe system in which it is flowing, used as a basis for estimating pipe friction loss.

collapse of timber A flattening of the cells of timber during drying, which is manifested by excessive or uneven shrinkage. It is liable to occur in certain Australian hardwoods, such as brush box, mountain ash and messmate stringybark. In quarter-sawn timbers it produces a washboard effect, and in back-sawn

timbers it produces an unusually high degree of shrinkage. *Reconditioning* is a steam treatment, carried out in a sealed chamber for about six hours at about 90 °C (195 °F), which restores the timber to its normal condition.

collapsible forms Formwork which collapses to a reduced volume in order to be removed.

collar beam, collar tie The horizontal member in a timber roof, connecting the two opposite rafters at points which are much higher than the wall plate (*see figure*). A *collar-beam roof* thus gives more headroom than one with conventional trusses, but less than a rigid frame. Its purpose is to prevent the rafters from spreading, but the higher it is placed, the less efficient it is for this purpose. If the walls are massive enough to prevent the spreading, the collar beam goes into compression.

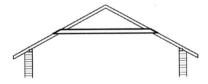

Collar beam

collector (solar energy) A device which converts incoming solar radiation to heat. *See also* PHOTOVOLTAIC CELL.

collector efficiency The ratio of the useful (heat or electrical) energy converted by a solar collector, to the radiation incident on the device.

collector plate *See* ABSORBER PLATE.

collector tilt angle The angle between the horizontal plane and the surface of a solar collector.

collimation line The line of sight, or optical axis, of a telescope, *e.g.* in a survey instrument. When properly adjusted, it passes through the *cross hair* or *reticule*.

colloid A substance consisting of very fine material, 10^{-9}–10^{-7} m (1–100 nm) in diameter. When mixed with water, the particles are too fine to settle. If undisturbed, they remain in suspension to form a GEL. CLAYS are partly colloidal.

colloidal grout A grout which has an artificially induced ability to retain the dispersed solid particles in suspension.

colonnade A series of columns, normally spaced at a uniform distance. In classical and neo-classical architecture the columns supported an ENTABLATURE, but the term is used in modern architecture for any regular arrangement of columns.

colophony *Same as* ROSIN.

color US spelling for *colour.*

colorimeter A device for measuring the colour attributes of light or reflective surfaces.

colorimetry The process of measuring the attributes of colour.

colour *See* CIE CHROMATICITY SYSTEM *and* MUNSELL BOOK OF COLOR.

colour appearance (of a lamp) The name (usually representing a band of CORRELATED COLOUR TEMPERATURES) that describes the appearance of a light source.

colour lookup table (CLUT) The range of colours available to most graphics programs is organised as a mixture of primary colours assigned specific numbers in a table. Whenever a particular colour is chosen from a colour palette, the program consults the colour lookup table to find the actual mixture of primary colours to reproduce it.

colour rendering index (CRI) *See* CIE GENERAL COLOUR RENDERING INDEX.

colour rendition The effect which the spectral characteristics of a light have on the appearance of coloured objects illuminated by it.

colour temperature The absolute temperature of a black-body radiator having a chromaticity equal to that of the light source (*see* CORRELATED COLOUR TEMPERATURE).

colouration The noticeable change in sound quality that occurs when a signal passes through an imperfect transmission system such as an enclosed space or a sound reinforcement system.

coloured cement Portland cement blended with a pigment, which does not chemically react with any of the components of concrete. Certain pigments, which are suitable for internal use, fade if used externally. Ordinary (grey) cement is satisfactory for the darker colours. WHITE or OFF-WHITE CEMENT is required with some lighter pigments.

Colt ventilator A proprietary device for the improvement of ventilation in a building by assisting the natural circulation of air.

column An upright structural member, generally square, rectangular or round, designed to carry a compressive load, often in conjunction with bending. *See also* PILLAR *and* STANCHION.

column analogy An analogy between the equations for SLOPE DEFLECTION and those for load and moment in short, eccentrically loaded columns, published by Professor Hardy Cross in the USA in 1930. It was used for the design of rigid frames.

column capital *(a)* The head of a column. In Classical and Gothic architecture it was elaborately decorated. *(b)* In modern concrete construction, the enlargement at the head of a column, built as an integral unit with the column and the FLAT SLAB. It is designed to increase the shear resistance of the flat slab. *See also* COLUMN STRIP.

column head *Same as* COLUMN CAPITAL.

column loudspeaker A linear array of interconnected loudspeakers which, if arranged in a near vertical line, will produce a horizontal directivity pattern.

column strip The portion of a FLAT SLAB or FLAT PLATE over the column. Most building codes define the column strip as consisting of the two adjacent quarter panels on each side of the column centre line (*see figure*).

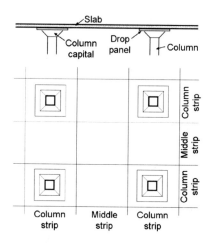

Column strip

column, long A column with a high SLENDERNESS RATIO. Its load-bearing capacity is reduced by BUCKLING.

comb filter Any device that produces a series of sharp attenuation notches in the output that resemble the teeth of a comb when plotted graphically. A reflecting surface or a reverberant room can act as a comb filter on sound.

comb joint An angle joint in timber formed by parallel tenons engaging matching slots.

combined footing A foundation supporting more than one column.

combined water Water in mineral matter which is chemically combined, and driven off only at temperatures above 110 °C.

combing *(a)* Smoothing the face of stone. *(b)* Creating a pattern in wet paint using a comb or stiff brush. *(c)* Top row of roof shingles protruding beyond the ridge.

combustible A material which burns. If placed in a hot furnace (usually at 750 °C) it raises the temperature of the furnace. A combustible material may or may not be *flammable, i.e.* burn with a flame. A material which does not support combustion is *non-combustible.*

combustion behaviour of upholstered furniture project (CBUF) A European project on classifying fire behaviour of furniture. Basically, four classes of furniture were classified based on their heat release rate curves.

comfort chart A graphical representation of the COMFORT ZONE. It usually has the dry-bulb temperature as an abscissa, and the wet-bulb temperature as an ordinate. The additional variable may be either the speed of the air movement, or the amount of radiant heat. The base of this may be the BIOCLIMATIC CHART, or the PSYCHROMETRIC CHART, and on this base the comfort zone is outlined.

comfort equation A heat balance relationship between the physical variables of ambient temperature, mean radiant temperature, humidity, and velocity of air, clothing insulation, metabolic rate and mechanical work performed by a human being, used to predict the sensation of thermal comfort.

comfort zone The range of temperature, humidity, air movement and radiant heat at which people may rest or work comfortably, where THERMAL COMFORT is possible. Normally a trapezoid shape on the psychrometric chart and an aerofoil shape on the BIOCLIMATIC CHART.

command language A user-interface language based on a restricted set of commands.

comment Notes included in a computer program amongst the code to clarify its operation for a human reader; however, they have no effect on its execution.

commitment rating A term applied to the commitment of a building owner to achieve a designated performance rating level prior to construction of a building.

common areas The unassigned space within a facility available for all users, such as lobbies, toilets and stairs.

common bond A brick BOND in which all courses are STRETCHERS, except the fifth, sixth or seventh course, which is a HEADER course. *Also called American bond*, or *Scotch bond.*

common brick An ordinary brick, as opposed to a FACE BRICK.

common mode (CM) Electrical interference which is measurable as a ground referenced signal. In true common mode, a signal is common to both the current-carrying conductors.

common rafter A RAFTER carried by the PURLINS, as opposed to a *principal rafter.*

common wall A wall forming part of two properties, and equally owned or leased by both parties. *Also called a party wall.*

community title A form of property title in which some common areas of a subdivision are owned jointly by all the property owners, while the separate houses or commercial premises are individually owned. *See also* CONDOMINIUM, OYO *and* STRATA TITLE.

commutator Segments on the rotor of a motor or generator that switch current at the correct instant to generate direct current or permit a motor to run from a source of direct current.

compact disk A disk on which information is recorded physically in digital code and read by a LASER beam.

compact disk read-only memory (CD-ROM) Compact disks that are created by a mastering process. Once the CD-ROM disks are mastered and pressed, the data is permanent and can be read by standard CD-ROM drives employing reflective laser technology. The popular audio CDs are examples of CD-ROM disks.

compact disk-recordable (CD-R) Compact disks that can be written directly by a computer using the appropriate software, as opposed to the mastering process used to create CD-ROM disks. Once the CD-R disks are written, the data is permanent and can be read by most standard CD-ROM drives.

compacting factor test A method for determining the WORKABILITY of freshly mixed concrete. The concrete is placed in a container of standard size, and allowed to fall under standard conditions into another container. Fully compacted concrete has a factor of one. The test is more precise, but also more time-consuming, than the SLUMP TEST. *See also* BALL TEST.

compatibility Two computers are said to be compatible if the same programs will run on both without alteration. Two components of a computer system (*e.g.* the computer and the printer) are said to be compatible if they can be used together without an intervening converter.

compensated balance A spring balance in series with a turnbuckle, used to measure a force in a structural *model*. As the spring balance extends or contracts, the turnbuckle is adjusted to keep the geometry of the structure correct.

compensating chain A chain used to offset the varying weight effect of the hoisting ropes of a lift system, which is connected at one end to the underside of the car frame, and at the other to the COUNTERWEIGHT.

compensating error An error due to an *accidental* cause, which may be either positive or negative, and is therefore likely to be self-compensating if sufficient data are taken. By contrast, an error due to a *systematic* cause is always in the same direction, and therefore *cumulative*.

compile To translate an algorithm written in a program language into machine code for a particular computer. The compiled version can then be run in full.

compiler A program that COMPILES. *See also* INTERPRETER.

complementary angle An angle that equals the difference between a given angle and a right angle (90°). For example, 60° is the complementary angle to 30°.

complex number The sum of a REAL and an IMAGINARY NUMBER.

component of a force *See* RESOLUTION OF A FORCE.

composite construction *(a)* A type of construction made up of different materials. *(b)* Specifically, structural steelwork and reinforced concrete designed as a single structural system.

composite girder *(a)* A PLATE GIRDER. *(b)* A girder of COMPOSITE CONSTRUCTION *(b)*.

compositing (keying) Compositing refers to superimposing part of one video clip on another. Keying is a general technique that places portions of one video in selected areas of another. Combining these techniques, one video scene can serve as a background for a foreground comprised of objects from an entirely different video clip.

composition roofing *Same as* BUILT-UP ROOFING.

compound (chemical) A substance in which several different types of *atoms* chemically combine to form new *molecules*, and thus a new substance, as opposed to a *mixture*, where different substances retain their own chemical identity.

compound curve Normally defined as a curve consisting of two (or more) circular arcs, which have different radii, and a common tangent at their point of junction.

compressed fibreboard *Same as* HARDBOARD.

compression (acoustic) The technique by which the DYNAMIC RANGE of the output of a device is less than that of the input (*see also* AUTOMATIC GAIN CONTROL).

compression (data storage) Transforming data for storage so that the stored data will take less memory space than the raw or uncompressed data. LOSSLESS COMPRESSION methods provide for recovery of the exact original data; whereas LOSSY COMPRESSION methods involve some loss of detail when the data is uncompressed.

compression (structural) A direct push in line with the axis of a body, and therefore the opposite of TENSION.

compression cycle *See* VAPOUR COMPRESSION CYCLE.

compression failure Failure under the action of a compressive force, either due to the material reaching its LIMITING STRENGTH, or due to BUCKLING, or due to a combination of both.

compression reinforcement Reinforcement used near the compression face of the concrete; it requires ties to prevent buckling.

compression wood A region of excessively dense wood; it is very brittle, and shows abnormal longitudinal shrinkage.

compressive strength of concrete *Same as* CUBE STRENGTH (in Europe) or CYLINDER STRENGTH (in the USA and Australia).

compressor *See* AIR, CENTRIFUGAL, HERMETIC, RECIPROCATING *and* SCREW COMPRESSOR.

computational fluid dynamics A computational technique that enables the detailed modelling of variations in temperature, velocity, contaminant distribution and similar phenomena in a fluid occupying a space by iterative solution of the transport equations.

computer An electronic device which receives, stores and operates on data according to a program and outputs the result. A computer is different from an electronic calculator due to the ability to change its program, *i.e.* altering its simulated behaviour. *See* DIGITAL COMPUTER *and* ANALOG COMPUTER.

computer architecture The way the components of a computer are organised.

computer graphics The use of computers to display information in pictorial form as opposed to textual form.

computer graphics interface *See* GRAPHICAL USER INTERFACE.

computer hardware, software *See* HARDWARE *and* SOFTWARE.

computer language A language whereby instructions are given to a computer.

computer memory The device where information is stored for retrieval by a computer. Usually reserved for main memory, *i.e.* memory which is directly accessible by the central processor of the computer.

computer model A representation of an object in a symbolic form that can be manipulated by a computer.

computer network *See* NETWORK *(c)*.

computer vision Intelligent hardware/ software systems that recognise features from and interpret visual images. A computer vision system, for example, may process photographs or video for objects of interest. An area of research in ARTIFICIAL INTELLIGENCE.

computer-aided The process of using computers to aid in some application domain, *e.g. computer-aided design, computer-aided engineering, computer-aided learning and computer-aided manufacturing.*

computer-aided facility management. The use of specific computer functions such as drawings and spreadsheets to provide FACILITY MANAGEMENT data.

computer-assisted design *See* CAD *and* CAAD.

computer-integrated construction The process of integrating all the information pertaining to the design and construction of a facility (a building) in a computer system.

computer-integrated facility management The use of interrelated computer databases, integrating specific facility information, which make FACILITY MANAGEMENT possible.

computer-integrated manufacturing *See* CAD/CAM.

computer-supported collaborative work A computer system for supporting collaboration between various participants, usually geographically distant from each other.

computing power The capacity of a computer, that may be designated by the speed (in MHz or GHz), of its CPU, and its architecture. Sometimes the size of its memory (RAM or 'cache'), and perhaps also its storage capacity, that of its HDD, are also considered.

concave A curve which bends inwards, like the inside of a circle, ellipse, etc. It is the opposite of *convex*.

concealed gutter *Same as* BOX GUTTER.

concealed lighting An artificial light

source, recessed into a ceiling or wall, or concealed behind a decorative facing or a *pelmet.*

concealed nailing *Same as* SECRET NAILING.

concentrated load A load acting on a very small area of the structure's surface, the opposite of a DISTRIBUTED LOAD.

concentrating collector A solar collector that reflects (or occasionally refracts) the direct solar radiation to an absorber surface to produce higher temperatures.

concentric column load A load which compresses a column without bending, as opposed to an ECCENTRIC column load. *Also called* an *axial load.*

concordant tendons Tendons in statically indeterminate prestressed concrete structures which do not produce secondary moments. They must be coincident with the line of pressure produced by the tendons.

concrete An artificial stone made from stone chips or gravel, sand and a cement (usually Portland cement). *See also* CAST IN PLACE, CELLULAR CONCRETE, GRANOLITHIC CONCRETE, GREEN CONCRETE, LEAN CONCRETE, NO-FINES CONCRETE, PLAIN CONCRETE, POLYMER CONCRETE, POLYMER–CEMENT CONCRETE, PRESTRESSED CONCRETE, READY-MIXED CONCRETE, REINFORCED CONCRETE, TRANSLUCENT CONCRETE *and* VACUUM CONCRETE.

concrete admixture *See* ACCELERATOR, AIR-ENTRAINING AGENT *and* RETARDER.

concrete aggregate The inert component of concrete. Heavyweight, or normal, aggregate consists of sand (FINE AGGREGATE) and gravel, crushed gravel, crushed stone or crushed recycled concrete (COARSE AGGREGATE). *See also* LIGHTWEIGHT AGGREGATE.

concrete block, brick A *block* or *brick* moulded from sand and cement, often with the addition of a mineral pigment.

concrete cancer A figure of speech describing the deterioration of concrete structures, usually associated with the penetration of moisture and chloride ions, and the corrosion of reinforcement.

concrete curing *See* CURING.

concrete hardener A chemical applied to a concrete floor to reduce wear and dusting. *See also* HARDENING OF CONCRETE.

concrete hardening *See* HARDENING OF CONCRETE.

concrete joist construction A floor structure consisting of a slab reinforced by joists (or ribs) in one direction, or in two directions at right angles to one another.

concrete mixer A machine for mixing the ingredients of concrete. *See* BATCH MIXER, CONTINUOUS MIXER, PAN MIXER, TILTING MIXER *and* TRANSIT MIXER.

concrete paint *See* CEMENT PAINT.

concrete pile A long, slender reinforced or prestressed concrete column embedded in the foundation. It may be driven, or cast in place. It may support the building as a BEARING PILE or as a FRICTION PILE.

concrete prestressing *See* PRESTRESSED CONCRETE.

concrete pump A pump that pushes concrete through a pipeline. It is widely used for transporting concrete from a TRANSIT MIXER to the place of pouring, particularly in a multi-storey building or over difficult ground. It may also be used in conjunction with a CEMENT GUN.

concrete quality control Statistical control of the COMPRESSIVE STRENGTH OF CONCRETE.

concrete retarder *See* RETARDER.

concrete terrazzo Concrete made with marble aggregate, and frequently with WHITE CEMENT, and subsequently ground smooth for decorative floor or wall surfaces. It may be precast or cast-in-place.

concrete vibrator A mechanical device which delivers energy to fluid concrete in order to assist compaction. *See also* VIBRATED CONCRETE.

concrete-encased beam A steel beam cast into concrete, generally MONOLITHIC with the floor slab, and completely encased by the concrete.

condensate Liquid formed by the condensation of vapour.

condensation The formation of water caused by the temperature falling below the DEW POINT of the air. It may occur on a cold surface or within the pores of a material (INTERSTITIAL CONDENSATION) or in the air itself, forming fog. Condensation is particularly likely in cool weather when the temperature drops at night, since the RELATIVE HUMIDITY then tends to be high, even in relatively dry climates.

condensation groove A groove to collect the condensation on the inside of windows, from which the moisture escapes to the outside by means of WEEPHOLES.

condenser *(a)* An apparatus for condensing vapours, *e.g.* in a steam engine, or in the refrigeration plant of an air conditioning unit. *(b)* A lens or mirror used in an optical system to collect light and direct it on to a projecting lens. *(c)* Non-preferred term for a CAPACITOR in an electrical circuit.

condenser microphone A microphone where the pressure fluctuations cause a displacement of a thin diaphragm which forms one plate of a capacitor. The change in capacitance is proportional to the magnitude of the pressure fluctuations. Condenser microphones are substantially omnidirectional in their response to sound.

condenser water Cooling water circulated as a heat transfer medium between a refrigerant gas condenser and a COOLING TOWER.

condenser water loop The piping loop connecting one or more refrigerant gas condensers to one or more cooling towers to form a system for the rejection of heat to atmosphere.

condensing boiler A boiler for heating water, in which the flue gases are cooled below dew point, and the recovered heat used in order to increase thermal efficiency.

condition appraisal A technical appraisal of the existing physical state of a facility's assets, including the building fabric, systems, services and functionality.

conditions of engagement The terms of contract between two parties, which set out each party's responsibility, such as fees, ownership of information and dispute resolution.

condominium US term for an APARTMENT which is sold and not rented. *See also* STRATA TITLE.

conductance, conduction, conductivity, thermal *See* THERMAL CONDUCTANCE, *etc.*

conductance, electrical *See* ELECTRICAL CONDUCTANCE.

conduction *(a)* The mode of heat transfer through a material (solid, liquid or gas) by the motion of adjacent atoms and molecules without gross displacement of the particles. *(b)* The transfer of electrical current by movement of free electrons within a material. *(c)* The transfer of sound through a solid by the propagation of a wave.

conduction band The energy band in which the electrons can move freely.

conductor A substance or body capable of readily transmitting electricity, heat or sound by CONDUCTION.

conduit *(a)* A natural or artificial channel for conveying liquids. *(b)* A tube, usually of plastic or metal, which encloses electrical wires or cables. Conduits are partly used for protection, and partly to allow cables to be pulled through after the concrete or other building material has been placed in position.

conduit box A junction box serving as an outlet and as a place from which to pull wires through the conduits.

cone *(a)* A figure whose base is a circle, with sides tapering uniformly towards a point. A *truncated cone* is one which is cut off before reaching the point (*see figure*). *(b)* One of the receptors in the retina of the eye, used in bright conditions, and capable of seeing in colour. *See also* ROD *(a)*.

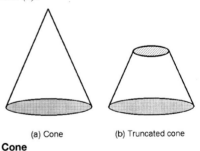

(a) Cone   (b) Truncated cone
Cone

cone calorimeter A bench-scale apparatus to measure heat release rate by oxygen consumption method under adjustable radiation heat flux.

confidence limits The limits within which a random sample of a set of data is presumed to be included, with a pre-assigned degree of confidence.

configuration factor A factor which

summarises the external obstruction to daylight at any given window, used in calculating the DAYLIGHT FACTOR.

confined compression test *Same as* TRIAXIAL COMPRESSION TEST.

conglomerate A rock composed of (usually rounded) pieces of pre-existing rock cemented together.

conic sections The CIRCLE, the ELLIPSE, the PARABOLA and the HYPERBOLA, produced by cutting a CONE at different angles.

conifer A tree belonging to the botanical group *Gymnospermae*, which bears cones. It includes all the softwoods used in building, particularly the pines and firs.

connecting rod The rod connecting the piston of a RECIPROCATING ENGINE to the crankshaft. It converts the backward-and-forward motion into rotary motion.

connection *See* BLACK BOLT, BOND, BRIGHT BOLT, GANG-NAIL, HIGH-TENSILE BOLT, MORTISE, NAILER, NAIPLATE, RIVET, SOLDERING, SPLIT-RING CONNECTOR, TOOTHED-PLATE CONNECTOR, TRUSS PLATE *and* WELDING.

conoid A SURFACE OF TRANSLATION generated by the motion of a straight line over a curve and a straight line, or two curves that are different, but of the same type. For example, a *parabolic conoid* is generated by a straight line moving over a flat parabola at one end and a more strongly curved parabola at the other. A conoid is a RULED SURFACE, and it can be utilised as a NORTHLIGHT SHELL.

conservatory *(a)* Same as GREENHOUSE. *(b)* US term for *conservatorium*, a school for teaching music or other arts.

consistency index A ratio for comparing the stiffness of cohesive soils. It is defined as

$$\frac{\text{liquid limit} - \text{water content of sample}}{\text{liquid limit} - \text{plastic limit}}$$

consistency limits The LIQUID and PLASTIC LIMITS of COHESIVE SOILS, which describe soils' range of workability. *Also called Atterberg limits.*

consistency of concrete The ability of freshly mixed concrete or mortar to flow, and fill the formwork without voids. *Also called workability.* It is measured with the

BALL TEST, COMPACTING FACTOR TEST and the SLUMP TEST.

console A manual control unit for a large computer, providing a display of information and a means of communicating with the computer. Now largely superseded by *terminals.*

consolidation The gradual settlement of a COHESIVE SOIL under the weight of the structure which it carries. It results from the squeezing of water from the pores of the soil, and is a problem only in clays and other soils of low water permeability.

consolidometer *Same as* OEDOMETER.

consortium A group of firms that jointly undertake a project while still retaining their separate identities.

constant air volume system A method of air distribution in an air conditioning system in which air is circulated at constant volume with the temperature varied to maintain the desired space condition, in contrast to a VARIABLE AIR VOLUME SYSTEM where temperature is held constant and air volume flow rate is varied for the purpose.

constantan An alloy of about 55 per cent copper and 45 per cent nickel. Junctions of copper and constantan are widely used in THERMOCOUPLES for temperature measurement.

constitutional diagram *Same as* PHASE DIAGRAM.

construction joint A joint (usually in in-situ concrete) to enable the building process to be interrupted, without detracting from the strength of the structure. It may or may not be masked with a DUMMY JOINT.

construction key A key which allows construction workers to access all parts of a new building. Upon handover to the owner, a simple procedure disables the construction key and allows the owner's keys to operate the locks.

construction loads The loads imposed on the building during construction due to the erection, assembly and installation of building components and building services.

construction management A method of procurement in which a head contractor is appointed as Construction Manager, to provide advice to the principal and to manage the construction phase of a project, including tendering of subcontract trade packages, award and administration of successful subcontractors.

constructive solid geometry A solid geometry representation using three-dimensional GEOMETRIC PRIMITIVES and BOOLEAN OPERATIONS. For example, a wall with an opening is constructed by subtracting a piece of wall from the wall.

contact adhesive An adhesive that adheres instantly upon contact.

contaminant (of air) A substance present in air causing it to be considered unclean.

contemporary Existing at the same time. This may be at the present time, or at the same historical time in a discussion of the architecture of the past.

contiguous piers A method of stabilising an excavation, by drilling and concreting a series of piers (usually 450–600 mm diameter) around the perimeter before excavating a basement. As the excavation proceeds, GROUND ANCHORS may be installed through the piers to prevent them from collapsing inwards.

continental seating Auditorium seating unbroken by aisles. Access is from aisles at the ends of the rows of seats.

contingency A sum of money identified contractually to provide for unforeseen activities during the course of a contract.

contingency planning The process of anticipating and developing alternative actions, should a preferred course of action be terminated.

continuity Structural continuity implies that the SLOPE at a rigid joint or the support of a continuous beam is altered by the same amount on each side of the joint or the support by elastic deformation.

continuous beam A beam which is continuous over intermediate supports (*see figure*), and thus *statically indeterminate*, as opposed to a *simply supported beam*.

continuous footing A COMBINED FOOTING which acts like a CONTINUOUS BEAM on the foundation.

continuous girder *Same as* CONTINUOUS BEAM.

continuous mixer A machine that mixes concrete in a continuous operation, as opposed to a *batch mixer*.

contract administration The management process of ensuring that all obligations of the contract are carried out during the contract period.

contract capacity The maximum legal load which a lift CAR is permitted to carry, measured in either a number of passengers or a specific mass in kilogram or pounds.

contract load Alternative term for CONTRACT CAPACITY.

contract speed The linear car speed in the lift well which the lift manufacturer has contracted to supply.

contraction joint A joint which allows shrinkage of concrete or brick to take place in a predetermined location, and so avoid objectionable shrinkage cracks elsewhere. It may be made by an insert or by a sawcut in a concrete slab. *See also* EXPANSION JOINT *and* CONTROL JOINT.

contraflexure A change in the direction of bending of a beam (*see figure*). The slope has a maximum value at this point, and therefore the differential coefficient of the slope $d\theta/dx = 0$. From NAVIER'S THEOREM and the geometry of the figure,

$$\frac{d\theta}{dx} = \frac{M}{EI}$$

so that the bending moment is zero at the point of contraflexure. Consequently it is possible to insert a hypothetical 'hinge' at this point and remove a REDUNDANCY. *Also called inflection or inflexion.*

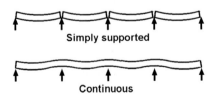

Simply supported

Continuous

Continuous beam

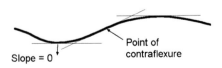

Slope = 0

Point of contraflexure

Contraflexure

contrast In illuminating engineering, the assessment of the difference in appearance of two parts of a field of view seen simultaneously or successively. More particularly as *luminance contrast*, a measure of the difference in the luminance or reflecting properties of sources or surfaces, respectively. It is usually expressed in terms relative to, say, the background luminance.

contrast (relative) The ratio of the luminance difference of an object, and that of its immediate background, to the background luminance.

contrast rendering factor (CRF) See CIE CONTRAST RENDERING FACTOR (CRF).

control joint A generic name for EXPANSION JOINT and CONTRACTION JOINT. A joint or separation in a building which permits its component parts to move relative to one another. The most common cause of such movement is thermal, but it may also be caused by shrinkage, creep, wind loads or seismic action. *See also* BRICKWORK MOVEMENT JOINT, CONTRACTION JOINT *and* EXPANSION JOINT.

control of lift systems *(a) Attendant*: the direction of travel, door closing and lift car starting are under the control of an attendant. *(b) Automatic pushbutton*: the travelling passengers are able to control the movement of a lift car without an attendant. Door control and starting are automatic. *(c) Collective*: landing calls are registered on a single set of pushbuttons, passengers being unable to indicate their desired direction of travel. *Also referred to as simplex collective control. (d) Directional collective*: landing calls are registered on a set of up and down pushbuttons. *Also referred to as full collective control. (e) Group collective*: a simple form of group control system. Two or three cars are collectively controlled, to allocate the best placed car to each landing call. *(f) Group supervisory*: a control system which commands a GROUP of interconnected lift cars (to improve the overall system performance). *(g) Non-collective*: the simplest form of control. A lift car will answer a landing call only if it is available. *(h) Scheduled*: a supervisory control system which dispatches lift cars to serve landing calls according to a fixed schedule. *See also* LIFT RECALL.

convection The transmission of heat by natural or forced motion of a liquid or gas, *i.e.* by movement of the particles, as opposed to THERMAL CONDUCTION or RADIATION.

convergent series An INFINITE SERIES whose sum is finite, *e.g.* the series $1 + \frac{1}{2} + \frac{1}{4} + \frac{1}{8} + \ldots$ adds up to 2. The sum of all the terms of a *non-convergent series* is infinity.

conversion factor A number which converts a unit of one system into that of another.

conversion of timber The process of sawing timber from the log.

convex A curve bending outwards, the opposite of *concave*. The curvature of the lens of a magnifying glass is convex.

conveyor A powered continuous belt for the horizontal or inclined movement of bulk materials, *e.g.* concrete, aggregate. A conveyor designed for the movement of discrete items is generally called a BRICK ELEVATOR, *tile elevator*, etc.

cookie A FILE sent to a WEB BROWSER by a WEB SERVER that is used to record one's activities on a WEB SITE. For example, when the browser requests additional files, the cookie information is sent back to the server. Cookies can remember other kinds of information about the user, so at the next visit to that site one is presented with customised information.

cool white fluorescent lamp A lamp that contains more light in the blue-green part of the spectrum than an ordinary white lamp.

cooling coil load The heat load that a cooling coil must remove from air in order to maintain a required room thermal condition. It includes the room sensible and latent heat gains together with gains from ventilation air and from transport of air between the room and the coil.

cooling load The quantity of heat required to be removed from air in order to maintain a desired thermal condition of air in a space.

cooling tower A device for cooling water to approximately the wet-bulb temperature of the outside air, to take heat away from the CONDENSER *(a)* of a heat engine.

cooling tower fill Material placed inside a cooling tower for the purpose of increasing the contact between the cooling water and the air flow through the tower.

coordinates *See* CARTESIAN COORDINATES *and* POLAR COORDINATES.

COP *Abbreviation for* COEFFICIENT OF PERFORMANCE.

copal A hard natural resin, derived from the gum of tropical trees or from recently fossilised gum. It is used for varnishes and paints.

coping A capping of stone, brick or concrete for the top of a wall. It frequently projects beyond either or both faces of the wall, partly for protection from the weather, and partly for decoration.

coping saw A bow saw with a narrow blade, which can be used for cutting sharp curves in timber.

copolymerisation Addition POLYMERISATION involving more than one type of MER.

copper A metallic element. Its chemical symbol is Cu, its atomic number is 29, its valency is 1 or 2, it has an atomic weight of 63.54, its specific gravity is 8.96, and it melts at 1083 °C. Copper is used in many alloys, notably brass, bronze and aluminium bronze. Because of its high electrical conductivity and good corrosion resistance it is used extensively as an electrical conductor.

coprocessor A computer processor which assists the CENTRAL PROCESSING UNIT (CPU) to carry out specialised tasks, usually much faster, *e.g.* a graphics coprocessor.

copy command, operation A commonly used command or operation in word processing and other environments. Using this operation, text, images, sounds, *etc.* can be *copied* (but not deleted) for temporary storage on the system's CLIPBOARD, then pasted into another location within the same document or to a location within another document.

corbel A projection of masonry, brick or concrete from a wall face, which serves as support for a lintel, beam or truss *(see figure)*. It is, in effect, a short cantilever.

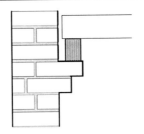

Corbel

corbelled arch ARCH formed by courses of brick or masonry uniformly advancing from each side of an opening until they meet in the middle. Its joints are horizontal, instead of being normal to the line of thrust as in a true ARCH *(see figure)*.

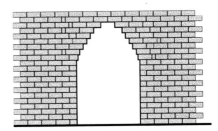

Corbelled arch

corbelling Masonry or brickwork consisting of a series of *corbels*, each projecting a little more than the one below. It is used for supporting ORIEL WINDOWS and forming chimney stacks. At one time it was used for forming CORBELLED ARCHes.

cord An obsolete measure for timber. 1 cord = 128 ft³ (4 ft × 4 ft × 8 ft).

cordless tools Electric tools powered by rechargeable batteries instead of a power lead.

core *(a)* The ferrous centre part of a transformer or inductor used to increase the strength of the magnetic field. *(b)* The central region of the Earth, having a radius of about 3470 km, outside of which lies the mantle and the crust. The radius of the Earth is 6370 km. *(c)* See SERVICE CORE.

core drilling Drilling holes with a hollow *bit* (usually a *diamond drill*), so that the cylinder of material inside the bit is recovered. It is often used to obtain samples of rock or concrete for testing, but it is also an economical way of drilling large holes because the amount of material to be cut is much less than with a solid bit.

core samples *See* BOREHOLE SAMPLES.

core saturation Condition when an inductor or transformer core has reached maximum magnetic strength.

Coriolis force The effect of the Earth's rotation, causing secondary rotational effects in air streams and ocean currents. It influences some of the large-scale meteorological patterns, particularly near the equator.

cork The bark of the cork-oak. It is used for stopping bottles, in granulated form as an insulating material, and as a floor-surfacing material which has good heat and sound insulation.

cork tiles Tiles made from compressed CORK. They form a floor-covering with good insulating properties.

cork wood *Same as* BALSA WOOD.

cornerstone *(a)* a stone at the corner of a building. *(b)* The FOUNDATION STONE of the building, if it is situated on a corner. *(c)* In colloquial use, a particularly important part of the building, or of some argument.

cornice *(a)* In Classical, Gothic and Renaissance architecture, the projecting top-most part of the ENTABLATURE (*see figure at* ENTABLATURE). It was usually decorated, but it had the functional use of throwing the rainwater that fell on the roof clear of the masonry wall. Because Modern architects would not use decoration, they generally failed to use cornices, even as simple rectangular projections. As a result the facades of many of their buildings were spoilt prematurely by streaks of dirty rainwater. The term *cornice* is also used in traditional architecture for a projecting moulding at the top of a door or window casing. *(b)* A moulding between the wall and the ceiling inside a building.

corps de logis The centre part of a large building. The outer parts are the WINGS.

corrected effective temperature (CET) EFFECTIVE TEMPERATURE as modified to include the effect of the mean radiant temperature.

corrective maintenance *See* MAINTENANCE, CORRECTIVE.

correlated colour temperature (CCT) (of a light source) In colorimetry, the temperature of the BLACK BODY (full radiator) that most closely resembles colour distribution of the light source. The light source, say, a lamp, may operate at a temperature much lower than its correlated colour temperature.

corrosion Destruction of material, particularly metal, by chemical means. *See also* DECAY *(a)*.

corrugated sheet Roof sheet which has been corrugated, partly for flexural stiffness and partly to provide drainage channels for rainwater. The most common type is 'corrugated iron', which is normally galvanised mild steel. Corrugated sheets are also made from aluminium, fibre cement, PVC, polycarbonate and glassfibre-reinforced translucent resin.

Corten steel A high-strength, low-alloy steel which does not need to be protected by paint because, like aluminium, it forms a protective oxide coating through weathering. The colour changes from light brown (after about one month) to dark brown or purple (after one to two years). However, the oxidation process may produce brown streaks on concrete or other materials at a lower level. *Called Austen steel in Australia.*

corundum Aluminium oxide (Al_2O_3) used as abrasive. Not to be confused with CARBORUNDUM. *See also* EMERY.

cos The COSINE of an angle.

cosec The COSECANT of an angle.

cosecant A CIRCULAR FUNCTION of an angle, the ratio of the length of the hypotenuse of a right-angled triangle to that of the side opposite the angle. *Abbreviated cosec.* The cosecant is the inverse of the SINE; cosec $\theta = 1/\sin \theta$.

cosh Hyperbolic cosine. *See* HYPERBOLIC FUNCTIONS.

cosine A CIRCULAR FUNCTION of an angle, the ratio of the length of the side adjacent to the angle in a right-angled triangle to that of the hypotenuse. *Abbreviated cos.*

cosine law of illuminance A law enunciated by J. H. Lambert in the eighteenth century, stating that the illuminance on a surface tilted at an angle θ is equal to the illuminance on a surface normal to the light source times cos θ.

cosine wave The same as a SINE WAVE, but displaced by one-quarter of a wavelength.

cost analysis An analytical technique involving an assessment of all costs and revenues in order to identify and assess as many costs and benefits as possible.

cost–benefit analysis A process of evaluation measuring expected financial benefits against present value.

cost planning A technique used to control the cost of a project within the budget during the design phase by reference to the historical costs of elements.

cost-plus contract The actual prime cost of labour, plant and materials is paid for at net cost to the contractor plus a fee, based on a percentage of these, or a fixed fee, to cover the contractor's overheads and profit. This type of contract is used if there is insufficient time to design the entire project and complete the drawings and specification. *Also called a cost-reimbursement contract.*

cot The COTANGENT of an angle.

cotangent A CIRCULAR FUNCTION of an angle, the ratio of the side adjacent to the angle (other than the hypotenuse) in a right-angled triangle, to that of the side opposite the angle. *Abbreviated cot.* The cotangent is the inverse of the TANGENT; $\cot \theta = 1/\tan \theta$.

cotter A wedge, pushed through a slot to hold two pieces together.

cotter pin A split pin used as a COTTER. After it has been placed in position, its ends are bent outwards to keep the pieces securely in place.

coulomb (C) Unit of electrical charge, named after the eighteenth-century French scientist and military engineer. It is the quantity of electricity transported by 1 ampere in 1 second.

Coulomb's equation A relation between the shear strength of a cohesive soil, v, and the normal (foundation) pressure, f; devised by the French engineer C. A. Coulomb in 1776.

$$v = c + f \tan \theta$$

where c is the cohesion of the soil, and θ is its *angle of shearing resistance*. This is a straight limiting line, inclined at an angle θ, for a series of MOHR CIRCLES. The

equation can also be applied to the compression failure of concrete as a failure criterion; the cohesion is contributed mainly by the cement paste, and the shearing resistance mainly by the aggregate.

counterclockwise The opposite of CLOCKWISE. *Also called anticlockwise.*

counterfeit architecture *See* TROMPE L'OEIL.

counter-flow Term used to describe the arrangement of flow through a HEAT EXCHANGER when fluids enter with maximum difference and leave with minimum difference in temperature.

counterfort A pier at right angles to a RETAINING WALL, on the side of the retained material and therefore not visible. It can only be used to strengthen a structure capable of tensile resistance, such as reinforced concrete, since the earth pushes the wall away from the counterfort (*see figure*). A BUTTRESS can also be used to strengthen a plain concrete or masonry retaining wall.

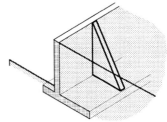

Counterfort

countersink To make a depression just sufficient to receive the head of a screw, rivet, or some other part of a joint which normally projects. It can be done in timber, metal or any other material, using a conically shaped cutting tool, or *bit*.

counterweight *(a)* A component of a lift system used to ensure TRACTION between the drive SHEAVE and the hoisting ropes, comprising a set of weights to balance the car and a proportion of the car load, usually 50 per cent of the CONTRACT CAPACITY. *(b)* Any heavy weight used, temporarily or permanently, to prevent the uplift of part of a structure.

counterweight guard A screen installed in the pit of a lift system, and sometimes at the mid-point of the lift well, to prevent inadvertent encroachment into the COUNTERWEIGHT runway space.

counterweight safety device A mechanical device attached to the counterweight frame of a lift system, designed to stop and hold the COUNTERWEIGHT in the event of an overspeed, free fall, or the slackening of the suspension ropes.

couple A pair of equal and parallel forces, not in line and oppositely directed. The moment of a couple equals the magnitude of one of the forces, F, times the perpendicular distance between them, a (*see figure*).

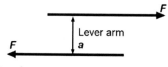

Couple

coursed ashlar ASHLAR laid in regular horizontal courses.

coursed rubble RUBBLE arranged to form courses by using small pieces, or mortar, to fill up the interstices between them.

cove A concave quadrant moulding, *i.e.* a hollow CORNICE, or a concave junction between a wall and a floor, to facilitate cleaning.

cover In reinforced concrete, the thickness of concrete overlying the steel bars nearest to the surface (*see figure*). An adequate layer is needed to protect the reinforcement from rusting and from fire.

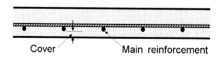

Cover

cover fillet or strip A moulding used to cover a joint.

covering power The HIDING POWER of a paint for a given spreading rate.

cowl A metal cover, often capable of rotating, and fitted with louvres. It is fixed on a roof ventilator or chimney to improve the natural ventilation or draught.

CPM *Abbreviation for* CRITICAL PATH METHOD.

cps *Abbreviation for* Cycles Per Second. Since the introduction of SI UNITS, this is called HERTZ, *abbreviated* Hz.

CPU *Abbreviation for* CENTRAL PROCESSING UNIT.

CPVC *Abbreviation for* Chlorinated Polyvinyl Chloride.

Cr Chemical symbol for *chromium.*

crack *See* CRAZING, GRIFFITH CRACK *and* MICROCRACK.

cracked section In reinforced concrete design, a section which is designed on the assumption that the concrete has no resistance to tensile stresses, and that the tension is taken by the reinforcement.

cracking load The load at which cracks occur in a concrete structure because the tensile strength of the concrete is exceeded. The term generally refers to the appearance of visible cracks, not to the appearance of MICROCRACKS.

cramp *(a)* A U-shaped metal cramp used since Ancient Roman times to fasten adjoining stones to one another. It was generally inserted in recesses cut in the top of the stones, and often secured with molten lead. *(b)* A clamp with a tightening screw used to hold a frame in place during construction, or to compress two pieces of wood during gluing.

crane *See* CLIMBING, GANTRY, HAMMER-HEAD, MOBILE, SCAFFOLD, SELF-CLIMBING *and* TOWER CRANE, DERRICK *and* SHEAR LEGS.

crane, box girder A crane consisting of one or two box girders, supported on end carriages, which allows the rope and pulley to move along the box girders.

crank A bar with two right-angled bends, which gives it leverage, *e.g.* a crank handle for starting an internal combustion engine, or a crank shaft in a RECIPROCATING ENGINE.

crash bar The cross bar of an exit door, which operates its opening device, so that the door can be opened from the inside, but not from the outside.

crashed time The fastest time in which an activity in a building project can be performed by making more labour and materials available than would normally be done. If the activity lies on the CRITICAL PATH, it may be more economical to perform the activity in crashed time than in normal time. The critical path must be recalculated if any operation is speeded up, since it may no longer lie on it; however, this would not necessarily imply that the use of crashed time is uneconomical.

crawl space The space under a suspended floor needed for access to services.

crazing The development of fine, random cracks caused by shrinkage on the surface of plaster, cement paste, mortar or concrete. They are particularly noticeable if the material is finished to a smooth surface with a steel trowel. Crazing is more likely to occur in concrete if the cement is brought to the surface by excessive trowelling.

creep Time-dependent deformation due to load. It can be represented by a RHEOLOGICAL MODEL. *(a)* In structural metals, creep occurs only at elevated temperatures (in steel above 300 °C). It is caused by the increased mobility of atomic particles at higher temperatures. *(b)* In concrete, a sustained load squeezes water from the cement GEL at ordinary temperatures. Creep deformation may be two or three times as great as the ELASTIC DEFORMATION, and it causes a substantial redistribution of stress, often transferring load from the concrete to the steel reinforcement. Because of creep, the EFFECTIVE MODULUS OF ELASTICITY of concrete is reduced. Creep is a major cause of LOSS OF PRESTRESS in both POST-TENSIONED and in PRE-TENSIONED concrete.

creep deflection Deflection of a beam due to CREEP. Elastic deflection occurs instantly, whereas creep deflection requires time to develop; it may be several months before it becomes noticeable.

creosote oil A liquid distilled from coal tar between 240 and 270 °C, which is used as a timber preservative.

crest factor The ratio of the maximum value to the RMS value of a signal measured over a given period of time. For instance the crest factor of a sinusoidal signal is √2.

CRF *Abbreviation for* CIE CONTRAST RENDERING FACTOR.

CRI *Abbreviation for* CIE GENERAL COLOUR RENDERING INDEX.

cricket US term for roof flashing behind a chimney or wall that diverts the water away.

crimping Deforming metal to produce a series of (usually flat) ridges.

cripple stud A wall stud that does not run the full height of a wall, *e.g.* at a doorway.

crippling load (of a column) The load at which a slender column BUCKLES.

critical activity An ACTIVITY which lies on the CRITICAL PATH.

critical angle The maximum angle of a ramp or a staircase which is considered safe.

critical distance In a room, the sound field can be divided into a DIRECT SOUND FIELD, where the direct sound from the source dominates, and the REVERBERANT SOUND FIELD, where the reflected sound dominates. The critical distance is the distance from the source at which the contribution from the direct and reflected sound is equal.

critical load (electrical) Devices and equipment whose failure to operate satisfactorily jeopardises the health or safety of personnel, and/or results in loss of function, financial loss or damage to property deemed critical by the user.

critical path The route through the NETWORK, from starting point to terminal point, which is critical for the project. The *critical time path* is the longest route through the network. The *critical resources path* may also have to be determined, if either labour or materials are limited.

critical path method (CPM) A method of scheduling complex building contracts to determine the critical operations which would, if neglected, lead to delays, and to determine the cost of finishing the work more quickly, or the saving in cost if it were finished more slowly. As in a progress chart, the normal time required for all operations is worked out, and the interrelation of the various operations is plotted as a NETWORK. The CRITICAL PATH through the network is then determined, which gives the completion period if all operations are performed on time. The operations which lie on this path are critical, and it may be worthwhile to perform them in CRASHED TIME, by making more material or labour available; this may, however, alter the critical path. *See also* PERT.

critical slope The slope corresponding to the ANGLE OF REPOSE of a soil.

critical temperature In metallurgy, the temperature at which a critical transformation occurs in the heating or cooling curves of a PHASE DIAGRAM.

critical velocity The velocity at which fluid flow changes from streamline to turbulent.

CRO *Abbreviation for* Cathode-Ray Oscilloscope.

crocodiling The formation of cracks on the surface of paint or other finishes, somewhat resembling crocodile skin.

cross flow cooling tower A COOLING TOWER in which the air flow is horizontal across the falling stream of water.

cross flow ventilation *See* NATURAL VENTILATION.

cross grain Wood in which the fibres deviate from a line parallel to the sides of the piece.

cross hairs *(a)* Threads fixed across the diaphragm of a *level* or a *theodolite*. Modern instruments use a GRATICULE, a glass plate with lines engraved in it. *(b)* In computer graphics, two lines orthogonal to each other and extending over the full screen. The intersection defines the CURSOR position.

cross vault A vault resulting from the intersection at right angles of two BARREL VAULTs of identical shape (*see figure*). *Also called* a *groin vault*.

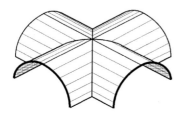

Cross vault

cross ventilation *See* NATURAL VENTILATION.

crossbanding The layers of veneer in plywood that are perpendicular to the core.

crosscut saw A saw whose teeth have

been set and sharpened to cut *across* the grain of the wood, rather than with it.

cross-headed screw A screw with a cross-shaped recess in the head (instead of a slot), such as a *Phillips head* or a *Pozidriv*. It is preferred for use with power screwdrivers, since the bit tends to slip out of a conventional slotted screw-head. *See also* ALLEN HEAD.

cross-linking of polymers The tying together of adjacent polymer chains.

cross-over network An active or passive electronic network used to ensure that each loudspeaker driver, in a loudspeaker unit, receives only the frequency band for which it was designed. For example a cross-over network allows only frequencies above 2–4 kHz to be handled by a TWEETER.

cross-platform capabilities Software with versions available on more than one type of computer hardware (*e.g.* Macintosh and PC) and designed so that files created by the software on one hardware platform can be opened by the software on the other platform.

cross-sectional area The area of a cross-section, *i.e.* of a section cut transversely to the longitudinal axis of a member.

cross-talk *(a)* The transmission of sound between two rooms through a supply or return duct that is common to the two rooms. *(b)* The pick-up of a signal from one channel of an electronic system by another channel.

crotchwood The portion of a tree where a large limb branches from the trunk. The fibres of the branch produce a curly grain, and a veneer cut from crotchwood is highly FIGUREd. *See also* BURL.

crown The highest point, or *vertex*, of an arch or dome. The stone at the crown of a masonry arch is called the KEYSTONE.

crown glass *(a)* Glass made by blowing a mass of molten material, which is then flattened into a disc, and spun into a circular sheet. It is limited in size to about 1.4 m (4 ft 6 in.) diameter. Since the glass does not come into contact with any other material during manufacture it is free from the defects which occur in CYLINDER GLASS. The process was introduced into England in the seventeenth century, and the sash window with brilliantly clear, often slightly curved crown glass became one of the characteristics of Georgian architecture. The centre of the disc, or *bull's eye*, was originally used for inferior work. Later it was employed deliberately, often using cast imitations, for the windows of 'rustic' cottages. The crown glass process became obsolete in the nineteenth century. *(b)* GLASS of the alkali-lime-silica type, as opposed to FLINT GLASS.

crown post *Same as* KING POST.

crown silvered lamp A kind of REFLECTOR LAMP, in which the outer half of the glass bulb is internally silvered, thus the filament is not visible and the light is reflected back onto a PARABOLIC REFLECTOR.

CRT *Abbreviation for* CATHODE-RAY TUBE.

crucks Pairs of large curved timbers used for the principal framing of barns and primitive houses. They form a pointed arch, taking the place of both the posts and the rafters. Called *crutches* in the USA.

crushing failure The compression failure (due to diagonal shear) of many brittle materials which results in the production of crushed material or debris. Since this takes time, it is much slower than a CLEAVAGE FRACTURE. The compression failure of concrete is a typical example.

crushing strength of concrete This is measured as CUBE STRENGTH or CYLINDER STRENGTH.

crutches *See* CRUCKS.

crypt Cellar space below the choir or nave of a church.

cryptocrystalline Having a structure too small to be discerned with an optical microscope, for example in natural stone.

crystal A body whose atoms are arranged in a definite pattern. The regular arrangement gives rise to the characteristic crystal faces.

crystal chandelier A glass CHANDELIER with additional glass prisms. These were originally intended to improve the illumination by reflecting the light of the candles, but with the advent of ELECTRIC LAMPS they became mainly decorative.

crystal structure *See* BODY-CENTRED CUBIC LATTICE, CLOSE-PACKED HEXAGONAL LATTICE *and* FACE-CENTRED CUBIC LATTICE.

crystalline fracture Fracture taking place between crystals, and exposing their faces. In a tension test particularly, this is evidence of *brittleness*.

crystalline silicon A type of PHOTO-VOLTAIC CELL made from a single crystal or polycrystalline slices of silicon.

CSA Canadian Standards Association, Missisauga.

CSG *Abbreviation for* CONSTRUCTIVE SOLID GEOMETRY.

CSIR Council for Scientific and Industrial Research, a term employed in India, Pakistan, South Africa and, formerly, in Australia.

CSIRO Commonwealth Scientific and Industrial Research Organisation, Australia.

CSTB *Centre Scientifique et Technique du Bâtiment*, Paris.

CT (colour temperature) *See* CIE CORRELATED COLOUR TEMPERATURE.

ctg Continental abbreviation for CO-TANGENT.

Cu Chemical symbol for *copper*.

cube One of the five regular *polyhedra*. It is bounded by six squares, and hence is *also called* a *hexahedron*.

cube strength (of concrete) In most European countries the compressive strength of concrete is ascertained by crushing a cube; this is expressed as the ultimate load per unit cross-sectional area. The size of the cube varies from 100 mm (4 in.) to 200 mm (8 in.). Because of the greater probability of the presence of flaws in large pieces of a brittle material, the average cube strength decreases as the size of the cube increases. *See also* CYLINDER STRENGTH.

cubic lattice *See* BODY-CENTRED CUBIC LATTICE *and* FACE-CENTRED CUBIC LATTICE.

cubit The principal measure of length used in Ancient Egypt, Babylon, Israel and Greece. It was based on the length of the forearm, and varied from 525 to 445 mm. The forearm measure was called *braccia* in Medieval and Renaissance Italy, and it varied from city to city.

culls *(a)* In forestry, trees which are removed individually, because they are deformed, too closely spaced, etc. They provide one source of raw material for

FIBREBOARD. *(b)* Any pieces (such as bricks) rejected from a production run as inferior.

culvert A large drain below ground level, built in place of a small bridge. It is generally formed by a box or a large-diameter pipe.

cumulative error An error due to a *systematic* cause, which is always in the same direction, as opposed to a *compensating error*.

cup Curvature across the face of a wood plank.

cup head The rounded head of a bolt or screw, several times the diameter of the shank, but much flatter than a hemisphere. *See also* COACH BOLT.

cup-and-cone fracture The typical fracture of a DUCTILE material, *e.g.* structural steel, in tension (*see figure*). The bar first elongates plastically, and the consequent *necking* reduces the cross-sectional area until the ultimate tensile stress of the material is reached, when a brittle fracture across the bar occurs. After failure, one of the two parts of the bar is cup-shaped and the other cone-shaped.

Cup-and-cone fracture

cupola *Same as* DOME.

curing *(a)* The maintenance of an appropriate humidity and temperature in freshly placed concrete to ensure the satisfactory hydration of the cement, and proper hardening of the concrete. It may be necessary to provide a source of heat in very cold weather, or some cooling in very hot conditions. Evaporation of water is reduced by placing covers over the concrete, applying a *curing membrane* (a liquid sealing compound) to the exposed surface, or sprinkling the concrete periodically with water. *(b)* The chemical change, resulting in additional linkages between the molecules, which occurs when an ACCELERATOR is added to a COLD-SETTING RESIN, or when a THERMOSETTING

plastic is heated above the critical temperature. The material gains the required strength and hardness through curing.

curl A fine, curved FIGURE in the grain of wood, frequently obtained by the conversion of CROTCHWOOD.

current The flow of electrons through a CONDUCTOR.

current balance The (nearly) equal flow of current on each leg of a THREE-PHASE power system. With this flow balanced, the theoretical flow of current in the neutral will be zero.

current distortion DISTORTION in the AC line current.

current transformer (CT) A TRANSFORMER used in instrumentation to assist in measuring current. It utilises the strength of the magnetic field around the conductor to form an induced current that can then be measured.

cursor A special symbol on a computer screen indicating the location of the next operation to be performed.

curtain wall A thin wall supported by the structural frame of the building, as opposed to a BEARING WALL.

curtaining Sagging of wet paint on a surface (when applied too thickly) to produce an uneven and unsatisfactory coat. Refers to sagging in wide areas, as opposed to thin *runs* from local concentrations of paint.

curvilinear Consisting of or bounded by curved lines.

cusec Cubic feet per second.

cusp *(a)* A point where two branches of a curve meet, have a common tangent, and terminate. *(b)* An ornament of roughly this shape, used in Gothic tracery.

cut command, operation A commonly used command or operation in word processing and other environments. Using this operation, text, images, sounds, etc. can be *removed from* a document and temporarily stored on the system's CLIPBOARD. Later, the removed data can be pasted into another location within the same document or to a location within another document.

cut nail A heavy rectangular nail made by cutting or shearing from steel plate.

cut-off angle The critical viewing angle beyond which a light source can no longer be seen because of an obstruction (such as a baffle or overhang).

cut-off frequency The cut-off frequency of a MODE in a duct is the frequency below which a given mode of a travelling wave cannot be maintained. It is usually taken as the frequency at which the only mode which can propagate is a plane wave.

cutting-in When painting a wall or piece of trim, carefully finishing the paint against the boundary of the adjoining surface.

CV *Abbreviation for* COEFFICIENT OF VARIATION.

C-weighting A weighting scale occasionally used for high intensity sound level measurements or measurements that require an almost flat frequency response over the frequency range of the human ear.

CWT *Abbreviation for* Copper Water Tube (refers to nominal pipe size).

cwt Abbreviation for *hundredweight*, an obsolete British mass of 112 lb or about 50 kg.

cyanide hardening CASE HARDENING of steel by immersion in a bath of molten sodium cyanide (NaCN).

cybernetics The science of automatic control.

cyberspace Term coined by William Gibson in his novel *The Neuromancer* to describe the dimension of digital communication enabled by computer networks.

cybrarian Cyber-librarian.

cybrid Hybrid of physical and CYBER-SPACES. (Term coined by Peter Anders.)

cycle A full repetition of a regular wave. The time it takes for the wave to complete a cycle is called the *period* of the wave's motion.

cycles per second The frequency of alternating current, or any other repetitive waveform. The SI term for frequency is Hertz (Hz), which is cycles per second.

cycloid A curve generated by a point on a circle rolling over a straight line. It can be rotated to form a dome which, like a semielliptical dome, has vertical springings. *See also* EPICYCLOID.

cyclone A large-scale wind event, mainly limited to certain tropical regions, and characterised by destructive winds and rotation of the air mass. A wind of force 12 on the BEAUFORT SCALE. *Also called hurricane* (in the Caribbean) *and typhoon* (in East Asia).

cyclopean concrete Mass concrete containing a large number of PLUMS.

cyclopean masonry *(a)* Masonry composed of very large irregular blocks, particularly in prehistoric architecture. *(b)* RUSTICATED masonry in squared blocks, popularised by the Renaissance in the fifteenth century, which either have the rough hewn texture resulting from quarrying, or an artful imitation thereof.

cylinder A solid bounded by a curved surface terminating in two parallel and equal plane figures (which are generally, but not necessarily, circles).

cylinder glass Glass made by blowing a mass of molten material into a hollow cylinder which, while soft, was cut lengthwise, laid out on a preheated iron table, and placed in an annealing furnace to flatten. The process became obsolete in the 1930s.

cylinder lock A lock with a central cylinder which rotates when the key lifts the internal tumblers.

cylinder strength (of concrete) In most parts of the USA and Australia the compressive strength of concrete is ascertained by crushing a 150mm (6in.) diameter cylinder, 300mm (12in.) long, and expressed as the ultimate load per unit cross-sectional area. The cylinder strength of concrete is about 84 per cent of its 150mm CUBE STRENGTH.

cylindrical shell A roof structure, which forms a part of a cylinder. Its cross-section is generally a circular arc, although elliptical and CATENARY cylindrical shells have been built. Cylindrical shells are DEVELOPABLE and RULED SURFACES, and SURFACES OF TRANSLATION. *See also* BARREL VAULT *and* NORTHLIGHT SHELL.

cyma A moulding whose profile has a double curvature. In a *cyma recta* the curvature is concave at the outer edge and convex at the inner edge; in a *cyma reversa* it is convex at the outer edge and concave at the inner edge. The cyma reversa is also known as an *ogee* moulding *(see figure)*.

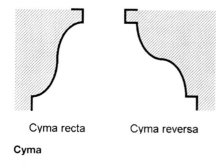

Cyma recta   Cyma reversa

Cyma

D

d *Abbreviation for deci*, one-tenth.
D1S Timber dressed one side only.
da *Abbreviation for deka*, ten times.
DAC *Abbreviation for* digital-to-analog converter. DACs are used to convert digitised analog information (such as digitised sound waves) back to analog form, which is a process referred to as playback. Contrast with an ANALOG TO DIGITAL CONVERTER (ADC).
dado In Classical architecture, the portion of the pedestal between the base and the cornice. In modern buildings, any border or panelling over the lower half of the walls of a room, which is above the skirting.
dado rail A moulding on the wall at the top of a DADO.
DAI Distributed Artificial Intelligence.
daily noise dose The ratio of the noise exposure experienced by a person during a working day to a reference value of noise exposure. A daily noise dose of less than unity usually indicates that the subject is unlikely to suffer noise-induced hearing loss.
dais A raised platform at one end of a large room.
Dalton's law of partial pressure 'The total pressure exerted by a mixture of different gases is the sum of the pressures each would exert if they alone occupied the container.'
damage risk criterion (DRC) An empirical curve, relating the frequency to the upper limit of sound pressure (in

DECIBELS), above which loss of auditory acuity or deafness is likely to result.
damp course *See* DAMPPROOF COURSE.
damped oscillation A mechanical (*e.g.* acoustical) or electrical oscillation in which there is an appreciable diminution of amplitude during successive cycles. Reducing vibrations by damping is analogous to reducing movement by friction. Damping is measured by the DECAY FACTOR or DAMPING RATIO.
damper An adjustable metal plate inside a flue or air duct, used to restrict the flow. Also a plate inside a duct, operating automatically in the event of a fire to close off the duct completely.
damping The dissipation of energy from a vibrating system that results in a reduction in amplitude of the vibration. *See also* DAMPED OSCILLATION.
damping of structural vibrations Wind and earthquake loads may set up excessive vibrations, particularly in tall buildings of flexible construction. These can be damped by *viscoelastic* devices.
damping ratio A measure of decay rate of a decaying oscillating system: it is the ratio of the actual damping to the critical damping.
damping, critical The least value of the damping that will allow a displaced oscillatory system to return to its rest condition without oscillation.
dampproof course (DPC) An impervious layer inserted into a pervious wall (such as a brick wall) to exclude water. A DPC is required above ground level (below the level of a timber floor) and below a roof parapet (above the roof level). Traditional materials for a DPC are slate, vitrified brick and lead. BITUMEN with a core of lead, copper, zinc, aluminium or plastic is now more common. A DPC is sometimes, misleadingly, called a *damp course*. *See also* FLASHING.
DAR Dressed All Round (all four sides of a piece of timber dressed).
Darcy's law 'The velocity of percolation of water in saturated soil = HYDRAULIC GRADIENT × coefficient of PERMEABILITY.'
dark adaptation *(a)* The process by which the retina becomes adapted to lower light levels. *(b)* Adaptation to luminances less than 10^{-3} cd/m^2.

DAT *Abbreviation for* Digital Audio Tape, a small, 4 mm tape which has a very good signal quality. DAT in computers is used for ARCHIVING or backing up data and may be referred to as DDS (Digital Data Storage).

data Items of information. Strictly, *data* is the plural of *datum*, so that it implies a number of items of information. In practice, the singular is only used in a few special situations, such as a *datum level*.

data bank A large electronic store of data. *See also* DATABASE.

data decompression *See* COMPRESSION (data storage).

data exchange The process of transferring DATA between different applications.

data exchange standards Standards for the representation of data to allow transfer between different graphic programs, *e.g.* STEP, IGES, DXF.

data file *See* FILE.

data link The medium over which data are transferred.

data logger An electronic device to record data on a tape or disc, in digital form, where often analog (*e.g.* millivolt or milliamp) output from sensors is passed through an A–D CONVERTER.

data network *See* NETWORK *(c)*.

data transfer rate The rate at which data are transferred. Usually measured in bits per second (BPS).

database Collection of interrelated data stored on files, to facilitate the addition, modification and removal of data, usually by computer.

database management system SOFTWARE which controls the operations on a DATABASE.

datum line or level A reference *line* or *level*, used to locate other lines or levels in a survey. *See also* BENCHMARK.

daub *See* WATTLE-AND-DAUB.

day labour A system of payment where employees are paid by the day (or hour), rather than by PIECEWORK.

daylight *(a)* Direct, diffused or reflected sunlight and skylight. Sometimes the term is used to refer only to *skylight* with sunlight being treated separately. *Also called natural light.* *(b) (colloquial)* The visible clearance between two parts.

daylight factor A factor describing the efficiency of a window in a particular room, used in the design of rooms for daylight. It is defined as the ratio of the ILLUMINANCE at a point in a room to the illuminance at the same instant on a horizontal plane exposed to the unobstructed sky.

daylight protractor A transparent mask which is used in the graphical determination of the DAYLIGHT FACTOR.

daylighting Generally, the lighting of a space using daylight, either from skylight alone or with direct or indirect sunlight. Daylighting is usually used in combination with ELECTRIC LIGHTING.

day–night sound level (L_{dn}) A 24-hour L_{Aeq} where 10 dB is added to night-time noise levels between 22:00 and 07:00 hours to account for increased annoyance caused by noise at night.

dB *Abbreviation for* DECIBEL.

DB *Abbreviation for* DRY BULB. Sometimes used incorrectly as an abbreviation for DECIBEL.

dB(A) A-weighted SOUND PRESSURE LEVEL in DECIBELS. *See also* A-SCALE ON A SOUND LEVEL METER.

DBCE Division of Building and Construction Engineering, now part of CSIRO Manufacturing and Infrastructure Technology (CMIT).

DBMS *Abbreviation for* DATABASE MANAGEMENT SYSTEM.

DBR Division of Building Research *(a)* Melbourne, part of CSIRO, *(b)* Ottawa, now Institute for Research in Construction (IRC).

DBT *Abbreviation for* DRY-BULB TEMPERATURE.

DC *Abbreviation for* DIRECT CURRENT.

dead level This normally means perfectly level; but a very small slope is sometimes tolerated within that definition.

dead light A window which does not open, as opposed to an *open light*.

dead load A load which is permanently applied to a structure, and acting at all times, as opposed to a LIVE LOAD.

dead man A heavy weight used for anchorage, or a pole set in the ground for anchorage.

dead room A room which has very high sound absorption.

dead shore A temporary vertical support.

dead wall *Same as* BLANK WALL.

dead window *Same as* BLANK WINDOW.

dead-burnt gypsum *Same as* ANHYDRITE.

deadend anchorage The anchorage opposite to the jacking end of a tendon when POST-TENSIONING is carried out from one end only.

deadlock *(a)* A lock which can only be closed or opened by a key (from outside) or a snib (from the inside). It usually has a rectangular tongue, as distinct from a NIGHTLATCH that has a spring-loaded, wedge-shaped tongue, so it can be slammed shut and can also be forced open from the outside by a thin flexible tool. *(b)* A lock as above, but capable also of being key-locked from the inside. Therefore an intruder who gains access, *e.g.* through a window, cannot exit through the door.

debugger A program or part of a program which aids in locating and correcting BUGS in program CODE.

debugging The process of eliminating errors from a computer program or system.

deca *See* DEKA.

decagon A ten-sided POLYGON. The angle included between the ten equal sides of a regular decagon is 144°.

decal An image or pattern, printed in reverse onto a plastic or paper sheet and then transferred onto a glass or other surface.

decarburisation Removal of carbon from the surface of steel.

decay *(a)* The decomposition of timber, particularly by fungi. *(b)* The damping of an oscillation, particularly a sound wave. *(c)* Spontaneous transformation of an atomic particle into two or more different particles.

decay factor The factor expressing the rate of decay of oscillations in a DAMPED oscillatory system, defined as the natural logarithm of the ratio of two successive amplitude maxima, divided by the time interval between them. It is a measure of the damping, for example, of acoustical RESONANCE.

deci Latin prefix for $\frac{1}{10}$, *e.g.* 1 decimetre = 0.1 m.

decibel, dB *(a)* A scale unit used in the comparison of powers mainly in electronics and acoustics. The logarithm (base 10) of the ratio of two power quantities (W) is named Bel (after Alexander Graham Bell) but as this is a large unit, one-tenth of it is commonly used, the deci-Bel (1 bel = 10 dB). *See* SOUND POWER LEVEL. *(b)* The sound intensity level in dB is 10 times the logarithm (base 10) of the ratio of a given intensity to a reference intensity (10^{-12} W/m^2), whilst the SOUND PRESSURE LEVEL is 20 times the logarithm (base 10) of the ratio of given sound pressure to a reference sound pressure, as the square of pressure is proportional to intensity (W/m^2) or power (W).

deciduous tree A tree which loses its leaves in winter. In Northern Europe the term is largely synonymous with hardwood, since all native hardwoods lose their leaves and none of the commercially used softwoods lose their needles in winter. However, most hardwoods native to the tropics and subtropics are evergreen.

decimal arithmetic Arithmetic based on the ten digits, 0, 1, 2, 3, 4, 5, 6, 7, 8, 9. It originated from counting on the ten digits of one's fingers. Since the only factors of 10 are 2 and 5, this is not the most useful arithmetic system, and DUODECIMAL ARITHMETIC has evident advantages. Electronic digital computers use BINARY ARITHMETIC.

decimal logarithm A LOGARITHM to the base 10. This is the logarithm normally employed. It is denoted by the abbreviation *log*. The other commonly used logarithm is the NATURAL LOGARITHM, or logarithm to the base *e*, designated *ln*.

decimal system (of measures) The system originally introduced by the new republican government of France in 1793, based on DECIMAL ARITHMETIC. The original CGS UNITS have now been replaced by the slightly different SI UNITS.

decking *(a)* Timber boards forming an elevated, outdoor platform, usually spaced apart to allow rainwater to escape and to assist in drying after rain. *(b)* By extension, the upper surface of any elevated outdoor balcony or roof.

declarative language A programming language that operates with logical relationships. In a declarative language a problem is expressed by describing it rather than how to solve it as in a PROCEDURAL LANGUAGE. *Prolog* is a well-known example of a declarative language.

declination The vertical coordinate of the sun, moon or a star at any given time, measured from the Earth's equatorial plane. It is listed in the NAUTICAL ALMANAC. *See also* ALTITUDE *and* RIGHT ASCENSION.

decrement factor The attenuation ratio between the magnitudes of internal and external diurnal temperature swings either side of a massive construction element, resulting from its thermal mass.

deemed to satisfy A procedure or technical solution which is deemed to satisfy requirements of a building regulation, as opposed to *demonstrating* that it meets a PERFORMANCE SPECIFICATION.

deep discharge battery A type of rechargeable battery that is not damaged when a large portion of its energy capacity is repeatedly removed (*i.e.* motive batteries).

defects liability period The period following practical completion of the works during which the contractor must rectify or repair defects due to faulty materials or workmanship.

deferred maintenance *See* MAINTENANCE, DEFERRED.

defibration Separating fibres, for example of timber, by chemical or mechanical means to create a new material, such as FIBREBOARD.

defibrator Machine for disintegrating wood into fibres.

definition In acoustics, the degree to which individual sounds in a musical performance stand apart one from another. *Also called clarity.*

deflected tendon A tendon whose eccentricity, with reference to the CENTROID of the section, varies along the length of the beam. The object of deflecting, or *draping*, the tendon is to set up a bending moment which opposes the moment due to the imposed load, and thus reduces the stresses in prestressed concrete under load by LOAD BALANCING.

deflection The flexural deformation of a structural member. Although ELASTIC

DEFORMATION is recoverable, it may damage brittle finishes, such as plaster, if it is excessive. The deflection of concrete and timber increases over a period of time due to CREEP.

deflectometer An instrument for measuring deflection. The most common device is a DIAL GAUGE.

deformation Change of shape. It may be ELASTIC (instantly recoverable), PLASTIC (permanent) or VISCOUS (recoverable over a time interval).

deformed bar A reinforcing bar with surface deformations which provide an anchorage with the surrounding concrete, and thus increase the BOND with the concrete (*see figure*). The deformed surface is produced during the hot rolling of the bars from indentations in the rolls of the steel mill. The deformations must provide sufficient anchorage without setting up excessive stress concentrations in the concrete.

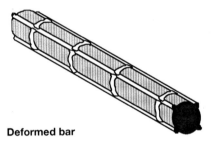

Deformed bar

deformeter *See* BEGGS' DEFORMETER.

deg *Abbreviation for* degree.

degradation Reduction of polymers to smaller molecules, *also called depolymerisation.*

degree of compaction The degree of density of a soil sample, given by the ratio $(V_1 - V_s)/(V_1 - V_d)$, where V_s = VOIDS RATIO of sample, V_1 = voids ratio of soil in its loosest state and V_d = voids ratio of soil in its densest state.

degree of polymerisation Measured in MERS per average molecular weight.

degree of saturation A measure of the VOIDS in a soil which are filled with water (the remainder being filled with air). It is the ratio of the volume of waterfilled voids to the total volume of voids.

degree-day A unit employed in estimating the total heating requirement for a building in a particular climate. For any one day, when the temperature is below a specified value (usually 15 °C (59 °F) in Europe and 18 °C (65 °F) in the USA), there exist as many degree-days as the mean temperature for the day is below the specified value. The total for the month or heating season is then compiled in Kd (Kelvin-days) or Fahrenheit degree-days. The base temperature can be taken as the BALANCE-POINT TEMPERATURE of the building.

degree-hour A more accurate unit similar to the DEGREE-DAY, but defined in terms of hours. It is used mainly for estimating the cooling loads for air conditioning.

degrees of freedom The number of variables, defining the state of a system, which may be fixed at will.

dehumidification of air Removal of moisture from the air. In AIR CONDITION-ING plants it is accomplished by cooling the air below the DEW POINT, normally with a spray of chilled water, and draining off the condensate. In order to reduce the humidity to the desired level, it is usually necessary to cool the air below the temperature ultimately required and then reheat it. This is one reason why air conditioning is more expensive than heating. For small quantities of air, for example in instruments sensitive to moisture, the water vapour may be removed by an adsorbent, such as SILICA GEL. *See also* ABSORPTION CYCLE *and* COMPRESSION CYCLE.

dehumidifier Component of an AIR CONDITIONING plant which reduces the moisture content of the air by cooling and condensation. *See also* HUMIDIFIER.

dehydration of air Dehumidification of air. It generally refers specifically to the removal of moisture by ADSORPTION.

deka (da) The Greek word for ten. Prefix for 10 times, *e.g.* 1 dekagram (a unit popular in Austria) = 10 gram. *Also spelled* deca (not to be confused with deci).

delamination Separation of layers in a laminated assembly, either through failure in the adhesive or through failure at the interface of the adhesive and the lamination.

deliquescence The liquefying of certain salts due to their absorption of water from the air. Bricks or plaster containing chlorides may show an appearance of dampness due to this property.

delta connection In THREE-PHASE electrical systems, a *three-wire system* of connecting a balanced electrical load making use of the higher line voltages. *See also* STAR CONNECTION.

delta–delta The connection between a DELTA source and a delta load.

delta–star The connection between a DELTA source and a STAR load (*see figure*).

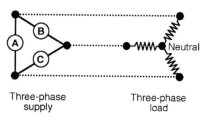

Three-phase   Three-phase
supply   load

Delta-star

delta–wye *Same as* DELTA–STAR.

deluge system Automatic fire sprinkler system consisting of open sprinkler heads controlled by a quick opening valve which is activated by detectors installed in the same area as the open sprinklers. This system is employed for fire risks requiring total or zoned water coverage.

demand factor A factor (less than unity) by which the actual wattage of an electrical installation may be multiplied in designing the wiring system, to allow for the fact that the larger the premises, the less likely it is that all lights, etc. will be switched on at the same time. Demand factors are generally specified in electrical codes.

demand unit A standardised unit of demand related to fixture type used for the estimation of peak demand in a water supply system.

demand-side abatement Action designed to reduce emission of greenhouse gases or other pollutants to the atmosphere by improving the efficiency of utilisation of energy, thus reducing the demand.

demand-side management (DSM) The planning and implementation of strategies designed to encourage consumers to improve energy efficiency, reduce energy costs, change the time of usage or promote the use of a different energy source.

demec strain gauge A demountable STRAIN GAUGE which consists of a long bar with one fixed and one movable point which operates a DIAL GAUGE through a lever. The points engage plugs glued to the structure under test.

demised premises Premises held under the terms of a lease.

demolition hammer A heavy hand-held machine with a reciprocating chisel-pointed bit, used for breaking up concrete, masonry, etc. *Same as jackhammer*, although a demolition hammer is more commonly electrically operated and jackhammer is more commonly applied to a pneumatic tool.

demountable partition A PARTITION which can be easily installed, removed, and relocated without damage to its pre-fabricated components.

dendrite A tree-shaped crystal, caused by the tendency of some metals to grow by branches developing from a nucleus. The secondary branches growing from the primary branches produce the dendritic structure.

dense concrete Concrete made in the conventional way, as opposed to LIGHT-WEIGHT CONCRETE. It generally weighs 1900–2600 kg/m³ (120–160 lb/ft³).

density Mass per unit volume. SPECIFIC GRAVITY is the ratio of the mass of a substance to the mass of an equal volume of water. In the metric and SI systems it has the same numerical value as the density in g/cm³ or tonne/m³.

depolymerisation Reduction of polymers to smaller molecules, *also called degradation.*

depreciation The reduction in the value of an asset through wear, tear and obsolescence.

depth of discharge A measure of the amount of energy removed from a battery during a cycle of use, as a percentage of its total charge.

derrick Originally the gallows at Tyburn in London, named after a sixteenth-century hangman. Now a crane consisting of a jib set up obliquely, with its head steadied by guy ropes. There are many different types ranging from small, hand-operated derricks to large, power-operated derrick cranes. *See also* SCOTCH DERRICK, TOWER CRANE *and* GANTRY CRANE.

desalination Producing drinking-quality water from salty water, by processes such as DISTILLATION or REVERSE OSMOSIS.

desiccant A chemical substance with the property of adsorbing moisture from air. Used in desiccant air driers.

desiccation Drying, *e.g.* of timber in a kiln.

design and construct contract A contract between a client and construction contractor to provide both design and construction services for an agreed financial return.

design heat load The total heat loss from a building during the most severe winter conditions for which the building is designed.

design load The working or service load for which a part of the building is designed.

design month The month having the most adverse conditions, around which a heating, cooling or solar energy system is designed.

design review The formal review of a design proposal by independent reviewers, required as part of QUALITY ASSURANCE accreditation.

design sky A term used in DAYLIGHTING calculations, usually meaning the diffuse (or sky-) ILLUMINANCE (excluding beam sunlight) of an unobstructed horizontal surface outdoors that is exceeded for 90 per cent of the annual daylight hours (usually taken from 09:00 to 17:00 h), that is determined for a given location and would be used for converting a DAYLIGHT FACTOR into indoor illuminance. It can also mean the luminance distribution assumed for the sky (uniform, CIE sky, *etc.*).

design tools May mean any implement or method used in design, but in modern usage it means computer-based tools, CAD systems or various software used for design calculations, such as lighting, daylighting, acoustics or thermal response prediction.

design-build *Same as* DESIGN AND CONSTRUCT CONTRACT.

desktop The term for the screen background in most graphical user interfaces (GUIs) on which WINDOWS, ICONS, and *dialog boxes* appear.

despatcher panel An assembly of INDICATORS showing up/down and landing calls, direction, status and position for each car in a lift system, with key-controlled switches. *See also* ANNUNCIATOR.

destructive distillation DISTILLATION of a solid substance, accompanied by its decomposition.

detached A freestanding building, as distinct from one with one or more COMMON WALLS.

detector *See* FIRE DETECTOR.

detention basin Part of a stormwater drainage system formed by a constructed or natural basin in the ground which receives flow from the site and regulates the outflow to achieve the rate of discharge that would be expected from the site if it had retained its natural ground cover of vegetation. *See also* RETENTION BASIN.

determinant (of a matrix) A square array of quantities, and the sum of the products formed by evaluating it in accordance with certain mathematical rules.

detritus tank A settling tank through which SEWAGE is passed for the settlement of the heavier solids.

detrusion Shear strain.

developable surface A curved surface which can be flattened into a plane surface without shrinking, stretching or tearing. Cylindrical, SINGLY CURVED SURFACES are developable. DOUBLY CURVED SURFACES are non-developable. Developable surfaces have zero GAUSSIAN CURVATURE.

development length In reinforced concrete, the length of reinforcing bar required to develop the stress at the critical section.

deviation *(a)* The amount by which one observation of a set of observed values differs from their mean. The STANDARD DEVIATION is a measure of the spread of the observations. *(b)* The bending of a ray of light as it passes through a prism or lens, or is reflected by a mirror.

deviation angle The total angular deviation by a ray after a series of refractions and/or reflections, through an optical system.

devitrification In glass, deterioration through crystallisation.

dew point The temperature at which CONDENSATION of water vapour in the air takes place, *i.e.* the temperature at which the air is fully saturated.

dewatering Keeping a building site dry and the soil in stable condition during construction by pumping the water from the excavation. *See also* WELLPOINT DEWATERING.

dewpoint hygrometer An instrument which measures the humidity of the atmosphere by determining the dew point. A refrigerating effect is produced on a silvered bulb by evaporating ether inside it, until dew appears on the silvered surface, where it can easily be recognised. The best-known type is the *Regnault hygrometer.*

dextrin A water-soluble gum made from starch, used as an adhesive.

dezincification The leaching of zinc from BRASS and other zinc alloys, resulting in loss of strength and integrity of the item. It can occur in plumbing fittings in acidic environments.

DF *Abbreviation for (a)* DEGREES OF FREEDOM, *or (b)* DAYLIGHT FACTOR.

DHW Abbreviation for Domestic Hot Water system or supply.

diagnostic program A program, usually an expert system, for the diagnosis of faulty performance. May also include a prescription for remedial actions.

diagonal *(a)* A straight line connecting two non-adjacent angles of a quadrilateral, polygon or polyhedron. *(b)* A strut or tie running at an angle to both the horizontal and the vertical in a TRUSS or a LATTICE STRUCTURE.

diagonal bracing See DIAGONAL *(b).*

diagonal compressive stress One of the PRINCIPAL STRESSES resulting from the combination of horizontal and vertical SHEAR STRESSES in a beam. Beams with slender webs such as steel plate girders must be provided with STIFFENERS to prevent web BUCKLING due to the diagonal compression.

diagonal crack An inclined crack caused by the DIAGONAL TENSILE STRESSES in a brittle material, such as concrete. It starts on the tension face and gradually disappears as it passes into the compression zone of the beam (*see figure*). Small diagonal cracks are acceptable in concrete, but when the permissible shear stress is exceeded, SHEAR REINFORCEMENT must be provided across the cracks.

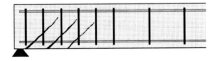

Diagonal crack

diagonal Flemish bond A brick BOND in which a course of HEADERS alternates with a course of headers and STRETCHERS; it shows a diagonal pattern (*see figure*).

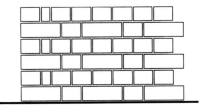

Diagonal Flemish bond

diagonal member Member used for BRACING.

diagonal tensile stress One of the PRINCIPAL STRESSES resulting from the combination of horizontal and vertical SHEAR STRESSES in a beam or slab. In brittle materials, such as concrete, it causes DIAGONAL CRACKS.

dial gauge An instrument for measuring deflection. It consists of a plunger whose movement is enlarged by a train of gears, operating a rotating pointer. It can readily measure a deflection of 1×10^{-3} mm or 1×10^{-4} in. A dial gauge may be used as a DEFLECTOMETER, as a measuring device in a STRAIN GAUGE or in a PROVING RING.

dial-up The process of accessing a computer via a telephone line using a MODEM.

diamagnetic Pertaining to bodies which are *repelled* by a magnet.

diametral compression test *Same as* SPLITTING TENSILE TEST.

diamond The crystalline form of CARBON. It is one of the hardest materials on Earth and is classified 10 on the MOHS' SCALE.

diamond drill A drilling machine with a hollow cylindrical bit, coated on the cutting edge with industrial diamonds, used for CORE DRILLING in concrete, rock, etc. Water is usually used to cool the bit and remove the material.

diamond mesh *Same as* EXPANDED METAL.

diamond pyramid hardness test *See* VICKERS DIAMOND HARDNESS TEST.

diamond saw A circular saw, with industrial diamonds on the cutting edge of the blade. It is commonly used for cutting brick and other hard materials.

diaphragm A relatively thin, usually rectangular element of a structural member which is capable of withstanding shear in its plane. It serves to stiffen the structural member.

diaphragm pump A pump in which a flexible partition (or diaphragm) of rubber, leather or canvas is operated by a rod. The diaphragm takes the place of the piston in the usual *reciprocating* pump. The pump is very robust, and it can be used for pumping water containing mud, sand and even small stones.

diatomaceous earth A whitish powder consisting mainly of the frustules of diatoms (which are microscopic plants). It is nearly pure hydrous amorphous silica, and is resistant to heat and chemical action. It is used in insulating materials and fireproof cements, in filters, and also as an absorbent in the manufacture of explosives. Nobel's discovery of the 'safe' explosive dynamite consisted of the observation that nitroglycerin is absorbed by diatomaceous earth. *Also called kieselguhr.*

diatonic scale The scale used in most Western music, ascribed to J. S. Bach, which consists of eight notes per OCTAVE. In a major scale the frequencies of the notes are in the ratios 1, $2^{2/12}$, $2^{4/12}$, $2^{5/12}$, $2^{7/12}$, $2^{9/12}$, $2^{11/12}$ and 2. In a minor scale the third and sixth notes are reduced by a semitone. *See also* CHROMATIC SCALE.

dicalcium silicate One of the principal components of PORTLAND CEMENT. Its chemical composition is $2CaO.SiO_2$, or

C_2S in the notation used by cement chemists. It is the component named *Belite* by Tornebohm in 1897, before the chemical composition of cement had been properly established.

dichroic Literally, 'having two colours': in lighting, referring to the properties of filters and reflectors employing thin films of metal oxides to alter the spectral composition of reflected or transmitted light and infrared radiation. Dichroic reflectors are used with some incandescent lamps to reflect the visible light in the desired direction but allow much of the heat to escape.

die *(a)* (plural *dies*) A tool for drawing wire, extruding rods, cutting threads or stamping metal. *(b)* (plural *dice*) A cube whose faces are marked with one to six spots used in games of chance, or any small cube into which food is cut.

dielectric *(a)* A non-conducting material. *(b)* Capable of sustaining an electric field.

dielectric heating The process of generating heat at high frequencies in nonconducting materials by placing them in a strong alternating electric field.

dielectric strength Electric breakdown potential of an electrical insulator, per unit thickness.

differential amplifier Amplifier that has two input signal connections and a zero signal reference lead. The output is the algebraic sum of the instantaneous voltages appearing between the two input signal connections.

differential mode voltage The voltage between any two of a specified set of active conductors.

differential pulley block A lifting tackle consisting of two pulleys of slightly different diameters and an endless chain

Differential pulley block

(see figure). The closer the diameter of the two pulleys, the greater the lifting power of the tackle, and the slower its speed of operation.

differential settlement Uneven sinking of different parts of a building. It endangers the safety of a building if it causes it to tilt (the Leaning Tower of Pisa is a classical example), or if it places severe strain on some of the structural members. Differential settlement may be due to a clay foundation of variable consolidation characteristics, or to grossly uneven load distribution (*e.g.* due to a tower block) on a compressible clay.

diffraction *(a)* The deviation of a ray (or wave) of light at an edge of an obstacle in its path, sometimes breaking up the ray into colours or dark and light fringes due to interference, *e.g.* when a ray passes through a narrow slot. *(b)* The similar breaking up of other types of electromagnetic waves. *(c)* The modification of a progressive acoustical wave due to the presence of an obstacle in the sound field.

diffuse irradiance (or irradiation) That radiation, scattered by the atmosphere, received from all directions within a hemisphere the surface is exposed to, excluding the beam (or direct) component.

diffuse reflection The scattered reflection (as opposed to SPECULAR REFLECTION) of light or sound from a rough surface.

diffuse solar radiation The solar radiation reaching a surface due to reflection and scattering effect.

diffuse sound field A sound field where the properties of the field are the same throughout. *See also* REVERBERANT SOUND FIELD.

diffuser *(a)* A device used to alter the spatial distribution of the luminous flux from a source by DIFFUSION. A perfectly *matt* surface is one in which the whole of the incident light is redistributed uniformly in all possible directions in such a way that the LUMINANCE is the same in all directions. *(b)* A cone or wedge placed in front of a loudspeaker to obtain a more uniform polar distribution of sound with varying frequencies. *(c)* Any surface or surface irregularity introduced into a room in order to attain a more uniform distribution of sound. *(d)* A device used to introduce supply air to a conditioned space in such a way that it is gradually diffused into the space without creating a draft.

diffusing panel A translucent panel in a luminaire, used to reduce the brightness of the lamps by distributing the radiant flux over a larger surface area.

diffusing surface A surface that redistributes some of the incident flux by scattering in all directions (*also known as a Lamberian surface*).

diffusion *(a)* The movement of atoms or molecules of one material in another without chemical combination. *(b)* Alteration of the spatial distribution of light or sound which, after reflection at a surface or passage through a medium, travels on in numerous directions.

diffusion coefficient A measure of the scattering of light or sound by a surface.

diffusivity *See* THERMAL DIFFUSIVITY.

digit *(a)* One of the terminal divisions of the hand or foot (*i.e.* a finger or toe). *(b)* One of the first ten numbers (represented by the numerals 0 to 9) which can be counted on the fingers of one's hands. *(c)* A symbol used in a system of enumeration; *see* BINARY ARITHMETIC *and* DECIMAL SYSTEM. *(d)* As a Roman measure of length, $\frac{1}{16}$ of a Roman FOOT.

digital Consisting of discrete elements (which can be represented numerically by INTEGERS), as opposed to ANALOG.

digital calculator A portable electronic calculator, which superseded the SLIDE RULE. A calculator differs from a COMPUTER by having little or no MEMORY; and by dealing with numbers but not alphabetical characters.

digital camera A camera which records images in digital form, and may be used as input to computer graphics systems.

digital computer A COMPUTER which operates on data represented in digital form, *i.e.* as a series of discrete elements, based on BINARY ARITHMETIC, as opposed to an ANALOG COMPUTER.

digital image Image generated on a computer screen, either by digitising a real scene or photograph, or by using a drawing, painting or illustration program.

digital signal processor (DSP) Fast digital processor used to filter, add reverberation, synthesise, modify and analyse acoustic signals in real time.

digital sound Sound waves (which are ANALOG INFORMATION) are digitised by temporal sampling. The sampling is accomplished by dividing the time interval of interest into small subintervals. The amplitude of the wave at each sample point is stored using either 8 or 16 bits. The number of bits used determines the dynamic range of the digitised sound. The number of sample points per unit of time is called the SAMPLING RATE (usually measured in number of sample points per second). *See* ANALOG TO DIGITAL CONVERTER *and* DAC (DIGITAL TO ANALOG CONVERTER).

digital video Digital video is created by sampling continuous analog video sources. The sampling is done in two dimensions. The first is a temporal sampling of captured still images (usually called FRAMES) which will in turn be played back at a rate sufficient to appear as continuous motion. The second phase is the sampling of the individual still images. (It can also be produced by creating a series of digital images, from an analog source; or by using images already digitised in a video camera.)

digitisation The process of converting ANALOG information (continuous information) to DIGITAL (discrete, finite) form.

digitise To convert an analog representation into a digital form.

digitiser Any device which converts a physical quantity into a coded character form. Commonly used for a device for converting shapes drawn on a GRAPHICS TABLET into digital data, usually by pointing to the vertices of the shapes with a STYLUS or digitiser pen.

dihedral angle The angle of inclination of two meeting or intersecting planes.

dilution ventilation Supply of clean air to a space for the purpose of diluting contaminants that are or may be released as a result of occupation and use.

dimension *(a)* The measured distance between two points. *(b)* A measure shown on a drawing which is intended to become a precise distance between two points in a building. *(c)* The unit attached to a measurement (length, mass, etc.).

dimensional analysis Analysis of structures, fluid flow, heat transfer, acoustics and other problems by means of dimensional similarity using the PI-THEOREM and involving DIMENSIONLESS NUMBERS. *See also* ACOUSTIC MODEL ANALYSIS *and* DIRECT MODEL ANALYSIS.

dimensional coordination Design of building components to conform to a dimensional standard, which may be a MODULE.

dimensional stability The term usually implies that a material has little MOISTURE MOVEMENT and CREEP, since thermal and elastic deformation are unavoidable.

dimensional tolerance *See* TOLERANCE.

dimensioned lumber US term for lumber (timber) sawn to a range of standard larger sizes, *e.g.* 4 in. (100 mm) by 12 in (300 mm).

dimensioned stone Stone cut to specific dimensions, *e.g.* as ASHLAR.

dimensionless *(a)* In mathematics, referring to a point, as distinguished from, say, a line which has one dimension (length). *(b)* In physics and metrology, a quantity without any measurement (length, mass, etc.), *i.e.* a pure number. For example, *efficiency* is the ratio of two quantities with the dimensions of power, but their ratio has no dimensions.

dimensionless number A ratio of two quantities, with the same dimensions, or a grouping of several variables whose product has no dimension, used in DIMENSIONAL ANALYSIS and for experimental data. *See* for example REYNOLDS' NUMBER.

dimetric projection An AXONOMETRIC PROJECTION in which the two horizontal axes are drawn at the same angle.

dimmer *See* LAMP DIMMER.

DIN *Deutsche Industrie Normung* (German Standard).

diode A two-terminal electronic device that allows current to flow through in only one direction. Hence it can be used as a RECTIFIER. Four diodes are required to make a *full-wave* rectifier.

dioptre A measure of the power of a lens; it is generally the reciprocal of its focal length in metres.

diorite An IGNEOUS rock formed by plutonic intrusion; it contains no quartz and is more basic than GRANITE. In the industry classification of stone, diorite is called a granite.

direct current (DC) A current which flows in one direction without significant pulsations, as opposed to an ALTERNATING CURRENT.

direct expansion An air conditioning system where the refrigerant is expanded (and therefore causes a cooling effect) in a coil located in the air handling plant (as opposed to a CHILLED WATER system).

direct gain method The oldest and most common method for PASSIVE SYSTEMS of solar energy utilisation, by allowing sunlight penetration through windows in cool weather, while shading the windows in warm weather.

direct lighting Lighting using luminaires which direct most of the flux toward the surface being lit, as opposed to INDIRECT LIGHTING.

direct model analysis Analysis of structural problems and studies of lighting, ventilation or acoustics by means of models which are accurately scaled in accordance with the theory of DIMENSIONAL ANALYSIS. In the case of *structures*, the loads are accordingly reduced to a magnitude which can be easily handled in a laboratory. Measurements of deformations are usually made with DIAL GAUGES and with ELECTRIC RESISTANCE STRAIN GAUGES. The rules of dimensional analysis also apply to ACOUSTIC MODEL ANALYSIS, to the analysis of lighting problems in an ARTIFICIAL SKY, and to the investigation of air flow in a WIND TUNNEL.

direct modulus of elasticity The MODULUS OF ELASTICITY, as opposed to the MODULUS OF RIGIDITY.

direct solar gain Solar energy obtained directly through a window.

direct solar radiation The part of the solar radiation that reaches a surface without having been scattered, as opposed to *diffuse solar radiation.*

direct sound The sound received directly from the sound source, as opposed to the sound *reflected* from the boundaries of the auditorium.

direct sound field That part of a sound field where the effect of reflections from the room surfaces may be neglected.

direct strain Elongation or shortening per unit length, caused by tensile or compressive stresses, respectively.

direct stress A STRESS due to a tensile or compressive force.

direct view storage tube (DVST) A type of CATHODE-RAY TUBE whose screen surface is coated with a phosphor capable of retaining an image for some time. Changing this image requires erasing the entire screen, and redrawing it.

directional lighting Lighting coming mainly from one direction, and therefore emphasising three-dimensionality by casting shadows and/or highlights.

directivity factor The ratio of the intensity of sound from a source, at a position in a *free field*, relative to the intensity generated at the same point by a spherical source radiating the same sound power.

directivity index Defined as $10 \log_{10}$ (DIRECTIVITY FACTOR).

directory In computing, an index giving the addresses of data, for example the location of files or other directories on a DISK.

dirt resistance The ability of a surface, particularly a painted surface, to resist the accumulation of foreign material.

disability glare GLARE which impairs the vision without necessarily causing DISCOMFORT. It is a physiological effect.

disaster recovery plan A procedure or set of actions required to manage recovery from a catastrophe (fire, etc.) occurring within a facility.

DISC *Abbreviation for* Discomfort Index, developed by A. P. Gagge. It predicts how people would vote on the seven-point ASHRAE scale. Conceptually similar to Fanger's PMV. It can be calculated from skin wettedness or from a pre-calculated SET.

disc *Same as* DISK.

discharge The removal of electric energy from a BATTERY.

discharge lamp A LAMP in which light (or ultraviolet radiation) is produced by an electrical discharge through a vapour. *See* FLUORESCENT LAMP, COLD-CATHODE LAMP, HOT-CATHODE LAMP *and* SULPHUR LAMP.

discharging arch An arch placed above the LINTEL of a door or a window to carry the weight of the wall above, that is, discharge it to each side. *Also called* a *relieving arch*. These arches were frequently used in masonry and brick construction from Ancient Roman times until the early twentieth century, when reinforced concrete lintels were introduced. *See also* ARCHING *(c)*.

discomfort glare GLARE which causes discomfort without necessarily impairing the vision of objects. It is a psychophysical effect.

discontinuous construction Construction which avoids continuous sound paths, particularly through a steel frame, to provide the greatest amount of IMPACT SOUND insulation with the least amount of insulating material, *e.g.* by the use of a FLOATING FLOOR. This sometimes conflicts with the structural requirements of the building.

discounted cash flow method A capital investment project is evaluated by considering all net receipts from the venture, and all necessary operating payments. Future receipts and payments are discounted at an appropriate rate.

discrete Distinct and finite, as opposed to continuous and infinitely variable. *See* DIGITAL.

dishing Grading of a pavement or a floor surface to form a shallow dish, generally with a drain at the lowest point.

disk (computing) A non-VOLATILE magnetic storage device containing addressable tracks. Data may be written to and read from these tracks by means of read/write heads. *See* FLOPPY DISK, HARD DISK *and* DISKETTE.

disk drive The device in a computer which controls the operations to and from magnetic DISKS.

diskette Once synonymous with a 5.25 in., and later a 3.5 in. FLOPPY DISK. Now generally regarded as an obsolete term.

dislocation in a crystal An imperfection caused by a failure of the crystal planes in two portions to match *(see figure)*. Dislocations are closely related to slipping action. In an *edge dislocation* there is a linear displacement accompanied by zones of tension and compression. In a *screw dislocation* there is a distortion, with associated zones of shear. The dislocation can be demonstrated with a BUBBLE MODEL.

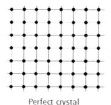

Perfect crystal

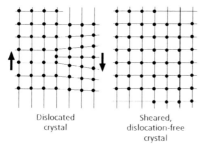

Dislocated crystal

Sheared, dislocation-free crystal

Dislocation in a crystal

dispersion *(a)* The even distribution of finely divided drops in an EMULSION, *e.g.* in an emulsion paint. *(b)* The separation of electromagnetic radiation (light) into constituents of different wavelengths, by REFRACTION or DIFFRACTION.

displacement ventilation A ventilation system operated on the principle of introducing air that is slightly cooler than room air at floor level and allowing it to rise due to thermal buoyancy, to be released from the space at high level.

display device Any device capable of displaying information. If it is capable of displaying graphical information it is called a VISUAL DISPLAY UNIT.

dissipative muffler A MUFFLER (or *silencer*) which relies on the absorption of sound for attenuation while allowing the unimpeded flow of air or other gases. Dissipative mufflers are usually used to attenuate mid and high frequency sounds. An example of a dissipative muffler is an acoustically lined duct (*see also* REACTIVE MUFFLER).

dissolved solids Minerals and other impurities dissolved in water, as opposed to SUSPENDED SOLIDS. Dissolved solids cannot be removed by filtration. Common dissolved solids include calcium carbon-

ate (which causes HARD WATER), iron compounds (which cause discoloration), and others which may be toxic.

distemper A cheap paint with a binder of casein or some other glue; it is usually heavily pigmented, and thinned with water. *Washable distemper* contains some drying oil.

distillation Process of converting a liquid into vapour, condensing the vapour, and collecting the condensed liquid or *distillate*. It is used for separating a mixture of liquids with different boiling points.

distortion An undesired change in a waveform (*see also* COLOURATION).

distributed computing A system in which a number of computers are organised in a network to cooperate in performing a single task.

distributed load A load distributed over the length or surface of a structure. Unless described otherwise, it is usually considered *uniformly distributed*.

distribution board A switchboard, usually controlling the final sub-circuits in an electrical installation.

distribution rack A frame or cupboard housing PATCH PANELS.

distribution reinforcement Small-diameter bars placed in concrete slabs at right angles to the main reinforcement to spread a concentrated load. It also serves to control *temperature* and *shrinkage* cracking.

distribution temperature (of a light source) *See* CORRELATED COLOUR TEMPERATURE.

district heating A larger-scale CENTRAL HEATING system, where the centrally generated heat is distributed by a pipe network to many buildings, *e.g.* a hospital complex, a university campus or a housing estate.

diurnal Belonging to each day, *e.g.* the *diurnal motion* of the sun, or the *diurnal rhythm* of the human body.

dividers An instrument for transferring a length from one part of a drawing to another location. It consists of two legs with pointed ends, hinged together at the other ends, similar to a compass.

dividing screen (for lift well) A screen installed between the paths of travel of two lifts sharing a common lift well, to enable the safe maintenance of one lift while the other is still in operation.

DL *Abbreviation for* DEAD LOAD.

DLOR (downward light output ratio) The ratio of the flux emitted in the lower hemisphere below a luminaire to the total flux emitted by the lamp(s) installed in the luminaire.

DMM (digital multimeter) An instrument used to measure voltage, current and resistance. The output is in digital form.

DN *Abbreviation for (a)* down, *(b)* nominal diameter.

docking saw A CIRCULAR SAW mounted above the work and cutting by pulling down on it.

dodecagon A twelve-sided POLYGON. The angle included between the twelve equal sides of a *regular* dodecagon is 150°.

dodecahedron A regular POLYHEDRON, bounded by twelve regular PENTAGONS. It has 20 vertices and 30 edges.

DOE Department of Energy (USA).

DOE-2 The computer model developed by the Lawrence Berkeley Laboratory to calculate the energy intensiveness of buildings.

dog iron A short steel bar whose ends are bent at right angles, and pointed. It is hammered into adjacent pieces of timber to connect them. *See also* CRAMP *(a)*.

dog tooth course A STRING COURSE in brickwork with diagonally projecting headers.

dog-bone connection Engineered connection involving removal of portions of steel beam flanges near the column face to allow plastic hinges to form under extreme seismic loading. This limits the stress on the welds and prevents brittle fracture in the connection. *Also called* a *reduced beam section (RBS)* connection.

dogman A person directing a crane's operations from the ground, from other parts of the building, or while riding on the load.

Dolby noise reduction system An electronic system for increasing the signal to noise ratio of recordings which is based on *compressing* only the lower end of the dynamic range of the signal.

dolerite An igneous rock formed by MINOR INTRUSIONS or thick lava flows. It is a fine-grained rock of basic composition. In the industry classification of stone it is called a GRANITE.

dolly A block of hardwood used to cushion the blow from a PILE HAMMER.

dolomite The double carbonate of calcium and magnesium, $CaMgCO_3$. It is used for REFRACTORY MATERIALS and as a lime for *jointless flooring*. Dolomite limestone is also known as *magnesian limestone*.

dome A vault of double curvature, both curves being convex upwards. Most domes are portions of a sphere; however, it is possible to have a dome of non-spherical curvature on a circular plan, or to have a dome on a non-circular plan, such as an ellipse, an oval or a rectangle. In Classical architecture, domes were normally constructed of masonry. A spherical dome is subject to hoop tension when the angle subtended at the centre of curvature exceeds 104°; consequently hemispherical domes, which subtend 180°, are subject to HOOP TENSION for the lowest 38°, and this presents problems in masonry construction (*see figure*).

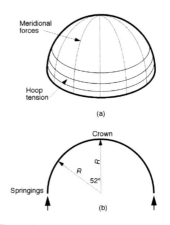

Dome

door buck US term for a timber or metal subframe to support a door frame.

door closer A spring or hydraulic device to close a door and control the speed of its closing.

door furniture Knobs, handles, cover plates, etc. used in conjunction with door locks or latches.

door jamb Same as DOORPOST.

door light The glass area in a door.

door louvres Blades or slats, which may or may not be adjustable, in a door to permit ventilation while the door is closed.

door schedule A tabulation of doors required for a project, showing location, type, etc.

door vane A mechanism mounted on a lift door which transmits the operating power to the landing doors.

doorpost The vertical post on each side of a door opening.

dopant A chemical impurity added usually in minute amounts to a pure semiconductor in order to alter its electrical properties.

doping The addition of DOPANTS to a semiconductor.

Doppler effect The change in the spectrum of a signal (sound or light) when the relative position of the source and receiver changes during the production of the sound. The phenomenon occurs because ahead of a moving source the waves bunch up on one another (causing an increase in frequency) while behind they spread apart (causing a reduction in frequency).

Doppler shift The change in frequency of a signal due to the relative motion of the source and receiver (due to the *Doppler effect*).

dormer window A vertical window inserted into a sloping roof. It usually has its own gable projecting through the main roof slope.

dot A dab of plaster, a nail or laths at intervals plumbed or levelled to establish the finished level of a final plaster or render surface. The nails or laths are removed on completion.

dot matrix printer A printer which prints by impacting an ink ribbon against paper using closely packed needles or pins.

double catenary A pair of CATENARY cables curved in opposite directions, commonly used to support a frameless glass wall. The two catenaries are needed to resist wind pressure, which may come from either side. Because of the efficiency of a catenary, the resulting structure can be lighter and more elegant than a system of beams or MULLIONS relying on bending strength.

double door Two single doors fixed to one door frame, meeting in the centre.

double Flemish bond Brickwork showing FLEMISH BOND on both faces (*see figure* under FLEMISH BOND). As this is the only practical use of Flemish bond for walls less than two bricks in thickness, *double* is usually omitted.

double glazing Glazing in which two layers of glass are separated by an air space for thermal and acoustic insulation. Used in climates where the indoor–outdoor temperature difference is large, in order to reduce window heat losses (or gains in hot weather). The two panes of glass are sealed around the edges with a spacer bar, or folded over and welded. The space between the two panes may be partial vacuum or partially filled with an inert gas (xenon, krypton, argon) to further reduce its U-value. LOW-EMISSIVITY coating can usefully be applied to the inner (protected) face of one of the panes. Such sealed, double-glazed units must be factory-made to size, to fit the given frame. *See also* DOUBLE WINDOWS.

double windows Used for the same purposes as DOUBLE GLAZING units, but these have two separate frames, separately hinged, each with a single glass pane. Sometimes the two frames may locked together for everyday operation, but can be separated for cleaning. A venetian blind may be located between the frames.

double-acting engine A RECIPROCATING ENGINE in which the working fluid (*e.g.* steam) acts on each side of the piston alternately, so that each stroke is a working stroke, as opposed to a *single-acting* engine.

double-acting hinge A hinge which allows a door to swing both ways, through 180°. It usually has a spring to make the door also self-closing.

double-acting pump A reciprocating pump in which both sides of the piston act alternately, giving two delivery strokes per cycle.

double-cut saw A saw which can cut on both pull and push strokes, because its teeth have been cut accordingly.

double-deck lift (or elevator) A two-storey lift, whose two compartments must stop at adjacent floors where both compartments can be unloaded and loaded simultaneously. This increases the capacity of the lift by about 25 per cent above that of a single-deck lift.

double-headed nail A nail with two heads, one above the other, used on temporary structures such as scaffolds and formwork. The lower head bears on the surface into which the nail is driven. The upper head is used to withdraw the nail. *Also called* a *scaffold nail.*

double-hung window A SASH WINDOW with two vertically sliding sashes, originally each balanced by a set of sash weights (*see figure*). Now generally balanced by *spring sash balances* instead of weights.

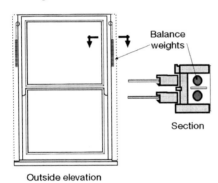

Outside elevation

Double-hung window

double-swing door A door with DOUBLE-ACTING HINGES.

double-walled shell A structure with two parallel MEMBRANES, joined by DIAPHRAGMS at regular intervals. It can be used for long spans, since the two membranes, separated by the space between, provide bending resistance. Doubling the shell also improves the waterproofing, since any water penetrating the first membrane can be drained off before entering the interior of the building.

doubly curved surface A surface curved in both directions, as opposed to a singly curved surface. Doubly curved surfaces are divided into domes, which have positive GAUSSIAN CURVATURE, and saddles which have negative Gaussian curvature.

Doubly curved surfaces are non-DEVELOPABLE. They may or may not be RULED.

doubly prestressed concrete Concrete prestressed in two mutually perpendicular directions. By this means the diagonal tensile stresses due to shear and torsion can be completely eliminated.

doubly reinforced concrete Concrete with both tension and COMPRESSION REINFORCEMENT.

doubly ruled A surface that is RULED in two directions.

doughboy An underburnt brick.

Douglas fir A softwood widely used in the USA and Canada, and exported in large quantities to Europe and Australia, because it is obtainable in large sizes which are straight-grained and free from knots. It is light (about 530 kg/m³ or 33 lb/ft³) and comparatively strong. *Also called British Columbian pine, Oregon pine* or just *Oregon.*

dovetail An interlocking joint between two pieces of timber in which the interlocking pins are fanshaped, like the tails of certain pigeons. Because of the shape, they are not easily pulled out. Dovetail joints are used for joinery, drawers and boxes (*see figure*).

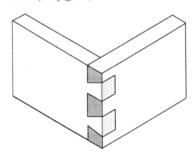

Dovetail joint

dowel A pin of wood or metal, used in timber, masonry or concrete structures, usually to resist shear.

down peak A down peak traffic condition exists in a lift system when the dominant or only traffic flow is in the downward direction, with all or the majority of the passengers leaving the system at the main terminal floor of the building.

down time The period during which an item of plant is unable to operate.

downconductor In a LIGHTNING PROTECTION SYSTEM, a conductor which connects the AIR TERMINATION with the EARTH TERMINATION.

downfeed system *(a)* In water supply, a system of water supply fed from a tank at the top of a building. *(b)* In hot water or heating, a type of central heating pipework, where either the boiler is at high level or the hot water flow pipe is taken to the highest point and it is the downward flow pipe which is branching out to all radiator panels or emitters, thence returning to the boiler.

downlight A LUMINAIRE which directs the majority of its flux downwards, usually within a restricted cone, as opposed to an UPLIGHTER.

download To transfer data or code from one computer to another, usually from a larger or remote SERVER to a smaller or local CLIENT system, especially a MICRO-COMPUTER or PERIPHERAL. To UPLOAD implies the opposite direction, but the distinction is not always precise.

downstand Any element projecting downwards from the underside of a floor or ceiling. In fire engineering, a smoke control device to limit smoke spreading along the ceiling.

dozer A general term for bulldozers, angle dozers, tilt dozers, etc., which are tractors, usually mounted on crawler tracks, with a blade mounted on the front in order to push material.

DP *Abbreviation for (a)* Data Processing, *(b)* Dynamic Programming.

DPC *Abbreviation for* DAMPPROOF COURSE.

DPI *Abbreviation for* Dots Per Inch. Describes the size of the PIXELS on a monitor or dots of ink from a printer.

DPM *Abbreviation for* Dampproof Membrane.

draft *See* DRAUGHT.

dragline An excavator with a toothed or cutting bucket suspended from a jib and filled by dragging toward the base of the jib.

dragon's blood A red resin, obtained from certain trees, which is insoluble in water, but soluble in alcohol and ether. It is used for tinting varnish.

drain, vertical sand A vertically bored hole, subsequently filled with granular material in order to assist the drainage of impermeable soils.

drainage An assembly of pipes and fittings, *in the ground*, used for the removal of waste water or rainwater from a building or a site.

drainage hole A hole or open joint, particularly in a RETAINING WALL, to drain unwanted water.

drained joint One method of waterproofing an external wall is to provide a RAIN SCREEN at the outdoor face, an *airseal* at the indoor face, and a *drainage system* between the screen and the seal. This equalises the pressure in the drainage cavity to that outdoors, and allows water that enters the joint to drain to the outside.

draped tendon *Same as* DEFLECTED TENDON.

draught A pressure difference in a room, and more particularly in a chimney or ventilator, which induces natural air movement. *Also spelled draft* (USA).

drawing program Program for creating two-dimensional illustrations and charts. Rather than create BIT-MAPPED GRAPHICS, most drawing programs rely on the use of VECTOR GRAPHICS or PARAMETRIC CURVES. This has the advantage of allowing editing at a higher level than PAINTING PROGRAMS which provide only pixel-by-pixel editing.

drawings *See* SHOP DRAWINGS *and* WORKING DRAWINGS.

DRC *Abbreviation for* DAMAGE RISK CRITERION.

drenchers Automatic fire devices similar to sprinklers which deliver a curtain spray, usually used to protect the external face of a building from some adjacent fire risk.

dressed lumber *See* DRESSED TIMBER.

dressed stone Stone which has been squared all round and smoothed or rusticated on the face.

dressed timber Timber which has been sawn and finished with a planing machine at the timber mill. It is customary to state the nominal size, which is the size of the timber *before* dressing and seasoning. The dressed timber is 5–13 mm ($\frac{3}{16}$–$\frac{1}{2}$ in.) smaller. Dressed timber is usually DAR (dressed all round, or dressed on all four faces) unless specifically ordered as dressed on one or two faces. *Also called dressed lumber.*

drier A compound which encourages oxidation of the DRYING OIL in a paint or varnish.

drift *(a)* Movement of air away from an exhaust of a building under the influence of wind. It may carry contaminants toward fresh-air intakes. *(b)* A tapered rod for enlarging or aligning holes in metal.

drilled pile *Same as* BORED PILE.

drip *(a)* A moulding or projection above an opening to shed water. *(b)* A groove on the underside of a sill, coping or cornice to interrupt water flow.

drive *See* DISK DRIVE.

driven pile A precast concrete, steel or timber pile that is driven into the ground with a pile driver.

driver *(a)* In a loudspeaker, the voice coil to which a speaker diaphragm is attached and the related magnetic assembly. *(b)* In computing, the software that allows the computer to communicate with a printer or other peripheral.

drop hammer See PILE HAMMER.

drop panel The portion of a FLAT SLAB or FLAT PLATE which is thickened throughout the area surrounding the column or COLUMN CAPITAL, to reduce the magnitude of the shear stress, and thus obviate the need for shear reinforcement. *See figures under* COLUMN STRIP *and* FLAT PLATE.

drop saw *Same as* DOCKING SAW.

dropout A discrete voltage loss. A voltage sag (complete or partial) for a very short period of time (milliseconds) constitutes a dropout.

dropout voltage The voltage at which a device will release to its de-energised position (or cease to operate).

dropped panel *Same as* DROP PANEL.

DRT *Abbreviation for* DRY RESULTANT TEMPERATURE.

drum A vertical wall supporting a dome or cupola.

drum plotter A plotter in which the drawing is held on a drum. Lines are drawn with a pen by a combination of rotating the drum and moving a pen along its surface parallel to its axis of rotation.

dry construction Building without the use of wet plaster, wet concrete or mortar on the site. However, the concrete may be precast, or the brickwork prefabricated; indeed a large proportion of dry construction consists of precast concrete units joined with dry fasteners which may or may not be sealed with mastic. Dry construction avoids damage to finishes through concrete and mortar droppings, and it is unnecessary to wait for the wet materials to dry; but the cost is often higher.

dry density The mass of soil or aggregate per unit volume, after it has been dried at 105 °C.

dry film thickness Thickness of the film of a liquid-applied coating (such as waterproofing membrane or paint) after the drying and curing process has finished.

dry glazing A method of securing glass, with a preformed gasket and without glazing compounds, *see* PATENT GLAZING.

dry ice Frozen carbon dioxide.

dry press brick A brick pressed from clay with a low (5 per cent to 7 per cent) moisture content.

dry resultant temperature A simple comfort index, often used in cool climates. It is the average of DBT and MRT, often stated as DRT = 0.5(DBT + MRT).

dry rot Timber decay caused by a fungus, which flourishes only if the timber is *damp.* It is usually caused by inadequate ventilation. *See also* WET ROT.

dry wall *(a)* Stones or blocks laid without mortar. Dry stone walls were used in prehistoric times before the invention of mortar, often by wedging small stones into the joints; they are still in use in some country districts, particularly for walls around fields. In recent years, a number of concrete BLOCK types have been designed for precision fitting without the use of mortar. *(b)* (*Also spelled drywall,* especially in the USA) DRY CONSTRUCTION using plasterboard on timber or steel studwork. (The joints and fixings may be finished with a small amount of wet plaster.)

dry-bulb economiser An outdoor air ECONOMISER CYCLE in an air conditioning system that is controlled by comparison of dry-bulb temperatures of outdoor and return air.

dry-bulb temperature The temperature

indicated by a normal thermometer, as distinct from the WET-BULB TEMPERATURE.

dry-bulb thermometer A normal thermometer, as opposed to a WET-BULB THERMOMETER, which has its bulb wrapped in a damp wick.

drying oil An animal or vegetable oil (the most common being linseed oil) which forms a tough film by oxidation when exposed to air in a thin layer. The process can be speeded up by the use of a DRIER.

drying shrinkage Contraction (of timber or concrete) caused by moisture loss.

dryness As an acoustic quality, the lack of LIVENESS.

dual flush A WC cistern arranged so that the user can choose to flush the pan using the full quantity of water, or a reduced quantity. A considerable saving in water consumption can be achieved.

DuBois area The surface area of a person's skin in square metres, determined from a formula derived in 1915 by D. and E. F. DuBois. It is used in THERMAL COMFORT calculations.

duct (a) A pipe, conduit or runway for electric or telephone wires. (b) A pipe or cavity used to convey air for ventilation or air conditioning. (c) A cavity within a building (usually running vertically through several storeys) containing water pipes, drainage pipes, wires, etc. (d) A hole formed in a concrete member to accommodate post-tensioning TENDONS.

duct lining An absorbent lining placed in an air conditioning duct to attenuate the noise caused by the equipment and air flow.

ductility The property of certain metals which enables them, when cold, to undergo large permanent deformations without rupture, as opposed to brittleness. See also PLASTIC MATERIAL.

ductwork An assembly of ducts and duct fittings, usually of sheet metal, arranged for the distribution of air in air conditioning and mechanical ventilation systems.

dumbwaiter A lift for the vertical transportation of materials only, with its size and controls limited to ensure that it cannot be used to transport people. See also LIFT TYPES (f).

dummy activity An arrow in a NETWORK which is used as a logical connector, but does not represent actual work items. It is usually shown as a dotted line.

dummy joint A groove formed or cut in concrete to imitate the appearance of a CONTROL JOINT, usually for aesthetic reasons to match other, genuine control joints, or to disguise CONSTRUCTION JOINTS.

dumpy level A level in which the telescope and the SPIRIT LEVEL are attached rigidly to the vertical spindle. LEVELLING is performed with three (in old instruments sometimes four) levelling screws, and the instrument is then level in any direction. This used to be the most commonly employed instrument. However, the QUICKSET LEVEL has now become more common.

duodecimal system A system based on 12 units, e.g. 12 inches = 1 foot. It was used by the Babylonians, and it is arithmetically versatile, since 12 is divisible by 2, 3, 4 and 6. From a mathematical point of view it may be superior to the DECIMAL system (10 being divisible only by 2 and 5), based on counting on ten human fingers, which became firmly established during the Roman Empire. However, since the 'digital' computer (which is really a BINARY calculator) has a keyboard based on the decimal system, duodecimal units are unlikely to survive, except for time and angle measurement.

duplex (a) A house with two separate two-storey dwellings, one on each side of a common party wall. (b) A two-storey house containing two separate apartments, one on each storey. (c) US term for MAISONETTE. (d) Two interconnected LIFT cars, sharing a common signalling system controlled under a simple group control system, operating under directional collective principles.

duplex receptacle US term for an electrical outlet with two places to plug in electrical cords.

duplex-head nail Same as DOUBLE-HEADED NAIL.

durability The ability of a material to resist ABRASION, CORROSION, weathering action and other conditions of normal service.

duralumin An aluminium alloy containing

3.5–5.5 per cent copper, 0.5–0.8 per cent magnesium, 0.5–0.7 per cent manganese and up to 0.7 per cent silicon. It is capable of AGE HARDENING at room temperature, and it can be cast, forged and rolled hot or cold.

dusting The application of dry Portland cement to a wet floor or deck mortar surface, to improve adhesion of tiles.

dutchman A cut tile used as a filler in the run of a wall or floor area. Usually the use of BALANCED CUTS is preferred on aesthetic grounds.

DVST *Abbreviation for* DIRECT VIEW STORAGE TUBE.

dwang *(a)* In New Zealand, a horizontal timber member to stiffen studs. *(b)* In Scotland, strutting between floor joists. *See* NOGGING.

dwell time The time during which the doors of a lift or elevator are fully open to unload and load.

DWV piping Drain, waste and vent piping.

dye A colouring material which, unlike a PIGMENT, colours materials by penetration.

dye test (drainage) A test whereby a strong dye (such as fluorescein) is introduced into a drainage system. Observation of the dye downstream demonstrates where the water flows, and it may identify the source of a leak.

dynamic energy modelling Simulation of energy flows in a building by software that takes account of dynamic hour-by-hour variations in internal and external boundary conditions.

dynamic head (velocity head) The energy possessed by a unit mass of a fluid due to its velocity (*v*). It is expressed as a height (H_v) and calculated using the equation

$$H_v = v^2/2g$$

where g = gravitational acceleration.

dynamic load A *live load* due to moving machinery, EARTHQUAKE or WIND, as opposed to a *static load*. Dynamic loads are frequently converted into equivalent static loads by means of an IMPACT FACTOR; however, where they exercise a controlling influence on the design of the structure, a dynamic analysis is required.

dynamic modulus of elasticity The MODULUS OF ELASTICITY determined from the vibration of a specimen or structure, or from the velocity of a pulse, which may be ULTRASONIC.

dynamic penetration test A PENETRATION TEST in which the testing device is forced into the soil with a specified number of blows with a standard hammer, as opposed to a STATIC test which employs a measured force.

dynamic pressure *(a)* The pressure in pipework under flow conditions. *(b)* The pressure resulting from a change in velocity of a fluid stream.

dynamic range A measure of the difference between the maximum and minimum signal that can be handled by a device or system. The upper limit is usually determined by the saturation of an amplifier and the lower limit by inherent noise.

dynamic smoke exhaust A system intended to remove smoke to the exterior of the building. The system may include smoke exhaust fans, purging by the introduction of clean air, and gravity venting systems, as well as normal exhaust fans operating to reduce the pressure in a smoke zone. *See also* STATIC SMOKE EXHAUST.

dynamic (thermal) response Whilst for very lightweight buildings the thermal response to variable outdoor conditions (temperature and solar radiation) is practically instantaneous, so that use of the steady state calculation method is acceptable, buildings with some mass or thermal capacity would have a delayed response, which can only be analysed as dynamic thermal response, in the simplest case by the ADMITTANCE PROCEDURE or by other sophisticated mathematical algorithms.

dynamics The branch of the science of mechanics concerned with the action of forces and the motions they produce; as opposed to STATICS, which deals with the case when there is no motion, and the forces are in equilibrium.

dynamo A direct-current generator. *See also* ALTERNATOR.

dyne The force required to produce an acceleration of one centimetre per second per second in a mass of one gram. In SI UNITS the dyne is replaced by the newton (1 dyne = 10^{-5} N).

E

E *(a)* The most common symbol for the MODULUS OF ELASTICITY. *(b)* Prefix meaning *exa*, one million million million times, or 10^{18}. *(c)* The symbol for ILLUMINANCE. *(d)* Symbol used for energy.
e The base of the NATURAL LOGARITHM; $e = 2.718\,28\ldots$
ear defender A device placed over the ear or in the ear canal to protect the wearer from loud sounds, *e.g.* ear muff, ear plug or ear canal cap.
ear plug *See* EAR DEFENDER.
early wood The lighter wood with thinner cell walls formed during the earlier stages of the growth of each GROWTH RING (*also called spring wood*). The denser wood with thicker walls, formed during the later stages, is called *late wood*, or *summer wood*.
earphone An electro-acoustic transducer, closely coupled to the ear, which transforms electrical signals into acoustic signals.
earth auger See AUGER *(b)*.
earth construction ADOBE, COB WALLING or PISÉ DE TERRE, as distinct from construction with hardburnt BRICKS. This form of construction, which goes back to prehistoric times, is still used in many developing countries. Because of its low EMERGY, the use of earth construction is advocated as being environmentally responsible.
earth ground A low impedance electrical path to earth for the purpose of discharging lightning, static, and radiated energy, and to maintain the main service entrance at earth potential.
earth leakage circuit breaker A CIRCUIT BREAKER designed to open (trip) a circuit when an imbalance of current is detected between the active and neutral (indicating a 'leak' to earth). *Also known as residual current detector.*
earth pressure The horizontal pressure

exerted by soil on a retaining wall, or vice versa. The *active*, or minimum, earth pressure is that exerted by a retained soil on the wall retaining it. The *passive*, or maximum, earth pressure is exerted by soil in front of a wall sunk in the ground; it is the resistance offered by that portion of the soil to the movement of the wall (which is pushed by the active pressure due to the retained soil). The pressure due to granular soil is given by the RANKINE THEORY.
earth termination The connection of a LIGHTNING PROTECTION SYSTEM to the earth by means of electrodes (rods) of sufficient number and depth to achieve a low electrical resistance to allow the dissipation of the energy of a lightning stroke.
earthed In reference to electrical wiring, connected to the earth, so as to ensure immediate and safe discharge of electricity. *Also called grounded.*
earthing electrode A grounding electrode, water pipe, or building steel, or some combination of these, used for establishing a building's earth ground.
earth-integrated construction Building partly or wholly underground, or with an earth-covered roof.
earthquake loading The forces exerted on a structure by earthquakes. Earthquakes occur mainly in regions where there are suitable GEOLOGICAL FAULTs, and many of these do not pass through centres of population; however, most of the West Coast of the USA, Japan, New Zealand and several Mediterranean countries are liable to severe earth tremors. Earthquakes consist of ground vibrations. When the ground is moved beneath a structure, the building tends to remain in the original position because of its inertia. The resulting vertical forces are usually within the load-bearing capacity of the structure, but it must be designed to resist the horizontal component of the earth's motion. Earthquake loading for small buildings may be treated as a static horizontal force, but for tall buildings a dynamic analysis is required.
earthquake scale *See* MERCALLI SCALE *and* RICHTER SCALE.
easement An area, across land or within

a building, over which someone (other than the owner or occupier) has the right of access for a specific purpose, such as a *services easement.*

eave used in the USA as the singular of EAVES.

eaves Projecting edges of the roof extending beyond the wall.

EBS Experimental Building Station, Sydney. Previously the Commonwealth Experimental Building Station. Now part of CSIRO Manufacturing and Infrastructure Technology (CMIT).

EC(UK) Engineering Council (UK), London. Succeeds the Council of Engineering Institutions.

eCAADE Education and research in Computer-Aided Architectural Design in Europe (Association).

eccentric bracing Structural bracing element in which the force vector lines do not intersect at a single point.

eccentric load A compressive or tensile load which does not act through the CENTROID of the cross-section. The *eccentricity* is the distance of the line of action of the load from the centroid.

echo Sound which can be distinguished as being a repetition of a sound just heard. Whether an echo is heard, or whether the delayed sound is integrated with the original sound, depends on the delay time between the original and repeated sounds as well as their relative intensities. If the two sounds are of approximately the same intensity, most people will hear the second as an echo if the delay is more than 70 ms.

ECL *Abbreviation for* Emitter Coupled Logic. Extremely high-speed electronic circuitry where changes in binary logic are determined by very fast switching between specific voltage levels, rather than by semiconductor saturation and cutoff.

ecological footprint A concept used to indicate the magnitude of environmental impact, the load or demand placed on the global environment by any activity or object (such as a building) in extracting and producing the materials and providing the energy used by it, in terms of a notional land area (the footprint) that would be required to support or sustain that activity.

ecologically sustainable construction Construction by methods and techniques that minimise ecological impacts and do not reduce the opportunity of future generations to satisfy reasonable lifestyle requirements.

ecologically sustainable design Building design that seeks to minimise ecological impacts and to maintain the opportunity of future generations to satisfy reasonable lifestyle requirements.

ecology The study of the Earth's life support systems.

economiser cycle Control cycle used in some air conditioning systems to save energy by circulating outdoor air instead of recycling return air when the heat content of the outdoor air is lower than that of the return air. *See also* OUTDOOR AIR CYCLE.

ecosystem The plants, animals and people living in a defined zone. The ecosystem includes the food chain, the energy flows and the biological cycles, and it thus has the means for the continuation of life.

eddy currents Currents introduced in surrounding masses of conducting material by circuits carrying alternating currents. They can result in a considerable loss of energy.

eddy flow *Turbulent flow* (in a fluid) in which there is unsteady motion of the particles, as opposed to STREAMLINE FLOW.

edge beam A beam at the edge of a shell or plate structure. The stiffness which it provides may greatly increase the loadbearing capacity of the structure. However, it may also complicate the BOUNDARY CONDITIONS. While some edge beams merely add to the stiffness and strength of the structure (often at the cost of making it appear unduly heavy), others are essential for stability.

Edison cap A LAMP BASE or cap used on electric lamps, particularly in the USA. It is screwed into the lampholder. *See also* BAYONET CAP.

editor In computing, a program which facilitates the editing of data in text or graphical form. A screen editor allows a cursor to move about on the screen and change characters directly.

EDT (early decay time) EDT is a measure of the reverberation time of a room based on the early part (e.g. −5 dB to −15 dB) of the decay of a sound.

effective depth of reinforced concrete beam or slab The distance of the *centroid* of the reinforcing steel from the compression face of the concrete (*see figure*).

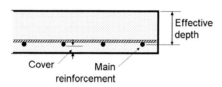

Effective depth of reinforced concrete beam or slab

effective flange width *(a)* The width of the concrete slab adjoining the rib, which is assumed to function as the flange element of a T-BEAM or L-BEAM section. *(b)* The width of plate adjoining the web, which is assumed to function as the flange element of a metal section in a LIGHT-GAUGE STRUCTURE.

effective length (or height) of column The distance between the points of inflection or CONTRAFLEXURE of a column when it buckles. It is the length used in the SLENDERNESS RATIO.

effective modulus of elasticity of concrete The deformation of concrete under load is partly due to (instantaneous) *elastic deformation* and partly due to (time-dependent) *creep*. To simplify calculations, an effective modulus of elasticity is introduced which is the SECANT MODULUS, *i.e.* the secant of the stress–strain diagram.

effective perceived noise level (EPNdB) The perceived noise level of a continuous reference sound, which in the same total time as a noise event (or a number of noise events) would give the same noise annoyance to a listener. It is used mainly for aircraft noise assessment.

effective prestress The stress remaining in the concrete due to PRESTRESSING after all LOSSES have occurred.

effective sound pressure The ROOT MEAN SQUARE value of the pressure of a sound wave.

effective span The span used in computing the bending moment in a beam. A common rule is to take the lesser of *(i)* the distance between the centres of the supports and *(ii)* the clear distance between the supports, plus the depth of the beam or slab.

effective temperature (ET) A *comfort index* or index of the thermal environment that describes the combined effect of temperature and humidity, developed by Houghten and Yaglou at the ASHVE laboratories in 1923, depicted by sloping 'equal comfort lines' plotted on the psychrometric chart (these are designated by the DBT lines met at the saturation curve), later modified in a nomogram to include the effect of air movement, adopted by ASHVE in 1932. If, on the temperature scale of the nomogram, GT (globe temperature) is used in lieu of DBT, the result is referred to as CET (CORRECTED EFFECTIVE TEMPERARTURE).

effective width (of flanges or slab) *See* EFFECTIVE FLANGE WIDTH.

efficacy Similar to EFFICIENCY but used where the output and input quantities have different units as in the *efficacy of a light source* which has the units lm/W.

efficiency The ratio of the energy or power output of a system to the input, usually expressed as a percentage. *See also* EFFICACY.

efflorescence A deposit, usually white, formed on the surface of a brick, block or concrete wall. It consists of salts leached from the surface of the wall. Although unsightly, it is harmless, and it can normally be removed by brushing. However, it is liable to lift any paint which has been applied to the area of wall where it occurs.

effluent Liquid discharge from a waste water treatment process.

effusivity A composite index of material properties, rarely used outside France, although the same concept is sometimes referred to as 'specific admittance'. It is the square root of the product of conductivity, density and specific heat capacity of that material:

$$\beta = \sqrt{\lambda \times \rho \times c}$$

It is a measure of the ability of the

material to absorb heat flow. Multiplied for the daily cycle by $\sqrt{(2\pi/24)}$ it gives the value of ADMITTANCE.

EFT *Abbreviation for* Earliest Finish Time (of an activity in a NETWORK).

EGA *Abbreviation for* Enhanced Graphics Adapter.

eggcrate A building shading device combining both horizontal and vertical elements.

eggshell gloss A painted surface intermediate between full gloss and a flat surface.

egress path The exit from a building or facility, to meet statutory requirements.

EIS *See* ENVIRONMENTAL IMPACT STUDY.

elastic constants The MODULUS OF ELASTICITY and POISSON'S RATIO.

elastic deformation Deformation that occurs instantly when a load is applied, and is instantly and fully recovered when the load is removed, as opposed to CREEP.

elastic design Structural design based on the assumption that structural materials behave elastically, and that the stresses therein should be as close as possible to, but not greater than, the MAXIMUM PERMISSIBLE STRESSES under the action of the SERVICE LOADS or WORKING LOADS. Also known as *working load design*. The main alternative approach is called *plastic design*, *ultimate strength design* or LIMIT STATE DESIGN.

elastic limit The limit of stress beyond which the strain is not wholly recoverable. In MILD STEEL, the elastic limit is slightly lower than the YIELD STRESS. In concrete, it is difficult to determine its precise location, because some CREEP occurs even under rapid loading.

elastic loss of prestress The LOSS OF PRESTRESS which is due to the elastic shortening of the concrete. It need be considered only for PRE-TENSIONED units. When members are POST-TENSIONED the elastic shortening occurs during the operation, and is automatically compensated.

elastic modulus *See* MODULUS OF ELASTICITY.

elastic shortening *See* ELASTIC LOSS OF PRESTRESS.

elastic strain STRAIN that is instantly and fully recovered when the load causing it is removed.

elasticity The ability of a material to deform instantly under load, and to recover its original shape instantly when the load is removed.

elasticity, modulus of *See* MODULUS OF ELASTICITY.

elastomer A synthetic material with rubber-like qualities, which result from its coiled molecular structure.

elbow A sharp corner in a pipe or conduit as opposed to a BEND, which has a larger radius of curvature. *See figure* under PIPE FITTINGS (water and gas).

electric arc welding *See* ARC WELDING.

electric current The passage of electricity through a body, caused by a drift of negatively charged IONS. It is measured in AMPERES.

electric eye A PHOTOVOLTAIC cell used as a detector.

electric lamp *See* ARC LIGHT, DISCHARGE LAMP *and* FILAMENT LAMP.

electric lock Lock operated by an electrical circuit, to enable the lock to be opened remotely. It is more difficult to install than an ELECTRIC STRIKE.

electric resistance strain gauge A STRAIN GAUGE based on OHM'S LAW. It consists of a zigzag wire (*see figure*) or a zigzag thin FOIL, attached to a paper or lacquer backing. This is glued to the part of the structure to be examined. Tensile strain causes the wire to elongate, become thinner, and consequently pass less current. Compressive strain causes an increase in current. The current is measured with a WHEATSTONE BRIDGE, or some other suitable circuit. With careful choice of wire and adhesive, strains as low as 1×10^{-6} can be determined. *See also* STRAIN ROSETTE.

Electric resistance strain gauge

electric strike Lock STRIKE, part of which can be withdrawn by an electrical circuit, to enable the door to be temporarily unlocked by remote control, *e.g.* for admitting visitors to a secure area. *See also* ELECTRIC LOCK.

electrical conductance The measure

of the ability of a material to conduct an ELECTRIC CURRENT, the reciprocal of RESISTANCE, with the unit *mho*.

electrical insulation The prevention of the flow of an electric current; or the material used to prevent the flow of current.

electrical resistance The ratio of electric VOLTAGE to ELECTRIC CURRENT. It is measured in OHMS.

electrical services The system of reticulation, required to deliver electrical energy within a facility.

electrochemical corrosion Corrosion caused by the gradual solution of the ANODE, when two electrochemically dissimilar metals are in contact in the presence of moisture. These then form a galvanic cell, which generates a direct current. Aluminium sheet used externally is subject to such damage if it is fixed with copper nails, or to a lesser extent with steel nails. Steel nails or bolts when used with aluminium should be plated with *cadmium* or *zinc*. The NOBLE METALS are resistant to electrochemical corrosion. *See also* GALVANISING *and* SACRIFICIAL PROTECTION.

electrochemical series The sequence of elements in order of the electrode potential developed when immersed in a solution of normal ionic concentration. For commonly used metals the series is: *(cathodic end)* gold, platinum, silver, mercury, copper, hydrogen *(zero)*, lead, tin, nickel, cadmium, iron, chromium, zinc, aluminium, magnesium, sodium, calcium, potassium, lithium *(anodic end)*. The use of dissimilar metals in contact in the presence of water may lead to ELECTROCHEMICAL CORROSION.

electrochromic glass Laminated glass that contains a layer of particles whose orientation can be changed by an electric current to vary the transparency and thus rate of transmission of solar gain through windows. Still under development.

electrode *(a)* The terminal through which a current is led into and out of an ELECTROLYTE. *(b)* A rod of metal, either bare or covered, used as a terminal in ARC WELDING.

electrodeposition The deposition of a layer of metal or alloy onto another while both are submerged in an ELECTROLYTE consisting of a solution of salts of the metal to be deposited. *See* GALVANISING.

electrolier An electrically operated LUMINAIRE that is styled to look like a CHANDELIER.

electroluminescent panel An electric light source consisting of a phosphor (usually zinc sulphide) contained in a sandwich panel, and excited by an alternating current. It can be used to illuminate large surfaces at a low, uniform brightness when the spatial requirements of the lighting system must be kept to a minimum.

electrolyte A conducting medium (usually a solution) in which an ELECTRIC CURRENT flows by virtue of chemical changes. The process is known as *electrolysis.*

electromagnet A magnet formed by winding a coil of wire around a core of *soft iron*. This becomes magnetic when an electric current flows through the wire, and loses its magnetism when the current is switched off. It is therefore a temporary magnet.

electromagnetic A magnetic field caused by an electric current. Power lines cause electromagnetic fields which can interfere with nearby data cables.

electromagnetic compatibility The ability of a device, equipment or system to function satisfactorily in its electromagnetic environment without introducing intolerable electromagnetic disturbances to anything in that environment.

electromagnetic induction A process in which a voltage is induced in a conductor whenever there is a relative motion between that conductor and a magnetic field.

electromagnetic radiation *See* RADIATION.

electromagnetic spectrum The entire range of wavelengths or frequencies of electromagnetic radiation extending from gamma rays to the longest radio waves, including visible light.

electromechanical A mechanical device which is controlled by an electric device. Solenoids and shunt trip circuit breakers are examples of electromechanical devices.

electromotive force (EMF) The force that

tends to cause the movement of electrons in an electric circuit. It is measured in VOLTS.

electron *(a)* The Greek word for an *alloy* consisting of four parts of gold and one part of silver. This was widely used by the ancient Greeks, partly because they found it difficult to produce a purer gold (modern 'pure gold' is generally 22 carat, *i.e.* 11/12 pure). *(b)* The Greek word for *amber*, which was thought to present an appearance similar to that of electron metal. In the sixteenth century Dr Gilbert, an English natural philosopher, coined the term *electricity* to denote attractions between certain bodies, including amber, after rubbing in a certain way. *(c)* Subatomic particle having a rest mass of 9.04×10^{-28} gram, *i.e.* 1/1840 that of the PROTON or NEUTRON, and bearing a negative electric charge. An electric current is a flow of electrons from the CATHODE to the ANODE.

electron gun The assembly of electrodes in a CATHODE-RAY TUBE which produces the electron beam. It comprises a cathode from which electrons are emitted, an apertured anode, and one or more focusing electrodes. Those electrons which pass through the aperture form the beam.

electronic digital computer *See* DIGITAL COMPUTER.

electronic mail *Also called* email. A potentially two-way communication for sending text and data over computer networks. It does not have to establish a simultaneous connection, because MAIL SERVERS will process and store messages and deliver them to the receiver when the receiver attaches to the network.

electronic whiteboard A device which converts markings on a whiteboard to digital information.

electro-osmosis Flow of liquid through the pores of a membrane due to a difference of electric potential. The term is also used for WELLPOINT DEWATERING assisted by the passage of an electric current. When a direct current is passed through water-logged silt, water flows to the *cathode*. Cathodes are placed in the silt at intervals of about 10 m (30 ft) and water is pumped away from there; *anodes* are placed at intermediate points.

electroplated Coated with a more precious or more corrosion-resistant metal by electro-chemical deposition.

electrostatic A potential difference (electric charge) measurable between two points which is caused by the distribution of dissimilar static charge between the points. The voltage level is usually in kilovolts.

electrostatic filter A machine which imparts a positive electrical charge to particles suspended in an air stream, which are subsequently collected on electrically negative plates.

electrostatic plotter A plotting device which uses electrostatically charged paper.

electrostatic shield A metallic barrier or shield between the primary and secondary windings of a transformer which reduces the capacitive coupling and thereby increases the transformer's ability to reduce high-frequency noise.

electrostatic spraying Spray painting in which the paint and the object are given opposite static electrical charges. The paint is attracted to the surface, even of awkward shapes, and loss by overspraying is greatly reduced.

element *(a)* A substance consisting entirely of atoms of the same atomic number. *(b)* The resistance wire constituting the heating unit of an electric heater. *(c)* One of the four elements of Aristotle (earth, water, air and fire), to which reference was commonly made in classical architectural and protoscientific texts.

elevation *(a)* The vertical distance of a point above or below the BENCH MARK or some other reference point. *(b)* Representation of an object as seen on a vertical plane, viewed from the front.

elevator A car or platform for the vertical transportation of persons or goods. Called a *lift* in the UK and in Australia. *See also* BRICK ELEVATOR.

elevator hoistway US term for *lift well*.

elevator recall *See* LIFT RECALL.

ell US term for ELBOW.

ellipse A closed loop obtained by cutting a right circular cone by a plane, if the whole of the section lies on one side of the vertex of the cone. It is also the locus of a point such that the sum of the distances of the point from two fixed points, or foci, is constant. Consequently an ellipse can be drawn by pinning the ends of a string at the foci, and running a pencil around with the string tightly stretched (*see figure*). The greatest and smallest diameters are the *major* and the *minor* axes. The equation of the ellipse is of the form

$$\frac{x^2}{a} + \frac{y^2}{b} = 1$$

where a and b are constants. *See also* OVAL.

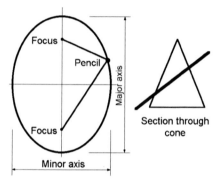

Ellipse

ellipse of stress *See* ELLIPSOID OF STRESS.
ellipsoid A SURFACE OF REVOLUTION generated by an ellipse.
ellipsoid of stress An ELLIPSOID representing the state of stress at a given point in a body. Its semi-axes are the vectors representing the PRINCIPAL STRESSES at the point, and any radius vector represents the resultant stress on a particular plane through the point. When one of the principal stresses is zero (which includes the *plane-stress* condition), the ellipsoid reduces to an *ellipse*. *See also* MOHR CIRCLE.
elliptical arch An arch whose elevation is half an ellipse. It comes vertically on to its SPRINGINGS. Whereas in a semicircular arch the rise must be half the span, an elliptical arch can have any ratio of rise to span.
elliptical paraboloid A surface of translation generated by a convex parabola moving over another convex parabola.

elongation *(a)* The extension of a structural member due to a tensile force. *(b)* The plastic extension of a metal test specimen at failure in a tensile test.
elutriation A method of separating grain sizes according to the velocities at which they sink in a liquid. The particle sizes are evaluated by STOKES' LAW.
email or e-mail ELECTRONIC MAIL.
embedded column A column that is partly, but not wholly, built into a wall.
embodied energy The energy consumed in the activities of the production of materials, their use and subsequent disposal.
embossed Ornamental designs or figures in RELIEF, *i.e.* raised above the surface.
emergency lighting Lighting which is essential for the safe evacuation of a building in the event of a failure of normal electric power, as distinct from *safety lighting* or *standby lighting*.
emergency power The power that is available within ten seconds of a normal power failure to operate emergency lighting or part of the normal lighting. *Standby power* is the power available within one minute.
emergy The embodied energy, the heat used or the energy required by machinery expended in making a building component.
emery An impure form of CORUNDUM. It consists mainly of alumina and iron oxide.
EMF *Abbreviation for* ELECTROMOTIVE FORCE.
EMI *Abbreviation for* Electromagnetic Interference. A term that describes electrically induced noise or transients.
emissions trading Trading between parties that allows an emitter of above-average quantities of restricted substances to the atmosphere to purchase credits from another who is a below-average producer.
emissivity Non-preferred term for EMITTANCE.
emittance The ratio of radiant heat emission by unit area of a surface to such emission by a unit area of a BLACK BODY at the same temperature and with the same surroundings.
emulsifier A substance which modifies the surface tension of COLLOIDAL droplets, keeping them suspended, and keeping them from coalescing.

emulsion A COLLOIDAL suspension of one liquid in another.

emulsion paint A paint consisting of small particles of synthetic resin (such as POLYVINYL ACETATE) and pigments suspended in water. When the water evaporates, the resin particles form a film that binds the pigments.

en suite Forming a suite of rooms with internally communicating doors.

enamel *See* VITREOUS ENAMEL.

enamel paint Hard-gloss paint which contains a high proportion of varnish, and consequently has less pigment. For that reason it requires one or two undercoats.

enamelled brick A glazed brick.

encased beam Iron and steel beams were at one time encased in a variety of materials for protection against fire. Today the term usually means a CONCRETE-ENCASED BEAM.

encastré BUILT-IN or fixed-ended, and consequently restrained from rotation. *Also called encastered.*

encaustic tiles Tiles whose coloured decoration has been fixed by the application of heat. They were much used in the Middle Ages, and subsequently in Neo-Gothic churches.

end block A section at the end of a POST-TENSIONED member, which has been enlarged to reduce the bearing stresses to permissible values.

end grain The face of a piece of timber exposed when the fibres are cut transversely. It easily deteriorates when exposed unprotected to the weather.

end joint Joint formed between the ends of two pieces of material which are in line. The term is commonly used for timber in preference to BUTT JOINT.

end lap The overlap of the ends of sheet material, as distinct from SIDE LAP.

end-bearing pile A BEARING PILE which is carried on a load-bearing layer, such as rock.

end-lap joint Joint formed between the ends of two pieces of timber, normally placed at right angles. Each piece is halved for a distance equal to the width of the other piece, so that the surfaces are flush in the assembled joint (*see* figure). *Also called a right-angled half-lap joint.*

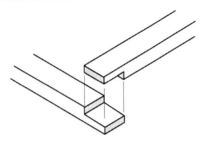

End-lap joint

end-matched board A timber board, usually flooring, with a matching tongue and groove at the ends.

endoscopy Remote viewing of the inside of pipes, cavities and the like, usually with a miniature television camera and fibre-optic lighting on the end of a flexible probe, similar to medical endoscopy.

endothermic reaction A reaction in which heat is absorbed, as opposed to an *exothermic* reaction.

endurance limit *See* FATIGUE STRENGTH.

energy The capacity for doing WORK. In classical physics, *mechanical energy* is divided into *kinetic energy*, due to motion of a mass, and *potential energy*, due to its position. The latter consequently includes the gravitational HEAD of water and the STRAIN ENERGY stored in a stressed material. Energy can be converted between the forms of mechanical, heat, sound, electrical, chemical energy, etc. Much of the energy used in buildings comes from the combustion of fuels, a form of chemical energy which can produce undesirable by-products.

energy audit Detailed and systematic investigation of energy use in a building or facility with a view to identifying opportunities to make savings.

energy intensity The ratio of energy use in a sector to activity in that sector, for example, the ratio of energy use to constant-dollar production in manufacturing.

energy management The management of the use and consumption of energy, to reduce its cost, or in response to a need for energy conservation.

energy modelling Dynamic computer simulation of energy flows to and from and within a building over time.

energy modelling software Software designed to simulate energy flows to and from and within a building over time.

energy rating The formal rating of a building in accordance with a defined series of energy levels to provide an indication of overall efficiency of energy consumption.

energy simulation Computational method of constructing and operating a mathematical model of a building and its energy systems in order to estimate energy consumption over a period of time, usually for comparison of design options.

energy source depletion The gradual consumption of material from a finite, non-renewable energy source.

energy, embodied *See* EMBODIED ENERGY.

engaged column A column that is partly, but not wholly, built into a wall.

English bond A brick BOND which consists of alternate courses of HEADERS and STRETCHERS (*see figure*). *Also called Old English bond.*

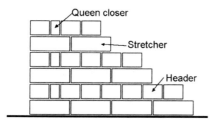

English bond

English cross bond An ENGLISH BOND which introduces a single header placed into alternate stretcher courses. This produces a diagonal pattern. *Also known as St Andrew's Cross bond or Dutch bond.*

English tile A ROOF TILE, moulded with a plain surface.

ensemble The ability of the performers at a concert to hear one another so that they can play in unison. If the stage or orchestra pit is very wide and shallow, the two sides of an orchestra may not be able to hear one another.

entablature In Classical architecture, the horizontal elements above a COLONNADE.

From top to bottom the entablature consisted of the CORNICE, the frieze and the ARCHITRAVE (*see figure*).

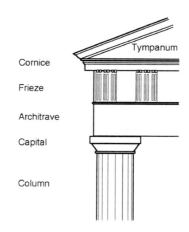

Entablature

entasis The deliberate, slightly convex curvature given to the vertical profile of a tapered column, used to correct the optical illusion that straight-sided columns are concave.

entering temperature The temperature of a fluid at the point of entry to a heat exchanger, *e.g.* air entering a cooling coil in an air conditioning system.

enthalpy The heat content per unit mass of moist air, due to both LATENT HEAT and SENSIBLE HEAT, relative to 0 °C dry air (0 g/kg AH), measured in kJ/kg (or BTU per lb).

enthalpy controlled economiser An ECONOMISER CYCLE in an air conditioning system which is designed to supply outdoor air without recirculation when the ENTHALPY of the outdoor air is lower than that of return air from the conditioned space.

entrained air Air incorporated in concrete by the use of an AIR-ENTRAINING AGENT.

entrapped air Air voids in concrete which are not purposely ENTRAINED.

entropy A name coined in 1865 by the German physicist R. Clausius for one of the quantitative elements of THERMODYNAMICS. He explained it as follows: 'A portion of matter at uniform temperature retains its entropy unchanged so long as no heat passes to or from it; but if it receives a quantity of heat without change of temperature, the entropy is increased by an amount of heat equal to the ratio of the mechanical equivalent of the quantity of the heat to the absolute measure of the temperature on the thermodynamic scale. The entropy of a system . . . is always increased by any transport of heat within the system; hence the entropy of the universe tends to a maximum.'

envelope *(a)* The line formed by a series of common tangents to a family of related curves *(see figure). (b)* Often used as a shortened term for BUILDING ENVELOPE.

Envelope

envelopment The sensation that sound appears to come equally from all directions.

environmental control glass Generic term for HEAT-ABSORBING, REFLECTIVE, LOW-EMISSIVITY and other types of glass intended to reduce solar heat gain or heat transmission.

environmental impact study An evaluation of the existing environmental conditions at a given location and the impact of subsequent development, required by statutory authorities as part of an approval process.

environmental temperature (EnvT) A comfort index, similar to DRT, more suitable for warm climates (lightly clad human bodies more exposed to radiation), where MRT is twice as important as DBT, often expressed as EnvT = ⅓ DBT + ⅔ MRT.

environmentally sensitive construction Construction according to environmentally sensitive design.

environmentally sensitive design Design with the objective of minimising impact of construction on the environment.

EPDM *Abbreviation for* Ethylene Propylene Diene Monomer, *also called* ethylene propylene terpolymer (EPT), an elastomeric material, used mainly in waterproofing applications.

ephemeris A table giving the computed position of a heavenly body. *See* NAUTICAL ALMANAC.

epicentre Point on the Earth's surface immediately above the focus of an EARTHQUAKE.

epicycloid A curve generated by a point on a circle rolling on another circle. It is particularly useful for the design of smoothly operating gears. *See also* CYCLOID.

epoxy resin A group of thermosetting plastics based on the epoxide grouping.

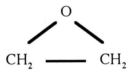

The uncured resin consists of short-chain polymer molecules with an epoxide group at either end. The epoxide group is very reactive, and many substances can be used as HARDENERS. The uncured resin and the hardener are kept separately and mixed just before use. Epoxy resins are appreciably more expensive than the POLYESTER RESINS, but they are better suited for many applications. They adhere strongly to metals, glass, concrete, stone and rubber, and thus make good glues, and solvents for paints. They are resistant to abrasion, weather, acids and alkalis, and to heat up to 100°C (212°F). In particular, they have been found useful for repairing damaged concrete, and for joining new concrete to old; for this purpose they can be mixed with sand into an epoxy resin mortar.

EPS (computing) *Abbreviation for* Embedded Postscript. A data format suitable for driving postscript printers.

EPS (materials) *Abbreviation for* Expanded Polystyrene. *See* EXPANDED PLASTIC.

equaliser An electronic instrument used to obtain a desired overall frequency response of a system. Mainly used in audio systems.

equation of time The difference between APPARENT SOLAR TIME and MEAN SOLAR TIME.

equator The PARALLEL OF LATITUDE

located midway between the poles of the Earth or other sphere. The only parallel of latitude which is a GEODETIC LINE.

equatorial comfort index Criterion for determining the COMFORT ZONE, evolved by C. G. Webb in Singapore in 1952, *also known as* the *Singapore index*. It takes account of wet-bulb and dry-bulb temperature, and air movement, but ignores radiation. Its application is confined to the conditions which exist in the hot-humid equatorial zone, and it is intended for indoor conditions for people acclimatised to wet-bulb temperatures above 24°C (75°F).

equatorial mounting A mounting tilted from the horizontal at the same angle as the geographical latitude (so that it would be horizontal at the equator). Used in astronomy, but also for concentrating mirror (parabolic trough type) solar collectors, for tracking, *i.e.* following the sun's apparent movement. One dimensional (east to west) rotation is sufficient.

equilateral Having all sides equal. An equilateral triangle has three equal sides, while an ISOSCELES triangle has only two equal sides.

equilibrant A force required to keep an unbalanced system of forces in equilibrium.

equilibrium In mechanics, the state of a body at rest, or moving with a uniform velocity. The resultant of all the forces acting on a body in equilibrium is zero.

equilibrium diagram *Same as* PHASE DIAGRAM.

equilibrium moisture content of timber The moisture content in the wood which balances that in the atmosphere, so that it neither gives off nor takes in any moisture from the surrounding air. It is expressed as a percentage of the oven-dry weight of the wood.

equinox When the length of day equals the length of night, due to the fact that the sun crosses the celestial equator. It occurs about 21 March and 23 September. *See also* SOLSTICE.

equipment event log A record that is kept of equipment problems and activity, to assist with maintenance.

equipment grounding conductor *See* SAFETY GROUND.

equivalent continuous sound level (L_{eq}) A constant sound level in dB(A) which would give the same total acoustic energy at a point as a fluctuating sound level of the same duration. It is used in occupational and environmental noise assessments.

equivalent sphere illuminance (ESI) Used mainly in North America, the illuminance which would produce, under reference lighting conditions, the same visibility as is found in the existing lighting system. *See also* CIE CONTRAST RENDERING FACTOR (CRF).

equivalent temperature Criterion for determining the COMFORT ZONE, evolved by A. F. Dufton in 1929. It takes account of temperature, air movement and radiation, but ignores humidity. Dufton, in 1932, devised the EUPATHEOSCOPE for assessing the thermal environment in terms of equivalent temperature for research at the British Building Research Station. *See also* EFFECTIVE TEMPERATURE.

ERC *Abbreviation for* EXTERNALLY REFLECTED COMPONENT (of the daylight factor).

erection stresses Stresses caused by the CONSTRUCTION LOADS, particularly by the self-weight of components while being lifted into position.

erg The unit of energy in CGS UNITS. It is the work done when a force of one DYNE moves one centimetre in the direction of the force. In SI UNITS the erg has been replaced by the JOULE, which equals 10^7 erg.

ergonomics The study of the interaction between work and people. *Also called human factors engineering.*

ERW *Abbreviation for* Electric Resistance Welding.

escalator A moving staircase, consisting of an endless belt carrying a series of steps. It can be used for upward or downward movement; however, sometimes an escalator is used for transporting people up, while a conventional stationary stair may be provided for downward movement.

escutcheon A protective plate surrounding a keyhole in a door.

ESD *Abbreviation for (a)* Ecologically Sustainable Design; *(b)* Electrostatic

Discharge (static electricity). The effects of static discharge can range from simple skin irritation for an individual to degraded or destroyed semiconductor junctions for an electronic device. *(c)* Ecologically Sustainable Development.

ESI *Abbreviation for* EQUIVALENT SPHERE ILLUMINANCE.

ET *Abbreviation for* EFFECTIVE TEMPERATURE.

ET* (pronounced ET star) The New Effective Temperature, developed in 1971 by Gagge *et al.* at the J. B. Pierce Laboratories, based on their two-node model of heat exchange between the human body and its environment. It is indicated on the PSYCHROMETRIC CHART by isotherm lines which coincide with DBT up to 14 °C, but are increasingly sloping above this, designated by the DBT line crossed at the 50 per cent RH curve.

etching *(a)* The process of biting lines into a metal plate by means of acid, and producing a picture from the plate. *Also* the picture produced by this process. *(b)* Revealing the structure of metal by selective chemical attack. In PERLITE, for example, the ferrite lamellae are electropositive to the cementite, so that they can be shown up by etching. *(c)* Chemically cleaning a surface in preparation for painting or other coating. *See also* PICKLED.

ethanol Ethyl alcohol (C_2H_5OH) intended for industrial use, rather than human consumption.

ethernet A network transmission protocol in which the transmitting device waits for a moment when the transmission medium is idle before transmitting a packet of data. This protocol works well on relatively low-load networks, with sufficient idle time to allow it to operate without noticeable delay.

eucalypt An evergreen genus of trees which sheds its bark. Many Australian hardwoods, with names such as white ash and red mahogany, are in fact eucalypts. *Also called gum tree.*

Euler formula A formula for the BUCKLING of slender columns, published by the French mathematician Leonard Euler in 1757. The buckling load of a column

$$P = \frac{\pi^2 EI}{L^2}$$

where π = circular constant, 3.1416…, E = modulus of elasticity, I = second moment of area, L = effective length. *See also* RANKINE COLUMN FORMULA *and* SHORT COLUMN FORMULA.

eupatheoscope A black, electrically heated cylinder, designed to have the same surface temperature as a clothed human under comfortable conditions; the heat input required for comfort was measured to determine the EQUIVALENT TEMPERATURE.

eutectic The alloy with the lowest melting temperature in its range of composition. It is readily apparent on the PHASE DIAGRAM as a point of intersection between two descending LIQUIDUS curves in a binary system, or three descending liquidus curves in a ternary system. The eutectic thus solidifies out of the liquid as a mixture with a definite composition.

eutectoid A mixture of two or more constituents that forms on cooling from a *solid solution*, and transforms again on heating. PERLITE is a typical eutectoid. The process is similar to the formation of a EUTECTIC, which solidifies from the liquid, or melt.

evacuated tubular collector Solar energy collector suitable for temperatures up to 150 °C (300 °F). The tubes are given a SELECTIVE SURFACE coating to increase the efficiency, and evacuated to limit convective heat loss.

evacuation (of a building) The removal of people from a building or part of a building, which is usually the first life-safety measure in case of fire or other emergency. It involves an alarm or communication system to initiate the evacuation, the provision of safe exit routes, and the organisational procedures to manage it. *See also* FIRE ACTION PLAN and REFUGE FLOOR.

evaporation Conversion of a liquid into a vapour, without necessarily reaching the boiling point.

evaporative cooling A simple method of air conditioning which can be employed in hot-arid climates. The latent heat of the water evaporated is absorbed from the hot dry air, which is thus cooled. The humidity is increased by the evaporation of the water.

evaporative shower tower A tower equipped with shower heads which entrain air at the top and cool it by evaporation of water as it falls. Cooler air flows to occupied spaces from the bottom of the tower.

event A point in time representing the intersection of two ARROWS in a NETWORK, *i.e.* the start or finish of an activity. An event has no time duration.

exa Prefix meaning 10^{18}, or one million million million times, used particularly in SI UNITS. *Abbreviated* E, for example 1 EJ = 10^{18} joule.

excavator Earthmoving machine mounted on wheels or tracks, used for digging in a stationary position (*see figure*). The bucket digs toward the machine by the combined movement of a *boom* and *dipper arm*, and by crowding the bucket. The whole superstructure rotates to dump the material. The action is similar to a BACKHOE.

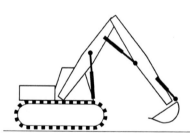

Excavator

exfiltration Opposite of *infiltration*. *Leakage* is a more common word.

exfoliation Swelling, peeling or scaling of mineral surfaces in thin layers, *e.g.* exfoliated VERMICULITE.

exhaust fan Fan which withdraws air and delivers it to the outside, as opposed to RETURN AIR, which is returned to the central air treatment system.

exhaust ventilation Circulation of air through a space by means of a fan or fans located at or near the outlet to produce a slight negative pressure. May be localised at a piece of process equipment such as a

food fryer to prevent the general spread of contaminants.

exittance The ratio of luminous (radiant) flux leaving a surface to that arriving.

exosphere *See* ATMOSPHERIC LAYERS.

exothermic reaction A reaction that occurs with the evolution of heat, as opposed to an *endothermic* reaction.

expanded clay An artificial LIGHTWEIGHT AGGREGATE.

expanded metal Metal network formed from sheet metal by cutting a pattern of slits, followed by pulling the metal into a diamond pattern. It is used as a metal *lath*, as concrete reinforcement, and for the making of screens. *Also called diamond mesh.*

expanded plastic A very light insulating material, obtainable as a loose fill, in sheets or in blocks. *Polystyrene*, for example, can be expanded 40 times by foaming. The density of expanded polystyrene or of rigid *polyurethane* foam is from 16 to 64 kg/m^3 (1 to 4 lb/ft^3), its compressive strength is between 100 and 400 kPa (15 to 60 psi), and its thermal conductivity is between 0.014 and 0.043 W/mK (0.1 to 0.3 Btu in./h/ft^2/°F). *Also called cellular plastic, foamed plastic or rigid foam.*

expansion bolt An anchor into masonry which consists of a bolt operating inside a split cone. As the bolt is tightened, the cone expands and wedges into the hole.

expansion joint A CONTROL JOINT forming a separation between adjoining parts to allow for small (positive or negative) relative movements, such as those caused by temperature change. It requires a gap between the adjacent parts, usually filled with compressible material. *See also* CONTRACTION JOINT.

expansion loop A loop or horseshoe bend inserted in a pipe to provide for its expansion and contraction due to temperature change.

expansion sleeve A tube covering a DOWEL bar, to allow its free longitudinal movement at a joint.

expansive cement A cement which, on setting, expands instead of shrinking. Depending on the amount of additive, the expansion may be merely sufficient to counter the shrinkage of PORTLAND

CEMENT, or it may be sufficient to induce tensile stresses in the reinforcement, and thus POST-TENSION the concrete. The additives most commonly used to produce expansive cements are calcium sulphate ($CaSO_4$), free lime (CaO) and anhydrous aluminosulphate ($4CaO. 3Al_2O_3. SO_3$).

experiential Relating to or derived from experience, empirical; as opposed to *experimental*.

experimental stress analysis *See* BRITTLE COATING, DIRECT MODEL ANALYSIS, INDIRECT STRUCTURAL MODEL ANALYSIS, MOIRÉ FRINGES *and* PHOTO-ELASTICITY.

expert system A KNOWLEDGE-BASED SYSTEM which captures human expertise and emulates human experiential reasoning in specialised applications.

expert system shell A computer program which allows the input of knowledge to create an EXPERT SYSTEM. An expert system without the KNOWLEDGE BASE.

exploding In computer graphics, the process of decomposing a complex object into its constituent components.

explosion hazard Risk of explosion in a space due to accumulation of combustible gaseous or particulate matter in sufficient quantity to create an explosive atmosphere.

explosive rivet A type of BLIND RIVET with a hollow shank which contains an explosive charge. The rivet shank is expanded by exploding the charge with a hammer blow after the rivet has been inserted. It is used particularly in aluminium structures, but seldom in the building industry.

explosive-powered tools Tools used for driving hardened nails and threaded fasteners into hard materials such as concrete and steel, using an explosive cartridge as the power source.

exponential function A function of the type $y = e^x$, where e is the base of the NATURAL LOGARITHM. It is thus the inverse of the natural logarithm. Exponential functions occur as a result of integration of terms containing $1/x$, and also in HYPERBOLIC FUNCTIONS.

exponential horn A horn, the cross-sectional area of which increases exponentially with axial distance. Such horns

are sometimes used on loudspeakers, loud-hailers and musical instruments, as ACOUSTIC IMPEDANCE matching devices, to increase the acoustical output.

exposed aggregate A decorative finish for concrete. The aggregate may be exposed by removing the outer skin of cement mortar from the surface before it has hardened, or the 'exposed' aggregate may be sprinkled on the wet concrete after placing.

exposure meter A device for estimating the exposure required for photography. It usually incorporates a PHOTOVOLTAIC CELL.

express language An information modelling language developed for STEP for the description of entities.

express run The non-stop run of a lift car from its departure floor to its destination floor, ignoring any possible stops on the way. *See also* SKY LOBBY.

express-G The graphic representation for the EXPRESS LANGUAGE.

extender pigment Pigment which provides very little hiding power but is useful in stabilising suspension, improving flow, lowering gloss, and providing other desirable qualities of a paint or coating.

extensibility The maximum tensile strain of which a material is capable. It is much lower in BRITTLE than in DUCTILE materials.

extension *(a)* *See* FILE EXTENSION. *(b)* Extension of time under the conditions of a contract. *(c)* A special file used on Macintosh computers to add extra functionality to the system.

extension of time An extension of a contract period to provide for delays arising from conditions over which the contractor has no control.

extensive property A property of a substance, that depends on mass or 'extent' of the substance, *e.g.* volume.

extensometer *Same as* STRAIN GAUGE.

external insulation The use of resistive (bulk) insulation on the outside of a massive layer (*e.g.* brick or block or a concrete roof slab). It tends to produce a more stable indoor temperature, utilising the thermal capacity of the massive layer, than the more usual internal insulation.

Especially important in passive solar (direct gain) systems.

external memory A memory which is under the control of a computer, but not necessarily permanently connected to it, such as a FLOPPY or HARD DISK.

externally reflected component (ERC) (of the DAYLIGHT FACTOR) The component due to the external reflecting surfaces.

extrados The outer or upper curve of an arch.

extrapolate To infer the position of a point belonging to a graph *beyond* the last known point, assuming that the curve is smooth. This is inherently less accurate than *interpolation.*

extruded brick A BRICK produced from a stiff but cohesive clay–shale mixture, which is extruded through a die. It may contain a series of holes, so that the bedding faces of the bricks are perforated. After extrusion, the ribbon of clay is cut to the height of the bricks with a set of taut wires.

extruding In computer graphics, the process of creating three-dimensional graphic objects by sweeping a two-dimensional form in two axes through a specified distance in the third axis. *Also called* 2½D.

extrusion Producing a linear shape by pushing material through a die (*see figure*). The process is used for the manufacture of sections in aluminium, as an alternative to hot-rolling. It is also used for plastics.

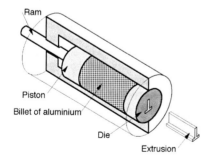

Extrusion

eye bolt A bolt with a ring forged on one end, or welded to one end.

eye of a dome An opening at the top of a dome to admit light. It may be glazed or open to the sky. *See also* LANTERN.

F

°F Degree Fahrenheit.

F Symbol for the unit of electrical capacitance, the FARAD.

fabric *See* MESH REINFORCEMENT.

fabric energy loads Cooling or heating loads imposed on space in a building by energy flows through external walls, floor and roof.

facade The face or front wall of a building.

facade engineering Engineering design of a building envelope so that it can maintain its integrity despite action of wind and weather.

facade system The system of elements that make up an external wall. It may include separate elements for resisting wind forces, for controlling water and air penetration and vapour transmission, for insulation, and for admission of daylight and vision.

face brick A BRICK especially made to have an agreeable colour and texture. It is often weaker than a common brick.

face brickwork Brickwork made using FACE BRICKs and laid with a good standard of workmanship and jointing.

face veneer Wood VENEER selected for its decorative qualities, rather than its strength.

face-bedded Natural stone built into wall with the BEDDING PLANEs parallel to the wall surface.

face-centred cubic lattice A crystal structure which has an atom at each corner of a cube and one at the centre of each face. It may be imitated by packing spheres to line up both vertically and horizontally.

face-sealed facade system A FACADE SYSTEM where the waterproofing and control of air infiltration all occur primarily at the outside surface.

faced plywood Plywood faced with metal, plastic or any material other than WOOD VENEER.

facia *Same as* FASCIA.

facility A physical environment designed to service an organisation's objectives, ranging from open space (parks and gardens) and infrastructure (roads, etc.) to built premises (offices, factories, schools, hospitals, residences, etc.).

facility audit A survey of a facility portfolio to establish the condition of the fabric and systems, and the functionality and risk associated with any part that does not comply with the requirements.

facility management The management of resources (people and assets), place and process to optimise an organisation's business.

facility plan A planning tool for managing a facility's operations and maintenance to plan for current and future activities and requirements in a cost-effective manner.

factor analysis Statistical procedure for grouping associated variables.

factor of safety Factor used in ELASTIC DESIGN to provide a margin of safety against collapse and serious structural damage. It includes an allowance for inaccurate assumptions in the loading conditions, for inadequate control over the quality of materials, for imperfections in workmanship, and for minor approximations made in the structural theory. It does not allow for arithmetical errors.

fader A device for gradually attenuating the intensity of an audio signal.

Fahrenheit scale Temperature scale, now used mainly in the USA. The scale was originally intended to run from 0 for the freezing temperature of a mixture of water and common salt to 100 for the blood temperature in the human body. However, it is now defined by the freezing point of water (+32 °F) and the boiling point of water (212 °F). To convert to the CELSIUS scale (°C) we subtract 32 and then divide by 1.8.

faience Originally the French word for *porzellana di Faenza*, a fine painted and glazed earthenware made in Faenza in Italy. In buildings, prior to the twentieth century, the term generally denoted glazed TERRA COTTA, which had been fired once without and once with the glaze. The term is now used for any decorative glazed tiles and even for glazed plastic floor mosaic.

fail safe An automatic protective response initiated in the event of a failure.

failure (of materials) The condition when a structure or material ceases to fulfil its required purpose. The failure of a structural member may be caused by *elastic deformation, fracture, cracking* or excessive *deflection*. The non-structural failure of a material may be due to *weathering, abrasion* or *chemical action*.

fair market rent *See* MARKET RENT.

fall-arrest system System of harness or safety belt, together with ropes, anchorage points and energy-absorbing devices, to arrest the fall of a worker from an elevated location and bring the person to a controlled stop without injury.

false ceiling A ceiling *suspended* or *hung* from the floor above which hides its SOFFIT, and which provides a space for cables and ducts (*see figure*). See also RAISED FLOOR.

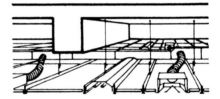

False ceiling

false header A half-brick, which completes the visible bond, but is not a header.

false set The rapid development of rigidity in freshly mixed cement paste, mortar or concrete, with little evolution of heat. Plasticity can be regained by further mixing without addition of water. *See also* SETTING *and* FLASH SET.

false window A walled-up window.

falsework A temporary structure erected to support work during construction, and subsequently removed.

fan *See* AXIAL-FLOW FAN, BOOSTER FAN *and* CENTRIFUGAL FAN.

fan coil unit A device used in air conditioning systems consisting of a container, usually of metal, in which are installed a fan and cooling and/or heating coils for the purpose of cooling, heating and circulating air in a space. May also contain an air filter to remove contaminants.

fan noise The noise caused by fans used in ventilating and air conditioning equipment. Fan noise can be attenuated by DUCT LININGS.

fan vault Gothic stone vaulting system decorated with fan tracery, formed by a convex line rotated in a semicircle around a vertical axis. The bottom of this convex line is tangential to the face of the column, which has numerous clustered shafts, and the top merges into an almost flat stone ceiling. Because flexural tension may develop in the flat parts of the vault, it often has stone pendants whose weight reverses any tension that occurs.

fanlight Originally a fan-shaped window, with sash bars radiating like the ribs of a fan, located over a door. It was much used in Georgian and Colonial architecture, and in their revivals. The term is now sometimes applied to any window located over a door (*see figure*).

Fanlight

fanning Gradual increase in the spacing of tile joints so they will conform to an area that is not parallel.

FAO *Abbreviation for* Finish All Over.

FAR *Abbreviation for* Floor Area Ratio.

far field That part of a FREE FIELD generated by a source where the SOUND PRESSURE and the air velocity (due to the passage of the sound) are in phase. In most cases the far field will exist at distances greater than one representative dimension of the source, where the INVERSE SQUARE LAW may be used to predict the sound pressure.

farad (F) Unit of electrical capacitance, named after Michael Faraday, an English scientist who discovered the laws of electromagnetic induction, and first produced electromotive power in 1831. The capacitance is 1 F if a capacitor is charged with 1 coulomb, and the difference of potential between the plates is 1 volt.

Faraday shield A grounded metallic barrier which can be used for: *(a)* general electromagnetic shielding of equipment and communications; *(b)* shielding from lightning or other high voltage discharges; *(c)* improved isolation between the windings of a transformer. In this application, the shield basically reduces the leakage capacitance between the primary and secondary.

fascia A plain horizontal band on the surface of a building. In Classical design, fascias were employed both in the CORNICE and in the ARCHITRAVE. In modern usage, the same as FASCIA BOARD. *Also spelled facia.*

fascia board In timber construction, a wide board fixed to the wall, the wall plate, or the ends of the RAFTERS. It usually carries the gutter.

fast Fourier transform *See* FFT.

fast track A phasing technique between design and construction whereby construction starts before design is complete.

fast tripping The common practice in which a circuit breaker or line recloser on an electrical supply line operates faster than a fuse can blow. *Also called fuse saving.* Effective for clearing transient faults without a sustained interruption, but is somewhat controversial because industrial loads are subjected to a momentary or temporary interruption.

fat clay A clay having a high PLASTICITY INDEX and a high LIQUID LIMIT.

fat concrete Concrete containing a high proportion of cement mortar.

fat mortar A mortar which sticks to the trowel, as opposed to a *lean mortar.*

fathom A nautical measure equal to 6 ft or 1.829 m. It originated as the distance between the outstretched fingertips of a man.

fatigue (in materials) The tendency of materials to fracture under many repetitions of a stress considerably lower than the ultimate static strength. The term *fatigue* is reserved for a large number of repetitions, while *repeated loading* is commonly used for a small number of load repetitions.

fatigue strength The greatest stress which can be sustained without failure for a given number of stress cycles. *Also called endurance limit.*

faucet US word for a water tap.

fault *(a) See* GEOLOGICAL FAULT. *(b)* In electricity, a defect in a circuit, component or line, especially referring to the effect of the defect, as in *fault current* or *fault level.*

fault, transient A short circuit on the power system usually induced by lightning, tree branches, or animals that can be cleared by momentarily interrupting the current.

Fe Chemical symbol for *iron* (ferrum).

FEA *Abbreviation for* FINITE ELEMENT ANALYSIS.

feasibility study A study conducted in the initial stage of a project in order to determine physical, economic and legal viability.

feather edge A fine taper.

feature In product modelling, an important characteristic, usually regarding an aspect of the shape, *e.g.* a slot, chamfer, etc.

feed and expansion tank A small tank connected to a system circulating a heat transfer liquid in heating and cooling systems to accommodate expansion or contraction of the fluid and make up any losses from the system.

feedback *(a)* A report on the production of an item which shows defects by comparison with the required standard and how errors can be corrected. *(b)* The return of the output of a system to its input. Used to monitor and control the behaviour of a system. *(c)* In audio systems, feedback is the howling which occurs when the sound from a loudspeaker causes a self-reinforcement of the sound at the microphone.

feeder Transmission line supplying electrical power to a distribution system.

feeler gauge An instrument for measuring the clearance in a gap, consisting of a series of blades of different thickness.

felspar A group of minerals consisting mainly of aluminium silicates. They are contained in granite and other rocks, and decompose into clay. *Also spelled feldspar.*

felt *See* ROOFING FELT.

felting *See* AIR FELTING.

FEM *Abbreviation for* Finite Element Modelling.

fenestration The arrangement of the windows and other openings on the walls of a building, particularly with reference to the appearance of the facade.

ferrite A solid solution in which ALPHA IRON, as distinct from GAMMA IRON, is the solvent. It may contain in solid solution up to 30 per cent of chromium and up to 15 per cent of silicon, but no more than 0.03 per cent of carbon. Ferrite is the principal constituent of low carbon steels and of many alloy steels. *See also* AUSTENITE. Ferrite also has magnetic properties which make it useful in electronic applications.

ferrocement Concrete made with several layers of finely divided reinforcement, instead of the conventional larger bars. It is usually made in thin panels, about 12–25 mm (½–1 in.) thick. The maximum aggregate size is about 5 mm (³⁄₁₆ in.). It can be used for curved surfaces such as boat hulls or small domes, the concrete being applied to the reinforcement with a trowel in several layers, without the need for formwork. *Also spelled ferrocemento*, sometimes hyphenated.

ferroconcrete An obsolete term for reinforced concrete.

ferroresonance Resonance resulting when the iron core of an inductive component of an LC circuit is saturated, increasing the inductive reactance with respect to the capacitance reactance. This is an undesirable effect in electrical distribution systems.

ferroresonant transformer A voltage regulating transformer which depends on core saturation and output capacitance.

ferrous metal A metal in which iron is the principal constituent.

ferruginous stone or sand Stone or sand

containing iron. It generally has a reddish or brown colour.

festoon *(a)* A carved decoration on pilasters and panels, and suspended in a curve between rosettes, typically in the form of hanging clusters of fruit, tied in a bunch with leaves and flowers. *Also called garland* or *swag. (b)* An arrangement of the FILAMENT in a linear electric lamp, where the filament hangs in a series of shallow loops along its length.

FFR *Abbreviation for* FLUX FRACTION RATIO.

FFT *Abbreviation for* Fast Fourier Transform. A digital method of obtaining the SPECTRUM of complex signals in real time.

FHA Federal Housing Administration, Washington, DC.

fiber US spelling for *fibre.*

Fibonacci series An infinite series, credited to the twelfth-century Italian mathematician Leonardo Fibonacci of Pisa, in which successive pairs of numbers are added together to form the next number. The intervals increase rapidly. Thus the simplest Fibonacci series is 1, 1, 2, 3, 5, 8, 13, 21, 34...

fibre cement Building board made using cement reinforced with fibres, usually of cellulose obtained from wood. *Also called fibre-reinforced cement* or *FRC.* When glass fibres are used, it is called glass-reinforced cement or GRC. *See also* ASBESTOS CEMENT SHEET.

fibre optics *See* OPTICAL FIBRE.

fibre stress A term used to denote the longitudinal direct (tensile or compressive) stress in a beam. The *extreme fibre stress* is the stress in the fibre most remote from the NEUTRAL AXIS, and it is thus the maximum tensile or compressive stress. *See* NAVIER'S THEOREM.

fibreboard Building board made from felted wood or other fibres, and a suitable binder. It is a generic term which includes ACOUSTIC BOARD, FLAXBOARD, HARDBOARD, INORGANIC FIBRE BOARD, INSULATING BOARD, MEDIUM-DENSITY FIBREBOARD, PARTICLE BOARD, PEGBOARD and SOFTBOARD. Some of these terms overlap.

fibreglass Strictly, the fibre made from glass. However, the term also denotes

glassfibre-reinforced plastic (commonly *polyester*), abbreviated FRP or GRP. The fibres are finely distributed in the plastic as reinforcement, either as a woven fabric or as a random mat. *See also* OPTICAL FIBRE.

fibro *(a)* Formerly, Australian term for ASBESTOS CEMENT SHEET. *(b)* Hence, low cost house built with a timber frame and an external lining of FIBRE CEMENT sheet, usually with an internal plasterboard or particle board lining.

fibrous concrete Concrete containing fibres of glass, rockwool or steel to improve its tensile strength.

fibrous plaster Gypsum plaster reinforced with *sisal* fibres or with canvas. In Australia, large sheets capable of supporting their own weight were at one time made from fibrous plaster by specialist craftsmen, called *fibrous plasterers.*

FIBTP *Fédération Internationale du Bâtiment et des Travaux Publics*, Paris.

FIC *Abbreviation for* Foundation Industry Classes.

Fick's law of mass diffusion 'The mass flux across a fluid layer is directly proportional to the local concentration gradient.' If one fluid is unevenly distributed as a mixture within another fluid (in the absence of other effects), some of it will gradually diffuse toward the more dilute areas, until it eventually becomes evenly distributed.

FID *Fédération Internationale de Documentation*, The Hague. Now *Fédération Internationale d'Information et de Documentation.*

fidelity A concept used in acoustic systems, particularly for sound reinforcement, transmission, recording and reproduction systems. It is a composite index based on dynamic range (in dB) and frequency range (in Hz). Ordinary AM radio transmission would be around 18, the best sound systems today around 70, whilst the range of a large symphonic orchestra in live performance may be approaching 100. Anything above about 40 would be referred to as *high fidelity* or hi-fi.

field (in data management) A constituent part of a data RECORD, which is in turn a component of a data FILE. Each field holds some specific data about the entity whose information is stored in the RECORD.

field moisture equivalent The minimum moisture content at which a drop of water placed on a smoothed soil surface is not immediately absorbed, thus giving the soil a shiny appearance.

field sound transmission class The SOUND TRANSMISSION CLASS of a wall or partition measured in situ rather than in a laboratory. Field sound transmission class values are usually lower than laboratory measured values because of FLANKING TRANSMISSION.

field welding, field bolting, field riveting *Same as* SITE WELDING, etc.

fieldstone Irregularly shaped pieces of rock that can be used to cover the surface of a building or pathway.

fifth-generation computing A project to produce computers and programs using ARTIFICIAL INTELLIGENCE and *parallel processing*.

figure The natural grain of timber, particularly when it is cut as a veneer. Highly-figured timber, although it makes attractive veneer, is often structurally weak. *See also* BURL *and* CROTCHWOOD.

figure 8 microphone A MICROPHONE where the polar response is a maximum in two opposite directions and the response is zero on an axis perpendicular to that of the maximum response.

filament Electrical conducting material in the form of a fine wire.

filament lamp An electric lamp in which a filament in a glass bulb, filled with an inert gas, is raised to incandescence by the passage through it of an electric current.

file In computing, an organised collection of data, such as a computer program or a piece of text, stored in a computer's memory.

file extension A label added to the end of a file name, after a period, to denote the type of file, *e.g.* '.doc', '.jpg'.

file manager A program which controls operations on files such as creating, deleting and copying of files.

file server A computer attached to a network which provides high-capacity mass storage space for files and programs. Software for instance may be downloaded from a file SERVER for execution. This scheme saves disk storage space on the user's local system and also provides a central location for software updates.

fill Material of varying sizes and degrees of preparation used to raise levels or fill voids.

filler metal *See* BASE METAL.

fillet weld A weld of approximately triangular cross-section joining two surfaces approximately at right angles to one another. The strength of the fillet weld depends on its THROAT.

film *(a)* A thin, not necessarily visible, layer of material. *(b)* A photo-sensitive emulsion, before or after processing, on a flexible base.

film conductance Outside (f_o) or inside (f_i), same as SURFACE CONDUCTANCE.

filter *(a)* A device to separate particles from air or from liquids. *See also* HEPA FILTER. *(b)* A device to remove odours from the air. *(c)* A device which transmits energy at some frequencies differently to others. *See also* BANDPASS FILTER.

final certificate A certificate issued to the contractor when all the obligations under the contract have been fulfilled.

final set (of cement mortar) Measured by the VICAT TEST.

fine aggregate The smaller size of aggregate used for mixing concrete, as opposed to COARSE AGGREGATE. It usually consists of SAND, but small-size crushed stone is sometimes used.

fine grained soil Soil consisting predominantly of fine sand, silt or clay.

fine stuff The LIME PUTTY used in the finishing coat of a plastering operation. *See also* COARSE STUFF.

fineness modulus A measure of the fineness of sand, cement or paint. It is obtained by adding the total percentage of a granular sample retained on each of a specified series of sieves, and dividing the sum by 100.

fines Naturally occurring or crushed rock particles, ranging in size from dust to sand.

finger joint An END JOINT made up of several meshing tongues or fingers of wood, made with a fingerjointing machine and normally glued (*see figure*).

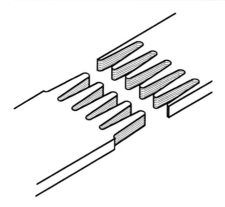

Finger joint

finial *(a)* A decorative ornament, especially at the peak of an arching structure or the APEX of a tiled roof. *(b) See* AIR TERMINATION.

finishing coat Final coat of render or plaster ready for decoration.

finite difference method A numerical method to used to solve a variety of fluid flow problems. A flow field is dissected into a set of grid points and the continuous functions (velocity, pressure, etc.) are approximated by discrete values of these functions calculated at the grid points, and the differential equations are thereby solved by appropriate numerical techniques. The principle is comparable to FINITE ELEMENT ANALYSIS.

finite element analysis (FEA) A method of analysis (usually for structural problems) based on modelling continuous elements as a large series of interconnected elements of various shapes.

finite element modelling (FEM) *See* FINITE ELEMENT ANALYSIS.

fink truss A commonly used roof truss, suitable for spans of 12 to 15 m (40 to 50 ft). It has two trussed rafters, each divided into four parts *(see figure). Also called* a *Belgian* or *French truss.*

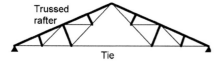

Fink truss

finned coil A bundle of tubes for the exchange of heat between fluids. The tubes have metal fins to extend the heat transfer surface.

fire action plan A plan of procedures to be followed when there is a building fire, a part of the *fire safety plan* in fire safety management.

fire and life safety management A plan for the protection and safety of building occupants in the event of life-threatening emergencies, such as fire and bomb threats.

fire barrier Any element of a building, such as a wall, floor or ceiling, so constructed as to delay the passage of fire from one part of a building to another.

fire brick A brick that will resist high temperatures in furnaces, chimneys and fireplaces; a REFRACTORY BRICK.

fire compartment A part of a building bounded by FIRE-RESISTING walls and fire-resisting doors that close automatically in case of a fire.

fire control Limiting the size of a fire by the use of water or other extinguishant, in order to decrease the rate of heat production, pre-wet adjacent combustible materials, and limit the resulting gas temperatures to avoid structural damage. *See also* FIRE EXTINGUISHMENT.

fire control room A room containing systems controlling a facility's fire services. In an emergency it must be accessible directly by the emergency services.

fire curtain A fire-resisting curtain capable of being lowered into the proscenium opening of a theatre to protect the audience from the effects of a fire in the stage area. Originally made of ASBESTOS fabric, it is now made of other fire-resisting fibres.

fire damper A DAMPER held open by a fusible link that melts at a predetermined temperature.

fire detector An automatic device which detects a fire by the *rise of temperature* in a BIMETALLIC STRIP, or by an element melting at a low temperature, or by solid state electronics; or by the *rate of rise of temperature* in an expanding sealed chamber; or which detects the flickering of a *flame. See also* SMOKE DETECTOR.

fire door A SELF-CLOSING DOOR made of fire-resisting material. It delays or prevents the spread of fire and smoke by confining it to one compartment.

fire endurance The time taken to cause the failure of a structure in a fire.

fire engineering A traditional term dealing with active fire protection systems and fire fighting, different from the modern terms of FIRE SAFETY ENGINEERING and FIRE PROTECTION ENGINEERING.

fire extinguishment The complete suppression of a fire until there is no burning material, and no parts hot enough to re-ignite a fire.

fire field model Application of COMPUTATIONAL FLUID DYNAMICS to study fire-induced convective flow.

fire hydrant A connection to a water main for extinguishing a fire.

fire indicator panel A control panel which indicates a signal from an alarm, and the zone where the signal was activated.

fire isolation See ISOLATION *(b)*.

fire load The amount of heat generated if the contents and combustible parts of a building were to be *completely* burnt. It is calculated in J/m^2 (Btu/ft^2) of floor area, assuming the burning material to be spread uniformly over the floor. The fire load depends on the type of occupancy.

fire prevention plan A plan of procedures to prevent an accidental fire occurring, part of the fire safety plan in fire safety management.

fire protection engineering The application of science and engineering principles to protect people and their environment from destructive fire. It includes: analysis of fire hazards; mitigation of fire damage by proper design, construction, arrangement, and use of buildings, materials, structures, industrial processes and transportation systems; the design, installation and maintenance of fire detection and suppression and communication systems; and post-fire investigation and analysis.

fire protection of steel structures Although steel does not support combustion, it is more vulnerable to fire than a heavy timber section (which burns, but is protected by the charcoal formed). At about 400 °C (750 °F) it suffers significant

loss of strength; at 540 °C (1000 °F) only 50 per cent, and at 650°C (1200 °F) only 20 per cent of its cold strength remains. The most common protection is a layer of reinforced concrete, SPRAYED MINERAL WOOL or sprayed VERMICULITE.

fire resistance grading (or level, or rating) The grading of building components according to the minutes or hours of resistance in a *standard fire test*. The higher the FIRE LOAD, the higher the fire-resistance grading required.

fire safety engineering A new branch of engineering to provide fire safety in buildings, a key part in engineering performance-based fire codes.

fire safety manager The person who is charged with the duties and responsibilities of providing and maintaining fire safety for a facility or institution.

fire separation A construction assembly that acts as a barrier against the spread of fire.

fire sprinkler system See SPRINKLER SYSTEM.

fire stop A fire-resisting barrier at an opening, *e.g.* around a pipe penetration of a FIRE-RESISTING floor or wall.

fire suppression The reduction of the size and heat output of a fire, and preventing it from re-establishing, by applying water or other extinguishants to the burning surfaces. Suppression may be achieved before there is enough access for FIRE EXTINGUISHMENT.

fire test A standard test used to determine the FIRE RESISTANCE GRADING of a structural element.

fire wall *(a)* A fire-resistant wall constructed to subdivide a building into smaller units. *(b)* A wall on the outside of a building to resist the spread of fire to other buildings. *(c)* (in computing, *spelled firewall*) Security software that examines all transmissions between a computer and the Internet, intended to prevent unauthorised access.

fire warden A person, normally present during working hours, trained and assigned to perform certain duties in the event of a fire emergency.

fire zone model A mathematical model for simulating fire based on physical observation. There are one-zone model, two-layers zone model, and multi-layers zone model.

fire-resisting Attribute of a material which resists fire for some length of time. The term has replaced *fireproof*, since no material is completely proof against the effect of fire. *See also* SLOW-BURNING CONSTRUCTION.

fire-retardant Chemical treatment used to reduce flammability or to retard spread of a fire.

fire-retardant coating A coating that will reduce flame spread, resist ignition when exposed to high temperature and insulate the substrate.

fire-retardant paint A paint based on silicone, casein, borax, polyvinyl chloride, urea formaldehyde or some other substance. A thin coating reduces the rate of flame spread of a combustible material, usually by intumescence under the effect of heat.

firedamp *Same as* METHANE.

fireman's switch A key switch, which when operated brings the designated FIREMEN'S LIFT car(s) under the control of the fire fighting service. *See also* LIFT RECALL.

firemen's lift *See* LIFT TYPES *(e).*

fireproof Now replaced by FIRE-RESISTING, as no construction is completely fireproof.

firing Controlled heat treatment in a kiln, particularly of bricks and other ceramics.

first floor In the USA, the floor at ground level. In Europe and Australia, the first floor above ground level.

first moment of area *Same as* MOMENT OF AN AREA.

first-angle projection *See* ORTHOGRAPHIC PROJECTION.

fishplates Plates on each side, making a connection between the two pieces of a BUTT JOINT. They are *fixed* with nails or with *fish-bolts.*

fishtail burner *Same as* BATSWING BURNER.

fitout The stage of the building process after the structure and enclosure are completed, and finishing trades such as the installation of trim and fittings, and painting and carpet-laying, are being carried out.

five-axis milling An extension of CNC (computer control of machine-shop equipment) to allow automatic milling of certain complicated and undercut forms.

fixed glazing Glazing held in a frame or SASH that does not open.

fixed price contract A contract in which the work will be carried out for a fixed lump sum without rise and fall cost adjustments, usually used for minor and short-duration projects.

fixed-ended beam A BUILT-IN BEAM, or *encastré* beam.

fixture *(a)* A LUMINAIRE, especially in the USA. *(b) See* PLUMBING FIXTURE.

fixture unit A unit of measure based on the rate of discharge, time of operation and frequency of use of a plumbing fixture. It expresses the hydraulic load imposed by that fixture on the plumbing installation.

flaking Separation of a paint layer from the layer beneath due to loss of adhesion.

flame cutting Cutting with an oxyacetylene torch. The flame first heats the steel to a high temperature, then additional oxygen is introduced to oxidise the metal in the line of the flame.

flame spread The rate at which a flame spreads under intense radiant heat. The flame spread on wall and ceiling linings is classified by a standard test.

flame-retardant paint *Same as* FIRE-RETARDANT PAINT.

flammable A material that burns with a flame.

flange *(a)* The top or bottom member of a rolled steel beam, or of a plate girder. *(b)* A projecting flat rim. *(c)* A disc-shaped rim at the end of a tube.

flanging Modulation of the frequency and duration of a sound.

flanking transmission The transmission of sound from one space to another by paths other than the common wall or floor between them.

flash An intentional or unintentional random vitrification or fusion on the surface of a brick, producing colour variation.

flash point The lowest temperature at which a substance ignites when a flame is put to it.

flash set The rapid development of rigidity in freshly mixed cement paste, mortar or concrete, usually with considerable evolution of heat. Plasticity cannot be regained by further mixing without the addition of water. *See also* SETTING OF CONCRETE *and* FALSE SET.

flash welding A resistance welding process. After the electric supply has been turned on, the two parts are brought together. This produces arcing which expels small particles of metal (flashing), and thus protects the metal from oxidation.

flashing Sheet metal or other sheet material used to cover open joints in exterior construction, such as joints in parapets or roof valleys, and above and below window openings, to prevent ingress of water. Flashing depends mainly on gravity to shed water. When there are high windspeeds causing large differences in air pressure, flashing alone may not be sufficient to guarantee waterproofness.

flashover (electrical) Flashing due to unwanted high current flowing between two points of different potential. Usually due to insulation breakdown resulting from arcing.

flashover (fire) During a fire, hot gases are formed that rise to the ceiling. When these have accumulated in sufficient quantities and ignite, a flashover occurs, after which a fire cannot be extinguished with simple equipment.

flat *(a)* A painted surface without sheen. *(b)* British and Australian term for a rented APARTMENT. The building is known as a *block of flats*. *(c)* A steel bar of a rectangular cross-section.

flat arch An arch with a level *extrados* and *soffit* made from wedge-shaped stones or bricks; *Also called* a JACK ARCH. It has been superseded by steel and reinforced concrete lintels (*see figure*).

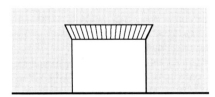

Flat arch

flat bed plotter A pen plotter in which the paper is held on a flat surface, while the pen moves along both axes.

flat jack A hydraulic jack consisting of light gauge metal, bent and welded to a flat shape, which expands under internal pressure. It is particularly useful for pre-stressing concrete in confined locations, *e.g.* the springings or the crown of an arch.

flat plate A concrete slab reinforced in two directions, and supported directly on the columns without column capitals or beams (*see figure*). By contrast, a FLAT SLAB has column capitals.

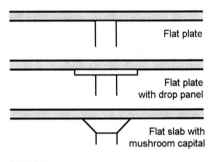

Flat plate

Flat plate with drop panel

Flat slab with mushroom capital

Flat plate

flat plate collector Solar energy collector suitable for temperatures up to about 85°C (185°F). It is particularly suitable for heating water for the hot water supply. It consists of a black flat plate, which may be given a SELECTIVE SURFACE coating to increase its efficiency, connected to tubes containing water; or the water may circulate between two plates.

flat roof A roof with a slope just sufficient to ensure drainage, usually less than 1:25 (approximately 2°), or (rarely) a roof without any slope at all.

flat slab A concrete slab reinforced in two or more directions, and supported directly on COLUMN CAPITALS without beams; *Also called mushroom slab* because of the shape of the enlarged capitals. In contrast, a FLAT PLATE has no column capitals. (*See figures at* COLUMN STRIP *and* FLAT PLATE.)

flax A plant whose blue flowers are succeeded by seed pods from which *linseed oil* is made. *Linen* is made from flax fibres. *See also* MINERAL FLAX.

flaxboard FIBREBOARD manufactured from flax.

Flemish bond A brick BOND which consists of alternate HEADERS and STRETCHERS in each course (*see figure*). *See also*

DIAGONAL, DOUBLE *and* SINGLE FLEMISH BOND.

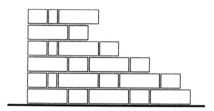

Flemish bond

Fletton A common English brick made from Peterborough shale.

flexibility method *Same as* MATRIX-FORCE METHOD.

flexural rigidity Measure of the stiffness of a member in resisting bending. It is usually taken as the product *EI*, where *E* is the MODULUS OF ELASTICITY, and *I* is the SECOND MOMENT OF AREA.

flexure *Same as* BENDING.

flicker *(a)* In lighting, the visible fluctuation in the light emitted from lamps when operated on alternating current supplies. *(b)* In photometry, an obsolete method for determining luminance matches, flicker photometry. *(c)* Generally, any fluctuation of brightness from any cause that produces a visual sensation.

flight A series of stairs unbroken by a landing.

flint Concretions of SILICA found in some limestone and dolomite beds. They are believed to be organic in origin, deriving from siliceous sponges. Flints were used extensively in stone-age tools. In certain parts of Europe, particularly in Southern England, split flints (called *knapped flints*) were used in a characteristic vernacular architecture. *See also* CHERT *and* OBSIDIAN.

flint glass GLASS containing lead, as opposed to CROWN GLASS. It was traditionally used for cut glass, because it was easier to engrave, and for this reason the best source of silica, *i.e.* FLINT, was used. The name is today often used for any high-quality glass, of whatever chemical composition. The difference in the chemical composition of crown and flint glass gives them different refractive indices, and the two materials have been used in

conjunction to produce ACHROMATIC LENSes.

flitch A large piece of converted timber, suitable for re-sawing into smaller sizes.

flitched beam A steel plate sandwiched between two pieces of timber, and connected to them with bolts.

float The difference between earliest *(EFT)* and latest *(LFT)* finish times of an activity in a NETWORK. The *free float* is the amount of time by which the start of an activity may be delayed without interfering with the start of any subsequent activity.

float coat In multi-coat plastering, the final mortar coat over which the skim coat of HARD PLASTER is applied.

float finish A rather rough concrete finish, obtained by finishing with a wooden float.

float glass Sheets of glass made by floating the molten glass on a surface of molten metal, which produces a smooth, polished surface.

float valve *See* BALL COCK.

floating floor Separation of the floor-wearing surface from the rest of the building to provide locally DISCONTINUOUS CONSTRUCTION for insulation against impact sound. A concrete floor may be insulated from the supporting structure by an insulating layer, such as mineral wool, and a wooden floor may be similarly insulated by resilient packing (*see figure*).

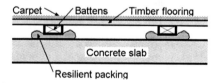

Floating floor

floating-point number In computing, a representation for a REAL NUMBER consisting of a mantissa, an exponent and base, *e.g.* 2.15E3 (= 2150).

flocculation Clumping together of minute particles by means of coagulant chemicals to promote their sedimentation, *e.g.* in purifying water or sewage.

flooded suction The location of a pump so that the inlet is below the level of the liquid being pumped. Therefore the pump does not need PRIMING. A SUBMERSIBLE PUMP is in this category.

floor cavity ratio A ratio used to represent the size of the space below the WORKING PLANE, used in the lumen or flux method of illuminance calculation.

floorspace ratio The ratio of the total floor area of a building to the site area on which the building is located. *Same as* PLOT RATIO.

floppy disk A small magnetic disk used for the external storage of computer data, as against the HARD DISK of a computer. Originally made of flexible material, hence the name.

FLOPS FLoating-point OPerations per Second.

flow meter An instrument for measuring the quantity of a fluid, such as water or gas, which flows through a pipe in a unit of time. A common type is based on the VENTURI TUBE.

flow rate, pedestrian *See* PEDESTRIAN FLOW RATE.

flowchart, flow diagram A diagram that employs both writing and standardised graphical symbols to indicate the flow of an operation required to solve a particular problem. It is useful for planning any complicated operations, but is mainly used in writing computer programs.

flue A chimney used to take combustion products from a burner.

flue gas The waste gaseous products of the combustion of fossil fuels.

fluid A substance which flows, *i.e.* a liquid, a gas or a vapour.

fluid dynamics The science of dynamic effects giving rise to the motion of fluids.

fluidity The ability of a material to flow readily; the opposite of *viscosity.*

Fluon Trade name for POLYTETRAFLUOROETHYLENE.

fluorescence A process by which radiant flux of certain wavelengths is absorbed and reradiated non-thermally in other, usually longer, wavelengths.

fluorescent lamp An electric DISCHARGE LAMP, consisting of a tube coated inside with a fluorescent powder (*see figure*). A current passing through a low pressure mercury vapour emits ultraviolet radiation. The fluorescent coating on the tube changes the invisible radiation into visible

light. Fluorescent lamps have a higher LUMINOUS EFFICACY than INCANDESCENT LAMPS.

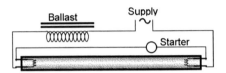

Fluorescent lamp

fluorescent paint A pigment which converts invisible to visible radiation, and therefore appears brighter than surrounding surfaces. Certain organic dyes, tungstates, borates and silicates have this property; but the brilliance of some of them dulls after a period of time due to weathering. Unlike PHOTOLUMINESCENT PAINT, it does not exhibit an afterglow.

fluorinated hydrocarbons *See* CFC.

flush joint A flat JOINT IN BRICKWORK or masonry.

flush switch A switch which has been recessed so that its front is flush with the wall.

flush valve A valve which, when opened, allows a set quantity of water to pass through to flush a water closet. In some countries the water may be supplied directly from the building's water supply system; but in others it must be fed from a separate supply tank, either because of a perceived danger of contamination of the water supply, or to avoid the sudden, heavy demand for water which could reduce the pressure available to other outlets.

flushing (of pipe systems) Circulation and discharge of fluid through a new pipe system to remove debris left by the processes of fabrication and installation.

fluting A vertical series of curved channels used to decorate columns and pilasters in Classical architecture.

flutter *(a)* Undesirable forms of frequency modulation due to irregular motion of the recording or reproduction sound system. *See also* WOW. *(b)* Rapid vibration of small amplitude.

flutter echo A rapid repetitive succession of sounds from an impulsive source (*e.g.* hand clap) usually as a result of reflections from large flat reflective parallel surfaces.

flux *(a)* The lines of force of a magnetic field. *(b)* The time rate of flow, *e.g.* volume per hour is the flux of a fluid. *(c)* See LUMINOUS FLUX. *(d)* See SOLDERING.

flux fraction ratio (FFR) The ratio of upward light flux fraction of a luminaire to the downward light flux fraction. The FFR is numerically equal to the ratio (ULOR/DLOR).

fly ash The finely divided residue resulting from the combustion of ground or powdered coal, which is transported from the fire box through the boiler by flue gases. It has POZZOLANIC properties, and is sometimes blended with cement for this reason.

fly-ash concrete Concrete containing FLY ASH.

flying buttress A BUTTRESS suspended in the air to resist the thrust of a roof structure.

flying shore A horizontal SHORE.

fly-jib An auxiliary jib which may be fitted to the end of the BOOM or JIB of a crane.

FM *Abbreviation for* Frequency Modulation.

f-number A measure of the light-gathering power, or speed, of a lens by reference to its focal length. The exposure time is proportional to the square of the f-number.

foamed concrete CELLULAR CONCRETE made with a FOAMING AGENT, such as detergent.

foamed plastic *Same as* EXPANDED PLASTIC.

foaming agent A substance which creates a foamy structure to reduce the weight of a material, such as concrete, gypsum, various plastics and rubber. The bubbles may be formed physically, as in detergent, or chemically by generating a gas.

focusing collector *See* CONCENTRATING COLLECTOR.

fog room *Same as* MOIST ROOM.

foil *(a)* Thin metal SHEET, generally less than 0.1 mm (0.005 in.) thick. *(b)* A rounded ornament, once widely used as a decoration. It is a stylised leaf, commonly divided into three (*trefoil*), four (*quatrefoil*) or five (*cinquefoil*) divisions.

foil strain gauge ELECTRIC RESISTANCE STRAIN GAUGE made from thin foil printed on a thin lacquer film.

FOK *Abbreviation for* Free Of Knots.

folded-plate roof A roof structure formed by flat plates, usually of reinforced concrete, joined at various angles (*see figure*). It has many of the properties of SHELL CONSTRUCTION, but since the component parts are not curved, they do not act in accordance with the MEMBRANE THEORY, and the structure is subject to substantial bending moments. Folded plates can be designed to perform the same function as DOMES *(a)*, BARREL VAULTS *(b)*, and NORTHLIGHT SHELLS *(c)*.

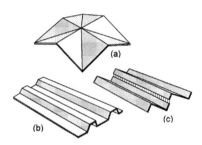

Folded plate roof

folder *Also called* DIRECTORY. A level of organisation in a HIERARCHICAL FILE STRUCTURE. Folders/directories can be nested to create complex file organisational schemes. In GRAPHICAL USER INTERFACEs, folders are usually represented on the computer desktop by ICONS in the shape of ordinary office file folders.

font In printing, a typeface or style of letters. The broad categories are fonts with or without serifs, and those with proportionate or fixed (typewriter) spacing. With the latter, the I would occupy the same width as the M.

food waste disposal unit Appliance mounted between the outlet of a sink and the waste pipe, fitted with grinding blades driven by an electric motor. Food and other soft waste can be washed into the disposer, ground to a slurry, and washed into the sewer.

foot (ft) A traditional measure of length based on the human foot. Its length varied from country to country, and in medieval times from city to city. The British/US foot equals 0.3048 m. The Roman foot was 0.2956 m.

foot, super *See* SUPER FOOT.

foot-lambert An obsolete British unit for LUMINANCE, equivalent to the APOSTILB. $1 FL = 1/\pi \text{ cd/ft}^2 = 0.318 \text{ cd/ft}^2$.

foot-pound The FPS UNIT of ENERGY or work. The SI equivalent is the JOULE. (The unit of bending moment or twisting moment is generally called *pound-foot*. Although dimensionally the same, the two units represent different physical concepts.)

footcandle An obsolete British unit for ILLUMINANCE equal to 1 lm/ft^2. 1 foot-candle = 10.76 lux.

footing The base under a wall or column, immediately in contact with the ground. The ground which supports the footing is the FOUNDATION.

footprint The projected area of a building or equipment on a horizontal surface.

force Defined as anything which changes or tends to change the state of rest of a body, or its motion in a straight line. The forces most commonly acting on buildings are the weight of the materials from which they are built, the weight of the contents, and the forces due to snow, wind and earthquakes. STATICS is the branch of science which deals with forces in EQUILIBRIUM.

force transmissibility *See* TRANSMISSIBILITY.

forced circulation Circulation of fluid by pumping, as opposed to *gravity circulation.*

forced draught cooling tower A COOLING TOWER in which the air flow is forced upward through the falling stream of water by a fan or fans at the entry point, rather than flowing by natural means.

forced vibration The vibration imparted to a body by a periodic force. If its period is the same as that of the NATURAL FREQUENCY of vibration of the body, its effect is cumulative, and RESONANCE results.

forged A wrought metal product formed by hammering or pressing between dies (usually while hot).

form lining The lining of concrete FORMWORK can be utilised to impart a smooth

or patterned finish to the concrete surface; to absorb moisture in order to obtain a drier consistency at the surface; or to apply a set-retarding chemical which enables the aggregate to be exposed.

form tie A device which both holds vertical forms apart before concrete is poured and holds them together when fresh concrete is poured.

form, slip FORMWORK which can be moved upward progressively as the work proceeds, rather than being dismantled and re-erected.

formaldehyde A gas (H.CHO) of pungent odour, readily soluble in water. The *amino-plastics* phenol formaldehyde and urea formaldehyde are condensation products of formaldehyde with phenol or urea; they are THERMOSETTING. BAKELITE, one of the earliest synthetic resins, is phenol formaldehyde.

format *(a)* To prepare a DISK for use by an operating system. *Also called* INITIALISING. When the computer initialises a disk, it also destroys any information already there. *(b)* The way text is set up on a page (underlining, bold, indenting, etc.). *(c)* The way information is structured in a file, often specific to a particular application.

formwork The mould for freshly placed concrete (which gives it its shape), as well as the supporting structure and bracing required to support its weight. *Also called shuttering.*

forward transfer impedance The amount of impedance placed between the source and load with the installation of a power conditioner.

fossil fuel Flammable hydrocarbons such as coal or oil recovered from non-renewable underground source(s), formed from ancient plant or animal remains.

foul sewer Same as SOIL DRAIN.

foundation The portion of the ground on which the FOOTINGS of a building are supported. *Foundation* is sometimes used interchangeably with *footing.*

foundation pressure *See* BOUSSINECQ PRESSURE BULB, COULOMB'S EQUATION *and* EARTH PRESSURE.

foundation stone *(a)* A stone in the foundations of a building. *(b)* A stone on which information is recorded on the formal opening of the building. It may cap a small vault in which contemporary records are preserved for later generations.

Fourier analysis A method of analysing a steady continuous signal into its frequency components. *See* FOURIER SERIES.

Fourier equation A differential equation, which is the basis of all non-STEADY-STATE heat transfer calculations (*see also* FOURIER SERIES).

Fourier series The sum of an infinite number of SINE and COSINE waves of successively higher orders, which can be made to represent any periodic function with an accuracy depending on the number of terms used. It is named after the French physicist and Egyptologist who developed it in 1822 for his work on heat transfer. *Fourier analysis* and *fast Fourier transforms* are important for the frequency analysis of sounds.

four-in-one bucket Earthmoving bucket for a tractor, in which the front (cutting) part of the bucket can be rotated independently of the remainder. It can be used closed as a normal digging and loading bucket, with the front raised as a bulldozer blade, (in reverse) with the front partly open as a scraper, and by closing over a pile of spoil, as a clamshell bucket (*see figure*).

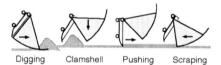

Digging   Clamshell   Pushing   Scraping

Four-in-one bucket

fourth-power law of radiation *See* STEFAN–BOLTZMANN LAW.

four-wire system *See* STAR CONNECTION.

fovea The small region (pit) in the retina of the eye, on the optical axis, containing CONES but no RODS, and capable of the clearest vision in good lighting conditions.

foyer An entrance hallway or lobby.

FPS Forest Products Society, Madison, WI.

FPS units The units of the traditional British system, based on foot, pound and second, as opposed to those used in the METRIC SYSTEM. They are used in the US CUSTOMARY UNITS.

fraction The ratio of two integers, *e.g.* ¼. A fraction is a RATIONAL NUMBER. Some fractions become *approximate numbers* when expressed in decimal form.

fracture Failure caused by breaking of the material into two parts. It causes a sudden failure of a structural member, as distinct from the gradual failure caused by PLASTIC DEFORMATION or CRUSHING FAILURE. *See also* BRITTLE FAILURE, CLEAVAGE FRACTURE *and* GRIFFITH CRACK.

frame (structural) An assembly of structural members. Most frames are *rectangular, i.e.* they consist of horizontal and vertical members only. Most frames are also *plane, i.e.* they can be designed as two-dimensional structures, connected by additional members at right angles. Frames which cannot be so designed are called SPACE FRAMES.

frame (video) A single still image, sequenced together in rapid succession to form a video presentation.

frame construction Any type of construction in which the building is supported mainly by a frame, and not mainly by load-bearing walls. BALLOON FRAMEd timber houses, BRICK VENEER houses, steel-framed buildings, and reinforced concrete framed buildings all belong to this type.

frame grabber A device which allows the capture, storage and display of a FRAME of information, *e.g.* a single frame of video.

framed tube structure *Same as* TUBE STRUCTURE.

frameless glass A system of single or multiple glass panes in which one or more edges are not supported by normal continuous framing. The panes may be supported on SPIDERS, or the edges may be stiffened by structural glass fins. The joints between panes can be sealed with clear SILICONE.

framing bracket or framing anchor A type of TIMBER CONNECTOR formed by folding a piece of galvanised steel sheet, with prepunched holes to enable nails to be driven in three mutually perpendicular directions. Used for making connections in three dimensions, *e.g.* joining a roof truss to the top of a wall.

frass Dust made by wood-boring insects, and one way of identifying them.

FRC *See* FIBRE CEMENT.

free address Non-assigned workspace available for use by employees on a first come, first served basis, usually located in OPEN PLAN offices.

free cooling The use of outdoor air without mechanical cooling to remove heat from a building space or spaces when its condition is suitable. *See* ECONOMISER CYCLE.

free field A sound field where the effects of the boundaries are negligible.

free float *See* FLOAT.

free surface (in fluid mechanics) A surface separating a GAS from a LIQUID.

free-body diagram A diagram obtained by making an imaginary cut through a structure, and considering the STATIC equilibrium of one or both parts separately as, for example, in the METHOD OF SECTIONS. Since the conditions of equilibrium must be satisfied by every stationary structure, the diagram can be drawn even for highly complex, statically indeterminate structures. It is sometimes possible to obtain a simple answer for the critical forces by this approach, without having to analyse the entire structure.

free-field room *Same as* ANECHOIC CHAMBER.

freedom *See* DEGREES OF FREEDOM.

freestone A building stone which can be freely carved in any direction. Most LIMESTONES and the finer-grained SANDSTONES are in this category.

freeware SOFTWARE that is provided without charge, as opposed to SHAREWARE and commercial software.

freezer Cabinet or room maintained for the storage of frozen food at a temperature of about −12 °C (+10 °F).

freight elevator US term for *goods lift*.

French chalk Finely ground TALC.

French door *See* FRENCH WINDOW.

French polish SHELLAC dissolved in methylated spirits.

French roof *Same as* MANSARD ROOF.

French tile Flat roof tiles moulded with drainage channels and side interlock. The MARSEILLES PATTERN TILE has, in

addition, interlocks with the tiles above and below.

French truss *Same as* FINK TRUSS.

French window or door A long window reaching to floor level, and opening in two leaves like a pair of doors.

Freon The trade name for CFC refrigerants.

frequency The number of cycles of a periodic phenomenon which occur in a given time interval. Frequency is measured in HERTZ (cycles per second). The product of frequency and *wavelength* equals the wave velocity. Thus the wavelength of any kind of electromagnetic RADIATION, multiplied by its frequency, equals the SPEED OF LIGHT. Similarly, the wavelength of sound, or of any other vibration in air, multiplied by its frequency, equals the SPEED OF SOUND.

frequency analyser An instrument for measuring the FREQUENCY BAND, SOUND PRESSURE LEVELS or determining the SPECTRUM of a sound. Frequency analysers have traditionally used either proportional bandwidth filters (*e.g.* OCTAVE-BAND) or constant bandwidth filters but with the advent of fast Fourier transform (FFT) methods, many frequency analysers are now capable of both.

frequency band A limited continuous range of frequencies. *See also* OCTAVE-BAND.

frequency deviation A variation from nominal frequency of an AC power supply system.

frequency distribution curve A curve relating the magnitude of a test result (or an observed variable characteristic) to its frequency (or the number of times it occurs). If the phenomenon varies only

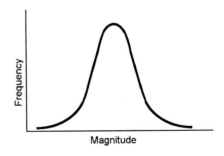

Frequency distribution curve

within a narrow range (as, for example, the test results for carefully controlled concrete), the curve is narrow and steep. As quality control declines, the curve becomes wider (*see figure*). A normal frequency distribution produces a GAUSSIAN CURVE.

frequency modulation (FM) A method of encoding a signal on a carrier wave (for the purpose of recording or transmitting it) by varying the frequency of the carrier. *See also* AMPLITUDE MODULATION.

frequency, resonant *See* RESONANCE.

fresco Painting on wet lime plaster with pigments mixed with water. The colours dry and set with the plaster. The range of pigments is restricted to a small range which is sufficiently alkali-resistant. The plasterer and the painter must work together since the plaster does not absorb colour after it has reached a certain degree of dryness. Later alterations are impossible. The technique is now rarely employed, but it was the medium of the greatest wall and ceiling paintings of the Renaissance. Hence the term 'fresco painting' is sometimes used, incorrectly, for painting on dry plastered walls and ceilings.

freshness The opposite of STUFFINESS. It is produced by air movement and cooler temperatures.

Fresnel lens A near-flat, convex lens, as if a plain/convex lens were cut into circular rings, the central rings cut thinner and put together again, to form circular grooves of various prismatic cross-sections. This can be cast or machined into glass or a transparent plastic sheet. Used in downlights, spotlights, signal lamps or overhead projectors. Linear Fresnel lenses are also possible.

Fresnel number A DIMENSIONLESS NUMBER (wavelength/distance) used in acoustics to define the degree of DIFFRACTION of a sound.

friction The resistance to motion that is brought into play when one body is moved over another. When the two surfaces are examined under a microscope, it is found that they touch only at a few points; hence the true area of contact is independent of the nominal area of contact. The contact area is, however, increased by the contact pressure. Frictional resistance is therefore proportional to the pressure between the bodies, and independent of the overall surface area of the bodies in contact. *See also* ANGLE OF FRICTION *and* COEFFICIENT OF FRICTION.

friction loss (in post-tensioning) The loss of stress resulting in curved TENDONS due to friction with the concrete or duct lining. Some friction loss occurs also in nominally straight cables due to the unavoidable imperfections of construction, which causes slight bends where the tendons touch the ducts.

friction pile A BEARING PILE whose load is carried by friction between the pile and the surrounding soil.

friction stay Window hardware used in lieu of hinges; a sliding friction mechanism; if used for push-out type (AWNING) sashes, it will form also a narrow opening at the top edge and will hold the sash in an open or semi-open position, which is said to improve natural ventilation.

friction, internal *See* ANGLE OF INTERNAL FRICTION.

friction-grip bolt A HIGH-TENSILE BOLT tightened to a carefully controlled tension with a calibrated torsion wrench. This ensures on the one hand that the bolt is not damaged by overtensioning, and on the other hand it provides high frictional forces between the two pieces of steel to be connected. This form of jointing is more convenient than site *riveting* or *welding*, and more reliable than the use of BLACK BOLTS.

frieze *(a)* The ornamented, central part of an ENTABLATURE. *(b)* A sculptured or ornamented band in a building, on the upper part of the walls.

frigidarium The cool room in a Roman bath.

frit Finely ground friable particles for glazing bricks.

frog A depression on one or both of the larger faces of a brick or block. It provides a key for the mortar, and reduces the weight of the brick. The frog is not necessarily filled with mortar.

front end loader A tractor with a bucket mounted on the front; the tractor may be rubber tyred or crawler mounted.

frost heave Swelling of soil due to the expansion of the ground water when it turns into ice. It usually causes uplift, since the soil is restrained in other directions.

frozen-stress method *Same as* THREE-DIMENSIONAL PHOTOELASTICITY.

FRP *Abbreviation for* Fibre-Reinforced Plastic. *See* FIBREGLASS.

frustum of a cone or pyramid The portion left after cutting off the upper part by a plane parallel to the base.

ft *Abbreviation for* FOOT.

FTE *Abbreviation for* FULL-TIME EQUIVALENT.

FTP *Abbreviation for* File Transfer Protocol. This protocol is a standard set of rules that allows users on different computer platforms to send files to one another across a network connection.

fuel cell A device combining a fuel with oxygen in an electrochemical reaction in the presence of a catalyst, to generate electricity directly without combustion.

fuel-controlled fire An early stage of a fire; whether the fire can sustain or not depends on the availability of fuel and the temperature.

fulcrum The point of support, or pivot, of a lever.

full radiator A perfect, non-selective surface previously termed a *black body radiator*. The radiation produced by the surface, BLACK-BODY RADIATION, conforms to the STEFAN–BOLTZMANN LAW. *Also called* a *Planckian radiator*.

full-time equivalent (FTE) A measure of the equivalent total number of employees, based on the hours worked by a full-time employee.

fully fixed *Same as* BUILT-IN.

fume cupboard An enclosure connected to an exhaust ventilation system and used to enclose a workspace where a process will cause the production of hazardous or noxious gases or vapours.

function key A key on a keyboard which allows a specific operation to be carried out, as opposed to the normal character keys.

functional area An area in a building set aside for a designated specific use, *e.g.* a ward in a hospital.

fundamental frequency The lowest resonant frequency (also known as the first harmonic) of a vibrating system.

fungicidal paint A paint which discourages fungal growth, *e.g.* by the inclusion of a metallic salt. It is particularly used in the tropics.

fungus Cryptogamous plant without chlorophyll. DRY ROT and mould are caused by the growth of fungi.

funicular arch An arch which is purely in compression under a series of point loads. It is the reverse of a string carrying the same load system as a suspension cable (*see figure*). *Also called* a *linear arch*.

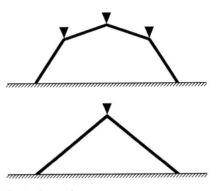

Funicular arch

funicular polygon *Same as* LINK POLYGON.

furnace A chamber used for the combustion of fuel for the production of useful heat.

furniture calorimeter A medium-scale burning test facility to measure the heat release rate of furniture by the oxygen consumption method.

furring Timber strips or metal channels fixed to joists, studs, walling or floors to provide support or a guide for an accurate finished surface.

fuse A safety device for preventing the overloading of a circuit (which might start a fire), and for protecting electrical apparatus from excess current. It consists of a short length of metal, which conducts a safe current, but melts when the current is above the specified value. *See also* CIRCUIT BREAKER.

fusible link A link that melts at a predetermined temperature, used for fire dampers, fire-resistant doors and sprinklers. *See also* FIRE DOOR *and* SMOKE VENTING.

fusion welding The WELDING of metals or plastics solely by melting the edges of the pieces to be joined, without mechanical pressure. Additional weld metal may be provided by a filler rod. *See* ARC WELDING.

fuzzy controller An element in an automatic control system arranged to apply FUZZY LOGIC to the state of a controlled variable.

fuzzy logic Control logic applied when there is a degree of uncertainty about input variables, *e.g.* comfort indices, and when there is more than one control parameter.

fuzzy logic algorithm An algorithm designed to apply FUZZY LOGIC to a task in a control system.

G

G Abbreviation for *giga*, one thousand million times (10^9).

g The symbol for the acceleration due to gravity, about $9.8 \, \text{m/s}^2$ at the Earth's surface.

gabbro An IGNEOUS rock formed by plutonic intrusions; due to their slow cooling, the crystals are relatively large. It is of basic composition, and dark in colour. In the industry classification of building stones, gabbro is called a GRANITE.

gable The triangular part of the end wall of a building with a sloping roof; it is frequently of a material different from the rest of the wall.

gable roof A sloping roof with gables. It has inclined slopes on two sides, and vertical gables on the other two (*see figure*). By contrast, a HIP ROOF has four inclined slopes.

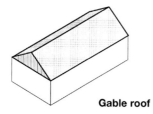

Gable roof

gable wall A wall of which a gable forms a part.

gable window A window built into a gable. The room behind usually has a sloping ceiling. *See also* DORMER WINDOW.

gage US spelling for GAUGE.

gain *(a)* The increase in the power of a signal as a result of processing, *e.g.* by an AMPLIFIER. *(b)* The inverse of the proportional band in an automatic control system.

gale A wind of force 8 on the BEAUFORT SCALE. Its speed is approximately 65 km/h (40 mph) 10 m (30 ft) above ground. A gale blowing steadily on a vertical face exerts a pressure of about 200 Pa (4 psf).

galleria A shopping ARCADE, named after the Milan Galleria.

gallery An elevated floor projecting from an interior wall.

gallon (gal) Liquid measure in FPS UNITS. The British gallon equals 4.546 litres and the US gallon equals 3.785 litres.

Galton whistle An instrument for producing ULTRASONIC vibrations of constant amplitude and frequency.

galvanic cell A cell containing two dissimilar metals and an ELECTROLYTE.

galvanic corrosion *Same as* ELECTRO-CHEMICAL CORROSION.

galvanic protection SACRIFICIAL PROTECTION given to a metal by making it the cathode to a sacrificial anode.

galvanic series The ELECTROCHEMICAL SERIES, named after the eighteenth-century Italian physicist Luigi Galvani who discovered the generation of electricity by chemical means.

galvanised iron Normally GALVANISED STEEL (not iron) sheet. *Also spelled galvanized.*

galvanised steel Steel sheet, often corrugated, which has been protected against corrosion by GALVANISING.

galvanising The coating of steel or iron with ZINC, either by immersion in a bath of zinc covered with flux at a temperature of about 450°C or by ELECTRODEPOSITION from cold sulphate solutions. The zinc is capable of protecting the iron from atmospheric corrosion even when the coating is scratched, since the zinc is preferentially attacked by carbonic acid, forming a protective coating of basic zinc carbonates. A less brittle and more durable coating is formed by combining ALUMINIUM with the zinc. The resulting alloy cannot be soldered as readily as pure zinc, but it has become popular since plastic sealants have been available to take the place of soldered joints. *See also* ZINCALUME *and* ZINC PLATING.

galvanometer Precision instrument for measuring *small* electric currents. A *galvanoscope* is an instrument capable of detecting, but not measuring, small currents. *See also* AMMETER.

gambrel roof A sloping roof similar to a HIP ROOF, but with the addition of small gables part-way up the end sloping portions (*see figure*).

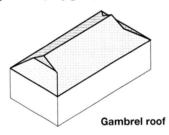

Gambrel roof

gamma iron Unalloyed iron in the temperature range from 910–1405 °C (1670–2560 °F). It has a FACE-CENTRED CUBIC space lattice. *See also* ALPHA IRON.

gamma rays Electromagnetic RADIATION produced by radioactive materials. It is similar to X-RAYS, which are produced both naturally and by high-voltage apparatus.

Gang-nail Trade name for a type of TIMBER CONNECTOR having preformed nails.

gantry crane A portal crane with four legs. Normally the whole crane runs on rails as a TRAVELLING GANTRY. It can pass over railway tracks, motor vehicles or even complete buildings under construction. This is the most expensive type of crane, used only for large building projects or permanent installations (*e.g.* in PRECAST CONCRETE factories). *See also* CLIMBING CRANE, CRANE, TOWER CRANE *and* DERRICK.

Gantt chart A BAR CHART which shows, for example, the duration of the various processes in a building operation by the length of a bar. It is named after Henry L. Gantt, who popularised its use in the early 1900s.

gap-graded aggregate Aggregate characterised by a particle-size distribution in which certain intermediate sizes are wholly or substantially absent. It is more common to use *continuous grading*. An extreme case of gap grading is NO-FINES CONCRETE.

garderobe *(a)* The French word for wardrobe, also sometimes used in English with that meaning. *(b)* A euphemism for an unsewered toilet, particularly in the era when both water closets and unsewered toilets co-existed.

gargoyle A water spout projecting from the gutter of a building, so that it throws the rainwater clear of the wall. It generally terminated in a grotesquely carved animal or human head with an open mouth, through which the water discharged. Neo-Gothic buildings of the nineteenth and twentieth century frequently used gargoyles for decorative purposes only, and avoided the discharge of the water on passers-by by connecting the gutters to downpipes.

garret A room in the ATTIC.

gas One of the states of matter, in which there is no shear strength, and therefore the material is formless. The volume, pressure and temperature are interdependent in accordance with CHARLES' LAW. (The other forms of matter are LIQUID and SOLID.)

gas booster A mechanical device used to increase the pressure of gaseous fuel from a mains supply to suit the requirements of a burner.

gas burner The tip of a gas lighting or heating fixture. See BATSWING BURNER and WELSBACH MANTLE.

gas concrete CELLULAR CONCRETE made with a gas-forming agent, such as aluminium powder.

gas cutting *Same as* FLAME CUTTING.

gas jet Same as GAS BURNER.

gas laws *See* BOYLE'S LAW *and* CHARLES' LAW.

gas mantle *See* WELSBACH MANTLE.

gas protection system Fire safety system based on discharging gas agents like nitrogen, carbon dioxide, HALON or its substitutes. There are TOTAL FLOODING SYSTEMS and local application systems.

gas welding Fusion welding with an oxy-ACETYLENE flame.

gas, coal Gas obtained from coal, originally for lighting, but later also used for heating and for operating gas engines. It has been largely replaced by NATURAL GAS.

gas, natural *See* NATURAL GAS.

gas-filled glazing DOUBLE GLAZING in which the two panes are sealed together in the factory, the gap between them being filled with a dry gas such as *nitrogen* or *argon*.

gas-filled panel Panel made with thin polymer films and low-conductivity gas to create a device with exceptional thermal insulation properties.

gaseous phase The state of a substance when its internal energy content is such that it can exist only as a GAS.

gasket A piece of material placed around a joint to make it leakproof. An *inflatable gasket* is used around windows in some curtain walls; it is deflated by the maintenance crew, and filled again with air after cleaning the window.

gasolier A CHANDELIER for GAS BURNERS.

gate valve A casting machined to receive a gate which closes the opening. The gate may be lifted and lowered by turning a screw. For high fluid pressures a GLOBE VALVE is used.

gauge *See* BOURDON GAUGE, DIAL GAUGE *and* ELECTRIC RESISTANCE STRAIN GAUGE. *Also spelled gage* (USA).

gauge length The length on a test piece or structural model over which a STRAIN measurement is made.

gauge pressure The pressure in a fluid as measured by a MANOMETER or BOURDON GAUGE. It is really the *difference* in pressure between the fluid and the surrounding atmosphere. For a fluid at standard atmospheric pressure, the gauge reads zero, whereas the *absolute* pressure is 1 ATMOSPHERE, or about 101.3 kPa.

gauged arch An arch built from gauged bricks, which are made with a taper to form a circular arch.

gauss The unit for measuring magnetic flux density, named after the nineteenth-century German scientist.

Gaussian curvature The product of the two principal curvatures at a point on a curved surface, *e.g.* a SHELL ROOF. The term is commonly used in differential geometry to classify surfaces (*see figure*). A *dome-type* surface has positive Gaussian curvature, because the curvature is the same way in two mutually perpendicular directions. A *saddle-type* surface has a negative Gaussian curvature, because the curvature is upwards in one direction and downwards at right-angles to that direction. A singly-curved surface has zero Gaussian curvature because the curvature in one direction is zero. A surface with zero Gaussian curvature is, by definition, DEVELOPABLE.

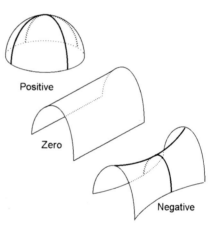

Positive

Zero

Negative

Gaussian curvature

Gaussian curve An exponential curve fitting the normal FREQUENCY DISTRIBUTION, named after the early nineteenth-century German physicist:

$$y = Ke^{-\frac{1}{2}t^2}$$

where $t = (x - \mu)/\sigma$ is the *standardised normal variate*, σ = STANDARD DEVIATION, μ = MEAN, x = magnitude of phenomenon, y = frequency of phenomenon, K = a constant and e = the base of the natural logarithm.

GAX *Abbreviation for* Generator Absorber heat eXchange.

Gay-Lussac's law *Same as* CHARLES' LAW.

gazebo A turret on top of a house, a bow window or a garden house commanding an extensive view.

gel The apparently solid material formed from a COLLOIDAL solution which is undisturbed. The major part of hydrated PORTLAND CEMENT is in gel form.

gel coat A smooth, hard and usually coloured layer of synthetic RESIN placed next to the mould before a FIBREGLASS reinforced plastic item is laid up. On completion, the item is removed from the mould and the gel coat is the surface exposed to view. The other side is rough and unsightly.

general conditions of contract Clauses included as part of a contract to establish the legal and contractual relationship between parties to the contract.

general-purpose computer A programmable computer capable of performing a large variety tasks under program control. (The normal office computer, as opposed to special-purpose computers installed in machinery and vehicles.)

generator *See* ALTERNATOR *and* DYNAMO.

gentrification The phenomenon of high-income earners moving into low-income housing because of its central location, and renovating or restoring it.

geodesic dome Originally a dome formed by structural members in the form of GEODETIC LINES intersecting to form spherical triangles. Later, any dome whose structure consisted of light linear elements. *See also* SCHWEDLER DOME.

geodesy The branch of surveying concerned with the mapping of extensive areas, in which allowance must be made for the curvature of the Earth's surface (which is neglected in *plane surveying*).

geodetic construction Originally construction of a STATICALLY INDETERMINATE *space frame*, particularly in aircraft design, whose members follow GEODETIC LINES, each compression being braced by an ORTHOGONAL tension member. The term now generally implies STRESSED-SKIN CONSTRUCTION, in which the skin of the aircraft or other structure forms a statically indeterminate space frame with the ribs, which prevent the skin from BUCKLING.

geodetic line The shortest possible line that can be drawn from one point of a curved surface to another. The geodetic lines of a sphere are called GREAT CIRCLES, because they are the circles with the greatest diameter which can be drawn on a sphere. They correspond to straight lines on a plane surface. The *equator* and all the *meridians of longitude* on the Earth's surface are great circles. The *parallels of latitude* (other than the equator) are SMALL CIRCLES, and travelling along them is not the shortest distance between two points. They correspond to curved lines on a plane surface (*see figure*).

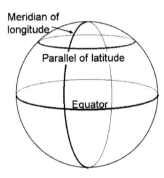

Geodetic line

geo-exchange energy Energy extracted by a heat exchange process from beneath the surface of the Earth, where the temperature is stable over time. Heat can be extracted from the earth when the air is cooler and can be rejected to earth when the air is warmer. *See also* GROUND COUPLED ENERGY SYSTEM.

geographical information system (GIS) A computer system for handling data related to positions on the Earth's surface. Used for handling maps, *e.g.* the manipulation of land features.

geography The science of the Earth's surface.

geological fault A fracture in a rock formation, accompanied by displacement of one part relative to another. The displacement, or *throw*, may be a few millimetres or several metres. Faults are a source of weakness in foundations, since they may cause movement of the entire building, or of one part relative to the other. Movement along major faults is a common cause of EARTHQUAKES.

geology The science that describes the

Earth's crust. A *geological map* is one which shows the outcrops of all *rocks* and sedimentary deposits, without the top soil. *See also* PETROGRAPHIC MICROSCOPE.

geometric mean The geometric mean of *n* values is the *n*th root of their product.

geometric primitive A building block of SOLID MODELLING, such as a cube, cone, sphere and cylinder.

geometrical stair A winding staircase formed by cantilevered stone treads built into the wall, which support one another by shell action.

geotechnical analysis The technical testing and reporting on the composition and condition of the soil and rock below the ground.

geotextile A textile material used to filter suspended solids from groundwater, to assist in drainage; or to provide reinforcement to stabilise ground.

geothermal energy Energy derived from the heat of the Earth's interior, generally by tapping reservoirs of steam in geothermal regions to drive steam turbines.

Gerber beam A continuous beam that is made statically determinate by the insertion of two hinges in alternate spans (*see figure*). It thus consists of cantilevered beams alternating with short spans simply supported from the ends of the cantilevers. Gerber beams are useful where continuous structures are assembled from heavy precast concrete elements, or where differential settlement of the foundations is a possibility, as in CANTILEVER BRIDGES.

Gerber beam

gesso A hard white surface, prepared to serve as a basis for painting or bas-relief. It usually consists of PLASTER OF PARIS, or WHITING and glue. *See* TEMPERA PAINTING.

GFCI (ground fault circuit interrupter) A life safety device commonly used in outdoor, bathroom and kitchen locations which limits ground fault current to 5 milliamp. *See also* RESIDUAL CURRENT DEVICE.

GFI (ground fault interrupter) A device whose function is to interrupt the electric circuit to the load when a fault current

to ground exceeds some predetermined value that is less than that required to operate the overcurrent protective device of the supply circuit.

GIF *Abbreviation for* Graphic Interchange Format. An image file format used primarily for data transmission of DIGITAL IMAGES. Introduced by CompuServe, GIF files are much more compact in size compared to conventional images. Besides using image DATA COMPRESSION methods to reduce their file size, GIF images also employ INDEXED COLOUR to reduce the amount of data stored.

giga Prefix denoting one billion (one thousand million, 10^9), e.g. *gigajoule*.

gigabyte Roughly, a quantity of measurement that is just over a billion bytes. Specifically, a gigabyte is 2^{30} bytes.

girder A deep BEAM. It is generally a PRIMARY BEAM which supports secondary beams, as opposed to a JOIST. A *steel girder* may be a single large steel section, a PLATE GIRDER or a lattice girder (such as a HOWE, PRATT or WARREN TRUSS).

GIS *Abbreviation for* GEOGRAPHICAL INFORMATION SYSTEM.

GKS *Abbreviation for* GRAPHICAL KERNEL SYSTEM.

gland A seal placed around a shaft where it passes through the wall of a vessel containing a fluid under pressure, such as the spindle of a tap. It allows the shaft to rotate or reciprocate, while maintaining the seal. Traditionally, a gland was packed with a mixture of fibrous material and grease, squeezed together by a mechanical sealing ring. In low to medium pressure applications, now largely replaced by O-RINGS.

glare A condition of vision in which there is discomfort, or a reduction in the ability to see significant objects, or both, due to an unsuitable distribution or range of luminance, or to extreme contrasts in space or time. *See* DISABILITY, DISCOMFORT *and* REFLECTED GLARE.

glare index (GI) In lighting, one of a number of systems for indicating the possibility of discomfort glare from lighting. The most common are the British Glare Index (BGI), the CIE Glare Index (CGI) and the CIE Unified Glare Index (UGI).

glass A hard and brittle amorphous substance, made by fusing silica (sometimes in combination with the oxides of boron or phosphorus) with certain basic oxides (notably those of sodium, potassium, calcium, magnesium and lead) and cooling the product rapidly to prevent crystallisation or devitrification. Most glasses melt between 800°C and 950°C. Heat-resisting glass generally contains a high proportion of boric oxide. Glasses occur naturally, due to the rapid cooling of molten rock, *e.g.* OBSIDIAN. *See also* BULLET-RESISTING, CROWN, CYLINDER, FLOAT, HEAT-ABSORBING, INSULATING, LAMINATED, OBSCURE, OPAL, PLATE, REFLECTIVE, ROLLED, SAFETY, SHEET, SOLAR CONTROL, TEMPERED *and* TRANSLUCENT GLASS.

glass brick A hollow block of glass, which is translucent but not transparent. It can be used in brick and block walls, or in GLASS–CONCRETE CONSTRUCTION.

glass fibre *See* FIBREGLASS.

glass paper An abrasive paper.

glass wool MINERAL WOOL made from molten glass.

glass, actinic Glass that screens out ACTINIC LIGHT, which is damaging to fabrics and some finishes.

glass, electrochromic *See* ELECTRO-CHROMIC GLASS.

glass, photochromic A glass whose transmittance varies with the incident light flux. Used in some spectacle lenses and experimentally in window glazing.

glass–concrete construction Reinforced concrete into which blocks of glass, capable of transmitting compressive stresses, have been cast. The glass may be in the form of hollow translucent blocks, which provide diffused white light, or it may be coloured, to provide a decorative pattern in the manner of stained glass. *See also* BÉTON TRANSLUCIDE.

glaze *(a)* To install glass panes in window or door frames. It normally implies the traditional method of using PUTTY to hold the glass in position. *(b)* To produce a shiny surface on photographic prints. *(c)* A brilliant glass-like surface given to tiles or bricks. It may be transparent or opaque, white or coloured. *See also* SALT GLAZE. *(d)* A nearly transparent thin coat of colour put on paint to enhance the original colour.

glazed tile A glazed *clay tile*, which facilitates cleaning.

glazing bar *Same as* SASH BAR.

glazing bead A strip which presses the glass against the glazing bar. The glass is bedded and sealed either in window PUTTY or an elastomeric strip such as NEOPRENE. It is an alternative to the use of window putty alone to secure the glass.

global irradiance (or irradiation) All the radiation that is received from a full hemisphere, the sum of beam, diffuse and reflected components.

global warming *See* GREENHOUSE GASES *and* GWP.

globe temperature Measured by a GLOBE THERMOMETER, which gives a combination of air temperature and radiation effects. In still air, GT = MRT and for a known air velocity the relationship can be calculated.

globe thermometer Instrument devised by H. M. Vernon in 1930 as a means of indicating the combined effects of radiation and convection, as they influence the human body. It consists of a black, hollow copper sphere containing an ordinary thermometer at the centre of the sphere. The temperature of the instrument depends on a combination of the air temperature, air movement and the mean radiant temperature. Recently, black-painted ping-pong balls have been shown to give equally reliable results. *See also* WET-BULB GLOBE THERMOMETER INDEX.

globe valve A casting machined to receive a bulbous circular disc which closes a circular opening between the two chambers. The disc is operated by a screw, and it can resist a higher fluid pressure than that of a GATE VALVE.

globoscope A paraboloidal mirror in which a distorted image of all the surrounding buildings is seen in STEREO-GRAPHIC PROJECTION, as observed from above. The image can be viewed, or photographed. It is possible to study sunlight penetration by superimposing a transparent sunpath diagram on a globoscopic view.

gloom In lighting, an interior that

appears to be underlit either as a result of inadequate surface luminances or due to excessive contrasts, as from bright windows.

gloss The reflection of light from a painted surface. It ranges from full gloss (the smoothest mirror-like surface attainable), through semi-gloss, eggshell gloss and eggshell flat, to flat (a matt surface without sheen, even when viewed from an oblique angle).

GLS lamp General Lighting Service, the range (from 25 W to 150 W) of INCANDESCENT LAMPS used for general lighting purposes. They are usually spherical and can be clear, frosted (etched) or diffusing.

glue Sticky substance for joining two pieces, particularly of wood, by bonding of the contact surfaces. The traditional carpenter's glue is made from bones and other animal waste products. Other traditional glues are fish glue, casein glue and vegetable glues such as soya glue and cassava glue. These have now been largely superseded by *synthetic resins*, particularly for exterior and other waterproof applications. *See also* HYDRAULIC GLUE.

glulam Structural glued LAMINATED TIMBER used as load-carrying framing for roofs, floors and other structural portions of buildings.

glycerin A trihydric alcohol (CH_2OH. $CHOH$. CH_2OH). It is a constituent of many paints and varnishes.

GMT *Abbreviation for* Greenwich Mean Time. The internationally accepted datum for calculating times around the world is based on the time at the meridian through the Greenwich Observatory, near London, but it is now known as *Universal Time*. *See* UTC.

gneiss A coarse-grained metamorphic rock, predominantly dark coloured, and characterised by mineral banding. In the industry classification of building stones, gneiss is called a GRANITE.

gnomon The upstanding element on a sun-dial, which casts the shadow.

gnomonic sunpath diagram Similar to a sun dial of the horizontal plate type, where the tip of the shadow cast by the pin or GNOMON describes the sun's path for a day. That path, drawn on a chart and repeated for various dates of the year, constitutes this sunpath diagram.

going The horizontal distance from NOSING to nosing on a staircase. *See figure under* STAIR.

gold A metallic element; highly resistant to corrosion, one of the few to be found as a metal in the native state. Its chemical symbol is Au, its atomic number is 79, its atomic weight is 197.2, its specific gravity is 19.3, and its melting point is 1063 °C.

golden section A geometric construction used by Euclid to draw the regular pentagon. From it can be derived the golden number [$\phi = 0.5 (1 + \sqrt{5}) = 1.618$], which was widely claimed in the nineteenth and twentieth centuries to be the key to the beautiful proportions of Greek and other Classical architecture. It has not been proved that the golden section was used in Greek architecture, or even that it was known in Pericles' lifetime. It was used in the revival of Greek and other Classical architecture in the nineteenth century.

goods lift A lift designed mainly for the transporting of goods, with large doors and robust finishes, but capable also of carrying people. Called a *freight elevator* in the USA.

gooseneck A flexible tube, usually metal, which retains the position to which it is bent; often used on desk and machine-mounted luminaires. *See also* ANGLEPOISE.

governor A mechanical device which controls automatically the speed of a machine. In LIFT systems, it is used to detect overspeed.

GPF *Abbreviation for* Gallons Per Flush.

GPM *Abbreviation for* Gallons Per Minute.

GPS *Abbreviation for* Global Positioning System, using input from multiple satellites to calculate a position. Under ideal conditions, current commercial systems can achieve absolute positioning to about 5 m, and relative positioning to about 5 mm. In the latter mode it can be used for setout and surveying, where line-of-sight optical surveying is difficult. It is more widely used (in relative mode) to control earthmoving machinery. It has similar uses in agriculture and transportation.

grab A bucket which is split and hinged and which can dig into loose material.

grade *(a)* At grade, at ground level. *(b)* To reduce a slope to an easy or uniform gradient. *(c)* A system of angular measurement, in which a right angle is divided into 100 grade, instead of 90 degrees of arc. (The grade is divided into 100 *centigrade* instead of the 60 *minutes* of a degree. To avoid confusion, the term *Celsius* is preferred over *Centigrade* for the temperature scale.) *See also* STRESS GRADING OF TIMBER.

grade (wood) *See* STRESS GRADING OF TIMBER.

grade beam or slab Reinforced concrete beam or slab which is normally placed directly on the ground.

grade stamp The stamp on timber indicating its *stress grade. Also called* a *grade mark.*

grader Wheeled earthmoving machine with a long wheelbase, and an adjustable blade mounted between the axles, used for accurate spreading and levelling of earthworks (*see figure*).

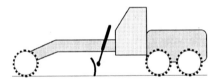

Grader

gradient The slope of a line or curve given by the ratio of rise to run of a tangent line drawn to the curve.

grading curve The graph obtained by PARTICLE-SIZE ANALYSIS.

grading of timber The sorting of timber according to the type and the number of defects. *See also* STRESS GRADING OF TIMBER.

graffiti Unwanted, deliberate writing or painting on building surfaces by unauthorised persons. Removal of graffiti can be a costly and ongoing expense for building owners and operators. Removal is facilitated if a special graffiti-resistant coating has been applied to the surfaces beforehand.

graffito *(a)* A plaster surface decorated by scoring a pattern while it is still wet. The plaster is normally applied in two or more layers of different colour, and the lower coats are exposed by the graffito work. *Also spelled sgraffito and scraffeto.* *(b)* *(rare)* singular of GRAFFITI.

grain The direction, size, arrangement or quality of the fibres in wood. When applied to the *appearance*, the preferred term is *figure. See also* CLOSE GRAIN *and* COARSE GRAIN.

grain boundary The boundary between two CRYSTALS.

graining The now obsolete art of painting a surface to look like the grain of wood or marble.

gram molecule Obsolete term for MOLE.

granite An IGNEOUS ROCK formed by plutonic intrusions (consisting of relatively large crystals due to slow cooling). It is of acid composition, its main constituents being QUARTZ, FELSPAR and MICA. Granite is a little heavier than concrete, and generally much stronger (up to 140 MPa or 20 ksi); however, its fire resistance is poor. In the industry classification of building stones, the term 'granite' is also applied to other high-strength igneous rock, such as DIORITE, DOLERITE, GABBRO, trachyte and GNEISS.

granolithic concrete Concrete mixed with specially selected aggregate, whose hardness, surface and particle shape make it suitable for a wearing surface on a heavy-duty floor.

granular soil Consisting of GRAVEL, SAND and SILT, as distinct from a COHESIVE SOIL.

granulated cork Cork broken down into small particles for thermal insulation or for the manufacture of cork tiles.

granulated glass OBSCURE GLASS with a roughened surface finish.

graphic image A DIGITAL IMAGE generated artificially, or digitised from another source, on a computer system.

graphical kernel system (GKS) A device-independent software standard for graphics.

graphical user interface A user interface to communicate with computers based on a graphic form rather than a textual form.

graphics attribute A property of an object defining one of its geometric or graphical properties, *e.g.* shape, colour, line style, etc.

graphics tablet A device for inputting graphics into a computer, in the form of a *digitiser board*, often used with a STYLUS and superimposed MENU, as a means of indicating commands to the drafting system of a computer.

graphite One of the allotropic forms of CARBON. It is present in grey CAST IRON. Colloidal graphite is an excellent lubricant which can be used at high temperatures. *Also called black lead.*

grate, grating A two-dimensional grid of bars, usually steel, cast iron or aluminium, used to cover a drainage trench or sump to allow surface water to pass through.

graticule A graduated scale placed in the eyepiece of a telescope or microscope; *see also* CROSS HAIR.

gravel Naturally occurring deposits of unconsolidated sediment, ranging from about 75 to 5 mm (3 to ⁵⁄₁₆in.), and resulting from the disintegration of rock. Larger samples are called boulders, and smaller material SAND. Most gravel consists of SILICA. Gravel, either whole or crushed, is used as COARSE AGGREGATE for concrete, and as a protective layer on top of built-up roofing.

gravitation The force of nature that causes a mutual attraction between masses. According to Newton's law, 'Any two particles of matter attract one another with a force inversely proportional to the square of the distance between them.' *See also* g.

gravity circulation Circulation of fluid due to gravity, as opposed to *forced circulation* due to pumping.

gravity retaining wall RETAINING WALL that relies for its stability on the weight of the masonry or concrete (*see figure*).

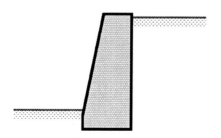

Gravity retaining wall

gravity tank system A water supply system that utilises an elevated storage tank to provide the necessary water pressure, as opposed to a HYDROPNEUMATIC TANK SYSTEM.

gray US spelling of *grey.*

GRC *Abbreviation for* Glassfibre Reinforced Cement. *See* FIBRE CEMENT.

grease trap A device for removing grease from waste water by allowing it to collect on top of the water in the trap, from which it can be removed.

great circle The shortest possible line that can be drawn on the Earth's surface between two points. It corresponds to a straight line on a plane surface. A great circle is also the circle with the largest diameter that can be drawn on the Earth's surface. The equator and the meridians are great circles. Parallels of latitude are SMALL CIRCLES.

green architecture Design that encourages energy conservation and minimises the use of fossil fuels and other non-renewable resources.

green brick A moulded brick prior to baking.

green concrete Concrete which has SET, but not sufficiently HARDENED.

green power Energy (mostly electrical) produced from renewable sources, such as wind or solar, rather than the burning of fossil fuels.

green wood Timber that still contains most of the moisture which was present in the living tree; this is reduced by SEASONING.

greenhouse A building or room containing large areas of glass, which transmits solar radiation, but not the long-wave radiation produced by the surfaces of a building after absorbing solar radiation. In consequence, a greenhouse exposed to sunshine becomes much hotter than a room with smaller windows. *Also called a conservatory or orangery.*

greenhouse abatement certificate A certificate issued by a recognised authority in recognition of reduction of greenhouse gas emission below an industry norm. For use in a CARBON TRADING system in which high emitters can offset a part of emissions by purchase of rights from low emitters.

greenhouse effect The warming effect achieved in a GREENHOUSE. By extension, the warming effect on the Earth's surface due to certain gases in the atmosphere which similarly transmit short-wave solar radiation but retain long-wave re-radiation. Changes in these gases may lead to excessive heating or cooling of the Earth.

greenhouse efficiency level Level of GREENHOUSE EMISSIONS by an organisation expressed as a proportion of the norm or benchmark for the industry in which it is operating.

greenhouse emissions Emissions of GREENHOUSE GASES to atmosphere.

greenhouse gas abatement Reduction of atmospheric content of greenhouse gases by human intervention.

greenhouse gases Gases such as carbon dioxide and methane which accumulate in the atmosphere and reduce the loss of heat to space, giving rise to global warming.

grey body A surface whose *emissivity* is the same at all wavelengths, but is significantly less than unity. *See also* BLACK BODY.

grey cast iron CAST IRON that contains some free carbon in the form of GRAPHITE as distinct from WHITE CAST IRON.

grey scale A range of different shades of grey in a continuous tone image between black and white.

grey water Non-potable SULLAGE with minor pollution, and contaminated surface water. It can be collected, filtered, stored and recycled for flushing toilets, car washing and irrigation.

greyscale (greylevel) image Image that is the digital equivalent of black-and-white photography. Each pixel sampled from the continuous tone image represents a specific shade on a GREY SCALE.

Griffith crack An ideal crack postulated in the theory of the fracture of brittle materials, particularly GLASS.

grillage foundation A foundation formed by a framework of cross beams of timber or steel.

grille A slotted or louvred opening to allow the passage of air through a wall or barrier from a space to another space or a duct.

gritstone SANDSTONE composed of large sand particles.

groin The curved line at which the soffits of two intersecting vaults meet. *See* CROSS VAULT.

groin vault *Same as* CROSS VAULT.

grommet A metal or plastic lining for a hole, to protect cables passing through it from damage on sharp edges.

groove *(a)* In building, a narrow channel, moulded into a concrete surface or machined into timber, either as a DRIP to interrupt the flow of water, or to disguise or accentuate a joint. *(b)* In machinery, a narrow channel, machine-cut into a surface, for example to locate the ropes in a lift machine.

gross building area The gross floor area for development purposes, in accordance with individual authority definitions.

gross energy requirements The measure of all energy inputs in the processes of manufacturing materials for use in construction, from extracting raw materials to delivery for construction, including associated transport and facilities.

gross lettable area The total area available for lease, calculated by adding the NET LETTABLE AREA and the COMMON AREA of a floor or building.

ground (electrical) Connection of one side of a circuit to the earth or a body that serves in place of the earth, through low impedance paths. Sometimes confused with bonding. Grounding should always conform to the relevant Electrical Code.

ground anchor A device inserted into the ground, by screwing in like an auger, or by excavation and backfilling. It is used for stabilising a retaining wall, or for resisting uplift.

ground coupled energy system A system designed to exchange heat with the earth as required, *e.g.* for operation of an air conditioning system.

ground electrode A conductor or group of conductors in intimate contact with the earth for the purpose of providing a connection with the ground. *Also called earth electrode.*

ground fault Any undesirable current path from a current-carrying conductor to ground.

ground grid A system of interconnected bare conductors arranged in a pattern over a specified area, on or buried below the surface of the earth. The primary purpose of the ground grid is to provide safety for workers by limiting potential differences within its perimeter to safe levels in case of high currents which could flow if the circuit being worked became energised for any reason or if an adjacent energised circuit faulted. Metallic surface mats and gratings are sometimes utilised for the same purpose.

ground loop The condition of having two or more ground references in a common electrical system. When two or more grounds have a potential difference between them, current can flow. This flow of current is a new circuit or loop which can interfere with the normal operation of the system.

ground source heat pump A heat pump system designed to extract heat from the ground for use in a building.

grounded (in reference to electrical wiring) *Same as* EARTHED.

group (in lift systems) A number of lift cars located adjacent to each other, using a common signalling system and a common CONTROL system.

group address A space in a building assigned periodically to a team for working activities.

grout A cement, mortar or concrete slurry which is sufficiently fluid to penetrate into rock fissures, masonry joints or pre-stressing ducts without segregation of the constituents. A commonly used mixture consists of equal volumes of cement and sand, with an appropriate amount of water.

grout injection Stabilising or waterproofing the ground by injecting a liquid cement slurry under pressure. Grout-injected *piers* are made by drilling into sandy or unstable soil with an *auger*, and injecting the grout through the hollow drill-stem as the auger is withdrawn. This prevents the pier-hole from collapsing as the auger is withdrawn. If the grout is sufficiently fluid, a reinforcing cage can be inserted into it after the auger is withdrawn.

growth rings Rings on the transverse section of a trunk or branch of a tree which mark successive cycles of growth. *Also called annual rings. See also* COARSE GRAIN *and* CLOSE GRAIN.

GRP *Abbreviation for* Glassfibre Reinforced Plastic. *See* FIBREGLASS.

GT *Abbreviation for* GLOBE TEMPERATURE.

GUI *Abbreviation for* GRAPHICAL USER INTERFACE.

guide rails A set of vertical machined rails installed in a lift well to guide the travel of a lift car or counterweight.

guide shoes Devices to guide the movement of lift cars, counterweights and doors along their associated GUIDE RAILS. *See also* LINER.

guide vane A blade placed in an air duct to influence the direction of flow, for example by turning vanes to assist air to turn around a bend or change of direction. *See also* SPLITTER.

gully trap An assembly used in a waste water system which provides a water seal to prevent odours and gases from escaping into a building or into the atmosphere.

gum arabic A white powder obtained from certain acacia trees grown mostly in the Sudan and Senegal. It is used for GLUE, and as a base for transparent paint. *See* TEMPERA PAINTING.

gum tree Australian term for EUCALYPT.

gum vein Local accumulation of natural resin, which occurs as a wide streak in certain hardwoods, particularly the eucalypts. It is a defect which can seriously weaken the timber.

gun metal An alloy containing about 90 per cent copper, 8 per cent tin and 2 per cent zinc.

gunite *Same as* SHOTCRETE.

Guojia Biazhun (National Standard for Buildings, China) A set of standards from the People's Republic of China.

gusset A piece of plate to which the members of a truss are joined, if they are too small or inconveniently shaped for a direct connection.

gutter A channel to catch water, leading it to a drain, *(a)* flowing from a roof, usually at the eaves, or as a BOX GUTTER; *(b)* at the edge of a paved area or roadway.

guy rope A rope that secures or steadies a DERRICK or a temporary structure.

GWP *Abbreviation for* Global Warming Potential.

gymnosperm One of the two main divisions of seed plants. It includes all CONIFERS.

gypsum Calcium sulphate dihydrate ($CaSO_4 \cdot 2H_2O$). It is a natural mineral which is the raw material of gypsum PLASTER. ALABASTER is a pure variety of gypsum.

H

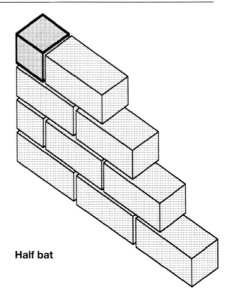

Half bat

H *(a)* Chemical symbol for hydrogen. *(b)* The symbol for the unit of electrical inductance, the HENRY.

h Abbreviation for *hecto*, one hundred times.

Haas effect Within certain limits of intensity and time difference all the sound from two sources will appear to come from the source from which the sound arrives at the listener first.

ha-ha A barrier in the form of a trench, particularly one used in country houses built in the eighteenth and nineteenth century, to prevent livestock from crossing into the garden. A fence is usually built at the bottom of the trench, and is not seen from a distance.

hair Used as reinforcement for lime and gypsum plaster. Hair from bullocks and goats was once used; however, manila fibre, sisal and glass fibre are now more common. *See* FIBROUS PLASTER.

hair cracks Fine cracks just visible with the naked eye.

hair hygrometer An instrument based on the experimental relation between the increase in the length of certain animal hairs and the relative humidity of the atmosphere, due to the absorption of moisture by the hair. They are used in HYGROGRAPHS.

half bat One half of a brick, cut in two across the length (*see figure*). *See also* KING CLOSER and QUEEN CLOSER.

half-lap joint *Same as* END-LAP JOINT.

half-round A semicircular moulding.

half-timbered Building constructed with a timber frame, the spaces between the frame timbers being filled with brickwork, plaster or WATTLE-AND-DAUB. This is still a vernacular form of construction in some rural districts of Europe. It was widely used in Tudor England, even for large urban buildings. Modern 'half-timbered' suburban houses are often of brick or brick-veneer construction, with thin vertical and diagonal pieces of timber superimposed.

halftone The simulation of different shades of grey using dots of a single shade of grey but of varying size. Used to reproduce photographs in print.

halides The binary salts (*chlorides, bromides, iodides* and *fluorides*) formed by the union of a *halogen* (chlorine, bromine, iodine or fluorine) with a metal. The best-known halide is common salt, NaCl.

hall In lift terminology, the word is synonymous with corridor, floor, landing or lobby.

halocarbons *See* CFC.

halogen *(a)* One of the monovalent elements (fluorine, chlorine, bromine, iodine) which readily form negative ions. *(b)* In lighting, the common term used for low voltage TUNGSTEN-HALOGEN LAMPS.

halon Various of the heavy CFC gases, which are very effective fire extinguishants, particularly in confined spaces. They can be used on liquid and electrical fires and evaporate, leaving the space unaffected. Being ozone-depleting chemicals, they are no longer manufactured, although recycled material is still available in some places.

halophosphate A class of fluorescent materials, having a broad emission spectrum over the visible part of the spectrum when excited, used in tubular fluorescent lamps. In high efficacy lamps, these have been replaced or used in combination with narrow band phosphors.

halving Cutting away two pieces of timber at their ends to half their thickness to form a LAP JOINT or an END-LAP JOINT.

hammer See BALL-PEEN HAMMER and CLAW HAMMER.

hammer, pile See PILE HAMMER.

hammer-beam roof A medieval timber roof without a tie. The hammer beams are supported on brackets projecting from the wall, but (unlike a modern tie) they do not meet. Instead, the forces are transmitted by arched braces and struts. A well-known example is the roof of Westminster Hall in London, the only surviving part of the old Westminster Palace.

hammered finish A paint finish that simulates hammered metal.

hammered glass Glass made translucent by embossing it on one side to resemble beaten metal.

hammerhead crane A crane with a horizontal jib along which the lifting hook travels, and a shorter counterbalancing jib, rotating on top of a tower. *Also called saddle jib, horizontal jib.*

hand See RIGHT-HAND.

hand level Same as CLINOMETER.

handling capacity (of a lift system) The number of people that a bank of lifts (elevators) can move in five minutes. This is usually expressed as a percentage of the population of the building.

handwinding The action of using a manual device to lower a lift car in an emergency.

hangar A building housing aircraft.

hanger A strap, rod or wire suspended from a structure to support a pipe, the framework for a suspended ceiling, etc.

hard copy A copy of the output of a computer on paper or film, as opposed to the visual display on a screen.

hard disk Non-flexible magnetic disk for the bulk storage of data. Usually an integral part of a computer. *See also* FLOPPY DISK, which has a much smaller capacity.

hard plaster Plaster usually of cement and sand, or PLASTER OF PARIS, trowelled to a smooth, hard finish.

hard solder Same as SILVER SOLDER.

hard water Water containing calcium or magnesium salts in solution. These are picked up if water passes slowly through LIMESTONE or DOLOMITE. The salts react with soap, and thus make washing and laundering difficult. They are also deposited on heating as scale, and thus tend to block the pipes of hot-water systems. Water which is too hard must be treated to remove some of the salt with a WATER SOFTENER.

hardboard A FIBREBOARD formed under pressure to a density of 500 to 1000 kg/m³ (30 to 60 lb/ft³). Most hardboards have one smooth and one textured surface; however, hardboards are also made with decorative and veneered surfaces, and they can be treated to be water-resistant. *Also called compressed fibreboard.*

hardener A CATALYST which increases the hardening rate of synthetic resins or glues. It is mixed with the resin immediately before use. *Also called accelerator. See also* CONCRETE HARDENER.

hardening of concrete The stage in the chemical reaction between cement and water when the concrete hardens and gains sufficient strength to bear its own weight and that of the construction loads. *See also* SETTING *and* AGEING.

hardening of metal See CASE HARDENING, COLD WORKING *and* QUENCHING.

hardness The resistance of a material to permanent deformation of its surface.

hardness scale See MOHS' SCALE.

hardpan An extremely hard soil containing gravel and boulders.

hardware The physical equipment of a computer, as opposed to the programs or SOFTWARE.

hardwood Timber from trees belonging to the botanical group *Angiospermae*, *i.e.* all trees but the CONIFERS, which are called *softwoods*. While some softwoods are moderately hard, some hardwoods are very soft (*e.g.* BALSA WOOD). However, taken as a group, the hardwoods are much harder than the softwoods. Practically all Australian native timbers are hard, and many can only be nailed in their green state. *See also* BOXED HEART.

Hardy Cross method *Same as* MOMENT DISTRIBUTION METHOD.

harmonic A tone whose frequency is an integer multiple of the fundamental frequency of a sound or vibrating system. *See also* OCTAVE.

harmonic distortion The introduction of harmonic components into a signal output, by a transducer, amplifier or other device, due to the imperfect behaviour of the device.

harmonic filter On power systems, a device for filtering one or more harmonics from the power system. Most are passive combinations of inductance, capacitance and resistance. Newer technologies include active filters that can also address reactive power needs.

hatchway A term historically used to describe a lift well, but now used only for the LIFT WELL of goods lifts and DUMB-WAITERS.

haunch (a) The part of an arch near the springing. (b) A section of a beam near the supports whose depth is increased because of an increase in bending moment.

haw-haw Same as HA-HA.

hawk A flat surface of metal or timber held by a handle underneath, to carry plaster or mortar while it is being applied to a surface.

haydite A LIGHTWEIGHT CONCRETE aggregate produced by heating shale.

H-beam or H-section *Same as* WIDE-FLANGE SECTION.

HCFC Hydrochlorofluorocarbons, a family of synthetic refrigerants with less severe OZONE DEPLETING potential than CFCs. *See also* HFCS.

HDD *Abbreviation for* HARD DISK Drive, a digital storage device of computers, its capacity measured in bytes (usually GB).

HDTV *Abbreviation for* High Definition Television.

He Chemical symbol for *helium*.

head (a) The energy possessed by a liquid due to its elevation above some datum, or due to any other cause, such as its velocity. (b) The enlarged part of a bolt. (c) The upper end of a column. (d) The upper part of a vertical timber. (e) The topmost member of a door or window frame.

header A brick, block or stone laid across the wall, to bond together the STRETCHER bricks (*see figure*). The shorter length, or head, of the brick is visible on the face of the brickwork. *See also* BOND (a).

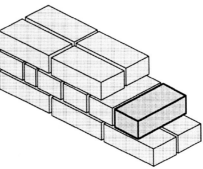

Header

header, lift door Used in the lift industry for a horizontal structural member located above, and on the lift-well side of an entrance, to support the door hanger.

headroom (a) The clear vertical distance between the ground or floor and the lowest point overhead. (b) In audio systems, headroom is the difference (in dB) between the average and peak sound levels. 10 dB is usually adequate for speech.

hearing threshold The sound level in dB, at a given frequency, which can just be heard in quiet conditions.

heart The centre of a wooden log. *See also* BOXED HEART.

heat (etc.) *See also* THERMAL, etc.

heat capacity The quantity of heat required to raise unit mass of a substance by one degree.

heat exchanger A device in which heat is exchanged between two fluids while the fluids themselves are kept separate. An automobile radiator is a water-to-air heat exchanger.

heat gain Heat migration into a substance or space by conduction, radiation or exchange of air.

heat gain, solar *See* DIRECT SOLAR GAIN *and* THERMAL CAPACITY.

heat gun A tool that produces a stream of hot air, at a temperature suitable for softening and removing paint, or heat-welding of THERMOPLASTIC materials.

heat insulation *Same as* THERMAL INSULATION.

heat island effect Higher temperatures in cities as opposed to nearby rural areas. Heat islands are created by several contributing factors, including waste heat from buildings and cars, reduced vegetation and non-porous paved ground surfaces.

heat load The quantity of heat required to be removed or added to the air in a space to maintain a desired condition of temperature and/or relative humidity.

heat loss Heat migration from a substance or space by conduction, radiation or exchange of air.

heat of hydration The quantity of heat liberated or consumed when a substance takes up water.

heat pipe A passive device for the efficient transfer of thermal energy, consisting of a closed metal pipe containing a liquid and a tubular perforated metal wick. It conducts heat by evaporation of the liquid at its base and condensation at the other end. The condensate then collects by gravity at the base for recycling.

heat pump An air conditioning installation which can act either as a heating or as a cooling unit. The refrigerant soaks up heat from the inside in summer, and from the outside in winter. After a COMPRESSION CYCLE, the heat is released (on the outside in summer, and on the inside in winter).

heat reclamation, recovery The process of recovery of heat, which would otherwise be wasted, from an effluent fluid for useful purposes.

heat rejection Discharge of surplus heat from a space to a sink such as the atmosphere by way of a cooling tower, air-cooled condenser or other arrangement.

heat sink A part of an energy system to which unwanted heat can be rejected, *e.g.* the atmosphere or a body of water.

heat source A part of an energy system from which useful heat can be extracted, *e.g.* a boiler, or the atmosphere.

heat stress A condition of distress arising from increase in deep body temperature due to inadequate heat loss.

heat transfer A generic term for THERMAL CONDUCTION, CONVECTION *and* RADIATION.

heat wheel A rotary device used to transfer heat from one moving air stream to another.

heat-absorbing glass Glass whose solar transmittance is reduced, particularly in the INFRA-RED end of the spectrum, by adding various colouring agents to the molten glass. The most common colours are bronze, grey and green. The visible light transmittance varies from 14 to 83 per cent, depending on the colour and the thickness. *See also* REFLECTIVE GLASS.

heating energy Energy available for the supply of required heat.

heat-reflective glass *See* REFLECTIVE GLASS.

heat-treated glass *See* TEMPERED GLASS.

heat-treatment of metal *See* ANNEALING, NORMALISING, TEMPERING *and* QUENCHING.

heavy metals In environmental terminology, those metals of a high atomic weight, which in certain concentrations can exert a toxic effect. The main 'heavy metals' are cadmium, chromium, copper, lead, mercury, nickel and zinc.

hectare A metric unit of area, equal to $10\,000\,m^2$ or 2.47 acres.

hecto (h) Prefix for 100 times, from the Greek word for hundred; *e.g.* 1 hectare = 100 are.

heel That part of the horizontal slab of a CANTILEVER RETAINING WALL which is under the retained soil, as opposed to the TOE.

held water Same as CAPILLARY WATER.

heliarc welding A form of SHIELDED-ARC WELDING in which the arc is protected by the inert gas *helium*. It is used mainly in the USA where helium is readily available. *See also* ARGON-ARC WELDING.

helical reinforcement Small-diameter reinforcement wound around the main, or LONGITUDINAL, REINFORCEMENT of columns. It restrains the lateral expansion of the concrete under compression, and consequently increases the column strength. *Also called* (incorrectly) *spiral reinforcement.*

helical stair A stair whose treads are arranged along a helix. Commonly (but incorrectly) called a *spiral stair.*

heliodon A term often used synonymously with SOLARSCOPE, but more accurately a particular type of solarscope, having a model table that rotates and tilts, to give solar AZIMUTH and ALTITUDE, with respect to a spotlight to simulate the sun, at some distance away. The model is fixed to the table.

heliostat A device to follow the sun's apparent movement, motorised, controlled by a sensor or programmed, most often referring to a mirror to reflect the sun's rays onto a stationary receiver.

helium The lightest of the inert gases, used in HELIARC WELDING. Its chemical symbol is He, its atomic number is 2, its atomic weight is 4.002, and its boiling point is $-268.9\,°C$.

helmet-mounted camera A camera mounted on a helmet which captures images and transmits them to a remote unit.

Helmholtz absorber *See* HELMHOLTZ RESONATOR *and* RESONANT ABSORBER.

Helmholtz resonator A resonant acoustical absorber, named after the nineteenth-century Prussian scientist. In its original form it consisted of a vessel with a narrow neck, within which the air resonated, which was connected to a large volume of air in the vessel which acted as the spring in the single degree of freedom system. The movement of the air in the neck of the vessel resulted in damping of the system and hence absorption of the sound at and around the resonant frequency.

hemihydrate A compound containing one-half of a molecule of water to one molecule of another substance. The hemihydrate most widely used in building is *calcium sulphate hemihydrate*, PLASTER OF PARIS.

hemispherical dome A DOME with a constant radius of curvature that comes vertically on its springings. Hence the horizontal component of the thrust is absorbed by HOOP TENSION.

henry (H) The unit for measuring electrical inductance, named after the nineteenth-century American scientist.

HEPA filter High Efficiency Particulate Arrestance air filter, used for removing very fine particulate matter from air.

heptafluoropropane A colourless, almost odourless, electrically non-conductive gas (HFC227ea in the system of coding refrigerants, or C_3HF_7), with a density approximately six times that of air, a candidate to substitute HALON in GAS PROTECTION SYSTEMS.

heptagon A seven-sided POLYGON. The angle included between the seven equal sides of a *regular* heptagon is $128.6°$.

hermetic compressor Refrigerant compressor which has the electric motor contained in the refrigerant circuit in a sealed vessel.

herringbone In masonry and carpentry, a zigzag pattern or bond.

herringbone strutting A form of LATERAL SUPPORT between deep, narrow timber or steel joists to prevent them from twisting. Small pieces, usually of timber about $38 \times 38\,mm$ or $1\frac{1}{2}$ in. $\times$ $1\frac{1}{2}$ in., are fixed as cross-bracing between each adjacent pair of joists. Now generally superseded by SOLID BRIDGING.

hertz Unit of frequency. 1 hertz (Hz) = 1 cycle per second, 1 kilohertz = 1000 cycles per second. The hertz has the units s^{-1}. It is named after the nineteenth-century German physicist.

hessian *Same as* BURLAP.

heuristic Originally: *serving to discover*, but in the theory of problem solving it means goal-oriented search (as opposed to SERENDIPITY), or problem solving by trial and error.

hexagon A six-sided POLYGON. The angle included between the six equal sides of a *regular* hexagon is $120°$.

hexagonal close-packed lattice *See* CLOSE-PACKED HEXAGONAL LATTICE.

hexagonally-recessed screw head *See* ALLEN HEAD.

hexahedron *Same as* CUBE.

HFC Hydrofluorocarbons, a family of synthetic refrigerants with no OZONE DEPLETING potential. They are replacing the CFCS and HCFCS.

hidden line removal The process of determining and removing HIDDEN LINES from a view, thus transforming a WIREFRAME display into a surface display.

hidden lines In computer graphics, in line drawings, such as WIREFRAME drawings, those lines that are hidden from view when the surfaces of the shapes are made opaque.

hidden surface removal The process of determining and removing HIDDEN SURFACES from view in a three-dimensional display.

hidden surfaces In computer graphics, surfaces which are obscured by other surfaces from a particular viewpoint.

hiding power The ability of a paint to obscure existing colours and patterns; it is a measure of its opacity. *Covering power* is the hiding power for a given spreading rate.

hierarchical file structure (HFS) A file organisation scheme in which related files can be associated or grouped for easy access, maintenance and recognition. Graphical user interfaces use folder icons to form such associations; command line oriented operating systems use directories and subdirectories for this purpose. In either case, groups can be organised within groups, providing a nested or tree-like hierarchy of file associations which greatly simplifies a user's task in keeping track of file collections.

hi-fi *Abbreviation for* HIGH-FIDELITY.

high gloss An enamel-like finish on paint or varnish.

high-alumina cement Cement manufactured from BAUXITE and limestone. It is chemically different from PORTLAND CEMENT and gains its strength more rapidly than high-early-strength Portland cement. *Also called calcium aluminate cement.*

high-bond bar *Same as* DEFORMED BAR.

high-carbon steel CARBON STEEL containing more than 0.5 per cent of carbon. *See also* LOW-CARBON STEEL.

high-density concrete Concrete of exceptionally high density, due to the use of very dense aggregates, such as BARITE or LIMONITE. It is used for radiation shielding. *See also* BARIUM PLASTER.

high-early-strength cement A PORTLAND CEMENT which gains strength more rapidly than the ordinary variety, and costs slightly more. It has a higher SPECIFIC SURFACE through finer grinding, and thus allows the chemical action to proceed more rapidly. *Also called rapid-hardening cement.*

high-fidelity Sound reproduction of a superior, but generally undefined quality.

high-intensity discharge lamp A DISCHARGE LAMP in which the radiant energy exceeds $3 \, W/cm^2$ of tube surface area. It includes MERCURY VAPOUR, METAL HALIDE and HIGH-PRESSURE SODIUM lamps.

high-level inversion *See* INVERSION.

high-level programming language Language which provides operations closer to the problem domain than the basic machine language operations that the computer must use to implement a task. High-level languages allow the programmer to write programs that are more readable and easier to debug than machine language programs. Special programs, called COMPILERS or INTERPRETERS, translate the high-level code to the appropriate machine language for execution.

high-light window A window set high in the wall. *Also called* a CLEARSTOREY window.

high-pass filter *(a)* In graphics, a filter to modify the pixel values (and hence the appearance) of a digitised image. High-pass filters are used to sharpen the image by increasing the contrast of nearby pixels. *(b)* In acoustics and signal processing, a filter which only allows the passage of signals above a certain frequency. *See also* LOW-PASS FILTER.

high-performance windows Windows made of glass treated to improve its control of heat exchange between the exterior and interior of a building.

high-pressure hot water Water raised to a high temperature under a pressure greater than atmospheric. *Also called high temperature hot water.*

high-pressure mercury lamp A HIGH-INTENSITY DISCHARGE LAMP using mercury vapour in the discharge tube. The light is 'white' but with a cold appearance due to the strong mercury lines in the blue/green part of the spectrum. The colour appearance and colour rendering are improved by using a red phosphor fluorescent coating on the inside of the outer bulb. This is now the common form of the lamp, often called a *mercury fluorescent lamp*. The other method for improving the colour is to add metals in the form of halides to produce the METAL HALIDE LAMP.

high-pressure sodium lamp A HIGH-INTENSITY DISCHARGE LAMP using sodium vapour in the discharge tube. The light is yellowish in colour (but not as yellow as the monochromatic LOW-PRESSURE SODIUM LAMP). The light can be made 'whiter' by increasing the pressure in the discharge tube, but at the cost of efficacy.

high-pressure steam curing *See* AUTO-CLAVE.

high-speed steel A high-alloy steel used in metal-cutting tools operating at high speeds. It contains 12–22 per cent of tungsten and is capable of intense hardening.

high-strength bolt *Same as* HIGH-TENSILE BOLT.

high-strength steel Steel with a high YIELD or PROOF STRESS, generally above 400N/mm^2 (60 ksi).

high-temperature hot water *See* HIGH-PRESSURE HOT WATER.

high-tensile bolt A bolt made of high-strength steel, and usually used as a FRICTION-GRIP BOLT.

high-velocity system An air distribution system that operates at high pressure and velocity to distribute conditioned supply air through ductwork of reduced size.

highway In computing and telecommunications, a channel over which information is transferred.

highway width Refers to the *bandwidth* and the capacity of a HIGHWAY to transmit information; the greater the width the faster the transmission.

hinge joint *See* PIN POINT *and* PLASTIC HINGE.

hip roof A roof with four inclined slopes, that meet at the *hips* (*see figure*).

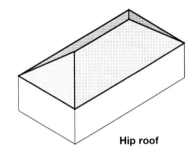

Hip roof

hipped plate roof HIP ROOF formed by folded plates.

histogram Literally, a diagram showing a web-like pattern. Its most common use is as a *frequency histogram*, which shows the relation between the magnitude of an observed variable characteristic and its frequency as a series of bars, or vertical rectangles; each rectangle is drawn so that its height corresponds to the frequency (*see figure*). *See also* FREQUENCY DISTRIBUTION CURVE.

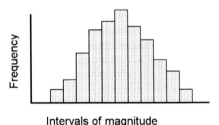

Histogram

HMSO *Abbreviation for* Her (or His) Majesty's Stationery Office, London.

Hoffmann kiln A continuous ring tunnel brick kiln of annular longitudinal arch design, as opposed to an INTERMITTENT KILN.

hog-backed *Same as* CAMBERed.

hogging moment A NEGATIVE BENDING MOMENT, such as occurs in a continuous beam at a support; it causes a 'hogging' deformation. A SAGGING MOMENT is positive.

hoist A platform for lifting people and/or materials. It is lifted by cables and within, or cantilevered from, an open frame supported by the building. It ranges in size from two storeys to any height. The platform can be open or enclosed.

hoisting The movement of a load vertically.

hoistway US term for LIFT WELL.

holding-down bolt A bolt built in to a concrete footing, with the threaded end projecting to secure another member, usually a steel column.

hole, effect on strength *See* STRESS CONCENTRATION.

hollow block An extruded BLOCK of concrete or burnt clay, which consists largely of voids, and is consequently a good insulator, but of limited strength. It is used for partitions and in floors. *Also called* a *hollow tile*.

hollow-core door A door formed of a light timber frame, faced on both sides with hardboard or plywood. It may have a hollow or a HONEYCOMB CORE.

hollow-tile floor A reinforced concrete floor which is cast over a soffit consisting of hollow blocks (of burnt clay or concrete) between narrow ribs (*see figure*). Its structural design is like that of a RIBBED SLAB; however, it presents a flat, uniform soffit after plastering, and its thermal insulation is superior to that of a solid slab. *Also called* a *pot floor*.

hollow-tile floor

hologram A three-dimensional image of an object created by a LASER.

home directory The starting point of the system of file organisation in a computer. *Also called root directory*.

home page The entry point to an organisation of documents in the WORLD WIDE WEB.

home unit Australian term for an APARTMENT which is sold and not rented. *See also* STRATA TITLE.

home working The process of engaging in work activities in the employee's home as the main place of work, with the agreement of the employer and with a contract which describes the employer's commitment to worker's compensation, occupational health and safety matters, and negotiated productivity outcomes.

homebase Assigned workplace from which most of an individual employee's work in a building is carried out.

homogeneous Having identical characteristics throughout.

honed Smooth texture produced by rubbing, particularly on natural stone.

honeycomb core A structure of air cells, resembling a honeycomb, placed between plywood panels. It has excellent insulating properties and adequate flexural strength. The honeycomb is commonly made of paper. *See also* HOLLOW-CORE DOOR.

honeycombed concrete Concrete with voids caused by failure of the cement mortar to fill all the spaces between the particles of the coarse aggregate. It reduces strength, and may reduce the protection of reinforcement against corrosion.

hooked bar A concrete reinforcing bar whose end is bent to improve its anchorage, generally through 90° or 180°. The minimum radius of the hook must be sufficient to avoid stress concentrations in the concrete, and a free length of bar is required at the end of the hook to prevent pull-out of the bar.

Hooke's law In 1678, Robert Hooke published his observation that all known ELASTIC materials had deformations which were directly proportional to the applied loads. Today the law is usually stated as 'STRESS is proportional to STRAIN'. Hooke's law is the basis of the ELASTIC DESIGN of structures, and of the principle of SUPERPOSITION.

hoop reinforcement Closed hoops around the main, or longitudinal, reinforcement of columns to restrain the BUCKLING of the longitudinal steel (*see figure*).

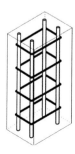

hoop reinforcement

hoop tension The tension which occurs in the lower portion of a hemispherical DOME, in a cylindrical or spherical water-tank, or in the *tension ring* which absorbs the horizontal components of the reactions of a shallow dome.

Hopkins–Stryker equation A theoretical equation for predicting the sound level at any position in a room due to a sound source in the room.

Sound pressure level (dB)
= sound power level (dB)
+ $10 \log_{10} (Q/4\pi r^2 + 4/R)$

where Q = *directivity factor* of the source, r = distance from source to receiver and R = room constant which is approximately equal to the total absorption in the room.

hopper window A window sash hinged at the bottom and opening inwards

horizon The circle, as seen by an observer, which has an ALTITUDE of zero. If the true horizon is obstructed, *e.g.* by mountains or buildings, it may be necessary to use an *artificial horizon*. The point above the observer, which makes an angle of 90° to the horizon, is the *zenith*.

horizontal Perpendicular to the direction of the gravitational forces.

horizontal shadow angle The angle measured in the horizontal plane between the position of the sun and the normal to a surface.

horn A projecting end of a timber member beyond a right-angled joint, *e.g.* the extension of a sash stile beyond the bottom rail of the top sash of a window.

horn loudspeaker Horns are used to increase the radiation efficiency of a loudspeaker driver and to give a more directional radiation pattern.

horsepower (hp) The performance of 33 000 foot-pounds of work per minute (= 746 W); originally intended to equal the capacity of a horse when rating the power of a mechanical vehicle. However, a horse can perform better than 1 hp, at least for a short time. The metric horsepower (force de cheval, *ch*, or Pferdestärke, *PS*) equals 4500 kgf m/min, which is 0.986 hp. In SI UNITS the horsepower is replaced by the watt, 1 ch = 735.5 W. *See also* POWER.

horseshoe arch An ARCH shaped like a horseshoe. The curve of the INTRADOS continues below the SPRINGINGS, so that the opening at the bottom of the arch is less than at the springings (*see figure*). *Also called* a *Byzantine arch* or a *Moorish arch*.

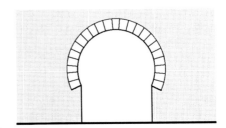

Horseshoe arch

host Any computer directly connected to a NETWORK that acts as a repository for services (such as EMAIL, Usenet newsgroups, FTP or WORLD WIDE WEB) available for other computers on the network.

hot desking The practice of sharing workplaces between individuals in different time periods.

hot dip galvanising Protecting ferrous metal by GALVANISING in a bath of molten zinc to form a coating, as opposed to *electroplating*.

hot gas line The pipeline that transports hot gas from a refrigerant compressor to a condenser.

hot restrike In lighting, the technique used to restart high pressure DISCHARGE LAMPS after an interruption to supply. These normally need a period of from 2 to 5 minutes for the arc materials to drop to a pressure sufficiently low for conventional starters/ignitors to restart the lamp.

hot smoke test A test conducted in a building to prove the effectiveness of the smoke management system. A controlled fire of nominated intensity is established and synthetic smoke is injected into the hot effluent gas stream so that the flow patterns can be visualised.

hot spots Areas within an air conditioned space, whose thermal performance is perceived to be unsatisfactory.

hot water *See* WATER HEATER.

hot working The mechanical working of a metal above the temperature for recrystallisation, as opposed to COLD WORKING.

hot-air seasoning Drying timber in a kiln.

hot-cathode lamp A DISCHARGE LAMP, usually low pressure, in which the electrodes are heated, either by the arc or by a separate heating current.

hot-rolled section Steel structural section produced by passing a red-hot *billet* through a series of rollers, gradually forming it closer to the desired shape. The surface finish is rough with *mill scale*, as opposed to a *cold-formed* section, which is of thinner material and has a smoother finish.

hot-wire anemometer A remote-reading instrument for measuring low air speeds. An exposed fine resistance wire is heated by the passage of an electric current, and the effect of air movement on its temperature is measured. The probe is small enough to be used for model analysis in a wind tunnel.

hotelling The practice of allocating non-assigned workplaces in a building by reservation.

housed joint Timber joint in which the end of one piece fits into a slot cut across the face of the other (*see figure*).

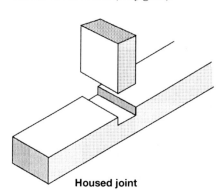

Housed joint

housekeeping Procedures for maintaining a building in a clean, uncluttered and well-operating condition, by attention to routine cleaning and simple replacement of items subjected to wear-and-tear. It does not usually include major maintenance of plant and equipment. In *fire safety management*, it includes keeping public areas clear of obstructions and flammable items.

Howard diagram A polar diagram which provides a graphical solution for the buckling of laterally loaded struts, developed by the British aeronautical engineer, H. B. Howard.

Howe truss A statically determinate truss consisting of top and bottom chords connected by diagonal *compression* members and vertical tension members (*see figure*), as distinct from a PRATT TRUSS. *See also* WARREN TRUSS.

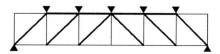

Howe truss

HSB colour A scheme for encoding colour in terms of three parameters: hue, saturation and brightness. HSB colour is often preferred by artists and designers since it defines colour attributes in terms that are closer to colour perception. *See also* RGB COLOUR, and CMYK COLOUR.

HSI *Abbreviation for* Heat Stress Index, developed by Belding and Hatch in 1955, the ratio of evaporative cooling that would be required to maintain the body's thermal equilibrium to the maximum evaporative cooling possible under the given conditions (rarely used today).

HSV *Abbreviation for* Hue, Saturation, Value, one of the methods of specifying a colour.

HT *Abbreviation for* High Tensile.

HTML *Abbreviation for* Hypertext Markup Language, the language used to compose web pages. The term 'markup' is taken from the traditional way pages were delivered to a typesetter, with special characters and fonts marked on plain text copy. HTML employs the same paradigm. Formatting information is marked using special TAGS that are inserted into the plain text. The interpretation of the tags can be left to different client browsers to format to suit the given display system. *See* CLIENT and MAIL SERVER.

HTML tags Formatting information that is inserted into plain text documents to transform them into web pages. *See* HTML.

HTTP *Abbreviation for* Hypertext Transfer Protocol. The standard protocol (set of communication rules) for exchanging information on the World Wide Web. Using this common set of communication rules, web clients can contact and request information from web servers worldwide, and web servers can then deliver documents composed in HTML which client browsers can interpret according to the local display system's capabilities.

HTTP servers (Web servers) Servers attached to the World Wide Web configured to communicate using the communication protocol HTTP.

hue In the MUNSELL BOOK OF COLOR, the hue describes the basic colour of a coloured material: red, yellow, green, blue and purple, and combinations identified by combinations of the letters R, Y, G, B and P.

Huggenberger tensometer A STRAIN GAUGE with a gauge length of 10–20 mm, employing a compound lever system giving a magnification of about 1200.

human factors engineering The study of the interaction of work and people. *Also called ergonomics.*

human tolerance of noise *See* DAMAGE RISK CRITERION, HEARING THRESHOLD *and* BACKGROUND NOISE.

humidifier Component of an AIR CONDITIONING plant which removes suspended dirt by spraying or washing, and raises the moisture content, if necessary. *Also called an air washer.* The spray equipment of an air conditioning plant may be used either for *humidification* or for DEHUMIDIFICATION, if its temperature is low enough.

humidistat A sensor used to measure relative humidity in air in an air-conditioned space and to signal the need for adjustment of it to meet a required condition.

humidity Water vapour within a given space. The *absolute humidity* is the mass of water vapour per unit volume. The *relative humidity* is the ratio of the quantity of water vapour actually present in the air, expressed as a percentage, to that present at the same temperature in a water-saturated atmosphere.

humidity ratio (HR) A non-dimensional expression of the moisture content of air, *e.g.* kg/kg, thus ABSOLUTE HUMIDITY of 10 g/kg = HR of 0.010.

humus The dark-coloured, fertile portion of the topsoil, which contains a large

proportion of rotting vegetation. It is excellent for growing plants, but a poor foundation material, and it is removed before construction commences.

hung ceiling *Same as* FALSE CEILING.

hung window *See* DOUBLE-HUNG WINDOW.

hungry joints *Same as* STARVED JOINTS.

hungry surface Highly absorbent surface, used to describe a surface to be painted, or bricks that absorb much water out of the mortar.

hurricane A CYCLONE, particularly when occurring in the Caribbean region.

Huygen's principle A geometrical method for finding the shape of a wavefront at some instant of time after an initial observation. The principle applies to light and sound waves.

HV *Abbreviation for* High Voltage.

HVAC *Abbreviation for* Heating, Ventilation and Air Conditioning.

hybrid A device which is a composite of differing technologies to create a better functionality.

hybrid computer A mixed computer system combining analog and digital computing devices.

hybrid ventilation A system that can ventilate a building by means of either wind and/or buoyancy-driven or forced air flows, depending on prevailing weather conditions.

hydrant A connection to a water main, usually for extinguishing a fire.

hydrated lime Calcium hydroxide $(Ca(OH)_2)$, *Also called slaked lime.* It is formed by slaking QUICKLIME, *i.e.* adding water to it. The old-fashioned product was made in a lime maturing pit, and the *lime putty* required some weeks to mature. It is now common practice to use *dry hydrate* (a dry powder supplied in bags) for *lime mortar.*

hydration Addition of water, particularly to cement, lime and plaster, and the subsequent chemical action.

hydraulic cement An old-fashioned term to distinguish cement proper from lime. Cement sets and hardens under water due to the interaction of the cement with the water. Lime is washed out if submerged for a long period in water, because hydrated lime is soluble.

hydraulic friction The loss of HEAD

caused by roughness or obstruction in a pipe or channel.

hydraulic glue An old-fashioned term for a glue which retains its adhesion under water. Few of the traditional glues satisfied this requirement but most synthetic RESINS do. *See also* MARINE GLUE.

hydraulic gradient The difference in the water level (in a pipe or in soil) between two points, divided by the shortest path between them.

hydraulic jack *See* JACK.

hydraulic lift *See* LIFT TYPES *(b), (d), (g)* and *(m)*.

hydraulic lime LIME that hardens under water because it contains 30–50 per cent of clay, which provides the necessary silica and alumina for the hydraulic properties.

hydraulic platform *See* CHERRY PICKER *and* SCISSOR LIFT.

hydraulic services The services required to deliver water to and within a facility, and to remove waste water and stormwater from the facility.

hydraulics The science of the flow of fluids.

hydrogen The lightest element. On burning it forms water (H_2O). Its chemical symbol is H, its atomic number is 1, its atomic weight is 1.008, it has a valency of 1, and its boiling point is −252.7°C.

hydrograph A curve showing the variation of water flow over a period of time.

hydrometer An instrument for measuring the specific gravity of a liquid.

hydronic system A heat transfer system that employs hot or cold water in a closed loop, to convey heat between a point of production and a point of use or disposal.

hydropneumatic tank system A water supply system that utilises a pressurised tank, containing pressurised air above the water, to provide the necessary water pressure, as opposed to a GRAVITY TANK SYSTEM.

hydrostatic pressure The pressure at any point in a liquid which is at rest. It equals the density of the liquid multiplied by the depth of the point under consideration.

hygrograph A recording hygrometer, which plots the change in RELATIVE HUMIDITY with time on a clock-driven drum. Many hygrographs are HAIR

HYGROMETERS combined with a clock mechanism.

hygrometer An instrument for measuring the humidity in the air. The simplest type is the WET-AND-DRY BULB THERMOMETER.

hygroscopic material A material which readily absorbs water vapour.

hypar *Abbreviation for* HYPERBOLIC PARABOLOID.

hyperbola The section of a right circular CONE by a plane which intersects the cone on both sides of the apex. Its equation is of the form

$$\frac{x^2}{a} - \frac{y^2}{b} = 1$$

where *a* and *b* are constants.

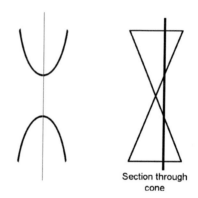

Section through cone

Hyperbola

hyperbolic functions A set of six functions *sinh, cosh, tanh, coth, sech* and *cosech*, which are analogous to the CIRCULAR FUNCTIONS, but are derived from the properties of the hyperbola instead of the circle. They can also be interpreted in terms of EXPONENTIAL FUNCTIONS:

$$\sinh x = \frac{1}{2}(e^x - e^{-x})$$

and

$$\cosh x = \frac{1}{2}(e^x + e^{-x})$$

hyperbolic paraboloid A geometric surface which has the equation $z = kxy$, where *x, y* and *z* are the Cartesian coordinates, and k is a constant (*see figure*). It has a negative GAUSSIAN CURVATURE, *i.e.* it is saddle-shaped. It is a RULED surface, and can be generated by moving a straight line over two other straight lines inclined to one another. Frequently abbreviated to *hypar*.

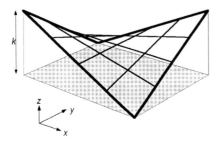

Hyperbolic paraboloid

hyperbolic paraboloid shell A shell in the form of a HYPERBOLIC PARABOLOID. Since the shape can be generated by two systems of straight lines, its formwork is more readily constructed from straight pieces of timber than that of a dome.

hyperboloid of revolution *See* SURFACE OF REVOLUTION.

hypermedia An extension of HYPERTEXT including graphics, sound and video.

hyperstatic structure *Same as* STATICALLY INDETERMINATE STRUCTURE.

hypertext An organisation of textual documents containing cross-references or links allowing a reader to move easily from one referenced subject to another in any order.

hyperthermia Condition of body overheating, of body temperature being substantially above the normal range.

hypo *(a)* A colloquial term for *sodium thiosulphate*, a material commonly used for fixing photographic film after developing. It removes the unreduced silver halide emulsion. *(b)* A prefix meaning 'below', as in *hypothermia*.

hypocaust A central UNDERFLOOR HEATING system used in Ancient Roman baths and (occasionally) villas. Hot air and gases from a fire were passed through masonry chambers and flues under the floors.

hypostyle A structure whose roof is supported by numerous columns.

hypotenuse The longest side of a right-angled triangle, which is opposite the right angle.

hypothermia Condition of body underheating, of body temperature below the normal range.

hypsometer An instrument in which water is boiled and the boiling temperature measured. It may be used at ground level for calibrating thermometers, or in conjunction with a calibrated thermometer to measure the altitude above ground level, since water has a lower boiling point when the air pressure is reduced.

hysteresis *See* MECHANICAL HYSTERESIS.

Hz *Abbreviation for* HERTZ.

I

i Symbol for $\sqrt{(-1)}$.

I *(a)* The most common symbol for the SECOND MOMENT OF AREA (MOMENT OF INERTIA). *(b)* The symbol for luminous intensity, the CANDELA.

I/O *(a)* *Abbreviation for* INPUT/OUTPUT DEVICE (of a computer). *(b)* Inspection Opening (in a drainage pipe).

I/O controller The component of an operating system consisting of primitive input/output routines to manage the input and output operations of a computer. *See* INPUT/OUTPUT DEVICE.

I²R The expression of power resulting from the flow of current through a resistance: $P = I^2R$, where P = Power, I = Current, R = Resistance.

IABSE International Association for Bridge and Structural Engineering, Zurich.

IAI International Alliance for Interoperability. An alliance of the building industry formed to integrate the AEC/FM industry through the specification of industry foundation classes (IFC) as a universal language.

IALD International Association of Lighting Designers.

IAQ *Abbreviation for* Indoor Air Quality.

I-beam, I-section A metal section, particularly a rolled steel JOIST, shaped like the letter I. Also a fabricated timber joist of similar section, usually with a plywood web.

IBIS *Abbreviation for* Issue-Based Information System. A design decision support system based on argumentation.

IC *Abbreviation for* INTEGRATED CIRCUIT.

ICE Institution of Civil Engineers, London.

ice house A building for storing ice blocks cut from lakes and streams in winter for use during the summer. Eighteenth-century British country houses generally placed a decorative pavilion above the underground storage chamber.

Iceland spar A pure, transparent and crystalline form of calcium carbonate ($CaCO_3$). It is noteworthy for its double reflection and perfect cleavage, and hence is utilised for producing plane-polarised light in the form of NICOL PRISMS.

ICOMOS International Council on Monuments and Sites, Paris.

icon In computing, a symbol used in a GRAPHIC USER INTERFACE to represent a command or an object. The icon usually depicts some object familiar to a user, for example a pen in a drafting system.

icosahedron A regular POLYHEDRON. It is bounded by 20 equilateral triangles. It has 12 vertices and 30 edges.

ICT *Abbreviation for* Information and Communication Technology.

ID *Abbreviation for* Internal Diameter.

IEA International Energy Agency, Paris.

IEAust Institution of Engineers, Australia, Canberra.

IEC The International Electrotechnical Commission, responsible for international standards in electrotechnology.

IEE Institution of Electrical Engineers, London.

IEEE Institute of Electrical and Electronics Engineers, Piscataway, NJ.

IES Illuminating Engineering Society. The shortened abbreviation used both by the Illuminating Engineering Society of North America (IESNA) and by the Illuminating Engineering Society of Australia and New Zealand (IESANZ).

IESANZ Illuminating Engineering Society of Australia and New Zealand.

IESNA Illuminating Engineering Society of North America.

IFC *Abbreviation for* Industry Foundation Class. Industry-defined classes of elements to be used universally in a shared project model.

IFE Institution of Fire Engineers, Leicester, UK, an engineering institution dealing with fire engineering, founded in 1918.

IFIP International Federation for Information Processing, Laxenburg, Austria.

IGES *Abbreviation for* Initial Graphics Exchange Specification. An ANSI-standard for the digital representation and exchange of information between CAD/CAM systems.

igneous rock Rock formed by the solidification of magma, injected from the Earth's interior into its crust, or extruded on its surface. Igneous rocks are classified according to whether they are predominantly acid or basic, and according to their grain size (which depends on the rate of cooling).

ignition temperature The temperature at which flammable material will ignite.

ignitor In lighting, a device used to start high pressure DISCHARGE LAMPS, particularly, metal halide and high pressure sodium, by means of very high voltage pulses usually generated electronically. In retrofit lamps these may be internal; however, it is usual to locate them externally but near to the lamp.

IL *Abbreviation for* INVERT LEVEL.

illuminance The area density of luminous flux. It is measured in LUX (LUMEN per square metre) in the SI system or (rarely) lm/ft^2 or FOOTCANDLES in the British system.

illuminance meter *Same as* LUX METER.

illuminance vector Light of the dominant direction, its magnitude and direction. Normally measured by a pair of back-to-back illuminance meters, on a goniometric mounting, with a circuit to give a readout of the difference between the two. The maximum difference (ΔE_{max}) is the vector magnitude, and the direction in which it occurs (with respect to a reference direction, measured on the horizontal plane and its altitude) is the vector direction.

illuminant *(a)* In colorimetry and photometry, the term used to describe one of the standard light sources, *e.g.* Illuminant D$_{65}$ (which simulates daylight with a CCT of 6500 K). *(b)* In lighting, the general term to refer to a light source or luminaire.

illumination *(a)* Until 1981, the Illuminating Engineering Society of North America used the term illumination for what is now called ILLUMINANCE. *(b)* The process of lighting.

illustration program *See* DRAWING PROGRAM.

image processing The processing of images using computer techniques, including image enhancement, etc.

image scale The relative size of the image compared with its actual size (usually expressed as a percentage). Most drawing and painting programs allow control over the scale of objects and entire images.

image size The actual size (measured as a horizontal quantity times a vertical quantity, usually in pixels, but sometimes in inches) of a digital image.

imaginary number A REAL NUMBER multiplied by $\sqrt{(-1)}$, usually represented by the symbol i (or j in electricity), *e.g.* i56. Thus the square root of a positive number is real, the square root of a negative number is imaginary. A COMPLEX NUMBER is the sum of real and imaginary numbers. *See also* IRRATIONAL NUMBER.

imaginary (reactive) power *See* REACTIVE (IMAGINARY) POWER.

imbricate To overlap in a regular pattern in tiles, shingles, etc.

IMechE Institution of Mechanical Engineers, London.

immersion heater An electric resistance heater immersed in a water tank.

immersion vibrator *See* VIBRATED CONCRETE.

immiscible Incapable of being mixed to form a homogeneous liquid, *e.g.* water and oil are immiscible.

impact drill A hand-held power drill that can provide a light longitudinal impact as well as rotary motion to the BIT. *Also called percussion drill. See also* ROTARY HAMMER.

impact factor A factor by which a DYNAMIC LOAD is multiplied to allow for the vertical impact which it makes on the floor. Impact factors for bridges generally range from 1.0 to 1.6. Impact factors are rarely used in the design of buildings.

impact insulation class (IIC) In acoustics, the single number rating of a floor which provides an estimate of the impact isolating performance of a floor/ceiling assembly.

impact resistance Capacity of a material to resist suddenly applied or shock loads. It is measured by the CHARPY TEST or the IZOD IMPACT TEST.

impact sound Noise transmitted through the structure of a building as a result of direct excitation by impacts on the structure, *e.g.* footsteps. Sound insulation against impact sound is best achieved by DISCONTINUOUS CONSTRUCTION. *See also* AIRBORNE SOUND, SOUND INSULATION and STRUCTUREBORNE SOUND.

impedance (electricity) Forces which resist current flow in AC circuits, i.e. resistance, inductive reactance, and capacitive reactance.

impedance tube An instrument for measuring SOUND ABSORPTION on small samples for normal (90°) sound incidence only. It consists of a long tube, with the test sample at one end. At the other end is a loudspeaker. The incident wave is partly reflected and partly absorbed by the sample, and the reflected wave interferes with the incident wave. The pressure distribution is examined with a travelling microphone which is small enough not to disturb the sound field. From the ratio of the pressures at the maximum and minimum positions, the sound reflection coefficient and the absorption coefficient can be determined. *Also called a standing-wave tube. See also* REVERBERATION CHAMBER.

impedance, acoustic *See* ACOUSTIC IMPEDANCE.

impeller The rotating element in a CENTRIFUGAL machine (pump, fan or compressor) that imparts energy to a fluid, thus increasing its pressure.

impermeable, impervious Resistant to the penetration of fluids into or through the material. *Impermeable* is commonly used to include resistance to both water and water vapour; *impervious* is commonly used to mean resistant to water.

impluvium A pool for receiving the water draining from the roof in an Ancient Roman ATRIUM. The term is not used for the pools sometimes placed in modern atria.

importance factor A building code term used to identify occupancies of importance, such as fire stations or hospitals, and apply appropriate safety factors to them.

imprecise control parameters Control parameters that cannot be defined exactly, *e.g.* comfort indices.

impregnation of timber The process of saturating timber with a preservative, such as CREOSOTE OIL.

impressed current corrosion protection CATHODIC PROTECTION of metals from corrosion by applying a small electric potential to them relative to a cathodic element, sufficient to reverse the natural direction of current flow.

impulse *See* TRANSIENT.

impulse noise A noise of short duration.

impulse response If a vibrating structure is subjected to an impulse, such as a tap from a hammer, or the air in a room is excited by a starting pistol, all the modes of vibration can be excited. A temporal record of the excitation of the modes and their decay is known as the impulse response of the resonant system.

impulse turbine A turbine which has fixed jets impinging on a moving wheel, as opposed to a REACTION TURBINE.

in situ *See* CAST IN SITU.

in-situ pile A concrete pile cast, with or without a casing, in its final location, as distinct from a pile which is precast and subsequently driven.

in. *Abbreviation for* INCH.

incandescence The production of light by a hot body, such as the filament of a lamp.

incandescent lamp *(a)* Originally a WELSBACH MANTLE impregnated with the oxides of thorium and cerium, made white-hot by a gas flame. *(b)* A small filament, usually of tungsten, placed inside a glass bulb in an inert gas, made white-hot by the passage of an electric current, *i.e.* the *electric* FILAMENT LAMP, as opposed to a FLUORESCENT LAMP or a DISCHARGE LAMP.

incentive A discount or contribution offered to a lessee of a property or facility.

inch (in.) As a measure of length, $\frac{1}{12}$ of a FOOT. The British-US inch equals 25.4 mm.

inching With manually controlled goods lifts, the use of a button or switch to move the car in small increments until it is level with the landing sill.

incident radiation The quantity of radiant energy striking a surface per unit time and unit area.

incise To cut into a material, *e.g.* masonry or wood. The term implies a shallow cut as in an engraving, rather than a sculptural carving.

inclinator A platform running on *(a)* an inclined rail for taking passengers, supplies, dustbins, etc. from the street to a house at a much higher or lower level otherwise accessible only by steps; or *(b)* internally on the side of a staircase. *See also* LIFT TYPES *(o)*.

inclinometer *Same as* CLINOMETER.

incombustible A material which does not burn in a standard test in a furnace (usually lasting 2½ hours). *Also called non-combustible.*

indented wire Wire with machine-made surface indentations. Unlike the hot-rolled deformations of DEFORMED BARS, the indentations can be cold-rolled, and therefore placed also on high-tensile wires. They are used to improve the bond, particularly in PRE-TENSIONING tendons.

index of plasticity *See* PLASTICITY INDEX.

index of thermal comfort Any of the single measures intended to provide an indication of the likelihood that the thermal condition of an enclosed space will satisfy the requirements for human comfort, for example EFFECTIVE TEMPERATURE, EQUIVALENT TEMPERATURE or PREDICTED MEAN VOTE.

indexed colour *See* COLOR LOOKUP TABLE (CLUT).

Indian standard clear sky A simple luminance distribution for the portion of a clear sky away from the sun. The luminance at any point of ALTITUDE θ is $L_\theta = L_z / \sin \theta$ for θ between 90° and 15°, and $L_\theta = L / \sin 15°$ for θ between 15°

and $0°$, where L_z is the luminance at the ZENITH. *See also* CIE STANDARD CLEAR SKY.

indicators for lifts *(a) Call accepted*: indicates when the call has been accepted. *(b) Car position*: shows the position of the car in the lift well. *(c) Car direction*: shows the direction of travel of the lift car. *(d) Next car*: indicates the next car, in sequence, to leave the floor. *(e) Car approaching*: indicates when the lift car is approaching the calling landing. Used in lift installations with very simple supervisory control systems. *(f) Lift in use*: indicates when the lift car is busy. Used in lift installations with very simple supervisory control systems. *(g) Excess load*: an indicator on the lift car operating panel, illuminated when the load exceeds the rated value. It may also give an audible alarm.

indirect evaporative cooler A device to provide EVAPORATIVE COOLING, without adding moisture to the supply air. Outdoor air is evaporatively cooled and passed through a HEAT EXCHANGER, where it cools the room air without mixing, then it is discharged. The room air is recirculated through the heat exchanger and back to the room.

indirect light sources Surfaces which, after being illuminated by other sources (direct sources such as the sun, sky or electric light, or other indirect sources), have measurable luminance and, in turn, become sources themselves.

indirect lighting Lighting reflected from a surface (usually the ceiling), rather than received directly from a luminaire, because the luminaire emits most of its light upwards.

indirect structural model analysis Analysis of a structural problem by means of a model which represents an analogy to the behaviour of the structure. It may be considered as an ANALOG COMPUTER, although the model bears a physical resemblance to the structure under investigation.

individual-mould pre-tensioning *See* PRE-TENSIONING.

inductance The ability of a coil to store energy and oppose changes in current flowing through it. A function of the cross-sectional area, number of turns of coil, length of coil and core material. Measured in henry, H.

induction box An air distribution terminal device used in some air conditioning systems in which discharge of primary air through a nozzle or nozzles induces a secondary circulation of air over a cooling or heating coil.

induction heating The production of heat utilising the principle that an eddy current is produced in an electric conductor which is subject to a changing magnetic field. The magnetic field is produced by a coil carrying an alternating current. The heater is placed within that coil.

induction unit An air distribution terminal device that uses a primary supply of conditioned air through a set of NOZZLES at comparatively high pressure to induce air flow from a room for mixing with the primary air stream.

inductive reactance A term used to describe the IMPEDANCE to alternating current offered by an inductive circuit.

inductor A coiled conductor which tends to oppose any change in the flow of current. Usually has coils wrapped around a ferrous core. *Also called choke*.

industrialised building Building with factory-made components (which may be small or comprise several rooms in one piece) to reduce the amount of work on the site. Work in the factory is deliberately increased to speed up construction and/or reduce cost. The term 'industrialised building' superseded *prefabrication* (with which it is practically synonymous) in the 1950s, after prefabricated houses had acquired a poor reputation in the late 1940s because of several unsatisfactory designs, which gave 'prefab' the quality of a term of abuse. Industrialised building may be in accordance with a CLOSED SYSTEM or an OPEN SYSTEM.

industry calorimeter A large-scale burning test facility to measure the rate of heat released by large objects, using the oxygen consumption method.

inelastic Not ELASTIC. Inelastic deformation is not immediately recovered when the load is removed. It may be permanent, *i.e.* it remains permanently when the stress is removed (*see* PLASTICITY), or it may be recoverable over a period of time (*see* CREEP).

inert gases HELIUM, NEON, ARGON and krypton, which do not react with other substances. Gases such as CARBON DIOXIDE and NITROGEN are also considered inert under some circumstances, as they do not support combustion.

inert pigment A pigment which does not undergo chemical change.

inertia The tendency of a mass to resist any change in its state of rest or motion.

inertia, moment of *See* MOMENT OF INERTIA.

infiltration of air The uncontrolled inflow of air, through openings in the building envelope caused by the dynamic pressure of the wind and the buoyant pressure of indoor–outdoor temperature differences; opposite of *exfiltration*.

infinite series A regular arrangement of mathematical terms which can be continued indefinitely. It may be CONVERGENT or non-convergent.

inflammable *Same as* FLAMMABLE, *not* the opposite. The word has been replaced by *flammable* in technical use to avoid confusion.

inflatable gasket *See* GASKET.

inflatable structure See PNEUMATIC STRUCTURE.

inflection, inflexion *Same as* CONTRA-FLEXURE.

influence line A diagram showing the effect of moving a load along a beam (frame, arch, etc.). Thus an influence line for bending moment shows the variation of bending moment *at one point* of the beam as the load (usually a concentrated unit load) is moved along the beam; by contrast, the bending moment diagram shows the variation of bending moment along the beam due to *one combination of loads.*

information Processed data in a meaningful form.

information technology A general term describing all areas of information processing using computers and telecommunications.

infrared radiant heating Heating, for human comfort or industrial processes, by exposure to infrared radiation generated by the elevated surface temperature of an emitter.

infrared radiation Radiation with wavelengths too long to be perceived by the human eye (that is, longer than 770 nm) and less than 1000 μm. Typical radiation from surfaces near room temperature is infrared radiation in the 9–10 μm region.

infrasound An acoustic oscillation where the frequency is below the lower audible limit of 16 Hz.

ingle-nook A corner by an open fire, usually with a built-in seat.

ingot A mass of metal cast into a mould. It is the raw material for rolling and forging.

inhibiting pigment A pigment which prevents corrosion of a metal surface. *See also* PRIMER.

initial flux *See* INITIAL LUMENS.

initial lumens The luminous flux emitted by a lamp when new or, in the case of discharge lamps, after about 100 hours' operation (when the lamps have stabilised). *Also called initial flux.*

initial prestress The force applied to the concrete by a TENDON at the time of the prestressing operation, before the LOSS OF PRESTRESS.

initial set Measured by the VICAT TEST.

initial stress *See* INITIAL PRESTRESS.

initial time delay gap The time between when a sound first reaches a receiving position in an auditorium and when the first reflection of the same sound reaches the same position. It is considered by some to be a useful indicator of the acoustics of an auditorium.

initialising (computing) Preparing a DISK or other storage medium to receive data, and creating a directory so that the data can be accessed. Initialising does not completely erase the disk, but it removes the information that enables any existing data to be accessed.

injection moulding The moulding of liquid plastics, liquid metal or other material by injection into a mould.

inkjet printer Computer output device in which tiny drops of ink (black and coloured) are deposited onto the paper to form a printed page or image.

inlay Forming a pattern or decoration in a wooden surface by inserting pieces of various materials including WOOD VENEER, metals, ivory, etc. *See also* MARQUETRY.

inlet guide vane control Control of the air handling capacity of a fan by adjustment of the alignment of INLET GUIDE VANES.

inlet guide vanes Guide vanes installed in the air stream at the inlet to a fan for the purpose of modifying the angle of approach of air to the impeller.

inorganic fibreboard Board made from inorganic fibres, such as fibreglass.

input In computing, information or data entered into a computer, using a keyboard, tape or graphic device.

input/output device A device for entering INPUT into a computer and/or receiving OUTPUT from it. In early computers, a *teletypewriter* often performed both functions, but now devices like keyboards and printers perform them separately.

insertion loss The difference in sound level at a receiver caused by the insertion of a device such as a duct silencer, barrier, wall, etc. between the source and receiver.

insolation The rate at which energy from the sun reaches the Earth's surface.

inspection station, lift car top *See* CAR TOP INSPECTION STATION.

instantaneous reclosing A term commonly applied to reclosing of an electric circuit breaker as quickly as possible after interrupting a fault current. Typical times are 18–30 cycles.

instantaneous water heater A non-storage water heating device. When water flow is detected, an electric element in the water stream, or a gas flame around a coil of piping, is activated to heat the water as it is needed. The control of temperature depends to some extent on the flow rate.

institutional building Building such as a hospital, school, prison, etc., occupied by a population which is neither an owner or renter (as in a house or office), nor 'general public' (as in a shop). Fittings and finishes in institutional buildings are often subject to more severe wear and tear.

insula In Ancient Rome, an apartment building occupying an entire city block.

insulating board FIBREBOARD of a density

not exceeding $400\,kg/m^3$ ($25\,lb/ft^3$), specifically designed to give good thermal insulation. *See also* ACOUSTIC BOARD.

insulating glass Two or more panes of glass that enclose hermetically sealed air spaces.

insulation *(a)* The prevention of the flow of an electric current, or the reduction of the flow of heat or passage of sound. *(b)* The material used to achieve insulation.

insulation, sound *See* SOUND INSULATION and DISCONTINUOUS CONSTRUCTION.

insulation, thermal *See* THERMAL INSULATION.

insulator A material that is a poor conductor of electricity, sound or heat.

intaglio Originally a design INCISED or carved into a material, as opposed to a design carved in RELIEF; now also used for a shallow design *pressed* into a surface.

integer A whole number, which may be positive, negative or zero. The term excludes fractions and imaginary numbers. In computing, an integer differs from a FLOATING-POINT or REAL NUMBER in the way it is stored.

integral number *Same as* INTEGER.

integral waterproofing Waterproofing concrete by an admixture to the cement or the mixing water, as opposed to using a SURFACE WATERPROOFER subsequently. It should be pointed out, however, that carefully placed concrete is often as waterproof as concrete with an admixture.

integrated building design A design procedure for a building which allows integration of input from specialist advisers to optimise performance of the whole building. For example, the lighting designer may select a high performance system at higher cost which will be offset by lower cost for a smaller refrigeration system and also a reduction in overall energy consumption.

integrated ceiling A ceiling in which the LUMINAIRES and the air conditioning ducts are integrated so that the air is exhausted through the light fittings and cools the lamps.

integrated circuit An imprint of a large number of electronic circuits, etched on to a single piece of *semiconductor* material, such as a silicon CHIP.

integrating sphere A sphere or poly-hedron with a non-selective white interior, which by inter-reflection produces a uniform illuminance on its surface. It is used to determine the LOR (light output ratio) of a luminaire.

intelligent (software) agent Software that makes the computer behave as if it has intelligence. These systems typically act as agents on behalf of the user, performing specific tasks. See ARTIFICIAL INTELLIGENCE.

intelligent building A building designed with extensive automated systems to detect, diagnose and control the response to varying environmental requirements.

intensity *(a) Radiant intensity* is the radiant flux per unit solid angle, emitted from a small radiant source in a particular direction; measured in WATTS per stera-dian. *(b) Luminous intensity* is measured in LUMENS per steradian, or in CANDELA. *(c)* In acoustics, intensity is the energy per unit area (watt/m^2) at a point in a sound field. Intensity in these instances is a VECTOR quantity having both magnitude and direction. See also MERCALLI SCALE *and* WIND LOAD. *(d)* In computer graphics, a characteristic of individual PIXELS in DIGITAL IMAGES. Intensity is a function of the reflective or luminous properties of the scene. In this instance, it is a SCALAR quantity. See also HSB COLOR.

intensive property A property of a sub-stance that is independent of mass, such as temperature or pressure. EXTENSIVE PROPERTIES can be made independent by expressing them per unit mass, *e.g.* specific volume.

interactive Relating to the use of com-puters, whereby the user and computer program interact with each other via commands, questions and answers, or graphic input.

intercolumniation The clear space between two adjacent columns, particu-larly in the Classical Orders.

interdome The space between the inner and the outer shells of a dome.

interface A connection or common boundary between two separate units, *e.g.* of a computer's HARDWARE and/or SOFTWARE, or two different modes of transportation.

interference The effect of superimposing two or more trains of waves of equal wavelength. The resultant amplitude is the algebraic sum of the amplitudes of the interfering trains. When two sets of circular waves interfere, a system of hyperbolic stationary nodes and anti-nodes is formed, which are known as *interference fringes* in the case of visible light. See also MOIRÉ FRINGES and ISOCLINICS.

interfloor distance The vertical distance between two adjacent landing floors of a lift installation.

interior span A span, other than the end span, in a CONTINUOUS BEAM. If the spans are equal, the positive bending moments are generally highest in the end span.

interior support A support, other than the end support, in a CONTINUOUS BEAM. If the spans are equal, the negative bending moment is generally highest at the first interior support.

interlayer The layer of plastic material used to join two sheets of glass in LAMI-NATED GLASS.

interlock of lift doors A device which prevents the operation of a lift-driving machine unless the car and landing doors are closed.

intermediate switch A switch used with TWO-WAY SWITCHES to alter the control of lighting from more than two locations.

intermittent kiln A *non-continuous* kiln for making bricks and other clay products, as opposed to a HOFFMANN KILN.

internal energy Energy that depends on the state of a system, *e.g.* energy con-tained in a gas stored at high pressure.

internal friction See ANGLE OF INTERNAL FRICTION.

internal memory or internal storage RAM and ROM memory contained within the main memory of a computer, as distinct from memory on removable or peripheral devices.

internal vibrator A poker CONCRETE VIBRATOR which is immersed in the con-crete.

internally reflected component The component of the DAYLIGHT FACTOR due to the internal reflecting surfaces.

International System of units *See* SI UNITS.

Internet A collection of diverse networks across the globe unified by certain communication protocols and standards. This aggregate of networks comprises a vast repository of digital information. *See also* WORLD WIDE WEB.

internetwork A collection of autonomous networks, usually having different protocols for communication. Internetworks exchange information via gateways. *See also* INTERNET.

interpolate To infer the position of a point on a graph defined by several other known points, by assuming that the curve is smooth. *Extrapolation* is the same process, continuing the graph at either end *beyond* the last known points.

interpreter Program that translates symbolic programs to binary or machine instructions for a given processor. An interpreter translates and causes the execution of one single instruction of a source program at a time, as opposed to a COMPILER. *See also* HIGH-LEVEL PROGRAMMING LANGUAGES.

interruption, momentary (power quality monitoring) A type of short duration variation. The complete loss of voltage on one or more phase conductors for a time period between 30 cycles and 3 seconds.

interruption, sustained (electric power systems) Any interruption longer than a momentary interruption.

interruption, sustained (power quality) A type of long duration variation. The complete loss of voltage (<0.1 pu) on one or more phase conductors for a time greater than 1 minute.

interruption, temporary A type of short duration variation. The complete loss of voltage on one or more phase conductors for a time period between 3 seconds and 1 minute.

interstitial condensation CONDENSATION which occurs within spaces inside the construction, as opposed to *surface* condensation. It is likely to dry out more slowly than moisture on the surface, and is therefore more likely to cause WET ROT or corrosion.

interval time (for lifts) *See* TIME INTERVAL.

intimacy A term used in concert hall acoustics to describe how close performers sound to the audience.

intrados The inner or lower curve of an arch.

intranet An organised collection of networks, usually restricted to a single organisation, for the sharing of information internally. Intranets are usually secure in that only members of the organisation may access their information and services (*see* INTERNET).

intrinsic insulation The thermal insulation provided by the actual items of clothing worn by an individual at any given time.

intruder detector A device used in a security system, to detect the presence of a person. Most of these devices cannot determine whether the person is an intruder or an authorised person.

intumescent paint A paint of normal appearance until a fire occurs, when the heat causes it to form a thick insulating layer. It is mainly used for the fire protection of steel.

inverse square law The intensity of sound or illuminance in a *free field* is inversely proportional to the square of the distance from the source.

inversion (of temperature) A meteorological state which causes the temperature to rise with height above ground instead of falling. Since the colder and heavier air is below, there is no tendency for the air to rise, and turbulence is suppressed. If inversion occurs at a high level above the ground (upwards of 300 m or 1000 ft), it acts as a lid, preventing the ascent of chimney plumes and the escape of automobile exhaust gases. This increases air pollution. *See also* SMOG.

invert level The level of the lowest portion at any given section of the inside surface of a drain, sewer or other liquid-carrying conduit. It determines the HYDRAULIC GRADIENT available for moving the liquid in the conduit.

inverter A device used to convert DC current to AC current. Inverters may be mechanical (motor), ferroresonant or solid state.

investment casting A method of casting complicated shapes accurately and with good surface finish. First, a wax model of the finished item is produced, and this is coated with a refractory slurry which sets at room temperature. Then the wax is removed by melting, and the molten metal is poured into the refractory mould. Often used to produce SPIDERS for frameless glass applications and NODES for cable networks.

invisible fixing Fixing of materials with adhesives or double-sided tape, or with brackets or other hardware attached to the back surface so as to be invisible on the face.

ion A molecule, atom, or group of atoms, which carries a charge, either positive or negative.

ionisation anemometer A remote reading instrument for measuring low air speeds which is less sensitive to natural convection than the HOT-WIRE ANEMOMETER. It consists of a sphere coated with radioactive material which is surrounded by a collecting cage and an earthed screen.

ionisation smoke detector A *fire detector* which monitors the electrical conductivity of ionised air, and detects the presence of smoke by comparing it with a sealed reference chamber.

ionosphere *See* ATMOSPHERIC LAYERS.

IPENZ Institution of Professional Engineers New Zealand, Wellington, formerly called NZIE.

IRC *Abbreviation for* Internally Reflected Component (of the daylight factor).

IRC Institute for Research in Construction, Ottawa, part of NRC.

iridescence The play of the colours of the spectrum on a surface. It is produced by interference of light reflected from the front and back of a very thin film.

iron A metallic element which exists in the three forms of ALPHA IRON, GAMMA IRON and *delta iron*. Its chemical symbol is Fe, its atomic number is 26, its atomic weight is 55.84, its specific gravity is 7.87, and its melting point is 1535 °C. *See also* WROUGHT IRON, STEEL *and* CAST IRON.

iron carbide A hard and brittle crystalline compound of iron and carbon (Fe_3C), *also called cementite*. It is a constituent of high-carbon steel and of cast iron.

iron oxides Apart from their use as a raw material from which metallic iron is made, the oxides also provide a number of traditional *mineral pigments*, mostly named after the place in Italy from which

they were originally obtained. Haematite (Fe_2O_3) provides *venetian red*. Magnetite (Fe_3O_4) provides purple and black pigments. Ferrous oxide (FeO) is the main ingredient of *ochre* (yellow), *sienna* (yellow) and *burnt sienna*. It is one of the ingredients of *umber* (dark brown), manganese oxide being the major constituent.

irradiance The (instantaneous) area density of radiant flux, with the units W/m^2.

irradiation The area density of incident radiant energy over a stated time period, or integration of irradiance over that time period, with the units of J/m^2 or Wh/m^2.

irrational number A REAL NUMBER which cannot be expressed as a fraction of two integers. $\sqrt{2}$ and π are irrational, but not IMAGINARY, numbers. *See also* RATIONAL NUMBER.

irreversible process A thermal process that can proceed in a given direction but cannot be reversed, *e.g.* the energy lost in overcoming friction in a thermodynamic process.

ISI Indian Standards Institution, Delhi. Now called Bureau of Indian Standards (BSI).

ISO International Organization for Standardization, Geneva. A worldwide federation of national standards bodies.

isobaric process A process that occurs at constant pressure.

isobars Curves relating points at the same pressure, *e.g.* atmospheric or barometric pressure.

isochromatics Lines of equal colour; in PHOTOELASTICITY the colour fringes denote lines of equal difference between the principal stresses. When MONOCHROMATIC light is used, the fringes are black and white, but the term 'isochromatic' is still applied; they can be separated from the ISOCLINICS with QUARTER-WAVE PLATES.

isoclinics Lines in a stressed body which connect the points at which the principal stresses have the same direction. In photoelastic analysis the light is extinguished when the direction of polarisation is the same as that of the principal stresses, and the isoclinics thus show up as dark lines superimposed on the ISOCHROMATICS.

isohyets Lines drawn on a map through places having equal amounts of rainfall.

isolation Separation of one part of a system from undesired influences of other parts. This can include: *(a)* the reduction of vibration or structure-borne sound, which usually involves resilient surfaces or mountings or discontinuous construction (*see also* VIBRATION ISOLATOR and RUBBER MOUNTING); *(b)* the separation of parts of a facility or building by FIRE-RESISTANT CONSTRUCTION; *(c)* the separation of parts of an electrical installation from other parts or from the electrical supply.

isolation transformer A transformer that contains electrostatic shields between primary and secondary windings, and no direct electrical path between primary and secondary, as opposed to an AUTO-TRANSFORMER.

isolator *See* VIBRATION ISOLATOR.

isolux (isofootcandle) line A line plotted on any appropriate set of coordinates to show all the points on a surface where the daylight illuminance is the same. A series of such lines for various illuminance values is called an isolux (isofootcandle) diagram.

isomers Molecules with the same composition, but with different structures.

isometric projection A pictorial PROJECTION in which the elevation, the plan and the side elevation are all drawn at an angle. Vertical lines remain vertical, but all lines which are horizontal in the ORTHOGRAPHIC PROJECTION are drawn at 30° to the horizontal in the isometric projection. While the plan, elevation and side elevation are all given equal prominence, the object frequently appears distorted. However, all dimensions on the vertical and on the 30° axes are accurately to scale.

isopleth A line on a chart or map connecting points of equal value, *e.g.* of a meteorological variable, such as temperature.

isosceles Equal-legged. An isosceles triangle has two equal sides. A triangle with three equal sides is *equilateral.*

isostatic line A line tangential to the direction of one of the PRINCIPAL STRESSES at every point through which it passes. *Also called stress trajectory.* It is useful for visualising STRESS CONCENTRATIONS.

isostatic structure *Same as* STATICALLY DETERMINATE STRUCTURE.

isothermal *(a)* A line on a thermodynamic, psychrometric or meteorological chart connecting points of equal temperature. *(b)* A reaction proceeding at a constant temperature. An isothermal change cannot normally be ADIABATIC.

isotopes Atoms of the same chemical element with identical chemical properties, but different atomic masses. The *atomic mass* of the entire element is determined by the proportions in which the various isotopes are present. Some isotopes are radioactive; but the term 'isotope' does not imply radioactivity as such, although it is often used that way.

isotropic Having the same properties in all directions, as opposed to AELOTROPIC. In structural theory, the term usually means having the same strength, MODULUS OF ELASTICITY and POISSON'S RATIO in all directions.

IStructE Institution of Structural Engineers, London.

IT *Abbreviation for* INFORMATION TECHNOLOGY.

Italian tile A type of PAN TILE.

ITBTP *Institut Technique du Bâtiment et des Travaux Publics*, Paris.

ITS *Abbreviation for* Index of Thermal Stress. A theoretically derived thermal comfort index, based on a biophysical model of the body-environment thermal system, developed by B. Givoni (1963).

I–V curve The plot of current versus voltage characteristics of a solar cell, module or array. I–V curves are used to compare various solar cell modules, and to determine their performance at various levels of insolation and temperature.

Izod impact test An impact test carried out on a notched specimen which is cantilevered from one end. The energy absorbed during fracture is measured with a pendulum.

J

J *Abbreviation for* JOULE.

jack A portable machine for lifting heavy loads through short distances. It may be operated by a square-threaded screw or by a hydraulic ram.

jack arch *(a)* A shallow arch of brick or plain concrete, spanning about 1 m (3 ft), used in the nineteenth century. *(b)* A FLAT ARCH.

jackblock method A method for erecting a multi-storey prestressed concrete building, while carrying out most of the construction at ground level. The ground-floor slab is cast first, and serves as a casting bed for the other floors. The roof slab is cast next, and jacked up one floor. The top floor and its load-bearing walls are then constructed and jacked up one floor, and so on.

jackhammer *See* DEMOLITION HAMMER.

jambs The vertical side posts used in the framing of a doorway or window. The outer part of the jamb, which is visible, is called the *reveal*.

Japanese lacquer An extremely durable glossy varnish obtained from tapping the sap of the Japanese varnish tree *(Rhus vernicifera)*.

Japanese mat *See* TATAMI.

Java An *object-oriented programming* language developed by Sun Microsystems, Inc. to create executable content (i.e. self-running applications) that can be easily distributed through NETWORKS like the INTERNET.

jib The (inclined) member of a crane from which the load is suspended, providing positioning of the load. *See also* BOOM.

jigsaw A narrow-bladed reciprocating saw for cutting thin material, and particularly for cutting curved shapes.

jockey pump A small pump used to replenish minor water loss, to avoid starting a large automatic suction or booster pump unnecessarily.

joggle *(a)* To bend a steel angle to make it fit as a web stiffener over the angles at the top and bottom of a built-up girder. *(b)* A form of tongue-and-groove joint in stone or precast concrete.

Johansen's method The YIELD-LINE THEORY for the ultimate strength of reinforced concrete slabs.

joinery Detailed woodwork for the finishing stages of a building, including doors and windows (if of timber), trim and shelving.

joint The space between two adjacent components, irrespective of whether it is filled with a jointing material or not.

joint in brickwork The principal mortar joints for brickwork are *(a)* flush joints, *(b)* RAKED JOINTS, *(c)* tooled joints, *(d)* STRUCK JOINTS and *(e)* weather-struck joints *(see figure).*

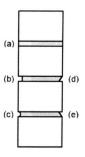

Joints in brickwork

joint sealant or filler Material used to exclude water and foreign solid matter from joints. *See also* MASTIC *(b)*.

jointer *See* PLANER.

jointing tape Tape used to reinforce a joint, such as the joints between sheets in DRY WALL construction.

jointless flooring A term used for MAGNESITE FLOORING.

joist A small BEAM. It is generally the member which directly supports the floor or roof, as opposed to a GIRDER. A *steel joist* may be a ROLLED STEEL JOIST or an OPEN-WEB JOIST.

joist hanger Formed steel stirrup used to support the end of timber joists and transmit loads to a beam.

joule (J) Unit of energy, named after the nineteenth-century English physicist, J. P. Joule. It is the energy dissipated in 1 second by a current of 1 ampere flowing across a potential difference of 1 volt. In SI UNITS the joule also replaces the erg and the calorie; 1 joule = 10^7 erg = 0.239 calories.

Joule's laws The three laws of the nineteenth-century English physicist, J. P. Joule, are as follows. *(a)* The intrinsic energy of a given mass of gas is a function of temperature alone; it is independent of the pressure and volume of the gas. *(b)* The molecular heat of a solid compound is equal to the sum of the atomic heats of its component elements in the solid state. *(c)* The heat produced by a current *I* passing through a conductor of resistance *R* for a time *t* is proportional to I^2Rt.

Joule's mechanical equivalent *See* MECHANICAL EQUIVALENT OF HEAT.

Jourawski's method The method of RESOLUTION AT THE JOINTS.

joystick A lever controlling the movement of a CURSOR on a screen.

JPEG A LOSSY COMPRESSION standard for digitised photographic images, standardised by the Joint Photographic Experts Group.

jump form A type of *formwork* system in which the formwork for the vertical surfaces of a wall or shaft are prefabricated, usually one storey high. After the concrete has gained sufficient strength, the forms are released and lifted to the next storey level without substantial dismantling. *See also* SLIPFORM.

K

K *(a)* Chemical symbol for *potassium* (kalium, the latinised version of the Arabic *alkali*). *(b)* (Degree) *Kelvin*. *(c) Abbreviation for* 1000.

k *Abbreviation for kilo*, 1000 times.

kalsomine A cheap white or tinted wash made of WHITING and glue mixed with water. *Also spelled calcimine.*

kaolin A pure white form of hydrated aluminium silicate, resulting from the decomposition of FELSPARS contained in igneous rock. It is the raw material for the best quality pottery (*porcelain*). *Also called china clay.*

kaolinite A finely crystalline form of hydrated aluminium silicate $(Al_2Si_2O_5(OH)_4)$.

kata thermometer Instrument devised by L. Hill in 1914 to measure the physiological effect of the environment, and determine the COMFORT ZONE; it can also be employed as an ANEMOMETER. It is an alcohol thermometer with a large bulb. It is now rarely used.

katabatic wind A local, cold wind flowing down a hillside. High-altitude ground cools more rapidly at night than that at lower altitudes due to virtually unimpeded radiation exchange to the sky. Thus, the air is chilled, becomes denser and flows down the hillside.

kathode *Same as* CATHODE.

Kb, KB or kb *Abbreviation for* KILOBYTE.

K-bracing Bracing for a TRUSS or wall in the form of a K. It is used in place of DIAGONAL bracing when door openings have to be accommodated (*see figure*).

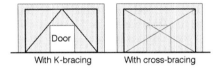

With K-bracing   With cross-bracing

K-bracing

KBS *Abbreviation for* KNOWLEDGE-BASED SYSTEM.

Keene's cement A hard plaster used for finishing coats. It consists of ANHYDRITE, *i.e.* anhydrous gypsum plaster $(CaSO_4)$, and an ACCELERATOR. It can be applied over Portland cement rendering, but should not be mixed with lime. *Also called Parian plaster.*

Kelly ball test *See* BALL TEST.

Kelvin (K) The temperature scale referred to absolute zero, which is $-273.15\,°C$.

kentledge Ballast used to give stability to a crane, provide a reaction for a jack, etc. It may consist of scrap iron, concrete, or any heavy building material.

kerf A slot or cut in a material, particularly the cut made by a saw.

kerosene A fuel oil originally distilled from coal and oil shale, and later from petroleum. It was widely used for lighting and heating before gas and electricity became available, and is still used for that purpose where an electrical supply is not readily available.

Kevlar The trade mark name of an aromatic POLYAMIDE fibre of exceptional strength, comparable to that of steel.

key *(a)* In construction, a mechanical bond, *e.g.* between old and new concrete. *(b)* In computing, an index used to identify an item such as a record in a file.

(c) A button on a keyboard used for entering a character.

key frames One of the techniques for video COMPRESSION is to choose selected frames (called 'key frames') and compute the differences between consecutive key frames, and compute (rather than store) the frames in between these frames upon playback.

keyboard A device containing a set of keys for entering characters.

keyed alike Indicates that two or more locks are designed to be opened by identical keys.

keypad A small keyboard, usually handheld, with a character set usually restricted to numerals and numeric operation keys.

keystone The stone at the CROWN of an arch. A VOUSSOIR arch becomes self-supporting only after the keystone has been placed in position. Hence it was frequently made larger, and especially decorated. Since the keystone need only resist the horizontal thrust, it is less heavily loaded than any of the stones lower down the arch.

keyway The profile of the opening or *broach* in a lock into which the key fits. It therefore defines the profile of the key.

kg *Abbreviation for* kilogram.

kgf *Abbreviation for kilogram-force*, also used for KILOPOND.

kick plate Plate used at the bottom of cabinets, doors, lift car enclosures and step risers to protect them from shoe marks. *Also spelled kickplate.*

kieselguhr *Same as* DIATOMACEOUS EARTH.

kiln A large oven used for the artificial seasoning of timber, for the firing of pottery, for the baking of brick, for the burning of lime, or for the burning of cement clinker. *See also* HOFFMANN KILN and INTERMITTENT KILN.

kiln dried Wood that has been seasoned mechanically in a kiln, as opposed to natural SEASONING.

kilo (k) Prefix for one thousand times, from the Greek word for 1000, *e.g.* 1 kg = 1000 gram.

kilobyte 2^{10} (= 1024) BYTES, which is approximately 1000 bytes. The power of 2 is used because computers employ BINARY ARITHMETIC.

kilomega Prefix meaning 10^9 (one thousand million). The prefix used in SI UNITS is GIGA.

kilometre (km) The metric measure for longer distances, 1000 metres. 1 km = 0.62137 miles.

kilopond The unit of force in CGS UNITS. It is not used in SI UNITS. It is the gravitational pull on a mass of 1 kilogram. The abbreviations *kp*, *kgf* (kilogram-force) and *kg* are all in use, and have the same meaning if applied to forces. 1 kp = 9.807 NEWTON.

kilowatt hour (kWh) A unit of energy, equal to 1000 WATT HOURS. 1 kWh = 3.6 MJ.

kinematic viscosity The ratio of viscosity to density.

kinematics The study of the geometry of motion in time and space. It is used to relate displacement, velocity, acceleration and time without reference to the cause of the motion.

kinetic energy The ENERGY which a body possesses by virtue of its motion.

kinetic friction, coefficient of The ratio of the FRICTION to the contact pressure required to *maintain* motion against frictional resistance.

king closer A three-quarter brick used as a closer. A diagonal piece is cut off one corner *(see figure). See also* HALF BAT *and* QUEEN CLOSER.

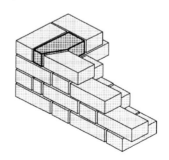

King closer

king post The vertical tie in a KING-POST ROOF TRUSS.

king-post roof truss A traditional timber truss consisting of a pair of rafters, held by a horizontal tie beam, a vertical *king post* between the tie-beam and the ridge, and usually also two struts to the rafters from the foot of the king post *(see figure)*. Contrary to first impression, the king post is usually in tension.

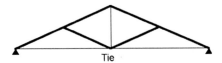

King-post roof truss

kiosk A small pavilion, usually without walls, originally in a Turkish garden. Now also used for small buildings selling newspapers and other merchandise.
kip An abbreviation popular in the USA for kilopounds (1000 lb).
kL *Abbreviation for* kilolitre, same as the volume m³.
knapped flint FLINT split in half and used with the split side showing.
kneebrace A diagonal member joining the top of a column to the roof truss, used to improve resistance to wind loading *(see figure)*.

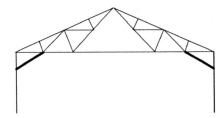

Kneebrace

knocked down Prefabricated, but not assembled.
knockout A removable section of a junction or outlet box to accommodate installation of a conduit.
knot *(a)* A branch or limb embedded in a tree, and cut through in the process of manufacture. It may be a source of weakness (comparable to a hole drilled into the timber) if it is *loose, hollow* or *decayed*. On the other hand, a *sound, tight* or *intergrown* knot may be relatively harmless. *(b)* A unit of speed, equal to 1 NAUTICAL MILE per hour.
knotting compound Sealer used to cover KNOTS *(a)* and other imperfections in timber, to stop natural resins from seeping out through the paint finish.
knowledge base That part of a KNOWLEDGE-BASED SYSTEM where the knowledge is stored without explicit control or procedures.
knowledge engineering The process of acquiring and representing knowledge in a form suitable for use by knowledge-based systems.
knowledge-based systems Computer systems which represent and manipulate knowledge explicitly. They separate the knowledge from its control as opposed to conventional (procedural) systems. *See* EXPERT SYSTEMS.
knurl To mill or otherwise roughen a surface to provide a better grip, *e.g.* on the head of a thumb screw.
Köppen–Geiger climate classification The system of climate classification, created by Köppen (1900), based on vegetation, but revised in 1918 on the basis of temperature, rainfall and seasonal variation. Later revised with the cooperation of Geiger (1936). Five main categories are distinguished: *(a)* tropical, *(b)* dry, *(c)* warm temperate, *(d)* snow climates and *(e)* ice, or polar climate. There are two further levels of subdivision, giving a total of 28 climate types.
kp *Abbreviation for* KILOPOND.
kraft paper A strong brown paper, made from wood pulp and sulphate.
ksi *Abbreviation for* kilo-pounds per square inch, or thousands of pounds per square inch.
kVA *Abbreviation for* kilovolt-amperes. kVA is the actual measured power (apparent power) and is used for circuit sizing. *See also* POWER FACTOR.
k-value An obsolete abbreviation for THERMAL CONDUCTIVITY (W/m.K) which is now denoted λ.
kW *Abbreviation for* kilowatt = 1000 watt.
kWh *Abbreviation for* kilowatt hour.
Kyoto Protocol An international agreement to reduce emissions of GREENHOUSE GASES by the developed nations. It is yet to be ratified by a sufficient number of the signatories to become international law.

L

λ **(lambda)** *(a)* Symbol for wavelength (both of light and sound). *(b)* Symbol for THERMAL CONDUCTIVITY of materials, that was in the past denoted as *k-value*.
L *Abbreviation for* litre.
labyrinth cooling A massive structural labyrinth arrangement, usually under a building, configured so that ventilation air is channelled through the passages. Heat is removed from the massive structure during cool summer nights and ventilation air is cooled by contact during hot days.
lac Purified SHELLAC.
lacquer A glossy finish which dries quickly by evaporation of the vehicle. *See also* JAPANESE LACQUER *and* VARNISH.
lag screw, lag bolt US term for a COACH SCREW.
lagging Insulating material applied to the outside of heating equipment and pipes to prevent heat loss.
lagging load An inductive electrical load, with current lagging voltage. Since inductors tend to resist changes in current, the current flow through an inductive circuit will lag behind the voltage.
laitance A layer containing cement and very fine aggregate brought to the surface of concrete by BLEEDING. It has poor durability and strength, and generally is removed if it forms.
lake A pigment which consists of a DYE precipitated on an inorganic base.
lambert An obsolete measure of LUMINANCE, equal to 3183 candela per square metre.
Lambert's cosine law *See* COSINE LAW.
lamella roof A roof frame consisting of a series of intersecting skew arches, made up of relatively short members, called lamellas, fastened together at an angle so that each is intersected by two similar adjacent members at its midpoint, forming a network of interlocking diamonds.
laminar flow *Same as* STREAMLINE FLOW.
laminated arch A wooden arch made from LAMINATED TIMBER.
laminated glass Two or more layers of glass bonded with polyvinyl butyral.
laminated plastic A stiff board made from sheets of paper, cloth, linen or silk, soaked with synthetic resin (*e.g.* MELAMINE RESIN) and sandwiched between layers of that resin. One side is usually given a glossy or matt decorative finish. Laminated plastics imitating wood are produced by printing the grain of the wood, from a photograph, on a sheet of paper, which forms the top lamination.
laminated timber Timber beam or arch manufactured from four or more wood layers, each about 25 mm (1 in.) in thickness, bonded together with waterproof adhesive. It differs from PLYWOOD, which is made from thinner layers, and in the form of sheets, some of them with the grain running in the cross direction.
laminated veneer lumber (LVL) Structural timber made of many layers of WOOD VENEER, laminated together with adhesive. Whereas PLYWOOD has the layers of veneer laid in alternate directions, LVL has them all laid in the long direction of the member. *See also* GLULAM.
laminating The process of bonding *laminations*, or thin plates, together with adhesive.
lamp An electrically energised source of light, commonly called a bulb or tube.
lamp base The means by which an electric lamp is supported by the LAMPHOLDER. It also makes the electrical connection. *See* BAYONET CAP *and* EDISON CAP.
lamp black *Same as* CARBON BLACK.
lamp dimmer Variable resistance or, more typically, other electronic device, which controls the amount of light by varying the voltage or waveform to the lamp.
lamp lumen depreciation The decrease over time of lamp lumen output, caused by bulb wall blackening, phosphor exhaustion, filament depreciation and other factors.
lampholder The device which mechanically supports and electrically connects a lamp.
LAN *Abbreviation for* LOCAL AREA NETWORK.
lancet arch An arch that is so sharply pointed that the centres of curvature of the two arcs are further apart than the width of the arch (*See figure*).

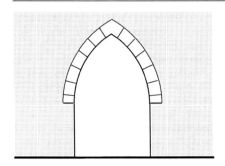

Lancet arch

landing *(a)* The portion of floor or corridor adjacent to a lift entrance where passengers enter or leave the lift cars. *(b)* A level space within a stair, usually at a change in direction, but also within a long straight flight to provide rest and safety for persons using the stair.

landlord and tenant A phrase used to refer to the contractual relationship between the two parties.

langley An obsolete unit of solar radiation measurement. 1 langley = 1 calorie per square centimetre = 41 868 J/m^2.

lantern *(a)* A LUMINAIRE, particularly a light in a street or garden. *(b)* A circular or polygonal turret with windows all around, crowning a DOME or other roof.

lap The length by which one piece of material overlaps another.

lap joint A joint between two pieces of material which overlap, as opposed to a BUTT JOINT. *(a)* In metal, the two pieces of material to be joined are generally not in line, and are joined by bolting or welding *(see figure)*. *(b)* In timber, the pieces are generally halved, which makes it possible to align them. For *timber lap joints at right angles see* DOVETAIL *and* END-LAP JOINT.

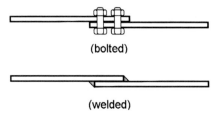

(bolted)

(welded)

Lap joint

lapis lazuli A decorative variety of calcite, stained a deep blue by three minerals (lazurite, sodalite and hauyne). It is used as a stone veneer, and in powdered form it is the original ULTRAMARINE pigment.

lapping of reinforcing steel The overlapping of steel bars or fabric to provide transfer of stress from one piece of steel to the next through BOND with the concrete. *Same as* SPLICE.

large calorie *Same as kilocalorie* = 1000 cal.

large numbers *See* LAW OF LARGE NUMBERS.

larry A long-handled hoe with a perforated blade, used for mixing plaster or mortar.

laser An intense monochromatic source of coherent radiation (either visible light or infrared), capable of being focused into a very narrow, non-divergent beam. Used in surveying for both alignment and distance measurement, and for communications. (The name is an acronym for Light Amplification by Stimulated Emission of Radiation.)

laser disc *See* COMPACT DISK.

laser-cut panel Usually a transparent acrylic sheet, with grooves cut by a laser beam at quite close spacings, almost throughout its thickness, to form a series of prisms to bend a light beam. Can be used for daylighting (to redirect the solar beam onto the ceiling), but also for solar control, to return the high angle solar beam to the outside, but admit a low angle beam.

laser-induced fluorescence A technique to measure the concentration of a particular chemical, based on fluorescence induced by a laser of a particular frequency.

latch A device for holding a door closed by means of a bolt which engages a STRIKE. The latch automatically engages when the door is closed. It can be opened by a knob or lever and does not lock.

late wood *Same as* SUMMER WOOD.

latent heat Thermal energy expended in changing the state of a body without changing its temperature, *e.g.* converting water to steam at 100°C. *See also* SENSIBLE HEAT.

lateral buckling BUCKLING of a deep, narrow beam sideways. It is prevented by limiting the ratio of depth to width, or by providing LATERAL SUPPORT.

lateral loading *See* EARTHQUAKE LOADING *and* WIND PRESSURE.

lateral reinforcement Ties, hoops, helical or other secondary reinforcement used in concrete columns, as opposed to the main or longitudinal reinforcement. *Also called transverse reinforcement.*

lateral support The horizontal propping of a beam or column to reduce its EFFECTIVE LENGTH. *See also* HERRINGBONE STRUTTING *and* SOLID BRIDGING.

latex Originally the viscous, milky fluid which is exuded when the rubber tree *(Hevea brasiliensis)* is tapped. It is a colloid of caoutchouc dispersed in water, which forms rubber by coagulation. The term is now also applied to artificial emulsions of natural or artificial rubber, or of certain synthetic resins (such as polyvinyl acetate), used in EMULSION PAINTS.

lath Originally a sawn strip of timber, 25–40 mm wide and 6–10 mm thick (1½ in. × ¼ to ⅜ in.), fixed to timber framing with small gaps between adjacent laths, used as a foundation for plastering. Now applied to other materials used for the same purpose, *e.g. metal lathing.*

lathe A machine for turning metal or wood. The piece to be turned is mounted on a face plate, in a chuck, or between two centres, and the cutting tool is stationary. The cutting speed is higher for small-diameter pieces and for soft materials (such as wood). *See also* MILLING MACHINE.

latitude The angle subtended by any point on the Earth's surface with the equator, measured along its MERIDIAN. Except for the equator, the parallels of latitude are SMALL CIRCLES, and thus not GEODETIC LINES. They correspond to curved lines on a plane surface, and travelling along them is not the shortest distance between two points.

latrine A TOILET, generally in military or institutional usage.

lattice structure An open girder *(open-web joist)*, column, cylindrical shell, dome *(geodesic dome)* or other structural type, built up from members intersecting diagonally to form a lattice.

Lattice structures may be built in any material, but lightness is usually a prime objective.

lattice window *Same as* LEADED LIGHT.

lava The molten IGNEOUS rock material which issues from a volcanic fissure or vent, and consolidates on the surface as OBSIDIAN or PUMICE.

lavatory Literally, a wash basin. By extension, a room containing a wash basin and a WC, and a room containing a WC without a wash basin.

law of large numbers 'If n successes are obtained in N trials of an event, then the ratio n/N approaches a fixed probability as N increases.' This is one of the basic postulates of STATISTICS.

lay The number of helix diameters in which the strand of a cable or wire rope makes one complete turn of 360° in its helix. The lay of a cable may be right-hand or left-hand, the former being the more common.

lay bar A horizontal SASH BAR.

lay light A window fixed horizontally in a ceiling.

layer In computer-aided drawing, a grouping of objects for convenience of display. Equivalent to a transparent overlay.

layer, neutral *See* NEUTRAL AXIS.

layering The process of dividing a drawing into separate LAYERS, each representing a different component of the whole drawing.

lazy susan *Same as* REVOLVING SHELF.

lb *Abbreviation for* POUND.

L-beam A beam whose section has the form of an inverted L. It is usually formed by the combination of an edge beam (or SPANDREL) and the adjacent portion of the floor slab. *See also* EFFECTIVE FLANGE WIDTH.

lbf Symbol for pound as a force, *i.e.* the gravitational pull on a mass of 1 lb. The symbol *lb* is frequently used both for mass and for force.

LC circuit An electrical network containing both inductive and capacitive elements.

LCD *Abbreviation for* Liquid Crystal Display.

lead A grey metal which is soft and easily deformed plastically at room temperature;

however, at a sufficiently low temperature it shows elastic behaviour. Because of its corrosion resistance and the ease with which it can be formed it was widely used for pipes, roofing, flashings and damp-proof courses. Due to its increasing cost, and recognition of its toxicity, it has largely been replaced by other less easily worked materials. Lead is an excellent insulator against radiation, including X-RAYS, and also a good sound insulator in the form of limp panels. Its symbol is Pb, its atomic number is 82, its atomic weight is 207.21, its specific gravity is 11.34, and its melting point is 327.3 °C. *See also* BLACK, RED *and* WHITE LEAD.

lead monoxide Litharge (PbO).

lead paint Usually synonymous with WHITE LEAD, an exterior undercoat containing basic lead carbonate. Now generally superseded by paints containing oxides of zinc or titanium. (Lead paints are considered to present a long-term health hazard.)

lead primer *Same as* RED LEAD, which contains red oxide of lead.

lead time The time between the ordering of a building component and its delivery to the building site.

lead-free paint Paint containing no lead compounds, in particular no WHITE LEAD.

lead-lined door A door lined internally with sheets of lead, as a protection from radiation. *See also* HIGH-DENSITY CONCRETE.

leaded light A window consisting of relatively small pieces of glass, often diamond shaped, held in lead strips of H-section (called *cames*). *Also called a lattice window.* The method evolved in the Middle Ages, because of the difficulty of making large sheets of glass; it became obsolete in the seventeenth century with the perfection of the broadglass process, but it was revived in the nineteenth century.

leading load A capacitive electrical load, with current leading voltage. Since capacitors resist changes in voltage, the current flow in a capacitive circuit will lead the voltage.

leaf In brickwork, *same as* WYTHE.

lean concrete A concrete with a low cement content, as opposed to a *rich concrete.*

lean-to roof *Same as* SHED ROOF.

learning curve A decrease in the cycle time due to increased experience.

lease An agreement granting possession of a property for a specified time period, usually for a specified payment or rent, without conferring ownership.

lease expiry The date on which the period of a lease ends and possession of the leased premises returns to the lessor.

lease proposal A preliminary offer of terms to be included in a LEASE.

lease term The period for which the tenant has possession of the premises.

leaseback A transaction that occurs when a property owner sells a property to another, who subsequently leases back possession of the property to the original owner.

leasehold improvements Improvements, such as repairs, maintenance, additions, made by the LESSEE during the lease period.

least squares *See* METHOD OF LEAST SQUARES.

leaving temperature The temperature of a fluid leaving a heat exchanger, *e.g.* air leaving a cooling coil.

LED *Abbreviation for* Light Emitting Diode. Originally used for small indicator lights, but now available with higher intensity suitable for some decorative lighting applications.

ledger A main horizontal member of wooden or steel formwork. It is normally supported on the vertical scaffold poles (uprights) and it in turn supports the SOFFIT of the formwork, or the PUTLOGS which support the soffit.

LEED *Abbreviation for* Leadership in Energy and Environmental Design, a voluntary, consensus-based national (US) rating system for developing high-performance, sustainable buildings.

leeward On the side sheltered from the wind, as opposed to *windward.*

Legionella pneumophila The micro-organism responsible for LEGIONNAIRES' DISEASE. It colonises places where warm water collects and it may be carried in aerosol drifts into fresh air intakes in buildings.

legionnaires' disease A disease of the lungs that can be fatal, caused by inhalation of aerosols bearing LEGIONELLA PNEUMOPHILA organisms.

lehr Furnace for melting or annealing glass.

lengthening joint A joint between two pieces of material, normally timber, which run in the same direction, as opposed to an *angle joint*. Most lengthening joints are END JOINTS.

lessee The recipient of the right to possession and use of a property under a LEASE agreement.

lessor The owner of a property granting the right to possession and use under a LEASE agreement.

level *See* DATUM LINE, DEAD LEVEL, DUMPY LEVEL, QUICKSET LEVEL, SPIRIT LEVEL *and* WATER LEVEL. *See also* SOUND PRESSURE LEVEL.

level 1 The lowest level in a multi-storey building. The FIRST FLOOR is generally at a higher level.

level, spirit *See* SPIRIT LEVEL.

levelling The determination of differences in level between various points on a site *(see figure)*. Sights are taken through a DUMPY LEVEL on a graduated staff placed vertically on the ground at various points where levels are required. The differences between the graduations on the staff, as seen through the telescope, equal the differences in level.

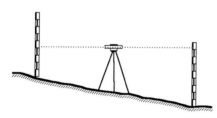

Levelling

levelling device (lift installations) A mechanism which moves a lift car at a reduced speed toward the landing, when it is in the LEVELLING ZONE, and stops it there. *See also* RE-LEVELLING.

levelling zone A distance near to each landing floor where a lift car slows and moves under fine control towards the floor.

lever arm The distance between the resultant tensile force and the resultant compressive force at a section. These two forces and the lever arm form the MOMENT OF RESISTANCE. *See figure under* COUPLE.

lever principle The principle used for the composition and resolution of parallel forces. If a lever is in equilibrium under the action of a number of parallel forces, then the sum of the moments of these forces about any point is zero. The principle was discovered by *Archimedes of Syracuse* ca. 250 BCE, and reputedly used by him to devise machines for throwing missiles in the defence of Syracuse when it was attacked by the Romans.

lewis A steel contrivance for gripping heavy blocks of stone for lifting. It consists of a DOVETAILed tenon, made in sections, which is fitted into a dovetailed recess in the stone *(see figure)*.

lewis bolt A steel anchor bolt with an enlarged conical lewis-shaped base, generally with a roughened surface *(see figure)*. It is fixed into concrete by casting it in during construction, or by leaving a hole in the concrete, and grouting it in later. It is fixed into stone by cutting a hole, and filling it with molten lead or with cement mortar.

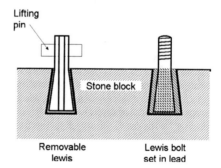

Lewis and lewis bolt

LFT *Abbreviation for* Latest Finish Time (of an activity in a NETWORK).

library *(a)* In computing, a collection of, usually standard, programs or sub-routines. *(b)* In CAD, a collection of common objects in design, *e.g.* a library of elements such as furniture elements, wall types.

lien *See* MECHANIC'S LIEN.

life safety See FIRE AND LIFE SAFETY.

life-cycle analysis An ENVIRONMENTAL IMPACT STUDY of the effect of a material, product or building process, or of an entire building, on its environment over its expected lifetime. An analysis of LIFE-CYCLE COST is concerned primarily with cost.

life-cycle cost The cost of a design feature that allows for prime capital cost, running cost and maintenance.

lift A car or platform for the vertical transportation of persons or goods. Called an *elevator* in the USA.

lift door types *(a) Advance opening*: the initiation of door opening while a lift car is slowing, usually when the car is 300 mm from the floor level. *(b) Centre opening*: a door with two horizontally sliding panels linked to operate simultaneously. *(c) Multiple panel* door: comprising two or more panels which telescope behind each other as the door opens. *(d) Side opening*: sliding door opening to one side of a lift well. *(e) Two-speed side-*, or *centre-opening* door: with one panel sliding behind another at double the speed, in order that both panels arrive at the open position simultaneously.

lift doors The movable portions of lift CAR and LIFT WELL entrances.

lift drive The power unit providing the energy required to raise and lower a lift.

lift drive types *(a) Basement drive*: a lift drive located adjacent to the bottom of the lift well. *(b) Belt drive*: an *indirect* drive, using a belt as the means of connection. *(c) Direct drive*: an *electric* drive whose motor is connected directly to the driving sheave, with or without intermediate gearing. *(d) Direct plunger drive*: a *hydraulic* drive whose cylinder is connected directly to the car frame. *(e) Electric drive*: a drive using an electric motor, in any given configuration. *(f) Geared traction drive*: a *traction* drive using gears. *(g) Gearless traction drive*: a *traction* drive without intermediate gearing. *(h) Indirect drive*: an electric drive whose motor is connected to the SHEAVE, shaft or drum by belts or chains. *(i) Hydraulic drive*: a drive utilising the energy from a hydraulic fluid. *(j) Overhead drive*: a lift drive located at the top of the lift well. *(k) Rack and pinion drive*: an *electric* drive whose lift car movement is achieved by power-driven pinions mounted on the car, running on a stationary rack fixed to the structure, or the lift well wall. *(l) Roped hydraulic drive*: a *hydraulic* drive whose cylinder is connected to the lift car frame by ropes. *(m) Screw drive*: a drive by a screw assembly, whose power is supplied by an electric motor. *(n) Traction drive*: a *direct drive* through friction between the suspension ropes and the driving sheave. *(o) Worm-geared drive*: a *direct drive* connected to the sheave or drum through worm gearing.

lift machine See LIFT DRIVE.

lift of concrete The concrete placed in a wall or column between two successive construction joints. In columns, it is generally the height of one storey.

lift passenger journey time The TIME INTERVAL that a passenger spends travelling to a destination floor, measured from the instant the passenger registers a landing call until the instant the passenger alights at the destination.

lift recall A fire control system for lifts. In Phase I all lifts are automatically recalled to the ground floor in the event of a fire, and they remain there. In Phase II the lifts are operable by the fire brigade.

lift round trip time The average TIME INTERVAL, usually during an up peak traffic condition, for a single lift car trip through a building, measured from the time the car doors open at the main terminal, until they reopen there after the car has completed its trip.

lift slab A reinforced or prestressed concrete FLAT PLATE cast at ground level, and jacked up to its correct level after the concrete has hardened. Also, an entire system of floor slabs and roof cast on top of one another at ground level, and hoisted into position by the lift-slab method.

lift types *(a) Bed*: a lift for the movement of patients on beds or stretchers in hospitals, etc. with a narrow and deep platform, capable of carrying a load of at least 20 passengers. *(b) Direct plunger hydraulic*: a *hydraulic* lift having a plunger or cylinder attached directly to the car frame. *See also roped hydraulic.*

(c) Electric: a lift using an electrical drive machine for the movement of the car. *(d) Electro-hydraulic*: a *hydraulic* lift; the hydraulic pressure is produced by an electrically driven pump. (A *hydraulic* lift now implies *electro-hydraulic*, but early in the twentieth century, many cities had hydraulic mains in the streets to reticulate hydraulic power.) *(e) Firemen's*: a lift with controls that enable it to be used under the direct control of the fire brigade during an emergency. *See also* FIREMAN'S SWITCH and LIFT RECALL. *(f) Goods*: a lift designed primarily for the transport of freight and goods. *See also* DUMBWAITER. *(g) Hydraulic*: a lift using hydraulic pressure as the motive force. *(h) Inclined*: a lift which moves at an inclination of 15° or greater to the vertical. *(i)Multi-deck*: a lift having two or more compartments located to form a vertical stack. *See also* DOUBLE-DECK LIFT. *(j) Observation*: a lift designed as an architectural feature to provide a panoramic view for passengers, while travelling in a partially enclosed or glazed well. *(k) Passenger*: a lift designed to carry passengers. *(l) Passenger/goods*: a lift designed to carry goods and/or passengers. *(m) Roped hydraulic*: a *hydraulic* lift whose piston is connected to the car frame by means of wire ropes. *See also direct plunger hydraulic*. *(n) Service*: a lift designed to carry goods and service personnel. *(o) Stair*: a lift installed on a stairway. *See* INCLINATOR.

lift well The vertical opening through a building in which lifts travel. It extends from the lift PIT at the bottom to the underside of the lift machine room (if it is on top), or the roof. Called an *elevator hoistway* in the USA.

lifting frame A purpose-made steel frame for the lifting by crane of prefabricated components, *e.g.* PRECAST CONCRETE.

lifting tackle *See* DIFFERENTIAL PULLEY BLOCK, DERRICK *and* WHIP.

light Synonym for window; *see* DEAD, LAY *and* OPEN LIGHT. *See also* VISIBLE SPECTRUM.

light alloys Alloys of low specific gravity. They include the aluminium alloys; the others are too expensive for use in buildings at the present time.

light loss factor (LLF) A factor used in calculating the illuminance after a given period of time and under given conditions. It takes into account temperature and voltage variations, lamp depreciation (of electric luminaries), dirt accumulation on luminaire and room surfaces, maintenance procedures and atmospheric conditions. *Also called maintenance factor.*

light output ratio *See* LUMINAIRE EFFICIENCY.

light pen A form of INPUT device which is used in conjunction with a CATHODE-RAY TUBE to enter graphical information into a digital computer.

light pipe A hollow tube with a reflective surface used to 'pipe' light from a source to where needed. Different from FIBRE OPTICS since *total internal reflection* is not used. Light pipes can be used to light coolrooms and hazardous locations from outside.

light shelf A horizontal shelf positioned (usually above eye level) to reflect daylight onto the ceiling and to shield direct glare from the sky.

light source The generic term for any source of light: electric, gas, oil or natural.

light timber frame *See* BALLOON FRAME.

light well A small court commonly placed in large buildings before artificial light of adequate brightness was developed. It admitted daylight through windows opening on to it. An ATRIUM is similar, but is roofed at the top.

light/air fitting A recessed fluorescent light fitting to which is attached an air supply terminal device which delivers conditioned air through a linear diffuser or pair of diffusers at the side(s) of the fitting.

light-gauge structure Structure built up from thin cold-rolled steel or aluminium sheet. *See also* LOCAL BUCKLING.

lighting *See* ARTIFICIAL LIGHT, COLOUR, DAYLIGHT *and* GLARE.

lighting level A commonly used term for ILLUMINANCE.

lightness The attribute of visual sensation by which a body is judged to transmit or reflect a greater or smaller proportion of the incident light. It is the visual correlate of REFLECTANCE. This is the property called VALUE in the MUNSELL BOOK OF COLOR.

lightning arrester A device used to pass large electrical impulses to ground. It is vital that this device be placed upstream from the ground for any computers or other sensitive electronic equipment.

lightning protection system A system of conductors and other components to reduce the injurious and damaging effects of lightning, comprising at least AIR TERMINATIONS, DOWNCONDUCTORS and EARTH TERMINATIONS.

lightwatt A term sometimes used to describe the LUMEN.

lightweight aggregate Concrete aggregate which weighs less than gravel or crushed stone. Natural materials include VERMICULITE and PUMICE. Artificial materials include expanded clay or shale, and products made from FLY ASH or BLAST-FURNACE SLAG.

lightweight concrete *(a)* Concrete made with LIGHTWEIGHT AGGREGATE. Usually sand is used as FINE AGGREGATE, but the weight can be reduced further by using small-size lightweight aggregate also for the fines. The concrete may have almost the same strength as normal concrete, and the consequent saving in space may be more significant than the higher cost of the lightweight aggregate. *(b)* CELLULAR CONCRETE made without lightweight aggregate. In this case the concrete has little structural strength.

lightweight structure *See* CABLE STAYS, GEODESIC DOME, LIGHT-GAUGE STRUCTURE, MEMBRANE STRUCTURE, PNEUMATIC STRUCTURE, SADDLE SURFACE, SCHWEDLER DOME *and* SUSPENSION ROOF.

lignin The most important constituent of wood after cellulose, consisting of resins which bind the wood fibres together. It can be recovered from wood pulp, and is used as a binder in PARTICLE BOARD, in the manufacture of some PLASTICS, and in some anticorrosive coatings.

lime A generic term for calcium oxide (CaO) which is QUICKLIME, and calcium hydroxide (Ca(OH)$_2$) which is HYDRATED LIME.

lime mortar Mortar made of lime and sand. It was the general medium for laying stone and brick until the nineteenth century. However, it is water-soluble, and it has now been largely superseded by

PORTLAND CEMENT mortar, which is water-resistant, and also stronger. However, as cement mortar is stronger than many types of stone and brick, cracks due to foundation settlement, temperature and moisture movement are liable to pass through the stone or brick, rather than through the mortar joints. This causes irreparable damage, whereas a crack in a joint can be repaired by repointing. Thus an admixture of lime with cement mortar is often favoured. *See also* MASONRY CEMENT.

lime putty *Same as* HYDRATED LIME.

limestone SEDIMENTARY rock containing a large proportion of calcium carbonate (CaCO$_3$). It is formed by the consolidation of calcareous ooze, which may be formed by organisms, by chemical precipitation, or by the weathering of pre-existing limestone. Most limestones are easily carved (*see* FREESTONE *and* PORTLAND STONE). In the building industry classification of building stones, the polishable limestones are called MARBLE. Limestone is a raw material for LIME mortar and for PORTLAND CEMENT. *See also* MARBLE *and* TRAVERTINE.

limewash *Same as* WHITEWASH.

limit design Design based on the *limiting loads* at which the structure collapses. PLASTIC HINGES are reached first at the sections subjected to the greatest curvature. Formation of these hinges allows redistribution of bending moments, and the formation of further hinges with increase in load. The limit is reached when sufficient hinges have formed

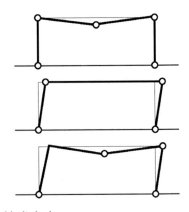

Limit design

to turn the STATICALLY INDETERMINATE STRUCTURE into a MECHANISM. It then collapses (*see figure opposite* for alternative collapse mechanisms). A separate ELASTIC DESIGN is needed if deformations need to be determined.

limit of liquidity, plasticity *See* LIQUID, PLASTIC LIMIT.

limit of proportionality *See* PROPORTIONAL LIMIT.

limit states design A structural design which considers both the *ultimate limit states*, which determine the ultimate load-carrying capacity of the structure, and the *serviceability limit states*, relating to the criteria governing the normal use of the structure.

limiting strength of material The strength above which a material ceases to contribute to the strength of the structure. It is usually defined, for convenience, in terms of standard tests which approximate to the limiting strength. In structural steel, it is taken as the YIELD STRESS, since the steel suffers very large deformations above that point, which are liable to cause structural collapse. In concrete, it is the CYLINDER STRENGTH or the CUBE STRENGTH. The limiting strength is used directly in LIMIT DESIGN. In elastic design, MAXIMUM PERMISSIBLE STRESSES are used, which are derived from the limiting strength.

limits of size The range of TOLERANCE of a dimension.

limonite Iron ore composed of a mixture of hydrated ferric oxides.

limp Behaving as an inelastic material, *e.g.* lead, that does not recover from its deformation after the deforming force is removed. Such materials are good for *sound insulation*.

line *(a)* In graphics, a graphic element defined by a sequence of points. A straight line is defined by its start and end points. *(b)* In telecommunications, a channel for the transmission of signals. *(c)* In electricity, an active conductor. Hence, in three-phase systems, *line voltage* is measured line-to-line. *See also* PHASE *(b)*.

line drawing A drawing whose graphic elements are all LINES.

line imbalance Unequal loads on the phase lines of a multiphase feeder.

line of thrust The curve produced by the points through which the resultant THRUST passes, *e.g.* in an arch.

line printer Printer which formats and prints entire lines at a time. These printers were often used for printing program source code and program output in earlier days of computing. They can operate at significant speeds, but are limited to printing text only.

line source A sound source formed by numerous *point sources* in a continuous line.

line spectrum A spectrum whose components occur at one or more discrete frequencies

line-to-line A term used to describe the voltage, or other conditions, between conductors of a multiphase feeder.

line-to-neutral A term used to describe the voltage, or other conditions, between a phase conductor and a neutral conductor.

lineal foot A foot, as distinct from a square foot or a cubic foot.

linear arch *Same as* FUNICULAR ARCH.

linear diffuser A terminal device used in air conditioning which distributes air to a space from a linear slot.

linear equation An equation which can be plotted as a straight line. A linear algebraic equation is one of the type $y = ax + b$, where a and b are constants.

linear heat loss coefficient Used to allow for the additional heat loss due to THERMAL BRIDGES, over and above that accounted for by the U-value of the overall construction. Dimensionally it is W/m.K, and it is multiplied by the length of the thermal bridge. Its use is part of most building energy codes in Europe.

linear load (electrical) A load in which the current relationship to voltage is constant, based on a relatively constant load impedance.

linear programming A mathematical programming technique for OPTIMISATION, where the objectives and constraints can be expressed as linear functions of variables.

linear regression Statistical technique that predicts the most likely association between variables assuming a linear relationship.

liner *(a)* The replaceable part of a sliding GUIDE SHOE, sometimes called a *gib*, which slides against the guide rail and steadies a lift car in its travel. *(b) Hydraulic*: an insert placed inside the original cylinder of a hydraulic JACK to stop leaks. *(c)* The liner of BRAKE SHOES. *(d)* An impermeable sheet placed inside a dam, pond, etc. to prevent water leakage.

link *(a)* An obsolete measure of length, equal to 1/100 of a surveyor's 66-foot chain, or 201 mm. *(b)* In computing, a connection for transmitting signals between two terminals. *(c)* In HYPERTEXT documents, any highlighted words or phrases that allow a jump to another location (a *target*) in the same document or to another document on the WORLD WIDE WEB.

link polygon A graphical construction for solving problems of static equilibrium, based on the POLYGON OF FORCES. It can be used for determining the forces in roof trusses, drawing bending moment diagrams, and determining the line of thrust in an arch. *Also called a funicular polygon.* Instead of a graphical construction, an experimental solution can be obtained with a freely hanging string, which produces a *string polygon.*

linoleum Floor covering made from jute or similar fabric, impregnated with oxidised linseed oil, resin and a filler, such as cork.

linseed oil A vegetable oil obtained by crushing the seeds of FLAX. When exposed to the air, it thickens and darkens through oxidation, forming a tough skin. It is used for paints and varnishes, for linoleum and for glazier's putty.

lintel *(a)* In Classical architecture, the horizontal member which spans between the posts in TRABEATED construction. *(b)* A short beam, particularly one spanning across a door or window opening, and carrying the wall above it.

liquefied petroleum gas (LPG) The gaseous fraction remaining after the catalytic cracking process used in refining crude oil. Stored as a liquid under high pressure and used as a portable source of gaseous fuel. It consists mainly of propane and butane.

liquid A state of matter in which the shape of a given mass depends on the containing vessel, but its volume is independent thereof; liquids are practically incompressible, but their shear strength is zero. The other states of matter are GAS and SOLID.

liquid chiller A self-contained refrigeration machine which incorporates a refrigerant compressor and a heat exchanger to produce chilled liquid (often water) for distribution to air handling unit(s) in an air conditioning system or to other systems where cooling may be required. *Also called water chiller.*

liquid crystal display (LCD) Display system commonly used in laptop computers. LCDs offer the advantage of a full-colour display with low power consumption, light weight, and compact (flat) size. However, the present generation of LCDs have lower contrasts and accommodate a narrower viewing angle compared to CRT MONITORS.

liquid limit The water content of a (clayey) soil which marks the boundary between its plastic and liquid state as determined by a standard test. The wet soil is placed in a cup, which is raised by a cam and allowed to drop to close a groove over a specified length. The liquid limit is the water content corresponding to 25 drops of the cup. *See also* PLASTICITY INDEX.

liquid line The pipeline that carries liquid refrigerant from the condenser to the pressure-reducing device in a refrigeration circuit.

liquid phase The state of a substance when its internal energy content is such that it exists only as a LIQUID.

liquid-glass Same as WATER-GLASS.

liquid-membrane curing CURING of concrete with a liquid sealing compound to slow the evaporation of the mixing water.

liquidus line The line separating the liquid from the liquid–solid phase. In a PHASE DIAGRAM it shows the variation of the composition of an alloy with the temperature at which solidification is complete.

L-iron *Same as* ANGLE IRON.

liter US spelling for LITRE.

litharge Lead monoxide (PbO).

lithium bromide Absorbent used in the ABSORPTION CYCLE for refrigeration.

lithopone An opaque white pigment, which is non-poisonous, unlike WHITE LEAD. It is a co-precipitated mixture of zinc sulphide (ZnS) and barium sulphate ($BaSO_4$).

litmus An organic colouring matter used as a reagent to test the alkalinity or acidity of liquids. It turns red in acid solutions, and blue in basic solutions.

litre (L or l) The metric measure for capacity. 1 L = $0.001\,m^3$ = 0.220 British gallons = 0.264 US gallons (= 1 US quart approx.).

live load A load which is not permanently applied to a structure, as opposed to a DEAD LOAD. It may or may not be acting at any given time. *See also* SUPERIMPOSED LOAD.

liveness The reverberant quality of an auditorium. A hall which reflects too little sound back to the listener is called dead or *dry*. *See also* REVERBERATION TIME, DEFINITION *and* WARMTH.

LL *Abbreviation for* LIVE LOAD.

ln *Continental abbreviation for* NATURAL LOGARITHM ($\log_e$).

LNG *Abbreviation for* Liquefied NATURAL GAS, as distinct from LPG, liquefied petroleum gas. It is principally methane, and is transported in insulated pressure vessels at low temperature.

LOA *Abbreviation for* Length Overall.

load *(a)* In structures, *see* DEAD LOAD, LIVE LOAD, EARTHQUAKE LOADING, SUPERIMPOSED LOAD *and* WIND LOAD. *(b)* In computing, to enter data or program instructions into the memory of a computer. *(c)* In electricity, the driven device that uses the power supplied from the source. *(d)* In air conditioning, the quantity of heat to be removed or supplied by a cooling or heating coil.

load balancing (electricity) Switching the various loads on a multi-phase feeder to equalise the current in each line.

load balancing (prestressed concrete) Arranging the prestressing tendons in concrete so that the load is completely balanced by the prestress, and the member is subject purely to compression. For example, a beam or slab carrying a uniformly distributed load (which produces a parabolic bending moment diagram) requires a parabolic cable for load balancing *(see figure)*.

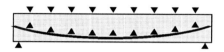

Load balancing

load factor *(a)* In limit design of structures, a factor used to provide a margin of safety against collapse. It is possible to apply a different factor to each type of load; for example, the dead load which can be accurately predicted requires a factor only a little above 1, whereas a much higher factor is required for live loads. *See also* CAPACITY REDUCTION FACTOR. *(b)* In an electrical installation, a factor to allow for the probability that only a portion of the whole load will be in use at any one time.

load fault A malfunction that causes an electrical load to demand abnormally high amounts of current from the source.

load platform A platform cantilevered from a building frame to receive crane loads.

load shedding Reduction of electrical load by turning off non-essential plant or equipment in order to avoid exceeding a predetermined level of electricity demand and thus save cost.

load switching Transferring an electrical load from one source to another.

load tails In an electrical installation, the conductors extending from a part of the installation back to the supplier's meters or protective devices.

load unbalance Unequal loads on the phase lines of a multi-phase electrical system.

load-bearing wall *See* BEARING WALL.

load–extension curve *See* STRESS–STRAIN DIAGRAM.

load-indicating bolt A high-tensile bolt embodying a small projection, which is compressed as the bolt is tightened. The gap thus indicates the tension in the bolt, and it can be measured with a feeler gauge.

loading dock The area of a building accessible by vehicles, which provides for loading and unloading, convenient to transportation systems within the building. The floor is usually elevated above the roadway, to be level with the tray of a truck.

loadstone A form of MAGNETITE which exhibits polarity, and was used by the early navigators as a magnetic compass. It points to magnetic north and south when freely suspended. *Also spelled lodestone.*

loam A soil which contains sand, silt and clay in roughly equal proportions.

lobby *(a)* The entrance of a public building giving direct access from the street to the building's circulation systems for building occupants and visitors. *(b)* A room or space which gives access to other rooms and spaces, or to a bank of LIFTS. *See also* SKY LOBBY.

local application system (fire protection) A type of GAS PROTECTION SYSTEM to discharge gas at a specific area.

local area network (LAN) A network linking electronic equipment within a single geographic location, as opposed to a WIDE AREA NETWORK (WAN).

local buckling Crinkling of a strut or of the compression flange of a beam because it is too thin. Local buckling is particularly liable to occur in *thin-walled sections* and LIGHT-GAUGE STRUCTURES, and it can be prevented by the corrugation of excessively long straight runs of sheet.

local filter mask (template) A filter used in image processing. A local filter mask is a template defining how a pixel will be transformed in relation to its neighbours.

local filtering Processing the pixels of an image based on their relation with neighbouring pixels. For example, sharpening increases the contrast for pixels that occupy boundaries between different regions of the image.

local time The legal time of day at a particular location, calculated by applying the local TIME ZONE (adjusting for daylight saving if necessary) to UTC. It is the same across a whole time zone, while *mean solar time* depends upon the exact location.

lock *See* CYLINDER LOCK *and* DEADLOCK.

lock nut A secondary nut used to prevent the first nut from working loose.

lock-washer A washer ring, with furred edges, used on a bolt to prevent the nut being loosened (*e.g.* by vibration).

lodestone *Same as* LOADSTONE.

loess Silt deposited by wind *(aeolian action).*

log A rough, unshaped piece of tree trunk.

log LOGARITHM. Unless otherwise stated it means $\log_{10}$, *i.e.* a *decimal logarithm.*

$\log_e$ NATURAL LOGARITHM, to the base e. The symbol ln is also used, principally in Europe, but increasingly elsewhere.

log cabin A small house with walls constructed of horizontal logs laid on top of one another, and held in place by notches at the corners *(see figure).*

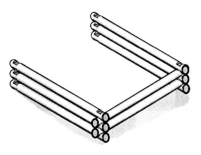

Log cabin

log file A file which keeps records of all of a series of transactions.

logarithm A mathematical function. If a and b are two numbers, and $a = 10^b$, then the decimal logarithm of a, $\log_{10} a = b$, and the *anti-logarithm* of b is a. The suffix 10 is generally omitted for decimal (or common) logarithms. It follows that the logarithm of the product cd

$$\log cd = \log c + \log d$$

so that the process of multiplication can be reduced to the simpler operation of adding the logarithms. This was utilised in *logarithmic tables* and in SLIDE RULES, and it was the common method of calculation before the invention of DIGITAL CALCULATORS and COMPUTERS. *See also* DECIMAL *and* NATURAL LOGARITHM.

logarithmic scale A scale plotted to the logarithm of the variable. An increase of one unit of the scale represents a tenfold increase in the quantity. *Logarithmic* *graph paper* (log paper) has logarithmic scales for both the ordinate and the abscissa. *Semi-logarithmic paper* (semi-log paper) has one logarithmic and one ordinary scale.

loggia A gallery or arcade open on one side, typically on the upper floors of a building.

logical AND The logical or BOOLEAN operator which connects two statements in such a way that the compound statement is true only when both component statements are true.

logical OR The logical or BOOLEAN operator which connects two statements in such a way that the compound statement is true when either or both component statements are true.

long column A column whose SLENDERNESS RATIO is sufficiently high to make it liable to a BUCKLING failure.

long throw sprinkler A SPRINKLER SYSTEM commonly used in atrium levels, which can discharge water to cover a long horizontal distance.

long ton The British TON of 2240 pounds.

long-line prestressing *See* PRE-TENSIONING.

long-term deflection Total deflection over a long period of time. It consists of both the *elastic deflection* and the *creep deflection*.

long-term lease Generally, a LEASE agreement whose lease period exceeds ten years.

long-wave radiation In the context of solar design, radiation with a wavelength exceeding 3 μm, emitted from low-temperature surfaces on the Earth's surface as a result of absorbing SHORT-WAVE SOLAR RADIATION.

longitude *See* MERIDIAN OF LONGITUDE.

longitudinal reinforcement The main reinforcement parallel to the long dimension of a structural member, as opposed to the *lateral reinforcement.*

longitudinal wave When sound propagates in air, the movement of the air particles due to the passage of the sound is in the direction of the propagation of the sound. This wave is known as a longitudinal or *compressional* wave.

LONWORKS Proprietary computer communication protocol that allows con-forming elements of a control system to communicate with each other and with the central processor.

loop In computing, a sequence of instructions that is carried out repeatedly until some specified condition terminates it.

loop antenna A flat loop of wire, *e.g.* buried in a roadway to detect the presence of a vehicle by a change in its INDUCTANCE; or located around the perimeter of a room to broadcast a low-powered audio-frequency signal that can be received by people with hearing aids within the loop, but not beyond it.

LOR (light output ratio) The ratio of the flux from a luminaire to the total flux emitted by the lamp(s) installed in the luminaire. LOR = DLOR + ULOR.

LOSP *Abbreviation for* Light Oil Solvent Preservative, a timber preservation treatment in which the preservative is dissolved in a mineral oil solvent, which carries it into the pores of the timber. As the oil evaporates, the preservative crystallises out and is left behind.

loss of prestress The loss of INITIAL PRESTRESS by the SHRINKAGE of the concrete, and by CREEP in the steel and the concrete. The reduction in the prestressing force due to friction between the tendon and the duct, and the ELASTIC LOSS OF PRESTRESS, are often considered separately.

lossless compression *See* COMPRESSION (DATA STORAGE).

lossy compression *See* COMPRESSION (DATA STORAGE).

lost-head nail A thin nail whose head is only slightly larger than its diameter, so that it can be driven below the surface of the timber.

loudness The loudness of a sound is an auditory sensation of the intensity of a sound that depends on the sound level and the frequency of the sound. The unit of loudness is the *sone*.

loudness level The loudness of a sound expressed on a logarithmic scale is known as the loudness level. The loudness level of a sound is expressed in *phons*. The loudness level of a 1000 Hz tone at 40 dB is 40 phons.

loudspeaker An electroacoustic TRANSDUCER for audition by a number of people.

louver US spelling for LOUVRE.

louvres Long, thin strips of glass, wood or other material, either fixed or adjustable, placed so as to allow passage of air or light between them. Used particularly in the hot-humid tropics where ventilation is important for COMFORT. Horizontal louvres permit the passage of air with as little obstruction as possible, while controlling vision and excluding rain or sunlight. The term 'louvre' is also applied to the grilles covering the openings in the overhead ducts of an air conditioning, heating or ventilating installation. *See also* SUNSHADING, PUNKAH LOUVRE *and* VENETIAN BLIND.

low-alloy steel Steel containing less than 10 per cent of alloying elements.

low-carbon steel CARBON STEEL containing less than 0.25 per cent of carbon.

low-emissivity glass Glass coated very thinly with metallic salts which reduce its emissivity in the infrared spectral range. *Also called Low-e glass.*

low-heat cement A PORTLAND CEMENT in which the generation of heat during setting is reduced by a modification of its chemical composition. It is used in dams and other massive concrete structures where the heat cannot easily be dissipated.

low-pass filter *(a)* In acoustics and signal processing, a filter which only allows the passage of signals below a given frequency. *(b)* In image processing, a filter to modify the pixel values (and hence the appearance) of a digitised image. Low-pass filters are used to blur the image by decreasing the contrast of nearby pixels. *See also* HIGH-PASS FILTER *and* LOCAL FILTERING.

low-pressure sodium lamp A DISCHARGE LAMP using sodium vapour at low pressure in the discharge tube. It produces a monochromatic orange-yellow light of high LUMINOUS EFFICACY but without any colour-rendering properties.

low-pressure steam curing Steam curing at normal atmospheric pressure, as opposed to AUTOCLAVING.

LP *Abbreviation for* LINEAR PROGRAMMING.

LPG *Abbreviation for* LIQUEFIED PETROLEUM GAS.

LSI *Abbreviation for* Large Scale Integration.

Lucite Trade name of an ACRYLIC RESIN.

Lüders' lines Lines that appear on the polished surface of a crystal, or a polished metal surface that is polycrystalline, after it has been stressed beyond the elastic limit; first reported by W. Lüders in 1860. They represent the intersection of the surface by planes on which the shear stress has produced plastic slip. *Also called slip lines.*

luffing The raising or lowering of a crane boom.

lumber In the USA, the product derived from LOGS of timber in a sawmill. Elsewhere the word *timber* is used for both the round logs and the rectangular pieces.

lumen (lm) *(a)* The unit of luminous flux. *(b)* The quantity of luminous flux emitted within a unit solid angle (one steradian) by a point source with one CANDELA intensity.

lumen maintenance *(a)* The ability of a lamp to maintain its INITIAL FLUX over time. *(b)* The curve or table that shows the depreciation of lamp flux with time.

lumen method The method commonly used for calculating illuminances in interiors from regular arrays of luminaires. Also used to determine the number of lamps required. Also a method for the design of daylit rooms, particularly favoured in the USA. *Also called the flux method.* The calculations require tables of UTILISATION FACTORS, usually produced by manufacturers of luminaires.

lumen-second The unit of luminous energy, the radiometric equivalent of the Ws or J.

luminaire A device for providing mechanical support and electrical connections to a lamp or lamps, together with any light control materials and a means of fixing the luminaire to a support (such as a ceiling). *Also called* a *light fitting,* a *fixture* (in the USA), a *lantern* (in roadlighting) or a *lamp* (as in table and floor-mounted luminaires).

luminaire efficiency The ratio of the luminous flux emitted by a luminaire to the luminous flux emitted by the lamps inside it. It is the same as the *light output ratio.*

luminance The area density of luminous intensity, equivalent to the radiometric quantity, RADIANCE. Luminance has the units candela per square metre, cd/m². Luminance is sometimes referred to as the photometric brightness of an illuminated surface or a light source.

luminance contrast See CONTRAST.

luminance factor The ratio of the luminance of a reflecting surface, to that of a perfect diffuse reflector, similarly illuminated. With perfect and near-perfect diffusers it is usual to use REFLECTANCE; the luminance factor takes into account the degree of specularity and the direction of the illuminant.

luminescence The emission of light as a result of any cause other than high temperature, e.g. the effect of ultraviolet light on certain chemicals. See also ELECTROLUMINESCENT PANEL.

luminosity Same as APPARENT BRIGHTNESS.

luminous ceiling A lighting system in which the whole ceiling is translucent (or louvred), with lamps above it. The ceiling becomes an approximately uniform luminous source.

luminous efficacy Whilst 'efficiency' is a non-dimensional number, efficacy is the ratio of unlike quantities, in this case the emission of light per unit of power consumed, measured in lumens per watt (lm/W).

luminous flux The light flux (power) from a light source. It is measured in LUMENS. It is distinguished from radiant flux by weighting the radiant flux from the source by the response of the human visual system V(λ) and applying the luminous efficacy of vision, 683 lm/W.

luminous intensity The LUMINOUS FLUX per unit solid angle, in a particular direction, measured in CANDELA (LUMEN per steradian).

luminous paint See FLUORESCENT PAINT and PHOSPHORESCENT PAINT.

luminous reflectance The ratio of reflected to incident luminous flux.

luminous transmittance The ratio of transmitted to incident luminous flux.

lump sum tender A tender at a fixed, but not necessarily firm, price for which a contractor undertakes to carry out specified work.

lux (lx) The SI unit of ILLUMINANCE. It is the same as LUMENs per square metre (lm/m²).

lux meter A meter, usually portable or hand-held, used for measuring illuminance, often called, generically a PHOTOMETER.

LVL Abbreviation for Laminated Veneer Lumber.

lx Abbreviation for the unit of luminous flux, the LUX.

lyctus borer A wood borer of the family Lyctidae, which attacks the SAPWOOD of certain seasoned hardwood species. Also known as the powder-post borer, because the FRASS is a fine smooth powder. Unless the susceptible sapwood is treated, the borer will eventually destroy that part of the member, but will leave the HEARTWOOD untouched. See also ANOBIUM BORER.

M

μ (mu) Abbreviation for micro (one millionth).

M Abbreviation for mega (one million times), or for the basic module.

m Abbreviation for milli (one thousandth) and metre.

macadam Uniformly sized stones rolled to form a surface, a process developed by the Scottish road-builder J. L. McAdam in the early nineteenth century. Macadamising is the process of laying the surface. Tarmacadam is a waterproof surface whose stones are bound together by tar, bitumen or asphalt, as distinct from waterbound macadam.

macerator Machine for grinding up contaminated disposable items and flushing them into the sewer.

Mach number The ratio of the velocity of an object to the local speed of sound, named after the nineteenth-century Austrian physicist, Ernst Mach. A Mach number below 1 means subsonic flow, and a number above 1 means supersonic flow.

machine bolt A straight shank bolt with a conventional head and a full length thread.

machine language The language defined by the primitive tasks a given processor can perform. Each kind of processor will have its unique associated machine language. All programs must eventually be translated to the machine language of a computer before they can be executed on that computer.

machine learning A sub-area of the field of ARTIFICIAL INTELLIGENCE whose goal is to discover techniques whereby computer programs can learn to solve problems by inferring new information and strategies.

machine room A room or space which houses machinery and equipment, usually for lifts.

macro A code in which a single instruction will generate several computer instructions. For example, a macro for a helical stair will generate all the instructions for drawing such a stair.

macro library A LIBRARY of MACRO routines.

macroscopic Visible to the naked eye, as opposed to *microscopic. Also called megascopic.*

made ground or made-up ground Ground built-up with excavated material or refuse, as distinct from the natural, undisturbed soil. Its load-bearing capacity is often very low.

magnesia Magnesium oxide.

magnesian limestone Limestone containing DOLOMITE.

magnesite Carbonate of magnesium ($MgCO_3$).

magnesite flooring A composition of OXYCHLORIDE CEMENT with a filler of sawdust, wood flour, sand or ground silica. It is used to cover concrete floors, and is commonly floated in a layer about 40 mm (1½ in.) thick. *Also called jointless flooring.*

magnesium A very light, silvery-white metal which burns in air with a brilliantly white light when ignited. It is produced for commercial purposes by electrolysis from seawater. Its alloys weigh less than aluminium alloys and have comparable strength. They are used in aircraft and automobile design, but are too expensive for use in building.

magnet steel A steel capable of retaining its magnetism after removal from an external magnetic field, and therefore useable for *permanent magnets.* It is usually an alloy steel containing tungsten, cobalt or nickel, quenched from about 900°C. By contrast, an ELECTROMAGNET is a *temporary magnet.*

magnetic declination or magnetic deviation See TRUE NORTH.

magnetic disk See DISK.

magnetic field The lines of force that exist around an energised electrical conductor, magnet or inductor.

magnetic floppy diskettes, drives See FLOPPY DISK, DISKETTE.

magnetic hard disks, drives See HARD DISK.

magnetic north See TRUE NORTH.

magnetic tape Non-volatile data storage medium consisting of thin Mylar or similar tape with a magnetic coating. Unlike DISK storage, tape only allows sequential access to the data. It is a useful, low-cost REMOVABLE STORAGE medium for backing up computer data, as well as sound and video recording.

magnetite Ferrous ferric oxide (Fe_3O_4). It is a black iron ore, which is attracted by a magnet, but does not attract particles of iron to itself. The LOADSTONE is a form of magnetite which exhibits polarity. Red, purple and black pigments are produced from some magnetite ores.

mahogany A large hardwood tree, *Swietenia mahogoni,* found originally in the American tropics. Its straight-grained yellowish to reddish brown wood was much in demand for fine furniture and panelling. Similar timber from other trees is now often called mahogany.

Maihak strain gauge A type of ACOUSTIC STRAIN GAUGE.

mail server The hardware/software that sends and receives electronic mail over a network.

main memory See COMPUTER MEMORY.

main service entrance The enclosure containing connection panels and switchgear, located at the point where the utility power lines enter a building.

main tie The tension member joining the feet of a roof truss, generally at wall-plate level.

mainframe Powerful computers capable of performing all the computing needs of a large enterprise are referred to as mainframe computers. Note that definitions of categories of computers change rapidly as computing technology advances, and future desktop machines may have equivalent performance to today's mainframe computers.

maintenance The work required to keep buildings and assets at a standard appropriate and adequate for use. *See also* BREAKDOWN REPAIRS.

maintenance factor The ratio of the FLUX in a lighting installation after a period of time to the initial flux in the same installation. It is usually the product of the maintenance factors for lamps, luminaire surfaces and room surfaces. *Also called light loss factor.*

maintenance plan in fire safety management Part of a FIRE SAFETY PLAN to carry out HOUSEKEEPING and maintaining of fire safety provisions, both active and passive.

maintenance, breakdown Maintenance undertaken to return damaged components or equipment to satisfactory operation.

maintenance, comprehensive A form of lift maintenance contract, whereby the system is inspected, lubricated and adjusted. In the event of breakdown of equipment it is repaired only during normal working hours.

maintenance, condition based A form of maintenance where work is performed only when the asset's monitored performance falls below pre-determined levels.

maintenance, corrective The restorative maintenance of an item which has ceased to be of adequate quality.

maintenance, deferred The maintenance works that are not carried out as planned and are carried forward to the next financial year as a backlog of maintenance items.

maintenance, performance guaranteed A lift maintenance contract which guarantees a certain performance of the lift system; for example, the number of lifts in service at any time, the lowest periods of down time, and the longest mean time between failures.

maintenance, periodic Maintenance carried out to a repeated schedule.

maintenance, planned/scheduled Preventative maintenance scheduled to be performed at specific intervals, or after a number of operations.

maintenance, preventive Maintenance to prevent deterioration below the level of adequate quality.

maintenance, programmed Maintenance to be implemented and completed within a specified time period.

maintenance, replacement The replacement of components and equipment which may be faulty through wear, or may be at the end of their useful life.

maintenance, routine Short-term maintenance activities to maintain operations to an adequate quality level.

maintenance, running Maintenance implemented while an item is still functioning.

maintenance, shutdown Maintenance requiring that an item is removed from service for implementation.

maintenance, statutory Maintenance required to maintain conformance with statutory requirements.

maisonette British term for a two-level APARTMENT, with the bedrooms at the upper level. *See also* DUPLEX *(c).*

make good *(a)* To restore the condition of parts of a building damaged during other work, such as cutting a new doorway into a wall. *(b)* The LESSEE's obligation to return premises to their original condition at the end of the LEASE period.

make-before-break Operational sequence of a switch or relay where the new connection is made prior to disconnecting the existing connection.

make-up air Air introduced to a space either by infiltration or by forced supply, to replace that removed by a process of exhaust ventilation or air leakage.

make-up water Water added automatically to a closed loop for circulation of chilled or hot water to make up for leakage losses.

malachite A variety of copper carbonate, used in buildings as a highly polished veneer. It is bright green, and harder than most marbles. In the industry classification of building stones, it is called a MARBLE. *See also* SERPENTINE.

malleable Able to be shaped by the application of compressive force, by hammering or rolling. Generally synonymous with DUCTILE.

mallet A hammer made of wood, rubber, leather or a soft metal, but not of steel.

management information system A computer system for providing management with organisational information, such as annual reports.

mandrel A former over which a material such as sheet metal is manipulated or formed into a shape. Also the internal former for a hollow EXTRUSION.

manganese A hard and brittle metallic element. Its chemical symbol is Mn, its atomic number is 25, its atomic weight is 54.93, its specific gravity is 7.39, and its melting point is 1245 °C. It is used in alloy steels for toughness, and also in the alloys of aluminium and copper.

man-hour Unit of human work. The input of work by one person for one hour.

manifold A pipe or chamber with several outlets or inlets for smaller pipes.

man-made mineral fibres Fibres manufactured from molten glass, furnace slag or natural stone. Their popularity increased rapidly when the carcinogenic properties of ASBESTOS became widely known in the 1970s. Like asbestos before them, they are used for fire protection, for INSULATION, and as reinforcement for cement-based materials or plastics. They are normally used as short fibres, but some can also be woven into fabrics. *See also* FIBRE CEMENT and FIBREGLASS.

manometer A PRESSURE GAUGE. It commonly takes the form of a U-tube filled with water, oil or mercury. One limb is connected to the air or other fluid whose pressure is to be measured, and the other is open to the atmosphere or connected to some other standard pressure.

mansard roof A roof, similar to a GABLE ROOF, with two slopes on each side. The lower slope is longer and steeper than the upper (*see figure*). It was named after the French architect François Mansart. *Also called a French roof.*

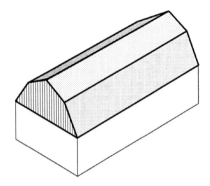

Mansard roof.

MAP *Abbreviation for* Manufacturing Automation Protocol.

marble A granular crystalline calcareous rock, formed *metamorphically* from limestone; greatly esteemed by sculptors because it can be polished to a smooth finish, and used in modern architecture because of the ease with which it can be cut by machine into thin slabs and polished. The term 'marble' is also used in the industry classification, for non-metamorphic limestones and for other decorative rocks capable of taking high polish. *See also* LIMESTONE, MALACHITE *and* SERPENTINE.

marbling The now obsolete art of painting a surface to look like marble.

margin The addition to the direct costs and overhead to cover risks and profit.

margin of safety *See* FACTOR OF SAFETY.

marine glue Waterproof or HYDRAULIC GLUE, originally consisting of about three parts of pitch, two parts of shellac, and one part of rubber. The term now refers to the most water-resistant of the synthetic RESINS.

market rent The current rental value of a property, which varies according to market conditions.

market valuation A valuation of the current capital value or market rental value of a property, obtained by comparison with equivalent properties. *See also* VALUE ANALYSIS *and* VALUE MANAGEMENT.

mark-up The MARGIN added to an estimate in order to determine the tender price.

mark-up language *See* HTML.

marl A clay which contains a substantial quantity of calcareous material. It is particularly suitable for making bricks without the addition of other substances.

marquetry The covering of a wooden surface with a layer of WOOD VENEERS, using different timbers cut into shapes to form a pattern or picture. *See also* INLAY.

Marseilles pattern tile Moulded clay tile with drainage channels. It interlocks at the sides, as well as above and below. Originating in France, it was at one time very common in Australia. *Also called a French tile.*

marsh gas A form of METHANE.

martensite A constituent of steel which appears needle-shaped under the microscope. It is produced when steel is cooled very rapidly from the hardening temperature, *i.e.* at a speed greater than its critical cooling rate, so that the transformation of AUSTENITE occurs at 400 °C or lower. It is essentially ALPHA IRON in non-equilibrium condition, formed directly from the undercooled austenite. It is the hardest of the decomposition products of austenite, and very BRITTLE. *See also* TEMPERING.

masking (image processing) *See* LOCAL FILTERING.

masking noise/sound A sound or noise that raises a listener's HEARING THRESHOLD for another sound. The masking sound may be detrimental, as in the case of air conditioning noise in a lecture theatre or concert hall, or beneficial, as in the case of sound or music purposely introduced (sometimes referred to as *acoustic perfume*) to prevent conversations being overheard.

masking tape Adhesive paper tape used to cover surfaces adjacent to new paintwork, to keep them free from paint. The adhesive is designed to be removed easily without damaging the surface.

masonry Originally work consisting of blocks of carved stone laid in mortar. Now also work consisting of bricks or blocks.

masonry cement A cement which has greater plasticity and water retention than can be obtained with Portland cement mortar (*see also* LIME MORTAR). In addition to Portland cement it may contain hydrated lime, pulverised limestone, pozzolan, clay, gypsum or talc. It may also contain an AIR-ENTRAINING additive.

mass A property of the amount of matter in an object. Unlike weight, it is not dependent upon the presence of a gravitational field. In SI UNITS the unit of mass is the KILOGRAM; in CGS UNITS, the gram; and in FPS UNITS it is the POUND.

mass centre *Same as* CENTROID.

mass concrete PLAIN CONCRETE placed in considerable thickness, so that the dissipation of the heat of hydration generated by the cement may become a problem. It often uses COARSE AGGREGATE of very large size, and also PLUMS.

mass law of sound insulation For a single wall the average INSULATION against AIRBORNE SOUND is largely determined by its mass per unit area. For sound normally incident on a wall the mass law can be written in the form of the following equation:

$$TL = 10 \log_{10}[1+(\pi fm/\rho c)^2] \text{ decibels}$$

where TL is the SOUND TRANSMISSION LOSS of the wall, f is the frequency of the sound, m is the surface density of the wall, ρ is the density of air, and c is the velocity of sound in air. The mass law predicts a 6 dB increase in the transmission loss for a doubling of the frequency of the sound or a doubling of the mass of the wall. In practice, for random incident sound, the increase is approximately 5 dB, as edge fixing and other factors have some effect.

mass retaining wall *Same as* GRAVITY RETAINING WALL.

mass spectrometer A device to measure the concentration of chemical species in a sample.

mass transfer Usually combined in the study of *heat and mass transfer*, in building thermal analysis it refers particularly to the transfer of air and water vapour through the fabric, as distinct from the transfer of heat alone by CONDUCTION, etc.

mass transfer wheel A device to transfer moisture from one air stream into another. A wheel packed with some sorbent (absorbent or adsorbent) material (such as silica gel, activated alumina or calcium chloride, CaCl; but wool has also been used) between two wire meshes, slowly rotating. When in the path of moist air this will pick up some of its moisture and when it turns into the path of dry (possibly solar heated) air, it will give off this moisture, thus it will be reactivated.

masterkeying An arrangement whereby individual locks are operable by separate, different keys; but in addition groups of these locks can all be operated by a single key, thus creating a hierarchy of access.

mastic *(a)* The resin of the mastic tree, a small evergreen tree found near the Mediterranean Sea, which is used in chewing gum and, dissolved in alcohol, as a varnish. *(b)* A jointing compound which dries on the surface, but remains permanently plastic underneath. The term covers a variety of compounds used in DRY CONSTRUCTION for sealing joints between precast concrete facing panels, curtain walls, windows, pipes, etc. It is usually inserted into the joint with a pressure gun. *(c)* A thick adhesive, consisting of asphalt, bitumen or pitch, and a filler, such as sand. It is used for bedding wood-block floors, bedding and pointing window frames, and for laying and repairing flat roofs.

matched veneer A sliced WOOD VENEER made in successive cuts, which are used left-face and right-face, so that the figure of the wood is repeated, in mirror image, in the matched pair.

materials science Application of the physics and chemistry of the internal structure of materials to the interpretation of their engineering behaviour. *See also* STRENGTH OF MATERIALS.

mathematical model A mathematical formulation which describes the known behaviour of a structure or other physical process. *See also* MODEL ANALYSIS.

matrix *(a)* A rectangular array of numbers or mathematical terms, used in the solution of simultaneous equations. Because large matrices are easily handled by computers, a substantial proportion of mathematical theory (*e.g.* for structural design) is now written in *matrix algebra*. *(b)* The cement which binds together the aggregate of concrete. *(c)* The principal constituent of an alloy or mechanical mixture, in which the other constituents are embedded. *(d)* The mould from which

printers' type was formerly cast. *See also* STEREOTYPE.

matrix-displacement method A matrix solution for STATICALLY INDETERMINATE STRUCTURES, intended for evaluation by computer, in which the equations are framed in terms of the unknown joint displacements. *Also called stiffness method.*

matrix-force method A matrix solution for STATICALLY INDETERMINATE STRUCTURES, intended for evaluation by computer, in which the equations are framed in terms of the redundant actions. *Also called flexibility method.*

matt surface *(a)* A surface without sheen, even when viewed from an oblique angle. *(b)* A surface which redistributes the incident light uniformly in all directions, so that the LUMINANCE is the same in all directions.

maximum allowable stress *Same as* MAXIMUM PERMISSIBLE STRESS.

maximum permissible stress The greatest stress permissible in a structural member under the action of the SERVICE or WORKING LOADS. It is usually defined as (LIMITING STRESS OF MATERIAL)/(FACTOR OF SAFETY).

mb *Abbreviation for* MILLIBAR.

Mb or MB *Abbreviation for* MEGABYTE.

MDF *Abbreviation for* Medium Density FIBREBOARD.

mean Unqualified, the mean is the average of all values (their sum, divided by the number of values). This is *also called* the *arithmetic* or *algebraic* mean. The *geometric mean* of *n* values is the *n*th root of their product. *See* ARITHMETIC MEAN for an alternative definition. *See also* MEDIAN *and* MODE.

mean radiant temperature The weighted average of the surface temperatures of all elements in a room in line of sight of an occupant.

mean solar time The time shown by a watch that operates at a uniform rate set to the annual mean local solar time, rather than the legal time zone of the region. Since the Earth's actual movement around the sun is not entirely uniform, it differs slightly from the APPARENT SOLAR TIME, the difference being given by the EQUATION OF TIME and shown by the

ANALEMMA. It may differ significantly from the LOCAL TIME.

means of access The paths for fire fighters to enter the fire sites of a building.

means of escape (or egress) The paths for occupants in a building to leave in case of fire.

measuring band Flexible steel ribbon, usually with widely-spaced graduations and a finely-graduated *reader* at one end. It is wound onto a reel when not in use, but fully removed when in use. For accurate surveying work, it is suspended as a CATENARY and pulled with a known force.

measuring tape *(a)* Graduated tape, of flexible steel ribbon curved to remain stiff when straight, wound into a spring-loaded case. Length usually 3–10 m, widely used in building trades. *Also called a pocket rule. (b)* Flat flexible graduated ribbon of steel or sometimes fibreglass, hand-wound onto a reel. Length usually 20–50 m, used in setting-out and site-works. In use, both types are pulled out as far as necessary but remain attached to the case, as opposed to a MEASURING BAND.

mechanical advantage The ratio of the load raised by a machine, such as a lifting tackle or a lever, to the force required to operate it. The *velocity ratio* is the ratio of the distance through which the operating force has to be moved, to the distance moved by the load. In an ideal machine the two ratios would be equal; however, due to friction the mechanical advantage is less. The *efficiency* of the machine is

$$\text{efficiency} = \frac{\text{mechanical advantage}}{\text{velocity ratio}}$$

mechanical analysis of particles PARTICLE-SIZE ANALYSIS by sieving.

mechanical equivalent of heat In FPS UNITS, 1 BTU = 778 ft-lb. In the old metric units, 1 calorie = 4.18 J. In SI UNITS the same unit, the joule, is used both for mechanical and for thermal energy. *See* THERMODYNAMICS, *First Law.*

mechanical hysteresis The dissipation of energy as heat during a stress cycle. It shows as a loop when the STRESS–STRAIN DIAGRAM is plotted for successive loading and unloading. If the ascending and descending branches coincide, then there is no hysteresis.

mechanical services The part of the BUILDING SERVICES involving mechanical power, and heating and cooling devices.

mechanical strain gauge A gauge for measuring strains by levers or other mechanical means, as opposed to an electrical, an acoustical or an optical gauge.

mechanic's lien A LIEN on real property in favour of persons supplying labour or materials for a building or structure, for the value of labour or materials supplied by them.

mechanisation The substitution of machinery for human labour.

mechanism A frame which is capable of movement. In terms of structural mechanics, a mechanism may be considered as a STATICALLY DETERMINATE STRUCTURE from which one or more members have been removed. The removal of each member gives a DEGREE OF FREEDOM, just as the addition of each member adds one redundancy.

media *See* MEDIUM.

media wall A wall, usually in a public building, completely or substantially covered with either one large video screen, or many smaller ones abutting each other. The images presented can be the equivalent of a mural, or advertising, or information panels.

media, removable *See* REMOVABLE MEDIA.

median The middle item of a group of observations, arranged in order of magnitude. For example, if there are 21 observations, it is the eleventh, and if there are 20, it is the mean of the tenth and eleventh. *See also* MEAN.

medium, media *(a)* a medium is a vehicle for communicating information. The *mass media* consist of the technologies of television, radio, press, etc. In the use of computers for communication, media include text, numbers, images, sounds and video (as in MULTIMEDIA). In terms of computer *hardware*, see also REMOVABLE MEDIA. *(b)* The liquid part of a paint, in which the pigment is suspended. After the paint has hardened it becomes the binder of the paint film. *Also called vehicle.*

medium-density fibreboard Fibreboard with a density of $480–800\,\text{kg/m}^3$ (30–50 lb/ft^3), used for building and furniture applications. *See also* INSULATING BOARD *and* HARDBOARD.

medium-temperature solar collector A solar thermal collector designed to operate in the temperature range of 60–80 °C.

mega (M) A metric prefix meaning $1,000,000$ or 10^6.

megabyte 2^{20} ($= 1\ 048\ 576$) BYTES, which is approximately $1\ 000\ 000$ bytes. The power of 2 is used because computers employ BINARY ARITHMETIC.

megaflops A million floating-point operations per second. A measure of computing performance for numerical work.

megahertz (MHz) A measure of the frequency of cyclical phenomena, equal to one million HERTZ. Microcomputer clock speeds are usually measured in MHz or GHz. *See also* CPS.

megascopic *Same as* MACROSCOPIC.

melamine resin A material used in LAMINATED PLASTICS. It is produced by the reaction of melamine $(C_3H_6N_6)$ and formaldehyde (H.CHO) with a suitable catalyst. Melamine resin-bonded laminates are characterised by extreme hardness.

melt The molten portion of the raw materials in a furnace.

membrane *(a)* A thin, sheet-like structure. *(b)* A thin, impervious sheet.

membrane analogy An analogy between the mathematical equations for the elastic *torsion* function and the transverse deformation of a stretched membrane, proposed by the German physicist L. Prandtl in 1903. It was utilised as an ANALOG COMPUTER for the torsional strength of complex shapes. The apparatus consists of a rubber membrane stretched over an opening shaped like the cross-section under investigation, and its slope and volume are determined. *See also* SANDHEAP ANALOGY.

membrane curing CURING with a liquid sealing compound.

membrane forces Three distinct internal forces are possible in a membrane: N_x and N_y, which are direct forces and may be either tensile or compressive, and the membrane shear V *(see figure)*. It is rarely possible to achieve equilibrium with membrane forces alone near the boundaries of the structure.

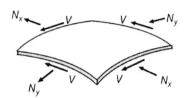

Membrane forces

membrane structure A roof of flexible membranes of canvas or plastic, supported by cables or ropes.

membrane theory Theory for the design of *thin* shell structures, based on the assumption that all forces are MEMBRANE FORCES that act *within* the membrane.

memex The first hypertext device, envisioned by Presidential Science Advisor Vannevar Bush in the 1930s and published in 1945. The machine was never actually built, but 20 years later the concept would be realised using electronic computers and a new input device called a MOUSE.

memory *See* COMPUTER MEMORY.

Memory Stick Proprietary name for a removable, compact, solid-state storage device capable of holding up to 512 MB (and probably several GB in the near future) used mainly for transferring data between different computers and other devices such as digital cameras.

memory, main The memory on chips installed inside the computer with direct bus lines to the CPU. *See also* RANDOM ACCESS MEMORY (RAM).

memory, secondary *See* SECONDARY MEMORY.

MEN *Abbreviation for* MULTIPLE EARTH NEUTRAL.

meniscus The curved surface formed when a liquid touches the surface of a solid, caused by SURFACE TENSION. The water at the edges of a glass tube rises above the general water level, and this must be allowed for when making sensitive measurements.

menu In computing, a list of options displayed on a screen, usually as a PULL-

DOWN MENU, from which the user can select the next program action. *See also* PALETTE.

MEPS *Abbreviation for* Minimum Energy Performance Standard; applied in Australia to enforce minimum energy efficiency standards for electrical appliances.

mer The smallest repetitive unit in a POLYMER.

Mercalli scale Scale for classifying the *effect* of an earthquake devised by G. Mercalli and modified in 1931 by H. O. Wood and F. Neumann. It is a 12-point scale based on the observed symptoms. Number 1 on the scale is not felt, number 6 causes some structural damage, and number 9 destroys weak masonry structures and damages frame buildings; number 12 causes nearly total destruction. The RICHTER SCALE measures the *magnitude* of an earthquake.

merchant bar A smoothly finished steel bar, as distinct from a *mill bar*, which has a rough surface that may be covered with MILL SCALE.

mercury A white metallic element, *also called quicksilver*, with a melting point of −38.5 °C, and a boiling point of +356.7 °C. Its chemical symbol is Hg *(hydrargyrum)*, its atomic number is 80, its atomic weight is 200.61, and its specific gravity is 13.56. It is a solvent for most metals, and the resulting alloys are called AMALGAMS. These played a prominent part in medieval alchemy. Mercury BAROMETERS are used for measuring air pressure, which is consequently often expressed in millimetres of mercury. At a temperature of 0 °C, 760 mm of mercury = 1 atmosphere = 14.7 psi = 101.3 kPa.

mercury fluorescent lamp A HIGH-INTENSITY DISCHARGE LAMP using mercury vapour in the discharge tube with an outer bulb coated with fluorescent material to convert some of the ultraviolet to visible light at the red end of the spectrum. *See also* HIGH-PRESSURE MERCURY LAMP.

mercury vapour lamp An electrical DISCHARGE LAMP that employs mercury at a higher pressure than in domestic fluorescent lamps to produce visible radiation. It is also the basis of other discharge lamps such as *mercury fluorescent* and *metal halide lamps*. *See also* HIGH-PRESSURE MERCURY LAMP.

meridian of longitude A GREAT CIRCLE on the Earth's surface, ORTHOGONAL to the equator, which passes through the north and south poles. The observer's meridian is the great circle passing through his or her location and the poles.

mesh The open spaces of a net; hence the net itself. Wire mesh is used in *sieves* and *screens* to separate materials, such as sand, into sizes. The larger sizes are specified by the size of the opening; the smaller sizes by a standard number. The Test Sieve Numbers standardised by the ASTM and the BSI are similar, but not quite the same.

mesh reinforcement Welded-wire fabric used as reinforcement for concrete, particularly in slabs. *See also* EXPANDED METAL.

met The unit of measure for the METABOLIC RATE for various activities, used in determining the COMFORT ZONE. 1 met = 58 W/m² (of body surface area) is the metabolic rate of an average person who is sitting up, but not working.

metabolic rate The rate at which heat of metabolism is produced by the body. It is an important component of cooling load in air conditioning design practice.

metabolism The chemical and physical processes continuously going on in living organisms, whereby food is assimilated and energy released.

metal *(a)* An element which is malleable, conducts heat and electricity, and can replace the hydrogen of an acid. Metals are electropositive, and their atoms readily lose their ELECTRONS. When untarnished, metals have a characteristic 'metallic' lustre. *(b)* Broken stone used as a COARSE AGGREGATE for concrete, tarmacadam, etc. *(c)* The liquid glass during the process of manufacture.

metal coating *See* GALVANISING, SHERARDISING *and* CADMIUM PLATING.

metal halide lamp A HIGH PRESSURE MERCURY LAMP using *metal halides* in the discharge tube to add spectral lines to those of the main mercury discharge. By suitable combination of halides, colour rendering properties are improved.

metal lath *See* LATH *and* EXPANDED METAL.

metal leaf Very thin sheet of metal, usually of gold or silver, used for decoration. After application, silver leaf may be protected against oxidation by a thin coat of lacquer.

metal oxide varistor (MOV) A voltage-sensitive breakdown device which is commonly used to limit overvoltage conditions (electrical surges) on power and data lines. When the applied voltage exceeds the breakdown point, the resistance of the MOV decreases from a very high level (thousands of ohms) to a very low level (a few ohms). The actual resistance of the device is a function of the rate of applied voltage and current.

metal primer *See* PRIMER.

metal roofing Roof covering with metal sheets of steel, aluminium, copper, lead or zinc. Flat sheets can be supported on closed sheathing; profiled steel or aluminium sheets are self-supporting on purlins. Steel sheet must be GALVANISEd or ZINCALUMEd for corrosion protection.

metallic paint A paint which contains flakes of metals, which reflect natural or artificial light.

metamorphic rock IGNEOUS or SEDIMENTARY ROCK which has been changed by chemical or physical action in the Earth's crust into a distinctly new type. *Marble* is metamorphic limestone, and *slate* is metamorphic shale.

meter *(a)* A measuring instrument, particularly for fluids, *e.g.* flow meter. *(b)* US spelling of METRE.

methane The name of the shortest hydrocarbon chain, CH_4. It is a colourless gas which occurs in *natural gas*, and is given off in marshes as *marsh gas* and in coal mines as *fire damp.*

methanol Methyl alcohol ($CH_3.OH$), generally produced from the fermentation of woody plant materials.

method of least squares A method for fitting the best linear equation to a set of experimental results by making the squares of the residuals a minimum. The 'squaring' is necessary to eliminate the effect of positive and negative signs.

method of sections A method for the design of STATICALLY DETERMINATE trusses, proposed by the German engineer, A. Ritter, in 1862. It is particularly useful if the magnitude of the force in only one member is required. If the truss shown in the figure is cut across the main tie, the force in it T_1, can be obtained in one operation by taking moments about A. The two other unknown forces pass through A, and therefore have no moment about it. This is a simple example of a FREE-BODY DIAGRAM. In the figure:

$$T_1 y = \sum Wx$$

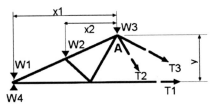

Method of sections

methyl ethyl ketone (MEK) A strong, flammable solvent used in paint and varnishes.

methyl methacrylate *See* ACRYLIC RESINS.

methylated spirits ETHANOL to which some METHANOL has been added to make it poisonous, and therefore undrinkable.

metre The unit of length in the metric system, introduced by the French Academy in 1791. It was originally defined as 1×10^{-7} of the distance from the north pole to the equator of the Earth's MERIDIAN passing through Paris, but it has since been redefined in terms of the wavelength of light at a particular frequency. 1 m = 39.37 in. *See also* SI UNITS.

metric system The system based on the *metre* used in CGS UNITS and SI UNITS.

metrication The act of converting any other unit to its metric equivalent, and of converting an industry or a national system to the SI system.

mezzanine An intermediate storey of lower height. It is usually a gallery between the main floor and the floor above it.

MF *Abbreviation for* Melamine FORMALDEHYDE.

MFLOPS *Abbreviation for* MEGAFLOPS.

Mg Chemical symbol for *magnesium*.

mho Unit of conductance. It is the reciprocal of the OHM.

mica A group of minerals found in igneous rocks; some are characterised by perfect cleavage, so that they can be split into thin sheets. Different types vary in chemical composition. Some micas are excellent electrical or thermal insulators and some are transparent.

micro (μ) *(a)* Prefix for one millionth, from the Greek word for small, *e.g.* 1 μs = 1 microsecond = 1 × 10^{-6} second. *(b)* Used commonly to signify smallness, as in microfiche, microcomputer.

microbar (μbar) A unit of pressure commonly used in acoustics. 1 μbar = 10^{-6} BAR = 0.1 Pa.

microchip A small CHIP.

microclimate The local climate of a small area.

microcomputer Term used to describe the desktop computers of today's technology. These machines typically depend upon a processor on a single chip for their processing power.

micro-concrete Concrete for use in small-scale structural models. Its aggregate is scaled down.

microcrack A crack too fine to be visible with the naked eye, but detectable with ultrasonic pulses.

microfiche A type of film for storing and archiving photographically reduced documents. Many pages are stored on a small rectangular film similar to a card index sheet.

microfilm A type of film for storing and archiving photographically reduced documents. Many pages are stored on a roll of 35 mm or 16 mm film. Accessing individual pages is less convenient than from MICROFICHE.

microlam Manufactured structural wood beam constructed of pressure- and adhesive-bonded strands of wood; it has a higher strength rating than solid sawn timber.

micrometer *(a)* An instrument for the precision measuring of length which consists of a G-shaped frame, one of whose legs is a round bar accurately threaded. A nut running on it is marked in 10^{-2} mm

or 10^{-3} in. *See also* VERNIER. *(b)* 1 μm = 10^{-6} m when US spelling is used.

micrometre In the SI SYSTEM 1 μm = 10^{-6} m. Previously called a *micron*.

micron One-millionth of a metre; an obsolescent unit, now called a *micrometre*.

microphone A transducer which responds to variations in pressure in the air due to sound, and converts them to an electrical signal. It also responds to hydrodynamic pressure fluctuations. *See also* CARDIOID MICROPHONE, CONDENSER MICROPHONE, FIGURE 8 MICROPHONE, MOVING-COIL MICROPHONE and UNIDIRECTIONAL MICROPHONE.

microprocessor A general-purpose computer PROCESSOR, contained within a CHIP.

microscopic Visible with a microscope only, as opposed to *macroscopic*.

microwave An ultra-high-frequency radio wave in the electromagnetic *spectrum* with a wavelength of less than 300 mm, *i.e.* a frequency of more than 1000 MHz.

middle strip The portion of a flat slab or flat plate between the COLUMN STRIPS (*where there is an illustration*). Most building codes define the middle strip as the middle half of the slab.

middle-third rule 'Provided the resultant force lies within the middle third, no tension is developed in a wall or foundation.' It is true only for rectangular sections.

MIDI *See* MUSICAL INSTRUMENT DIGITAL INTERFACE.

MIG welding Metal-inert-gas, a form of SHIELDED-ARC WELDING using an inert gas such as argon or helium, to surround the electrode, which is a wire continuously fed into the arc to provide the weld metal.

mil One thousandth: *(a)* of an inch; *(b)* of a right angle; *(c)* of a radian; *(d)* of a litre.

mild steel Steel with a carbon content of 0.1–0.2 per cent. It is ductile and has a yield stress of 200–250 N/mm^2 (30–35 ksi).

mildew A fungus that grows on fabrics and on paint, and feeds on them. It causes discoloration, and ultimately decomposition.

mile A measure of length. 1 British/American mile = 5280 ft = 1.609 km; 1

Admiralty NAUTICAL MILE = 1.853 km; 1 international nautical mile = 1.852 km.

milk of lime SLAKED LIME in water.

mill bar *See* MERCHANT BAR.

mill scale The oxide layer formed on structural steel sections and reinforcing bars during hot rolling. If it is loose, it must be removed before concreting or painting, to ensure proper adhesion.

milli (m) Prefix for one thousandth, from the Latin word for 1000, *e.g.* 1 millimetre = 0.001 metre.

millibar (mb) Unit of pressure used in meteorology. 1 mb = 100 NEWTONS per square metre = 100 PASCALS = 0.750 mm of mercury (measured with a mercury barometer at 0 °C). Widely replaced by the hectopascal (hPa), which has the same value.

milling machine A machine which removes shavings from a surface by pushing it on a moving table past a *rotating* cutter. Because both the work and the tool move, it can be used for making complex parts, such as gears. *See also* PLANING MACHINE.

millwork US term for building materials made of finished wood and manufactured off site, such as doors, frames, mouldings, wall panels, mantels and stairs . Typically, millwork does not include flooring or ceilings.

mime *Abbreviation for* Multipurpose Internet Mail Extensions. A format for transferring non-textual data such as graphics, video and audio through EMAIL.

MIMS cable Mineral Insulated Metal Sheathed, a cable having compressed powder mineral insulation enclosed in solid-drawn metal sheathing. Cables may be either single-core or multicore, and have greater fire resistance than plastic-insulated cables.

mineral flax Fiberised asbestos or mineral wool.

mineral pigment Pigment made by processing materials mined from the earth.

mineral spirits A petroleum distillate used as a solvent.

mineral turpentine Hydrocarbon solvent, widely used for thinning and cleaning up ENAMEL paints. It is different in composition from *gum turpentine*, which is distilled from tree products.

mineral wool An aggregate of fine filaments, which can be formed into a flexible and resilient mat. It is produced by blowing air or steam through molten blast-furnace slag *(slag wool)*, through molten rock *(rock wool)*, or through molten glass *(glass wool)*. It has excellent thermal insulating properties, particularly in loose form, and it does not support vermin or rot.

minimal surface The shortest surface which can be formed between a given set of boundaries. It can be obtained experimentally by forming the boundaries out of wire, and then dipping them into a solution (*e.g.* detergent or latex) which contracts to a minimal surface by surface tension. The minimal surface is always a SADDLE SURFACE.

minor intrusions IGNEOUS ROCKS formed by intrusions in fissures, etc. and consequently much finer grained than PLUTONIC INTRUSIONS.

MIPS *Abbreviation for* Million Instructions Per Second. A measure of computing power.

mirror A surface capable of reflecting light (or sound) without appreciable diffusion. The *angle of reflection* equals the *angle of incidence*. *See also* PARABOLIC REFLECTOR, SOUND MIRROR *and* SPECULAR SURFACE.

mirror glass *Same as* REFLECTIVE GLASS.

mirroring *(a)* In computer graphics, the process of copying and rotating graphic elements 180° around an axis so as to produce a reverse-image copy. Generally referred to as *flipping (vertically or horizontally)*. *(b)* In Internet hosting, reproducing information from one server on another, so that it can be accessed by a third party via a shorter route.

MIS *Abbreviation for* MANAGEMENT INFORMATION SYSTEM.

mission tile Roof tile of approximately semi-cylindrical shape, laid alternately up and down. *Also called Roman tile* and *Spanish tile.*

miter US spelling of *mitre*.

mitre *See* MITRE BOX, JOINT *and* SQUARE.

mitre box A U-shaped open box with cuts at 45°, which facilitate the making of 90° mitred joints. The piece of timber to be mitred is placed in the box, and the cuts guide the saw to cut at an angle of 45°. *Also called* a *mitre block.*

mitre joint A joint formed by fitting together two pieces of material in the same plane, on a line bisecting their junction. *Mitring* is the operation of cutting the boards and fitting them together at an angle, usually a right angle.

mitre square A square for setting out timber. It has one edge of the handle set at 45°, so that it can be used for laying out right-angled mitre joints. *Also called* a *combination square.*

mix proportions The ratio in which the various components of a composite material, such as concrete, mortar or plaster, are mixed together. Mix proportions may be specified by volume, which merely requires the filling of a bucket or gauge box, or by weight which is more accurate for materials subject to BULKING. *See also* BATCH BOX, WATER–CEMENT RATIO *and* WEIGH BATCHER.

mixed mode climate control A system of indoor climate control in which natural ventilation is supplemented by mechanical cooling and/or heating when considered necessary by the occupant(s) of a space.

mixer *See* CONCRETE MIXER.

mixing box A device for the controlled mixing of air from hot and cold air distribution systems to provide the correct supply temperature to suit transient cooling/heating loads in air conditioned space.

mixing chamber The section of an air handling unit where outdoor air is mixed with return air from conditioned space prior to treatment in filters and cooling and/or heating coils.

mixing desk or mixer (acoustics) A set of controls allowing several microphone signals to be adjusted and fed into a common sound distribution system such as an equaliser, power amplifier and loudspeakers.

mixture Two or more ingredients, intimately mixed together but each retaining its own chemical identity, as opposed to a COMPOUND.

MKS units The units of the metric system, based on the metre, kilogram and second. Some of its units, such as the CALORIE

and the units of stress, have been further rationalised in the SI system.

ML Megalitre = $1000 \, m^3$.

MLSA *Abbreviation for* Maximum Length Sequence Analyser. A digital technique used to measure acoustic characteristics of rooms using a repeated digital sequence excitation via a loudspeaker correlated with the received microphone signal from the room.

MMMF *Abbreviation for* MAN-MADE MINERAL FIBRES.

Mn Chemical symbol for *manganese*.

mobile crane A crane, usually with an extending jib and outriggers, but able to travel on normal roads under its own power.

Möbius' law A rule defining the number of members required for a STATICALLY DETERMINATE STRUCTURE, published by A. F. Möbius in 1837. The simplest plane PIN-JOINTed frame consists of three members and it has three joints. Each additional joint requires two additional members. Consequently the number of members required is

$$n = 2j - 3$$

where j is the number of joints. The simplest SPACE FRAME is a tetrahedron, which has six members and four joints. Each additional joint requires three additional members, so that

$$n = 3j - 6$$

modal analysis A method of predicting the behaviour of vibrating systems. It involves breaking complex vibrations into component modes of vibration in order to produce a useful mathematical model.

mode *(a)* The most common item of a group of observations. If these are plotted as a bar chart, or HISTOGRAM, the mode is the observation corresponding to the longest bar. *See also* MEAN and MEDIAN. *(b)* The *mode of vibration* of a system is the displacement amplitude pattern of the system. In a linear system the natural mode of vibration is such that every particle is in a state of simple harmonic motion with the same frequency.

model A representation of an aspect of reality which illustrates its properties. It

may be a physical model or a MATHE-
MATICAL MODEL.

model analysis Analysis of structural,
lighting, ventilation, acoustic or other
problems by means of physical as
opposed to MATHEMATICAL MODELS. *See*
ACOUSTIC MODEL ANALYSIS, ARTIFICIAL
SKY, DIRECT MODEL ANALYSIS, INDIRECT
STRUCTURAL MODEL ANALYSIS, PERISCOPE,
SOLARSCOPE *and* WIND TUNNEL.

modelling *(a)* The process of producing a
representation of some abstraction of a
situation. *(b)* In computing, the process
of producing a computer representation,
e.g. a building product model. *(c)* In
lighting, a description of the ability of
a lighting system to reveal form.

modelscope A PERISCOPE for viewing
models.

modem *Abbreviation for* MOdulator/
DEModulator, *i.e.* a device used to
convert *digital* signals to analog signals
(modulate) and vice versa (demodulate).
It is used, for example, to enable a *digital*
signal, as produced by a computer, to be
transmitted over a telephone network.

modern architecture *(a)* Buildings
designed in the currently fashionable style
of architecture. *(b)* Buildings designed
in accordance with the principles of
the Modern Movement, *also called* the
International Style. In that case, Modern
is commonly spelled with a capital M.
See also CONTEMPORARY.

Moderne *See* ART MODERNE.

modular coordination Design of building
components to conform to a dimensional
standard based on a modular system.

modular grid A *reference grid* in which
the grid lines are spaced at exact multiples
of the MODULE.

modular ratio (of reinforced concrete)
The ratio of the MODULUS OF ELASTICITY
of the reinforcing steel to the EFFECTIVE
MODULUS OF ELASTICITY OF CONCRETE.

modular size A dimension which is a
multiple of the basic MODULE M, *i.e. nM*,
where n is an integer. The modular size
nM is normally considered to include
allowances for joints and TOLERANCES.

modulating control Automatic control
device, continuously variable through
an operating range for the control of a
variable such as the quantity of chilled
water flowing to a cooling coil, as
opposed to an on–off control.

modulation *See* AMPLITUDE MODULATION
and FREQUENCY MODULATION.

module A unit of length particularly
specified for MODULAR COORDINATION.

modulus of elasticity The ratio of direct
STRESS to STRAIN in an elastic material
obeying HOOKE'S LAW. *Also called
Young's modulus*, after Thomas Young,
a British scientist who introduced the
concept in 1807. *See also* MODULUS OF
RIGIDITY *and* SECANT MODULUS.

modulus of rigidity The ratio of SHEAR
STRESS to SHEAR STRAIN in a material
obeying HOOKE'S LAW.

modulus of rupture The nominal stress

$$f = \frac{M}{Z}$$

(where M is the ultimate BENDING
MOMENT and Z the SECTION MODULUS) at
which a beam breaks. It is a common test
for the tensile strength of brittle materials,
such as concrete, whose flexural strength
is controlled by tension. Stress distribution at rupture is no longer elastic, and
consequently the true tensile stress is
lower than M/Z.

modulus of section *See* SECTION MODU-
LUS *and* PLASTIC SECTION MODULUS.

modulus, bulk *See* BULK MODULUS.

Mohr circle A graphic construction
devised by the nineteenth-century German
engineering professor, Otto Mohr, which
enables the stresses acting on a cross-
section oriented in any desired direction to
be determined if the PRINCIPAL STRESSES
are known. It can be used either for
two-dimensional or, with an additional
construction, for three-dimensional stress
problems. *See also* ELLIPSOID OF STRESS.

Mohr's theorem The theorem proposed
by Professor Otto Mohr at Dresden
Technical University in 1868, states that
the slope and deflection bear the same
relation to the bending moment as the
shear force and bending moment respectively do to the load. Consequently the
slope and deflection can be determined
from a fictitious load, which equals the
bending moment divided by EI (where E
is modulus of elasticity and I is the second

moment of area); this is the *moment–area method*.

Mohs' scale A hardness scale defined by Friedrich Mohs, a German mineralogist, in 1812. It consists of a comparison with 10 standard minerals: (1) talc, (2) gypsum, (3) calcite, (4) fluorite, (5) apatite, (6) orthoclase, (7) quartz, (8) topaz, (9) corundum and (10) diamond. A material of number 8 hardness is scratched by corundum, but scratches quartz.

moiré fringes Patterns produced by interference between two series of lines: an undistorted parallel grid, and a similar grid distorted by a loaded MODEL. This can be achieved either by reflection from the surface of the model, in a manner similar to the PHOTOSTRESS METHOD, or by refraction, *i.e.* by light passing through the model. The patterns resemble those of PHOTOELASTICITY, but the technique measures slope, and consequently *flexural curvature*. (Isochromatics give the difference between the two principal stresses.)

moist room A room in which the relative humidity is kept above 98 per cent, and the temperature is kept constant (usually $23\,°C \pm 2°$). It is used for curing test specimens of building materials (particularly concrete) under standard conditions. *Also called a fog room.*

moisture barrier Either a VAPOUR BARRIER or a DAMPPROOF COURSE.

moisture content The mass of water in a material, such as a soil, divided by the mass of the solids.

moisture content of air A more accurate term for what is generally referred to as ABSOLUTE HUMIDITY, *i.e.* grams of water vapour present in 1 kg of dry air.

moisture equivalent, field *See* FIELD MOISTURE EQUIVALENT.

moisture gradient The variation in moisture content between the outside and the inside of a piece of material, particularly wood.

moisture meter Instrument for determining the moisture content of a material (commonly of timber) by measuring the electrical resistance between two points on its surface.

moisture movement *(a)* The movement of moisture through a porous material. *(b)* The effect of changes in moisture content on the dimensions of the material. In concrete it causes mainly SHRINKAGE. In timber it may cause shrinkage, swelling or distortion, particularly if it is inadequately SEASONED. *(c)* Moisture movement due to a sustained load. It causes CREEP in concrete.

molding US spelling for MOULDING.

mole The amount of a substance whose mass in grams is numerically equal to the molecular mass of the substance. *Abbreviated mol.* The same as *grammolecule*, which it replaces in the SI system.

molecular heat The product of the SPECIFIC HEAT of a substance and its molecular weight.

molecular weight The sum of the ATOMIC WEIGHTS of all the atoms in a molecule.

Mollier diagram Graphic representation of conditions of moist air. Originally the '*i–x*' diagram, with humidity ratio on the abscissa and ENTHALPY (heat content) as the ordinate, followed by the '*t–x*' diagram, with the humidity ratio or vapour pressure on the abscissa and dry-bulb temperature on the ordinate (*see figure*). Generally used in Europe, as the PSYCHROMETRIC CHART is used in English-speaking countries.

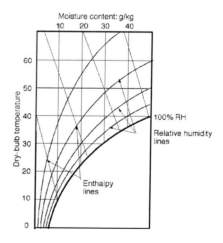

Mollier diagram

moment *See* BENDING MOMENT, COUPLE, MOMENT OF A FORCE *and* TWISTING MOMENT.

moment arm *Same as* LEVER ARM.

moment distribution method A technique devised by Professor Hardy Cross at the University of Illinois in 1930 for the solution of the bending moments in rigid frames and continuous beams by successive approximations. It was widely used until less laborious computer methods were devised, such as the MATRIX-DISPLACEMENT METHOD.

moment frame *Same as* RIGID FRAME.

moment of a force The moment of a force about a given point, or briefly 'the moment', is the turning effect, measured by the product of the force and its perpendicular distance from the point. *See also* COUPLE.

moment of an area The sum of the products obtained by multiplying each element of area, dA, by its distance from the reference axis, y. It is therefore

$$\sum y \, dA \text{ or } \int y \, dA$$

The CENTROIDAL AXIS is the axis about which the moment of an area vanishes.

moment of inertia *(a)* A measure of the resistance offered by a body to angular acceleration. It is the SECOND MOMENT OF AREA of the body, multiplied by its density. *(b)* The term 'moment of inertia' is also commonly used as a synonym for the SECOND MOMENT OF AREA. *See also* POLAR MOMENT OF INERTIA.

moment of resistance The moment produced by the internal forces in a beam. For equilibrium, it must equal the BENDING MOMENT due to the external forces.

moment–area method *See* MOHR'S THEOREM.

momentum The product of the mass of a body and its velocity.

monitor *(a)* A series of windows on both sides of a single storey factory roof, which admit daylight, and sometimes also provide ventilation. The monitor is a linear version of the LANTERN used in classical domes. Monitor frames *(see figure)*, and roof trusses are shaped to include the monitor as an integral part of the steel frame. *See also* NORTHLIGHT ROOF. *(b)* Any device or process which inspects the state of some other device or process. *(c)* Commonly used for the visual display unit of a computer.

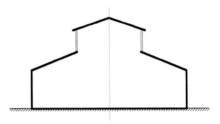

Monitor

monochromatic light Light of a single colour, produced by a filter (which absorbs the other colours), or by a monochromatic lamp, *e.g.* a sodium lamp.

monolith A single block of stone or concrete. Hence *monolithic construction*, which is concrete cast with no joints other than construction joints.

monomer A molecule containing a single MER, as opposed to a *polymer*.

Monte Carlo method A procedure that utilises the techniques of statistical sampling to obtain an approximate solution of a mathematical or physical problem.

monthly mean daily insolation The average solar energy per square metre available per day of a given month.

montmorillonite A mineral consisting of finely divided hydrous aluminium or magnesium silicate, characterised by a sheet-like molecular structure. Its expansion and contraction on wetting and drying are exceptionally high. It is the main constituent of BENTONITE.

Montreal Protocol An international agreement to limit the discharge of ozone-depleting substances to the atmosphere, reached at a meeting in the city of Montreal in 1987.

Moon–Spencer sky The CIE STANDARD OVERCAST SKY proposed by Parry Moon and Domenica Spencer.

Moorish arch *Same as* HORSESHOE ARCH.

mortar A mixture of sand and a cementing medium, such as PORTLAND CEMENT or LIME.

mortice A rectangular slot cut into one piece of timber, into which a tenon or tongue, from another piece is fitted to form a *mortice-and-tenon joint* (*see figure*). A *mortice lock* is one which fits into a mortice in the edge of a door, as opposed to a RIM LOCK. *Also spelled mortise*, especially in the USA.

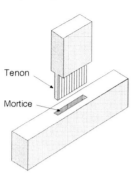

Mortice

mosaic Inlaid surface decoration for floors and walls formed by small pieces (or *tesserae*) of tile, glass or marble. Present-day mosaics are generally laid in geometric patterns, but representational designs were common in earlier days.

motion detector A sensing device used to detect motion in a space. May be used in a security system to detect an intruder or in an electric lighting or an air conditioning system to turn off an appliance to save energy when a space is not occupied.

motor alternator A MOTOR GENERATOR in which the output is AC, from an alternator.

motor generator An electrical generator mechanically linked to an electric motor which is driven by utility power or by batteries. The output may be AC or DC, depending on the application.

motor generator set A set that controls the speed of large electric motors, such as those for lifts (elevators). It consists of an induction or shunt motor which drives a variable voltage direct-current generator, and this in turn drives a direct-current motor, whose speed is thus infinitely variable, and whose direction of driving can be reversed. *Also called Ward Leonard control.* Now largely superseded by solid-state electronic controls.

mould *Also spelled mold* (USA): *(a)* FORMWORK: *(b)* a FUNGUS.

moulding A strip of wood, stone, metal or plastic, either plane or curved, used to cover a joint, or used for decoration. Hand-carved mouldings played an important part in classical architecture. Mass-produced mouldings can now be bought in many different shapes and sizes.

mouse A hand-held POINTING DEVICE used by moving it across a surface. It has one or more buttons allowing a number of functions such as selecting, dragging and drawing on the computer screen.

movement *See* MOISTURE MOVEMENT *and* TEMPERATURE MOVEMENT.

moving stair An ESCALATOR.

moving walk A continuously moving endless belt on which passengers can stand or walk; an ESCALATOR without steps.

moving-coil microphone A microphone in which the diaphragm exposed to sound pressure is connected directly to a movable coil. The movement of the coil in the magnetic gap produces a voltage.

MPEG *Abbreviation for* Motion Picture Experts Group. A COMPRESSION (DATA STORAGE) protocol for video, analogous to JPEG for still pictures.

mph *Abbreviation for* Miles Per Hour.

MRT *Abbreviation for* Mean Radiant Temperature.

MS *Abbreviation for* MILD STEEL.

MTBF *Abbreviation for* Mean Time Between Failure. A statistical estimate of the time a component, subassembly, or operating unit will operate before failure will occur.

MTTR *Abbreviation for* Mean Time To Repair. A statistical estimate of the repair time for a failed item.

mu (μ) *Abbreviation for micro.*

mud A colloquial term for mortar, or for gypsum board joint compound products.

mud brick construction *Same as* ADOBE.

muffler (*also known as a silencer*) A device for attenuating sound while allowing air to flow through largely unimpeded. *See also* REACTIVE MUFFLER *and* DISSIPATIVE MUFFLER.

mullion A vertical dividing member of a traditional window, capable of supporting weight. The corresponding horizontal member is a *transom*. Windows may be further subdivided by *glazing bars*.

multi-element prestressing Assembly of an integrated structural member from several individual units by means of PRESTRESSING.

multimedia The integration or combining of various forms of information such as text, graphics, sound and video. Multimedia documents are often richer, more expressive and engaging than conventional forms.

multiple earth neutral system A system of earthing used in electrical distribution systems in which the neutral is bonded to the earth at each point of connection (to a property). This provides parallel earth connections, via the neutral, reducing the impedance to earth. It also ensures that the neutral does not 'float' above earth potential.

multipurpose auditorium An auditorium used for a variety of performances such as theatre, cinema, music and dance. The acoustics of such a space are therefore a compromise between the different acoustics required for these activities.

multi-session optical drive A CD-R or DVD with the ability to record portions of the disk at different times (in different sessions). Early CD-ROM recorders could only record to a disk once; more recent CD-ROM drives have multi-session capability.

multispeed optical drive A CD or DVD drive with the ability to use different spin speeds to maintain a higher transfer rate when reading from a disk. Newer CD-ROM drives have multispeed capabilities (12×, 24×, etc.).

multiuser computer system Computer system designed to allow the shared use of its resources by multiple users. To the users of such system, it appears that they have exclusive control of the system. *Same as time-sharing system.*

multi-zone system An air conditioning system in which the thermal condition of air supplied to separate zones within a space is independently controlled.

Munsell Book of Color One of the standard methods for specifying physical (surface) colours by means of an atlas of colour chips. Munsell arranges colour according to HUE, VALUE and CHROMA. The colours are matched against the standard colours in the *Book of Color* for identification. This was first published by A. H. Munsell in 1905, and is now produced by the Munsell Color Co., Baltimore.

muntin *Same as* SASH BAR.

Muntz metal An alloy of three parts of copper and two parts of zinc, named after the English metallurgist, George Frederick Muntz.

muqarnas Concave three-dimensional shapes used in Islamic construction, generally formed by SQUINCHES.

muriatic acid Hydrochloric acid (HCl).

mushroom column A column with an enlarged head in a FLAT SLAB. (*See figure under* FLAT PLATE.)

musical instrument digital interface (MIDI) A standard set of commands enabling the communication between a computer and a MIDI-compatible electronic musical instrument. For example, computer synthesised music can be played under computer control on a MIDI instrument, and vice versa, music played on a MIDI instrument can be captured, digitised and converted to musical notation by the computer.

myopia Short-sightedness, caused by excessive convexity of the eye's lens, which reduces visual acuity; hence people with uncorrected myopia require a greater illuminance.

N

N *(a)* Chemical symbol for *nitrogen*. *(b) Abbreviation for newton.*

n *Abbreviation for nano*, one thousandth of a millionth, or 10^{-9}.

Na Chemical symbol for *sodium* (natrium).

nadir The opposite of zenith. If the hemisphere of sky is assumed to continue below the horizon plane it is the point vertically below the observer at the same distance as the zenith. It is used as the centre of projection for STEREOGRAPHIC PROJECTION sunpath diagrams.

nail A fastener hammered into a softer material, such as timber, and held in position by surface friction. Today nails are invariably of metal, but before the Industrial Revolution hardwood nails were commonly used with softwood. *See also* SCAFFOLD NAIL *and* SCREW NAIL.

nail gun A hand-held machine for driving nails. The nails are automatically fed from a magazine attached to it. The power is usually supplied by compressed air (from an air hose attached to the gun) driving a piston, but there are also self-contained gas-powered guns, using a small gas cylinder and a battery for ignition. A *framing gun* drives thick nails from about 50–100 mm in length, for structural work; a *finishing gun* and a BRADDER drive progressively smaller nails for finer work.

nail-glued roof truss A glued roof truss with plywood gusset plates. The nails hold the truss together until the glue dries; thereafter the strength of the joints is presumed to depend on the glue alone.

nailable concrete Concrete into which nails can be driven. It usually contains LIGHTWEIGHT AGGREGATE, often with the addition of SAWDUST.

nailer A strip of wood attached to steel, built into a brick wall, or cast into concrete, so that other building elements can be fixed with nails. *Also called nailing strip.*

nailplate A type of TIMBER CONNECTOR. It is variously used to mean a galvanised steel plate with prepunched holes through which nails are driven, or with preformed nails punched from the sheet (*see figure*). *Also written nail plate.*

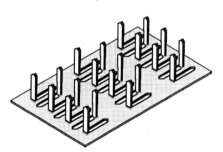

Nailplate

nano Prefix for one thousandth of a millionth (from the Greek word for dwarf), *e.g.* 1 nm = 1 nanometre = 1×10^{-9} metre.

nanocomposite fire retardant Fire retardant in nano-scale.

Naperian logarithm An alternative name for NATURAL LOGARITHM, named after the sixteenth-century mathematician, John Napier, who invented logarithms.

nappe A sheet of water flowing over a weir.

natatorium Building enclosing a swimming pool.

natural asphalt *See* ASPHALT.

natural cement A cement obtained by grinding calcined argillaceous limestone burned at a temperature no higher than is necessary to drive off the carbon dioxide. In contrast to PORTLAND CEMENT, it is produced from a natural mixture of argillaceous and calcareous material. Natural cements were common before the manufacture of Portland cement was perfected. The earliest example is the *Roman cement* patented by J. Parker in England in 1796.

natural convection The natural movement of heat through a fluid that occurs when warm, less dense fluid rises and cold, dense fluid sinks under the influence of gravity.

natural frequency The frequency of free oscillation of a system, when acted upon by no external forces other than an original excitation. *Also known as* the *resonant frequency* or frequency at which the system resonates.

natural gas Hydrocarbon gas obtained from underground deposits. Its main constituent is METHANE.

natural language processing (NLP) In computing, the process by which a computer understands and generates natural language.

natural light *Same as* DAYLIGHT.

natural logarithm A logarithm to the base $e = 2.71828\ldots$, also called a *Naperian logarithm*. This is of practical importance because the solution of the integral

$$\int \frac{\mathrm{d}x}{x} = \log_e x$$

See also EXPONENTIAL FUNCTION.

natural refrigerant(s) Naturally occurring substances with properties that render them suitable in appropriate circumstances for use as non-ozone-depleting refrigerants. Substances of interest include air, ammonia, butane, carbon dioxide and water.

natural seasoning The drying of timber by stacking it so that it is exposed to the flow of air, but is sheltered from rain and sun. It is an older method than KILN seasoning, and it takes much longer to achieve the same result. Since sufficient time is not always allowed, the extent of the seasoning is open to doubt.

natural stone Stone which has been quarried and cut, but not crushed into chips and reconstituted as *cast stone.*

natural ventilation Ventilation without the use of mechanical power, by the suitable location of windows and doors. It is more effective if the openings are placed on opposite sides of a room (to achieve *cross ventilation*), or at significantly different levels (to achieve *stack effect*).

Nautical Almanac A book of tables, published annually, of the daily movements of the sun, moon and stars. Since 1960 the *British Nautical Almanac* and the *American Ephemeris* have been published in the same form.

nautical mile One international nautical mile = 1852 m. One British Admiralty and US Coast Survey nautical mile = 6080 ft = 1853.2 m. Originally defined as one minute of arc on a GREAT CIRCLE on the Earth's surface.

nave The middle AISLE of a church.

nave arcade An open ARCADE between the central AISLE (or NAVE) and one of the side aisles.

Navier's theorem The simple theory of bending. It is based on the experimental result that sections that were plane before bending remain plane after bending, but converge on a centre of curvature. Consequently the relation between STRAIN (and therefore STRESS) and distance from the NEUTRAL AXIS is linear. In 1826 L. M. H. Navier, Professor at the *École des Ponts et Chaussées* in Paris, published the solution in the now accepted form:

$$\frac{M}{I} = \frac{f}{y} = \frac{E}{R}$$

where M is the BENDING MOMENT at the section, I is the SECOND MOMENT OF AREA of the section, f is the extreme fibre stress, y is the extreme fibre distance, E is the MODULUS OF ELASTICITY, and R is the radius of curvature at the section. The equation is often quoted in two different forms:

$$M = FZ$$

where F is the MAXIMUM PERMISSIBLE STRESS for the material in the beam and Z is the SECTION MODULUS of the beam, and

$$R = \frac{EI}{M}$$

which is used for determining the slope and deflection of the beam.

Navier–Stokes equations The set of fluid flow equations based on momentum conservation, derived from Newton's second law of motion for Newtonian fluids.

NBRI National Building Research Institute, Pretoria or Haifa.

NBS National Bureau of Standards, Washington, DC, *now* NIST, the National Institute of Standards and Technology.

NC *Abbreviation for*: *(a)* NOISE CRITERIA CURVES; *(b)* NUMERICAL CONTROL.

near field That part of a sound field, produced by a source in a FREE FIELD, where the SOUND PRESSURE and the air velocity (caused by the passage of the sound) are not in phase, *i.e.* at a distance which is usually within one representative dimension of the source. The INVERSE SQUARE LAW does not apply in this region and SOUND PRESSURE LEVEL measurements cannot be used to predict SOUND INTENSITY or SOUND POWER of the source.

near infrared (or solar infrared) The region of the electromagnetic spectrum between 0.77 to 1.4 μm. Most of the infrared solar radiation falls into this region. This region is transmitted, absorbed and reflected in a similar manner to visible light by most glazing and non-metallic building materials.

near-critical activity *See* ACTIVITY.

neat cement Cement used without sand, as opposed to cement mortar.

NEC *Abbreviation for* National Electrical Code.

neck velocity The velocity of a fluid as it passes through the neck of an air diffuser.

necking The contraction in area that occurs when a ductile material, such as mild steel, fails in tension. *See* CUP-AND-CONE FRACTURE.

needle A short, stout timber or steel beam which is passed horizontally through a wall, to support the end of a SHORE.

needlepoint screw A screw with a sharp point, intended for use with a power screwdriver, to penetrate thin sheetmetal without pre-drilling. *See also* SELF-DRILLING SCREW.

NEF *Abbreviation for* NOISE EXPOSURE FORECAST.

negative bending moment A BENDING MOMENT which causes hogging, or convex, curvature *(see figure)*. In continuous beams and frames, the negative moments occur over the columns, and the positive moments near mid-span.

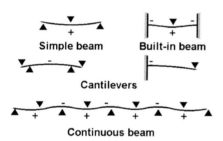

Simple beam   Built-in beam

Cantilevers

Continuous beam

Negative bending moment

negative reinforcement Reinforcement placed in concrete beams to resist the NEGATIVE BENDING MOMENT, *i.e.* near the top face.

negative resistance The characteristic of a circuit in which current varies inversely with applied voltage.

NEMA National Electrical Manufacturers Association.

neon A colourless, odourless and inert gas. Its chemical symbol is Ne, its atomic number is 10, its atomic weight is 20.183, and its boiling point is $-245.9\,°C$. It is used in lamps as both a source of light and as part of a starting mixture of gases.

neon lamp or tube A lamp containing neon at low pressure. A discharge of electricity through neon produces an intense orange-red glow, which is used for neon signs and glow DISCHARGE LAMPS. The term 'neon' is used generically for COLD CATHODE lamps containing other gases or fluorescent coatings.

neoprene An oil-resistant synthetic rubber.

NERDCC National Energy Research, Development and Demonstration Council, Australia (no longer in operation).

net lease A LEASE under which the LESSEE agrees to payment of all property charges such as taxes, insurance and maintenance as well as rent.

net lettable (or rentable) area The net area available for rental to a tenant. Usually excludes public access spaces, plant rooms and the like.

net occupiable area The area occupied in a LEASE agreement. It is generally the same as the NET LETTABLE AREA.

network *(a)* Generally any set of interconnected elements which form an overall organisation. *(b)* A diagram representing a series of interconnected events, as in the representation of a building project *(see figure)*. It forms the basis of both the CRITICAL PATH METHOD and PERT. A network must have one starting point and one terminal point. However, it may have many branches between, and become so complex that the CRITICAL PATH can be determined only with the aid of a computer. In the figure, the EVENTS are indicated by the circles, and the ACTIVITIES by arrows, with their duration shown. DUMMY ACTIVITIES are shown by dotted lines, and have no duration. The CRITICAL PATH is shown by the double line. *See also* ACTIVITY, CRASHED TIME, DUMMY ACTIVITY, EVENT *and* FLOAT. *(c)* In computing and information *technology*, it refers to a system of physically distributed computers interconnected by telecommunication channels.

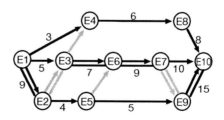

Network

network analysis An analysis of operations in which the logical relationships between activities are shown in terms of precedence, the times of activities and the resources required. *See* CRITICAL PATH METHOD.

neural network A model for constructing computer programs to emulate the action of the brain's neurons in learning to solve certain categories of problems (*e.g.* classification problems, image recognition problems).

neutral (electricity) The junction point of the legs of a STAR circuit, or the centre point of one coil of a DELTA transformer secondary. The neutral point is usually GROUNDED.

neutral axis The line in the cross-section of a beam where the flexural stress changes from tension to compression, *i.e.* the line where the direct stress is zero. In sections subject to pure bending, the neutral axis passes through the CENTROID. Also called *neutral layer* (of the beam).

neutral conductor The electric conductor in a single-phase or polyphase system which is at a uniform electric potential, usually by *earthing*. (In a balanced three-phase system it carries no current.)

neutral file A FILE written in a format which is common to many applications. Used for transferring data from one application to another without having to write specific translators for each pair of applications.

neutrality temperature (Tn) *Also called thermal neutrality.* The theoretical optimum (not too warm or too cold) temperature, usually determined as 'group neutrality', the mean of numerous votes in a comfort study and expressed as a linear function, *e.g.*

$$T_n = 17.8 + 0.31 \times T_{o'av}$$

where $T_{o'av}$ is often taken as the mean outdoor temperature of the month considered.

neutron Sub-atomic particle of the same mass as a PROTON, but having no electric charge.

newel An upright post supporting the hand-rail at the top and bottom of a staircase, and also at the turn on a landing.

newton (*abbreviated* N) In the system of SI UNITS, the unit of force and weight; it is named after the seventeenth-century English scientist. 1 newton is the force which, applied to a mass of 1 kilogram, produces an acceleration of 1 metre per second per second. Unlike the units of force used in the CGS and FPS UNITS, it is independent of the Earth's gravity. The newton is a small unit, and it is frequently necessary to use the kN or MN. *See also* KILOPOND.

NFPA National Fire Protection Association, Quincy, MA, USA, and National Forest Products Association, Washington, DC (formerly NLMA).

NIBS National Institute of Building Sciences, Washington, DC.

nickel A bright silvery metal, used as an alloying element to increase the strength, ductility and corrosion resistance of steel, and for electroplating metals which require corrosion protection. It is a major component of many STAINLESS STEELS. Its chemical symbol is Ni, its atomic number is 28, its atomic weight is 58.7, its specific gravity is 8.85, and its melting point is 1450°C.

Nicol prism A device for obtaining plane-polarised light, *e.g.* for PHOTOELASTICITY. It consists of a crystal of ICELAND SPAR, cut and cemented together in such a way that a plane-polarised ray of light is freely transmitted, while an ordinary ray of light is reflected out at the side of the crystal.

night cooling Cooling interior space in a building in hot weather by circulating outdoor air overnight when its temperature is lower than that of the air in the building. Sometimes referred to as 'night flush cooling'.

night sky radiation A method of cooling through radiant energy exchange. Relatively warm surfaces are exposed directly to the colder night sky to which they radiate the heat they collected during the day.

nightlatch A door lock which can be opened from the outside only by a key, and by a knob from the inside. The bolt has a tapered end, so that it will engage if the door is slammed shut. (Originally intended so that an employee could lock up the premises at night, but not gain re-entry without a key. Less secure than a DEADLOCK, and less convenient because of the danger of being locked out accidentally.)

nipple (plumbing) A (straight) pipe fitting having a male thread or surface at each end, which may be the same or different diameters. Used mainly for connecting to other fittings, since the pipes themselves usually also have male ends. *See figure under* PIPE FITTINGS (water and gas).

NIST National Institute of Standards and Technology, Washington, DC, *previously* the NBS.

nitrocellulose Produced by the action of a mixture of nitric and sulphuric acid on cellulose. Nitrocellulose with a low nitrogen content is not explosive, and it is used as a solvent of LACQUER. Nitrocellulose with a high nitrogen content is the explosive *gun cotton.*

nitrogen A colourless and odourless gas. It constitutes about 78 per cent by volume of the atmosphere. Its chemical symbol is N, its atomic number is 7, its atomic weight is 14.008, it has a valency of 3 or 5, and its boiling point is $-195.8\,°C$. *See also* OXIDES OF NITROGEN.

NLMA National Lumber Manufacturers' Association, Washington, DC (now NFPA).

NLP *Abbreviation for* NATURAL LANGUAGE PROCESSING.

nm Nanometre, one billionth of a metre. $1\,nm = 10^{-9}m$. Now replacing the ÅNGSTRÖM unit ($1\,nm = 10Å$).

NNI *Abbreviation for* Noise and Number Index; an index for the measurement of disturbance from aircraft noise, developed in Britain in 1961.

noble metals Metals, such as silver, gold and platinum, which have a high positive electrode potential in the ELECTROCHEMICAL SERIES, and consequently are resistant to most types of corrosion, and specifically to atmospheric oxidation.

node *(a)* The point where several members of a TRUSS, or SPACE FRAME or CABLE NETWORK meet; also a jointing device used at that point. *(b)* An intersection or end point on a computer network, being a computer or a distribution hub. *(c)* A point of minimum displacement in a system of stationary waves.

no-fines concrete Concrete made without sand. It therefore contains a high proportion of communicating pores, which provide thermal insulation and drainage.

nogging *(a)* Horizontal short timbers which stiffen the vertical studs of a framed partition. *(b)* Brick infilling in the spaces between the studs of a timber frame.

noise *(a)* (electrical and communications) An undesirable irregular, oscillatory signal which is superimposed on the desired signal. See COMMON MODE NOISE and NORMAL MODE NOISE. *(b)* An undesirable sound. *See also under* ACOUSTIC *and* SOUND.

noise absorption *See* SOUND ABSORPTION.

noise criteria (NC) A numerical rating of broad-band noises, developed by L. Beranek (1956) or prescription for noise limits depicted by a series of curves. These curves are designated by the sound pressure level at 1000 Hz. If a given noise is measured for octave-band sound pressure levels and the resulting sound spectrum is plotted, the NC rating will be given by the NC curve just touched by the lowest point of the spectrum, i.e. by the NC curve which does not cross to above the spectrum at any octave. Largely replaced by the NR curves or rating.

noise dose (*see also* DAILY NOISE DOSE) A measure of the noise exposure a person experiences over a given time. For example, a person exposed to the maximum allowable occupational noise level over a working day is said to have a noise dose of unity. The same noise exposure over twice the length of time would give a noise dose of 2. The reference value is often taken as $3.2\,Pa^2h$.

noise exposure The time integral of the square of the A-weighted sound pressure received by a person, in any stated measuring period.

noise exposure forecast (NEF) A calculated value of the noise climate near an airport, based on forecast estimates of the various numbers of different aircraft using the airport at some future stated dates, and the flight paths that will be used.

noise pollution level (L_{np}) A measure of the energy equivalent sound pressure level which takes into account the variability of the sound level over the time in which the measurement is made.

$$L_{np} = L_{eq} + 2.56\sigma \text{ dB}$$

where σ is the standard deviation of the sound level during the measurement period.

noise rating (NR) A numerical rating of broad-band noises, or prescription for noise limits depicted by a series of curves, developed by C. W. Kosten (1962); very similar to the NC curves, but slightly more stringent at high frequencies. Generally used in Europe. Whilst dB*(a)* is the weighted average of octave-band sound pressure levels, NR is tangential to the highest point of the octave-band spectrum.

noise reduction The difference in SOUND PRESSURE LEVEL between two adjacent rooms when the source of sound determining the sound level in both rooms is in one of the rooms.

noise reduction coefficient The arithmetic mean of the SOUND ABSORPTION COEFFICIENTS of a material at the frequencies of 250, 500, 1000 and 2000 Hz.

noise, background See BACKGROUND NOISE.

noise, fan See FAN NOISE.

nominal diameter (DN) A numerical designation of size which is common to all components in a piping system. The mating diameters or thread size of the connections are defined by the nominal diameter, which is a convenient round number for reference purposes and only approximates the manufacturing dimensions.

nominal rent A rent agreed between two parties for mutual benefit which is not necessarily related to market value.

nominal size of timber The size of timber before it is DRESSED, and usually before it is SEASONED. Sizes of dressed timber are usually given as nominal sizes, and the actual size is 5–13 mm (¾₆–½ in.) smaller.

nominal voltage (Vn) A nominal value assigned to a circuit or system for the purpose of conveniently designating its voltage class (as 208/120, 480/277, 600).

nominated subcontractor A supplier selected by the principal to carry out work or supply materials, specifically defined in the contract documents. The subcontractor then enters into a contractual agreement with the head contractor.

nomogram A diagram used for the evaluation of an equation. Its simplest form consists of three straight lines, each graduated for one variable. By joining any two of them with a straight edge, the third can be read off. However, more complicated forms can be constructed, using more lines, including curved and inclined lines.

nonagon A nine-sided POLYGON. The angle included between the nine equal sides of a *regular* nonagon is 140°.

non-bearing wall See PARTITION.

non-combustible *Same as* INCOMBUSTIBLE.

non-critical activity See ACTIVITY.

non-destructive testing Testing which does not destroy the test piece. It is often performed on the actual structure. X-RAYS, ULTRASOUND, magnetic particles and BRITTLE COATINGS have been employed for non-destructive strength tests. Tests based on elastic deformation, as in the STRESS-GRADING OF TIMBER, in the testing of concrete with the SCHMIDT HAMMER, or in experimental stress analysis with STRAIN GAUGES, are also non-destructive.

non-developable surface A curved surface that cannot be flattened into a plane surface without shrinking, stretching and tearing. Most DOUBLY CURVED SURFACES are non-developable.

non-ferrous metal A metal which does not contain iron, or only a little iron.

non-graphic attribute An attribute of an object defining a property which is not graphic in nature, *e.g.* material, cost, supplier, thermal properties, function, etc.

non-habitable area The area of a building that cannot be utilised. It includes the structure, partitions, and ducts, and storage and service areas which are not suitable to accommodate people on a regular basis.

non-linear load (electrical) Electrical load which draws current discontinuously or whose impedance varies throughout the cycle of the input AC voltage waveform.

non-recoverable costs The leasing

commission, legal fees and owner's contribution to marketing funds that are not charged to tenants.

non-renewable fuels Fuels that cannot be easily made or 'renewed'. Oil, natural gas and coal are non-renewable fuels.

non-return (reflux) valve A valve used in pipework, which allows flow in one direction only.

non-sinusoidal A waveform that is not capable of being expressed mathematically by using the sine function.

normal direction Direction perpendicular to the cross-section under consideration.

normal frequency distribution curve *Same as* GAUSSIAN CURVE.

normal incidence absorption coefficient There are two commonly used measures of sound absorption properties of materials: normal and random-incidence absorption coefficients. Normal incidence values, which are measured using an impedance tube, are mainly used for quality control and product development purposes. A material with an absorption coefficient of 0 is a perfect reflector while a material with a coefficient of 1 is a perfect absorber. *See also* RANDOM INCIDENCE ABSORPTION COEFFICIENT.

normal mode (NM) The term refers to electrical interference which is measurable between line and neutral (current-carrying conductors). Normal mode interference is readily generated by the operation of lights, switches and motors. *See also* COMMON MODE.

normal mode (of vibration) One of several possible ways in which an elastic system, such as air in a room, will vibrate naturally when subjected to a momentary disturbance.

normal stress A direct stress, as opposed to a shear stress.

normalised level difference The value of noise reduction between two rooms in a given frequency band, if the reverberation time in the receiving room is 0.5 seconds.

normalised noise isolation class A noise isolation class determined from measured values of noise reduction between two rooms where the receiving room has a reverberation time of 0.5 seconds.

normalising Heating steel to about 50 °C above the TRANSFORMATION TEMPERATURE, followed by cooling in still air at room temperature, so that moderately rapid cooling occurs. The object is to eliminate internal stresses, refine the grain size and render the structure of the metal more uniform.

Norris–Eyring equation An equation for estimating the *reverberation time* in a room. The equation is a more accurate version of the *Sabine formula*.

north *See* TRUE NORTH.

northlight roof A term originating in the northern hemisphere for a sloping factory roof, having one gentle slope without glazing, and a glazed roof face pointing north. In the temperate zone this has a slope to admit more daylight, but in the subtropics it is usually vertical to exclude direct sunlight. *Also called* a *sawtooth roof.* In the southern hemisphere a *southlight roof* is used instead. *See also* MONITOR.

northlight shell A shell designed as a NORTHLIGHT (or in the southern hemisphere, southlight) ROOF. It may take the form of a parabolic *conoid*, with the parabolas facing north, or a cylindrical shell which has been cut *(see figure).*

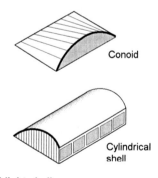

Conoid

Cylindrical shell

Northlight shell

nosing Any edge which projects beyond the general plane of a surface, but particularly the leading edge of a stair TREAD. *See figure under* STAIR.

no-sky line A line separating all points on the WORKING PLANE at which the sky is directly visible from those at which the sky is not directly visible.

no-slump concrete Concrete with a SLUMP of 25 mm (1 in.) or less.

notch A negative or subtractive impulse.

notch effect A locally increased stress in a section due to a notch, or sharp change in section. It is normally employed to test IMPACT RESISTANCE.

novated contract A contract with parties (such as design consultants), transferred from an original client to another participant, who may be the project manager or the head contractor.

nozzle A device for controlling and directing the discharge pattern of a fluid from a pipe or duct, and determining its shape. A nozzle has a smaller outlet than the pipe feeding it, to increase the velocity of the fluid. An air conditioning REGISTER *(a)* is larger, and does not significantly increase the velocity.

NPL National Physical Laboratory, Teddington, England.

NR *Abbreviation for* Noise Rating.

NRC *Abbreviation for (a)* Noise Reduction Coefficient; *(b)* National Research Council (USA or Canada).

NSFNET One of the direct precursors of the INTERNET. Originally conceived as a world-wide network for scientists, it evolved into today's Internet.

N-truss *Same as* PRATT TRUSS.

nudging When automatically operated lift doors remain open for longer than a specified time, the doors are made to close at a reduced speed in order to remove the obstruction.

numeric range The range of numbers available for numerical work on a computer is limited by the fact that only a finite representation of the real number line can be used. *See* FINITE PRECISION *and* OVERFLOW ERROR.

numerical control The automatic control of machines by means of numerical instructions which can be generated by computers.

nylon The generic name of a group of *polyamides*; it is derived from the initial letters of New York and London. Nylons are among the stronger plastics. They have good resistance to wear and corrosion, and are used in buildings for hardware, *e.g.* door fittings.

NZIA New Zealand Institute of Architects, Auckland.

NZIE New Zealand Institution of Engineers, Wellington, now called IPENZ.

O

Ω **(omega)** Symbol for OHM.

O Chemical symbol for *oxygen*.

O & M *See* OPERATION AND MAINTENANCE MANUALS.

OA On drawings, *abbreviation for* Overall.

oakum Loose fibre, which was once produced by picking old rope, used in CAULKING.

object-oriented graphics A model for constructing and storing graphic images in which some image components are treated as separate objects (as opposed to treating the entire image as one overall collection of pixels). For example, lines, circles, polygons, *etc.* would be individual objects which could be edited separately in an object-oriented graphics package. Most DRAWING PROGRAMS employ object-oriented graphics, whereas PAINTING PROGRAMS typically employ BIT-MAPPED GRAPHICS.

oblique parallel projection A pictorial PROJECTION in which the elevation is drawn as for the ORTHOGRAPHIC PROJECTION, and the plan and side elevation are then attached to the same picture at an angle of 45°. The object invariably looks too deep if drawn this way, and consequently an artificially foreshortened scale is sometimes used along the 45° lines.

obscure glass Glass which has been patterned so that it allows light to pass through, but it does not allow clear vision. If objects can be discerned at all, they are less distinct than through TRANSLUCENT GLASS.

obsidian A natural GLASS of granitic composition, originating as a LAVA. It is generally black with a vitreous lustre. It fractures with a sharp, hard edge, and has therefore been used in building tools by civilisations which did not have metal tools, *e.g.* the Aztecs and the Incas.

OC or O.C. *Abbreviation for* On Centre (*i.e.* the centre-to-centre spacing).

occupancy cost The total cost of occupying space, including rent, operating and capital costs, taxes, insurances and depreciation allowances.

occupancy rate The number of persons or users per unit of space, such as a room or a building.

occupied zone Zone within building space that is occupied by users. For the purposes of air quality, etc., usually considered to extend upward from the floor to a height of 2000 mm from the floor and horizontally to within 600 mm of walls.

ochre A yellow mineral pigment. It consists of ferrous oxide (FeO).

OCR *Abbreviation for* OPTICAL CHARACTER RECOGNITION.

octagon An eight-sided POLYGON. The angle included between the eight equal sides of a *regular* octagon is 135°.

octahedron A regular POLYHEDRON bounded by eight equilateral triangles. It has six vertices and twelve edges.

octave A range of eight notes on the DIATONIC (*i.e.* the conventional) musical scale. The FREQUENCY of the octave is precisely twice that of the base note, and it is the first HARMONIC of the base note.

octave-band A range of frequencies where the ratio of the highest frequency to the lowest frequency is 2.

octave-band analyser *See* FREQUENCY ANALYSER.

octave-band sound pressure level The SOUND PRESSURE LEVEL measured in a given OCTAVE-BAND.

oculus A round window, especially one in the EYE OF A DOME.

OD *Abbreviation for* Outside Diameter.

oedometer A machine for determining the CONSOLIDATION characteristics of COHESIVE SOILS. An *undisturbed* sample is loaded between two porous stone plates which allow free passage of water in and out of the sample, and the settlement is measured.

offcut wastage Many materials are produced in standard sheet or unit sizes, and if the dimensions needed in a building are not coordinated with the standard sizes, the wastage caused by cutting may be significant. This has implications both for cost and for efficient usage of resources.

office automation The use of electronic devices to replace manual processes, *e.g.* to produce a paperless or electronic office.

office space utilisation rate The ratio of the total number of office workers to the total number of offices and workstations, expressed as a percentage.

offline storage Data stored on a SECONDARY MEMORY medium that is routinely disconnected and stored separately from a computer system. This would include media such as magnetic tape and floppy disks.

off-peak tariff A reduced price charged for electricity at times of day when demand is comparatively low.

off-peak water heater A STORAGE WATER HEATER in which water is only heated during the electricity supplier's off-peak hours, usually at night, but at a lower cost.

off-premises workplace A workplace which is remote from the principal organisation workplace, requiring alternative work practices.

offset error A deviation from the desired set point for a controlled variable inherent in proportional control. The amount of offset increases in proportion to the departure of the controlled variable from the set point.

off-the-form The finish to in-situ and precast concrete made by the formwork surface.

off-white White, with the addition of a small amount of another colour, but insufficient to identify any colour other than white. *Also called broken white.*

off-white cement Cement which has very little of the grey colour of normal Portland cement. It is not as 'white' as WHITE CEMENT, but it is much cheaper, and suitable for many applications.

ogee A doubly-curved line, made up of a convex curve passing without a break into a concave. Same as CYMA *reversa.*

ohm (Ω) The unit of *electrical resistance.* It is defined by OHM'S LAW.

Ohm's law Law governing the flow of a steady current in an electric circuit, enunciated by the German physicist G. S. Ohm in 1827. It states that the voltage drop produced by the current is proportional to the magnitude of the current. The resistance is defined as the ratio of voltage to current, and its unit is the *ohm* (Ω).

oil paint Paint with a binder of DRYING OIL, as opposed to water paint.

oil stain A thin oil paint with very little pigment, used for staining timber. *See also* SPIRIT STAIN.

oil–alkyd paint *Same as* OLEORESINOUS PAINT.

old English bond *Same as* ENGLISH BOND.

oleoresinous paint A paint whose vehicle consists of a mixture of drying oil and resin (such as phenolic or alkyd resin), combined by a cooking process. *Also called oil–alkyd paint.*

on grade At ground level or supported directly on the ground.

one-axis tracking A solar energy system capable of rotating about one axis to track the sun east to west.

one-dimensional heat flow For a relatively thin large area (*e.g.* a wall or a slab), when a temperature difference exists between two uniform temperatures at the two faces, it is reasonable to assume that the heat flow will take place in one direction only: perpendicular to the area of the slab, without any sideways flow within the slab. This greatly simplifies all building envelope heat loss (or gain) calculations. Exceptions to this are thermal bridge effects (*see also* LINEAR HEAT LOSS COEFFICIENT).

one-way slab Slab designed to span in one direction only, as opposed to a *two-way slab.*

on-line Describes any device which is under direct control of the central processor of a computer.

online storage Data stored on a SECONDARY MEMORY medium that is continuously available to the computer system. Online storage supports transactional processing.

on-premises workplace A workplace located at the organisation's place of work.

onyx A banded variety of silica, consisting of very small quartz crystals. The bands are straight, not curved as in AGATE, and as a result it has been widely used for CAMEOS.

oolitic limestone A limestone formed by the agglomeration of oolites. These are tiny spherical concretions (less than 2 mm in diameter) of calcium carbonate, usually showing a concentric-layered or radiating fibrous structure. The structure resembles the roe of fish cemented together. The best-known oolitic limestone is PORTLAND STONE.

opacity The opposite of *transparency.* In painting, it denotes HIDING POWER of a paint.

opal Amorphous hydrous silica ($SiO_2.nH_2O$). Apart from the gemstone, there are less precious varieties, *e.g.* in opaline cherts, which find application as building materials.

opal glass Glass containing calcium phosphate derived from bone ash. This renders it white and opaque. *Also called milk glass.*

open circuit voltage (V_{OC}) The maximum voltage produced by a solar array, battery or generator when no current is being drawn from it.

open cooling tower A COOLING TOWER in which the circulating condenser water makes direct contact with the cooling air stream.

open cut Excavation from the ground downwards, as opposed to *tunnelling.*

open cycle cooling system A generic term for a family of cooling systems, the simplest of these being the evaporative cooler, in which the substance which is evaporated to produce cooling is not recycled. (Both the compression and the absorption type cooling machines use a refrigerant fluid, circulated in a *closed* loop or cycle.)

open drained joint *See* DRAINED JOINT.

open drive chiller A water CHILLER in which the electric motor is located outside the refrigerant circuit.

open light A window that can be opened, as opposed to a *dead light.*

open loop A pipe circuit for circulating water as a heat transfer medium that is at some point open to the atmosphere, *e.g.* a pipe loop between a refrigerant condenser and an open cooling tower.

open plan An office space designed without partitions.

open stairs Stairs without risers.

open stairway Stairway with one or both sides open to a room.

open system *(a)* A system whereby an

INDUSTRIALISED BUILDING is assembled from stock components, which may be produced by different manufacturers. *(b)* In computing, a system which allows any computer HARDWARE or SOFTWARE from any manufacturer to communicate with each other.

open-cell foam Cellular plastic in which the cells are interconnected; it is not resistant to water or vapour, as opposed to a *closed-cell* material.

open-frame girder *Same as* VIERENDEEL GIRDER.

open-hearth process Steel made in an open hearth from iron and limestone. The process was developed in 1858 by William Siemens, and it is also known as the Siemens Martin process.

open-web joist A lattice JOIST welded from light steel sections, which directly supports the roof or floor. It is mass produced to certain standard lengths. It permits the passage of plumbing and electrical conduits.

open-well stair A stair built around a well, leaving an open space.

operable walls Walls or partitions which can be opened or closed to combine or separate spaces to suit a variety of activities.

operating costs The total costs associated with operating a facility, comprising total fixed costs and total variable costs.

operating profit The difference between operating revenue and operating costs, excluding abnormal adjustments.

operating revenue The income minus deductions, including taxes and monies collected on behalf of a third party.

operating system In general, any program which controls a data processing system. More usually, the program in a computer which controls the running of other programs.

operation and maintenance manuals Manuals provided by the services contractors following the installation of building services, describing operation and maintenance (O&M) requirements.

operations research The analysis and solution of problems through the development of mathematical models, usually using computer-based methods.

operative temperature An index of thermal comfort, produced by Winslow, Herrington and Gagge (1937). It is the average of MRT and DBT, weighted by the radiation and convection heat transfer coefficients. Later modified to include air movement effects. The *humid operative temperature* is a more recent change, to include humidity effects.

opposite hand A mirror-image of the original. Sometimes used as a note on a drawing 'one as drawn, one opposite hand' to avoid having to draw an item twice.

optical axis *Same as* COLLIMATION LINE.

optical character recognition The recognition of printed characters by an optical scanning device. The images of the characters are converted into the digital representation of the characters.

optical fibre Very thin fibre of glass allowing for very high-speed transmission of data and for multiplexing of a large number of data channels on one single glass fibre, using light rather than electrical impulses.

optical smoke detector See PHOTO-OPTICAL SMOKE DETECTOR.

optimal control A control algorithm designed to optimise the start and stop times of air conditioning machinery so as to provide comfortable conditions only between the hours when the premises are in use.

optimisation An approach for finding the maximum efficiency of a system, *i.e.* its OPTIMUM value for some purpose. This may entail finding a minimum or maximum value as in the lowest cost, lowest energy consumption or maximum load-bearing capacity. *See* LINEAR PROGRAMMING.

optimum The best or most favourable solution for a particular purpose. This may be a minimum or maximum value as in the lowest cost, lowest energy consumption or maximum load-bearing capacity. *See also* PARETO OPTIMUM.

option In a lease, a clause proffering a right to a lessee to renew their lease for a further term, or to take up additional space at some future date.

opus incertum Ancient Roman masonry consisting of small stones set irregularly in mortar.

opus quadratum Ancient Roman term for ASHLAR, frequently laid with dry joints.

opus reticulatum Permanent formwork for Ancient Roman concrete, consisting of stones or bricks set diagonally.

opus signinum Ancient Roman STUCCO, which had very low water penetration because of its HYDRAULIC properties.

opus spicatum Ancient Roman brickwork in herringbone pattern.

opus testaceum Ancient Roman facing of broken tiles set horizontally in mortar.

orange-peeling A surface defect in paint that looks like the rough texture of orange peel.

orangery A term used for a GREENHOUSE, particularly in the eighteenth and nineteenth centuries. Since orange trees, which were highly esteemed for the scent of their flowers, could not be grown outdoors throughout the year in France, England and Northern Italy, they were grown in tubs which were put in a greenhouse for the colder time of the year. However, the term was also used for greenhouses that were never intended to accommodate orange trees.

orbital sander A powered SANDER in which the face plate oscillates with an orbital motion.

order of magnitude A number rounded to the nearest power of 10.

orderly shutdown The sequenced shutdown of units, particularly in a computer system, to prevent damage to the system and subsequent corruption or loss of data.

ordinality A characteristic of numeric (and sometimes other) data that allows the data to be ordered.

ordinary Portland cement PORTLAND CEMENT used for general construction, as opposed to WHITE CEMENT, OFF-WHITE CEMENT, HIGH-ALUMINA CEMENT, etc. *Also called Type 1 cement.*

ordinate The *y*-axis, or vertical axis, of a CARTESIAN COORDINATE system.

Oregon or Oregon pine *Same as* DOUGLAS FIR.

organic chemistry The study of those compounds of carbon which form chains or rings. Many organic materials are POLYMERS.

organic clay or silt A clay or silt that contains the remains of plants or animals. It is normally recognisable by smell when the soil is moulded. Its bearing capacity is generally very low.

organic coating A coating such as paint, the ingredients of which are derived from animal or vegetable matter.

oriel window A projecting window on an upper floor, CORBELLED from the wall. A BOW WINDOW usually projects from the ground floor.

orientation The arrangement of a building in relation to the north point.

oriented strand board (OSB) A panel composed of strands of wood which are purposefully aligned in directions which make a panel stronger than a panel with random strand orientation.

orifice plate An obstruction to a fluid flow (as in the outlet from a stormwater DETENTION BASIN), consisting of a plate with a hole of appropriate size to regulate the flow.

origin The point of intersection of CARTESIAN COORDINATES, *i.e.* the zero point for the *x*-, the *y*- and (in three dimensions) the *z*-axes. Also used with a similar meaning in computer graphics.

O-ring A toroidal ring of rubber or similar material, used to seal the gap between a circular shaft and a hole in which it can move. O-rings have replaced GLANDS in the spindles of taps and many other applications.

ormolu From the French for powdered gold; this was dissolved in mercury. Hence article or furniture decorated with mercury-gilded bronze.

orthogonal curves Curves crossing one another at right angles.

orthographic projection The PROJECTION most commonly used for drawing buildings. It shows the object by means of three separate drawings: the *plan*, the *elevation* and the *side elevation*. In the *first-angle* projection (commonly used in the UK) each view is placed so that it represents the side of the object remote from it in the adjacent view. In the *third-angle* projection (commonly used in the USA and Australia) each view is placed so that it represents the side of the object near to it in the adjacent view. While the orthographic projection is true to scale in every respect, it fails to give a pictorial representation of the object.

orthotropic Having physical properties which vary at right angles, *e.g.* the strength of timber along and across the grain. It is a special case of AEOLOTROPIC.

oscillation *See* VIBRATION.

osmosis The diffusion of a solvent or of a dilute liquid through a skin, permeable only in one direction, into a more concentrated solution.

OT *Abbreviation for* OPERATIVE TEMPERATURE.

OTTV *Abbreviation for* Overall Thermal Transfer Value, an average heat transfer rate for the whole of the building envelope (in W) including opaque elements and windows, both air-to-air and solar radiation transmission.

outage *See* BLACKOUT.

outdoor air Air introduced to the supply to air conditioned space for the purpose of dilution of contaminants which have their origin within the space.

outdoor air cycle A control cycle on an air conditioning system arranged to replace recycled return air with outdoor air when the heat content of the outdoor air is lower than that of the return air. The purpose is to save cooling energy. *See also* ECONOMISER CYCLE.

outlet *(a)* A point at which current can be taken from an electric wiring system, an electric SOCKET. *(b)* A connection to which a gas-burning appliance can be attached. *(c)* A ventilator. It could be a louvred opening in an attic or in the upper part of a window, or a discharging air duct.

out-of-plumb Not aligned with the plumb line, not perfectly vertical.

out-of-square Not at right angles.

output The results produced or the information transmitted by a computer or other data-processing system, using a printer, graphic display unit, PLOTTER, etc.

outsourcing The process of contracting with an external party to provide services traditionally performed by employees within an organisation.

oval Any plane figure resembling the longitudinal section of an egg. The term is commonly used for closed curves resembling an ELLIPSE, but not precisely conforming to its mathematical definition.

oven-dry soil Soil dried in an oven at 105 °C.

oven-dry timber Timber which does not lose moisture in a ventilated oven heated to 100 °C.

overall heat transfer coefficient A heat transfer coefficient calculated for a composite surface such as a wall that includes opaque panels and viewing panes. Usually applicable only to the building for which it has been calculated. Sometimes used as an indirect index of energy efficiency of the building envelope.

overcast sky *See* CIE STANDARD OVERCAST SKY.

overcharging Leaving BATTERIES on charge after they have reached their full (100 per cent) state of charge.

overcloak That part of metal roof sheeting or flashing that overlaps an adjacent lower sheet.

overflow error The condition that results when the scale of a numeric result is too big to be represented with the number of bits available to encode it. For example, integer overflow results when the value falls outside the normal positive–negative range allowed for that representation.

overhand work Bricklaying an outer part of a wall from within a building.

overhang A horizontal building projection, usually above a window, for the purpose of shading or otherwise.

overheated period A term used in the design of SUNSHADING devices to denote the period when the temperature exceeds a specified limit (such as 21 °C or 70 °F). This period can be shown on a STEREOGRAPHIC PROJECTION of the sunpath, or incorporated into a computer program.

overlay A sheet of transparent paper or film used to represent some aspect of a building, *e.g.* the electrical layout, the furniture layout, etc. Several sheets can be placed over each other so that interactions between the various aspects can be seen. The same result is achieved by LAYERING in a computer-generated drawing.

over-reinforced section A reinforced concrete section with more steel than is needed for a BALANCED DESIGN.

overrun The space provided, for example in a LIFT WELL, to allow for the OVERTRAVEL of the lift car.

oversail To project beyond the general face of a building or part.

overtravel The safe distance that a moving object, such as a lift, may travel past its normal range of movement without striking any fixed object. *Also called runby.*

overvoltage A voltage greater than the rating of a device or component. Normally overvoltage refers to long-term events (several AC cycles and longer). The term can also apply to transients and surges.

oxidation The chemical combination of an element with oxygen. A fire is caused by rapid oxidation. Corrosion of some materials, *e.g.* steel, is caused by slow oxidation. The opposite process is called *reduction.*

oxides of nitrogen (NOX) Trace contaminants of air arising from the combination of nitrogen with oxygen during the combustion of fuels. They are an irritant of the human respiratory system.

oxides of sulphur Trace contaminants of air arising from the combination of atmospheric oxygen with sulphur during the combustion of fuels. They are an irritant of the human respiratory system, and cause corrosion of some building materials. They are soluble in water, and a cause of ACID RAIN.

oxy-acetylene welding and cutting *See* ACETYLENE and FLAME CUTTING.

oxychloride cement A composition of magnesium chloride ($MgCl_2.6H_2O$) and magnesia (MgO). *Also called Sorel's cement.* The magnesia is derived from MAGNESITE; hence the floor finish in which this cement is used, is called MAGNESITE FLOORING.

oxygen A colourless and odourless gas which supports combustion. It is the most abundant of all chemical elements, since it forms 21 per cent by volume of the Earth's atmosphere, 89 per cent by weight of water, and almost 50 per cent of the weight of the rocks in the Earth's crust. Its chemical symbol is O, its atomic number is 8, its atomic weight is 16, its valency is 2, and its boiling point $-183\,°C$.

oxygen consumption calorimetry Measurement of heat release rate by measuring the depletion of oxygen in the fan-duct system with an exhaust hood to collect flue gases from burning objects.

oxygen index The minimum concentration of oxygen, in a mixture of oxygen and nitrogen, that will just support combustion of a material under specified test conditions. The *limiting oxidant concentration*, LOC, has a similar meaning but allows materials other than oxygen to be considered as oxidants.

OYO 'Own-Your-Own', a form of STRATA TITLE in which each apartment in a block is separately owned. *Also called home unit* (Australia) and *condominium* (USA).

ozone A toxic, unstable form of oxygen, which contains three atoms per molecule (O_3), instead of the normal two (O_2). It occurs naturally in the stratosphere where it plays an important part in screening out ultraviolet radiation. It also occurs in minute concentrations at lower levels.

ozone depletion Reduction in concentration of stratospheric OZONE due to complex reactions with the chlorine that originates from manufactured substances such as CFCs and HCFCs.

ozone depletion potential An index used to rank the potential of substances to cause reduction of OZONE in the upper stratospheric ozone layer.

P

π **(pi)** The circular constant 3.1416. . .

P *Abbreviation for peta*, a prefix for SI units, meaning 10^{15}.

p *Abbreviation for pico*, one millionth millionth, or 10^{-12}.

P4SR *Abbreviation for* Predicted 4-hour Sweat Rate. A comfort index suitable for temperatures about $28\,°C$ and higher, developed by McArdle (1947).

Pa *Abbreviation for* PASCAL.

PA *Abbreviation for* Polyamide, more commonly called *nylon.*

PA system A system of microphones, signal processors, amplifiers and loudspeakers for amplifying and distributing sound to an audience. Where the audience is in the vicinity of the source, the term *sound reinforcement system* is often used.

being parallel to one another. In a *right parallelepiped* all edges are parallel or perpendicular to the base. The CUBE is a special case of a right parallelepiped.

parallelogram A QUADRILATERAL with two pairs of parallel sides.

parallelogram of forces 'If two forces acting at one point be represented in magnitude and direction by two sides of a parallelogram, their resultant is represented by the diagonal drawn from that point.' In structural design two sides of the parallelogram are usually omitted, leaving the other two sides and the diagonal forming a *triangle of forces*. The parallelogram of forces was published by Stevinus of Bruges in 1586.

parameter A variable in a mathematical relation, which is kept constant for a particular investigation. Variation of the parameter thus produces a family of curves or surfaces.

parametric curve Curve that is defined by mathematical equations (as opposed to pixel-by-pixel definitions). As an example, one class of such curves, called Bezier curves, are used to construct very smooth attractive FONTS, which are capable of being scaled to any size.

parapet The portion of a wall which extends above roof level and conceals the roof.

parasol roof A 'roof above the roof', usually of some light sheet material, to provide shading for the roof itself. Usually the parasol roof is designed also to take on the role of rain protection, but thermal insulation would be provided by the lower roof, which may be combined with the ceiling.

parcel A small piece of land as part of a SUBDIVISION.

Pareto optimum Where there is more than one objective for a design there is rarely a single optimal solution. A Pareto optimum, named after an early twentieth-century Italian professor of political economy, is a solution such that no other solution can be found that is better in at least one objective and no worse in the others. There may be many Pareto optimal solutions to a design problem. Which one is used depends on a TRADE-OFF decision.

parge coat *(a)* A coat of cement mortar often containing waterproofing material applied to rough masonry. *(b)* A smooth coat of cement render applied to the inside of a flue.

Parian plaster *Same as* KEENE'S CEMENT.

Paris white *Same as* WHITING.

Paris, plaster of *See* PLASTER OF PARIS.

parity error An unintentional change in the bit structure of a data word due to the presence of a spurious pulse or transient.

parking area An area set aside for the parking or storage of vehicles.

parking of lift The act of moving a lift car to a specified floor, or leaving it at the last served floor, whenever there is no further service assigned to it.

parking ratio The number of car parking spaces required per unit area of developed floor area. It is generally determined by the requirements of the building or planning authority.

parquetry Small pieces of wood, sometimes of different species, fitted together to form a geometrical design. They are usually glued to a floor.

parsing, data The process by which programming data INPUT is broken into smaller, more distinct chunks of information that can be more easily interpreted and acted upon.

part load Operation of a machine to provide less than 100 per cent of its rated power output. It will be less efficient than when fully loaded.

partial prestressing Prestressing to a lower level than full prestressing (which eliminates all possibility of cracking under service or working loads). In partially PRESTRESSED members, tensile stresses exist in the precompressed tensile zone of the concrete at the working load.

partially fixed joint *Same as* SEMI-RIGID JOINT.

particle board A FIBREBOARD formed with only a small amount of pressure (unlike HARDBOARD), or by EXTRUSION. The binder is usually urea or phenol resin, and only a small amount (>12 per cent) is required. It can be joined and veneered like plywood, but is cheaper and has better insulation. *Also called chipboard.*

particle-size analysis Determination of the proportion of particles of each size in a granular mixture, such as soil or aggregate. When the result is plotted on semilogarithmic graph paper, the particle *grading curve* is obtained. The larger particles are separated by *sieving* or *screening*. For those particles too fine to pass through a sieve (74 μm), the SPECIFIC SURFACE is determined, usually by STOKES' LAW; or a TURBIDIMETER may be used. *See also* GRAVEL, SAND, SILT *and* CLAY.

particulates, particulate matter Very small particles of solid matter suspended in air.

parting bead, parting strip A narrow vertical strip between the sashes of a DOUBLE-HUNG WINDOW.

partition An internal wall which supports its own weight, but not the weight of the building above it.

partly cloudy sky A sky that has between three-tenths and seven-tenths cloud cover.

party wall *Same as* COMMON WALL.

pascal (Pa) Unit of pressure in SI UNITS. It equals 1 NEWTON per square metre, and is named after the seventeenth-century French mathematician. The pascal is also used as the unit of *stress* (which is equivalent to pressure) in some countries, whereas others use N/m^2 and its multiples.

passageway A narrow pedestrian access path within a building or between buildings.

passenger detector An automatic electronic device which causes a lift's doors to re-open whenever a passenger is detected in the doorway, using photoelectric, electromagnetic, electrostatic or ultrasonic detection means. *See also* SAFE-EDGE.

passive cooling Cooling of a building interior by passive means such as shading to exclude direct solar radiation in hot weather, cooling of massive structural elements during unoccupied periods, circulating cool night air to pre-cool space in hot weather.

passive downdraft evaporative cooling (PDEC) *See* EVAPORATIVE SHOWER TOWER.

passive earth pressure *See* EARTH PRESSURE.

passive filter (electrical) A combination of inductors, capacitors and resistors designed to eliminate one or more har-

monics. The most common variety is simply an inductor in series with a shunt capacitor, which short-circuits the major distorting harmonic component from the system.

passive heating Heating of a building interior by passive means such as release of heat from direct solar radiation, which has been stored in massive structural elements.

passive solar energy An incorrect term often used for PASSIVE SYSTEMS of solar energy utilisation.

passive systems (of solar energy utilisation) Systems where the building itself (or some special components of it) are used for the collection of solar radiant heat, its storage and distribution, without the need for circulating pumps, etc. as opposed to ACTIVE SYSTEMS.

paste command, operation A commonly used command or operation in word processing and other environments. Using this operation, text, images, sounds, etc. that have been removed from a document and temporarily stored on the system's CLIPBOARD, can be copied from the clipboard and placed in another location within the same document or in a location within another document.

patch panel (or rack) A system terminating in-coming communication cables and connecting them with the local distribution system.

patent glazing Any system of dry glazing, *i.e.* without the use of putty.

paternoster lift A passenger lift consisting of a series of open compartments that proceed slowly up or down in an open lift shaft without stopping. Most were installed on the European continent in the 1930s.

patina Surface alteration due to the aging process: *(a)* green or greenish-blue deposit forming on copper or brass as copper oxide gradually changes to copper sulphate due to atmospheric contamination; *(b)* gloss produced by aging on woodwork.

patio An open area adjacent to a building and accessible from it, with a floor but no roof, used for outdoor sitting or eating.

patio lock (or balcony lock) Lock designed for access to a private balcony.

It can be locked or unlocked from the inside only. Once unlocked (to allow access to the balcony) there is no danger of being accidentally locked out.

pattern staining Discoloration of plaster ceilings of composite construction, caused by the different thermal conductances of the backing. The air circulates more freely over the warmer parts, and deposits more dust on them.

pavement light A window of GLASS BRICKS built into a pavement surface, to admit natural light to a space below ground level.

pavilion *(a)* Originally a large tent. *(b)* A light ornamental structure, roofed but only partially enclosed in a garden or sports ground. *(c)* A projecting sub-division of a building, often elaborately decorated.

pawl A single tooth which engages a RATCHET.

Pb Chemical symbol for *lead* (plumbum).

PC *Abbreviation for* PRIME COST.

PCA Portland Cement Association, Skokie, IL, USA.

PCB *Abbreviation for (a)* Poly-Chlorinated Biphenyl, a compound used in plastics and paint manufacture, the effect of which is similar to DDT, in that it becomes increasingly concentrated in the food-chain and can cause environmental harm; *(b)* Printed Circuit Board.

PDES *Abbreviation for* Product Data Exchange Specification. A US industry group formed for the development of product data exchange standards. Now allied with the STEP effort.

PDU *Abbreviation for* Power Distribution Unit. A portable electrical distribution device that provides an easily expandable and flexible electrical environment for a computer and its associated peripherals.

PE *Abbreviation for* POLYETHYLENE.

pea gravel Screened gravel, from which particles larger than 10 mm and smaller than 5 mm have been removed by sieving.

peak The maximum instantaneous measurement of a continuous variable.

peak line current Maximum instantaneous current during a cycle.

peak power Power generated by a utility unit that operates at a very low capacity factor; generally used to meet short-lived and variable high demand periods.

peak sun hours The number of hours per day during which solar irradiance averages 1000 W/m² at the site. A site that receives six peak sun hours a day receives the same amount of energy as would have been received if the sun had shone for six hours at an irradiance of 1000 W/m².

peak tariff Electricity tariff applied for a part of each day when demand is at peak levels.

peak watt Unit used for the performance rating of photovoltaic converters. The amount of power a solar cell module can be expected to deliver at noon on a sunny day (*i.e.* at Standard Test Conditions) when it is facing directly towards the sun.

pearl lamp An electric light bulb etched to diffuse the emitted light. The etching is generally applied to incandescent lamps on the inside, and to tungsten-halogen lamps on the outside. Called a *frosted lamp bulb* in the USA.

pearlite *Same as* PERLITE *(b)*.

peat Dead, gelatinous, compressible vegetable matter preserved by humic acid in the ground. It is unsuitable as a foundation material. However, it can be used as a fuel after drying.

pebble-dash An external plaster that has been surfaced with small stones, thrown on while the plaster is still wet.

pedestal The base of a classical column or superstructure. In modern construction, a short column, whose height does not exceed three times its least lateral dimension.

pedestrian flow rate The movement of persons in passages and on stairs depends on the crowd density and the walking speed. If the crowd density exceeds 0.3 persons per square metre (0.03 persons per square foot), the walking speed is reduced.

pediment In Classical architecture, a low-pitched GABLE above a PORTICO.

peen *See* BALL-PEEN HAMMER.

pegboard A perforated hardboard. A pattern of holes is drilled during manufacture. These may serve a decorative or acoustic purpose, or they may, with special hooks, be used to support shelves and other fixtures.

pelmet A built-in head to a window for hiding the curtain rail.

Pelton wheel An impulse turbine, consisting of a wheel carrying buckets on its perimeter which are struck by a fast-flowing water jet.

pencil rod US term for small steel reinforcing bars.

pencil round The rounding of an ARRIS to a radius approximating the size of a pencil (*see figure*). *See also* BULLNOSE.

Pencil round

pendant *(a)* A hanging ornament. *(b)* A suspended LUMINAIRE. *(c)* A decorated boss in stone, stucco or timber, elongated so that it hangs down.

pendentive A set of spherical wall surfaces. These provide a transition from a dome to its supporting structure, which may be a set of walls or a set of arches. In Roman, Medieval and Islamic construction the pendentives were built of brick or stone, but they can also be built of concrete or reinforced concrete in modern construction. *See also* SQUINCH.

penetration The intersection of two vault surfaces. *See also* PILE PENETRATION *and* VICAT TEST.

penetration test Test of undisturbed soil with a *penetrometer*. It may be either STATIC or DYNAMIC. The information obtained supplements that collected from BOREHOLE SAMPLES.

penetrometer An instrument used for conducting a PENETRATION TEST.

pentagon A five-sided POLYGON. The angle included between the five equal sides of a *regular* pentagon is 108°.

penthouse A room, apartment or separate dwelling built on the roof of a building.

penumbra *(a)* A partly shaded region around the total shadow (UMBRA) of the moon or earth in eclipse. *(b)* The partly lit region around any area of full shadow.

perceived noise level (PNDB) The sound pressure level of a reference sound, which is judged to be equally *noisy* (not to be confused with equally *loud*) as the observed sound.

per cent exceedance level The level of a fluctuating sound in the environment which is exceeded for N per cent of the observing time is called the N per cent exceedance level, L_N. The two most commonly used per cent exceedance levels are the L_{10} (used mainly for road traffic noise) and the L_{90} (usually taken as the BACKGROUND NOISE level).

percentage ALcons A method of specifying the intelligibility of speech transmitted (usually in a telephone or other electronic verbal communications system) using the ARTICULATION LOSS of consonants.

percentage reinforcement One hundred times the cross-sectional area of the reinforcement in concrete, divided by the width and the EFFECTIVE DEPTH.

percentage rent Rental income calculated according to a percentage clause in the lease document.

percolation test Measures the ability of the soil to absorb liquid, especially used for septic system design.

percussion drill *See* IMPACT DRILL *and* ROTARY HAMMER.

perforated hardboard *Same as* PEG-BOARD.

performance bond A written form of security from a surety (bonding) company to the owner, on behalf of an acceptable main contractor or subcontractor, guaranteeing payment to the owner in the event the contractor fails to perform all labour, materials, equipment or services in accordance with the contract.

performance indicator A measure of some aspect of the performance of activities, which enables a comparison to be made, for management purposes, against a standard target or norm.

performance specification A detailed description which sets criteria of performance of an item, but does not state how these are to be achieved.

performance testing Testing carried out on completion of building engineering services systems to demonstrate compliance with design intent as specified.

performance-based approach A performance-based approach relies upon measurable or calculable outcomes (*i.e.* performance results) to be met, but provides flexibility as to the means of meeting those outcomes, as opposed to a *prescriptive* approach.

perigee Point in the orbit of the moon, planet or satellite that is nearest to the earth (opposite of *apogee*).

perihelion Point in a planet's or comet's orbit that is nearest to the sun (opposite of *aphelion*).

perimeter air conditioning or heating A system which feeds air through registers located along the outer walls, supplied through ducts from a central plenum chamber.

perimeter grouting Injection of grout at low pressure around the periphery of an area. When the area is subsequently grouted at a higher pressure, the grout injection is confined by the perimeter, with consequent saving in grout.

perimeter zone Part of occupied space in a building adjacent to an external wall, treated as a separate zone for air conditioning purposes.

period In cyclical analog data such as waves, the time it takes for the wave to cycle through one complete repetition.

period contract A fixed-term contract for services or goods which is re-tendered or re-negotiated at the expiry of the contract.

periodic table of the elements A classification table of the chemical elements, arranged in ascending order of atomic weight (the ATOMIC NUMBERS). The table is arranged in nine vertical columns, and the properties show periodicity in accordance with these nine groups. The system was initiated by the Russian chemist Dimitri Mendeleev in 1869.

peripheral Hardware device (such as input/output devices and secondary storage devices) attached to a computer system.

peripheral vision The seeing of objects displaced from the primary line of site and outside of the central visual field.

periscope An apparatus consisting essentially of two prisms or two inclined mirrors which enable an observer to obtain a view of objects at a different level. Although it is best known for its use in submarines to see objects above while remaining below water, the process can be reversed. The observer can insert a periscope into a model, and thus obtain from above the view which a person would get if it were possible to stand inside the model *(model scope)*. The periscope can be used visually, or in conjunction with a television camera *(urban scope)*.

peristyle A COLONNADE surrounding the outside of a building, or an interior space inside a building, such as a court.

perlite *(a)* A volcanic glass, usually with a higher water content than OBSIDIAN. It can be expanded by heating. *Expanded perlite* is used as an insulating material, and as LIGHTWEIGHT AGGREGATE. *(b)* A EUTECTOID composed of alternate laminae of iron and iron carbide, formed at about 720°C when steel is slowly cooled. The etched section has a pearly appearance. The proportion of perlite in carbon steels increases with the carbon content. *Also spelled pearlite.*

permafrost Permanently frozen ground, which exists in the northern parts of Russia, Canada and Alaska. Buildings erected on it must be specially insulated to prevent the heat generated by the building from melting the frozen soil and turning it into mud.

permanent memory Memory which is not lost when power is switched off, as opposed to *volatile memory.*

permanent supplementary lighting *See* PSALI.

permanent threshold shift A permanent hearing loss due to noise exposure or other causes.

permeability For vapour movement, analogous with *conductivity* for heat flow. A material property, indicating how readily the material (per unit thickness) would allow the penetration of water vapour. Its SI unit is $\mu g/m.s.Pa$, *i.e.* the mass of vapour that would flow through unit area of unit thickness of the material in one second with 1 Pa difference in vapour pressure between the two sides. (Its reciprocal is *vapour resistivity.*)

permeameter A laboratory instrument for measuring the coefficient of permeability, using DARCY'S LAW. The head of water has to be kept constant for highly permeable materials, such as sand or gravel; however, for the slowly permeable clays and silts it can be allowed to drop from an initial head *(falling-head permeameter)*.

permeance Vapour conductance, indicating to what extent a material layer would allow the penetration of water vapour; for a homogeneous layer it is the PERMEABILITY of the material divided by its thickness, its SI unit being $\mu g/m^2.s.Pa$. (Its reciprocal is *vapour resistance.*)

permissible stress *See* MAXIMUM PERMISSIBLE STRESS.

permutation The number of permutations of *n* things, taken all at a time, is *n!*. The number of permutations of *n* things, taken *r* at a time, is *n!/(n–r)!*.

perpendicular A line or plane which meets another at right angles.

perpends The vertical joints on the face of brickwork.

Perry–Robertson formula A formula for the design of columns, which is more sophisticated than the RANKINE COLUMN FORMULA; the work of J. Perry (who derived it) and A. Robertson (who checked it experimentally in 1924). It is assumed that every slender strut has an unavoidable slight curvature, which is defined by the empirical constant in the formula.

perspective projection A pictorial PROJECTION in which the object is drawn the way the eye sees it. Lines which are parallel in plan are drawn to converge on a vanishing point, and lines which are parallel in the elevation and side elevation are also drawn to converge on their vanishing points.

perspex Trade name of an ACRYLIC RESIN.

perspiration Moisture on the skin produced by sweating as part of the human thermo-regulatory system. It is an important contributor to metabolic heat loss in conditions of high ambient temperature or when a person is subject to high rates of metabolic activity.

PERT Originally *Program Evaluation Research Technique*, now interpreted as *Performance Evaluation and Review Technique*. This form of network analysis,

developed mainly for military and aerospace work, differs in terminology, rather than in substance, from the CRITICAL PATH METHOD, developed for the construction industry.

PERT schedule A diagram that illustrates, charts and reports a project's estimated start and completion times, and work in progress.

Petersburg standard or Petrograd standard An obsolete measure of timber which equals 1980 BOARD FEET ($165 ft^3$ or $4.67 m^3$).

petrographic microscope A microscope fitted with a pair of NICOL PRISMS, one serving as a polariser and the other as an analyser. The characteristic colours produced by polarised light help to identify the minerals, particularly in igneous rocks.

petrography Descriptive PETROLOGY.

petrology The science of rocks.

pewter An alloy consisting predominantly of TIN.

PF *Abbreviation for* Phenol Formaldehyde.

PFA *Abbreviation for* Pulverised Fuel Ash, *i.e.* FLY ASH.

pH See PH VALUE.

pH value The logarithm to the base 10 of the reciprocal of the concentration of hydrogen ions in an aqueous solution, in moles per litre. Water has a pH value of 7; basic solutions are higher than 7 and acid solutions lower than 7. It is normally measured with an electrical instrument and used particularly to express small differences in the alkalinity or acidity of neutral solutions.

phase *(a)* A physically and chemically homogeneous portion of an alloy system, as shown in a PHASE DIAGRAM. *(b)* One of the windings or circuits of a polyphase electrical apparatus; also the recurring sequence of the electric wave. *See also* THREE-PHASE SYSTEM. *(c)* State of existence of a substance, *i.e.* solid, liquid or gaseous. The chemical composition is the same in all phases.

phase balancing The practice of placing equal electrical loads on each leg of a three-phase system. *See* NEUTRAL.

phase change material A substance which undergoes a reversible phase change from the solid to the liquid state within a useful temperature range. It may be employed for the storage and subsequent release of heat.

phase diagram A diagram which shows the temperature as ordinate, and the composition range of an alloy as the abscissa. Although its main use is in metallurgy, it can be used to show the variation of the phases in non-metallic solutions and solid solution. The phase diagram can be used to illustrate the temperatures at which alloys made of any proportion of two or three elements exist in the liquid and the solid state, the temperatures at which transformations occur, the manner in which solubility changes with temperature, and other features of the behaviour of an alloy system *(see figure)*. It is also called a *constitutional diagram*, an *equilibrium diagram* or an *alloy diagram*. *See also* LIQUIDUS *and* SOLIDUS LINE. The *figure* shows the phase diagram for iron and carbon, which is important because it deals with carbon steel, cast iron and wrought iron.

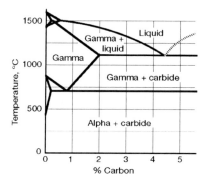

Phase diagram

phase rotation The sequence in which a comparable voltage appears in all three phases: A, B and C of a three-phase electrical system.

phenol formaldehyde *See* FORMALDE-HYDE.

Phillips head A type of BOLT or SCREW head with crossed slots perpendicular to one another.

phon A unit of the LOUDNESS of a sound.

phosphor A material capable of emitting light when irradiated by particles or ELECTROMAGNETIC RADIATION.

phosphorescent Emitting light due to the decay of materials containing *phosphorus*. Sometimes used to mean PHOTOLUMI-NESCENT.

photocell *See* PHOTOVOLTAIC CELL.

photochemical reaction A chemical reaction aided by radiation, particularly from the visible and ultraviolet spectrum.

photochromic glass Glass that has the property of reduced transparency when exposed to higher levels of incident light. Currently under development for use in buildings, but in use for smaller items such as spectacle lenses.

photodetector *See* PHOTOVOLTAIC CELL.

photoelastic material A material which has the property, when stressed, of breaking up light into two components polarised in the directions of the principal stresses. It is possessed by several glasses, thermoplastics and casting resins, such as BAKELITE, PERSPEX, PLEXIGLAS, Catalin and Araldite. *See also* THREE-DIMENSIONAL PHOTOELASTICITY *and* PHOTOSTRESS METHOD.

photoelasticity The property of certain transparent materials to break up the incident light, ordinarily oriented at random, into two components polarised in the directions of the PRINCIPAL STRESSES. By inserting a POLARISING FILTER, only light in one plane is transmitted. A model is placed between two filters at right angles, and no light is transmitted when the model is unstressed. When the model is stressed, coloured fringes (ISOCHROMATICS) appear which connect points of equal difference between the two principal stresses *(see also* MOIRÉ FRINGES). Although the colours give a clear visual picture, and often make fascinating patterns, they make precise measurement difficult, and MONOCHROMATIC light is used for numerical analysis. The photoelastic effect was discovered in 1816 by David Brewster and first applied to model analysis by E. G. Coker in the 1920s.

photoelectric cell *Same as* PHOTO-VOLTAIC CELL.

photoelectric effect The ejection of electrons from a solid by sufficiently energetic electromagnetic radiation.

photogrammetry Measurement and representation of three-dimensional geometry using multiple photographs, viewed using a *stereoscope*. Can be used with two cameras on a tripod to record building facades, and from aircraft for large-scale topographical surveying.

photoluminescent Able to emit light as a result of being exposed to light. Commonly referred to as 'glow-in-the-dark' materials. Photoluminescent coatings have been used for emergency exit signage. *See also* FLUORESCENT PAINT.

photometer An instrument for measuring light, but the term is used to describe one measuring ILLUMINANCE. A photometer can be adapted for the measurement of LUMINANCE.

photometric Referring to LIGHT (visible ELECTROMAGNETIC RADIATION) as opposed to *radiometric*.

photometry The branch of physics concerned with the measurement of light; the measurement of lighting quantities.

photomicrography The production of photographic negatives and prints of very small objects, obtained by attaching a camera to a microscope.

photon The elementary particle of electromagnetic energy; light. (Greek *photos*, light.)

photo-optical smoke detector A *fire detector* which 'sees' the presence of smoke by means of a photo-optical device, such as a PHOTOVOLTAIC CELL.

photostress method PHOTOELASTIC analysis by means of photoelastic coatings, applied to a model in sheet form or as a solution backed by a reflective surface. The method was developed by the French engineer F. Zandman in the 1950s for determining surface strains. It does not require a transparent model.

photosynthesis The production of carbohydrates from carbon dioxide and water in the green cells of plants, using light as the source of energy.

phototropic Strictly, the response of plant growth to light, but extended to apply to people's attraction to light.

photovoltaic array A number of PHOTOVOLTAIC CELL modules that are electrically connected in series and/or in parallel so as to provide the desired power and voltage.

photovoltaic cell A conversion device that changes light into electrical energy.

The cell consists of layers of semiconductor materials fabricated to form a junction (adjacent layers of materials with different electronic characteristics) and electrical contacts. Most PHOTOMETERS, EXPOSURE METERS of cameras, and PHOTO-OPTICAL SMOKE DETECTORS employ photovoltaic cells. By using a large enough array of cells it is possible to generate sufficient electricity from solar energy to operate electric equipment and lights. *Also called photoelectric cell.*

photovoltaic conversion efficiency The ratio of the electric power produced by a photovoltaic device to the power of the sunlight incident on the device.

physical depreciation The reduction in property value due to deterioration of the physical fabric because of wear and tear, inadequate maintenance and weathering and decay.

pi (π) The circular constant 3.1416. . .

PI control Proportional plus Integral control. The integral function acts to eliminate OFFSET ERROR in simple proportional control. *See also* PID CONTROL.

piano nobile In Renaissance and neo-Renaissance architecture, the storey containing the reception rooms, usually one flight of stairs above ground level.

pica *See* POINT.

pickled The state of a metal surface that has been cleaned by an acid treatment.

pico (p) Prefix for one millionth millionth, from the Spanish word for a little bit, *e.g.* 1 pm = 1 picometre = 1 $\times$ 10^{-12} metre.

PICT *Abbreviation for* PICTure files, a particular file format.

picture rail A moulding fixed to an interior wall. Pictures may be suspended from it by means of metal hooks which fit over the top of the moulding.

picture window A large window whose bottom ledge is less than waist high.

PID control Proportional plus Integral plus Derivative control. The *derivative* function acts to oppose the rate of change of deviation. If the control point is moving away from the set point, derivative action increases the control action to slow the rate of change.

piecework A scheme for payment of a uniform price per unit produced, rather than by DAY LABOUR.

pier A massive compression member.

piezo-electric effect The production of electricity as a result of the distortion of some crystalline materials. This effect is used in inexpensive gramophone cartridges and MICROPHONES and in load cells for measuring forces. The term is also used for the reverse effect where an electric field will distort a crystal: hence piezo-electric transducers are used in ULTRASONIC and audio applications, such as alarms.

piezometer An instrument for measuring pore water pressure.

pig A mass of metal, such as cast iron, lead or copper, cast into a simple shape, which is subsequently remelted for purification, alloying or processing. The term originated with the now obsolete method of running the liquid metal from the blast furnace into a channel in a bed of sand, called a *sow*. From there it ran into smaller lateral channels, called *pigs*.

pigment An *opaque* colouring agent (for paints, etc.), as distinct from a *dye*, which is a transparent colour. *See also* BLANC FIXE, CADMIUM YELLOW, CARBON BLACK, CHINESE WHITE, IRON OXIDES, LAKE, LITHOPONE, MINERAL PIGMENT, PRUSSIAN BLUE, RED LEAD, RED OXIDE, ULTRAMARINE, VERMILION, WHITING *and* WHITE LEAD. *See also* FLUORESCENT and PHOSPHORESCENT PAINT.

pigtail A short wire connected to another wire, for the purpose of making connections to multiple objects.

pilaster A rectangular column built into a wall, and projecting slightly from it.

pile *(a)* A long slender column of timber, concrete or steel embedded in the foundation. It may be driven, jacked, jetted or (in the case of concrete) cast in place. *See also* BEARING PILE, IN-SITU PILE *and* SHEET PILE. *(b)* The raised fibres of a carpet or velvet surface. Hence also the raised fibres of a paint roller.

pile cap *(a)* A protective cap fitted over the head of a pile during driving. *(b)* A structural member designed to distribute the load from a column or wall to a group of piles.

pile hammer A hammer for driving piles into the soil. Drop hammers, which depend purely on gravity, go back to

Roman times, but are still commonly used because of their reliability. Power-operated double-acting hammers, however, are faster since they can deliver up to 300 blows per minute.

pile head The top of a pile. Since the penetration of piles driven to REFUSAL cannot be accurately predicted, the heads are often cut off after driving.

pile penetration The depth reached by the tip of a pile. It generally refers to the depth at REFUSAL.

pile shoe A point of cast steel or cast iron at the foot of a driven pile of timber or precast concrete.

pillar A vertical compression member. In Classical architecture, a vertical compression member which was not circular.

pilot hole A guide hole for a larger diameter nail or screw.

piloti One of a number of massive piers supporting an elevated ground floor of a building, a name familiarised by buildings designed by Le Corbusier in the 1920s.

pin joint A joint between two or more members of a structure which transmits no moment, as opposed to a RIGID or SEMI-RIGID JOINT. Pin joints are so called because in the mid-nineteenth century they frequently consisted of pins pushed through a hole in each of the members to be joined. True pin joints are rare today, except for very large spans where complete certainty of freedom to rotate is required. Normally 'pin joint' denotes a flexible joint, or a joint at the end of a flexible member, which transmits only a negligible moment. Pin joints may be deliberately introduced into structures to render them STATICALLY DETERMINATE. *See also* PLASTIC HINGE.

pink noise Broadband noise which randomly varies in phase and intensity at each frequency and which has equal energy per *unit* bandwidth. *See also* WHITE NOISE.

pinna The part of the hearing system, that holds on the spectacles, which is commonly known as the 'ear'.

pipe column A column made from steel tubing. It is sometimes filled with concrete to increase its stiffness and strength.

pipe fittings (drainage) When these fittings are used in clay pipes, the joints are bulky and sealed with either rubber rings or cement mortar. When used with PVC pipes, the joints are a neat fit and are sealed with a PVC SOLVENT CEMENT. *See* SPIGOT AND SOCKET JOINT, SLOPE JUNCTION and SQUARE JUNCTION (*See figure*).

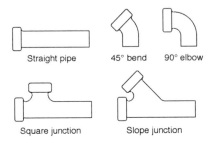

Pipe fittings (drainage)

pipe fittings (water and gas) When used with galvanised steel pipes, and sometimes with other materials, these fittings use a TAPERED THREAD connection. Copper tubes use smooth mating surfaces with a very close tolerance, sealed with SOFT or HARD SOLDER. Polythene and stainless steel pressure pipes often use *compression* fittings. *See* BEND, BUSH, ELBOW, NIPPLE, SOCKET *and* TEE. (*See figure*).

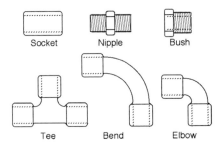

Pipe fittings (water and gas)

pipe wrench An adjustable spanner in which the grip is tightened by load application.

pipework An assembly of pipes and fittings used for the conveyance of fluids.

pisé de terre Wall of unburnt clay or chalk, rammed in a damp condition into formwork without reinforcement, except sometimes straw. This is a vernacular

form of construction in several arid regions. With a protective coating it can also be used in areas of moderate rainfall. *See also* COB *and* ADOBE.

pit *(a) Lift pit*: the part of a LIFT WELL situated below the lowest landing served. *(b) Drainage pit*: a SUMP formed below ground level, of concrete or masonry, to collect drainage from the surface through a GRATING, and/or from underground pipes, and to direct it out through another pipe. *(c) Brick pit, etc.*: an excavation from which brickmaking materials or other minerals have been removed.

pit sawing A method for sawing large pieces of timber before the development of power-operated saws. It was done by two men using a straight saw about 2 m long. One sawyer stood across the log pulling the saw up with a horizontal handle, the other stood below the log in a pit pulling the saw downwards with a vertical tiller.

pit switch An isolating switch located in the lift PIT to remove the electrical supply from the drive machine and brake.

pit-sawn Timber sawn lengthwise by PIT SAWING.

pitch (acoustics) Subjective assessment of the frequency of a tonal sound.

pitch (material) Dark viscous residue remaining after distillation of wood tars, petroleum or coal.

pitch mastic *See* MASTIC *(c)*.

pitch of a roof The angle of a sloping roof, usually defined by the *ratio* of rise to span.

pith A soft core in the centre of a wooden log.

pi-theorem (π-theorem) A theorem published by E. Buckingham in 1914, which establishes the number of dimensionless ratios (πs) required for dimensional similarity between two physical phenomena (*e.g.* a prototype and its model). If the two phenomena are determined by *r* parameters, which can be expressed in terms of *n* primary dimensions (length, mass, time, etc.), then the number of πs is $(r - n)$. *See also* DIMENSIONAL ANALYSIS.

pitot-static tube An open-ended tube within a closed outer tube with holes in the circumference near the end (*see figure*). The open end faces in the direction of motion of a fluid and provides a measure of total (*i.e.* static plus velocity) pressure in the fluid. The holes in the circumference of the outer tube provide an indication of static pressure; the difference indicates the velocity pressure. The two tubes can be connected to a manometer to provide direct readings of static, velocity or total pressure as required.

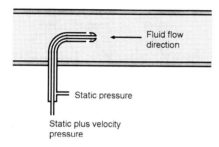

Pitot-static tube

pivot window A SASH that has two pivots near the middle of opposite sides, which allow tilting: vertically, or at top and bottom to allow pivoting horizontally.

pixel *Abbreviation for* picture element, the smallest part of an image on a screen.

pixel image An image on a screen comprised of a number of PIXELS.

plain bar or wire A reinforcing bar or wire without deformation to improve bond, as opposed to a DEFORMED BAR or an INDENTED WIRE.

plain concrete Concrete which is neither reinforced nor prestressed.

plain tile *See* ROOF TILE.

plan Representation of an object as seen on a horizontal plane, viewed from above.

planar Lying in one plane; flat.

Planckian radiator *See* FULL RADIATOR.

Planck's radiation law An expression for the spectral distribution of radiant energy from a FULL RADIATOR, in terms of its temperature. WIEN'S LAW gives the wavelength corresponding to the maximum ordinate of the Planck curve, and the STEFAN–BOLTZMANN LAW gives the area under the curve.

plane A hand tool for smoothing timber. A sharp blade, inclined to the surface of the timber, projects by a small and adjustable distance below the sole of the tool. *See also* PLANER.

plane angle An angle measured in two dimensions, as distinct from a SOLID ANGLE.

plane frame *See* FRAME.

plane of saturation The water table in soil.

plane table A device for plotting the results of a survey directly from the observations. It consists of a drawing board mounted on a tripod, a SPIRIT LEVEL and a ruler (called an *alidade*) with two sights which are pointed at the object to be observed. If the distances are substantial, an alidade with a telescope is used.

planer A powered tool for smoothing timber. Several sharp blades, attached to a rotating drum, remove small shavings as they pass over the timber: *(a)* in the case of a hand planer, the blades are mounted in the tool which is pushed over the (stationary) timber; *(b)* in the case of a floor-mounted machine, also called a *thicknesser* or *jointer*, the timber is pushed by hand or driven by rollers, past the rotating blades.

planimeter An instrument for measuring areas by mechanical means. It is a simple type of integrator.

planing machine A machine which removes shavings from a metal surface by pushing it past a stationary tool. *See also* PLANER, which usually describes a woodworking machine, *and* SHAPING MACHINE.

planned maintenance *See* MAINTENANCE, PLANNED.

planning grid A network of horizontal and perpendicular lines, to assist the designer with a layout plan.

plant Machinery installed as part of a building services system.

plant redundancy Ability of plant to continue to provide full or part service in the event of a breakdown of part of it.

plant room A room set aside for the installation of the equipment used for the engineering services of a building.

plaster Any pasty material of mortar-like consistency, used for covering the walls or ceilings of a building. The traditional plasters based on lime, gypsum and animal hair are now rare. Portland cement, mixed with lime, sand and water, is the common material for plastering over masonry. Gypsum (plaster of Paris) is the basis of PLASTERBOARD sheets, and is still used when a very smooth surface is required over concrete or cement render.

plaster lath *See* LATH.

plaster of Paris Hemihydrate of GYPSUM ($CaSO_4.\frac{1}{2}H_2O$). It occurs naturally, and there were large deposits near Paris, hence the name. It is more commonly made from gypsum by driving off some of its water by heat. When mixed with water it sets rapidly with formation of heat, and expands in the process. Hence it is particularly useful for making accurate casts. *Also known as hemihydrate* plaster. The setting is too rapid for many building applications, and *retarded hemihydrate plaster* contains a retarder, usually *keratin*. If plaster is to be used in conjunction with iron or steel reinforcement, it is necessary to add about 5 per cent of hydrated lime to prevent corrosion.

plasterboard A building board made of a core of gypsum or anhydrite plaster, faced with two sheets of heavy paper.

plastic cracking Cracking which occurs on the surface of fresh concrete soon after it is placed. It is often confused with SHRINKAGE CRACKING; however, plastic cracks can be filled in by trowelling, while shrinkage cracks occur during the HARDENING stage.

plastic deformation Continuous permanent deformation in metals, which occurs above a critical stress, the YIELD or PROOF STRESS. The ELASTIC DEFORMATION results from straining of the crystal lattice. Plastic deformation normally occurs by slipping action at a DISLOCATION IN A CRYSTAL when the interatomic forces become too high. It depends on the ability of the metal to sustain distortion of the crystal structure without fracture.

plastic design LIMIT DESIGN based on the formation of PLASTIC HINGES.

plastic hinge After structural steel has reached its LIMITING STRENGTH, which is the YIELD STRESS, it continues to deform at a constant stress until its deformation is several times as much as the total elastic deformation. Once it becomes a fully PLASTIC MATERIAL *(see figure)*, a hinge forms, which can be rotated without further increase in the bending moment.

When sufficient hinges have formed to turn the structure into a mechanism, it collapses. *See* LIMIT DESIGN.

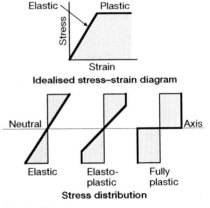

Plastic hinge

plastic limit The water content at which a damp clayey soil just begins to crumble when rolled into a thread approximately 3 mm (⅛ in.) diameter. *See also* PLASTICITY INDEX.

plastic material A term which is often confusing in discussions between architects and engineers. In materials science and in rheology, plasticity denotes the ability of a material to deform at a constant stress without fracture. Thus structural steel is the plastic material *par excellence*, from an engineer's point of view. In sculpture, a plastic material is one which can be freely moulded; unlike stone or steel, which must be finished by cutting. From this point of view, concrete is the ideal plastic material of architecture because it can be cast into any mould chosen by the designer. However, as an engineering material, concrete is BRITTLE, which is the very opposite of plastic. *See also* PLASTICS.

plastic mortar A mortar of a consistency which allows it to be readily deformed during bricklaying or blocklaying without disintegrating. Plasticity is sometimes improved by additives, called plasticisers.

plastic paint *(a)* A vague term for a paint whose medium is a *plastic, i.e.* a synthetic resin. *(b)* A *texture paint, i.e.* a paint that can be used plastically for relief modelling.

plastic section modulus (S) The SECTION MODULUS used in PLASTIC DESIGN, which is tabulated in section tables. The *shape factor* is the ratio

$$\frac{\text{plastic section modulus}}{\text{elastic section modulus}}$$

and its value for structural steel sections is about 1.15.

plastic tile A tile made from plastic, commonly PVC, as opposed to a ceramic tile.

plastic wood A paste of wood flour, synthetic resin, and a volatile solvent. It is used for filling holes and cracks in timber. Its surface can be painted about an hour after application, so that the stopping of holes is frequently undertaken by the painter, and not by the carpenter.

plasticiser *(a)* An admixture to mortar or concrete that increases its workability. However, some plasticisers also reduce the strength. *(b)* A non-volatile substance mixed with the medium of a paint, lacquer or varnish to improve the flexibility of the hardened film.

plasticity index The numerical difference between the LIQUID LIMIT and the PLASTIC LIMIT. It is indicative of the range of water content through which a soil remains plastic.

plastics A generic term for organic substances, mostly synthetic and formed by condensation or polymerisation, which become plastic under heat or pressure. They can then be shaped by moulding or extrusion. They are also used for laminates, paints, lacquers and glues. The main distinction is between THERMOPLASTIC and THERMOSETTING plastics.

plate compactor A machine consisting of a flat metal plate on which is mounted an internal combustion engine with an eccentric flywheel, to cause vibration. It is pushed over the surface of sand, gravel or other filling material in order to compact it.

plate girder A steel girder built up from vertical web plates and horizontal flange plates. *Also called* a *welded beam.*

plate glass Glass of better quality than ordinary SHEET GLASS. It is usually thicker, with a smoother polished surface

free of blemishes. Now superseded by FLOAT GLASS.

plate heat exchanger A HEAT EXCHANGER formed by a number of plates with small gaps between, allowing two separate fluid flows in alternate gaps, so that the many plates provide a large surface area for heat flow. It is often used in INDIRECT EVAPORATIVE COOLERS.

plate, flat *See* FLAT PLATE.

plate, metal Thicker than metal SHEET.

plate, timber A continuous horizontal piece that distributes the vertical loads from STUDS or RAFTERS. It could be used as a *ground sill plate*, as a *wall plate* or as a *top plate.*

platen *(a)* The plate in a printing machine that presses the paper against the inked type. *(b)* A hot steel plate used in presses that make plywood with thermosetting glues. *(c)* A smooth steel plate used to compress a specimen in a testing machine.

plenum This term is used with two different meanings. It may denote a duct maintained at a pressure slightly above atmospheric, so that it can be used for the supply of air but return air is kept out by the excess pressure. The term is also used for the air space in an INTEGRATED CEILING, above atmospheric pressure, used for the air supply. Sometimes also used, contrary to its original meaning, for the same space below atmospheric pressure, used for the air exhaust.

plenum chamber An air compartment maintained at a pressure slightly above atmospheric, to distribute that air to one or more ducts or outlets.

plenum system A method of heating or air conditioning whereby the air forced into the building is at a pressure slightly above atmospheric.

Plexiglas Trade name of an ACRYLIC RESIN.

plinth In Classical architecture, the projecting base of a wall or column PEDESTAL, moulded or chamfered at the top. The term is now used for a platform, or a slight widening at the base of a wall or column.

plinth brick A special shaped brick formed with one splayed long edge, suitable for use at the top of a PLINTH (*see figure*).

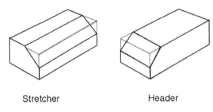

Stretcher   Header

Plinth brick

plot ratio The gross floor area of a building divided by the area of its site. The basic ratio permitted is frequently modified by providing a bonus for arcades, setbacks, plazas and the incorporation of existing buildings of architectural significance.

plotter An output device for computer graphics on paper or film, usually in larger format than a *printer*. *See* DRUM PLOTTER, FLAT BED PLOTTER *and* ELECTROSTATIC PLOTTER.

plugging Filling a drilled hole in masonry with a timber, fibre or metal plug into which a screw can be driven.

plug-in A module of computer program, which extends the capabilities of an application.

plum A random-shaped stone weighing 50 kg (100 lb) or more, which is dropped into MASS CONCRETE to economise on cement and reduce the generation of heat. *Cyclopean concrete* is mass concrete containing a large number of plums.

plumb *(a)* To determine the direction of the vertical with a line weighted with lead *(plumbum)*. *(b)* Any other method of lining up a building element in the vertical direction. *(c)* Vertical.

plumb bob A weight of any material at the end of a line to give it a vertical alignment.

plumbago *Black lead*, an obsolete term for GRAPHITE.

plumber's solder An alloy of lead and tin. *Coarse solder* consists of 3 parts of lead to 1 of tin; it melts at 250 °C. *Fine solder* consists of equal parts of lead and tin; it melts at 188 °C.

plumbing An assembly of pipes, fittings and fixtures used for: *(a)* the supply and distribution of water under pressure, whether in the ground or within a building; *(b)* the removal of waste water or

rainwater by gravity flow, within a building. The system for removal of this material in the ground is called *drainage*.

plumbing fixture *See* BALL COCK, BIDET, CISTERN, FAUCET, GREY WATER, WATER CLOSET, WATER HAMMER, WATER HEATING *and* WATER SEAL.

plume A column of hot gases, flames, and smoke rising above a fire or discharged from a chimney.

plunge test for sprinkler heads A hot wind-tunnel test at constant air speed and temperature to study thermal sensitivity of sprinkler heads. The output is *response time index* (RTI). *See also* RAMP TEST FOR SPRINKLER HEADS.

plutonic intrusions IGNEOUS ROCKS that have cooled slowly at great depth below the Earth's surface, and are therefore coarse-grained.

ply A thickness of material, used for building up several layers, as in plywood and built-up roofing.

plywood Material consisting of three or more plies of wood, with the grains of adjacent plies usually at right angles to one another. The outer plies may be veneers of decorative timber, while thicker and cheaper timber may be used inside. Plywood overcomes the inherent weakness of timber across the grain by lamination at right angles.

PMMA *Abbreviation for* Polymethyl Methacrylate, an ACRYLIC RESIN.

PMV *Abbreviation for* PREDICTED MEAN VOTE.

pneumatic caisson A CAISSON whose working chamber is kept sealed so that work may proceed inside under compressed air.

pneumatic loading *Same as* AIR-BAG LOADING.

pneumatic structure A structure held up by a slight excess of internal air pressure above the pressure in the atmosphere outside. It must be sufficient to balance the weight of the roof membrane, and must be maintained by air compressors or fans.

pneumatic tool A tool worked by compressed air.

pneumatically applied mortar *Same as* SHOTCRETE.

POE *Abbreviation for* POST-OCCUPANCY EVALUATION.

point As a measure of length: *(a)* 1 point of rainfall = 1/100 in. (0.254 mm); *(b)* 1 printer's point = 1/72 in. (0.351 mm); 12 printer's points = 1 pica (4.2 mm).

point cloud In computer modelling, a set of three-dimensional points typically captured by photo-scanning techniques. Can be used to help reconstruct detailed carving or moulding through CAD/CAM.

point load A concentrated load, as opposed to a distributed load.

point method A method of estimating the illuminance at various locations in a building using photometric data.

point of contraflexure *See* CONTRAFLEXURE.

point of inflection *Same as* POINT OF CONTRAFLEXURE.

point source A source of radiant energy of negligible dimensions compared with the distance between source and receptor.

point-bearing pile An END-BEARING PILE.

pointed arch A multi-centred ARCH, whose INTRADOS curves meet at an angle of less than 180° (*see figure*).

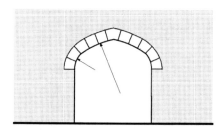

Pointed arch

pointing *(a)* Pressing surface mortar into a RAKED JOINT. Pointed mortar joints are not as durable as joints made with the original bedding mortar; however, the practice of pointing joints in white, black or coloured mortar was once common. *(b)* The finishing operation on a mortar joint, without the addition of surface mortar.

pointing device A generic name for a device which moves a CURSOR on a computer screen, such as a MOUSE, TRACKBALL or TRACKPAD.

poise A unit for measuring dynamic viscosity; it equals 0.1 pascal-second.

Poisson's ratio The ratio of lateral unit STRAIN to longitudinal unit strain, when a piece of material is subjected to a uniform and uniaxial longitudinal stress, defined by S. D. Poisson, a French mathematician, in 1829. For a fully plastic material it is 0.5. For steel it is about 0.25, and for concrete about 0.12. *See also* MODULUS OF RIGIDITY.

poker vibrator An internal vibrator which is immersed in the wet concrete.

polar coordinates A system of coordinates based on the radial distance r from a reference point and the angle θ with a reference axis, in place of the conventional CARTESIAN COORDINATES x and y. It is useful for problems framed in terms of circular functions. Polar graph paper greatly facilitates a graphical solution.

polar curves Curves based on a system of POLAR COORDINATES, giving a two-dimensional indication of vectorial quantities, such as distribution of light from a luminaire or sound from a speaker.

polar moment of inertia Moment of inertia about an axis *normal* to the plane of the section or area. The term 'moment of inertia' without prefix implies a moment about an axis *in* the plane of the section.

polariscope An instrument for showing phenomena connected with PHOTOELASTICITY. It consists of two POLARISING FILTERS or NICOL PRISMS, a MONOCHROMATIC light source and a holder or testing device for the model. QUARTER-WAVE PLATES are frequently added.

polarised light Light whose waves are confined to a single plane. Normal light, whose waves vibrate in space, can be polarised in a plane by passing it through a NICOL PRISM or a POLARISING FILTER or by reflecting it from a glass plate at a particular angle.

polarising filter A filter for producing POLARISED LIGHT.

polarising microscope *See* PETROGRAPHIC MICROSCOPE.

polarity *(a)* The negative and positive terminals in an electric circuit. *(b)* The north and south poles of a magnet.

polaroid *(a)* A trade name for a type of plastic that can (plane) polarise a transmitted beam of light as a result of the orientation of the long molecules. *(b)* A camera *(Polaroid Land camera)* capable of producing finished photographs 'in the camera' using a sandwich of negative, chemicals and print paper.

pole A round timber column or post, usually set into the ground and extending one or more storeys in height.

poles The two points where the MERIDIANS OF LONGITUDE intersect.

polyamide (PA) A group of plastics better known by their trade name NYLON.

polycarbonate A thermoplastic used for moulded parts and in sheet form where high impact strength and heat resistance are required. Often in clear form, as a glazing material or as PROFILED ROOF SHEETING.

polychromous Having more than one colour on its surface.

polyester resins A group of resins that contain an ester (—COO—) link. Some are used with FIBREGLASS reinforcement.

polyethylene (PE) A low-cost thermoplastic polymer of ethylene. It is an ELASTOMER, which is completely waterproof, and is therefore widely used for bags, protective wrapping and pipes. It forms a cheap waterproof membrane, but must be protected against puncture. *Also called polythene.*

polygon A many-sided plane figure. A *regular* polygon is one which is equiangular and equilateral. The included angle of a regular (commonly called equilateral) *triangle* is 60°; and that of a regular *quadrilateral (square)* is 90°. Other included angles are:

regular pentagon	108°;
regular hexagon	120°;
regular heptagon	128.5°;
regular octagon	135°;
regular nonagon	140°;
regular decagon	144°;
regular dodecagon	150°.

polygon of forces A figure analogous to the TRIANGLE OF FORCES, representing the statical equilibrium of more than three forces.

polyhedron A solid figure bounded by plane surfaces. There are only five *regular* polyhedra, bounded by identical poly-

gons: the TETRAHEDRON, the CUBE, the OCTAHEDRON, the DODECAHEDRON and the ICOSAHEDRON. In addition there are a large number of semi-regular polyhedra which are bounded by two or more types of regular polygon, but are otherwise symmetrical. These are important for the design of GEODESIC DOMES.

polyline In computer graphics, a single linear entity composed of a series of connected LINE elements.

polymer *See* POLYMERISATION.

polymer concrete A concrete in which a plastic is used as a binder, instead of Portland cement.

polymer–cement concrete A concrete in which a blend of cement and plastic is used as a binder.

polymerisation The combination of several molecules to form a more complex molecule, having the same empirical chemical formula as the simpler ones. It is often a reversible process (*see* DEPOLYMERISATION). Some of the most successful plastics used in buildings are produced by polymerisation (which is also called CURING *(b)*).

polymethyl methacrylate (PMMA) An ACRYLIC RESIN.

polymorphism The existence of more than one *crystal structure* for a single composition.

polynomial An expression consisting of many terms, but all of the type ax^n where a is a constant, x is the variable and n is a positive integer.

polyphase An alternating current supply with two or more active conductors. Voltage is measurable between the conductors and the voltage waveforms for each conductor are usually displaced 120° (in which case it is called three-phase). When a neutral is present, the voltage from each active conductor to neutral is equal. *Also called multiphase.*

polypropylene (PP) A low-cost thermoplastic material, whose properties are similar to those of high-density polyethylene.

polystyrene (PS) A *thermoplastic* material formed by the polymerisation of styrene ($C_6H_5.CH:CH_2$). It is resistant to moisture, strong alkalis, several acids and alcohol, but softens at 60°C (140°F).

In transparent form it is brilliantly clear. Expanded polystyrene is one of the EXPANDED PLASTICS used as an insulating material.

polysulphide A thermosetting resin, used as a building sealant. It is usually polymerised by mixing it with a catalyst immediately before application and is then poured in place.

polytetrafluoroethylene (PTFE) A crystalline, linear polymer, unique among organic compounds in chemical inertness. It is resistant to all alkalis and acids, even to AQUA REGIA. It does not have a melting point, but undergoes a phase transformation at 330 °C (620 °F), with a sharp drop in strength. It is marketed under the trade names *Teflon* and *Fluon*.

polythene Trade name of a make of POLYETHYLENE.

polyurethane A group of plastics used mainly as a light insulating material in the form of flexible or rigid foam (*see* EXPANDED PLASTIC); also as a high-gloss waterproof paint finish and as a sealant.

polyvinyl acetate (PVA) A thermoplastic material formed by the polymerisation of vinyl acetate ($CH_3.COOCH:CH_2$). It is the binding agent in many EMULSION PAINTS.

polyvinyl chloride (PVC) A low-cost thermoplastic material formed by the polymerisation of vinyl chloride ($CH_2:CHCl$). It is a rubbery material, used for insulating electrical cables. It does not sustain combustion and is resistant to water, oil and many chemicals. Thus it can be used for cold water pipes, as a flooring material (particularly in the form of tiles), as a waterproof membrane and as an expansion joint.

ponding Accumulation of water on a *flat roof* due to an insufficient slope or inadequate drainage. It may cause excessive loads, producing additional and progressive deflection.

pop rivet See BLIND RIVET.

population (a) In statistical terminology, the totality of all possible values of a particular characteristic for a UNIVERSE. A universe could have several populations associated with it. (b) In computing, used in evolutionary programming to denote a set of individuals to be evolved.

population factor The average floor space occupied by a person in a building; that is, the total floor space available divided by the number of people who use it.

pop-up menu A MENU which appears during execution.

porcelain Glazed pottery made from CHINA CLAY, used for fine table ware, for electric insulators and for dielectrics.

porcelain enamel *Same as* VITREOUS ENAMEL.

pore One of the small interstices between the particles of permeable solids (*e.g.* masonry materials, soils, timber, etc.). The term usually applies to spaces into which water will penetrate by capillary attraction.

pore-water pressure The pressure of water in a saturated soil.

porosity The ratio of the volume of voids to the total volume of a sample of soil. It equals $v/1+v$, where v is the VOIDS RATIO.

porous absorber A material which absorbs sound by the damping of the air movement, due to the passage of the sound through pores or over fibres of a material.

porphyry A generic term for IGNEOUS ROCKS which contain a few large crystals in a fine-grained groundmass.

port A hardware or software socket in a computer for connecting an input/output device.

portal (a) A monumental door or gateway. Hence a frame consisting of two columns and a member which may be horizontal, sloping or arched. (b) The entrance to a tunnel.

porte cochère A porch which can be entered by a vehicle.

portfolio management The acquisition, use and disposal of an organisation's property assets in accordance with strategic requirements.

portico A roofed space, open or partly enclosed, which forms the entrance to a building.

Portland blast-furnace slag cement Cement consisting of a mixture of PORTLAND CEMENT and BLAST-FURNACE SLAG in specified proportions. It can be produced by mixing the Portland cement clinker with granulated blast-furnace slag before grinding, or by blending the ground cement with finely granulated slag.

Portland cement The most common form of cement. It is made by burning together chalk or limestone and clay or shale, and grinding the resulting clinker into a fine powder. The result is a complex mixture of calcium silicates (*see* DICALCIUM and TRICALCIUM SILICATE) and calcium aluminates, which sets into a hard paste when it comes into contact with water. Portland cement, mixed with sand and AGGREGATE, forms CONCRETE. The name *Portland cement* is due to J. Aspden, who patented the first artificial cement in England in 1824.

Portland stone An OOLITIC LIMESTONE, quarried on the Isle of Portland, off the coast of Southern England. Because of its durability and the ease with which it can be carved, it has been a particularly popular stone for monumental and residential buildings in London.

Portland–pozzolan cement A blend of PORTLAND CEMENT with finely ground POZZOLANA, or a cement made by grinding a mixture of Portland cement clinker and pozzolana.

positional notation The conventional notational system for representing numbers, where a digit's value depends not only upon the digit itself but also its position in the number. Hence in the decimal system, we speak of the ones digit, the tens digit, the hundreds digit and so on.

positive bending moment A BENDING MOMENT which causes sagging or concave-up curvature. In simply supported and continuous beams the maximum positive bending moments occur near mid-span. *See figure* under NEGATIVE BENDING MOMENT.

positive reinforcement Reinforcement placed in concrete beams to resist the POSITIVE BENDING MOMENT, *i.e.* near the bottom face.

post-and-beam construction A system of construction in which posts and beams are the main load-bearing members.

posterising A technique in IMAGE PROCESSING in which the complexity of a colour (or greyscale) image is reduced by mapping similar colour (or grey) tones to a select small number of levels.

postern gate A small gate beside a large one; a small gate at the back of a building or compound.

post-hole auger An AUGER for boring holes in soil, usually implying a hand-operated or portable powered device, rather than a vehicle-mounted EARTH AUGER.

post-occupancy evaluation The process of evaluating an occupied facility, considering factors such as conformance to brief, user satisfaction, functionality, technical performance and cost efficiency.

post-stressing Obsolete term for *post-tensioning.*

post-tensioning PRESTRESSED CONCRETE in which the TENDONS are tensioned *after* the concrete has hardened, as opposed to PRE-TENSIONING.

postulate A simple proposition of a self-evident nature, which requires no proof, and generally cannot be proved. *Also called axiom.*

pot floor *Same as* HOLLOW-TILE FLOOR.

pot life Time interval after mixing during which a liquid material is useable, *e.g.* an adhesive mixed from a resin and a HARDENER. *See also* SHELF LIFE.

potable water Water that is suitable for human consumption.

potassium A very reactive ALKALI metal. Its chemical symbol is K, its atomic number is 19, its atomic weight is 39.096 and its specific gravity is 0.86. It has valency of 1, a melting point of $+62.5\,°C$, and a boiling point of $762\,°C$.

potential energy ENERGY due to position, as opposed to *kinetic energy.*

pound The unit of mass and weight in FPS UNITS, abbreviated lb, and sometimes lbf for pound-force.

poundal An obsolete unit of force in the FPS system, which causes a mass of 1 pound to accelerate at 1 ft per second per second.

pound-foot, pound-inch The unit of bending moment and twisting moment in FPS UNITS. The unit of energy and work is usually called FOOT-POUND.

powder coat A form of surface decoration in which a fine powder is applied to the surface of the item by *electrostatic attraction*; the item is then baked in an oven to cause the powder to melt, coalesce and adhere to the surface. The result is a smooth and durable coating, but since it must be done in a factory before installation, any subsequent damage is difficult to repair to the same standard.

powder metallurgy The technique of agglomerating metal powders into engineering components.

powder post borings Worm holes filled with a fine, dust-like flour from the boring of worms. *See* LYCTUS BORER.

power (in electrical systems) The vector product of voltage and current. Hence, in direct current systems, it is identical to watts. In alternating current systems, it has two components; the REAL POWER (measured in watts) and the IMAGINARY or REACTIVE POWER (measured in VAR or volt-amps-reactive).

power (in mechanics) The rate of doing *work* or converting ENERGY from one form to another. The SI unit of power is the watt (W), which is one joule per second (J/s). *See also* HORSEPOWER.

power (of a colour) In the MUNSELL BOOK OF COLOR the power scale is the composite of VALUE and CHROMA; thus 4/14 means a colour slightly darker than the middle value between black and white, and 14 arbitrary steps from the equivalent grey.

power factor The ratio of REAL POWER to APPARENT POWER. Power factor will be 'leading' or 'lagging' depending on which way the load shifts the current's phase with respect to the voltage's phase. Inductive loads cause current to lag behind voltage, while capacitive loads cause current to lead voltage.

power float A powered machine, the base of which consists of a three-bladed propeller-like device, about a metre (3 ft) in diameter. The blades rotate on a fresh concrete surface to act as trowels. Their angle of inclination is adjustable to achieve the desired finish. *Also called trowelling machine* or, colloquially, *helicopter.*

power line monitor A measuring device which reports information on the changing conditions of electrical power.

power outage *See* BLACKOUT or OUTAGE.

power spectrum level The sound power level per unit frequency (Hz) band.

Pozidriv head screw A type of CROSS-HEADED SCREW.

pozzolana (also pozzolan, Pozzuolana) *(a)* A volcanic dust, first discovered on the slopes of Mount Vesuvius near Pozzuoli, called *pulvis puteolanus* by Vitruvius. When mixed with lime mortar, it produces a waterproof or HYDRAULIC CEMENT. It was used in Ancient Rome for high-quality work. *(b)* Any natural deposit, usually of volcanic origin, which has pozzolanic properties. *See* SANTORIN EARTH *and* TRASS. *(c)* An artificial substance, usually a siliceous, or a siliceous and aluminous material, with pozzolanic properties. Although it possesses little cementitious value by itself, it reacts, in finely divided form and in the presence of water, with HYDRATED LIME $(Ca(OH)_2)$ to form a HYDRAULIC CEMENT. The reaction takes place at ordinary temperatures, whereas the manufacture of PORTLAND CEMENT requires burning of the silica and the lime.

PP *Abbreviation for* POLYPROPYLENE.

PPD *Abbreviation for* Predicted Percentage Dissatisfied, an index of thermal comfort used in conjunction with the PMV (predicted mean vote), as developed by P.O. Fanger (1982), based on analysis of body/environment thermal relations and observations. Included in ISO Standard 7730:1994, but now considered to be an expression of the 'constancy theory' and gradually replaced by the ADAPTABILITY MODEL.

PPM *Abbreviation for* Parts Per Million.

practical completion The point in the execution of a contract where the works are deemed to be essentially completed and ready for use, subject to minor defects, acknowledged by the issue from the superintendent of the works of a certificate of practical completion to the contractor.

Prandtl number A non-dimensional ratio used as a criterion for the similarity of temperature gradients in fluids. It is the ratio

$$\frac{\text{specific heat} \times \text{viscosity}}{\text{thermal conductivity}}$$

Prandtl's membrane analogy *See* MEMBRANE ANALOGY.

Pratt truss A STATICALLY DETERMINATE truss, *also called N-Truss*, consisting of top and bottom chords, regularly spaced vertical compression members and diagonal *tension* members, as distinct from a HOWE TRUSS. It is used for medium to long spans in buildings and for small bridges *(see figure)*. See also WARREN TRUSS.

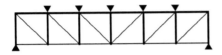

Pratt truss

precast concrete Concrete cast and cured and subsequently placed in its final location, as opposed to CAST IN PLACE concrete.

precast pile A concrete pile which is cast and subsequently driven, as opposed to a BORED PILE which is cast in place.

precast stone *Same as* ARTIFICIAL STONE.

precedence effect *See* HAAS EFFECT.

precipitation *(a)* Separation and deposition of a substance in solid form from solution in a liquid. *(b)* Condensation and deposition of moisture from water vapour held in the air or in clouds. *(c)* That which is so deposited, *i.e.* a collective term for dew, rain, hail and snow.

precipitation hardening *Same as* AGE HARDENING.

pre-cooling The cooling of air prior to mixing with return air in an air conditioning system. Air may also be pre-heated.

predicted mean vote (PMV) A concept developed by P. O. Fanger in Denmark, about 1970, as an index of thermal comfort. It is a number calculated from the physical variables that influence human thermal comfort that represents the mean vote likely to be recorded from a large sample of building occupants when required to indicate thermal sensation by voting on a seven point scale from −3 (cold) to +3 (hot). It is the basis of ISO Document 7730 which is widely used in Europe as a standard for defining thermal comfort. *See also* PPD.

predictive control Automatic control that acts to anticipate a movement of a controlled variable away from set point.

prefabrication *Same as* INDUSTRIALISED BUILDING.

preferred angle The preferred angle of inclination of stairs, ramps, etc. Building codes specify the acceptable range of angles for stairs and ramps, and industrial regulations control the use of ladders.

premature stiffening (of mortar and concrete) *See* FALSE SET.

premises The property, including the buildings, structures and grounds which are included in a title to ownership, or a deed of conveyance.

presbycousis Diminished hearing due to age, usually starting with hearing loss at high frequencies. In critical cases acoustic design should make provisions for listeners of an advanced age, for example by providing a LOOP ANTENNA for those with hearing aids.

presbyopia Often used as the opposite of myopia, but in its narrower sense meaning old-age vision, when the eye can no longer focus on near objects (*e.g.* in reading), but it may include loss of visual acuity due to deterioration of the eye lens or the cornea. This would increase the illuminance requirements.

preservation *(a)* The protection of a building material from deterioration caused by the natural elements or by human activity *(b)* Hence the process of the protection of heritage or historic buildings and sites by physical, financial or legal action.

preservative A substance which inhibits decay, infection or attack by fungi, insects, marine borers, etc. (as distinct from corrosion by chemicals), *e.g.* in timber. *See also* PRIMER.

pressed brick A brick without holes made by pressing a relatively dry clay mix in a mould, as opposed to an EXTRUDED BRICK.

pressure Force per unit area (dimensionally the same as STRESS). The SI unit is the N/m^2 also named Pa (pascal). Frequently used multiples are kPa, and hPa (hecto-pascal) in meteorology. Note that 1 hPa = 1 mbar.

pressure bulb *See* BOUSSINECQ PRESSURE BULB.

pressure differential A difference in pressure of air maintained between adjoining spaces to control direction of flow, *e.g.* from a clean to a dirty area in a hospital; or between inside and outside air pressure, which may assist or resist the entry of water through construction.

pressure drop The reduction in pressure due to friction when a fluid flows in a pipe, duct or conduit.

pressure gauge *See* BOURDON GAUGE *and* MANOMETER.

pressure gradient Average rate of pressure drop due to flow of a fluid in a pipe, duct or conduit.

pressure reducing valve Used in water circuits connected to the mains, to protect parts which cannot be exposed to full mains pressure (or peaks of a fluctuating mains pressure), such as medium pressure DHW systems, or solar water heater collectors.

pressure vessel A closed tank designed to hold a fluid under a pressure higher than that of the atmosphere in which it is located.

pressure, atmospheric The pressure exerted by the weight of the air at the surface of the earth at sea level is 1 atmosphere = $101.325\,kPa$ = $14.7\,psi$ = $760\,mm$ of mercury = $1013.25\,mb$ = $1013.25\,hPa$. *See also* ATM, MERCURY *and* MILLIBAR.

pressure, hydrostatic The pressure of a fluid at rest where all forces act normally to a boundary surface and are independent of viscosity. In the case of an incompressible fluid in contact with the atmosphere, the gauge pressure is a product of the specific weight of the fluid and the vertical depth below the free surface; pressure varies linearly with depth.

pressure-treating Application of a chemical preservative treatment such as copper-chromium-arsenic, pentachlorophenol and zinc to conditioned wood to increase its resistance to insects or decay. *(a)* The *empty-cell process* involves placing an initial air pressure into the wood cells prior to filling the treating retort with preservative. *(b)* The *full cell process* involves pulling a vacuum on the treating retort prior to filling with preservative.

pressurisation The maintenance of a pressure in a contained fluid above that of the surrounding atmosphere.

prestressed concrete Concrete which is precompressed in the zone where tensile stresses occur under load; consequently cracking of the concrete due to tension is avoided. The prestressing can be accomplished by jacking the concrete against a rigid abutment; but the usual technique is to tension TENDONS of high-tensile steel. Prestressing is classified as PRE-TENSIONED or POST-TENSIONED, depending on whether the tendons are tensioned before or after the concrete has hardened.

prestressed shell A SHELL containing some prestressing TENDONS in addition to normal reinforcement, *e.g.* in edge beams. It is uncommon to prestress the membrane surface of the shell.

prestressing cable A cable or TENDON of high-tensile steel, used to impart prestress to concrete when the cable is tensioned.

pre-tensioning PRESTRESSED CONCRETE in which the TENDONS are tensioned *before* the concrete has hardened, and generally before it is cast, as opposed to POST-TENSIONING. Pre-tensioning may be carried out *individually* for each mould, or a *long line* of wire may be tensioned against fixed anchorages, the concrete units being cast around the wires which are flame-cut after the concrete has hardened.

preventive maintenance *See* MAINTE-NANCE, PREVENTIVE.

primary air Air delivered to a terminal device and used to induce entrainment of SECONDARY AIR from the conditioned space.

primary beam A main beam, supported on columns or walls, and supporting smaller beams or JOISTS. *Also called* GIRDER.

primary circulation space Those parts of the building or floor that are aisles, lobbies or corridors; as well as space required for access to stairs, lifts, toilets and building exits.

primary colours *(a)* The colours of three *coloured lights* or *pigments* from which many transmitted or nearly all reflected colours can be produced by colour mixing. These colours are usually identified as red, green and blue (in additive colour mixing; mixing lights); or sometimes as magenta, yellow and cyan (in subtractive colour mixing; mixing pigments and printing). *(b)* In colorimetry, the three theoretical colours from which all other colours, including the spectral colours, can be created using additive colour mixing.

prime cost sum (PC) A sum entered in a BILL OF QUANTITIES by the architect or consulting engineer. Its original purpose is to specify the quality of the item, and not allow any choice to the contractors tendering for it. However, prime cost items are also inserted for parts of a building which have not yet been fully designed, and therefore cannot be priced.

prime mover *(a)* A machine which converts natural energy into mechanical power, *e.g.* a water turbine or an internal-combustion engine. *(b)* The powered section of an articulated vehicle.

primer or priming coat *(a)* Ground coat of paint applied to timber and other materials as a PRESERVATIVE and as a filler for the pores, which serves as a base for the further coat(s) of paint. *(b)* ANTI-CORROSIVE PAINT applied to steel.

priming Filling a SIPHON or a pump with water so that it can be operated.

princess post Used in large roof trusses, particularly QUEEN-POST ROOF TRUSSES. It is a short vertical post between the queen post and the support of the truss.

principal The party in a contract to whom the contractor is legally bound, also known as the client or proprietor.

principal planes Three mutually perpendicular planes on which the stresses are purely normal tension or compression. The stresses on these planes are the PRINCIPAL STRESSES.

principal rafter *See* RAFTER.

principal stresses The stresses acting across the *principal planes*. They are the greatest and smallest direct (tensile or compressive) stresses. The greatest shear stresses occur at an angle of 45° to the principal planes. *See also* MOHR CIRCLE.

principle of Archimedes 'If a body floats in a liquid, its weight is equal to the weight of the liquid displaced.'

principle of superposition *See* SUPER-POSITION.

prism A POLYHEDRON consisting of two parallel and equal faces (the *bases*),

connected by parallelograms. The best known example is the *right triangular prism*, consisting of two right-angled triangles connected by rectangles, which is used in optics. The *cube* is the only prism which is also a regular polyhedron.

prismatic glass ROLLED GLASS which has parallel prisms on one face. These refract the transmitted light, and thus change its direction.

prismoid A solid which has two parallel polygonal faces, which need not be the same. The volume of a prismoid is $\frac{1}{6}h$ $(A_b + 4A_m + A_t)$, where h is the height of the prismoid, A_b and A_t the areas of the polygons on the parallel top and bottom faces, and A_m is the area at mid-height. This formula is used for the computation of the volume of excavation of earthworks by the *prismoidal rule*, also known as SIMPSON'S RULE.

prismoidal rule *See* SIMPSON'S RULE.

privacy lock A door lock which can be locked from the inside by a pushbutton, but can be unlocked from the outside by a simple method (often a screwdriver) to allow emergency access. Used on bathrooms and the like.

privy A TOILET, particularly a primitive toilet in an outhouse.

probability A measure of the likelihood of the occurrence of a chance event. If the event can occur in N mutually exclusive and equally likely ways, and if n of these possess a characteristic E, then the probability that the event has this characteristic E is the fraction n/N.

probable simultaneous demand (in plumbing) The probable maximum flow rate for a pipe network based on the usage pattern of the PLUMBING FIXTURES.

procedural language A programming language whose statements are instructions of procedures the computer is to execute, as opposed to a DECLARATIVE LANGUAGE.

process A general term for any operation which transforms an item from one state to another in a period of time.

processor The component that does the actual computing in a computer. Depending on the context, the name may be short for CENTRAL PROCESSING UNIT (CPU) or MICROPROCESSOR.

profile A sectional drawing, usually vertical.

profiled roof sheeting A generic term for CORRUGATED sheeting, and various other shapes which generally provide greater strength and greater water-carrying capacity than the simple corrugated pattern.

program (a) A series of statements or instructions that direct a computer to perform a sequence of operations. (b) A plan or schedule of operations to be conducted over a period of time. (Sometimes spelled *programme* in non-computing applications.)

programming In computing, the activity of writing a PROGRAM.

progress certificate A certificate issued to both the principal and the contractor at identified stages of the works confirming the percentage or agreed stage of work completed against which payment may be made by the principal to the contractor.

progress chart A graph or, more commonly, a BAR CHART, showing the time when the various operations required for the construction of the building should commence and finish. The actual times can be shown on the same chart to see how far the progress made conforms to the original intention. *See also* CRITICAL PATH METHOD.

progress payment The payment made by the principal to the contractor upon the issuance of a PROGRESS CERTIFICATE.

project management The practice of developing, planning, procuring and controlling the services and activities required in the satisfactory completion of a project according to an agreed time, cost and brief.

project management contract The agreement for a person or organisation to be responsible for the PROJECT MANAGEMENT of a project.

projection A method of representing a three-dimensional object on a sheet of drawing paper. The most common projection is the ORTHOGRAPHIC PROJECTION, which shows the object by means of three separate drawings, all true to scale; but it fails to give a pictorial representation of the object. The most common pictorial projections are the ISOMETRIC, the AXONOMETRIC and the PERSPECTIVE PROJECTION.

Different projections are needed to represent the surface of a sphere. The STEREOGRAPHIC PROJECTION is commonly used in the design of SUNSHADING devices.

prompt In computing, a message given by a program to an operator requiring some information before it can proceed.

proof stress The nominal stress (*i.e.* load per unit of original cross-sectional area) which produces a specified permanent STRAIN, *e.g.* of 0.1 per cent (1×10^{-3}) or 0.2 per cent. It is specified for metals which exhibit significant PLASTIC DEFORMATION, without showing a marked YIELD STRESS.

propane The third of the gases in the hydrocarbon series, C_3H_8, the main component of LIQUEFIED PETROLEUM GAS. Its boiling point is $-42\,°C$ ($-43\,°F$). It is stored and transported as a liquid under moderate pressure in cylinders, and can be evaporated to a gas for use in all but the coldest of climates.

propeller fan *Same as* AXIAL-FLOW FAN.

property (of an energy system) A measurable quantity such as volume, mass, pressure, temperature, etc.

property portfolio The collection of facilities or buildings which are an organisation's assets.

proportional band The range within which a proportional controller maintains a required condition.

proportional bandwidth filter A frequency filter where the ratio of the upper to lower frequency limit is constant. *See also* FREQUENCY BAND.

proportional control Control of a variable by means of a device which operates a control element in proportion to the demand for change necessary to maintain a desired condition.

proportional limit The greatest stress which a material can sustain without departing from a proportional stress/strain relationship in accordance with HOOKE'S LAW.

proportioning of mixes *See* MIX PROPORTIONS.

propped cantilever A beam with one built-in and one simple support. It is STATICALLY INDETERMINATE.

proscenium The portion of a theatre stage between the curtain and the orchestra.

Also used to describe the opening *(proscenium arch)* between the stage and the auditorium.

protective finish of metals *See* ANODISING, CADMIUM PLATING, GALVANISING *and* SHERARDISING.

protocol A set of rules or conventions specifying the format of information to be exchanged between communication systems.

proton A positively charged subatomic particle of mass 1.66×10^{-24} gram. Its charge is equal and opposite to that of an ELECTRON. Its mass is 1840 times that of an electron.

protractor An instrument, usually in the form of a graduated circle or semicircle, for plotting and measuring angles.

proud Projecting forward from the surface.

proving ring A device for accurately measuring a load, or for calibrating a testing machine. It consists of a steel ring whose deflection under a diametral compressive force is measured, *e.g.* with a DIAL GAUGE. The ring is calibrated in a standard testing machine.

provisional sum A financial sum allowed for items of work not described or specified at the time of tendering. The actual sum payable is adjusted when the details of that part of the work are known.

proximity *See* ADJACENCY.

Prussian blue Ferric ferrocyanide. $Fe_4.[Fe(CN)_6]_3$.

prussic acid A highly poisonous solution of hydrogen cyanide (HCN) in water.

PS *Abbreviation for: (a)* POLYSTYRENE; *(b)* the metric *horsepower (German Pferdestärke).*

PSALI *Abbreviation for* Permanent Supplementary Artificial Lighting in Interiors. The deliberate use of electric light in daytime, introduced in the 1940s. Rooms could be made deeper if the back part was lit by luminaires, and the windows were required only to light part of the room.

psf *Abbreviation for* Pounds per Square Foot.

psi *Abbreviation for* Pounds per Square Inch.

psychophysics The study of the relationship between physical stimuli and their effects on an organism. Often called HUMAN FACTORS ENGINEERING when the study involves people.

psychrometer Instrument for measuring relative humidity. The simplest type is the WET-AND-DRY BULB THERMOMETER. *See also* ASSMAN PSYCHROMETER, DEW-POINT HYGROMETER, HAIR HYGROMETER, HYGROGRAPH, THERMOHYGROGRAPH *and* WHIRLING PSYCHROMETER.

psychrometric chart Graphic representation of thermodynamic properties of the atmosphere, of the air–water vapour mixture *(see figure)*, constructed by William Carrier in 1911–23. It shows the relationship of DBT, WBT, RH, absolute humidity (moisture content), vapour pressure and ENTHALPY. Almost exclusively used in English language literature and practice, especially in air conditioning design and thermal comfort studies. The MOLLIER DIAGRAM is commonly used in Europe.

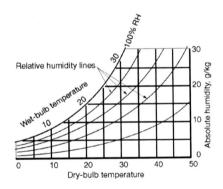

Psychrometric chart

psychrometry The study of the properties of a mixture of air and water vapour. *Psychros* is the Greek word for 'cold'.

PTFE *Abbreviation for* POLYTETRAFLUOROETHYLENE.

P-trap A plumbing TRAP constructed with the inlet leg vertical and the outlet leg inclined below the horizontal within specified limits. The shape of the trap resembles the letter 'P' on its side.

public address system *See* PA SYSTEM.

puddle A mixture of clay, water, and sometimes sand, worked while wet into a water-impervious layer of foundation material. It is used as a cut-off wall to prevent the ingress or egress of water.

pugging Material placed in a wall or floor cavity to provide fire resistance and/or sound insulation.

pull-down menu A MENU that is displayed when selected from a menu bar or a higher-level menu. This enables many menu items to be available without filling up the screen when they are not in use.

pulse An abrupt variation of short duration of a physical quantity followed by a rapid return to the initial value.

pulverised-fuel ash *Same as* FLY ASH.

pumice A vesicular glass formed from the froth on the surface of gaseous LAVAS. It has a high silica content, and is thus classed as an acid rock. Its highly porous structure makes it suitable as a lightweight aggregate for concrete. The sharp edges of the gas vesicles enable pumice to be used as an abrasive.

pump *See* BOOSTER, CENTRIFUGAL, CONCRETE, DIAPHRAGM, DOUBLE-ACTING, HEAT, RECIPROCATING *and* ROTARY PUMP.

pumped concrete Concrete that is transported through a pipe or hose by a pump.

pumping The ejection of water or mud from the joints between paving slabs under load, due to the accumulation of water in the subbase.

punch A small hand tool for directing the blow of a hammer onto a particular point. *(a) Nail punch*, has a slightly concave end, for driving a nail head below the surface. *(b) Centre punch*, has a pointed end for making a permanent mark on metal, and particularly for marking the centre of a hole so that the drill will not wander. *(c) Pin punch*, has a flat end and a parallel shaft, for driving a pin out of a hole, as in a *loose-pin hinge. See figure.*

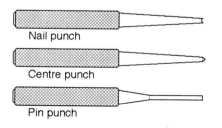

Nail punch

Centre punch

Pin punch

Punch

punching shear The shear caused by the tendency of a column, column head or column base to punch through a foundation slab, a FLAT SLAB or a FLAT PLATE *(see figure).*

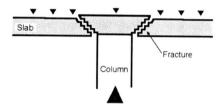

Slab

Fracture

Column

Punching shear

punkah A large swinging fan, traditional to the hot-humid regions of Asia. It is usually made of cloth stretched on a rectangular frame, hinged at the top, suspended from the ceiling or the rafters, and worked by a cord. *See also* CEILING FAN.

punkah louvre A circular air supply nozzle which can be rotated about a joint, used particularly for ventilating ships. If the temperature is high it can be directed on the occupant of a cabin. At other times the air can be admitted without causing undue draughts.

pupil The opening in the iris of the eye that admits light.

purlin A horizontal beam in a roof, at right angles to the trusses or rafters. It carries the roofing material, if it is in sheet form, or the COMMON RAFTERS, if the roof consists of tiles, shingles or slates. A purlin supporting common rafters is more correctly called an *underpurlin*, but the distinction is rarely made.

putlog Cross piece in a scaffold. It normally rests on the LEDGERs and supports the SOFFIT boards or sheets.

putty Compounds used for glazing windows and filling small holes in wood prior to painting. The most common form is made from powdered chalk and linseed oil.

PV *See* PHOTOVOLTAIC.

PVA *Abbreviation for* POLYVINYL ACETATE.

PVC *Abbreviation for* POLYVINYL CHLORIDE.

pycnometer An instrument for measuring

density. The most common type is a jar or bottle of known volume. It is weighed with and without its contents.

pylon In Ancient Egyptian architecture, one of a pair of monumental masonry towers at the gateway of a temple. In modern usage, a tall supporting structure, generally of steel, for supporting high tension electric lines in the open air, or for carrying lights in a theatre.

pyramid A solid bounded by plane surfaces, one being a polygon with any number of sides, and the others being triangles. The most elementary pyramid is the *tetrahedron*, which is a regular *polyhedron*, bounded by four equilateral triangles. The most common type of pyramid has a square base. The top of the pyramid is called the *apex*.

pyranometer An instrument for measuring total hemispherical (beam + diffuse) solar radiation. If fitted with a shadowband or occulting disc, to exclude the beam component, it will measure the diffuse radiation only.

pyrheliometer An instrument for measuring beam radiation from the sun and a small circumsolar area, usually with a tubular receiver, which is kept aimed at the sun by a motorised drive.

pyrometer Instrument for measuring temperatures. The term is used for instruments that measure high temperatures beyond the range of thermometry, and (less commonly) for instruments that measure temperature by electrical means.

pyrometric cone A small, pyramid-shaped cone whose composition is adjusted so that it melts at a definite temperature. The cones are made in series to cover a range of furnace temperatures, and the series constitutes a high-temperature thermometer. The SEGER CONE is a commonly used type.

Pythagoras' theorem 'The square on the longest side of a right-angled triangle equals the sum of the squares on the other two sides.' This theorem is credited to the Greek philosopher who lived in the sixth century BCE.

Q

Q-factor A measure of the sharpness of a RESONANCE.

quadrangle A rectangular space or court, the sides of which are occupied by a large building, such as a college.

quadrant An arc of a circle, forming one-quarter of its circumference. It subtends an angle of 90° or $\pi/2$ radians at the centre. Hence an instrument for measuring ALTITUDES with a graduated quarter circle; this has now been superseded by the *sextant*, a reflecting instrument which measures angles up to 120°.

quadratic equation An algebraic equation that contains the square, but no higher powers, of an unknown quantity.

quadratic residue diffuser A type of sound DIFFUSER where the diffuser profile is an array of troughs of constant width with depths defined by a mathematical sequence to maximise the diffusion of sound.

quadrilateral Plane figure bounded by four straight lines. If two of the lines are parallel, it is called a *trapezium*. If two pairs of lines are parallel, it is called a *parallelogram*. A right-angled parallelogram is a *rectangle*. An equilateral parallelogram is a *rhombus*. A right-angled rhombus is a *square*.

quadruplex A group of four lift cars sharing a common control system.

quality assurance The management of quality at all stages in the manufacture of product and delivery of services as standardised internationally by ISO 9000.

quality control Statistical control of the performance of products. *See also* FREQUENCY DISTRIBUTION CURVE *and* COEFFICIENT OF VARIATION.

quality factor (Q) The DAMPING of a MODE in a vibrating system is often defined in terms of the quality factor. The greater the damping of the mode, the greater will be the bandwidth of the mode. $Q = f/\Delta f$ where f is the modal frequency and Δf is the bandwidth of the mode.

quality management The management of systems developed to deliver a quality policy.

quality of lift service The passenger perception of the effectiveness of a lift system, measured in terms of passenger waiting time. *See* TIME INTERVAL.

quantising Converting to numerical or digital form. In order for information to be stored and manipulated in a computer it must first be represented in a numerical form. *See* DIGITAL.

quantity of lift service The handling capacity of a lift system.

quantity surveyor Building professional who is responsible for the technical accountancy of building contracts, particularly in the UK and South Africa. The quantity surveyor undertakes the preparation of the BILL OF QUANTITIES and the final measurement of the work.

quantum The minimum, indivisible quantity of radiant energy.

quarry tile A hard-burnt unglazed CLAY TILE.

quarter bend A bend through an arc of 90°.

quarter closer A brick which has been cut to one-quarter of its normal length.

quarter round A moulding which presents a profile of a quarter of a circle, inserted into corners.

quarter sawing Sawing a log into rectangular sections so that the longer dimension of the cross-section is roughly *radial* to the log (as opposed to BACK SAWING, where there is an illustration). Quarter sawing provides sections that are less subject to distortion during drying.

quarter-inch cartridge tape (QIC) A popular tape storage medium used for backup of desktop systems. Tape storage employs a sequential data organisation, and is sometimes referred to as a streaming tape, since the tracks store bytes contiguously along the track. *Also called digital linear tape (DLT)*.

quarter-turn tap Tap incorporating a CERAMIC DISC, capable of being fully opened or closed by a 90° turn of the spindle.

quarter-wave plates Crystal plates inserted into a POLARISCOPE at 45°. The first plate produces a retardation of a quarter of the wavelength of the MONO-CHROMATIC light. A second plate imparts a retardation by the same amount, but in the opposite sense. It is thus possible to show the ISOCHROMATICS without the ISOCLINICS (which are liable to cause confusion). Quarter-wave plates are usually cut from mica or quartz which has been split down to the required thickness.

quartz A mineral consisting of crystalline silica (SiO_2). It is a major component of many igneous and sedimentary rocks. Although pure quartz is colourless and transparent *(rock-crystal)*, it is commonly coloured by impurities. Many varieties are used as gemstones, *e.g.* AGATE, *amethyst*, *cairngorm*, ONYX and *tiger-eye*. Most SAND consists of small quartz grains with some impurities.

quartz (halogen) lamp A common name for a TUNGSTEN–HALOGEN LAMP.

quartzite A rock consisting of firmly compacted quartz grains.

queen closer *Also called queen closure*. A brick cut in half along its length to keep the BOND correct at the corner of a brick wall *(see figure)*. *See also* HALF BAT *and* KING CLOSER.

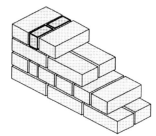

Queen closer

queen closure *Same as* QUEEN CLOSER.

queen-post roof truss A traditional timber truss similar to the KING-POST truss, except that it has no central king post, but instead a queen post on each side of the centre *(see figure)*. It does not satisfy MÖBIUS' LAW, and therefore relies on the stiffness of the bottom chord under asymmetrical loading. *See also* PRINCESS POST.

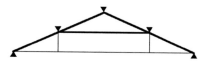

Queen-post roof truss

quenching Rapid cooling of steel from an elevated temperature, normally by immersing it in oil or water. The usual effect of quenching is to produce a hard steel, by suppressing the formation of PERLITE from austenite, and forming MARTENSITE instead. Quenching is often followed by TEMPERING.

quicklime Calcium oxide (CaO). It is the raw material for HYDRATED LIME, which is used in lime mortar.

quicksand A sand through which water moves *upwards* at sufficient speed to hold it in suspension. It has therefore negligible bearing capacity. The remedy is to reduce the flow of water. Although quicksand is due to water flow, the condition is more likely to occur with sand which is uniformly-grained and also fine-grained.

quickset level An instrument for LEVELLING, whose vertical spindle is adjusted only approximately, and the telescope is levelled for each sight. If only two readings are required at one station, it is quicker to use than the DUMPY LEVEL.

quicksilver *Same as* MERCURY.

quoin An outer corner of a wall. Hence dressed natural stone placed at the corners of a brick building, or face brick placed at the corners of a building with stone rubble walls. The quoins may be for additional strength, or for decoration, or both. *Also spelled coin.*

QWERTY keyboard The keyboard used in normal English typewriters.

R

R Symbol for THERMAL RESISTANCE.

R-value The measure of THERMAL RESISTANCE.

rabbit or rabbet *Same as* REBATE.

raceway An enclosed metal channel, usually fire-resistant, installed in a building to hold electrical wiring.

rack rent The rent that a tenant might reasonably be expected to pay in the open market.

racking The effect of lateral forces on a building, tending to push the walls out of square.

radial arm saw A circular saw sliding on an arm above the work, and cutting by pulling horizontally over the work. Usually adjustable for horizontal and vertical angles.

radial shrinkage The drying SHRINKAGE of timber at right angles to the growth rings. It is less than the *tangential shrinkage* which is normally considered; for many timbers the ratio is about 1:2.

radian (rad) The angle subtended between two radii of a circle on the circumference by an ARC equal in length to the radius. 1 radian = 57.296 degrees. 1 degree = 0.017 453 radians. *See also* STERADIAN.

radiance The area density of radiated power, per unit projected area of the source and per unit solid angle ($Wsr^{-1}m^{-2}$). The equivalent term in photometry is LUMINANCE.

radiant asymmetry An asymmetric sensation of warmth or coolness on one side of the body due to a radiant heat exchange with a surface that is warmer or cooler in one direction to the body.

radiant energy Energy in the form of electromagnetic waves that travel outward in all directions from the source. Measured in JOULES or equivalent units.

radiant heat Heat transmitted to a body by electromagnetic waves, as distinct from heat transferred by THERMAL CONDUCTION or CONVECTION. *See also* INFRARED RADIATION *and* STEFAN–BOLTZMANN LAW.

radiation Energy transmitted by electromagnetic waves. It ranges in decreasing order of wavelengths from radio waves, heat rays, infrared rays, visible light, ultraviolet rays, X-rays, gamma rays, to cosmic rays.

radiation barrier A device designed to reduce or stop the flow of radiant energy.

radiator A device for the transfer of heat to a space, ostensibly by radiation. When used as a terminal device in a central heating system a large proportion of the transfer may be by CONVECTION.

radiocarbon dating The scientific dating of an old building or artefact by analysing the rate of decay of carbon 14, which is radioactive. It is possible only if the building or artefact contains sufficient carbon.

radiography The production of photographs of invisible features, *e.g.* defects in welds, by means of X-RAYS.

radiometry The measurement of radiant energy. *See also* PHOTOMETRY.

radius of gyration A convenient shorthand notation for $\sqrt{(I/A)}$, where I is the second moment of area, and A is the cross-sectional area. The radius of gyration is required for certain dynamic problems, and for computing the SLENDERNESS RATIO in buckling problems.

radon A chemical element, the heaviest of the inert gases. It is formed by the radioactive decay of radium, and is emitted by some soils and rocks in small quantities as a natural process. However, it may collect in buildings if there is insufficient ventilation, and may then become a health hazard.

raft foundation A slab of concrete, usually reinforced, extending under the whole area of a building. It is used when loads are heavy and/or the bearing capacity of the soil is low.

rafter A sloping timber extending from the WALL PLATE to the ridge of a roof. The roofing material may be supported on BATTENS (small horizontal members placed on top of the rafters), or on PURLINS (larger horizontal members spanning between widely-spaced *principal rafters*). In some traditional roof constructions, the principal rafters support large purlins, which in turn support intermediate rafters or common rafters. These are smaller and more closely spaced than the principal rafters. The battens are carried by the common rafters.

rag bolt *Same as* LEWIS BOLT.

rag felt An asphaltic ROOFING FELT made from fibres or rag.

RAIA Royal Australian Institute of Architects, Canberra.

RAIC Royal Architectural Institute of Canada, Ottawa.

rain cap A cover over the upper termination of a vent or chute to prevent the entry of rain. It often includes a screen to prevent the entry of birds.

rain gauge An instrument for measuring rainfall. It usually consists of a funnel from which the water drips into a cylinder, graduated in inches or millimetres of rainfall per funnel area.

rain screen A system for the construction of external walls in which durable panels form the outer surface, intercepting the force of wind-driven rain; but the narrow joints between them are not waterproofed. Behind the panels is a cavity, and the face of the inner wall is made sufficiently waterproof to resist the small amount of moisture that penetrates the joints. This waterproofing material is not exposed to the weather, and is not seen. *See also* DRAINED JOINT.

rainwater head An enlarged receptacle attached to a wall at the top of a downpipe, to collect a concentrated discharge of rainwater from a roof and direct it into the pipe. There is usually provision for water to overflow harmlessly from the top, or from a slot partway down the rainwater head, in the event of a blockage (*see figure*).

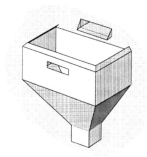

Rainwater head

raised floor A false floor which provides a space for cables or ducts above the structural floor, in the same way as a FALSE CEILING.

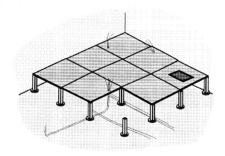

Raised floor

rake The slope, or angle of inclination. The context usually indicates whether it is measured from the vertical or the horizontal.

rake beam The beam that supports the roof on a gable or the top two sides of the triangle that form the gable.

raked joint A mortar JOINT IN BRICKWORK (where there is an illustration), or blockwork which has been scraped clean of mortar for about 12 mm (½ in.) back from the face. It may be left raked, or else it may subsequently be POINTED.

raking shore A sloping SHORE.

RAM *Abbreviation for* RANDOM ACCESS MEMORY.

rammed earth construction *Same as* PISÉ DE TERRE.

ramp test for sprinkler heads A hot wind-tunnel test to study thermal sensitivity of sprinkler heads under hot air with constant speed but temperature increasing linearly with time. *See also* PLUNGE TEST FOR SPRINKLER HEADS.

random access memory (RAM) Computer memory available for the storage of programs and data. Its memory cells are accessed directly by their addresses, rather than sequentially. Its contents can be altered, as distinct from *read-only memory*. RAM is usually volatile, *i.e.* it is lost when the power is turned off.

random ashlar *See* ASHLAR.

random incidence sound absorption coefficient The absorption of sound by a material depends on the angle of incidence of the sound. The sound absorption coefficient of a material as measured in a reverberant room where the sound is assumed to be DIFFUSE (as opposed to being measured in an IMPEDANCE TUBE where the sound is normally incident on the sample) is the random incidence sound absorption coefficient. The random incidence absorption coefficient is usually used to calculate the effect of an absorbent material in a room.

random noise Noise due to a large number of elementary disturbances with random occurrence in time. *See also* WHITE NOISE *and* PINK NOISE.

random numbers *(a)* A set of numbers obtained by chance. *(b)* A set of numbers, generated by an algorithm in a computer or given in a *table of random numbers*, which may be considered free from any statistical bias.

random sample A SAMPLE selected without bias. *See also* REPRESENTATIVE SAMPLE.

range of measured data The difference between the largest and the smallest measurement.

Rankine column formula One of the oldest formulas for the practical design of SLENDER columns *(see figure)*. The EULER FORMULA gives the correct load P_e for very slender columns, but it is unsafe for the buckling of columns with intermediate slenderness ratios (which includes most of the practical problems in the design of buildings). Similarly the *short-column* load P_s is unsafe for slender columns. The Scottish engineering professor, W. J. M. Rankine proposed in 1858 a gradual transition for the column load P:

$$\frac{1}{P} = \frac{1}{P_s} + \frac{1}{P_e}$$

See also PERRY–ROBERTSON *and* SECANT FORMULA.

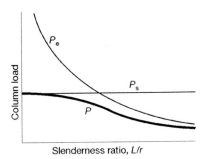

Rankine column formula

Rankine cycle An ideal cycle for a steam engine, proposed by W. J. M. Rankine in Scotland in the mid-nineteenth century. It can also be used for the analysis of refrigeration machines.

Rankine theory A theory for the EARTH PRESSURE developed by a granular soil (loose sand or gravel) on a retaining wall, proposed by W. J. M. Rankine in 1857. It gives the magnitude of the *active earth pressure* as

$$\frac{1 - \sin\varphi}{1 + \sin\varphi} \, ph$$

where ρ is the soil density, φ its ANGLE OF INTERNAL FRICTION, and h is the depth of the soil below the surface. For most granular soils, φ is approximately $35°$, and the active earth pressure is then 0.27 ph. The magnitude of the *passive earth pressure* is

$$\frac{1 + \sin\varphi}{1 - \sin\varphi} \, ph$$

which is 3.7 ph approximately. The theory does not apply to COHESIVE SOILS.

rapid-hardening cement *Same as* HIGH-EARLY-STRENGTH CEMENT.

raster A grid of a visual display unit dividing the display area into discrete units, *i.e.* PIXELS.

raster graphics A form of computer graphics employing a matrix of PIXELS, as opposed to VECTOR GRAPHICS.

raster image *See* PIXEL IMAGE.

raster scan The process of sweeping a display screen line by line to read or produce an image.

rasterised video display A technique for displaying images on a CRT that translates bit-mapped images to horizontal scan lines. Contrast with VECTOR GRAPHICS. *See also* BIT-MAPPED GRAPHICS.

RASTI *Abbreviation for* RApid Speech Transmission Index. A simplified form of the SPEECH TRANSMISSION INDEX (STI) that uses a limited frequency range to measure speech intelligibility in an auditorium.

ratchet A wheel with saw-like teeth, which a *pawl* (or single tooth) may engage for the purpose of preventing reversed motion.

ratchet clause A clause in a LEASE agreement that provides for periodic increases in rent in line with market conditions without provision for decreases.

rational number An INTEGER or a FRACTION. *See also* IRRATIONAL NUMBER *and* REAL NUMBER.

raw data Data that have not been processed.

ray tracing *(a)* A technique for predicting acoustic qualities of rooms by considering sound to travel as rays rather than waves. There are several commercially available software packages, using ray tracing, for predicting most acoustical parameters in a room. *(b)* A computer graphics technique for creating realistic images by calculating paths of *light rays*. Used to display various visual properties of objects, *e.g.* shadows, specular properties, etc. Also applies to the determination of hidden surfaces by tracing 'rays' emanating from the viewer's eye.

rayon A continuous-filament synthetic cellulose fibre. It is cheaper, but not as hard-wearing as NYLON.

RC *Abbreviation for* REINFORCED CONCRETE.

reactance Opposition to the flow of alternating current. *Capacitive* reactance is the opposition offered by a capacitor, and *inductive* reactance is the opposition offered by a coil or other inductance.

reaction The opposition to an action, *e.g.* to the downward pressure of a loaded beam. For static equilibrium the reaction must balance the action.

reaction turbine A turbine in which the jets or nozzles are on the moving wheel, as opposed to an *impulse turbine*.

reactive concrete aggregate Aggregate that is capable of combining chemically with Portland cement, under normal conditions, due to ALKALI–AGGREGATE REACTION, and may thus cause harmful expansion.

reactive muffler A MUFFLER (or *silencer*) that relies on the reflection of sound for attenuation (*e.g.* a sudden change in cross-section) while allowing the unimpeded flow of air or other gases. Reactive mufflers are usually used to attenuate low frequency sounds. (*See also* DISSIPATIVE MUFFLER.)

reactive (imaginary) power In alternating current electrical systems, the imaginary component of the vector product of voltage and current. It has the units of volt-amps-reactive or VAR. *See also* REAL POWER *and* POWER FACTOR.

read-only memory (ROM) *(a)* The memory in a computer used by the microprocessor manufacturer to permanently store programs to boot the computer upon startup. *(b)* The term ROM (as in CD-ROM) is also used to describe the disk drives that read information stored on CDs (compact disks).

reading (memory) Accessing information stored in memory for transfer to the CPU. The read operation is non-destructive, meaning that it has no impact on the information stored. *See also* WRITING MEMORY.

ready-mixed concrete Concrete mixed at a central plant and transported to the building site. Some or all of the mixing water may be added during transportation. *Also called transit-mixed. See also* TRANSIT MIXER.

real estate *See* REAL PROPERTY.

real number One of the infinitely divisible range of values between minus and plus infinity. A real number may be RATIONAL or IRRATIONAL, but not IMAGINARY nor COMPLEX. In computing, a difference is made between a REAL NUMBER and an INTEGER in that real numbers are represented (approximately) as FLOATING-POINT NUMBERS.

real power In alternating current electrical systems, the real component of the vector product of voltage and current. It has the units of watts. It is also the product of voltage, current and the POWER FACTOR. *See also* POWER, IMAGINARY POWER, POWER FACTOR *and* REACTIVE POWER.

real property Land with or without buildings, fences and other fixtures. *Also called real estate.*

real time processing Any processing where the response to an input happens almost instantaneously.

reamer A tool used for finishing or enlarging holes which have previously been drilled.

rebar US abbreviation for a REINFORCING BAR.

rebate A recessed timber edge, designed to receive a door, window sash or some other piece. *Also spelled rabbet and rabbit.*

recall *See* LIFT RECALL.

receiver A device configured to receive (and perhaps interpret) a transmission (electrical signal, wave, etc.) emitted by a TRANSMITTER.

recessed luminaire A LUMINAIRE recessed into a ceiling, so that its lower edge is flush with the ceiling, as opposed to *surface mounted.*

reciprocal diagram A graphical solution for the design of STATICALLY DETERMINATE trusses, proposed by the British physicist, Clerk Maxwell, in 1864. It consists of a series of triangles and polygons of force, drawn together so that all have at least one line in common. BOW'S NOTATION is commonly used for this construction.

reciprocal theorem A theorem published by the British physicist, Clerk Maxwell, in 1864, which relates the deflection of a structure at two points, and the reciprocal (or corresponding) loads at the same points. It is the basis of several methods for the analysis of STATICALLY INDETERMINATE structures.

reciprocating compressor A machine used for raising the pressure of a gas by the reciprocating action of a piston in a cylinder. Commonly used for compressing air, or the refrigerant in refrigeration systems, but increasingly superseded by *centrifugal* or *screw compressors.*

reciprocating engine An engine consisting of a piston moving *backward and forward* in a cylinder. The reciprocating motion is converted into rotary motion by means of a connecting rod and a crankshaft or flywheel. A *rotary engine* produces rotary motion directly.

reciprocating pump A pump in which a reciprocating piston draws liquid into a chamber and expels it through valve action.

reclosing The common utility practice on overhead power lines of closing the circuit breaker within a short time after clearing a fault, taking advantage of the fact that most faults are transient, or temporary.

reconditioning of collapsed timber A steam treatment for the COLLAPSE OF TIMBER.

reconstituted stone *Same as* ARTIFICIAL STONE.

record Files in a database are organised as a sequence of records, each having the same structure. Records in turn each contain a number of fields containing data about a single entity (like a student, a customer, etc.).

record drawings Copy of the contract drawings, marked up to reflect changes made during the construction process. *Also called as-built drawings.*

recoverable outgoings The difference between the total operating costs and non-recoverable operating costs.

recrystallisation The formation of new crystals, *e.g.* ANNEALed crystals from previously strain-hardened crystals.

rectangle A right-angled PARALLELO-GRAM.

rectangular coordinates *Same as* CARTESIAN COORDINATES.

rectifier An electrical device used to change AC power into DC power. A battery charger is a rectifier. A *full-wave* rectifier requires four DIODES to rectify both halves of an AC wave *(see figure).*

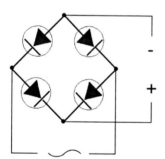

Rectifier

rectifier/charger A subassembly of a UPS that performs the function of converting the incoming AC into DC for driving the inverter and charging the batteries.

recurrent costs The expenses that can be expected annually in the general operation of a business.

recyclable material A material that can be wholly or partially put back into productive use by decomposition or disassembly.

recycled concrete Hardened concrete that has been crushed for re-use as concrete aggregate or gravel.

recycling The collection and reprocessing of materials to produce new products, instead of throwing them away. The con-

cept can be applied to the refurbishment and re-use of buildings.

red lead Red oxide of lead (Pb_3O_4). It was commonly used as a rust-inhibiting PRIMER on steel, but has been largely superseded by zinc-rich primers because of the toxicity of lead, and because of the *electrochemical protection* provided by the zinc.

red oxide Red IRON OXIDE, a pigment which does not inhibit corrosion. *See also* RED LEAD.

redirection In lighting, referring to the change of direction of light flux by reflection, refraction or diffraction.

reduced level (RL) Surveying term used for the level of a position with respect to a datum.

reducing power The strength of a white pigment in reducing the colour of a coloured pigment. It is a measure of the paleness of tint produced, and is the opposite of STAINING POWER.

reduction A chemical process involving a decrease in the state of OXIDATION.

reduction in area The contraction in cross-sectional area which occurs when a ductile material is tested in tension. It is one of the quantities normally measured during the test. *See* CUP-AND-CONE FRACTURE.

redundancy *(a)* In structural engineering, a structural member or restraint in excess of those required by MÖBIUS' LAW. A structure with redundancies is statically indeterminate, one without redundancies is statically determinate. *(b)* In mechanical and electrical installations, the inclusion of additional equipment or circuits, with provision for automatic switchover from a failing unit to its backup.

re-entrant angle An angle of less than 180° on the observer's side of a wall, the opposite of a *salient angle.* It forms the equivalent of a *concave* as opposed to a *convex* surface.

re-entrant corner An internal angle or corner, the opposite of a *salient corner.*

reference longitude The MERIDIAN of longitude which corresponds to the TIME ZONE of a region. Each 15° east of the Greenwich meridian represents a time zone 1 hour ahead of UTC. The reference longitude usually passes through part of the region, but it is not necessary for it to do so, especially when *daylight saving* is in operation.

reflectance The ratio of total reflected to total incident flux for a surface. It is a scalar quantity, so a non-matt surface's reflective properties are described by its *luminance factor*.

reflectance factor The REFLECTANCE of a surface, expressed as a percentage.

reflected ceiling plan A PLAN showing the underside of a suspended ceiling, but drawn as if reflected in a mirror on the floor, so that the whole layout can be easily related to the normal floor plan.

reflected glare GLARE produced by specular reflections of luminous objects, especially reflections appearing on or near the object viewed *(see figure)*.

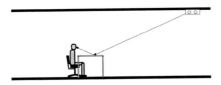

Reflected glare

reflected sound Sound that has undergone at least one reflection from a surface in a room, as opposed to DIRECT SOUND, which reaches an observer without undergoing a reflection.

reflection The process whereby energy reaching a surface partly or fully leaves that surface without change of wavelength, on the same side as it arrived. Reflection may be DIFFUSE or SPECULAR.

reflective glass Glass coated with a thin layer of metal or metal oxide, which reflects some of the solar radiation. *See also* HEAT-ABSORBING GLASS.

reflective insulation Metal that reflects infrared radiation, and therefore reduces the amount of heat entering a building, particularly via the roof. It commonly takes the form of aluminium foil, 0.15 mm (0.006 in.) or less in thickness, backed by KRAFT PAPER.

reflectivity The ratio of radiant energy reflected by a body to that falling upon it, expressed as a percentage. Preferred term is *reflectance*.

reflectometer A PHOTOMETER for measuring REFLECTANCE.

reflector lamp An electric lamp that has a reflective metal coating applied directly to part of the inside of the lamp.

reflector, parabolic *See* PARABOLIC REFLECTOR.

refraction The change in direction that occurs when a ray of light passes from one medium to another with a different density or impedance. The ratio of the sine of the angle of incidence to the sine of the angle of refraction is the *refractive index*. *See also* REFLECTION.

refractory brick A brick made from a REFRACTORY MATERIAL.

refractory material One that can withstand a high temperature, and is thus suitable for lining a furnace. CHINA CLAY, ALUMINA, SILICA, DOLOMITE and *chromite* make suitable refractories.

refrigerant The fluid circulated in a REFRIGERATION system that acts as the heat transfer medium in the cooling process.

refrigeration The process of mechanically extracting heat from a thermodynamic system in order to cool it by transferring the heat to another place.

refrigeration cycle The most commonly used refrigeration cycles are the ABSORPTION CYCLE and the VAPOUR COMPRESSION CYCLE.

refuge floor A protected floor that serves as a refuge for the occupants of the building to assemble in case of fire.

refusal A term applied to the resistance offered by a FRICTION PILE to continued driving. It is often defined as the failure to penetrate more than 10mm (0.4 in.) in four blows.

regeneration of energy The transformation of mechanical kinetic energy from a lift or escalator on a *down* run into electrical energy that is fed back into the electrical supply system.

regenerative heating Utilisation of heat that has been rejected in another part of the cycle, by heat transfer.

register *(a)* An air grille with a damper in a ventilating or air conditioning duct or in a chimney. *(b)* In computing, a storage location which holds data, instructions or addresses on a temporary basis.

Regnault hygrometer A type of DEW-POINT HYGROMETER.

reheat Heat supplied to previously cooled air to bring it to the condition necessary to meet comfort requirements in a part of a building.

reinforced brickwork or masonry Brickwork or masonry that has reinforcement embedded (in the joints, or through the holes in the units) to increase the resistance to flexural tension.

reinforced concrete Concrete that contains reinforcement, normally of steel, to improve its resistance to tension. It is designed on the assumption that the two materials act together in resisting the stresses in the composite material due to the loads. PRESTRESSED CONCRETE, in which the concrete is prestressed by steel before the loads are applied, is often considered to be a separate form of construction, although in current practice they can be used in combination. *See also* BALANCED DESIGN, COMPRESSION REINFORCEMENT *and* T-BEAM.

reinforced glass Glass in which a wire mesh was embedded during manufacture. *Also called wired glass*. Largely superseded by LAMINATED and TOUGHENED GLASS.

reinforcement for concrete *See* COLD-DRAWN WIRE, COLD WORKING, DEFORMED BAR, DIAGONAL CRACK, DISTRIBUTION REINFORCEMENT, EFFECTIVE DEPTH, EXPANDED METAL, HELICAL REINFORCEMENT, HOOP REINFORCEMENT, LATERAL REINFORCEMENT, LONGITUDINAL REINFORCEMENT, MESH REINFORCEMENT, REINFORCED CONCRETE, SECONDARY REINFORCEMENT *and* TENDON.

reinforcing bar *See* COLD-DRAWN WIRE, DEFORMED BAR, MESH REINFORCEMENT *and* TENDON.

relamping In lighting, the process of replacing ELECTRIC LAMPS by either SPOT REPLACEMENT (when a lamp has failed) or BULK REPLACEMENT (as part of a planned maintenance programme).

relative density *Same as* SPECIFIC GRAVITY.

relative humidity The ratio of the quantity of water vapour actually present in the air, to that present at the same temperature in a water-saturated atmos-phere, expressed as a percentage. *See also* ABSOLUTE HUMIDITY *and* WET-BULB TEMPERATURE.

relaxation of steel Decrease in the stress of steel due to CREEP in the steel under prolonged strain. The term is also applied to the LOSS OF PRESTRESS due to shrinkage and creep of the concrete, which results in a decreased steel strain.

relay A device in which a small electrical power is used to control a larger electrical power. Many relays employ electromagnets to operate switches.

re-levelling An operation permitting the stopped position of a lift car to be corrected during loading and unloading by successive small car movements. *See also* LEVELLING DEVICE.

reliability The statistical probability of trouble-free operation of a given component or assembly. Used principally as a function of MTBF and MTTR.

relief The elevation or projection of a design out from a plane surface in order to give a solid appearance, as opposed to INTAGLIO. Relief may be high, middle or low *(bas relief)*.

relief air Air that is allowed to escape to the atmosphere from an air conditioning system in order to be displaced by outdoor air for ventilation.

relieving arch *See* DISCHARGING ARCH.

remoulded clay Clay whose internal structure has been disturbed. Its SENSITIVITY RATIO is the ratio of the strength of an undisturbed to that of a remoulded clay sample.

removable hard disk *Also called cartridge disk*. In these devices, a disk enclosed in a cartridge can be inserted/removed from the hard disk drive. The advantage of such devices is that the total available disk space is limited only by the number of hard disk cartridges available.

removable media Any of the memory-containing devices, such as floppy disks, CDs, memory sticks and magnetic tape that can be inserted into a computer to transfer data, and then easily removed to allow the data to be physically transferred to another computer or stored in another location.

rendering *(a)* The application of mortar or plaster to a surface by means of a float or trowel. *(b)* In computer graphics, the application of colour, texture and shading to an image usually to simulate photo-realism.

renewable A resource that can be renewed or replenished at a rate equal or greater than its extraction rate.

renewable energy Energy produced from virtually inexhaustible resources such as the sun. For example, solar radiation, biomass, wind, water or heat from the Earth's interior are regarded as renewable energy resources.

rent The payment for the use or occupation of land or premises: categories of rent include contract, economic, ground and gross rent.

repeated loading Normally interpreted as a much smaller number of repetitions than are needed to produce a FATIGUE failure.

repeater Hardware device that boosts the strength of a SIGNAL along a transmission line (*e.g.* network connection). Repeaters are often used to increase the number of nodes allowed in a LAN.

repetition The ability of the computer system to perform more complicated tasks by organising a smaller set of simpler tasks that are repeated over and over. For example, multiplication can be achieved by repeated additions.

repose *See* ANGLE OF REPOSE.

repoussé Raised in relief by embossing.

representative sample A SAMPLE selected to be representative of the whole POPULATION.

residual current device A device to interrupt an electric circuit before a fault current to ground reaches a value that would endanger life. Used in many industrial situations, and required under Australian wiring rules for most domestic circuits. *See also* EARTH LEAKAGE CIRCUIT BREAKER.

resilience The ability of a material to absorb and return strain energy without permanent deformation.

resin *(a)* The produce from the secretion of certain plants and trees, consisting of highly POLYMERISED substances. They are insoluble in water, but soluble in certain organic solvents, and fusible. Most resins are hard and brittle. *(b)* Synthetic imitation of a natural resin. The term 'synthetic

resin' is often used as a synonym for a THERMOSETTING plastic. *See also* ROSIN.

resistance *See* ELECTRICAL RESISTANCE, MOMENT OF RESISTANCE *and* THERMAL RESISTANCE.

resistance arm *Same as* LEVER ARM.

resistance strain gauge *See* ELECTRIC RESISTANCE STRAIN GAUGE.

resistance welding Welding two parts by holding them in tight contact with electrodes through which a heavy current flows momentarily, causing them to fuse together.

resistor A discrete electronic component designed to produce a DC voltage drop when current passes through it.

resolution In computing, the number of PIXELS in the horizontal and vertical rows of a screen. *See also* PICTURE RESOLUTION *and* DIGITAL SOUND.

resolution at the joints A method for the design of statically determinate trusses, proposed by the Russian engineer D. J. Jourawski in 1850. Since each joint (as well as the whole truss) is in equilibrium, it is possible to resolve horizontally and vertically to produce *2j* equations for *j* joints. According to MÖBIUS' LAW, the truss has *2j – 3* members, in which we must determine the forces. The method thus produces three check equations. *See also* RECIPROCAL DIAGRAM *and* METHOD OF SECTIONS.

resolution of a force Determination of the *components* of a FORCE, usually horizontally and vertically.

resonance Resonance occurs when a system oscillates, with minimum impedance, in response to an excitation at a given frequency. The maximum response is at the *resonant frequency*. The phenomenon occurs in acoustics, and in the vibration of buildings subject to vibrations from machinery, earthquake or wind. *See also* DECAY FACTOR.

resonant absorber An object or construction that absorbs sound due to the physical RESONANCE of part or all of its structure or the medium associated with it. Two examples of resonant absorbers are HELMHOLTZ RESONATORS and panels of wood, glass, plasterboard, etc.

resonant frequency *See* NATURAL FREQUENCY.

resorcinol A high strength and water-resistant phenol adhesive used for glue-lamination and other structural timber adhesive applications. Leaves a dark brown glue line which may not suit decorative applications.

respirable particulates Particles suspended in air that may be inhaled deep into the lungs due to their very small size.

response time index (RTI) of sprinkler heads Product of time constant of a sprinkler head and square root of hot air speed in a wind tunnel. This is a property of the sprinkler head itself, independent of the hot air flow.

restricted area An area whose access is limited to identified persons.

restrictive covenant A requirement to adhere to a specified restriction on the use or development of real property.

restrike The process of restarting an electric DISCHARGE LAMP. *See also* HOT RESTRIKE.

resultant The vector sum of two or more forces.

resultant temperature A thermal comfort index developed by Missénard in France (1935), very similar to the original EFFECTIVE TEMPERATURE.

retaining wall A wall that retains a weight of earth or water. It may rely for its stability on the weight of the masonry or concrete, usually with a batter (GRAVITY RETAINING WALL), or on the cantilever strength of the wall (which may be of steel or timber, but is usually of reinforced concrete). In a CANTILEVER RETAINING WALL the weight of soil lying above the *heel* is utilised to improve the stability of the wall.

retarded hemihydrate plaster PLASTER OF PARIS with the addition of a retarder, usually keratin.

retarder A substance that slows down a chemical reaction, as opposed to an ACCELERATOR. In concrete, an additive which delays the setting of the cement, and thus allows more time for placing the concrete.

retention The holding of a percentage of a progress payment to cover possible defects or other contingencies.

retention basin Hydraulic structure designed to retain stormwater for the purpose of improving water quality and/or recharging the ground water table. *See also* DETENTION BASIN.

reticulate To divide so as to form a network.

reticulated work *See* OPUS RETICULATUM.

retina The membrane lining the interior surface of the back of the eye, containing photoreceptors (RODS and CONES) and the ends of the optic nerve.

retrofit *(a)* To make an improvement, for example to thermal insulation or sunshading, to an old building. *(b)* In lighting, to replace one type of lamp with another (newer) type having the same electrical and optical characteristics.

retro-reflective *(a)* A material that reflects light back along the same or similar path to the incident light, usually employing tiny spheres in a carrier. Used as a reflective material on safety clothing, in road signs and road marking paints. *(b)* 'Cats-eyes'.

return *(a)* A return circuit, pipe or duct. *(b)* A change in the direction of a wall or other building component, usually at right angles.

return air The air returned from an air conditioned space and recirculated in order to reduce energy consumption by the air conditioning system.

return moulding Moulding which RETURNS around a corner. When using prefabricated units such as special bricks with a moulding along one long edge, two separate special types are required at corners: a left-hand and a right-hand return.

reveal *(a)* The part of the JAMB between the frame and the outside wall, which is revealed, inasmuch as it is not covered by the frame. *(b)* The visible side of an open fireplace. *(c)* The entire JAMB or vertical face of an opening.

reverberant distance *See* CRITICAL DISTANCE.

reverberant sound field The sound field in an enclosure resulting from sound which has been reflected from the enclosure boundaries and where the DIRECT SOUND has an insignificant effect. The reverberant sound field approximates a *diffuse sound field* where the properties of the sound field are the same throughout.

reverberation chamber A room for acoustic testing in which a DIFFUSE SOUND FIELD exists because all the surfaces are highly reflecting. Reverberation chambers are used for measuring the SOUND ABSORPTION COEFFICIENT and SOUND TRANSMISSION LOSS of materials amongst many other things. *See also* ANECHOIC CHAMBER.

reverberation radius *See* CRITICAL DISTANCE.

reverberation time The time required for the average sound intensity, in a room or enclosure, to decrease to 10^{-6} of the initial value (60 dB) after the emission by the source has ceased. *See* SABINE FORMULA.

reverse brick veneer A wall construction in which a brick inner skin is placed inside a stud frame with an outer cladding of lightweight sheet material.

reverse cycle heating *See* HEAT PUMP.

reverse osmosis Whilst osmosis is the diffusion of a solvent (*e.g.* water) through a membrane into a more concentrated solution, a static electricity charge applied to the concentrated solution can reverse the process (by ionisation), and the solvent will diffuse from the concentrated solution. The process can be used for producing potable water from brackish or slightly salty water.

reverse video A display in which the background and foreground colours are reversed. For example, white characters on a black background.

reversed door A door opening in the direction opposite to that considered regular, *e.g.* a cupboard door opening inward.

reversible process An idealised thermodynamic process in which energy transferred from a system is returned to it without loss. In practice, no process is completely reversible due to friction losses.

revetment A protective covering to a soil or soft rock surface, to protect it against scouring by water or other effects of weathering. It may consist of grass or other plants, bundles of brushwood, asphalt, stone slabs or concrete.

revolution, surface of *See* SURFACE OF REVOLUTION.

revolving shelf A shelf designed to give access to inner corners where two cupboards meet, by rotating it on a vertical pivot. *Also called* a *lazy susan*.

Reynolds' critical velocity The velocity at which flow changes from *streamline* to *turbulent*.

Reynolds' number A non-dimensional ratio used for assessing the similarity of motion in viscous fluids, named after the British hydraulic engineer, who proposed it in 1883.

$$\text{Reynolds' number} = \frac{Lu}{v}$$

where L is any typical length, u is the velocity of the fluid and v is its KINEMATIC VISCOSITY. In model analysis, in order to satisfy the PI-THEOREM, the Reynolds' number must be the same for the prototype and the model. In practice it is often difficult to satisfy this condition, and some distortion may have to be accepted.

RF *Abbreviation for (a)* REFLECTANCE FACTOR. *(b)* Radio Frequency, the range of frequencies at which radio and TV signals are transmitted.

RFI *Abbreviation for* Radio Frequency Interference.

RFL *Abbreviation for* Reflective Foil Laminate. An aluminium foil can be used as insulation, particularly where the dominant heat transfer mechanism is radiation (*e.g.* downward summer heat flow in a roof), but it is very vulnerable, so it is bonded to building paper.

RGB colour A colour model used for representing colour images. The image is composed of three channels: the three additive primaries of Red, Green and Blue. This scheme maps directly for display on RGB COLOUR VIDEO MONITORS, where three phosphors are used to represent these three primary colours for each pixel. *See also* HSB COLOUR *and* CMYK COLOUR.

RGB colour video monitor Video display monitor in which three phosphors (one for each of the three primary colours red, green and blue) are used to represent each pixel in an image. *See also* CATHODE-RAY TUBE (CRT).

RH *Abbreviation for* RELATIVE HUMIDITY.

rheological model A physical model used to illustrate a theory in the field of RHEOLOGY *(see figure)*. Rheological models are mainly composed of: *(a)* springs for ELASTIC deformation; *(b)* dashpots for viscous or CREEP deformation, and *(c)* heavy weights resting on a rough surface which offer frictional resistance for PLASTIC DEFORMATION.

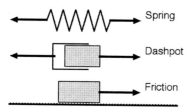

Spring

Dashpot

Friction

Rheological model

rheology The science of the flow of materials. In building science, rheological studies are valuable for determining the flow of liquid concrete, paint or mastics; and for the CREEP deformation of timber and concrete.

rheostat A resistance that can be adjusted to vary the total resistance in an electrical circuit.

rib *(a)* A small beam projecting from a concrete slab. *(b)* The vertical member of a T-BEAM. *Also called web.*

RIBA Royal Institute of British Architects, London.

ribbed slab A panel composed of a thin slab reinforced by ribs in one or two directions (usually at right angles to one another). The latter is also called *waffle slab* because of its appearance; it is commonly used with mushroom columns in a FLAT SLAB. When used in a FLAT PLATE, the ribbed slab is made solid in the area surrounding the column for extra shear resistance.

rich concrete A concrete with a high cement content, as opposed to a *lean concrete.*

Richter scale Scale devised by C. F. Richter in California for determining the *magnitude* of an earthquake. For this purpose 'standard earthquake' is defined as one providing a maximum trace amplitude of 0.001 mm on a certain type of seismograph at a 'standard distance' of 100 km. The magnitude on the Richter scale was originally defined as the log-arithm (to the base 10) of the ratio of the amplitude of any earthquake at the 'standard distance' to that of the 'standard earthquake'. To make the scale independent of the type of recording instrument it was later defined by the equation

$$\log E = 4.8 + 1.5\,M$$

where M is the magnitude on the Richter scale, and E is the energy released by the earthquake in joules. The smallest earthquakes recorded by very sensitive instruments at short distances have an energy of 0.01 J, and the largest an energy of 10^{18} J. The variation on the Richter scale is from 0 for the smallest earthquake to 8.6 for the largest recorded. The MERCALLI SCALE classifies the *intensity* of an earthquake.

RICS Royal Institution of Chartered Surveyors, London.

ridethrough The ability of a power conditioner to supply output power when input power is lost.

ridge A horizontal line caused by the junction of two sloping roof surfaces.

ridge board A horizontal board at the ridge of the roof, set on edge. The rafters are nailed to it.

ridge tile A tile moulded to cover the ridge of a roof and prevent entry of rainwater. Its moulding sometimes incorporates a decoration, particularly at the gable.

right angle An angle of 90°.

right ascension The horizontal coordinate of the sun, moon or a star at any given time, measured in the Earth's equatorial plane. It is listed in the NAUTICAL ALMANAC. The vertical coordinate is the *declination. See also* AZIMUTH.

right line Obsolete term for a straight line between two points.

right-angled half-lap joint *Same as* END-LAP JOINT.

right-hand Supposedly a fitting convenient to a right-handed person. A *right-hand screw* is one which tightens clockwise. A *right-hand stair* is one which has its handrail on the right going up. In the UK, a right-hand door is one whose hinges are on the right, when it swings *towards* the hand opening it. However, in the USA a *right-hand door* is one whose hinges are on the right, when it swings *away* from the hand opening it. A *right-hand lock* is one which fits a right-hand door, according to local convention.

rigid foam *See* EXPANDED PLASTIC.

rigid frame A FRAME with RIGID JOINTS, which are capable of transmitting moments. *See also* TUBE STRUCTURE.

rigid joint A joint which is capable of transmitting the full moment at the end of a member to the other members framing into the joint. *See also* SEMI-RIGID JOINT *and* PIN JOINT.

rigidity *See* MODULUS OF RIGIDITY.

RILEM *Réunion Internationale des Laboratoires d'Essais et des Recherches sur les Matériaux et les Constructions*, Paris.

rim lock A lock which is screwed to the face of the door, as opposed to a MORTISE lock.

ring shake A separation along or between the annual rings of a piece of timber.

ring, proving *See* PROVING RING.

ring, tension *See* TENSION RING.

ringing Vibrations or oscillations that continue after the removal of an external force. Ringing can occur in electrical or mechanical systems.

rip To cut timber parallel to the grain.

rise *(a)* The vertical height of an arch, roof truss or rigid frame. The vertical height of a cable structure is its *sag*. *(b)* The vertical distance from the top of one tread to the top of the next tread of a staircase. *See also* GOING. *(c)* The total vertical distance which a stair rises from floor to floor.

rise and fall Upward or downward cost adjustments, for unforeseen or unquantified variations in the cost of labour and materials.

riser *(a)* The vertical board under the TREAD of a step. *(b)* A vertical supply pipe for a SPRINKLER SYSTEM. *(c)* A pipe for water, drainage, steam, gas or venting which extends vertically through one or more full storeys and services other pipes. *Also called* a *rising main*. *(d)* An electrical cable which extends vertically through one or more storeys, and distributes power to electric panels on different floors of the building. *Also called* a *rising main*. *(e)* A vertical duct of a ventilating or air conditioning system which extends vertically through one or more storeys, and distributes air to branch ducts.

rise-time A measure of the time it takes an instrument or control system to respond to a sudden change in the input signal.

rising main *See* RISER *(c) and (d)*.

risk management The management of an activity, accepting a level of risk, which is balanced against the benefit of the activity, usually on the basis of an economic assessment model.

Ritter's method *See* METHOD OF SECTIONS.

rivet A headed shank for making a permanent joint between two pieces of metal. It is inserted into holes in the two pieces, and closed by forming a head on the projecting shank. In steel structures the head must be formed while the rivet is red-hot, and because of the inconvenience of handling the red-hot rivets, riveting has been gradually replaced by welding and by FRICTION-GRIP BOLTing. The heads of aluminium rivets can be formed cold, provided the diameter of the rivets is not too large. BLIND and EXPLOSIVE RIVETS can be used in inaccessible locations.

RL *Abbreviation for* REDUCED LEVEL.

RMS *Abbreviation for* ROOT MEAN SQUARE.

RMS line current The square root of the average of the squares of all instantaneous current amplitudes occurring during a given cycle.

RMS line voltage The square root of the average of the squares of all instantaneous voltage amplitudes occurring during a given cycle.

robotics A sub-area of ARTIFICIAL INTELLIGENCE in which the focus is on constructing computer hardware/software to control the actions of machines (robots). The ultimate goal is to create robots that will be able to sense and react to their environments in human-like ways.

rock *See* SEDIMENTARY, IGNEOUS *and* METAMORPHIC ROCK.

rock anchor *See* ANCHOR.

rock flour SILT-sized crushed rock.

rock wool MINERAL WOOL made from molten rock.

rockbreaker A hydraulically-operated

reciprocating hammer, attached to the arm of a backhoe or excavator, used for excavating in rock or breaking-up concrete.

Rockwell hardness test A method for determining hardness by indenting the test piece with a diamond cone or a hard steel ball, and measuring the depth of penetration. A smaller load is used for the *Rockwell superficial hardness* test.

rod *(a)* One of the receptors in the retina of the eye, used in low light conditions, not capable of seeing in colour. *See also* CONE *(b)*. *(b)* An obsolete measure of length, 16.5 ft or 5.03 m. *Also*, any stick of known length used for setting out the dimensions of a building, such as a *brick rod*.

rodding Using a system of flexible rods which may be progressively joined to clear blockages in sewerage and stormwater drains.

roll roofing *Same as* BUILT-UP ROOFING.

roll-formed sections Sheet metal sections, usually 1–3 mm ($\frac{1}{32}$–$\frac{1}{8}$in.) in thickness, formed from a continuous strip by passing longitudinally through successive sets of rollers, as opposed to *folding* in a *brake press*. The length of roll-formed sections is limited only by handling and transport.

rolled glass Molten glass from a furnace, passed through rollers to produce a pattern on one or both surfaces.

rolled steel joist (RSJ) A ROLLED STEEL SECTION of I-shape.

rolled steel section Any HOT-ROLLED SECTION of steel, including joists, angles, channels and rails.

rolling friction The frictional resistance offered when a body rolls over a surface. *See also* COEFFICIENT OF FRICTION.

ROM *Abbreviation for* READ-ONLY MEMORY.

Roman tile *Same as* MISSION TILE.

Röntgen rays *Same as* X-RAYS.

roof The surface enclosing the top of a building, generally including the top surface and the structure supporting it, but not the *ceiling*, which is considered separately. *See* CRUCKS, DORMER, FLAT ROOF, GABLE ROOF, HIP ROOF MANSARD ROOF, *and* RAFTER.

roof dormer *See* DORMER WINDOW.

roof space The space between the struc-ture of the ceiling of the highest storey and the underside of the roof structure and the roof cladding.

roof structure *See* DOME, FOLDED-PLATE ROOF, PNEUMATIC STRUCTURE, ROOF TRUSS, SHELL ROOF, SPACE FRAME, SUSPENSION ROOF, TOP-HAT STRUCTURE, *and* VAULT.

roof tile Clay or concrete tile used for covering sloping roofs; it may be moulded with a plain surface (sometimes called an ENGLISH TILE), or with drainage channels (*see* MARSEILLES PATTERN TILE, MISSION TILE, PAN TILE *and* S-TILE). *See also* SHINGLE *and* SLATE.

roof truss A TRUSS used as the supporting structure for a roof. *See* BELFAST, FINK, HOWE, AND WARREN TRUSS; KING POST, PRINCESS POST, QUEEN POST *and* HAMMER-BEAM ROOF; *also* KNEEBRACE *and* TRUSSED RAFTER.

roofing felt Waterproof felt, soaked in asphalt, bitumen or tar, used in BUILT-UP ROOFING. Largely superseded by fibreglass or synthetic fabrics sealed with various polymers.

rooflight Any glazed roof opening used for the purpose of admitting daylight.

room air A term used in air conditioning practice to denote the air in the occupied space as distinct from supply or return air.

room air conditioner A self-contained machine inserted in a window or external wall of a room and used to circulate air cooled by refrigeration in the room while rejecting heat outdoors. May be used as a HEAT PUMP to supply heat if appropriately circuited.

room cavity That portion of a room between the plane of the luminaires and the WORKING PLANE. *See also* ROOM INDEX.

room cavity ratio In lighting calculations, a measure of room proportion as determined by dimensions of length, width and height (used in the USA.) *See also* ROOM INDEX.

room constant The room constant of an enclosure is a measure of the sound absorption in the enclosure, given by the equation:

$$\text{Room constant} = A_{\text{TOTAL}}/(1 - AC_{\text{AVERAGE}})$$

where A_{TOTAL} = total absorption of the enclosure, and AC_{AVERAGE} = average absorption coefficient of the enclosure.

room index In lighting, in the LUMEN or FLUX METHOD, a number that indicates the largeness of a ROOM CAVITY. It is the ratio of the areas of the horizontal surfaces to those of the vertical surfaces. The symbol is usually K_R. In the IESNA system, it is called the *room cavity ratio* and it is proportional to the inverse of the room index.

room load The cooling load on an air conditioning system that is due to heat gains that originate in the room or result from external gains that appear directly in the room.

room radius The distance between a sound source and a position in a room at which the intensity of the direct sound is the same as the intensity of the reflected sound.

room-corner fire test A full-scale burning test to study the spread of fire on lining and partition materials.

root mean square The square root of the mean value of the squares of individual test results or statistical data. In the measurement of time-varying waveforms, especially in electricity, the root mean square represents the *effective* voltage, current or power, in terms of its ability to do work.

rosette *See* STRAIN ROSETTE.

rosin A RESIN obtained as a residue from the distillation of turpentine. It is used as a varnish, as a drier in paint and as a soldering flux. *Also called colophony.*

rot *See* DRY ROT *and* WET ROT.

rotary engine An engine which produces rotary motion directly, as opposed to a RECIPROCATING ENGINE.

rotary hammer A hand-held power drill that provides a hammer action as well as rotary motion to the BIT. It is usually possible to stop the rotation to use the tool as a chipping hammer. The impact action is usually more vigorous than that of an IMPACT DRILL, although the two terms are sometimes used interchangeably.

rotary heat exchanger (*also called heat wheel*) A device used to transfer heat from one air stream to another, by a wheel containing some porous, quick response heat storage material (*e.g.* metal turnings). When in the path of the warm air stream, this will be heated, but rotating into the path of the cool air stream, it will give off its heat to the air. The two air streams do not mix.

rotary pump A pump with a rotating impeller, as distinct from a *reciprocating pump.*

rotary veneer Wood veneer cut on a lathe as a thin continuous layer from the perimeter of a log, as opposed to SLICED VENEER.

rotational surface *Same as* SURFACE OF REVOLUTION.

roughcast Plaster mixed with small stones or shells, used on the outside of buildings.

rough-in To install the electrical cabling, plumbing pipework, etc. at an appropriate time during the construction, ready to have the switches, fittings, taps, etc. attached to them at a later stage.

router (computing) A hardware device or software system used to interconnect individual computers or computer NETWORKS. *See also* BRIDGE. (Pronounced ROO-ter.)

router (woodworking) A hand-held or fixed timber-working machine with a high speed rotating cutter for cutting grooves, or moulding the edges of timber. (Pronounced ROW-ter.)

routine maintenance *See* MAINTENANCE, ROUTINE.

rowlock *Same as* BRICK ON EDGE.

RPM *Abbreviation for* Revolutions Per Minute.

RSI *Abbreviation for:* (a) Repetitive Strain Injury, muscular pain due to repetitive work; (b) Relative Strain Index, a thermal comfort index, a further development by Lee and Henschel (1963) of the HSI (heat stress index).

RSJ *Abbreviation for* ROLLED STEEL JOIST.

RT *Abbreviation for:* (a) REVERBERATION TIME; (b) RESULTANT TEMPERATURE.

RTF (Rich Text Format) A FILE format for word processing documents which preserves many of the formatting features of a document and can be written and read by most word processing software packages.

rubbed finish A finish obtained by using a surface abrasive to remove irregularities.

rubber mounting A vibration-isolation mounting for a machine that is liable to transmit vibration to its supports.

rubber-banding In computer graphics, a dynamic process for drawing a series of straight lines in succession, where one point of a line segment is fixed on the screen and the other is attached to the moving CURSOR. This obviates the need to input two points for connected line segments (other than the first line).

rubble Rough stones of irregular shape and size. They may result from quarrying, from the demolition of old buildings or (more rarely) from the natural disintegration of large pieces of rock. Squared stone is called ASHLAR. *See also* COURSED RUBBLE *and* DRY WALL *(a)*.

ruled surface A surface on which it is possible to draw straight lines. Consequently such a surface can be generated by a straight line, and concrete formwork can be constructed from straight pieces of timber. A surface is *singly ruled* if at every point only a single straight line can be drawn. It is *doubly ruled* if at every point two straight lines can be drawn. CYLINDRICAL SHELLS and CONOIDS are singly ruled. HYPERBOLIC PARABOLOIDS and HYPERBOLOIDS OF REVOLUTION are doubly ruled.

ruler In computing, the display of a graduated scale at the top and/or side of an application. Used in word processing for setting margins, tabs, etc.

run hours The hours of actual operation of a machine exclusive of idle time.

runby *See* OVERTRAVEL.

rung A bar that forms a step in a ladder.

running maintenance *See* MAINTENANCE, RUNNING.

run-off The surface discharge of water derived from precipitation on a surface.

rupture *See* MODULUS OF RUPTURE.

rust Hydrated iron oxide $(2Fe_2O_3.3H_2O)$ formed on unprotected iron by exposure to air and moisture.

rustic brick A brick whose surface has been roughened by impressing it with a pattern, or by coating it with sand. *Also called texture brick.*

rusticated column A circular column whose shaft is interrupted by square blocks.

rustication *(a)* Construction of natural stonework with recessed joints. Rusticated stonework may be *smooth* or *diamond*

pointed (both with a dressed surface), *cyclopean* (rockfaced, with a finish as quarried, or an artful imitation thereof) or VERMICULATED. *(b)* Simulation of rusticated stonework in STUCCO. *(c)* Simulation of rusticated stonework in concrete, by moulding a groove in the concrete surface with a *rustication strip.*

rustication strip A strip of timber fixed to concrete formwork to produce a 'rusticated' surface, *i.e.* a series of grooves imitating the rustication of natural-stone blocks.

rutile *See* TITANIUM WHITE.

S

S *(a)* Chemical symbol for *sulphur.* *(b)* US symbol for the (elastic) SECTION MODULUS; in the UK and Australia, the symbol Z is used for section modulus, and S for the PLASTIC SECTION MODULUS.

s, sec *Abbreviation for second.*

SAA Standards Association of Australia, Sydney; now Standards Australia.

saber saw US term for JIGSAW.

sabin Unit of SOUND ABSORPTION, equal to 1 m^2 (metric units) or 1 ft^2 (foot units) of open window. It is named after W. C. Sabine, Professor of Natural Philosophy at Harvard University, who founded the science of architectural acoustics at the end of the nineteenth century.

Sabine formula An equation for predicting the REVERBERATION TIME of an enclosure which was determined empirically by W. C. Sabine:

$$T = 0.049 \frac{V}{A}$$

where T is the reverberation time in seconds, V is the volume of the enclosure in ft^3 and A is the total absorption in the enclosure in ft^2 SABINS. In SI units, the formula becomes

$$T - 0.16 \frac{V}{A}$$

SABS South African Bureau of Standards, Pretoria.

sack of cement *Same as* BAG OF CEMENT.

sacrificial protection GALVANIC PROTECTION given to a metal by making it the cathode to a sacrificial ANODE.

saddle stone The stone at the APEX of an arch, dome, gable or pediment. The KEYSTONE of an arch.

saddle surface A doubly curved surface of negative GAUSSIAN CURVATURE. The term is synonymous with *anticlastic surface*. If a DOME may be said to correspond to the top of a mountain, then a saddle corresponds to a mountain pass.

safe-edge A mechanically actuated device mounted on the leading edge of a LIFT DOOR, which when striking a passenger or other object, causes the car and landing doors to re-open. *See also* PASSENGER DETECTOR.

safetray A watertight tray fitted under an appliance to intercept condensation, spillage or leakage and provided with a waste pipe to direct any discharge to a safe location.

safety factor *See* FACTOR OF SAFETY.

safety glass *(a)* Glass containing thin wire reinforcement. *(b)* Glass laminated with transparent plastic; this prevents splinters flying if the glass is broken. *(c)* Glass, toughened by heat treatment, which breaks into small fragments without splintering.

safety ground *See* EQUIPMENT GROUNDING CONDUCTOR.

safety lighting Normally refers to STANDBY LIGHTING to allow processes to continue, or to be safely stopped, in the event of a power failure.

safety valve A pressure-relief valve fitted to a pressure vessel.

sag The LEVER ARM of a SUSPENSION CABLE.

sagging moment A positive bending moment, such as occurs in simply supported or continuous beams near midspan; it causes a 'sagging' deformation. A *hogging moment* is negative. *See also* NEGATIVE BENDING MOMENT *for a figure*.

Saint-Venant's principle 'Forces applied at one part of an elastic structure will induce stresses which, except in the region close to that part, will depend almost entirely upon their resultant action, and very little on their distribution.' The

principle was originally proposed by the French mathematician in 1864.

sal ammoniac Ammonium chloride (NH_4Cl).

salient corner Projecting corner, the opposite of a *re-entrant corner*.

salmon brick A relatively soft, underburnt brick of salmon colour.

salt A substance obtained by the union of an acid and a base radical, or by displacing the hydrogen of an ACID by a metal. In *double salts* the replacement is by two metals. Most salts are crystalline. *Common salt* is sodium chloride (NaCl) which crystallises in the cubic system.

salt glaze Glaze formed on stoneware by inserting common salt into the hot kiln.

Saltillo tile A simple fired earthen tile originally made in Saltillo, Mexico.

sample A group of members of large POPULATIONS, used to give information as to the larger quantity. A *random sample* is selected without bias, so that each member has an equal chance of inclusion. A *representative sample* is selected to be representative of the whole population.

sample, borehole *See* BOREHOLE SAMPLE.

samson truck Heavy-duty low-wheeled platform for transporting goods or equipment.

sand Naturally occurring deposits of COHESIONLESS SOIL, ranging from 10 mm (⅜ in.) to 0.1 mm (0.004 in.), and resulting from the disintegration of rock. Most sands are white or yellow and consist of SILICA; however, *black sands* occur naturally near volcanic rock deposits, and *coral sands* occur near coral reefs. Sand is used as FINE AGGREGATE for concrete, in cement and in lime MORTAR and in CALCIUM-SILICATE BRICKS.

sand-faced brick A facing brick coated with sand to give it a RUSTIC finish.

sand-lime brick *Same as* CALCIUM-SILICATE BRICK.

sandblasting Abrading a surface such as concrete, by a stream of sand ejected from a nozzle by compressed air. It may be used merely to clean up construction joints, or it may be carried deeper to EXPOSE the AGGREGATE, or to produce a sculpture. It is also used to clean metal surfaces prior to painting. *Gritblasting* is the term used when a material other than sand is used. *Wet* blasting implies the use of water instead of air, which has the advantage of controlling the dust. *See also* SANDING.

sander A machine for SANDING surfaces, usually of timber, and for smoothing the joints in soft materials such as PLASTER-BOARD. *See also* BELT SANDER and ORBITAL SANDER.

sandheap analogy An ANALOGUE for the plastic torsional resistance of a section, proposed by A. Nadai, which is an extension of the MEMBRANE ANALOGY. If the cross-section subject to torsion is suspended horizontally and covered with sand, the natural slope of the sand represents the constant plastic shear stress. The volume of the sand gives a measure of the section's plastic torsional resistance moment.

sanding The operation of finishing surfaces, particularly those of wood, with sandpaper or some other abrasive. It may be done by hand, or with a machine employing a belt or a revolving disc, faced with abrasive paper. *See also* SAND-BLASTING.

sandstone Sedimentary rock containing a large proportion of rounded silica grains, generally ranging from 1–0.1 mm in diameter. The sand is normally cemented into a solid mass by a matrix which may be composed of silica *(siliceous sandstone)*, of lime *(calcareous sandstone)* or of iron ore *(ferruginous sandstone)*. The finer-grained sandstones are easily carved if the matrix is sufficiently soft (*see* FREESTONE). Sedimentary rocks composed of larger sand particles are called *gritstones. See also* QUARTZITE.

sandwich panel A panel with two coatings of metal and a thermal insulating core, mainly used for partitioning systems requiring good acoustic and thermal insulation.

sanitary drainage or plumbing An assembly of pipes, fittings, fixtures and appliances that removes dirty water from kitchens, bathrooms, laundries, etc. *See also* STORMWATER.

Santorin earth A natural POZZOLANA found on the Greek island of Santorini (*also called* Thera). It has been used since antiquity.

sap The watery fluid circulating in trees, which is necessary for their growth.

sapwood The outer layers of the wood of a tree in which food materials are conveyed and stored during the life of the tree. They are usually of lighter colour than the *heartwood.*

sarking A continuous layer placed under tiles or other roofing, to keep out wind and wind-driven rain. Originally it was a layer of boarding, but now it is often a waterproof, fire-resistant plastic material. It may also have an aluminium foil facing to reduce radiant heat transfer.

sash A frame into which window panes are set. Originally a sliding frame in a *sash window*, but today it is used as a generic term for all opening frames, vertical or horizontal sliding, casement (side opening), awning or pivot windows or hopper (bottom hinged, 'drop-in') windows. Also used for a *fixed sash* when fixed glass is set into a separate sash rather than directly into the frame.

sash bars The strips of wood which separate the panes of glass in a window sash composed of several panes. *Also called muntins.*

sash window A window contained in a cased frame which slides, as opposed to a CASEMENT WINDOW. The traditional sash window (*also called* a *vertical sash* or *balanced sash*) slides up and down, and is supported by sash cords passing over sash pulleys and balanced by counterweights. It was introduced into England in the seventeenth century, and was a prominent feature of residential building from the Restoration to the Georgian period, and subsequently. *Also called* a DOUBLE-HUNG WINDOW, where there is an illustration. The less commonly used *sliding sash window* moves horizontally.

sashless window Window composed of panes of glass which slide along parallel tracks in the window frame towards each other to leave openings at the sides.

saturated air Air that contains as much water vapour as it is capable of absorbing, *i.e.* air at the DEW POINT. If the moisture content is increased, CONDENSATION or fogging occurs. The amount of water vapour that air can absorb decreases with temperature, so that air which is partly saturated may become fully saturated as it is cooled.

saturated solution A solution containing the maximum amount of a particular substance which it can dissolve at that particular temperature. If it is cooled further, PRECIPITATION *(a)* will occur.

saturation temperature The air temperature at which, for any given vapour content, air is saturated. Any further decrease results in CONDENSATION. The same as DEW POINT.

saturation vapour pressure The pressure of a vapour in contact with its liquid form. It falls as the temperature falls. Vapour pressure of water in the atmosphere at saturation, (vp_s) is an exponential function of DBT:

$$vp_s = 0.133322\ e^{\left(18.668 - \frac{4030.183}{DBT+235}\right)}$$

saw *See* BAND SAW, CHAIN SAW, CIRCULAR SAW, CROSSCUT SAW *and* PIT SAWING.

saw arbor The spindle on which a circular saw is mounted.

saw doctor A craftsman who sharpens, sets and maintains the saws in a sawmill.

sawdust concrete Concrete whose aggregate consists mainly of sawdust, *i.e.* the waste product of timber. It has a low strength, but it can be *nailed.*

sawn timber Timber reduced from the log by sawing, but not subsequently DRESSED. In North America, called LUMBER.

sawtooth roof *Same as* NORTHLIGHT ROOF.

Sb Chemical symbol for *antimony* (stibium).

SBS *Abbreviation for* SICK BUILDING SYNDROME.

SC *Abbreviation for* Sky Component (of the daylight factor).

scabble To rough-dress a surface of stone or concrete (or to roughen the surface with a sharp tool, to improve adhesion to an otherwise smooth surface).

scaffold A temporary structure of steel, timber or aluminium, to support workers and materials during construction, or for shoring concrete during hardening. Bamboo is widely used in Southern Asia.

scaffold crane A small self-contained motorised crane attached to scaffolding

for lifting relatively small loads, up to about 200 kg.

scaffold nail *Same as* DOUBLE-HEADED NAIL.

scagliola An imitation of ornamental marble, made from cement or lime, gypsum, marble chips and colouring matter. It was used in Ancient Rome, and its use was revived in the seventeenth and eighteenth centuries.

scalar A quantity which has magnitude, but no direction. A VECTOR has both magnitude and direction.

scale *(a)* Accumulation of salts deposited from HARD WATER on surfaces of a container such as a boiler or calorifier when the water is heated. *(b) See* MILL SCALE. *(c) See* CHROMATIC SCALE *and* DIATONIC SCALE. *(d)* Short for *scale rule.* *(e)* The scale at which a SCALE DRAWING is drawn.

scale drawing A drawing that shows all parts of the objects illustrated in the same proportion of their true size. Some pictorial PROJECTIONS do not result in scale drawings.

scanner A device for transferring printed, drawn or photographic material into a digital form suitable for manipulation by a graphics application in a computer.

scantling A piece of timber of comparatively small dimensions, used for framing.

scarf joint An END JOINT between two pieces of timber, tapered to form sloping surfaces which match. It may be glued or bolted. A *stepped* or *hooked* scarf joint is one in which the jointing plane is discontinuous, and both pieces are machined to form matching steps or matching hooks. This facilitates alignment of the two ends (*see figure*).

Scarf joint   Stepped scarf joint

Scarf joint

scarify To stir the surface of the soil to a prescribed depth.

scattering The effect of DIFFRACTION from an unordered array of discontinuities in a medium. In acoustics, sound scattering may occur because of objects in a room or because of surfaces which are irregular.

scenario analysis Identifying a hazard scenario and assessing the consequences, a key part in fire hazard assessment while implementing engineering performance-based fire codes.

Schmidt hammer An instrument used for the NON-DESTRUCTIVE TESTING of hardened concrete. It is based on the proposition that the rebound of the steel hammer from the concrete surface is proportional to the compressive strength of the concrete.

Schwedler dome A braced dome (devised by a German engineer of that name in the late nineteenth century) consisting of hoops and meridional bars, connected together to form a series of trapezia, lined up along horizontal polygonal rings. To stiffen the structure, each trapezium is divided into two triangles by a diagonal; however, symmetrical loading introduces no stresses in these diagonals, if the dome is pinjointed. *See also* GEODESIC DOME.

scima *Same as* CYMA.

scissor lift A work platform mounted on wheels, capable of rising vertically by a scissor-like mechanism (*see figure*). Often designed for indoor operation, for maintenance in tall rooms. *See also* CHERRY PICKER.

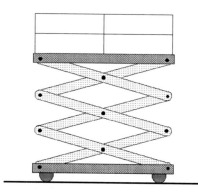

Scissor lift

sclerometer An instrument for the determination of hardness by means of a scratch with a diamond pyramid.

Scotch bond *Same as* COMMON BOND.

Scotch derrick A crane with a LUFFing and SLEWing jib pivoting at the base of a mast, the top of which supports jib cables, and which is supported by two rigid guys connected to each other and to the mast, with counterbalanced bases (*see figure*). *See also* DERRICK.

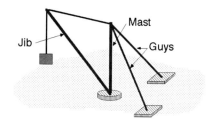

Scotch derrick

SCR *Abbreviation for* Semiconductor (or Silicon) Controlled Rectifier, an electronic DC switch which can be triggered into conduction by a pulse to a gate electrode, but can only be cut off by reducing the main current below a predetermined level (usually zero). Used as a RECTIFIER.

scraffeto or sgraffito *See* GRAFFITO.

scratch-coat The first coat of stucco or plaster applied to a surface in three-coat work.

screed *(a)* A heavy rule used for forming a concrete surface to the desired level or shape. *Also called screed board, tamper* or *strikeoff. (b)* The operation of striking off concrete lying above the desired level or shape. *(c)* A layer of concrete or mortar laid to finish a floor surface and hide the construction joints. This is sometimes called *jointless flooring. (d)* A bed of mortar laid as a base for ceramic or glass tiles. *(e)* A layer of concrete placed on a 'flat' roof to provide the correct gradient for drainage.

screen analysis PARTICLE-SIZE ANALYSIS for the larger particle sizes.

screen resolution *See* RESOLUTION.

screen size *(a)* A measurement of the diagonal size of a computer or television screen, usually in inches. *(b)* The measurement of the openings in a sieve screen.

screenings The rejects from screening a granular material. They may consist of either oversize or undersize particles.

screw A metal pin with a SCREW-THREAD. It may be a cylinder or pointed. It is generally screwed into a softer material, and has an enlarged head to hold the item to be fixed in position. Screws traditionally had a single slot in the head into which a screwdriver was inserted to drive the screw, but hexagonal- and CROSS-HEADED SCREWS are better suited to power screwdrivers. *See also* ALLEN HEAD.

screw anchor A shell which expands and wedges itself into a hole drilled for it when a screw is inserted into it.

screw cap (for a lamp) *Same as* EDISON CAP.

screw compressor A machine for compressing a gas or vapour by the action of two meshing helical rotors.

screw jack A lifting device actuated by means of a square-threaded screw. Its lifting capacity is more limited than that of a hydraulic JACK.

screw nail A fastening device used where the holding power required exceeds that of a nail. It is intended to be driven with a hammer, but removed with a screwdriver.

screw pile A pile with a helical-bladed shoe, which is twisted into the ground. Small screw piles of galvanised steel are used in place of *sleeper piers* or *stumps*.

screw-thread A helical cut in a pin or rod to enable it to be used as a BOLT or a SCREW.

scribe To mark a cutting line to accurately match with the profile of an adjoining piece.

scriber A tool for inscribing a mark on a surface: *(a) carpenter's scriber*, has one pointed end and one blade-like end, the latter for cutting a line into timber without tearing it; *(b) engineer's scriber*, has two hardened sharp-pointed ends, one of them turned at right angles.

scripts, scripting Scripts are short programs or sequences of instructions for accomplishing some specific task.

scroll bars Horizontal and vertical bars at the edges of windows on a computer screen, with sliding elements allowing the movement of displayed information, *e.g.* lines of text or graphics.

scrolling A type of PANNING restricted to horizontal or vertical movement using keys or SCROLL BARS.

scrubber A device for removing contaminants from a stream of air or gas(es) by passing it through a water spray.

scum A layer of froth and impurities on top of a body of liquid. In a SEPTIC TANK, the thick, stable froth layer which serves to exclude air and thereby aid the ANAEROBIC DIGESTION of sewage.

scupper *(a)* An opening in a parapet to drain rainwater. *(b)* A screen to prevent clogging of the drain.

Se Chemical symbol for *selenium*.

seal *See* TRAP.

sealing compound *See* JOINT SEALANT *and* MEMBRANE CURING.

seasoning The drying of timber by NATURAL SEASONING or in a KILN.

seasoning check Separation of wood extending longitudinally, formed during drying. It is commonly caused by the immediate effect of a dry wind or hot sun on freshly sawn timber. It usually extends only a few inches in length, whereas a longitudinal SHAKE may be several feet long.

sec Secant of an angle; sec θ = 1/cos θ.

secant *(a)* A straight line which intersects a curve. *See also* TANGENT. *(b)* A CIRCULAR FUNCTION of an angle, the ratio of the length of the hypotenuse of a right-angled triangle to that of the side adjacent to the angle. *Abbreviated* sec.

secant column formula A formula for the design of columns, which is more sophisticated than the RANKINE COLUMN FORMULA; it contains a secant term. The formula deals with the buckling of eccentrically loaded columns, treating the unavoidable imperfections in long, concentrically loaded columns as equivalent to an initial slight eccentricity of loading, defined by the empirical constant in the secant formula. *See also* PERRY–ROBERTSON FORMULA.

secant modulus of elasticity Many materials (*e.g.* concrete) do not conform strictly to HOOKE'S LAW because of deviations caused by INELASTIC behaviour. If the deviation is significant, it becomes necessary to define the MODULUS OF ELASTICITY as the tangent or secant to the STRESS–STRAIN CURVE.

second moment of area (*I*) The sum of the products obtained by multiplying each element of an area d*A*, by the square of its distance from the reference axis, drawn through the CENTROID of the section. It is therefore

$$\sum y^2 \mathrm{d}A \text{ or } \int y^2 \mathrm{d}A$$

The second moment of area is a geometric property essential to the solution of bending problems. It is frequently (incorrectly) called the MOMENT OF INERTIA.

secondary air Room air induced into a jet of PRIMARY AIR by its motion.

secondary beam A beam or joist carried by the main or PRIMARY BEAMS or girders, and transmitting its load to them.

secondary colour A colour obtained by mixing two or more PRIMARY COLOURS.

secondary floor (lift installation) A floor or platform, within a LIFT WELL, located just below the overhead machinery room. It gives access to the *diverter sheaves*, and may contain other items of equipment.

secondary memory (*also called external memory*) Non-volatile memory residing external to the computer's motherboard. The most popular secondary memory devices are hard disk drives and floppy disk drives. Tape drives and a variety of optical disk drives are also used frequently.

secondary reinforcement Reinforcement that is subsidiary to the main reinforcement, such as DISTRIBUTION REINFORCEMENT in slabs, STIRRUPS in beams and LATERAL REINFORCEMENT in columns.

secondary stresses Stresses that are of secondary importance, and do not determine the main dimensions of a structural member. The member may have to be checked for secondary stresses after it has been dimensioned for the primary stresses.

second-growth timber Timber grown after the virgin forest has been cut down.

secret gutter *(a) Same as* BOX GUTTER. *(b)* Roof gutter located behind a fascia, or a little way up the slope of a roof, rather than exposed as an eaves gutter (*see figure*).

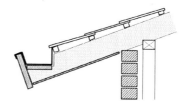

Secret gutter

secret nailing Driving nails (*e.g.* sideways into a joint) so that they cannot be seen. *Also called blind nailing or concealed nailing* (*see figure*).

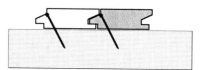

Secret nailing

section modulus (*Z*) A convenient notation for the ratio *I*/*y*, where *I* is the SECOND MOMENT OF AREA and *y* is the *extreme fibre distance*. It is used extensively in the design of beams (*see* NAVIER'S THEOREM). Section moduli for standard sections in steel, aluminium, timber and concrete are available in *section tables. See also* PLASTIC SECTION MODULUS *and* S *(b)*.

sector *(a)* Of a circle, a figure bounded by two radii and an ARC (*see figure*). *(b)* A pie-slice shaped portion of a circular MAGNETIC DISK. The disk contains a number of concentric circular tracks and the sectors divide each TRACK into a number of arcs. These small arcs are usually the addressable units when storing and retrieving data on a disk. *(c)* In lift industry terminology, a GROUP either of landings, or of landing calls considered together for lift car allocation or parking purposes.

Sector of a circle

security control system A system of automated locks and sensors arranged to monitor and control access to building spaces.

security glass *See* BULLET-RESISTING GLASS, SAFETY GLASS *and* TEMPERED GLASS.

sedimentary rock A rock produced as a sediment on the floors of oceans, lakes or rivers, or on land. It may consist of fragments of pre-existing rock, or the hard parts of organisms. *See* LIMESTONE, SANDSTONE *and* SHALE. *See also* IGNEOUS *and* METAMORPHIC ROCK.

sedimentation *See* STOKES' LAW.

Seger cone A type of PYROMETRIC CONE, made of a mixture of clay and salt of known melting point.

segment of a circle A figure bounded by a straight line (a SECANT) and an ARC. *See* SECTOR OF A CIRCLE *for figure*.

segmental arch A circular arch that has an INTRADOS that is less than a semicircle (*see figure*).

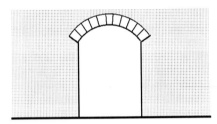

Segmental arch

seismic loading *See* EARTHQUAKE LOADING.

seismic restraint A device designed to limit movement of equipment and furnishings of a building during the motion set up by an earthquake.

seismograph An instrument for recording the magnitude and frequency of an earthquake. *See also* RICHTER SCALE.

SEL *See* SINGLE-EVENT NOISE EXPOSURE LEVEL.

selective surface A surface of which the absorptance (and emittance) varies with the wavelength of radiation. For an ordinary surface, absorptance = emittance at all wavelengths. Surfaces used for solar collector plates may have an absorptance for short-wave solar radiation much greater than the emittance at operating temperature (long-wave radiation). For radiant cooling, *e.g.* on roof surfaces, the opposite is desirable.

selective tender The invitation and receipt of tenders from a selected group of contractors who are considered suitable to perform the work.

selenium A non-metallic element, the first to be used in PHOTOVOLTAIC cells and in rectifiers. Its chemical symbol is Se, its atomic number is 34, its atomic weight is 78.96 and its specific gravity is 4.45. It has a melting point of 220 °C, and its valency is 2, 4 or 6. There are several allotropic forms. The grey (or 'metallic') selenium is a conductor of electricity when illuminated.

self-climbing crane A TOWER CRANE able to increase the height of the tower by lifting and adding sections without the aid of another crane.

self-closing door A door for fire or smoke control, which closes itself by the action of a spring or weight. It may be held open either by a fusible link, which melts in a fire, or by an electric circuit linked to the fire alarm system, causing the door to close in case of fire.

self-drilling screw A screw with a drill-point, intended for drilling its own hole when driven with a power screwdriver. Usually used for fixing to steel sections from 1 to about 6 mm ($\frac{1}{32}$–$\frac{1}{4}$ in.) in thickness, but screws with a modified point to assist drilling into timber are also available. (For fixing to steel less than about 1 mm in thickness, a NEEDLEPOINT screw is sufficient.)

self-embedding screw A screw whose head has a roughened underside. It is intended to embed the head flush into timber or other soft material, without first countersinking. *See also* BUGLE-HEAD SCREW.

self-priming pump Pump capable of generating enough suction when running dry, to raise the liquid from a distance below its inlet. The alternatives are to use a SUBMERSIBLE PUMP, or to manually prime the pump before starting whenever it runs dry.

self-stressing concrete PRESTRESSED CONCRETE which is post-tensioned by the use of EXPANSIVE CEMENT.

self-tapping screw A screw, usually of hardened steel, capable of cutting a thread when driven into metal. It may or may not also be SELF-DRILLING.

selvedge, selvage A thin margin at the edges of a length of fabric or other material that is produced in a linear manner. This portion is a result of the manufacturing process, is generally different from the body of the material and intended to be covered up or cut off.

semicircular arch A circular arch that forms a complete semicircle so that it comes vertically on its SPRINGINGS. Its rise therefore equals one half of its span (*see figure*).

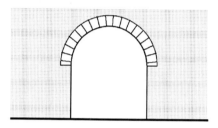

Semicircular arch

semiconductor An electronic conductor (*e.g.* silicon, selenium or germanium) whose resistivity can be controlled. It is used in transistors, integrated circuits and photovoltaic cells.

semi-detached house One of two houses erected as a single building separated by a COMMON WALL.

semidome One quarter of a sphere, used in traditional construction to cover a semicircular area, such as an apse.

semi-flexible joint *Same as* SEMI-RIGID JOINT.

semigloss *See* GLOSS.

semi-logarithmic graph paper (semi-log paper) Graph paper that has one LOGARITHMIC SCALE and one ordinary scale.

semi-rigid joint A joint that is designed to permit some rotation, either in steel or in reinforced concrete construction. It is intermediate between a RIGID JOINT and a PIN JOINT. *Also called a semi-flexible joint or a partially fixed joint.*

semi-specular The reflective properties of materials that exhibit a combination of SPECULAR and DIFFUSE reflection.

semitone Frequency interval that is

approximately 6 per cent of an OCTAVE. It is the interval between notes on the CHROMATIC SCALE.

sensible cooling Cooling of air in a building without changing the moisture content.

sensible heat The heat absorbed or emitted by a fluid or solid when temperature changes, without a change of state, as distinct from the LATENT HEAT.

sensible heat factor The ratio of sensible heat to total heat (sensible heat plus latent heat).

sensitivity ratio The ratio of the unconfined compressive strength of clay in its undisturbed state to that after REMOULDING. For some clays this is only slightly above unity, but for clays sensitive to remoulding, the ratio may be as high as eight.

sensor A device used to detect change in a variable of interest, *e.g.* a thermostat is a sensor used to detect temperature change.

septic tank A tank for the purification of domestic sewage, used in districts not served by sewer pipes. Disintegration of organic matter is effected by natural bacterial action, and the effluent is discharged into the ground.

sequential access storage devices (SASD), media Storage media constrained by their linear organisation of data, so that data items are stored sequentially on the media. To access an item, the device must read through the sequence of all the data preceding an item, as opposed to the direct access which is possible with RANDOM ACCESS MEMORY and HARD DISK drives..

serendipity Originally *happy discoveries by accident*, but in problem-solving theory it is used to denote random search, as opposed to HEURISTIC (goal-oriented) search.

serial port (computing) A connection socket for transferring information from a computer by a single pair of wires (the BITS of information flowing sequentially), as opposed to a PARALLEL PORT.

series connection An electrical or hydraulic connection in which the current or fluid passes sequentially through several elements (*see figure*). The total resistance to flow is the sum of the resistances of the separate elements. *See also* PARALLEL CONNECTION.

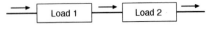

Series connection

serpentine Hydrated silicate of magnesium, found in ultrabasic IGNEOUS ROCKS. Some varieties, which are dark green and polishable, are called MARBLE in the building industry classification. *See also* MALACHITE.

server A HOST computer on a NETWORK (*c*) which acts as a reservoir of information. For example, World Wide Web (WWW) servers contain the information a client browser displays from a WWW site. *See* CLIENT and MAIL SERVER.

service agreement An agreement between service providers and principals that describes the scope of service, the standard of service and performance review.

service areas *(a)* Those areas of a building set aside for cupboards, plant rooms and risers. *(b)* Functional areas which support the operation of the building such as, loading, parking, tea rooms and waste collection.

service core A vertical element in a multi-storey building, containing the lifts (elevators), the vertical runs of most of the mechanical and electrical services and fire stairs. It is frequently the first part of the building to be erected, and is then used for vertical transportation during construction. The service core is usually a stiff element, contributing substantially to the building's resistance to horizontal forces such as wind loads. *See* TUBE STRUCTURE *and* TOP-HAT STRUCTURE.

service floor In high-rise buildings often an intermediate floor is used to accommodate much of the central service plant, such as boilers, chillers, air handling units or hot water service, thus substantially reducing service pipe or duct runs.

service life The period of time during which a building element is expected to provide satisfactory service with an acceptable return on investment.

service lift *See* LIFT TYPES *(f)*, *(m)*, *and (p)*, and DUMBWAITER.

service load The normal WORKING LOAD which the structure is required to support in service.

service riser *See* RISER *(e)*.

service stair A stair not in general use, giving access to specific areas such as roofspace and plant rooms, usually for maintenance purposes.

services easement *See* EASEMENT.

sesqui One-and-a-half times, *e.g.* Fe_2O_3 (ferric oxide) is *also called* iron sesquioxide.

SET *Abbreviation for* Standard Effective Temperature, a sub-set of the ET* (new effective temperature) scales. Whilst the slope of ET* isotherm lines varies with clothing and metabolic rate (with 'skin wettedness'), SET is standardised for 1.25 MET and 0.57 CLO and it is valid from 1–4 met and from 0.67–0.19 clo (a higher met being compensated for by a lower clo); thus it covers the most frequently occurring indoor situations.

set *(a)* As a mathematical concept, a group of different elements, having at least one common characteristic. *(b)* Strain remaining after removal of stress.

set point The value of a variable that is to be maintained by an automatic control system, *e.g.* temperature of air in a room.

set theory A mathematical theory dealing with the relationship between SETS *(a)*.

setback The withdrawal of the face of a building to a line some distance from the boundary of the property, or from the street. A building may be set back at the level of the ground floor, or merely at the upper floors.

setscrew A screw used to fix a detachable part to a machine, *e.g.* a collar to a shaft.

setting block A block used to position and support glass in glazing systems.

setting of concrete The initial stage in the chemical reaction between cement and water when the concrete stiffens and loses the fluidity necessary to fill the formwork. It gains significant strength only during the next, or HARDENING, stage. *See also* VICAT TEST.

setting time The time taken for a mixture to reach an acceptable strength.

settlement *See* CONSOLIDATION *and* DIFFERENTIAL SETTLEMENT.

sewage Human wastes, and the water used to carry them away. Any SANITARY DRAINAGE or rainwater added to the sewage is, from that point on, regarded as sewage.

sewerage A system of drainage used for removing SEWAGE. *See also* SANITARY DRAINAGE.

sextant A reflecting instrument for measuring ALTITUDES up to 120°. *See also* QUADRANT.

SfB *Samarbetskommittén för Byggnadsfrågor*, a Swedish committee that devised a classification system for building information, used internationally under the auspices of the CIB.

SFPE The Society of Fire Protection Engineers, Bethesda, MD, established in 1950 and incorporated as an independent organisation in 1971.

sg *Abbreviation for* Specific gravity.

sgraffito *Same as* GRAFFITO.

SGW *Abbreviation for* Salt-Glazed Ware, a fire-clay product, with salt introduced in the kiln during firing to produce a glaze; generally used for sewer drain pipes, particularly before the introduction of PVC pipes.

shading In computer graphics, the process of adding shadows and shade to surfaces taking into account light sources and surface characteristics.

shading coefficient (of a window) A measure of the reduction in the solar heat gain through the use of sunshades and/or of heat-absorbing or heat-reflecting glass. It is defined as the ratio on a particular day of the solar heat gain through the window under consideration, as glazed and shaded, to the solar heat gain through a similar unshaded window of clear glass 3 mm (⅛ in.) thick.

shadow angle protractor A transparent overlay for the SUNPATH CHART, used for the design of sunshades.

shake *(a)* A partial or complete separating between adjoining layers of wood, due initially to causes other than drying. A *felling shake* is one caused by the felling of the tree. A *water shake, ring shake* or *cup shake* is one occurring between two adjacent growth rings. A

heart shake or *star shake* is one extending from the pith of the tree, and existing in the log before conversion. A *wind shake* is one caused by wind action on the growing tree. *A transverse shake* runs across the fibres, and a *longitudinal shake* parallel to them. *See also* SEASONING CHECK. *(b)* A wood SHINGLE, particularly one made by splitting a short log into tapered radial sections.

shale A laminated and fissile sedimentary rock consisting primarily of clay and silt particles.

shape factor *(a)* In structural calculations, *see* PLASTIC SECTION MODULUS. *(b)* In radiation calculations, *see* ANGLE FACTOR.

shape grammar A set of rules based on shape, that can be used to generate designs.

shaping machine A machine that removes shavings from a metal surface fixed to a stationary table with a tool that moves backward and forward. *See also* PLANING MACHINE.

shared space A workplace shared between two or more employees, usually at different times.

shareware SOFTWARE of non-commercial origin, available freely on the Internet, for which the author requests a small payment.

shear box A laboratory SHEAR TEST that determines the strength of soil by applying a shear force directly to a soil sample, contained in a box split horizontally.

shear connector A welded stud, angle or spiral bar that transfers shear from concrete to steel in COMPOSITE CONSTRUCTION.

shear force (V) The resultant of all the vertical forces acting at any section of a beam (or slab) on one side of the section. This force tends to shear or cut through the beam. The shear force is the vertical resultant of the statical equilibrium equations at the section, while the BENDING MOMENT is the moment resultant (and generally the more important consideration).

shear legs A hoist consisting of two or more poles lashed together at the top, with a pulley hung from the lashing. Used for lifting moderately heavy weights. *See also* CRANE.

shear modulus of elasticity *Same as* MODULUS OF RIGIDITY.

shear reinforcement Reinforcement designed to resist the shear or diagonal tensile stresses in concrete.

shear strain *See* STRAIN.

shear stress *See* STRESS.

shear tests for soil *See* SHEAR BOX *and* TRIAXIAL COMPRESSION TEST (which are laboratory tests), UNCONFINED COMPRESSION TEST (a laboratory or site test) *and* VANE TEST (a site test).

shear wall A wall that resists shear forces in its own plane due to wind, earthquake forces, explosions, etc.

shearhead The COLUMN CAPITAL *(b)* in a FLAT SLAB.

sheath *(a)* An enclosure for post-tensioned tendons. The tendon is placed in the concrete enclosed in the sheath, and bond is prevented until after the tendon has been prestressed. *(b)* The tough plastic covering placed over the electrical insulation of cables to provide mechanical protection. *See* TPS CABLE.

sheave A wheel with a GROOVE or grooves in its circumference for receiving rope(s), particularly in LIFT systems. *See* WRAP, *single* and *double*.

shed roof A roof having one slope only. The one set of rafters has a fall from the higher to the lower wall. *Also called lean-to roof* or *skillion roof.*

sheet Material produced in thin layers. Sheet metal is thinner than metal *plate*, but thicker than metal *foil*. Metal *strip* is narrower than sheet metal.

sheet glass Drawn glass of the type used in windows. It is thinner than PLATE GLASS. It is specified either by thickness or by weight per unit area.

sheet pile A PILE in the form of a plank or steel in an open C-profile, driven in close contact with others to provide a tight wall to resist the lateral pressure of water, adjacent earth or other materials. It may be made interlocking if made of metal, or tongued and grooved if made of timber or concrete. *See also* WELLPOINT DEWATERING.

shelf life Maximum interval during which a perishable material, *e.g.* an adhesive,

may be stored, and remain in useable condition. *See also* POT LIFE.

shell roof A roof structure built with thin curved slabs. *See* BARREL VAULT, DEVELOPABLE SURFACE, DOME, DOUBLE-WALLED SHELL, EDGE BEAM, GAUSSIAN CURVATURE, HYPERBOLIC PARABOLOID SHELL, MEMBRANE THEORY, NORTHLIGHT SHELL, RULED SURFACE, SADDLE SURFACE, SURFACE OF REVOLUTION, SURFACE OF TRANSLATION *and* UMBRELLA SHELL.

shellac An encrustation, which is a natural resin, formed on certain tropical trees by an insect. The purified form is *lac*. It is soluble in alcohol, and is used in spirit varnishes and in *French polish*.

shell-and-tube heat exchanger A heat exchange device consisting of a series of parallel tubes inside a (usually cylindrical) vessel in which heat is exchanged between a fluid passing through the tubes and another surrounding fluid contained in the vessel (*see figure*).

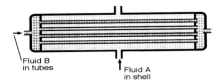

Shell-and-tube heat exchanger

sherardising A method of applying a protective zinc coating to steel. The steel parts are packed in boxes filled with sand mixed with zinc, and heated to a temperature below the melting point of zinc. *See also* GALVANISING.

SHF *Abbreviation for* SENSIBLE HEAT FACTOR.

shielded-arc welding ARC WELDING where the arc is surrounded by an atmosphere of an inert gas (argon, a mixture of argon and carbon dioxide, or helium). The gas is held under pressure in a cylinder and released around the electrode to exclude air, which would otherwise oxidise the weld metal and also allow nitrogen to combine with it. The process is used for stainless and other alloy steels, and for aluminium and magnesium alloys which oxidise readily, as well as for steel, especially in light gauges. *See also* ARGON-ARC, MIG, TIG and HELIARC WELDING.

shielding (of electronic equipment) The use of a conducting and/or ferromagnetic barrier between a potentially disturbing noise source and sensitive circuitry. Shields are used to protect cables (data and power) and electronic circuits. They may be in the form of metal barriers, enclosures or wrappings around source circuits and receiving circuits.

shielding (of utility lines) The construction of a grounded conductor or tower over the lines to intercept lightning strokes in an attempt to keep the lightning currents out of the power system.

shim A thin piece placed or driven into a joint to level or plumb a structural member.

shingle *(a)* Thin piece of wood, asphalt-impregnated felt or other material used for covering sloping roofs. *(b)* Rounded stone of variable size and shape, but coarser than SAND.

shoe *See* PILE SHOE.

shooting concrete Placing of SHOT-CRETE.

shop drawings Drawings, usually prepared by a specialist supplier or fabricator, showing sufficient detail to allow the off-site manufacture of a part of a building. The shop drawings show some different items of information from that required on site, but it is essential to ensure that they are compatible with the building drawings, before manufacture commences. *See also* WORKING DRAWINGS.

shop welding Welding carried out in the workshop, as opposed to work carried out on the SITE.

shore A temporary support, of timber or other material, used in compression as temporary support for excavations, formwork or propping of unsafe structures. It is usually sloping *(raking shore)*, but occasionally horizontal *(flying shore)* or vertical *(dead shore)*.

short circuit An accidental connection, of zero or low resistance, joining two sides of an electrical circuit.

short ton A TON of 2000 pounds.

short-column formula The strength of a column that has no tendency whatsoever towards BUCKLING,

$$P = fA$$

where A is the cross-sectional area and f is the failing stress, *i.e.* the yield stress of steel, or the crushing strength of concrete. Note that, unlike the EULER FORMULA, the SCF is independent of the modulus of elasticity. *See also* RANKINE COLUMN FORMULA.

short-term deflection Primarily elastic deflection that occurs over a short period of time, as opposed to LONG-TERM DEFLECTION.

short-wave solar radiation Radiation with a wavelength of 0.3–3 µm received directly from the sun, as distinct from LONG-WAVE RADIATION.

shot fixing Installing fixings using an EXPLOSIVE-POWERED TOOL.

shotblasting Cleaning a steel surface by projecting steel shot against it with compressed air or with a centrifugal steel impeller. *See also* GRITBLASTING *and* SANDBLASTING.

shotcrete Cement mortar or concrete placed under pressure through the nozzle of a CEMENT GUN. Also known as *gunite*, or as *pneumatically applied mortar*.

shoulder load Electrical loads generated in defined periods on either side of the defined peak period.

shoulder tariff Tariff charged for electricity used during defined shoulder periods on either side of the peak period.

shrinkage Contraction due to moisture movement. The two building materials most affected are timber and concrete. The maximum fractional shrinkage of timber is about 100×10^{-3} parallel to the growth rings, 50×10^{-3} at right angles to the rings (RADIAL SHRINKAGE) and 1×10^{-3} along its length. Timber is normally SEASONED before use to reduce shrinkage after the timber has been fixed in the building. The shrinkage of concrete is less, about 3×10^{-4}.

shrinkage cracking Cracking caused by SHRINKAGE when contraction is resisted by restraints.

shrinkage joint *Same as* CONTRACTION JOINT.

shrinkage limit The limiting water

content for a clay soil, below which a reduction in water content causes no further decrease in volume. It is often accompanied by a change in colour, and marks the limit between the plastic and the solid state.

shrinkage loss LOSS OF PRESTRESS caused by the shrinkage of the concrete.

shrinkage reinforcement Secondary reinforcement designed to resist shrinkage stresses in the concrete. *Same as* DISTRIBUTION REINFORCEMENT.

shrinkage stresses Stresses caused when the shrinkage of concrete (or timber) is resisted by restraints or (non-shrinking) metal reinforcement.

shrinkage-compensating cement An EXPANSIVE CEMENT, which on setting expands sufficiently to compensate for the contraction due to SHRINKAGE.

shunt trip A type of circuit breaker that can also be activated by a circuit other than the one it is protecting.

shuttering *Same as* FORMWORK.

shutters Protective covering for the outside of windows. Shutters usually consist of vertically hinged wooden frames, and are closed at night to prevent heat loss, and for privacy. *Louvred* shutters are used for ventilation, in conjunction with inward-opening *casement* windows. *Steel shutters* are used in fortifications, or in ordinary buildings if rioting or cyclonic winds are a frequent occurrence.

shuttle lift (elevator) An express lift from a street lobby to a SKY LOBBY, where transfer is made to local lifts.

Si Chemical symbol for *silicon*.

SI metric *See* SI UNITS.

SI units The units used in the *Système International d'Unités*. This modified version of the *metric system* has now been adopted by most countries. It differs from the traditional metric, or CGS UNITS: *(a)* by using millimetre and metre in preference to centimetre; *(b)* by using the NEWTON as the unit of force and weight; and *(c)* by using the JOULE as the sole unit of measuring work and energy.

sick building syndrome The incidence of complaints about illness in modern commercial buildings, which received widespread attention in the 1980s. The buildings were mostly sealed to prevent loss of energy, and were kept at the same temperature all day. Some of the problems were caused by pollutants, by humidity that was too high or too low, and by bacteria or viruses recirculated by the air conditioning system. However, boring work and the monotony of the constant temperature throughout the day may have been a contributing factor. Improvements in HVAC design have reduced the complaints.

side flash A discharge between nearby metallic objects, or from such objects to the LIGHTNING PROTECTION SYSTEM or to earth.

side lap The overlap required for two adjacent building components, such as two sheets of corrugated steel or two tiles, to prevent rain penetration.

side-hung window *Same as* CASEMENT WINDOW.

side-sway Sideways movement of a frame, or of a member of a frame, due to wind or other lateral loads, to the asymmetry of the vertical loads, or to plastic collapse (*see* LIMIT DESIGN).

siding Wall cladding for small frame building, other than masonry or brick. The term is particularly used in the USA, and includes CLAPBOARD (*also called weatherboard*), metal, fibre cement and asphalt.

Siemens Martin process *Same as* OPEN-HEARTH PROCESS.

sienna Yellow mineral pigment. It consists of ferrous oxide (FeO). *See also* BURNT SIENNA.

sieve analysis PARTICLE-SIZE ANALYSIS by passing material through successively finer sieves.

SIGGRAPH *Abbreviation for the* ACM's Special Interest Group for Graphics.

sight rail A horizontal board set at some specified height above, say, the INVERT LEVEL of a drain. With a vertical pole it is possible to set out the drain between two sight rails accurately without surveying instruments.

signal reference grid (or plane) A system of conductive paths among interconnected equipment, which reduces noise-induced voltages to levels that minimise improper operation. Common configurations include grids and planes.

signal to noise ratio (S/N) The ratio of

the magnitude of a signal of interest to the background noise level. It is usually expressed in dB.

signal (analog, digital) A vehicle for transmitting information. The form of the signal will be determined by the nature of the transmitting medium. An analog signal assumes a continuous form (waves, etc.) and a digital signal is discrete (a series of BITS).

SIGRADI *La Sociedad Iberoamericana de Gráfica Digital* (architectural computing association).

SIL *Abbreviation for* SPEECH INTER-FERENCE LEVEL.

silencer *See* MUFFLER.

silica *Silicon dioxide*, SiO_2. About 60 per cent of the Earth's crust consists of silica, and it is the chief constituent of sand and clay. Its crystalline form is QUARTZ.

silica brick *Same as* CALCIUM-SILICATE BRICK.

silica gel A colloidal form of silica made by treating sodium silicate with hydro-chloric or acetic acid. It has a high capacity for adsorbing water vapour, and it is used as a drying agent in instrument cases, etc.

silicon A non-metallic element, the second most abundant in the Earth's crust (next to oxygen). It is an amorphous brown powder, or a grey crystalline sub-stance; however, it commonly occurs as SILICA, or in the form of silicates which are constituents of most rocks, clays and soils. It is a major constituent of Portland cement, an alloying element for steel and aluminium, and the principal material used in PHOTOVOLTAIC CELLS. Silicon's chemical symbol is Si, its atomic number is 14, its valency is 4, its atomic weight is 28.06, its specific gravity is 2.4 and its melting point is 1420 °C.

silicon carbide In the form of CAR-BORUNDUM, used as an abrasive.

silicon chip A CHIP based on silicon SEMICONDUCTOR material.

silicon solar cell A solar cell made with the crystalline element silicon as part of its conductor.

silicone A heat-stable compound in which silicon atoms are linked up with oxygen atoms; the remaining valencies of the silicon atoms are saturated with hydrogen or organic radicals. There are many different silicones. All are chemi-cally inert, and they are used as sealants, insulators and lubricators, *e.g.* in water-resistant films, heat-resistant paints, synthetic rubbers, or resins for electrical insulation.

sill *(a)* The lowest horizontal member of a frame for a house or other structure. *(b)* The horizontal member below a door or window opening.

silt Natural deposit resulting from the disintegration of rock, whose particles are intermediate in size between sand and clay, ranging from about 2–50 μm in diameter.

silver A metal of characteristic 'silvery' colour. Its chemical symbol is Ag, its atomic number is 47, its atomic weight is 107.88, and its specific gravity is 10.50. It has a valency of l, and a melting point of 960 °C. *Sterling silver* is 92.5 per cent silver and 7.5 per cent copper.

silver solder A high-melting point SOLDER used where high strength is required. For plumbing work, it contains between 1 and 5 per cent silver. *Also called hard solder.*

silver steel Bright drawn steel containing about 1–1.25 per cent of carbon, but no silver.

similarity, dimensional *See* DIMENSIONAL ANALYSIS.

simple beam or simply supported beam A beam without restraint or CONTINUITY at the supports, as opposed to a *built-in beam* or a *fixed-ended beam.*

Simpson's rule A rule for the evaluation of an irregular area. Let the area be divided into an *even* number n of parallel strips of width x. The lengths of the boundary ordinates, or separating strips, are measured, and these are:

$$y_0, y_1, y_2, \ldots y_{n-1}, y_n$$

The area of the figure is then

$$1/3\, x\, [y_0 + y_n + 2(y_2 + y_4 + \ldots + y_{n-2}) + 4(y_1 + y_3 + \ldots + y_{n-1})]$$

The PRISMOIDAL RULE is an extension of Simpson's rule to solid geometry, and it is used for measuring the volume of an excavation. Simpson's rule is more accurate than the TRAPEZOIDAL RULE.

simulation The process of representing or modelling a situation. Used for analysing behaviour, usually using mathematical modelling, but the process is more general, *e.g.* visual simulation.

simultaneous equations A set of equations that are all satisfied by the same values of the variables. There must be as many equations as variables. A large number of simultaneous equations are most conveniently solved by *matrix algebra*.

sin *Abbreviation for* the SINE of an angle.

sine A CIRCULAR FUNCTION of an angle, the ratio of the side opposite to the angle to the hypotenuse of a right-angled triangle.

sine theorem A trigonometric theorem

$$\frac{a}{\sin \alpha} = \frac{b}{\sin \beta} = \frac{c}{\sin \gamma}$$

relating the sine of an angle to the length of the side opposite (*see figure*).

Sine theorem

sine wave A curve having the form $y = a \sin x$. Simple harmonic motion can be represented by the general equation

$$y = a \sin 2\pi \left(\frac{t}{T} - \frac{x}{\lambda} \right)$$

where x and y are the Cartesian coordinates of the curve, and t is the time. T (the period), λ (the wavelength) and a are constants. A *cosine wave* has the same shape, displaced by one-quarter of a wavelength. *See also* FOURIER SERIES.

Singapore index *Same as* EQUATORIAL COMFORT INDEX.

single Flemish bond A brick bond that shows FLEMISH BOND on one side only. *See also* DOUBLE FLEMISH BOND.

single phase An AC power source using one active and one neutral conductor, rather than the three phases that are available in normal commercial systems.

single point ground The practice of tying the power neutral ground and safety ground together at the same point avoiding differential ground potential between points in a system.

single-acting engine A RECIPROCATING ENGINE in which the working fluid acts on one side of the piston only. Most internal combustion engines are of this type, so that only 1 in 2 or 1 in 4 strokes are working strokes.

single-event noise exposure level The constant sound level L_{AX} which, if maintained for one second, would deliver the same A-weighted noise energy to the receiver as the actual event itself. It is therefore an *equivalent continuous sound level* (L_{eq}) normalised to a period of one second.

single-pitch roof A roof that slopes only in one direction, such as a *skillion roof*, *shed roof* or a *lean-to roof*.

single-sized aggregate Aggregate in which most of the particles lie between narrow limits of size. It is usually produced by removing larger and smaller particles by sieving. *See* PEA GRAVEL.

singly curved surface A surface with zero GAUSSIAN CURVATURE, as distinct from a doubly curved surface. It is DEVELOPABLE and RULED.

singly ruled *See* RULED SURFACE.

sinh *Abbreviation for* Hyperbolic Sine. *See* HYPERBOLIC FUNCTIONS.

sinusoidal waveform *See* SINE WAVE.

siphon A closed pipe that rises partly above the hydraulic gradient of the pipe. Provided the siphon has been PRIMED, the higher end is immersed in water, and no part of the pipe rises above the head due to atmospheric pressure (approximately 10 m or 30 ft), it conveys water. The term *inverted siphon* is often used for a sagging pipe, even though this presents no problems of siphonage. *See also* BACK SIPHONAGE.

S-iron An exposed S-shaped piece at the end of a TURNBUCKLE between two masonry walls in traditional construction.

sisal A coarse natural fibre, once used as reinforcement in a variety of building materials, now largely superseded by *plastics* fibres. *See also* FIBROUS PLASTER.

site contamination The degradation of land and buildings due to exposure to materials, processes or organisms detrimental to health.

site instruction An instruction delivered on site by the contract administrator or others authorised under the contract and subsequently confirmed in writing, itemising any variation to the contract.

site welding, site bolting, site riveting Welding, bolting or riveting carried out on the site, as opposed to work carried out in the SHOP. *Also called field welding*, etc.

site-cast concrete Concrete cast *monolithically* in its final position in the structure, as opposed to *precast concrete*.

size A thin, pasty substance used as a sealer, binder or filler. It generally consists of a diluted glue, oil or resin.

size analysis *See* PARTICLE-SIZE ANALYSIS.

skates Relatively small, low, wheeled platforms for transporting goods or equipment.

skeleton construction Construction in which the loads are transmitted to the ground by a FRAME, as opposed to construction with load-bearing walls. Now more commonly called *framed construction*.

skew Oblique, at an angle to the main direction.

skew nailing Driving a nail at an angle to the initial surface in order to permit it to penetrate into a second member. *Also called toe nailing* (mainly in the USA).

skid steer A small tractor having four wheels without any steering mechanism. The pair of wheels on each side is driven separately from those on the other side, so that steering is achieved by driving the two sides at different speeds (or in opposite directions). It is thus highly manoeuvrable.

skillion roof A roof with only one slope, formerly used when abutting another building, but now applied to any roof with a single slope other than a flat roof. *Also called* a *lean-to roof* or a *shed roof.*

skin wettedness The estimated fraction of the whole body surface that is covered by moisture during sweating.

skip *(a)* A moveable refuse container. *(b)* A bucket with a hinged handle and openable bottom for lifting concrete by crane.

skirting A finishing board that covers the joint between the wall and the floor of a room. *Also called baseboard* (mainly in the USA).

skirting heater A space convection heater installed at floor level against the wall(s) of a building in lieu of a skirting board. *Also called baseboard heater.*

sky *See* CIE STANDARD CLEAR SKY, CIE STANDARD OVERCAST SKY, INDIAN STANDARD CLEAR SKY *and* UNIFORM SKY.

sky component (of the DAYLIGHT FACTOR) The ratio of that part of interior daylight illuminance received directly from a sky of assumed or known luminance distribution, to the illuminance on a horizontal plane due to an unobstructed hemisphere of this sky. A special case of this component is obtained when the sky is of uniform luminance and the window apertures are unglazed; it is called the SKY FACTOR.

sky factor The ratio of the daylight illuminance that would be received directly through unglazed openings from a sky of uniform luminance, to the illuminance on a horizontal plane due to an unobstructed hemisphere of this sky; direct sunlight is excluded. The term has special legal significance in England.

sky lobby A lift (elevator) lobby at an upper floor. A 60-storey building, for example, could be divided into two sections of 30 storeys, each with its separate lift system and lift lobby. The sky lobby is served by express lifts. By stopping the upper lift units at the sky lobby, an appreciable amount of space is saved (*see figure*).

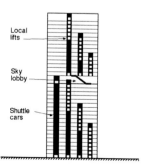

Sky lobby

sky-luminance distribution *See* CIE STANDARD CLEAR SKY, CIE STANDARD OVERCAST SKY, INDIAN STANDARD CLEAR SKY *and* UNIFORM SKY.

skylight A window placed in a flat or sloping roof.

skyscraper A term originally coined for the ten-storey Montauk Building in Chicago, built in 1882 with load-bearing walls. Buildings of this height were originally made possible by the development of the passenger lift (elevator), but soon rose much higher with the development of steel FRAME CONSTRUCTION.

slab In concrete construction, a flat surface that forms the floor or roof. Slabs may be directly supported on the ground (on GRADE); supported on beams as a BEAM-AND-SLAB FLOOR spanning *one way*; or spanning between supporting beams or walls (*see* TWO-WAY SLAB); or supported without beams on column capitals (FLAT SLAB); or supported directly on the columns without capitals or beams (FLAT PLATE). When the slab spans TWO-WAY, it is divided into MIDDLE STRIPS and COLUMN STRIPS in each direction.

slack The scheduling flexibility available for an activity in a PERT network. It is equivalent to the total FLOAT in a CPM network.

slag *See* BLAST-FURNACE SLAG.

slag wool MINERAL WOOL made from molten BLAST-FURNACE SLAG.

slake To moisten dry lime or clay with water.

slaked lime *Same as* HYDRATED LIME.

slate A fine-grained METAMORPHIC ROCK formed from clay, silt, shale or volcanic ash by high pressure. This gives the slate a CLEAVAGE PLANE across the original bedding planes. The material can be split into thin slabs. The terms *princess, duchess, countess,* etc. used in conjunction with slate for covering roofs, refer to the size of the pieces, not to their quality.

slats *See* VENETIAN BLIND.

sleeper pier Brick pier used to support a timber floor a small distance above ground. *See also stump.*

sleepers Strips of wood laid over concrete floor to which the finished wood floor is nailed or glued. *Also called nailing strips.*

sleeve *(a)* Conduit built into a structure of a building to allow another element to pass through, giving protection and allowing for relative movement. *(b)* A form of double SOCKET for joining two elements. *(c)* A flexible membrane used to protect the external surface of an element from corrosion or damage.

slenderness ratio The ratio of the EFFECTIVE LENGTH of a COLUMN to the least value of the RADIUS OF GYRATION. The longer the column, and the thinner it is, the more likely is it to BUCKLE.

slewing The action of horizontal rotation as applied to a crane jib.

sliced veneer WOOD VENEER cut as thin planar slices, as opposed to ROTARY VENEER.

slide rule An ANALOG calculator. The common slide rule has two scales, which may be slid past one another to perform addition or subtraction of the *scales*. Both scales are LOGARITHMIC, so that the slide rule actually performs multiplication and division. The slide rule was widely used until cheap DIGITAL CALCULATORS became available.

sliding formwork *See* SLIPFORM.

sliding sash window A SASH WINDOW that moves horizontally.

sling A wire, chain or flexible strap supporting a crane load.

sling psychrometer *Same as* WHIRLING PSYCHROMETER.

slip circle An assumed line of shear failure of a CLAY slope, which produces a rotational or cylindrical slide. The resistance of the slope to failure then equals the shear strength of the clay, multiplied by the surface of failure (the product of the length of the circular arc and the length of the slope).

slip lines *Same as* LÜDERS' LINES.

slipform Formwork that is raised or pulled in a continuous operation to speed the placement of the concrete. *Also called sliding formwork.*

slop hopper A plumbing fitting in the form of a large, low sink with a grating over it, into which human wastes are emptied from bedpans and the like. It drains into the SOIL DRAINAGE system, and is connected to the water supply for flushing and rinsing.

slope *(a)* The angle of inclination to the horizontal, expressed in degrees or as a ratio of rise to horizontal distance. *(b)* The rotation of part of a structural member, relative to its unloaded position, due to elastic deformation. This is usually expressed in RADIANS.

slope deflection A technique devised independently by G. A. Maney and A. Bendixen in 1914 for the solution of the bending moments in rigid frames and continuous beams by a series of simultaneous equations. Since all joints are assumed RIGID, the change in slope and the deflection are the same for all members framing into any one joint, and these equalities supply sufficient equations to solve the redundancies of the STATICALLY INDETERMINATE STRUCTURE. The concept is used in the MATRIX-DISPLACEMENT METHOD.

slope of timber grain The angle between the axis of a piece of timber and the general direction of the grain.

slot diffuser *See* LINEAR DIFFUSER.

slotted angle Steel angle prepunched with slotted holes. It is used for shelving and other utility structures, particularly those of a temporary nature.

slow-burning construction *(a)* Construction with materials chemically treated to make them more FIRE-RESISTING. *(b)* Construction with heavy timber sections; these are protected by the layer of charcoal formed during initial combustion, and are more fire-resisting than unprotected steel frames.

slow-burning insulation Insulating material that chars or burns without a flame or blaze. Some plastic materials used for thermal insulation are highly COMBUSTIBLE.

sludge Sediment settling to the bottom of a septic tank, ARRESTOR trap, etc.

slug An obsolete British unit of mass. It is defined as a mass in pounds numerically equal to g (the acceleration due to gravity), *i.e.* 32.2 pounds. *Also called a geepound.*

slump test A method of measuring the WORKABILITY of freshly mixed concrete. The concrete is placed in a mould, which consists of a truncated cone, 300 mm (12 in.) high, with a base diameter of 200 mm (8 in.) and a top diameter of 100 mm (4 in.). The mould is then lifted, and the subsidence measured. *See also* BALL TEST *and* COMPACTING FACTOR TEST.

slurry A finely ground solid suspended in a liquid, *e.g.* a fluid mixture of cement and water, or of sand, cement and water.

small circle A circle on the surface of a sphere that is smaller than a GREAT CIRCLE. The *parallels of latitude* (except the *equator*) are small circles on the Earth's surface. They are not GEODETIC LINES, and thus correspond to curves on a plane surface.

small power Power supplied to or consumed by items of electrical office equipment such as computer terminals, photocopiers and the like, as opposed to larger machinery.

SMF *Abbreviation for* SYNTHETIC MINERAL FIBRE.

smog Originally a mixture of smoke and fog; hence any objectionable mixture of air and pollutants. *See also* INVERSION.

smoke The products of combustion (usually of incomplete combustion) consisting of finely divided particulate matter and liquid droplets suspended in air and in gaseous products. In the atmosphere, smoke is one of the forms of air pollution. In a building fire, it is the principal hazard to life, because the smoke from some building materials is toxic; it contains little oxygen to sustain life; and thick smoke prevents people from finding their way to the exits.

smoke control system An engineered system that uses fans to remove smoke, and pressure differences across barriers to limit smoke movement.

smoke detector A device used to detect smoke in a part of a building, and then to operate an alarm procedure. Smoke detectors are often placed in the return air ducts, as this is a place where smoke from a fire within the building is likely to be detected early. *See* IONISATION SMOKE DETECTOR *and* PHOTO-OPTICAL SMOKE DETECTOR. *See also* FIRE DETECTOR.

smoke extractor A device that improves the draft of a chimney, such as a ventilator or a hood at its top.

smoke load That part of the FIRE LOAD which has the potential to produce smoke.

smoke management system All methods that can be used singly or in combination to modify smoke movement.

smoke test (drainage) A test in which smoke is introduced at a low level into drainage pipework. Observation of smoke may indicate a leak, and may also indicate that a stormwater drain or downpipe is illegally connected to a sewerage system.

smoke tunnel A WIND TUNNEL in which a smoke generator is used to indicate the movement of the air.

smoke venting Provision for allowing smoke from a building fire to escape rapidly to the atmosphere. In a single-storey building, smoke vents may be placed in the roof, where they remain closed until opened by a fusible link, or by the operation of a SMOKE DETECTOR. In a multi-storey building, the return air of the normal air conditioning system can be spilled to the outside, or a special set of ducts and fans can be installed to operate only in the event of a fire. The disadvantage of smoke venting is that it allows more air to enter and support the fire. This is outweighed by the removal of toxic smoke, and the clearing of the air to allow occupants to escape and firefighters to find the source of the fire.

smouldering The combustion of solid materials without a visible flame.

Sn Chemical symbol for tin (stannum).

snaphead An approximately hemi-spherical head used on rivets, bolts and screws. *Also called buttonhead.*

Snell's law 'When a plane wave strikes the boundary between two transparent media the ratio of the sine of the angle of the refracted ray to the sine of the angle of the incident ray is equal to the ratio of the two velocities in the media.'

Snellen notation *See* VISUAL ACUITY.

snow guard A board that prevents snow from sliding off a sloping roof.

snow load The superimposed load assumed to result from severe snow falls in any particular region. Snow loads range from zero in most parts of Australia to 3 kN/m² (60 lb/ft²) in Northern Canada.

soapstone *Same as* TALC.

socket *(a)* A point at which electric current can be taken from an electric wiring system. *(b)* The female end of a SPIGOT-

and-socket joint *(see figure)*. *(c)* A short metal tube with a female thread or mating surface both ends, for joining two metal pipes. See figure under PIPE FITTINGS.

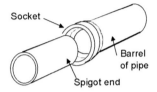

Socket

sodium A very reactive ALKALI metal. Its chemical symbol is Na (Natrium), its atomic number is 11, its atomic weight is 22.997 and its specific gravity is 0.98. It has a melting point of 97.7°C, and a valency of 1.

sodium lamp *See* LOW-PRESSURE SODIUM LAMP *and* HIGH-PRESSURE SODIUM LAMP.

sodium silicate Used as a waterproofer and surface hardener under the name of WATER-GLASS.

soffit The underside of any horizontal member of a structure, *e.g.* a beam or a slab.

soft solder A low melting point solder. *See* SOLDERING.

soft water *See* HARD WATER.

soft-start circuit Circuitry that limits the initial power demand when an electrical device starts up, such as a UPS which returns to commercial power after operating in emergency mode.

softboard A low-density FIBREBOARD.

software The computer programs for running a computer, as opposed to the HARDWARE.

software house An organisation that develops tailored SOFTWARE applications.

softwood Timber from *coniferous* trees, *e.g.* DOUGLAS FIR.

soil auger *See* AUGER *(b)*.

soil cement A mixture of Portland cement and locally available soil. It serves as a soil stabiliser.

soil classification *See* LIQUID LIMIT, PARTICLE-SIZE ANALYSIS, PLASTIC LIMIT *and* STOKES' LAW.

soil drain A drain that carries sewage, sanitary drainage and trade effluent to the sewer, as opposed to a STORM DRAIN.

soil mechanics A term coined in 1936 by Karl Terzaghi, who systematised the subject, to embrace all aspects of the scientific study of soils as engineering materials. *See* CONSOLIDATION, COULOMB'S EQUATION, DIFFERENTIAL SETTLEMENT, EARTH PRESSURE, RANKINE THEORY, SHEAR TESTS *and* SLIP CIRCLE.

soil profile A vertical section showing the variation of the soil below the surface of a site.

soil samples *See* BOREHOLE SAMPLES.

sol-air temperature The hypothetical external temperature, which would generate the same heat flow through the envelope element as the actual air temperature and solar radiation effects. It is the sum of the air temperature and the temperature equivalent of solar radiation.

$$T_{SA} = T_{air} + G \times \alpha/h_o$$

or more conveniently

$$T_{air} + G \times \alpha \times R_{so}$$

where T_{SA} = sol-air temperature, T_{air} = air temperature, G = global solar irradiance, α = absorptance, h_o = outside surface conductance, R_{so} = outside surface resistance. For walls faced by surfaces of similar temperature, radiant emission can be ignored, but for roofs facing the cold sky an emission term is included.

$$T_{SA} = T_{air} + (G \times \alpha - E) \times R_{so}$$

where the magnitude of E depends on sky conditions; it can be taken as 90 W/m² for a cloudless sky, but only 20 W/m² for an overcast sky. Values between these two can be estimated according to sky cloud cover.

solar absorber A sheet of material, usually copper, aluminium or steel that forms the surface of a solar collector.

solar altitude angle The ALTITUDE of the sun.

solar azimuth angle The AZIMUTH of the sun.

solar cell *See* PHOTOVOLTAIC CELL.

solar cell module Group of encapsulated solar cells framed in glass or plastic units, usually the smallest unit of solar electric equipment available to the consumer.

solar chart (or sunpath diagram) A two-dimensional representation of the sky, showing the sun's apparent path at various dates, used primarily for shading design or to determine sunlight penetration through openings. Circular charts may use three forms of representation of the altitude: *(a)* 'equidistant' charts, concentric circles of equal spacing, *e.g.* for each 10° altitude increment, where 90° (the ZENITH) is the centre point; *(b)* ORTHOGRAPHIC vertical PROJECTION, where the concentric circles are quite closely spaced near the horizon; *(c)* the STEREOGRAPHIC PROJECTION, where the imaginary NADIR point is used as the centre of radial projection, and the position (radius) of altitude circles is determined by projecting them to intersect the horizontal plane (*see figure* under STEREOGRAPHIC PROJECTION). Equidistant charts are used in the USA and the stereographic charts elsewhere. The GNOMONIC (perspective) SUN-PATH DIAGRAMS are rarely used.

solar collector A device that gathers and accumulates solar radiation to produce heat. *See* EVACUATED TUBULAR COLLECTOR, FLAT PLATE COLLECTOR, PHOTOVOLTAIC CELL *and* SOLAR WATER HEATER.

solar concentrator The part of a solar collector that focuses sunlight onto an absorber surface.

solar constant The average intensity of radiation arriving from the sun at the edge of the Earth's atmosphere. The accepted value is about 1350 W/m².

solar control *See* SUNSHADING *and* SOLAR CONTROL GLASS.

solar control glass *See* HEAT-ABSORBING, INSULATING *and* REFLECTIVE GLASS.

solar cooker A general term for the many types of cooking devices powered by solar energy.

solar cooling *See* SOLAR REFRIGERATION.

solar crop dryer A device that uses solar radiation to dry crops.

solar degradation *See* DEGRADATION *and* ULTRAVIOLET RADIATION.

solar distillation *See* SOLAR STILL.

solar energy The electromagnetic radiation generated by the sun. Often used in the context of that portion that reaches the Earth.

solar energy systems Systems for the application of solar energy, by thermal or photoelectric processes. *See* ACTIVE SYSTEMS, PASSIVE SYSTEMS, EVACUATED TUBULAR COLLECTOR, FLAT PLATE COLLECTOR, SOLAR GAIN, SOLAR WATER HEATER, PHOTOVOLTAIC CELLS *and* STE SYSTEMS.

solar envelope A set of imaginary boundaries over a site, derived from the sun's relative motion, used to define rules for regulating development. Buildings within this container will not overshadow their surroundings during critical periods of the day and year.

solar gain The part of a building's heat supply, or an additional load for cooling, due to solar radiation that strikes the building or passes into it through windows. *See* DIRECT GAIN METHOD, DIRECT SOLAR GAIN *and* THERMAL CAPACITY.

solar incident angle The angle between the incoming solar beam and the normal to a surface.

solar noon The moment the sun crosses the observer's MERIDIAN. At this moment the sun is at its greatest ALTITUDE for that day.

solar orientation The position of the building in relation to the north (or south), with particular reference to the amount of sunshine falling on the walls and windows, and the penetration of the sun through the windows into the building.

solar radiation The radiant energy received from the sun, from both direct and diffuse or reflected sunlight. *See also* SOLAR CONSTANT.

solar refrigeration A process in which solar radiation is used to provide heat energy to produce cooling.

solar spectrum The radiation received from the sun ranges approximately from 300 to 3000 nm (0.3 to 3×10^{-6} m). The spectrum of visible light ranges from 390 nm (violet) to 760 nm (red).

solar still A device consisting of one or several stages in which BRACKISH WATER is converted to potable water by successive evaporation and condensation with the aid of solar heat.

solar thermal electric power The indirect conversion of solar radiation into electricity by solar collectors, a heat engine and electrical generators.

solar toxic waste destruction Technique to destroy hazardous wastes with the aid of concentrated solar radiation.

solar water heater Water heated in pipes running through a solar collector is stored in a tank until required (*see figure*). *See also* THERMOSIPHON. A solar water heating system needs a subsidiary conventional heating system for use when there is insufficient sunshine, unless the user is willing to shower in cold water. In climates where water may freeze, the solar collector heats a non-freezing liquid, and the heat is then transferred from that to water. The *figure* shows two arrangements using the thermosiphon principle. The storage tank may also be located at ground level, with a circulating pump.

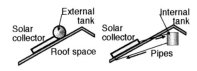

Solar water heater

solarimeter *See* PYRANOMETER.

solarium A room, terrace or balcony, generally with some glass walls, exposed to the rays of the sun. The term is particularly used for hospitals and sanatoria; for private houses *sunroom* is more common.

solarscope A device for model studies to simulate solar geometry, the effect of shading devices and sunlight penetration through openings. Many types have been developed, such as: *(a)* simple ones, with lamps along a large arc, mounted at 15° (hourly) intervals, individually switchable and the model table at the centre of the arc; *(b)* a lamp mounted at the end of a long arm (or a mirror at the end of this arm, with a spotlight at the base directed at the mirror, thus doubling the optical length), where the arm can be tilted and rotated to simulate the sun's apparent location; *(c)* lamps with a large diameter shallow parabolic searchlight mirror (to give a parallel beam) mounted on a motorised carriage which travels on a circular (about 2/3 circle) rail, which can tilt (for latitude) and slide (for calendar) adjustment. *See also* HELIODON.

soldering A process for joining two

pieces of metal by means of *solder*, *i.e.* an alloy which has a lower melting point than the pieces to be joined. For satisfactory jointing, the surfaces to be joined must be kept free from oxide films, and this is accomplished by using a *flux* which melts at a lower temperature than the solder. For the lower-strength solders, known as *soft solders*, *zinc chloride* or *rosin* can be used as a flux. PLUMBER'S SOLDER, an alloy of lead and tin, is in this category. For the higher-strength solders (*hard solder* or SILVER SOLDER), BORAX is a suitable flux.

soldier course A course of bricks laid each with their longest dimension vertical.

solenoid A multi-turn coil of wire wound on a cylindrical former. It behaves like a bar magnet when carrying a current. It is used in RELAYS, CIRCUIT BREAKERS, switches and brakes.

solid One of the states of matter, in which a material has shear strength, maintains its shape without external restraint, but can suffer breakage or permanent deformation under excessive stress. (The other states are GAS and LIQUID.)

solid angle An angle measured in three dimensions, as distinct from a PLANE ANGLE. *See also* STERADIAN.

solid bridging A form of lateral stiffening between deep, narrow timber joists to prevent them from twisting. Short lengths of material, similar to the joists but slightly shallower, are fixed between each adjacent pair of joists. It uses more material, but less labour, than HERRINGBONE STRUTTING.

solid door A flush door with a solid core, as opposed to a HOLLOW-CORE DOOR.

solid modelling In computer graphics, the process of representing solid objects by adding and subtracting primitive solids such as cubes, cones, spheres and cylinders, as opposed to SURFACE MODELS and WIREFRAME MODELS.

solid phase The thermodynamic phase in which a substance is in SOLID form.

solid state In electronics, referring to the use of TRANSISTORS, INTEGRATED CIRCUITS or CHIPS, but no thermionic valves.

solid-web joist A conventional joist with a solid web formed by a plate or a rolled section, as opposed to an OPEN-WEB JOIST.

solidus line The line separating the solid phase from the liquid + solid phase. In a PHASE DIAGRAM it shows the variation of the composition of an alloy with temperature when melting is complete.

Solomonic columns Twisted columns, like those cast by Bernini in the seventeenth century for the *baldachino* in St Peter's Basilica in Rome, and subsequently widely used in churches. They became a characteristic feature of the Spanish Mission style in the USA and in Australia. It is most unlikely that Solomon's Temple had twisted columns, but the story that it did gained wide credence in the sixteenth century when Raphael showed the Jerusalem Temple thus.

solstice The dates when the sun attains its maximum distance from the celestial equator; they occur about 21 June and 22 December. Consequently these are the longest and shortest days of the year.

solute A dissolved substance.

solvent A liquid used for dissolving a solid.

solvent cement Adhesive compound containing a solvent of the material being joined. It usually also contains some of the same material in solution. Upon evaporation of the solvent, the joint is homogeneous with the parts being joined.

sommer (*also spelled summer*) *See* BREASTSUMMER.

sone An obsolete unit of the loudness of a sound. One sone is defined as the loudness of a 40 dB tone at 1000 Hz. The loudness of a sound which sounds twice as loud as a 1 sone sound is 2 sones.

sonotube US term for a prefabricated circular cardboard tube used as formwork for concrete columns.

Sorel's cement *See* OXYCHLORIDE CEMENT.

sound A disturbance propagated in an elastic medium by a wave motion which is of such a character as to be capable of being heard by a listener. *See also* under ACOUSTIC *and* NOISE.

sound absorption The transformation of acoustic (sound) energy into heat by solid materials or the medium through which the sound is propagating. In rooms, the amount of sound absorption largely determines the amount of REVERBERATION and the SOUND PRESSURE LEVEL in the room. Sound absorption is often confused with SOUND INSULATION.

sound absorption coefficient The ratio of the sound energy absorbed by a surface to the energy incident upon the surface. Its value ranges from about 0.01 for a polished marble to 1.0 for the absorbing fibreglass wedges used in ANECHOIC CHAMBERS. *See also* NOISE REDUCTION COEFFICIENT.

sound attenuation Reduction in sound intensity.

sound digitiser A device (usually hardware and software) designed to SAMPLE analog sound waves and convert them to finite digital representations for storage and manipulation on a computer. *See also* DIGITAL SOUND *and* ANALOG TO DIGITAL CONVERTER.

sound frequency analyser *See* FREQUENCY ANALYSER.

sound insulation A term used to describe the ability of a wall or floor to ATTENUATE the sound passing through it. Good insulation against AIRBORNE SOUND requires a partition with high mass. Insulation against STRUCTUREBORNE and IMPACT SOUND is usually best achieved by a resilient floor covering, VIBRATION ISOLATOR or FLOATING FLOOR. *See also* SOUND ABSORPTION.

sound intensity *See* INTENSITY.

sound knot *See* KNOT.

sound level *See* SOUND PRESSURE LEVEL.

sound level meter An instrument having a microphone, amplifier and indicating device designed to measure a frequency-weighted and time-weighted value of the SOUND PRESSURE LEVEL (in DECIBELS). *See also* FREQUENCY ANALYSER.

sound mirror A plane or curved surface that reflects sound. *See also* ECHO *and* WHISPERING GALLERY.

sound mixer An electronic device that accepts a number of audio input signals, controls their relative power levels, and combines them into an output signal.

sound perfume A figure of speech for a MASKING NOISE.

sound power The sound power of a source is the total acoustic energy radiated per unit time.

sound power level Defined as ten times the logarithm (to the base 10) of the ratio of the SOUND POWER of a sound source to a reference sound power, (usually taken as 10^{-12} W). *See* DECIBEL *(a)*.

sound pressure The alternating pressure in an acoustic field due to the presence of a sound. The term sound pressure may be qualified by 'RMS', 'instantaneous', 'peak', etc. but where it is unqualified it is usual to imply the RMS or EFFECTIVE SOUND PRESSURE value.

sound pressure level A measure of the intensity of a sound. The sound pressure level (*also known as* SOUND LEVEL or just LEVEL) of a sound in DECIBELS is defined as 20 times the logarithm (to the base 10) of the ratio of the RMS sound pressure to a reference sound pressure (usually 20 µPa, the threshold of hearing at 1000 Hz, is used as the reference). Most environmental and occupational sound pressure levels are quoted in dB(A). These measurements are made using a SOUND LEVEL METER with an A-weighting filter which has a frequency characteristic similar to that of the ear. *See* DECIBEL *(b)*.

sound reduction index *See* SOUND TRANSMISSION LOSS.

sound reflector *See* SOUND MIRROR *and* ACOUSTICAL CLOUD.

sound reinforcement *See* PA SYSTEM.

sound shadow When sound propagates near the ground, air temperature or wind velocity gradients or barriers may cause a zone of low sound level. This is known as a sound shadow.

sound spectrum A graphical representation of a complex sound where energy or pressure is plotted as a function of frequency.

sound spectrum analyser *See* FREQUENCY ANALYSER.

sound transmission *See* SOUND TRANSMISSION LOSS.

sound transmission class The sound transmission class (STC) of a partition separating two spaces is a single-number rating of its ability to reduce the sound passing between the two spaces. For example, a single 110 mm unrendered brick wall has an STC rating of approximately 45. This is considered a minimum requirement for common walls separating dwellings, and some building codes require higher values.

sound transmission loss *Also known as sound reduction index. Abbreviated as* TL or SRI. A measure of the sound transmission of a partition at a particular frequency or frequency band. It is ten times the logarithm (to the base 10) of the ratio of the sound INTENSITY on the source side of the partition to the sound intensity on the receiver side of the partition. In practice, because sound intensity is difficult to measure, sound transmission loss (in decibels) is measured using:

$$TL = L_1 - L_2 + 10*\log_{10}(S/A)$$

where L_1 is the sound level on the source side of the partition, L_2 the sound level on the receiver side, S is the area of the partition common to both rooms and A is the total absorption in the receiving room. *See also* SOUND TRANSMISSION CLASS.

sound wave A disturbance in a medium whereby energy is transmitted by virtue of the inertial, elastic and other dynamic properties of the medium.

sound, airborne *See* AIRBORNE SOUND.

sound, impact *See* IMPACT SOUND.

soundness Freedom of a metal casting or of concrete from cracks, flaws and fissures; this is sometimes checked by listening to the sound which the casting makes when struck. The term is also used to denote freedom from excessive volume change, and from deterioration due to exposure to the weather.

soundproofing A non-technical term for reducing sound transmission into or out of a space.

southlight roof The equivalent of a NORTHLIGHT ROOF in the southern hemisphere.

sow *See* PIG.

sp gr *Abbreviation for* SPECIFIC GRAVITY.

spa (spa bath) A bath with the facility for injecting air and jets of turbulent water into the water contained in the bath.

space allocation The process of generating spatial designs by allocating units of functional spaces to physical space locations. Commonly a process of optimising a sum of distances between functional spaces.

space audit A physical survey and record of space occupied, and its functional use.

space frame A FRAME that can only be solved by considering its behaviour in space, *i.e.* in two mutually perpendicular planes at the same time (*see figure*). Space frames may be *statically determinate* or *indeterminate* (*see* MÖBIUS' LAW).

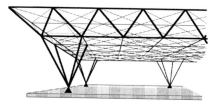

Space frame

space planning The definition of space requirements in terms of size, type, activity and adjacency for particular premises.

space utilisation The ratio of the number of people using a space to its potential use capacity, multiplied by the ratio of the hours of actual usage to the total available hours, and expressed as a percentage.

spaciousness *See* ENVELOPMENT.

spackle Proprietary name for a paste to fill holes, cracks and defects in the surfaces of various materials.

span The distance between the supports of the structure. *See also* CLEAR, BEARING *and* EFFECTIVE SPAN.

spandrel The part of the wall between the head of a window and the *sill* of the window above it. The term is also used as a synonym for *spandrel beam*, which is a beam placed within a spandrel, or a structural beam on the edge of a building frame. *Spandrel* also denotes the triangular infilling under the outer string of a stair, and the triangular infilling above the extrados of an arch, between the abutment and the crown.

Spanish tile A term used in some parts of the world for MISSION TILE, and in others for a type of PAN TILE.

spatterdash A rich mixture of cement and coarse sand thrown hard onto a brick or concrete wall, to form a thin, coarse-textured, continuous coat.

specific gravity The ratio of the MASS of

a given volume of a substance to the mass of an equal volume of water (at 4 °C, when water has its minimum volume). Since water weighs 1 kilogram per litre, the density of a substance in metric units is numerically equal to its specific gravity, which is a dimensionless ratio. In FPS units, the specific gravity must be multiplied by the density of water which is 62.4 lb/ft^3.

specific heat The ratio of the quantity of heat required to raise a substance through a given temperature range, to that required to raise the same mass of water through the same temperature range.

specific surface The total surface area of the particles contained in a unit mass or absolute unit volume of a material. The smaller the particle size, or the finer the powder, the greater the specific surface. *See also* STOKES' LAW.

specific volume The volume of a unit mass. It is the reciprocal of density.

specification A document accompanying the drawings, describing the materials and workmanship required to carry out the works for each particular trade.

specified compressive strength of concrete The strength of the concrete used in ULTIMATE STRENGTH DESIGN.

spectrophotometer A PHOTOMETER capable of reading the distribution of luminous flux across the visible spectrum. That can be done using prisms or gratings to disperse the spectrum prior to the measurement of narrow bands of light or by using three coloured filters, when the instrument is called a *tricolorimeter*.

spectrum A range of frequencies, and the way in which the energy of a particular source is distributed across those frequencies, particularly the VISIBLE SPECTRUM and SOUND SPECTRUM.

specular angle *Same as* ANGLE OF REFLECTION.

specular reflection The process by which incident light is redirected at the specular (mirror) angle.

specular surface A mirror surface (from the Latin for *mirror*).

specular transmission The process by which incident flux passes through a surface or medium without scattering.

speech transmission index (STI) A wide-band objective measurement of speech intelligibility. *See also* PERCENTAGE ALCONS (%ALCONS).

speech intelligibility The percentage of meaningful speech that is correctly interpreted by a listener or listeners. *See also* ARTICULATION.

speech interference level The arithmetic average of the octave-band sound pressure levels of a noise at 500 Hz, 1000 Hz and 2000 Hz (together with the level at 250 Hz if it exceeds the level at 500 Hz by 10 dB or more).

speech privacy A measure of the sound isolation between a speaker and a listener. High speech privacy corresponds to low speech intelligibility. For instance, a high degree of speech privacy is required between a doctor's consulting and waiting rooms, while a high degree of speech intelligibility is required *within* the consulting room. Speech privacy may be obtained by a high sound transmission loss partition between the two rooms or by a high background noise level in the waiting room.

speech recognition In information technology, the process of identifying human speech by electronic means.

speech synthesis Using a computer to convert text to simulated human speech. It normally involves identifying the basic phonemes of a language and programming the computer to recognise the text representing these phonemes in written text, sequence them together, and use recorded or simulated sounds to imitate the spoken word. *See also* VOICE RECOGNITION.

speed The ratio of the distance covered to the time taken. *See also* VELOCITY.

speed of light The speed of electromagnetic radiation, which includes light, is a universal constant. Its value in a vacuum is 299 796 km/s (186 293 miles/s).

speed of sound The velocity at which a disturbance is propagated in an elastic medium by a wave motion. In air, the speed of sound is approximately 343 m/s at normal temperature and pressure.

spelter An alloy containing about 99 per cent zinc.

spherical dome *See* DOME.

spherical trigonometry The TRIGONOM-ETRY of triangles drawn on the surface of a sphere.

spider A bracket used for connecting frameless glass panels to a supporting structure. It usually has four legs which terminate in screw-threaded fittings so that bolts can be passed through holes near the corners of the glass panels. Resilient washers and sleeves are used to prevent the glass from coming into contact with the metal spider (*see figure*).

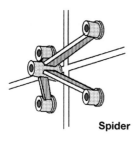

Spider

spigot The plain end of a length of pipe which is fitted into an enlarged *socket* or *bell* at the beginning of the next pipe. The *spigot-and-socket joint* (*also called bell-and-spigot joint*) is made tight by CAULKING.

spill air *See* RELIEF AIR.

spiral grain Growth of fibres in a helical direction around the trunk of the tree. The resulting timber is likely to warp.

spiral reinforcement More correctly called HELICAL REINFORCEMENT.

spiral stair More correctly called HELICAL STAIR.

spirit level An instrument for testing horizontal or vertical alignment. It consists of a straightedge incorporating a slightly curved glass tube filled partially with alcohol or other liquid. The horizontal position is indicated by the central location of the air bubble. *See also* WATER LEVEL.

spirit stain A dye dissolved in METHY-LATED SPIRITS, usually with SHELLAC or some other resin as a binder. It is used for darkening a wood surface, but emphasises the grain of the timber less than a *water stain* (in which water is the solvent for the dye). *See also* OIL STAIN.

spirits of alum Sulphuric acid.

spirits of salt Hydrochloric acid.

spirits of sulphur Sulphurous acid.

spirits of vitriol Sulphuric acid.

SPL *Abbreviation for* SOUND PRESSURE LEVEL. It is measured in DECIBELS.

splay An inclined surface, *i.e.* a large BEVEL or CHAMFER, running across the full width of the surface.

splice A joining of two structural pieces. The joint is generally designed to be as strong, or stronger, than the pieces to be joined.

splice of reinforcing bars Transfer of force from one bar to another. This may be achieved by welding or by mechanical connection. However, the normal procedure is to overlap the bars in the concrete, usually without touching; the force is transferred by bond between the concrete and the steel.

split ring connector A TIMBER CON-NECTOR in the form of a ring made from a flat steel bar, inserted into annular grooves in the mating faces of two timber members. The whole is held together by a bolt. It is now virtually superseded by NAILPLATES, which require much less labour.

splitter A metal plate or diaphragm arranged to divide the air stream in a duct or duct fitting to guide the flow in a desired direction. *See also* GUIDE VANE.

splitting tensile test Determination of tensile strength of concrete by testing a cylinder (*see* CYLINDER STRENGTH) on its side in compression. The cylinder splits across the vertical diameter. *Also known as Brazilian test* and *diametral compression test.*

spoil Material excavated which is in excess of the fill required.

spontaneous combustion A bursting into flames of a mixture of substances, due to the evolution of heat through chemical action between them.

spot cooling Supply of cool air at a local point in a building where a high local output of heat, often from a piece of equipment, may distress a worker or other person in its vicinity.

spot replacement (of lamps) The replacement of ELECTRIC LAMPS as they fail, compared with BULK REPLACEMENT.

spot welding Joining two or more overlapping pieces by local fusion of small areas or spots.

spotlamp Any lamp or luminaire that produces a narrow or near-parallel beam of light.

spray chamber An enclosure in an air distribution system in which the air stream is passed through a bank of water sprays for the purpose of humidifying and/or cleaning it.

spray gun A tool for applying paint, mortar, etc. through a nozzle under pneumatic or fluid pressure. *See also* CEMENT GUN.

sprayed mineral wool Mineral wool blown onto a surface with a spray gun, together with a binder. It provides thermal insulation and FIRE PROTECTION OF STEEL STRUCTURES that is rot-proof, vermin-proof and incombustible.

spread footing A footing made especially wide to reduce its pressure on the foundation.

spreader A fitting attached to the end of a rainwater pipe which has a slotted or perforated outlet, to spread the water.

spreadsheet Computer application used mainly for recording and calculating numerical data, as opposed to text, drawing or DATABASE applications.

spring Curvature of a piece of timber, in the plane of the longer side of the cross-section *see figure*.

Spring

spring washer A steel ring cut once and bent into a shallow helix. Used as a washer, it prevents the nut from unscrewing.

spring wood *Same as* EARLY WOOD.

springings or spring The level at which an arch springs from its supports. *See also* CROWN.

sprinkler head The temperature-sensitive element in a SPRINKLER SYSTEM. It is sealed by a metal plug, which melts at the predetermined temperature; or by a plastic plug which contains liquid bursting it at the predetermined temperature (*see figure*). This is usually 68 °C (155 °F), which is low enough to control a fire in its early stages, but also high enough to ensure that the system does not go off on a hot day without a fire.

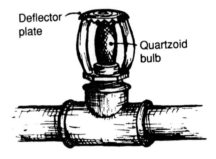

Sprinkler head

sprinkler system A system that sprinkles a fire with water soon after it breaks out, and thus extinguishes it, or controls it until the fire brigade arrives. It consists of pipes installed in or below the ceiling throughout the building. Branches projecting from these pipes are sealed by SPRINKLER HEADS which open at a predetermined temperature.

square *(a)* A surface measure exactly equal to 100 ft². It is equal to just under 10 m². *(b)* An equilateral RECTANGLE. *(c)* An L-shaped tool for setting out right angles.

square matrix A MATRIX *(a)* in which the number of rows equals the number of columns.

square metre The basic metric surface measure. It is approximately 10.76 ft², or one-tenth of a SQUARE *(a)*.

square wave inversion A method of converting a sinusoidal electrical signal into a square wave so that the current is either at maximum or zero. This is used in high efficiency variable frequency electrical motors such as in large electric lift systems.

squared log *Same as* BALK.

squared stone *Same as* ASHLAR.

squinch Corbelling at an upper corner of the structural bay of a brick or masonry structure to support a dome or its drum. It is an alternative to the construction of a PENDENTIVE.

squint brick A special shaped brick

formed with splays in the vertical plane on one end, suitable for turning a 45° corner (*see figure*).

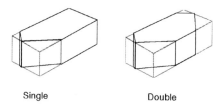

Single   Double

Squint brick

sr *Abbreviation for steradian.*
SRI Sound Reduction Index, *see* SOUND TRANSMISSION LOSS (TL). Some authors use the TL as the sound pressure level difference between the source room and the receiving room but use SRI as distinct from TL, adjusted for the absorption qualities of the receiving room.
SS *Abbreviation for* STAINLESS STEEL.
ST Subjective Temperature, a thermal comfort scale developed by McIntyre (1976), a composite of DBT and MRT.
St Andrew's cross bond *Same as* ENGLISH CROSS BOND.
St Petersburg standard An obsolete measure of timber which equals 1980 BOARD FEET (165 ft³ or 4.67 m³).
stabilised soil Soil which has been treated with a binder to reduce its movement. Suitable binders are Portland cement, waste oil, bitumen, resin or a more stable soil, but low cost is a prime consideration.
stability, dimensional *See* DIMENSIONAL STABILITY.
stability, elastic *See* BUCKLE.
stack *(a)* A vertical drainage or vent pipe within a building, or attached to the side of a building. *(b)* A freestanding industrial chimney.
stack effect Natural ventilation caused by air pressure differences due to variations in air density with temperature and with height.
stadia telemetry Measuring distances using a TACHEOMETER, so that the distance from the surveying instrument can be determined as a multiple of the intercept on a staff at the remote location.
staff Measuring rod, usually telescopic

for easy transport, used in a vertical position for LEVELLING.
stain *See* OIL STAIN, SPIRIT STAIN *and* WATER STAIN.
stained glass A decorative panel or window composed of pieces of coloured glass, joined by means of lead beads (*cames*) or concrete. The glass colouring is usually not a stain, but is fired into the glass.
staining power The amount of colour given to a white pigment by a given amount of coloured pigment. It is the opposite of REDUCING POWER.
stainless steel Steel that is highly resistant to atmospheric corrosion and attack by organic and dilute mineral acids. It is used for cutlery, facing panels for curtain walls, wash basins and urinals, as well as small structural items and fixings in corrosive environments. There are many different alloys, but all contain between 8 and 30 per cent CHROMIUM, in addition to a smaller amount of other elements, especially NICKEL.
stair One *step* in a flight of stairs; also the entire flight. *See also* BALUSTER, GOING, RISER, STRING *and* TREAD (*see figure*).

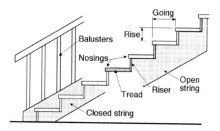

Stair

stair riser *See* RISER *(a)*.
stair well A space around which a staircase is disposed.
stairway pressurisation system A system whereby, in a fire situation, fresh air is supplied under pressure into the stairway by a system of fans and ducts. The pressure is intended to be enough to prevent the ingress of smoke when doors are opened, but not so great as to prevent opening of the doors.
stakeholder A person with an interest, not necessarily financial, in an outcome,

e.g. a neighbour to a building development site.

stanchion *(a)* A column, particularly of structural steel. *(b)* An upright bar placed intermediate between the MULLIONS to strengthen a LEADED LIGHT.

standard *(a)* A document prepared by a Standards Institution or a Government Agency prescribing methods or materials for safe use. *(b)* A STANDARD LAMP *(a)*, device, resistance, etc. used to calibrate those that are sub-standard. *(c)* An old measure of timber, *see* ST PETERSBURG STANDARD. *(d)* A term for anything standing upright, as in a STANDARD LAMP *(b)*.

standard atmosphere Air at the reference condition of standard temperature and pressure. *See* STP.

standard deviation The square root of the *variance*, *i.e.* the root of the average of the squares of the *deviations* of a number of observations from their mean value in a FREQUENCY DISTRIBUTION CURVE. It is a measure of the spread of the observations, and it is necessary first to square the variances, and then take the root of their mean, because otherwise the positive and negative variances would largely cancel out. By squaring the deviations, all values become positive. *See also* COEFFICIENT OF VARIATION.

standard fire test A standard test for determining the FIRE RESISTANCE GRADING.

standard hook A HOOKED BAR bent in accordance with the minimum radius and free length specified by the standard to prevent pullout. It is usually bent through 180°. A standard bend through 90° is often called a *cog*.

standard lamp *(a)* An ELECTRIC LAMP that has been calibrated for intensity or flux and used in photometric laboratories to calibrate instruments or to create *substandard lamps*. *(b)* A floor-mounted, portable luminaire used for local lighting.

standard section A metal section which has been standardised. In the case of hot-rolled sections, this is much cheaper than a section specially made to order; however, the difference is less marked for cold-formed and extruded sections.

standard sky *See* CIE STANDARD CLEAR SKY, CIE STANDARD OVERCAST SKY, INDIAN STANDARD CLEAR SKY *and* UNIFORM SKY.

standard temperature and pressure *See* STP.

standard test conditions A set of testing conditions laid down in a STANDARD *(a)* or commonly used by manufacturers to compare different products.

standardised normal variate *See* GAUSSIAN CURVE.

standby lighting A lighting system that supplies adequate illumination if the normal lighting system should fail.

standby power The power that is available within one minute of a normal power failure to operate life safety equipment and continuously operating equipment. *Emergency power* is the power available within ten seconds.

standing seam Seam formed between sheets of flat metal roofing, where the edge of each sheet is turned up at right angles. The seam may be completed by folding one of the edges over the other, or by adding a small third strip as a capping. Since the flat sheet needs continuous support from boarding or plywood sheets, the system has largely been superseded by the use of CORRUGATED or other PROFILED SHEET metal roofing, which is self-supporting between PURLINS (*see figure*).

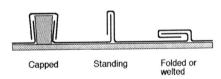

Capped   Standing   Folded or welted

Standing seam

standing-wave tube *Same as* IMPEDANCE TUBE.

standpipe A vertical pipe connected to an underground water pipe, and fitted with a tap. Used for general outdoor watering, or for fire fighting. In fire fighting, a removable standpipe can be connected to an underground *hydrant*.

staple A loop of bent wire, sharpened to two points, to be used as a fastener.

star connection In THREE-PHASE electrical systems, a means of obtaining or supplying PHASE voltages by means of a common connection (star) point for one terminal of each of the phase windings or loads. The phase voltages are $1/\sqrt{3}$ of the line voltages. The conductor connected to the common point is often called the *neutral* and results in a four-wire system. In a *balanced* three-phase system the neutral current is zero. *Also called a* WYE (Y) CONNECTION. *See also* DELTA CONNECTION.

star–delta connection Connection of a three-phase, four-wire (star, or wye) supply to a three-wire (delta) load. Each leg of the load is subject to a higher voltage than in a DELTA–STAR CONNECTION (*see figure*).

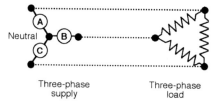

Three-phase   Three-phase
supply   load

Star–delta connection

starter *(a)* A device for starting an electric motor and enabling it to accelerate to operating speed. The starter limits the heavy current which would otherwise be drawn by some types of motor when starting. *(b)* A device for electrically heating the electrodes of a fluorescent lamp, to enable them to emit electrons at a sufficient rate to start the discharge process.

starved joints Glued joints that do not contain enough adhesive, due to the use of insufficient adhesive, excessive pressure, or adhesive of inadequate viscosity. *Also called hungry joints.*

static friction The limiting FRICTION when the body just starts to move.

static head The energy possessed by a liquid due to its elevation.

static load A load which is not a DYNAMIC LOAD, *i.e.* a normal DEAD or SUPERIMPOSED LOAD.

static moment A term used for the first MOMENT OF AN AREA.

static penetration test A PENETRATION TEST in which the testing device is pushed into the soil by a measurable force, as opposed to a DYNAMIC PENETRATION TEST

which employs a specified number of blows with a standard hammer.

static regain The regain of static pressure in accordance with BERNOUILLI'S THEOREM in an air stream contained in a duct after its velocity has been reduced by expansion of area or by the delivery of some of the air to a branch duct.

static smoke exhaust *Same as* SMOKE VENTING. *See also* DYNAMIC SMOKE EXHAUST.

statically determinate structure A structure that can be solved by the use of STATICS alone. *Also called an isostatic structure.* A statically determinate structure must have the appropriate number of members in accordance with MÖBIUS' LAW. If a structural member or restraint is removed, it becomes a MECHANISM; if one is added, it becomes a STATICALLY INDETERMINATE STRUCTURE.

statically indeterminate structure A structure that cannot be solved by the use of statics alone, unlike a STATICALLY DETERMINATE STRUCTURE. It is necessary in addition to consider its elastic deformation, as in the MATRIX-DISPLACEMENT METHOD or the *matrix-stiffness method*; or to consider its collapse mechanism, as in LIMIT DESIGN. *Also called a hyperstatic structure.*

statics The branch of the science of mechanics that deals with forces in equilibrium; as opposed to dynamics. The condition of plane static equilibrium is generally expressed in terms of three equations:

$$\Sigma H = 0$$

$$\Sigma V = 0$$

$$\Sigma M = 0$$

which means that the forces are zero in the *horizontal* and *vertical* directions, and the *moments* about any one chosen point are zero. If a structure can be solved with these equations alone, it is called STATICALLY DETERMINATE. If there are more unknown structural restraints than can be solved by these equations, it is STATICALLY INDETERMINATE.

statistical energy analysis (SEA) A method of analysing the transfer of vibrational energy from one part of a structure to another.

statistics Numerical data systematically collected; the science of collecting and interpreting numerical data. *See also* CHI-SQUARE TEST, GAUSSIAN CURVE, LAW OF LARGE NUMBERS, POPULATION, PROBABILITY, SAMPLE *and* STANDARD DEVIATION.

stator The stationary part of an electric motor or generator.

staunchion *Same as* STANCHION.

stave *(a)* A vertical plank, particularly in a traditional Scandinavian wooden church. *(b)* A narrow board used to build up a curved surface. *(c)* A rounded wooden step in a ladder.

STD *Abbreviation for* Subscriber Trunk Dialling, the now universal system of dialling long-distance telephone calls without the intervention of an operator.

STE systems *See* SOLAR THERMAL ELECTRIC SYSTEMS.

steady-state condition The condition of a heat-flow system or electrical circuit, after the initial effects of an impulse have settled down. Immediately after an impulse, heat or electrical energy may be stored within the system, but in the steady state there is no further storage, and the input of energy equals the output. Building heat loss calculations often assume steady state and use this calculation method. *See also* DYNAMIC RESPONSE.

steam Water converted into an invisible vapour by heating it above its boiling point. Steam containing some condensed water vapour becomes visible as a white mist.

steam boiler A boiler in which water is raised to or above saturation temperature at a desired pressure and the resulting steam is drawn off for use in process or heating equipment.

steam curing Accelerating the CURING of precast concrete or some adhesives by exposing it to steam in an oven at ordinary pressure, or at high pressure in an AUTOCLAVE.

steatite *Same as* TALC.

steel A malleable alloy of iron with a carbon content between 0.1 and 1.7 per cent. Iron with a lower carbon content is classified as WROUGHT IRON, and iron with a higher carbon content as CAST IRON. Prior to the invention of the BESSEMER PROCESS, steel could only be produced at great expense. ALLOY STEEL contains other elements in addition to carbon. *See also* ALPHA IRON, ANNEALING, AUSTENITE, CEMENTITE, FERRITE, GAMMA IRON, HIGH-SPEED STEEL, HIGH-STRENGTH STEEL, MARTENSITE, NORMALISING, OPEN-HEARTH PROCESS, PERLITE, PHASE DIAGRAM, QUENCHING, REINFORCEMENT FOR CONCRETE, STAINLESS STEEL *and* TEMPERING.

steel concrete Obsolete term for RE-INFORCED CONCRETE.

steel frame A FRAME assembled from structural steel members.

steel reinforcement *See* REINFORCED CONCRETE.

steel sheet *See* SHEET *and* CORRUGATED SHEET.

steelyard An instrument for weighing, which consists of a lever with unequal arms, with a single weight moving along a graduated scale. It was the type of balance used in Ancient Rome.

Stefan–Boltzmann law Derived by two Austrian physicists in the late nineteenth century. The total radiation from a BLACK BODY is proportional to the fourth power of the absolute temperature, or σT^4, where T is the temperature in degrees Kelvin, and σ is a constant which equals 5.67×10^{-8} W/m^{2}K^4. It also depends on the EMISSIVITY of the surface.

stemwall US term for the vertical part of a concrete or masonry retaining wall.

STEP *Abbreviation for* STandard for the Exchange of Product data. A standards development effort within the International Organisation for Standardisation (ISO).

steradian (sr) Unit of solid angle. 1 steradian is the SOLID ANGLE which, having its vertex in the centre of a sphere, cuts off an area of the surface of the sphere equal to that of the radius squared. A sphere subtends 4π steradians.

stereochemistry The study of the spatial arrangements of atoms in complex molecules.

stereogram A drawing or photograph that can be viewed three-dimensionally. One common method is to superimpose one print of a STEREOSCOPIC pair in one colour on the other in a different colour, and to view the composite picture through two appropriately coloured glasses.

stereographic projection Two-dimensional representation of the surface of a sphere. It is a PERSPECTIVE PROJECTION, whose perspective centre is on the point of the sphere diametrically opposite to the point where the pictorial plane touches the sphere (*see figure*). It has the remarkable property that all arcs of GREAT CIRCLES and SMALL CIRCLES are shown either as arcs of circles or as straight lines. Hence it is used for the analysis of SUNLIGHT PENETRATION. *See also* GLOBOSCOPE.

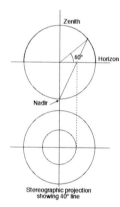

Stereographic projection showing 40° line

Stereographic projection

stereography The science of PERSPECTIVE PROJECTION.

stereolithography A three-dimensional computer output process that produces a solid plastic model.

stereometry Solid geometry.

stereophonic sound Sound reproduced from two channels, through two or more loudspeakers, which gives the illusion of auditory perspective.

stereopsis *See* STEREOSCOPIC VISION.

stereoscope An instrument for viewing a stereoscopic pair of photographs three-dimensionally. It consists of two lenses set at the correct distance apart to correspond with the separation of the STEREOSCOPIC CAMERA lenses.

stereoscopic camera A camera designed to give two displaced images (*called a stereoscopic pair*) by means of two matched lenses and shutters, so that the pair when viewed by both human eyes in a *stereoscope* gives a three-dimensional view of the object photographed.

stereoscopic vision The three-dimensional vision (*stereopsis*) due to the eyes being set a small distance apart.

stereotomy The science of making sections of solid bodies.

stereotype The printing process in which a solid plate of typemetal, cast from a papier-maché mould taken from the surface of a *forme* of type, is used for printing, instead of the forme itself. Hence something which is repeated constantly without change, like so many printed sheets run off the same stereotype. *See also* MATRIX *(d)*.

Stevenson screen A fully ventilated louvred enclosure used to measure the temperature of air in the shade. The enclosure is usually mounted at a height of 1.2–1.8 m above the ground.

stiffener A small member added to a thin section to prevent BUCKLING, *e.g.* an angle welded or riveted to the web of a deep steel or aluminium girder, which strengthens the web plate against buckling in diagonal compression due to the shear force.

stiff-jointed frame *Same as* RIGID FRAME.

stiffness Resistance to deformation. In rigid frames the flexural stiffness, which determines the moment distribution between members, is defined as EI/L, where E is Young's modulus, I is the second moment of area, and L is the effective length.

stiffness method *Same as* MATRIX-DISPLACEMENT METHOD.

stilb An obsolete unit for LUMINANCE. 1 stilb = 10 000 cd/m².

S-tile A strongly curved PAN TILE.

stile *(a)* A vertical member at the outer edge of a window, door or lift car frame. *(b)* A set of steps for crossing over a fence or a low wall.

still A vessel for the distillation of liquids.

stilt house A house built on stilts, to allow passage of air under the floor, and to provide shaded storage or living space. It is a traditional form of construction in many hot-humid countries.

stirrup In concrete construction, reinforcement to resist shear. It is normally a bar of U-shape, properly anchored to the longitudinal steel and placed perpendicular to it.

stock brick The brick type that is most widely used in any particular region.

stock size A size that is generally available from warehouse stock, and does not have to be especially ordered.

Stokes' law A formula developed by G. G. Stokes in 1851 for the velocity of sedimentation (or settlement) of spherical particles in a liquid. From the observed terminal velocity the particle diameter, and thus the SPECIFIC SURFACE, may be derived:

$$ d = \sqrt{\left(\frac{18\mu z}{\gamma_s - \gamma_l} t \right)} $$

where d is the particle diameter, z is the depth to which it has settled, t is the time taken for it to settle, μ is the viscosity of the liquid (for water at 20°C, 1 centipoise, or 1 mN.s/m^2) and γ_s and γ_l are the specific gravity of the solids (generally assumed to be 2.7) and of the liquid (1.0 for water). The sample is taken with a pipette at a depth z after a time t, and the amount of solid is measured. *See* PARTICLE-SIZE ANALYSIS.

stone *(a)* Natural stone; *see* ASHLAR, COARSE AGGREGATE, ROCK *and* RUBBLE. *(b)* A whetstone, usually of CARBORUNDUM, for sharpening tools. *(c)* Crystalline inclusion in glass.

stone sand Granular material in the particle-size range of sand, made from stone. It may be a quarry by-product, or deliberately manufactured.

stone slabs or slates Thin-bedded slabs of stone, generally limestone or sandstone, which are used as a roof covering, like SLATES. They were widely used in Europe in the Middle Ages in regions where they existed, but slates were not available until clay tile manufacture became common. Their use is rare today because their greater weight requires a heavier roof structure. Stone slates, being sedimentary rocks, split along their bedding planes, unlike true SLATES which, being metamorphic, split along their cleavage planes.

stone, cast *Same as* ARTIFICIAL STONE.

stonechips Broken stone used for road metal and for the COARSE AGGREGATE of concrete.

stopping Filling cracks and nail holes with putty before painting.

storage device Any device used for the storage of computer information in either MAIN MEMORY or in a backing store.

storage water heater *See* WATER HEATER, STORAGE.

storey In Europe and Australia the first floor or storey is normally the one above the ground floor. In the USA this is normally called the second story, the ground floor being the first story. Moreover, in large buildings the level of the 'ground' floor may depend on the door chosen. The terms 'floor' and 'storey' are therefore being displaced by *level*, level 1 being the lowest level served by a stair or lift (elevator); this is usually below ground.

storey height The vertical distance from the finished floor on one storey to the finished floor on the storey above.

storeypost A column, generally of timber, which rests on the floor structure and supports the beam of the floor above. (Steel and concrete columns are usually continuous through more than one storey.)

storm door An extra door for protection against bad weather.

storm drain Drain that carries only rainwater, as opposed to a SOIL DRAIN, *sanitary drain*, or SEWER.

storm window An additional window sash, generally placed on the outside of the existing window, particularly as a protection against heavy rain.

stormwater Water deposited on the ground by rainfall. In older cities it was drained in the general sewer with the SEWAGE, but modern practice uses a separate *stormwater drainage system* whose effluent requires less or no treatment.

story US spelling of STOREY.

STP *Abbreviation for* Standard Temperature and Pressure, which is 0°C and 1 atm. (101.325 kPa).

straight arch *Same as* FLAT ARCH.

straight grain Timber grain that is straight and in line with the axis of the piece, not *sloping*. *See also* FIGURE.

straight-line theory A theory based on a linear relationship; specifically, a structural theory based on HOOKE'S LAW.

straightedge A long piece of wood or metal whose edges are true and parallel. It is used for setting out, and for testing the accuracy of straight lines in buildings.

strain Change in the dimensions or shape of a body per unit length or angle. A *shear strain* is a distortion caused by shear STRESSES. A *direct strain* is an elongation or shortening caused by tensile or compressive stresses respectively. Strains may be ELASTIC or INELASTIC.

strain energy Mechanical ENERGY stored up in a stressed material. The elastic strain energy equals the work done by the external forces in producing the strains, and it is recoverable. It is divided into strain energy due to direct forces, shear forces, bending moments and twisting moments.

strain energy method The oldest method for the solution of STATICALLY INDETERMINATE STRUCTURES, published by the Italian engineer A. Castigliano in 1870. It is based on the assumption that the structure optimises its STRAIN ENERGY.

strain gauge An instrument for measuring strain, *also called* an *extensometer* or *tensometer. See* ELECTRIC RESISTANCE STRAIN GAUGE, HUGGENBERGER TENSOMETER, DEMEC STRAIN GAUGE, ACOUSTIC STRAIN GAUGE *and* CAPACITANCE STRAIN GAUGE.

strain hardening Increase in strength and hardness due to COLD WORKING.

strain rosette Device measuring strain at one point in three directions. The unknown quantities are the magnitude of the two (mutually perpendicular) PRINCIPAL STRESSES and their direction. If all three are unknown, then three measurements are required at each point. Strain rosettes are usually arranged along 60° (equilateral triangle), or two at right angles and the third at 45°.

strand Wires twisted around a centre wire or core; a TENDON made in the form of a strand.

S-trap A plumbing TRAP constructed with the inlet and outlet legs vertical. The shape of the trap resembles the letter 'S' on its side.

strata title A form of TITLE that enables each occupancy in a group to be separately owned. The boundaries between occupancies may be vertical or horizontal, and parts of the property are held in common for access or use by all the owners. *See also* CONDOMINIUM, HOME UNIT *and* OYO.

stratification The development of an equilibrium state in which horizontal layers form in a substance, for example hot water forming a layer above (denser) cold water in a storage water heater.

stratosphere *See* ATMOSPHERIC LAYERS.

straw bale A type of wall construction using baled straw, covered by stucco. The material is claimed to be low in cost, highly insulating and environmentally sustainable.

streamline flow Fluid flow that is continuous, *steady* and *laminar*, as in a viscous fluid. The upper limit is REYNOLDS' CRITICAL VELOCITY, above which it becomes TURBULENT FLOW, *i.e.* unsteady and eddying.

street furniture Civic accessories such as seating, rubbish bins, bollards and signage used in public places.

strength *See* LIMITING STRENGTH OF MATERIAL, STRESS *and* TESTING MACHINE.

strength of materials A conventional sub-division of the theory of structures, which deals with the calculation of stresses and strains due to tension, compression, shear, torsion and flexure, and any combination thereof. The *theory of structures* proper is then considered to cover the stresses and strains in structural members when they are combined into trusses, frames, etc. *See also* MATERIALS SCIENCE.

strength reduction factor *Same as* CAPACITY REDUCTION FACTOR.

stress Internal force per unit area, considering an infinitesimally small part of a body. (Dimensionally the same as PRESSURE and measured in the same units, Pa or N/m² and their multiples.) When the forces are tangential to the plane, they are called *shear stresses*; when they are perpendicular to the plane, they are called *direct stresses*. Direct stresses may be *compressive* or *tensile*, depending on whether they act towards or away from the plane of separation. The deformation caused by the stress is called STRAIN.

stress analysis *See* EXPERIMENTAL STRESS ANALYSIS *and* PRINCIPAL STRESSES.

stress circle *See* MOHR CIRCLE.

stress concentration A local high stress, or crowding of the ISOSTATIC LINES, caused by a sudden change in section, such as occurs at a NOTCH, the base of a screw thread, or a hole (*see figure*). Stress concentrations are particularly serious in brittle materials where they may lead to premature failure. In plastic materials local plastic yielding reduces the high stresses at the point of concentration, and raises them over a wider zone. Stress concentrations are shown up particularly well by PHOTOELASTICITY.

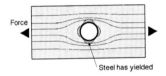

Stress concentration

stress corrosion Corrosion of a metal, accelerated by its being highly stressed.

stress diagram *See* STRESS–STRAIN DIAGRAM.

stress relaxation *See* RELAXATION OF STEEL.

stress relieving Heating of a metal or alloy, followed by slow cooling, to relieve internal stresses built up by hot or cold working. *See* ANNEALING, NORMALISING *and* TEMPERING.

stress trajectory *Same as* ISOSTATIC LINE.

Stresscoat A trade name for a BRITTLE COATING.

stressed-skin construction A form of construction in which the outer skin acts with the framework to contribute to the membrane and flexural strength of the unit, instead of being merely a cladding which protects the inside from the weather. The term was originally applied to aircraft frames, and later to prefabricated houses in LIGHT-GAUGE STRUCTURES. *See also* GEODETIC CONSTRUCTION *and* SANDWICH PANEL.

stress-grading of timber *(a)* Grading timber mechanically into several cate-gories of strength. The most common machine is based on an empirical relation between the strength and the deflection of timber. Each piece of timber is deflected at several points along its length, and the deflection category marked by means of a spot of dye. The timber is then classified by its colour markings. *(b)* Grading by visual inspection, observing knots and imperfections in the grain of the timber.

stress–strain diagram The diagram obtained by plotting the stresses in a test specimen against the strains (*see figure*, which shows the diagram for mild steel). It is used to assess the structural suitability of materials, since it shows the strength of the material, its elastic and inelastic deformation, and its ductility or brittleness. The *load–extension diagram* has the same shape.

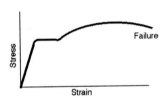

Stress–strain diagram

stretcher A brick, block or stone laid with its length parallel to the wall (*see figure*). Usually stretchers are interspersed with HEADERS to achieve a proper BOND.

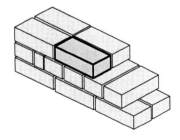

Stretcher

stretcher bond A bond in which all bricks are laid as STRETCHERS. It is the bond used in CAVITY WALLS and half-brick thickness walls.

strike The recess in a door JAMB into which the bolt of a lock or latch engages.

strikeoff *Same as* SCREED.

string In computing, a sequence of CHARACTERS.

string course A continuous projecting horizontal band set in the surface of a wall, sometimes moulded. Its function is partly decorative and partly to throw the water off the facade.

string polygon *Same as* LINK POLYGON.

stringer *(a)* A horizontal piece of steel or timber, connecting uprights in a framework and supporting the floor. *(b)* The inclined member that supports the treads and risers of a stair.

strip A metal strip is narrower than SHEET metal.

strip footing A footing for a wall, or a joint footing for a line of columns.

stroboscope Instrument for the inspection of objects rotating at high speed. It can be timed to light up the object only when it is in the same position, so that it appears stationary.

struck joint A mortar JOINT IN BRICKWORK (where there is an illustration), formed with a recess at the bottom of the joint, by pressing the trowel in at the lower edge. This work can be done as the wall goes up, and it is therefore more durable than POINTING. A *struck joint* is suitable only for interior work because it would collect water at the lower edge. For exterior work, a *weather-struck joint* or *weather joint* is produced by pressing the trowel in at the upper edge, so that the recess is formed at the top of the joint, and the water is thrown off the joint.

structural failure *See* FAILURE.

structural frame *See* FRAME.

structural insulated panel (SIP) An engineered laminate (a kind of SANDWICH PANEL) with a foam core 100–200 mm thick (4–8 in.) with a structural facing on each side. Common types of facings are plasterboard and/or structural wood sheathing such as plywood and oriented strand board (OSB).

structural model analysis *See* DIRECT MODEL ANALYSIS *and* INDIRECT STRUCTURAL MODEL ANALYSIS.

structural silicone glazing Glazing whose edges are fixed to the face of its supporting frame with a SILICONE adhesive, rather than being restrained by GLAZING BEADS.

structural steel STEEL rolled to one of the standard cross-sectional shapes, ready for fabrication into a structure.

structureborne sound Sound resulting from direct excitation of part of the structure of a building, as opposed to sound passing from the air in the building to the structure (AIRBORNE SOUND). Structureborne sound may be a result of TRANSIENT forces, such as the impact of a closing door or footsteps on a floor, or it may be from steady state excitation, such as that from a fan, pump or compressor attached to the structure. *See also* DISCONTINUOUS CONSTRUCTION.

strut A compression member that is liable to BUCKLE; the opposite of a tie.

stub mortise A MORTISE that does not pass entirely through a timber.

stub tenon A TENON cut to fit into a STUB MORTISE, or a short tenon used at the lower end of a post to prevent it from slipping out of position.

stucco External plastering. The term originally had a wider meaning, and in historical books it is used also for interior and decorated work. *See also* ROUGHCAST.

stud *(a)* An upright timber. *(b)* A threaded rod or bolt without a head. It may be fixed to a steel frame by resistance *welding*, or a pointed stud may be shot with a *stud gun* into timber, masonry or concrete.

stud wall A timber-framed wall. The studs, or vertical members, are usually spaced at 300–600 mm (12–24 in.) centres. Also a similar wall built with *steel studs*.

stud-and-track wall system Partition wall system using steel studs located in steel channel-section tracks top and bottom. The studs are spaced out to suit the sizes of the plasterboard sheets, which are fixed to them with adhesive and screws.

stuffiness A feeling of being in a close or ill-ventilated room. Thomas Bedford carried out experiments in the 1930s, which suggest that the sensation was more likely to occur in warm rooms, in the absence of ventilation touching the thermal receptors in the skin. By contrast, the sensation of FRESHNESS is associated with cooler conditions, and with sensations recognisable as those of touch, caused by air.

stuffy Unpleasant condition of air in a room; a sensation of excessive warmth associated with perceived lack of air movement and possibly an unpleasant odour. *See also* STUFFINESS.

stump A short post of timber or concrete, used to support a timber floor a short distance above ground level. *See also sleeper pier.*

stylus A hand-held pointer for computer input, such as a DIGITISER pen or LIGHT PEN.

styrene–butadiene coating A lacquer-type paint, which can be used on masonry and wood.

sub-basement A basement, other than the first one below ground level.

subcontractor A contractor whose contract is with the general contractor, not the owner.

subdivision The division of land into allotments with separate titles approved by a statutory authority.

subgrade The natural ground below a foundation, road or airport runway.

subjective brightness The subjective impression of the luminance of a surface. It will depend not only on the *objective* LUMINANCE, but also on the rest of the visual field, and on the previous exposure of the visual system. *Also called* LUMINOSITY.

sublimate or sublime Solid obtained by the direct condensation of vapour without passing through the liquid state. This is possible only for materials whose melting point and boiling point are very close together.

sublimation The process whereby a substance goes from the solid to vapour state without the liquid, as in the loss of TUNGSTEN from lamp FILAMENTS.

submerged-arc welding ARC WELDING, using a powdered flux deposited around the arc. The weld metal is supplied by a continuously-fed wire which also carries the welding current. Because of the equipment involved, and the fact that the arc is obscured from view, it is used for automatic welding. *See also* SHIELDED-ARC WELDING.

submersible pump Pump and electric motor sealed in a single unit, suitable for locating under water or other liquid. It provides FLOODED SUCTION to the pump inlet. Used to eject water from drainage sumps, etc.

subsidence Settlement caused by mining operations.

subsoil The soil below the TOPSOIL.

subsonic flow Airflow at a speed below the speed of sound. Its MACH NUMBER is less than 1.

sub-standard (in the context of standardisation and testing) An item used as a reference against which to check normal production items. It will have been calibrated against a STANDARD *(b)*. The official standards of length, mass, luminance, etc. are normally held in national laboratories, and sub-standard items are used for day-to-day calibration.

substation An enclosure for a TRANSFORMER (and associated switch and control gear) that changes the voltage of an AC electricity supply up or down.

substratum (substrate) A part that lies beneath and supports another.

substructure The foundation and footings, as opposed to the SUPERSTRUCTURE.

subsurface exploration Determination of ground conditions beneath a building to provide data for the design of the foundations.

sub-woofer *See* WOOFER.

suction line *(a)* The pipeline connecting a refrigeration evaporator to the compressor. *(b)* Any pipeline on the inlet side of a pump in which the fluid is below atmospheric pressure.

suction rate The amount of water absorbed by a brick in one minute. *Also called absorption rate.*

suction, wind A negative WIND PRESSURE.

sulfur US spelling for SULPHUR.

sullage Domestic wastes from bath, basins, showers, laundries and kitchens, including floor wastes from these sources.

sulphur A non-metallic element of yellow colour. Its chemical symbol is S, its atomic number is 16, its atomic weight is 32.06, and its valency is 2, 4 or 6. α-sulphur crystallises in rhombic form, has a lemon-yellow colour, melts at 112.8°C and has a specific gravity of 2.07. βsulphur crystallises in monoclinic form, has a deeper yellow colour, melts at 119.0 °C and has a specific gravity of 1.96. *Also spelled sulfur* (USA). *See also* OXIDES OF SULPHUR.

sulphur lamp An electric DISCHARGE LAMP using sulphur in a quartz glass sphere rotating in a microwave field.

sulphuric anhydride Sulphur trioxide (SO_3). It combines with water to form *sulphuric acid* (H_2SO_4).

summer (*also spelled sommer*) *See* BREASTSUMMER.

summer comfort zone *See* COMFORT ZONE.

summer wood Dense wood formed in summer, as opposed to EARLY WOOD.

sump Recess in the surface of a floor or roof, or in the bottom of a pit, into which water collects before entering a drainage pipe. *See also* RAINWATER HEAD, which is similar to a sump in a flat roof, but located outside the wall line.

sun bearing *See* AZIMUTH *and* HORIZONTAL SHADOW ANGLE.

sunlight Direct radiation from the sun. Strictly it includes only the visible portion of the spectrum, but the context may indicate that the whole solar spectrum is intended.

sunlight penetration The penetration of sunlight through windows can be predicted by model analysis with a SOLARSCOPE or HELIODON, by graphical methods using a STEREOGRAPHIC PROJECTION or by means of a computer program. *See also* PASSIVE SYSTEMS *and* DIRECT SOLAR GAIN.

sunlighting Lighting making use of sunlight directly, or indirectly by reflection. Direct use can be by refractor and reflector systems incorporated into the building, such as a LIGHT PIPE.

sunpath chart A chart that shows the ALTITUDE and the AZIMUTH of the sun at a particular location throughout the year. It can be used for the design of sunshades in conjunction with a SHADOW ANGLE PROTRACTOR.

sunroom *See* SOLARIUM.

sunshading Controlling the entry of the sun into a building by means of LOUVRES, projecting EAVES, projecting balconies, vertical slats or specially designed sunshading devices. As they are prominent features on the facade of the building, their visual aspect must be considered as well as their technical efficiency.

super foot *Same as* SQUARE FOOT.

supercomputer Term used for the fastest computers.

supercooling Cooling a liquid below its normal freezing point. In the case of a mixture, cooling below the LIQUIDUS LINE in a phase diagram.

super-flat floor A floor laid to much higher flatness tolerances than normal, usually for automated storage systems.

superheated steam Steam whose temperature exceeds its SATURATION TEMPERATURE.

superimposed load The load superimposed on the DEAD LOAD of the building. The term is generally synonymous with LIVE LOAD, although a distinction is sometimes made between the superimposed dead load caused by movable partitions, etc. and the live load caused by people.

superposition 'If a material is elastic and obeys HOOKE'S LAW, the relation between load and deformation is linear, and the effect of the various loads can therefore be computed separately and subsequently added, or superimposed on one another.' The *principle of superposition* greatly simplifies the design of elastic structures. It cannot, however, be used where the load–deformation relation is non-linear, as in some elastic problems relating to suspension structures or to buckling.

supersonic flow Air flow at a speed above the speed of sound. Its MACH NUMBER exceeds 1.

superstructure The structure above the main supporting level, as opposed to the foundation or *substructure*.

supplementary angle The difference between a given angle and 180° (the given angle should be less than 180°). *See also* COMPLEMENTARY ANGLE.

supplementary lighting Addition to the quantity or quality of general lighting, usually for specific work requirements.

supply air The air supplied to a space from an air conditioning plant at a thermal condition suitable to produce the required room condition.

support area A non-assigned functional

space catering for activities which complement the principal work activity.

support moment The negative bending moment at a fixed-ended or continuous support.

suppressor *See* ARRESTER.

surcharge *(a)* Overflow from a sewer or drain caused by overloading or blockage. Usually used in reference to wet weather infiltration or inflow. *(b)* Earth supported by a retaining wall, at a level above the top of the wall.

surface conductance A measure of heat transmission from air to the surface of an envelope element, or from the element to air, measured in W/m^2K. (Outside designated h_o and inside h_i.)

surface density The mass of a building element (wall, partition or floor) per unit surface area, measured in kg/m^2.

surface model In computer graphics: a model in which solid objects are defined by their surfaces, as opposed to SOLID MODELLING and WIREFRAME models.

surface mounted Mounted *on* the surface (of a wall, ceiling, etc.) and therefore projecting out rather than set in flush.

surface of revolution A surface generated by rotation. For example, a *sphere* is generated by the rotation of a circle, a *paraboloid* by a parabola, and an *ellipsoid* by an ellipse. A *hyperboloid of revolution* (*see figure*), is generated by a straight line at an angle to a vertical axis. *See also* TORUS.

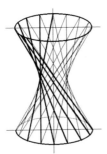

Surface of revolution

surface of translation A surface generated by the motion of a plane curve parallel to itself over another curve. A *cylinder* (*see* CROSS VAULT) is generated by a curve, such as a circle, moving along

a straight line. A HYPERBOLIC PARABOLOID is generated by an inclined straight line moving along two other inclined straight lines, or alternatively by a convex parabola moving along a concave parabola. An ELLIPTICAL PARABOLOID is generated by a convex parabola moving over another convex parabola. A *parabolic conoid* (*see figure*) is generated by a straight line moving over a flat parabola at one end, and a more strongly curved one at the other.

Surface of translation

surface resistance A measure of resistance to heat flow between surfaces of an envelope element and the adjacent air, measured in m^2K/W, the reciprocal of SURFACE CONDUCTANCE. (Outside designated R_{so} and inside R_{si}.)

surface retarder *See* RETARDER *and* EXPOSED AGGREGATE.

surface spread of flame *See* FLAME SPREAD.

surface tension A property possessed by liquid surfaces whereby they appear to be covered with a thin elastic membrane in a state of tension. It is due to the unbalanced molecular cohesive forces near the surface. CAPILLARY ACTION is due to surface tension.

surface water The run-off after rain, as opposed to soil or waste water. The two are often drained separately, and the surface water held in a DETENTION BASIN or discharged at a suitable place in the open to save sewer capacity.

surface waterproofer Waterproofing concrete and other materials by painting a liquid on the surface, as opposed to an INTEGRAL WATERPROOFER. The liquid may be colourless, or a pigmented paint. Many surface waterproofers contain silicone or epoxy resins.

surface-based 3-D graphics A SURFACE MODEL, which treats objects as only skin deep. The objective of surface-based techniques is to create the illusion of photorealism without worrying about the internal features of objects in a scene.

surface-water drain *Same as* STORM DRAIN.

surge *(a)* (electrical) A short duration high voltage condition. A surge lasts for several cycles where a transient lasts less than one half cycle. Often confused with *transient*. *(b)* (hydraulic) A short duration increase in pressure in a water piping system, due to the rapid closing of a tap. It is caused by the deceleration of a mass of moving water in the pipe. In extreme cases it results in WATER HAMMER.

surveyor's level *See* CLINOMETER, DUMPY LEVEL *and* QUICKSET LEVEL.

suspended absorber A prefabricated sound absorber suspended within a room to improve its acoustic performance. It may be hung from the ceiling, from the structural system, or from a secondary suspension system, such as stretched wires. *See also* ACOUSTIC REFLECTOR *and* ACOUSTICAL CLOUD, whose purpose is to *reflect*.

suspended ceiling A FALSE CEILING suspended from the floor above.

suspended formwork Formwork that is suspended from the supports for the concrete floor to be cast, and not propped from below.

suspended luminaire A luminaire, hung from a ceiling by rigid or flexible supports. There is a space, the CEILING CAVITY, between the luminaire and the ceiling.

suspended solids Small particles such as silt, suspended but not dissolved in water. They cause turbidity in the water, may interfere with industrial water uses and, depending on the material, may be harmful to health. Suspended materials can be removed by FILTRATION, or will eventually settle out if the water remains still (but will form a slimy layer in the bottom of the container).

suspended span A short span freely supported from the ends of cantilevers, as in a GERBER BEAM.

suspension cable A cable hanging freely. If carrying mainly its own weight, it assumes the shape of a CATENARY. If carrying mainly a load uniformly distributed in plan it assumes the shape of a *parabola*.

suspension roof A roof supported by suspension cables (*see figure*). The simplest geometric forms are: *(a)* a dished DOME, *i.e.* a series of cables hanging from an outer compression ring and terminating at a central tension ring; *(b)* a dished cylindrical shell (BARREL VAULT), which has parallel cables anchored to the banked seats; and *(c)* a saddle shell (HYPERBOLIC PARABOLOID) whose cables are anchored to crossed arches.

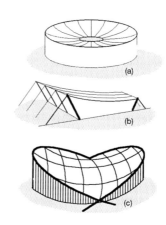

Suspension roof

sustainable Strategies for building and living that are capable of being maintained for a long period of time so that resources are not depleted or permanently damaged.

sustainable design Development that meets the need of the present without compromising the ability of future generations to meet their own needs (Brundtland Commission).

swage The spread of a tooth on each side of a timber saw to provide a clearance for the blade. *Also called set.*

swale A shallow depression in the ground, with a gentle slope, and usually covered in grass, to allow stormwater to run over the surface in a controlled manner without erosion.

swallow tail *Same as* DOVETAIL.

swarf Particles of metal removed by drilling or machining. When drilling screw-holes in sheet metal roofing, hot swarf may damage the surface, and if it is allowed to remain and corrode, it will cause unsightly staining.

sway *See* SIDE-SWAY.

sway brace A diagonal member, or a pair of diagonals, designed to resist wind or other horizontal forces acting on a light structural frame. *See also* SHEAR WALL.

swell A temporary increase in the RMS value of the voltage of more than 10 per cent of the nominal voltage for durations from 0.5 cycle to one minute.

SWG *Abbreviation for* Standard Wire Gauge.

switch gear A group of switches, relays, circuit breakers, etc. used to control distribution of power to other distribution equipment and large loads.

switching (communications) *See* CIRCUIT SWITCHING *and* PACKET SWITCHING.

synchronisation Maintaining a constant phase relationship between AC signals.

synchronous Having the same periodicity or occurring at the same time. In power transmission, having voltage waveforms in phase. In computing, having BITS of data transmitted and received according to a common time base.

synchronous motor An AC motor whose speed is exactly proportional to the power input frequency.

synclastic A surface with positive GAUSSIAN CURVATURE.

synthetic mineral fibre (SMF) Fibre produced from molten mineral material such as glass or rock as used in FIBRE-GLASS and MINERAL WOOL.

synthetic render Polymer compounds that are weatherproof and impact resistant, which can be applied with a trowel in a thin layer (3–5 mm), especially to the outside surface of a concrete block wall, or external insulation slabs.

synthetic resin *See* RESIN.

synthetic stone *Same as* CAST STONE.

system building INDUSTRIALISED BUILDING in accordance with a CLOSED or an OPEN SYSTEM.

system furniture Modular office furniture elements with provision for integrated electrical and data reticulation, including desktops, shelving, drawers and vertical screens. They can be interconnected in a variety of combinations to create appro-priate individual or linked WORKSTATIONS *(a)*.

systematic error An error that is always in the same direction, and therefore cumulative, as opposed to a COMPENSATING ERROR.

Système International d'Unités *See* SI UNITS.

systems analysis The definition and interpretation of problems, particularly for computer-aided solution.

T

T *Abbreviation for tera*, a million million times, or 10^{12}.

T&G joint *Abbreviation for* TONGUE AND GROOVE JOINT.

T&M *Abbreviation for* a contracting method called Time and Materials.

table form A formwork system for casting the floors of a building, resembling a series of tables butted together. After the concrete has gained enough strength, the legs are lowered and the tables are transferred by crane or hoist to the next floor.

tablet *See* GRAPHICS TABLET.

tacheometer A surveying telescope with two additional cross hairs, which make it possible to determine distance from a staff intercept, without running a tape or chain along the ground (by *stadia telemetry*).

tack weld A weld not designed to carry a load, but to make a non-structural connection.

tactile paving Paving with a distinctive pattern of small protrusions, designed to be easily recognisable by visually impaired people. Different patterns are used to warn of approaching steps, kerbs, etc.

tail The built-in end of a cantilevered stone.

tailing in Fixing the end of a member that is cantilevered from a wall by laying stones or any heavy weight on it.

tailings Stones that do not pass through a screen used to separate particle sizes. Generally, a residue.

talc Acid metasilicate of magnesium

($H_2Mg_3Si_4O_{12}$). It is a soft mineral, with a soapy or greasy feel, which can be used for intricate carvings. *Also called soapstone* or *steatite*. Finely ground talc is called *French chalk*.

tamper *Same as* SCREED *(a)*.

tan *Abbreviation for* the TANGENT of an angle.

tangent *(a)* A straight line that just touches a curve at a single point, but does not intersect it. *See also* SECANT. *(b)* A CIRCULAR FUNCTION of an angle, the ratio of the side opposite to the angle in a right-angled triangle, to the adjacent side. *Abbreviated tan.*

tangent modulus of elasticity Many materials (*e.g.* concrete) do not conform strictly to HOOKE'S LAW because of deviations caused by INELASTIC behaviour. If the deviation is significant, it becomes necessary to define the MODULUS OF ELASTICITY as the tangent or secant of the STRESS–STRAIN CURVE.

tangential shrinkage The shrinkage of timber that is normally considered, *i.e.* in the direction tangential to the growth rings. *See also* RADIAL SHRINKAGE.

tangential stress A shear STRESS.

tap *(a)* (electrical) A connection point brought out of a transformer winding to permit changing the turns ratio. *(b)* (plumbing) A controlled water outlet. *Also called cock* or *faucet. (c)* (tool) A tool for cutting an internal screw thread.

tap switcher A voltage regulator that uses power semiconductors to switch TAPS of a transformer, thereby changing the turns ratio and adjusting output voltage.

tape drive A drive designed to read and write MAGNETIC TAPE. Tape drives are used primarily as archival storage devices. They are limited by sequential access of data, but provide a relatively inexpensive storage option for large amounts of data.

taper The gradual reduction in size, *e.g.* the narrowing of a column towards the top or the bottom.

tapered thread A standard screw thread used on pipes and their fittings to ensure watertight, steamtight or gastight joints. The taper is generally 1 in 16, that is, the threaded portion is part of a cone whose length is 16 times its diameter.

tapered washer A bevelled washer for

use with, for example, a rolled steel joist which has non-parallel flanges.

tar A bituminous substance obtained from the destructive distillation of coal. It has a lower melting point than ASPHALT.

TAR *Abbreviation for* Thermal Acceptance Ratio, a thermal index developed by the US Quartermaster General (1945), thought to be a precursor of the HSI, later developed by Belding and Hatch.

tare The weight of a vehicle, as distinct from its load.

tarmacadam *See* MACADAM.

tarpaulin A covering of canvas impregnated with tar or paint, used to protect materials or unfinished work against rain.

task lighting Lighting provided specifically over an area at which a visual task is expected to be performed, in addition to AMBIENT LIGHTING.

tatami The Japanese mat, which provides the MODULE for the design of traditional Japanese houses. Each room is an exact multiple of the size of the mat which measures approximately 2 m × 1 m (6 ft × 3 ft).

T-beam *(a)* In metal, a section shaped like the letter T. It is an I-BEAM with only one flange. *(b)* In concrete, the T-beam is commonly formed by the RIB and the portion of the floor slab above it. It is part of a MONOLITHic beam-and-slab floor, not a separate T-shaped beam. *See* EFFECTIVE FLANGE WIDTH *and* L-BEAM.

TCP/IP (Transfer Control Protocol/ Internet Protocol) A PACKET SWITCHING network communication protocol that is the basis for the Internet's communication processes.

TCT *Abbreviation for* Total Coated Thickness. In galvanised or coated metal products, the total thickness of the product including the coating. It is easier to measure than the BMT.

tee A fitting for joining three pipes, one at right angles to the others. Called a tee when applied to water or gas pipes, and a *square junction* when applied to drainage pipes. *See figure* under PIPE FITTINGS (water and gas).

Teflon Trade name for POLYTETRAFLUOROETHYLENE.

telecommuting The use of technology that enables home-based employees to link directly with the principal office workplace by telecommunications. *See also* HOME WORKING.

teleconferencing The interconnection of a number of participants at remote locations using telecommunication links so that information is shared in real time. Teleconferencing includes computer and video conferencing as well as hybrid configurations.

telemetry Measurement with the aid of intermediate means that permit the measurement to be interpreted remotely from the primary detector.

temper *(a)* To moisten and mix to its proper consistency, especially MORTAR for bricklaying and plastering, or BRICK EARTH prior to its manufacture into bricks. *(b)* To modify the heat-induced hardness of a material. *See* TEMPERED GLASS, TEMPERED HARDBOARD *and* TEMPERING.

tempera painting A mural painting technique widely used in the Middle Ages and the Renaissance, which uses transparent colours on GESSO. The powdered pigment is bound with egg or GUM ARABIC, and thinned with water.

temperature The degree of hotness or coldness, measured with reference to an arbitrary zero (CELSIUS SCALE and FAHRENHEIT SCALE), or with reference to ABSOLUTE ZERO (KELVIN or *Rankine* scale).

temperature gradient The change in temperature per unit length, *e.g.* through a wall which is warm on one side and cold on the other.

temperature interval Temperature difference or increment. Whilst temperature as a point on the scale is denoted as °C (degree Celsius), or °K (degree Kelvin), by convention a temperature interval (without specifying its position on the scale) is denoted as K (Kelvin), hence wherever temperature occurs in the denominator of an expression or unit, it is denoted by K. (Not in US practice.)

temperature inversion *See* INVERSION.

temperature movement Thermal expansion and contraction.

temperature reinforcement *Same as* DISTRIBUTION REINFORCEMENT.

temperature reset Controlled variation of a SET POINT to achieve a desired operating condition appropriate to a particular set of circumstances.

temperature stress A stress caused by a change in temperature. All materials expand with rising temperature and contract with falling temperature. Stresses are caused only if the movement is restrained.

tempered air Air whose temperature has been raised or lowered in an attempt to provide a measure of thermal comfort without removing or adding the full quantity of heat required to meet strictly defined comfort conditions.

tempered glass Glass prestressed by heating followed by QUENCHING (with air); the rapid cooling produces a compressively stressed surface layer, which more than doubles the strength of the glass. *Also called toughened glass. See also* SAFETY GLASS.

tempered hardboard HARDBOARD that has been treated during manufacture to improve water resistance and strength. Its density usually exceeds 1000 kg/m^3 (60 lb/ft^3).

tempering Heating hardened steel to a few hundred degrees and cooling it slowly to reduce the brittleness induced by the MARTENSITE. The steel loses some hardness and strength in the process. Many bright steels acquire a characteristic colour on tempering, caused by an oxide film, which can be used to determine the temperature to which they have been heated. For plain carbon tool steels, heated for a normal period, these are: straw 225 °C, yellow-brown 255 °C, redbrown 265 °C, purple 275 °C, violet 285 °C, dark blue 295 °C and light blue 310 °C. At higher temperatures the skin turns grey. *See also* ANNEALING.

template or templet A sheet or light frame of wood or metal, used for marking out work to be done, or as a guide for a cutting tool.

temporary threshold shift (TTS) When exposed to a loud sound a person's *threshold of audibility* increases over a period which may last for many hours.

tenacity A term generally synonymous with the ultimate tensile strength.

tenancy The premises to which a tenant has access under the terms of a LEASE agreement.

tenant The party to a LEASE agreement responsible for paying rent.

tenant lighting Electric lighting equipment operated by a building tenant where electricity consumed is separately metered and paid for by the tenant.

tenant small power Electric SMALL POWER supplied for office appliances used by a tenant and paid for directly by the tenant.

tender An offer to execute a specified amount of work for a rate or price.

tendon A bar, wire, strand or cable of high-tensile steel, used to impart PRESTRESS to concrete when the element is tensioned.

tenon A tongue that fits into a MORTISE.

tension A direct pull in line with the axis of the body, and therefore the direct opposite of *compression*.

tension coefficient A shorthand notation for force divided by length.

tension ring A ring that absorbs the horizontal component of the thrust in a DOME.

tension structure *See* PNEUMATIC STRUCTURE *and* SUSPENSION ROOF.

tension wood Abnormal wood that may be formed on the upper sides of branches and inclined stems of hardwood trees.

tensometer *Same as* STRAIN GAUGE.

tensotast A demountable STRAIN GAUGE with one fixed and one movable point which engage plugs glued to the structure under test.

tera Prefix meaning 10^{12}, a trillion, or one million million, used particularly in SI UNITS. *Abbreviated* T.

terabyte Roughly, a quantity of measurement that is over a trillion bytes. Specifically, a terabyte is 2^{40} bytes.

teraflops *Abbreviation for* one TRILLION FLoating-point OPerations per Second.

terminal *(a)* Computer workstation attached to a remote HOST. Terminals are not typically fully functional computers, but rather depend upon the host for most, if not all, processing tasks, therefore sometimes called *dumb terminals*. Terminals are primarily input/output devices for the remote host. *(b)* An end-point or interchange on a transport system.

terminal reheat The supply of heat to conditioned air before delivery to a space to bring it to a suitable condition for the thermal requirement to avoid overcooling the space.

termite An insect that shuns light, and is highly destructive to seasoned timber, especially soft wood. Australian cypress pine and several eucalypts are naturally resistant, but in the tropics and subtropics most timbers require protection by TERMITE SHIELDS or IMPREGNATION. Termites are killed by arsenic or CREOSOTE OIL. *Also called white ant.*

termite barrier A barrier to prevent termites travelling from the ground, through holes or cracks in a concrete floor slab, into a building. It may be a TERMITE SHIELD or a *chemical* barrier, by impregnating the soil with a *termiticide*; but many previously-used chemicals are now banned. Other methods include the use of a fine stainless steel mesh, or a layer of fine compacted granite.

termite shield A protective shield placed between the foundation piers and a timber floor (*see figure*), around pipes, etc. It usually consists of galvanised iron, bent down at the edges. Termites cannot stand daylight and they can only get past the inedible iron by building an earthlike shelter tube; this shows up on the metal cap. Moreover, termites are very reluctant to pass over the downward bend.

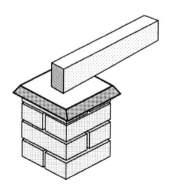

Termite shield

termiticide *See* TERMITE BARRIER.

terne coating A corrosion-protective coating for steel sheet used for roofing. It consists of 80–90 per cent lead and 10–20 per cent tin. Unlike *galvanising*, it does not provide GALVANIC PROTECTION.

terra cotta Burnt clay units for ornamental

work. Their colour varies from yellow to reddish brown. They are very durable, even when unglazed. The glazed terra cotta is called FAIENCE. *See also* CERAMIC VENEER.

terrace Originally a raised level earth surface for walking on sloping ground, sometimes provided with a balustrade. Hence an enclosed level platform in front of a house; a gallery or a balcony attached to a house; a row of houses on a raised platform; and any row of houses of uniform style.

terrazzo Marble-aggregate concrete that is either cast in place as a TOPPING or precast. It is subsequently ground smooth for decorative surfacing on floors or walls.

tessera A piece of glass or marble used to form a MOSAIC.

test cube or cylinder *See* CUBE STRENGTH *and* CYLINDER STRENGTH.

test pit Pit dug for SUBSURFACE EXPLORATION.

testing machine A machine used for loading test pieces, usually to destruction, to determine their *deformation* and *strength*.

TETD *Abbreviation for* Total Equivalent Temperature Difference, a notional temperature difference that includes daily average SOL-AIR TEMPERATURE effects and all other space heat gains, now replaced by the use of CLTD.

tetrahedron A regular POLYHEDRON bounded by four equilateral triangles. It has four vertices and six edges.

text editor Precursor of modern WORD PROCESSING PROGRAMS. Text editors provide primitive word processing capabilities, but none of the formatting tools expected of modern word processors.

texture brick *Same as* RUSTIC BRICK.

texture paint A paint that can be manipulated after application to give a textured finish.

tg Continental abbreviation for TANGENT.

thatch A roof covering of reed, straw or rushes. It has a high insulating value, but burns very easily. The fire risk can be somewhat reduced by soaking the thatch in a fire-resisting solution before laying.

the state postulate A statement that the thermodynamic state of a pure simple substance is fully determined by a know-

ledge of any two independent INTENSIVE PROPERTIES.

theatre dimmer *See* LAMP DIMMER.

theodolite A surveyor's instrument for measuring horizontal and vertical angles. It has a telescope rotating on a horizontal *(trunnion)* axis, to which is attached the vertical measuring circle. The trunnion axis is carried on a standard fixed to the upper plate, whose rotation relative to the lower plate measures the horizontal angles. The lower plate is fixed through levelling screws to a tripod. Modern theodolites almost invariably are capable of transiting about the trunnion axis, and in the USA the instrument is commonly called a TRANSIT. *See also* DUMPY LEVEL.

theorem of three moments A theorem, derived by the French mathematician B. P. E. Clapeyron in 1857, for calculating the redundant support moments in CONTINUOUS beams. Once these REDUNDANCIES have been determined, the problem becomes STATICALLY DETERMINATE.

therm An obsolete measure of thermal energy, equal to 100 000 BTU or 105.5 MJ.

thermal bridging A more general term that includes COLD BRIDGING, but also including warm climates, where air conditioned buildings may suffer (hot) thermal bridging effects.

thermal capacity A physical property of a body, the product of its mass and the specific heat capacity of its material (kg × J/kg.K). May be used for a multi-layer element, summing the capacities of all its material layers. In general, it may be used referring to a whole building, denoting its capacity to store heat. Loosely referred to also as *thermal mass*. The effect of thermal capacity is *thermal inertia*, a delay of heat flow. A heavy building (of 'massive' construction) would ensure a much more stable indoor environment than a lightweight one. *See also* TIME LAG.

thermal chimney A vertical duct attached to a building that employs buoyancy of heated air (STACK EFFECT) to drive a natural ventilation system.

thermal comfort A state of mind that expresses satisfaction (or the absence of dissatisfaction) with the thermal environmental conditions. *See* COMFORT ZONE *and* INDEX OF THERMAL COMFORT.

thermal conductance A thermal property of a body, given by the THERMAL CONDUCTIVITY of its material divided by its thickness $(W/m.K)/m = W/m^2K$, when the temperature difference is taken from one surface to the other, as distinct from THERMAL TRANSMITTANCE, taken from air to air (the latter takes into account the surface resistance effects).

thermal conduction The process of heat transfer through a material medium in which heat is transmitted from particle to particle, not as in convection by movement of particles, nor by radiation.

thermal conductivity (λ-value) A thermal property of a material, of its ability to conduct heat, measured as the rate of heat flow (W) over unit length (m) through that material over unit area (m^2), caused by unit temperature difference (K): $W.m/m^2K$, by cancellation: $W/m.K$. Metals have high conductivities, and low conductivity materials are used for thermal insulation.

thermal conductor A material that readily transmits heat by conduction.

thermal diffusivity The rate of propagation of temperature change through a material. It is the ratio of the thermal conductivity to the heat capacity per unit volume.

thermal diode A term used for any device allowing heat flow in one direction only (by analogy with an electronic diode): *e.g.* a solar water heater collector circuit fitted with a non-return valve, preventing backward flow, or aluminium foil lining to the underside of a roof skin, where heat flow downwards (in a hot climate) through the attic space would be dominantly radiant, strongly reduced by the foil, whilst offering no resistance to upward (convective) heat flow, thus allowing for quick cooling down of the building after sunset.

thermal expansion Increase in the length of members of a building due to an increase in temperature. Unless provision is made for EXPANSION JOINTS, thermal movement is liable to produce cracking.

thermal inertia *Same as* THERMAL CAPACITY.

thermal insulation The reduction of the flow of heat. Its measure is the THERMAL RESISTANCE (called the *R-value*).

thermal mass Materials of substantial THERMAL CAPACITY used to store heat for warming cool spaces or as a heat sink to accept thermal radiation from heated bodies. Usually a part of the building's structure, but containers of water or gravel are sometimes introduced specifically for this purpose.

thermal movement *See* THERMAL EXPANSION.

thermal performance A measure of the effectiveness of a construction element such as a wall or window in achieving a desired thermal behaviour, *e.g.* thermal conductivity.

thermal performance modelling Use of computer software to simulate the thermodynamic behaviour of a building and its contents.

thermal radiation *See* RADIANT HEAT.

thermal resistance A thermal property of a building element (m^2K/W). For a single layer element it is the thickness (in m) divided by the conductivity of its material: $R = b/\lambda$ (where b, for 'breadth', is thickness, λ is conductivity). For a multi-layer element, the air-to-air resistance (R_{a-a}) is the sum of its component resistances, including both surface resistances. The THERMAL TRANSMITTANCE (U-value) is the reciprocal of this R_{a-a}.

thermal response A general description of how buildings react thermally to various heat inputs and losses, and how the indoor temperatures will respond. Buildings of large THERMAL CAPACITY (heavyweight or massive buildings) will have a slow response; very lightweight buildings a quick response.

thermal response simulation Computer programs to calculate the DYNAMIC THERMAL RESPONSE of buildings at short time intervals (at least hourly). Used to evaluate a design from the thermal point of view, or as the basis of energy consumption calculations or energy rating.

thermal shock A very high THERMAL STRESS produced by a sudden large change of temperature.

thermal storage Any of several techniques to store heat energy by utilising

either the heat capacity of materials, the latent heat of phase change or the heat of chemical dissociation.

thermal storage wall Wall with high THERMAL CAPACITY used for the storage of heat or coolness in *passive solar* design. *See* TROMBE WALL.

thermal stress Stress produced by thermal movement which is resisted by the building. If the thermal stresses are higher than the capacity of the materials to resist them, expansion or contraction joints are required. Thermal stresses are particularly important in brittle materials, such as concrete and brick, because of their tendency to crack at comparatively small tensile stresses.

thermal transmittance (U-value) The ability of an envelope element to allow heat flow from air on one side to air on the other side, measured in the same units as THERMAL CONDUCTANCE (W/m^2K). Also referred to as air-to-air transmittance. Its reciprocal is the air-to-air resistance, R_{a-a}.

thermal unit *See* BRITISH THERMAL UNIT.

thermal, etc. *See also* HEAT, etc.

thermic boring A method of boring holes into concrete by means of a high temperature, produced by burning a steel lance packed with steel wool, which is ignited and kept burning by a gas such as an oxyacetylene mixture.

thermionic Relating to the emission of electrons from hot bodies. It generally concentrates on the subsequent behaviour and control of such electrons, particularly *in vacuo*. A *thermionic vacuum tube* was the principal means for the rectification, amplification or detection of electric currents, before the development of SEMICONDUCTORS. Thermionic emission is essential for the operation of low pressure DISCHARGE LAMPS.

thermistor A temperature-sensitive resistance element of metallic oxide, whose electrical resistance decreases with increase in temperature.

thermochromic glass Glass that has the property of reduced transparency when exposed to higher levels of incident heat.

thermocline Stratification layer separating hot and cold regions of a fluid.

thermocouple A thermometer consisting of a pair of electric wires so joined as to produce a *thermoelectric effect*. When the ends of two dissimilar metals are joined, an electric potential is produced by a change in temperature which is proportional to the temperature difference between the hot and the cold junctions. Thermocouples are remote-reading thermometers, but for room temperatures they are not as accurate as the conventional mercury-in-glass type. A cheap combination of wires consists of copper and CONSTANTAN. Precious metals, such as platinum and rhodium are required for high temperatures.

thermodynamics The study of the relation between heat and energy. The two often-quoted laws of thermodynamics are: *(a) First law*: 'Heat and mechanical energy are mutually convertible; there is a constant relation between the amount of heat lost and energy gained or vice versa, which is called the MECHANICAL EQUIVALENT OF HEAT.' *(b) Second law*: 'Heat can never pass spontaneously from a colder to a hotter body; consequently the ENTROPY of the universe tends to a maximum.'

thermograph *(a)* An instrument to measure and record temperature and its variation on a paper chart. Largely replaced by electronic devices and DATA LOGGERS. *(b)* A photographic instrument, operating at infrared wavelengths, which records surface temperatures with a colour code. The process is referred to as *thermography*.

thermohygrograph A clock-driven recording instrument that records both the dry-bulb and the wet-bulb temperature, or the dry-bulb temperature and the relative humidity.

thermopile An assembly of thermoelectric elements connected in series or in parallel, which can be used for measuring temperature, or by inference, the intensity of radiation on one side of the array.

thermoplastic Becoming soft when heated and hard when cooled. *See also* THERMOSETTING.

thermosetting Becoming rigid on heating due to chemical reaction, usually between a resin and a HARDENER. Thermosetting resins cannot normally be softened, and they do not soften significantly on heating.

See also THERMOPLASTIC *and* COLD-SETTING RESIN.

thermosiphon The circulation of water in a hot-water system by gravity without the use of a pump. The hotter fluid has a lower density and thus rises to the top.

thermostat A device, such as a BI-METALLIC STRIP, for maintaining a constant temperature. It is commonly used in conjunction with heating and air conditioning plants.

thermostatic valve A mixing valve that controls the mixing of hot and cold water such that water temperature will not exceed the temperature at which the thermostat is set.

THI *Abbreviation for* Temperature–Humidity Index, produced by the US Weather Bureau for warm-humid climates, a composite of DBT and dew point temperature.

thin shell A SHELL that can be designed using the MEMBRANE THEORY.

thin-walled section A section liable to LOCAL BUCKLING.

thinner Any volatile liquid which lowers the viscosity of a paint or varnish, and thus makes it flow more easily. It must be compatible with the medium of the paint. The most common thinners are TURPENTINE and WHITE SPIRIT.

third octave A commonly used frequency interval in acoustics for the analysis of sounds. A frequency ratio of one sound that is a third octave higher than another is $(2)^{1/3}$. The preferred third octave frequencies belong to the 100, 125, 160, 200, 250, 315, 400, 500 Hz, etc. progression.

third octave filter A filter whose ratio of upper to lower cut-off frequencies is $(2)^{1/3}$.

third-angle projection *See* ORTHO-GRAPHIC PROJECTION.

thixotropic Stiffening when left standing for a short period, and acquiring a lower viscosity on mechanical agitation. The process is reversible, and is characteristic of certain COLLOIDAL gels.

three-dimensional graphics In computer graphics, the process of drawing and manipulating graphical objects in three dimensions, and displaying three-dimensional views on a flat screen or on paper.

three-dimensional modelling The process of modelling three-dimensional objects using either surface modelling, *e.g.* CONSTRUCTIVE SOLID GEOMETRY, or solid modelling.

three-dimensional photoelasticity For certain PHOTOELASTIC MATERIALS, particularly phenol formaldehydes, the stress patterns can be frozen above room temperature at 75 °C. The model can therefore be stressed in an oven, and cooled while still under load. It is then cut into parallel slices which are examined in a POLAR-ISCOPE at room temperature to obtain the three principal stresses. *Also called* the *frozen-stress method.*

three-dimensional sound *See* STEREO-PHONIC SOUND *and* AMBISONICS.

three-dimensional vision *See* STEREO-SCOPIC VISION.

three-hinged arch *Same as* THREE-PINNED ARCH.

three-phase system An alternating-current system in which the currents, flowing in three independent circuits, are displaced in phase by 120 electrical degrees.

three-pin (or three-prong) plug An electric plug that has two pins connecting to the main circuit, and one to the earth.

three-pinned arch (or portal) An arch (or portal) with two pin joints at the supports and a third pin at the crown (or the centre of the beam). The third pin renders the structure *statically determinate.*

three-way divertor valve Used to control the flow of fluid, a diverting valve has one inlet and two outlets. A dual plug opens one outlet as it closes the other to balance the hydraulic forces (*see figure*).

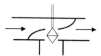

Three-way divertor valve

three-way mixing valve Used to control the flow of fluid, a mixing valve has two inlets and one outlet. A valve plug opens one seat while it closes another (*see figure*).

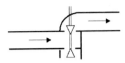

Three-way mixing valve

three-wire system *See* DELTA CONNECTION.

threshold *(a)* (of a door) A horizontal member or step, approximately flush with the floor surface, located at a doorway. It may form a junction between different floor finishes at either side of the door, and is of a hard-wearing material to resist the concentration of foot traffic at that location. *(b)* (of a physical stimulus) The lowest value of the stimulus that can be expected, with a certain level of confidence, to be detected by an observer.

threshold of audibility The minimum sound level, at a particular frequency, which an average young adult can hear.

threshold of pain The minimum sound level, at a particular frequency, at which an average young adult senses pain in the ear.

threshold shift A temporary or permanent alteration in a person's THRESHOLD OF AUDIBILITY due to noise or other causes.

thresholding A technique for simplifying complex colour images by reducing the number of colours displayed, perhaps exposing more of the underlying features in the image.

throat The minimum thickness of a FILLET WELD; it is the dimension that determines the strength (*see figure*).

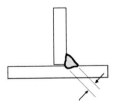

Throat

throttling range The change in the condition of the controlled variable that produces the full ouput range of a controller.

through car A lift car having two entrances at opposite ends of the car.

thrust A pushing force exerted by one part of a structure on an adjoining part. The term is more particularly used for horizontal or inclined forces in ARCHES, BUTTRESSES and RETAINING WALLS.

thrust bearing Support for a rotating shaft that is capable of resisting an end thrust.

thrust, line of The curve produced by the points through which the resultant THRUST passes, *e.g.* in an arch.

thumb nut *Same as* WING NUT.

thunderday A day on which thunder is heard, used in the determination of the need for a LIGHTNING PROTECTION SYSTEM.

tie *(a)* A tension member, the opposite of a *strut*. *(b)* In reinforced concrete columns, the lateral or HOOP REINFORCEMENT. *(c)* A WALL TIE.

tied arch *See* BOWSTRING GIRDER.

tied column A reinforced concrete column laterally reinforced with *ties* or HOOP REINFORCEMENT.

TIG welding Tungsten-Inert-Gas, a form of SHIELDED-ARC WELDING using an inert gas such as argon or helium, to surround a tungsten electrode. The weld metal comes from the parent metal plus a wire added to the arc zone; the tungsten is not consumed.

tile A thin slab used for covering a roof, a wall or a floor. It may be made of unglazed or glazed ceramics, of natural stone, concrete or various plastics.

tile, PVC *See* POLYVINYL CHLORIDE.

tile, roof *See* ROOF TILE.

tilt angle The angle at which a solar collector is tilted upward from the horizontal surface for optimum heat collection.

tilting mixer A small BATCH MIXER for concrete or mortar, which discharges its contents by tilting the entire drum.

tilt-up construction A method of precast concrete construction in which members are cast horizontally in a location adjacent to their final position, and tilted into place after removal of the moulds.

timber connector Originally, one of several types of steel device, used in conjunction with a bolt, to make connections between timber members which overlap each other. Now used to include connectors made of galvanised steel sheet, either with holes for nailing, or with pre-formed nails, used for connecting light timber members which lie in the same plane. *See* FRAMING BRACKET, GANG-NAIL, NAILPLATE, SPLIT RING CONNECTOR, TOOTHED PLATE CONNECTOR *and* TRUSS PLATE.

timber frame *See* FRAME CONSTRUCTION *and* BALLOON FRAME.

timber preservative *See* WOOD PRESERVATIVE.

timbre The quality of a musical sound that distinguishes it from other sounds of the same pitch. The timbre of a sound largely depends on the harmonic structure of the sound.

time constant A measure of the THERMAL RESPONSE of a building element. For a homogeneous element, it is the capacity/transmittance ratio (H/U) = capacity × resistance product $(H×R)$. Where H is the heat capacity in Wh/m²K and R is the resistance in m²K/W, then the product is h (hour), but if heat capacity is in J/m²K, then the result is in seconds.

time interval (for lifts) *(a) Down peak*: the average time between successive lift car arrivals at a defined floor during a DOWN PEAK condition. *(b) Loading*: the minimum time a lift car is held at a floor before it departs. *(c) Up peak*: The average time between successive lift car arrivals at a defined floor, during the up peak condition. *(d) Waiting*: the time a passenger waits for service. *See also* LIFT PASSENGER JOURNEY TIME *and* LIFT ROUND TRIP TIME.

time lag The time delay (measured in hours) of the peak of heat flow at the inner surface of an element of the BUILDING ENVELOPE from the time of peak heat flow at the outer surface. *See also* DECREMENT FACTOR.

time lapse photography The study of work processes by filming action by use of a series of photographs at intervals.

time of set The time taken for a mixture to reach an acceptable strength.

time sharing The apparent simultaneous use of a computer by several users or pro-grams. The processor shares its operating time between processes in small time slices.

time study The establishment of times for

a worker to carry out specific tasks under specified conditions.

time switch A switch controlled by an electrical clock, which opens and closes a circuit at a predetermined time.

time zone The legal definition of clock time in a geographical region, relative to UTC. Although MEAN SOLAR TIME is dependent upon an exact location on the Earth's surface, it is necessary for civic and commercial purposes to have the same time across a large region.

time, crashed or normal *See* CRASHED TIME.

timecode In video, a track which records timing and sequencing information which can be used for editing or for the insertion of interactive features.

tin A white metallic element, once widely used for tableware and other utensils (PEWTER), and one of the constituents of BRONZE; now mainly used as a protective coating for steel in *tin-plate*. Its chemical symbol is Sn (stannum), its atomic number is 50, its atomic weight is 118.7, its specific gravity is 7.3, its melting point is 232 °C and its valency is 2 or 4.

tin ceiling A ceiling formed by embossed panels of tin or tinplate nailed to the ceiling structure, and subsequently painted. They were popular from their introduction in the mid-nineteenth century until the First World War because of their durability, and some survive in old buildings.

tin roof Literally a roof covered with *tin-plated* steel sheet. In practice it usually means a roof covered with GALVANISED or ZINCALUME sheets (which are coated with zinc or a zinc-aluminium alloy).

tinnitus The 'ringing' of the ears that is due to a number of causes including exposure to loud sounds, diseases such as Meniere's disease and aging (*presby-cousis*).

tinted glass Generally a HEAT-ABSORBING GLASS.

tints Coloured pigments softened by white.

T-iron A section shaped like the letter T. It is an I-beam with only one flange.

titanium white A white pigment con-sisting mainly of titanium dioxide, which occurs naturally as *anatase* and as *rutile*. It has almost entirely replaced WHITE

LEAD, which is poisonous. Titanium white has good permanence and a high HIDING POWER.

TL *Abbreviation for* SOUND TRANSMISSION LOSS.

TNO *Nederlands Centrale Organisatie voor Toegepast Natuurwetenschappelijk Onderzoek*, the Dutch Government Organisation for Applied Scientific Research, which has several divisions interested in Building Research.

TOE *Abbreviation for* Tonne of Oil Equivalent, an energy unit used for large energy quantities, the product of a tonne mass of oil and its calorific value. 1 TOE $= 41.868 \times 10^9$ J ($9 \approx 42$ GJ approx.) or 11630 kWh.

toe Short horizontal slab of a CANTILEVER RETAINING WALL, on the side opposite to the retained soil.

toenailing US term for SKEW NAILING.

toilet A room containing a WATER CLOSET, and sometimes also a wash basin.

toldo A movable canvas courtyard covering used to admit or shield sunlight. At night it can be adjusted to regulate radiation cooling to the night sky.

tolerance The permitted variation from a given dimension. It is of particular importance when components are factory-produced by different manufacturers, since compliance with the specified tolerance is essential if the parts are to be fitted without cutting or filling gaps on the site. A tolerance may be negative (as for a partition to fit between two existing walls), or positive (as for a door frame to fit a given door), or both positive and negative (if there is no definite restriction either way). The *limits of size* are the two extreme sizes between which the actual size must lie, and the difference between them is the tolerance.

tolerance of noise *See* DAMAGE RISK CRITERION *and* BACKGROUND NOISE.

ton 1 long ton = 2240 lb; 1 short ton = 2000 lb. 1 metric ton (tonne) = 1000 kg = 0.984 long tons = 1.102 short tons. In the USA 'ton' usually means a short ton, but in most other English-speaking countries it commonly means a long ton. The metric ton is usually spelled 'tonne' in English, to distinguish it from the other two.

ton of refrigeration An obsolete unit for cooling power, used in air conditioning, the average power obtained when a (short) ton of ice at 0 °C melts to water at the same temperature (i.e. absorbing the latent heat of change of state) in 24 hours. Inherited from the time when ice was the only means of cooling. 1 ton of refrigeration = 12 000 BTU per hour = 3 516 W, for practical purposes 3.5 kW.

tonal sound A sound that is perceived as being dominated by one or more TONES.

tone *(a)* Strictly speaking, a tone is a sound composed of a single frequency, but the term is also applied to a sound that has a dominant single frequency. *(b)* A sound producing a sensation of PITCH. *(c)* Frequency interval that is approximately 12 per cent of an OCTAVE.

tone colour *See* TIMBRE.

tongue and groove joint (T&G joint) A joint in timber, and also in precast concrete piles, with projecting and grooved edges which provide a sliding fit (*see figure*). Floorboards, in particular, are frequently made with T & G joints, to allow the timber to move with change in moisture content while maintaining a satisfactory joint.

Tongue and groove joint

tonne A metric TON, equal to 1000 kilogram.

tooled joint A JOINT IN BRICKWORK (where there is an illustration), compressed and shaped with a tool.

toothed plate connector *(a)* A NAIL-PLATE with preformed nails punched from the sheet metal. It is normally fixed with a hydraulic press, but can also be formed with knuckle-shaped nails that can be driven in with a hammer. *(b)* A toothed ring, squeezed between two (soft) timber members as a TIMBER CONNECTOR.

top plate The horizontal member at the top of a stud wall.

topcoat The final coat of paint applied to a surface, over the PRIMER and/or UNDERCOAT.

top-hat section A light gauge metal section shaped ⌐⌐.

top-hat structure A tall building frame with a stiffened upper floor, generally used for accommodating building services. Connecting this floor to the perimeter columns reduces the cantilever deflection of the frame under lateral loading, and increases its strength, with consequent saving of structural material (*see figure*).

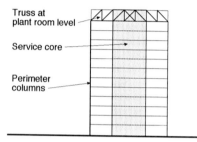

Truss at
plant room level

Service core

Perimeter
columns

Top-hat structure

top-hung window A CASEMENT WINDOW hinged at the top.

topology The arrangement of an object or network, having regard to the number and connectivity of its elements, but not to the dimensions or geometric shape.

topping A layer of high-quality concrete placed to form a floor surface on a concrete base.

topsoil The layer of soil that by its HUMUS content supports vegetation. It is valuable for agriculture and gardening, but must usually be removed before the foundation of a building is put down.

torque *Same as* TWISTING MOMENT.

torr Unit used in vacuum technology, equal to 1 mm of mercury, or 133 Pa.

torsion buckling Buckling of a column through rotation due to inadequate elastic stability.

torsion wrench A wrench (spanner) with an indicating dial so that the TORQUE applied to the nut can be accurately determined. Used for tightening FRICTION-GRIP BOLTS to the correct torque.

torsional moment *Same as* TWISTING MOMENT.

torsional rigidity A measure of the stiffness of a member in resisting torsion.

It is usually taken as the product GJ, where G is the MODULUS OF RIGIDITY and J is the POLAR MOMENT OF INERTIA.

torus *(a)* A surface or solid generated by the revolution of a circle or other conic section about any axis, *e.g.* a solid ring of circular or elliptical section. *(b)* A large convex moulding of approximately semicircular section, used especially at the base of a classical column.

total daily system energy requirement The amount of energy required to meet the daily electrical load plus the extra energy required to overcome system energy losses.

total equivalent warming potential An indicator of the likely influence of a substance on atmospheric warming. *See also* GREENHOUSE GASES.

total flooding system (fire control) Fixed fire extinguishing system consisting of storage, pipework and nozzles to distribute the extinguishant throughout the protected enclosure. The extinguishant is usually dry chemical, carbon dioxide or other heavy gas.

touch pad A POINTING DEVICE, *same as* TRACKPAD.

touch screen A computer screen which is sensitive to touch so that commands can be activated.

tough sheath *See* TPS CABLE.

toughened glass *Same as* TEMPERED GLASS.

toughness The ability to resist fracture by shock or impact.

tower crane A crane in which the lifting mechanism is mounted on top of a tower, totally or partially structurally independent of the building it is servicing.

TPS cable Tough Plastic Sheathed; a type of electrical cable in which each conductor is insulated in plastic, and the whole is then covered with a separate layer, usually of PVC. It is intended for use in building cavities and protected locations, without the need of a conduit.

TQM *Abbreviation for* Total Quality Management.

trabeated In traditional construction, spanning with stone lintels (*i.e.* beams), as opposed to ARCUATED construction.

track DISKS are organised into a series of concentric circular tracks for the storage of data. The read/write head is placed over a given track as the disk spins underneath to access specific locations on the track.

trackball A POINTING DEVICE consisting of a palm-sized, freely rotating ball. Rolling the palm of the hand across the ball causes a cursor to move on the computer screen, and one or more separate buttons are used for selecting, dragging and drawing.

tracking The movement of a (concentrating) solar collector to 'track' or follow the sun's path across the sky.

trackpad A POINTING DEVICE consisting of a small sensitive pad. Dragging a finger across the pad causes a cursor to move on the computer screen, and one or more separate buttons are used for selecting, dragging and drawing.

traction *See* LIFT DRIVE *(f)*, *(g)*, *and (o)*.

tractor-scraper Earthmoving machine with a large open body located between the axles. A cutting edge at the front of the body cuts and loads spoil as the machine moves forward. It can also discharge and spread the material while moving. Used to move and spread large volumes in siteworks and roadworks (*see figure*).

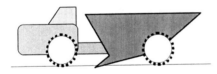

Tractor-scraper

trade-off The giving up of some desirable design characteristic (such as low energy consumption in a building) in return for improvement in another characteristic (such as low capital cost).

trajectory, stress *Same as* ISOSTATIC LINE.

trammel A beam compass used for scribing unusually large circular arcs.

transducer A device that senses one form of energy and converts it to another, *i.e.* temperature to voltage (for monitoring).

transfer column A column in a multi-storey building which does not go down to the foundation, but is supported by a *transfer girder*, which transfers its load to adjacent columns.

transfer duct A short duct used to transfer air through a solid wall from one space to another adjoining it.

transfer function A coefficient that expresses the relationship between a heat output function at a given time and the value of one or more heat input functions at a given time and for a period immediately preceding. Employed in the *transfer function method* of estimating space cooling loads.

transfer length The distance at the end of a pre-tensioned tendon necessary to develop the full tensile stress in the tendon by BOND. *Also called transmission length.*

transfer medium A fluid (air, water or antifreeze solution) that carries heat between two locations, such as a solar collector and a storage device.

transfer of prestress The process of transferring the anchorage of the prestress in the TENDONS from the POST-TENSIONING jacks, or from a PRE-TENSIONING bed to the concrete member.

transfer switch A switch used to transfer a load between a UPS and its by-pass source.

transformation temperature Temperature at which one phase of an ALLOY system changes to another.

transformed section A hypothetical section of one material which has the same elastic properties as a composite section of two materials. It is a device for simplifying calculations for composite materials.

transformer An electrical apparatus for converting from one AC voltage to another, either up or down. In a large building electrical power is received at a high voltage, and in a SUBSTATION this is transformed to the standard voltage used in the building (normally 220/240 V in Europe and Australia, 120 V in the USA). *Current transformers* are used in electrical measurements.

transient A high amplitude, short duration pulse superimposed on the normal voltage wave form or ground line.

transient response The ability of a power conditioner to respond to a change. Transient step load response is the ability of a power conditioner to maintain a constant output voltage when sudden load (current) changes are made.

transillumination In lighting, the process of lighting by means of transmission through a translucent material, as in X-ray viewing boxes.

transistor An electronic device that utilises *solid-state* SEMICONDUCTORS for rectifying, controlling or amplifying an electrical current.

transit *(a)* The apparent passage of a heavenly body across the meridian of a place, due to the Earth's daily revolution, *i.e.* the moment when it reaches its culmination or highest point. The sun's transit is *apparent noon. (b)* A TRANSIT THEODOLITE.

transit mixer A truck-mounted concrete mixer, used for transporting concrete from a central batching plant to a site. The mixer slowly rotates during the journey, mixing the concrete ingredients and preventing them from settling and segregating.

transit theodolite *(frequently abbreviated to transit)* A THEODOLITE that can be completely rotated about its horizontal axis. Virtually every modern instrument is designed to be able to do so.

translation Linear movement of a point in space without *rotation.*

translation, surface of *See* SURFACE OF TRANSLATION.

translucent concrete *See* GLASS–CONCRETE CONSTRUCTION.

translucent glass Glass which has been patterned so that it is *not* TRANSPARENT, but allows light to pass through. Objects on the far side can be discerned, but not clearly.

transmissibility The ratio of the response motion of a system to the input motion of the system when it is undergoing steady-state vibration.

transmission A general term for the passage of energy through a medium from one side to the other.

transmission length *Same as* TRANSFER LENGTH.

transmission line The conductors and supporting equipment used to carry electrical energy from one location to another, in the context of substantial distances.

transmission loss *See* SOUND TRANSMISSION LOSS.

transmission medium The medium over which SIGNALS may be transmitted.

Common network transmission media include copper wires (several different kinds) and optical fibre cable.

transmittance The ratio of transmitted energy to incident energy. *See also* THERMAL TRANSMITTANCE.

transom A horizontal dividing member of a traditional window. The corresponding vertical member is a *mullion.*

transparent *(a)* (of glass, etc.) Allowing light to pass with minimum interference, so that objects can be seen clearly through it. *See also* TRANSLUCENT GLASS. *(b)* (of technology assisting a user) Not obvious to the user, unobtrusive.

transparent insulation Transparent material that is able to transmit light while preventing the transfer of heat across a barrier. When applied to a well-oriented solid wall, it will allow the solar radiation to pass through with little reduction and heat the wall, but will reduce heat loss from the wall. Can also be used for windows, to fill the gap between two sheets of glass, where it would improve the window U-value, causing only a small interference with vision.

transverse loading Loading perpendicular to a structural member, *e.g.* vertical loading on a horizontal beam.

transverse reinforcement *Same as* LATERAL REINFORCEMENT.

trap A bend or dip in a SOIL DRAIN, so arranged that it is always full of water and provides a *water seal*, which prevents odours from entering the building *(see figure).*

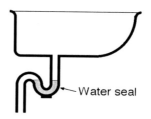

Trap

trap door A door, flush with the surface, in a floor, roof or ceiling, or in the stage of a theatre.

trapeze hanger A horizontal member suspended by rods. It is generally used to support pipes.

trapezium A QUADRILATERAL with two parallel sides. If the lengths of the two parallel sides are y_1 and y_2, and the height of the trapezium, at right angles to them, is x, then the area of the trapezium is $\frac{1}{2}x(y_1 + y_2)$. This is the basis of the TRAPEZOIDAL RULE.

trapezoidal rule A rule for the evaluation of an irregular area, or for graphical integration. Let the area be divided into a number of parallel strips of width x. The lengths of the boundary ordinates, or separating strips are measured and these are $y_0, y_1, \ldots, y_{n-1}$ and y_n. The area of the figure is then

$$x(\frac{1}{2}y_0 + y_1 + y_2 + \ldots + y_{n-1} + \frac{1}{2}y_n)$$

This calculation is quicker, but less accurate, than SIMPSON'S RULE.

trass A natural POZZOLANA of volcanic origin found in Germany near the River Rhine.

travel *(a)* The distance through which an item moves in its normal operation. *(b)* The vertical distance a lift can move, measured from the bottom to the top terminal floor or SKY LOBBY of a building.

travel distance The distance occupants need to travel to leave a building in case of fire. Building codes may specify the distance from a point on the floor to the entry of a fire-rated stairway, or to the exterior of the building.

travelator *Same as* MOVING WALK.

traveller gantry A stationary gantry that carries a traveller, *i.e.* a hoist moving on rails across the top.

travelling gantry A GANTRY CRANE built on wheels so that it can travel.

travertine A light-coloured TUFA; particularly the stone used in Ancient and Modern Rome, and exported worldwide.

tread *(a)* The level part of a step in a staircase. *(b)* The horizontal distance between one RISER and the next, exclusive of the nosing, *also called* the *going*.

treble ratio The ratio of high frequency (2–4 kHz) reverberation time to mid-frequency (500–1000 Hz) reverberation time.

tremie A hopper with a pipe at the bottom, used for placing concrete under water.

trestle A braced frame used to support horizontal working platforms.

triac An electronic device that provides switching action for either polarity of an applied voltage and can be controlled from a single gate. Usually composed of two SCRs connected back to back. Used for electronic switching of an AC circuit.

triangle A plane figure bounded by three straight lines. Its internal angles add up to 180°. A triangle with two equal sides is *isosceles*, and one with three equal sides is *equilateral*. A triangle with one angle of 90° is *right-angled*, and its longest side is called the *hypotenuse*.

triangle of forces The same as the PARALLELOGRAM OF FORCES, leaving out two sides of the parallelogram.

triangulation *(a)* A method used in the design of plane and space frames to ensure that they are isostatic. According to MÖBIUS' LAW, a truss whose members are all arranged in the form of adjacent triangles is statically determinate. *(b)* A method of surveying with ground stations forming a triangular network. One leg of one triangle is measured accurately on the ground. All other legs are then determined by angular measurement.

Triassic sandstone Sedimentary rock laid down about 200 000 000 years ago. It is found in abundance near Sydney and Hobart, where it was used for public and some private buildings in the nineteenth and the first half of the twentieth century, and it has been exported to other Australian cities because of its good workability and durability.

triaxial compression test A test on a sample (normally soil) contained in a rubber bag surrounded by liquid that exerts lateral pressure in two perpendicular directions. The vertical pressure (in the third direction) is applied by a piston. Unlike the UNCONFINED COMPRESSION TEST, it can be used on cohesionless soils.

tribophysics The physics of friction.

tricalcium silicate One of the principal components of PORTLAND CEMENT. Its chemical composition is $3CaO.SiO_2$, or C3S in the notation used by cement chemists. It is the main constituent of the component named *Alite* by Tornebohm in

1897, before the chemical composition of cement had been properly established.

trigonometry The mathematics of CIRCULAR FUNCTIONS. *Plane trigonometry* deals with triangles drawn on a plane surface. *Spherical trigonometry* deals with triangles drawn on the surface of a sphere.

trillion 1×10^{12}, a million million. Some Europeans, who equate 1×10^{12} to a BILLION, take a trillion to mean 1×10^{18}.

trim *(a)* The edging of an opening in a colour or material different from that of the wall surface. *(b)* A generic term for architraves, skirtings, etc. which cover open joints. *(c)* A generic term for all visible interior finishing work, including hinges and locks.

trimetric projection An AXONOMETRIC PROJECTION in which the two horizontal axes are drawn at different angles.

trip coil A SOLENOID-operated circuit breaker.

triphosphor In lighting, the term used to describe FLUORESCENT LAMPS employing narrow band phosphors. Sometimes *also called three-band lamps* or *multiphosphor lamps.*

triple bottom line A term used for the output from an accounting system which accounts for the financial, social and environmental performance of an organisation.

triple point of water The co-existing conditions of pressure and temperature that allow water to exist in the solid, liquid and gaseous phases simultaneously. The temperature at which this occurs is the practical datum for measurement of temperature (0°C or 32°F), since ABSOLUTE ZERO is not attainable.

triplex *(a)* Anything consisting of three layers. An obsolete term for LAMINATED GLASS, because of the two layers of glass and one of plastic. In North America, a set of three apartments (*see also* DUPLEX). *(b)* Three interconnected lift cars, sharing a common signalling system controlled under a simple group control system, operating under directional collective principles.

tripod A three-legged support.

tristimulus Referring to three colour receptors (types of *cones*) in the RETINA and, by extension, to COLORIMETRY.

troland The unit of retinal illuminance, used in experimental psychology and physiology.

Trombe wall A THERMAL STORAGE WALL, devised by Felix Trombe in France, for houses employing PASSIVE SYSTEMS of solar energy.

trompe l'oeil A two-dimensional painting that gives the impression of a three-dimensional part of the building, such as an additional room that does not exist. Sometimes called *counterfeit architecture.*

tropics The parallels of *latitude* 23° 26′ north and south that represent the furthest movement of the sun from the equator. The tropic zone is the region between the tropic circles.

troposphere *See* ATMOSPHERIC LAYERS.

trough collector A type of concentrating solar collector with one-axis tracking.

trough gutter *Same as* BOX GUTTER.

true north The direction of the geographic north pole from the observer. It is obtained from the *magnetic north* indicated by a magnetic compass by making a correction for the *magnetic declination.*

true volume of a porous material The volume excluding both the open and the closed pores. The BULK VOLUME includes the pores.

trunnion axis The horizontal axis of rotation of a THEODOLITE.

truss A structural member, acting like a beam, but made up of smaller members in a triangulated arrangement. *See also* BELFAST, FINK, HOWE *and* WARREN TRUSS; KING POST, PRINCESS POST, QUEEN POST, *and* HAMMERBEAM ROOF, *and* MÖBIUS' LAW.

truss plate *Same as* NAILPLATE.

trussed beam or purlin *(a)* A beam or purlin stiffened with a tie rod (*see figure*). *(b)* A beam or purlin in the form of a truss.

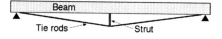

Trussed beam

trussed rafter A triangulated rafter in a roof truss. The FINK TRUSS is a large-span example.

try square A gauge consisting of two pieces of metal accurately set at right angles, used for laying out work, and for testing finished work for squareness.

TS *Abbreviation for* Thermal Sensation, a series of equations, with DBT and the VAPOUR PRESSURE, pv, as determinants of this thermal sensation, which is a ten-point scale (extension of the ASHRAE), from –4 (very cold) to +4 (very hot) and +5 (painfully hot).

TSI *Abbreviation for: (a)* Thermal Strain Index, developed by Lee (1958), represented by a series of equal strain lines on the psychrometric chart, very similar to the SET lines; *(b)* Tropical Summer Index, similar to the WBGT, developed at Roorkee and included in the Indian Standard for functional requirements of buildings, SP:4.

TTL *Abbreviation for: (a)* (in electronics) Transistor–Transistor Logic; electronic circuitry that defines a binary logic state when components are in saturation or cutoff; *(b)* (in photography) Through-The-Lens, referring to a single lens reflex camera, as opposed to one with a separate viewfinder.

tube structure or tube-in-tube structure Structural system for a tall building, which considers the columns and SPANDRELS on the facades as forming a pierced tube, cantilevered from the ground. The lift well (elevator shaft) forms another tube inside this outer tube.

tubular scaffolding Scaffolding built up from galvanised steel or aluminium tubes with clamps. The tubes are usually of 50 mm (2 in.) external diameter.

tuck pointing An obsolete method of emphasising the joints in brick and natural stone by grooving the mortar to form a *tuck*, which is then filled with mortar or putty of a distinctive colour, usually white or black.

tufa A porous limestone, deposited from solution around springs of water. *See also* TRAVERTINE. The term is also sometimes used as a synonym for *tuff*, a porous rock of volcanic origin.

tumbler switch A switch operated by pushing a short lever up or down.

tung oil An oil obtained from the seeds of *Aleurites cordata*, used in the manu-facture of paints, varnishes and enamels. It has excellent water resistance. Since the trees were found mainly in China and Japan, it is *also called China wood oil.*

tungsten A metallic element used as an alloy for hard steels, and as filaments and electrodes in electric lamps. Its chemical symbol is W (Wolframium), its atomic number is 74, its atomic weight is 184, its specific gravity is 19.3, and its melting point is 3300 °C.

tungsten–halogen lamp An INCANDESCENT LAMP that has a halogen (iodine, chlorine or bromine) added to the normal gas filling. This produces a regenerative cycle whereby the tungsten, sublimed from the filament and otherwise deposited on the glass, is kept in vapour form until it nears the filament when it is redeposited on the filament.

turbidimeter A device for the PARTICLE-SIZE ANALYSIS of finely divided material. Successive measurements are taken of the turbidity of a suspension of the fluid.

turbine A rotating PRIME MOVER, as distinct from a RECIPROCATING ENGINE.

turbulence index An index used to quantify the turbulence of air movement in a mechanically ventilated space. It is the ratio of the air velocity, measured as a time-weighted three minute average, to the standard deviation.

turbulent flow Unsteady flow with eddies, as opposed to STREAMLINE FLOW.

turnbuckle A coupling between the ends of two rods, one having a left-hand and the other a right-hand thread. Hence rotation of the buckle adjusts the tension in the rods. A simpler type has only one right-hand thread, and a swivel at the other end.

turning Making an object on a LATHE.

turnkey contract A contract where the contractor undertakes the complete design and construction and hands over the project ready for occupation. *See also* TURNKEY SYSTEM.

turnkey system A complete system supplied by a single supplier. *See also* TURNKEY CONTRACT.

turpentine A THINNER obtained by dis-tilling the sap of certain pine trees, some-times called *gum turpentine.* WHITE SPIRIT or MINERAL TURPENTINE is frequently used as a substitute.

tweeter A loudspeaker for reproducing high frequency sounds (> 2–4 kHz).

twisting moment The moment of all the forces acting on a member about its polar axis, *i.e.* the moment NORMAL to the section. *Also called torsional moment* or *torque.*

two-and-a-half-dimensional graphics The process of creating three-dimensional graphic objects by drawing them in two dimensions and adding the third dimension by EXTRUDING the two-dimensional object in the third dimension.

two-axis tracking A solar energy collection system capable of rotating independently about two axes so as to track the sun at all times.

two-dimensional graphics In computer graphics, the process of drawing and displaying graphical objects in two dimensions using graphic elements such as points, lines, polylines and polygons.

two-part adhesive Synthetic adhesive supplied in two parts, a resin and an accelerator, which are mixed only just before use. *Also called two-pot* adhesive.

two-way slab A SLAB spanning between beams or walls in two directions.

two-way switch An electric switch used to control a light or lights from two locations. Two two-way switches are required, one in each location (*see figure*).

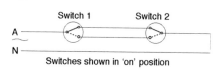

Switch 1   Switch 2

Switches shown in 'on' position

Two-way switch

U

U-bolt A steel bar bent into a U-shape, and fitted with screw threads and nuts on each end. *Also called* a *U-clip.*

UF *Abbreviation for* Urea FORMAL-DEHYDE.

U-gauge A U-tube MANOMETER.

UHF *Abbreviation for* Ultra High Frequency (frequencies 300–3000 MHz, corresponding to wavelengths 1–0.1 m).

UIA *Union Internationale des Architectes,* Paris.

UL Underwriters Laboratories, an independent US product safety assurance agency.

ULOR (Upward Light Output Ratio) The ratio of the flux emitted in the upper hemisphere above a luminaire to the total flux emitted by the lamps installed in the luminaire.

ultimate load In ULTIMATE STRENGTH DESIGN, the actual working load multiplied by the LOAD FACTOR.

ultimate strain The strain at which a material fails. In ULTIMATE STRENGTH DESIGN, the ultimate strain of concrete is assumed to be the same for all types of concrete, and equal to 3×10^{-3} (USA and Australia) or 3.5×10^{-3} (UK).

ultimate strength The highest load which a test piece can sustain before breaking.

ultimate strength design Design based on the ultimate strength of the structure, or of a structural member, as opposed to ELASTIC DESIGN.

ultramarine A characteristic blue pigment, originally made by grinding the semi-precious LAPIS LAZULI. It was synthesised in the 1820s by calcining china clay, soda, sulphur and coal, and its cost was greatly reduced.

ultrasonic *See* ULTRASOUND.

ultrasound Mechanical vibration in a solid, liquid or gas which has a frequency higher than that of audible sound (16 kHz), and a speed equal to that of sound in the same medium. It is reflected and refracted at the boundaries of a solid, and can therefore be used for the NON-DESTRUCTIVE detection of cracks and flaws in concrete structures, in metal castings, etc. or to determine the thickness of a piece of material when only one surface is accessible.

ultraviolet radiation Electromagnetic radiation with wavelengths shorter than 390 nm, *i.e.* beyond the violet end of visible light. It forms part of the radiation received from the sun, and it has a destructive effect on some materials, including a number of plastics. Hence ultraviolet radiation cycles are included in some WEATHEROMETERS. Short-wave UV produces erythema (reddening of the skin) and with sufficient exposure can trigger skin cancers.

umber Brown mineral pigment. It consists of iron oxide and manganese oxide. *See also* BURNT UMBER.

umbra Total shadow cast by an opaque body or by the earth or moon in eclipse. *See also* PENUMBRA.

umbrella shell A shell roof formed by four HYPAR shells (*see figure*), or by other suitable arrangements of hypar shells.

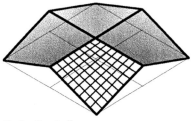

Umbrella shell

unbonded tendon A tendon in PRESTRESSED CONCRETE which is not bonded to the concrete by grouting after it is stressed.

unconfined compression test A compressive test on a sample of a material without lateral restraint, which is normal practice for structural materials. The term is mainly used for a soil test, to distinguish it from a TRIAXIAL COMPRESSION TEST.

unconfined compressive strength of clay This depends greatly on the water content, and it may range from less than $35 \, \text{kN/m}^2$ (5 psi) for a very soft clay to more than $275 \, \text{kN/m}^2$ (40 psi) for a very stiff clay. It may be seriously reduced by REMOULDING.

undercoat A coat of paint which is not the TOPCOAT. It may be the first coat, or applied over the PRIMER or another previous coat.

underfloor heating Heating provided below the finished floor by electric cables or hot-water pipes. These are frequently cast into a concrete slab. *See also* HYPOCAUST.

underlay Material laid directly on the floor to act as padding, generally for a carpet.

underlayment A layer of asphalt-saturated paper laid down before shingles are installed, to act as SARKING. *Also called tar paper.* (Some building codes do not permit flammable materials to be used in this location.)

underpin To provide a new foundation for a wall or column in an existing building without removing the superstructure.

under-reinforced section A reinforced concrete section with less steel than is needed for a BALANCED DESIGN.

undisturbed samples *See* BOREHOLE SAMPLES.

unidirectional microphone A microphone that picks up sound from one direction only. Extreme case of a CARDIOID MICROPHONE.

uniform gravel or sand Material retained between two adjacent sieves so that all particles are of approximately the same size. *See also* PEA GRAVEL.

uniform load A load that is uniformly distributed. For the sake of simplicity, this is usually assumed in structural calculations, even when there is some variation in distribution.

uniform sky An idealised sky whose luminance is the same at all altitudes. It is used in many daylight calculations because of its simplicity. *See also* CIE STANDARD CLEAR SKY, CIE STANDARD OVERCAST SKY *and* INDIAN STANDARD SKY.

unit stress A term generally synonymous with STRESS.

unit weight The density of a material, *i.e.* its weight per unit volume.

universal testing machine A TESTING MACHINE capable of exerting tensile, compressive or flexural forces on a specimen under test, as opposed to a machine designed for one kind of test only.

universe In statistical terminology, a specified group, *e.g.* of persons or concrete cylinders. A universe may have several POPULATIONS associated with it.

UNIX A MULTIUSER OPERATING SYSTEM developed by Bell Labs (AT&T) in the 1970s. It is available for use on a wide assortment of hardware platforms.

unreinforced concrete Concrete that is *plain*, neither REINFORCED nor PRE-STRESSED.

upfeed system A type of central heating pipework (the opposite of downfeed) where the boiler is at a low level (*e.g.* in the basement) and the upward flow pipe branches off to each radiator panel or other emitter. The cooled fluid will flow back to the boiler, assisted by gravity even in a pumped circulation.

upgrade A later release of a SOFTWARE program. Most software companies work to improve their existing software by upgrading it periodically by adding new features and functions.

uplift An upward force. *See also* FROST HEAVE *and* QUICKSAND.

uplighter A LUMINAIRE, usually floor-mounted or furniture-mounted, used to light the ceiling.

upload To load a file from one's computer onto a remote one. Contrast with DOWNLOADing.

uprights Vertical members, usually of timber, *e.g.* the sides of a door frame.

UPS *Abbreviation for* Uninterruptible Power Source (*or Supply*).

upstand beam A beam projecting above an adjoining slab.

UPVC *Abbreviation for* Unplasticised POLYVINYL CHLORIDE.

urea formaldehyde *See* FORMALDEHYDE.

URL *Abbreviation for* Uniform Resource Locator. The WORLD WIDE WEB (WWW) address of a document or resource that is stored on some computer system. Most URLs designate pages available from a Web server, although they may signify other types of services.

US customary units The system of FPS units as defined by the National Bureau of Standards, Washington. There are some differences between the customary units of the USA and those of the UK, *e.g.* in the GALLON and the TON.

USASI United States of America Standards Institute, now called American National Standards Institute Inc.

useable floor area The area of a space that can actually be occupied by a user; it is normally less than the NET LETTABLE AREA.

user-friendly A term describing an attribute of a system that can be used easily by untrained users.

USGBC The US Green Building Council,

a non-profit organisation dedicated to sustainable building design and construction.

UTC *Abbreviation for* Coordinated Universal Time, the international standard for reckoning time. Formerly known as GREENWICH MEAN TIME. Often a 'Z' is added to the time digits, *i.e.* 1800Z represents 6 pm in UTC convention. Local time at any location is calculated according to the legal TIME ZONE of the place, relative to UTC.

U-tie A U-shaped WALL TIE.

utilisation factor (*a*) A factor used in the LUMEN METHOD for the calculation of both daylight and electric light illuminances, which allows for both direct and inter-reflected light in interiors. (*b*) The proportion of available time during which a facility is used.

utility services The services traditionally provided for the community, such as water, gas, electricity, sewerage and garbage disposal.

U-tube *See* MANOMETER.

UV *Abbreviation for* Ultraviolet. *See also* ULTRAVIOLET RADIATION.

UV curing CURING of adhesives, plastics or paint by the application of ultraviolet light.

U-value The THERMAL TRANSMITTANCE of a building element, expressed as the rate of heat flow through a unit area for a unit temperature difference between the air on either side of the element.

V

VAC *Abbreviation for* Volts of Alternating Current.

vacancy rate The ratio of the currently vacant area to the total available area.

vacuum An empty space. A perfect vacuum is unobtainable on Earth, and a pressure of 10^{-4} Pa is considered a good vacuum.

vacuum concrete Concrete from which water is extracted with a vacuum mat before hardening occurs. The concrete has a water content adequate for placing in the formwork, but this is subsequently reduced to give a higher strength concrete; *see* ABRAMS' LAW.

vacuum gauge A gauge measuring the *reduction* in pressure below atmospheric pressure. The *absolute* pressure in the fluid cannot become negative.

vacuum lifting Raising an object, *e.g.* a precast concrete panel, with a suction attachment. It allows uniform distribution of the lifting force, but the cost of the capital equipment is appreciable.

valence band The highest energy band in a semiconductor that can be filled with electrons.

valency The combining power of an atom. Thus oxygen, which is bivalent, combines with two univalent hydrogen atoms to form water. Some elements have more than one valency, *e.g.* sulphur may have a valency of 2, 4 or 6.

valley The intersection between two sloping surfaces of a roof, the opposite of *hip*. A valley must itself have a slope so that it can discharge rainwater.

valuation *See* MARKET VALUATION.

value *(a)* Of a colour, in the MUNSELL BOOK OF COLOR, value correlates with the lightness of the colour perceived to belong to it, and it ranges from 0/ for ideal black to 10/ for ideal white. *(b)* In computing, a fixed constant, being a number or a STRING. *See* ATTRIBUTE.

value analysis A technique used to examine the evolving design in order to achieve design objectives as economically as possible; it involves criticisms of the design and subsequent analysis of alternative ideas.

value engineering Subjecting design proposals to systematic review to ensure that the final design meets user requirements at the lowest possible cost.

value management A review process to assess the impact of decisions made, usually during design or design development, with respect to cost, function and quality of the proposed building project.

valve *(a)* A device for regulating the flow of a liquid or gas in a pipeline. *(b)* A THERMIONIC tube used as an electronic rectifier or amplifier.

vane *See* DOOR VANE.

vane anemometer *See* ANEMOMETER.

vane test A SHEAR TEST for determining the strength of soil on the site. A four-bladed vane is inserted into the soil at the foot of a *borehole*. It is rotated by a rod at the surface and the force is measured when the soil shears.

vanishing point The point where parallel lines receding from the observer are drawn to meet in a PERSPECTIVE PROJECTION.

vapour A gas that is at a temperature below its critical temperature, and can therefore be liquefied by a suitable increase in pressure.

vapour barrier An airtight skin, *e.g.* of aluminium or polyethylene, which prevents moisture from the warm damp air in a building from passing into and condensing within a colder space. It is particularly needed in cool climates, at night and in winter, to protect the insulation from filling with condensation water or ice, and it is therefore placed on the inner, warm face of the insulation. A barrier that satisfactorily stops the ingress of liquid water is not necessarily sufficient to stop water vapour.

vapour compression cycle A refrigeration cycle. It utilises two phenomena: *(a)* the evaporation of a liquid refrigerant absorbs heat to lower the temperature of its surroundings; *(b)* the condensation of the refrigerant vapour gives off heat to raise the temperature of its surroundings. The refrigerant vapour has its pressure raised by a mechanical compressor, as opposed to the ABSORPTION CYCLE.

vapour diffusion If the vapour pressure is different on two sides of a partition it tends to equalise, and will cause diffusion through that partition. The magnitude of this diffusion (in $\mu g/m^2 s$) depends on the vapour pressure difference (Pa) and the permeance of that partition. A membrane or other layer with a permeance of less than $67 \mu g/m^2 s.kPa$ is considered as a VAPOUR BARRIER.

vapour phase A thermodynamic condition in which the internal energy of a substance is higher than can be sustained in it as a LIQUID but lower than one that determines its existence as a GAS.

vapour pressure Partial pressure of vapour in a gas mixture. *(a)* For water vapour in the atmosphere, it is proportional to the moisture content or absolute humidity. $pv = (AH \times pt)/(AH + 622)$, where pv is the vapour pressure in kPa, and pt = total atmospheric pressure, usually taken as 101.325 kPa for the standard atmosphere. *(b) See also* SATURATION VAPOUR PRESSURE.

vapour pressure gradient As a temperature gradient between inside and outside temperatures can be constructed through the cross-section of an element, as a function of the THERMAL CONDUCTIVITY of the material of each layer, so a VAPOUR PRESSURE gradient can be drawn, between the inside and outside vapour pressures, as a function of the PERMEABILITY of the material of each layer.

variable In computing, an element of a computer program whose VALUE can be changed during the execution of the program.

variable air volume system (VAV) Method of air distribution in an air conditioning system, in which air is circulated at a constant temperature and the volume flow rate is varied to maintain the desired condition, in contrast to a CONSTANT AIR VOLUME SYSTEM.

variable refrigerant flow The operating principle of a refrigeration system in which outdoor condensing supplies refrigerant to multiple indoor evaporator units used for space temperature control.

variance The square of the STANDARD DEVIATION.

variation An approved modification of the design shown in the contract documents, usually in the context of its effect of varying the contract sum.

varistor *See* METAL OXIDE VARISTOR, (MOV).

varnish A resin dissolved in oil or spirit, which dries to a brilliant, thin, protective film. Varnish may be applied to unpainted wood, applied over paint to increase its gloss or mixed with paint. The term LACQUER is usually reserved for finishes based on cellulose compounds.

vasoconstriction Narrowing of blood vessels to the skin, to preserve inner body heat when the body is cold.

vasodilation Expansion of blood vessels to increase heat transport to the skin surface, when the body is overheated.

vault *(a)* A vaulted roof, *i.e.* an arched masonry or concrete roof. *See also* BARREL VAULT, CROSS VAULT *and* GROIN VAULT. *(b)* A room or passage with an arched masonry roof. *(c)* A room below ground, of massive construction, not necessarily with a vaulted roof. *(d)* A safe room for the storage of valuables, usually below ground, but rarely with a vaulted ceiling.

VAV *Abbreviation for* VARIABLE AIR VOLUME.

VDC *Abbreviation for* Volts of Direct Current.

VDU *Abbreviation for* VISUAL DISPLAY UNIT.

vector *(a)* A quantity that has magnitude as well as direction. It may be represented by a straight line drawn from a point in a given direction for a given distance. A SCALAR has magnitude, but no direction. In vector algebra, vectors are usually distinguished from scalars by the use of bold typeface. *(b)* In computer graphics, a graphic element represented by a line allowing the addressing of such elements as whole elements rather than as a collection of PIXELS. *See* VECTOR GRAPHICS.

vector display monitor MONITOR that displays line drawings by exciting the phosphors between two defined end points. Contrast with RASTERISED VIDEO DISPLAY. *See also* CATHODE-RAY TUBE (CRT).

vector graphics A method of storing and representing images by mathematical equations or descriptions (as opposed to storing and mapping each BIT in the image individually). The images are recreated by calculating the points that compose them. Contrast with BIT-MAPPED GRAPHICS (*also called raster graphics*).

vector/scalar ratio (v/s) (of illumination) The magnitude of ILLUMINANCE VECTOR divided by the total spherical illuminance (E_s) measured at a point in space: $v/s = \Delta \bar{E}_{max}/E_s$. A value of 0 would indicate a completely diffuse uniform field of light without any directionality, whilst a purely monodirectional light would show $v/s = 4$. For everyday lighting tasks, v/s values between 1.2 and 1.7 are preferred, with a vector altitude between 30 and 60°.

vectorising Converting an image of a drawing, obtained from a SCANNER, into

VECTOR graphics. The vector drawing is much more economical to store, and individual lines can be manipulated easily.

vehicle The liquid part of a paint, as opposed to the pigment. *Also called medium.*

veiling reflection Reflections in a surface that partially or totally obscure other visual information contained in the surface.

velocity In common parlance, the same as SPEED. In physics, velocity is a VECTOR quantity, which determines direction as well as speed.

velocity head The energy possessed by a liquid because of its velocity. *See also* HEAD *(a).*

velocity of light, sound See SPEED OF LIGHT, SOUND.

velocity pressure Pressure in a fluid as a result of its motion.

velocity ratio In a lifting tackle, the ratio of the distance through which the force has moved to the distance moved by the load. In an efficient machine it is only slightly greater than the MECHANICAL ADVANTAGE.

veneer A thin layer of one material used as a facing to another: *(a) see* WOOD VENEER; *(b)* a thin layer of decorative LAMINATED PLASTIC such as melamine, used in a similar manner to a wood veneer; *(c) see also* BRICK VENEER.

Venetian blind A window blind composed of numerous thin slats that can be raised and lowered with ease. The slats (formerly of timber, now usually of aluminium or plastic) can be rotated by pulling a cord, to admit varying amounts of light and air. A Venetian blind is normally placed inside the window to protect it from the weather, and it is thus only partially effective in excluding *thermal radiation.* In air conditioned buildings with double glazing the blinds are therefore fixed between the inner and outer panes of glass. *See also* LOUVRE.

Venetian red Red mineral pigment made from haematite (Fe_2O_3).

ventilating brick *Same as* AIR BRICK.

ventilation The supply of fresh outdoor air to a space for the purposes of convective cooling of the space, convective and evaporative cooling of people, and diluting concentrations of undesirable contaminants that may be released in it as a result of occupation and use.

ventilation efficiency A series of indices or parameters that characterise: *(a)* the mixing behaviour of air; *(b)* the distribution and removal of pollutants within an enclosure. Some indices are based on room-averaged values, while others refer to specific points or locations. The latter may indicate regions where localised poor ventilation might occur, even when the average condition is satisfactory.

ventilation-controlled fire The later stage of a fire, when its sustainability and intensity depend on the amount of air supplied. *See also* FUEL-CONTROLLED FIRE.

venting *(a)* Of smoke produced by a fire: automatic vents are installed in single-storey buildings that cover large areas; these are operated by smoke detectors. *(b)* Of a gas explosion: the vents are provided by singly-glazed windows, or other panels that are blown out by the pressure of the explosion. This relieves the pressure and removes some of the flammable gases.

venturi tube A constriction inserted in a line of piping, together with a MANOMETER to measure the loss of pressure over the convergent part of the constriction. From this the rate of flow can be calculated by BERNOULLI'S THEOREM.

verdigris The green basic copper carbonate formed on copper roofs and statues exposed to the atmosphere. Although a corrosion product, it gives a highly esteemed *patina* if properly controlled.

verge The edge of a sloping roof that overhangs a GABLE.

verge board *Same as* BARGE BOARD.

vermiculation Literally, a worm-eaten state. Decoration of masonry with shallow, irregular channels, resembling worm tracks; it is one form of RUSTICATION.

vermiculite A generic name for hydrous silicates of aluminium, magnesium and iron, which occur as minerals in plate form, and show marked exfoliation on heating. The term often implies exfoliated vermiculite, which is used for thermal insulation and fire protection, often as an aggregate in lightweight plaster or concrete.

vermilion A brilliant red, slightly orange-coloured pigment, derived from cinnabar, which is mercuric sulphide (HgS). It is one of the traditional pigments, but is now too expensive for general use, and mercury is now known to be toxic.

vernier A device for measuring length more accurately than is possible with an ordinary scale. It consists of a subsidiary *(vernier)* scale that slides alongside the main scale. This carries one additional division, *i.e.* ten vernier divisions equal nine divisions on the main scale. By noting which division on the vernier scale is exactly in line with the main scale, the measurement can be taken to one more decimal place than is shown in the main scale *(see figure)*. *See also* MICROMETER *(a)*.

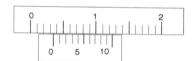

The 6th mark on the vernier aligns with a mark on the main scale. The reading is 0.36 units.

Vernier

versioning In computing, the process of generating, maintaining and displaying information from a number of versions for a project.

vertical In line with the direction of the gravitational forces, *i.e.* the dead loads. The *horizontal* direction is at right angles to the vertical. *See* PLUMB BOB *and* SPIRIT LEVEL.

vertical sash A normal sash in a SASH WINDOW.

vertical shadow angle The angle, measured in the plane normal to a surface, between the position of the sun and the horizontal.

vestibule A space located between the main entrance door and the remainder of the premises.

VGA *Abbreviation for* Video Graphics Array.

VHF *Abbreviation for* Very High Frequency (frequencies 30–300 MHz, corresponding to wavelengths 10–1 m).

vibrated concrete Concrete compacted by vibration during and after placing. Since vibration helps to place a comparatively dry concrete with satisfactory compaction *(see* ABRAMS' LAW*)*, it increases the effective concrete strength. On the other hand, displacement of the reinforcement is a possible danger. The vibrator can be fixed to the formwork, or an internal (or poker) vibrator can be immersed in the wet concrete.

vibration A periodic motion in a medium. There are two types of vibration: *(a) forced vibration* is where the motion of a system is maintained by one or more periodic forces and where the frequency is related to the frequencies of the forces; *(b) free vibration* is where the motion of a system results from a disturbance to the system and where the period of oscillation depends only on the properties of the system. *See also* DAMPING OF STRUCTURAL VIBRATIONS.

vibration isolator A spring and damper system designed to reduce the dynamic forces, from a machine or other vibrating object, transmitted to a building structure.

vibration transducer *See* ACCELEROMETER.

vibrator *See* CONCRETE VIBRATOR.

Vicat test Used to determine the onset of stiffening in Portland cement after water has been added. The Vicat test consists of placing a weighted test needle on the hydrated cement pat. The *initial set* is defined by failure of the initial-test needle to penetrate the pat. The *final set* is defined by failure of the final-test Vicat needle to make a 0.5 mm indentation on the cement pat.

Vickers diamond hardness test An indentation hardness test employing a diamond pyramid. The impression of the diagonal is converted into the hardness number from a table.

video adapter Hardware device that serves as an interface between the computer system's RAM and a VIDEO DISPLAY monitor. The video adapter translates the graphic information stored in memory to a video SIGNAL. *See also* VIDEO RANDOM ACCESS MEMORY.

video conferencing A form of TELECONFERENCING using video transmission so that participants can see as well as hear other participants.

video detection system A safety and security system operated by video camera with image processing software.

video digitiser Hardware device designed to convert a video SIGNAL to digital form for storage in a computer's memory. *See also* VIDEO CAPTURE *and* ANALOG TO DIGITAL CONVERTER (ADC).

video display monitor Hardware device designed to display information stored in a computer system. The primary component of a video display monitor is its CATHODE RAY TUBE (CRT). *See also* LIQUID CRYSTAL DISPLAY.

video random access memory (VRAM) Fast access memory that stores a direct digital representation of a graphic image intended for display on a video monitor. VRAM acts as a buffer between ordinary RAM and the video display monitor in order to speed the display of images on the monitor. VRAM is one of the components of a VIDEO ADAPTER.

Vierendeel girder A girder (named after a Belgian engineering professor) without diagonals, so that it can be used in walls which require openings for windows or doors. All the joints are rigid. *Also called an open-frame girder.*

viewpoint In computer graphics, a point in three-dimensional space that represents the observer's point of view.

viewport In computer graphics, that part of a WINDOW (*b*) which is visible at a given time.

viga Round logs used as ceiling beams in traditional American South-Western architecture.

vinyl *See* POLYVINYL.

virtual Pertaining to conceptual rather than physical.

virtual memory Dedicated hard disk space that is used as an extension to memory (RAM). The CPU treats the virtual memory space as if it were a part of RAM, switching information between actual RAM and the disk virtual RAM as needed and in a manner transparent to the user, but the access is slower.

virtual office A workplace that is determined by where the employee happens to be engaged in carrying out work at a particular time, remote from the main organisation workplace.

virtual organisation An organisation that exists only as a result of telecommunications. An electronic organisation existing in virtual space.

virtual reality The simulation of the real world in virtual space allowing for the virtual interaction of users, such as *walkthroughs, fly-bys.*

viscosity Internal friction (due to cohesion) in fluids, or in solids with flow characteristics. The opposite of *fluidity.*

viscous deformation Continuous deformation or flow over a period of time. It is generally proportional to the applied stress, and it may occur at quite low stresses.

visible fixing Fixing of materials with bolts, screws, etc. that penetrate the surface and are not hidden. In most cases this allows a simple fixing process. The layout of the fixings may be detailed to produce a neat pattern.

visible spectrum The visible range of electromagnetic RADIATION, ranging in wavelength from 760–390 nm (red to violet light).

vision panel The portion of a curtain wall containing glass for view and the admission of light, as opposed to the SPANDREL.

visionproof glass Glass that has been patterned, so that it is TRANSLUCENT or OBSCURE, but not TRANSPARENT.

visual acuity *(a)* The capacity of seeing distinctly objects very close together or of very small size; the ability to resolve fine detail. *(b)* The measure of the ability to see visual detail both *near* and *distant.* The *Snellen notation (e.g. 6/6)* is common for distance visual acuity.

visual angle The angle subtended by an object or a detail of an object, at the eye. Usually measured in minutes of arc.

visual display unit (VDU) A computer screen using a CATHODE-RAY TUBE or other form of electronic display.

visual field All the surfaces and objects that can be seen while the eyes are kept stationary.

visualisation The process of displaying realistic visual images of an object for evaluation. Visual simulation.

vitreous enamel Hard, impervious and

weather-resistant finish, *also called porcelain enamel*, applied to steel and aluminium sheet, particularly for CURTAIN WALLS. The process consists of fusing a thin coating of glass to the metal base at temperatures above 800 °C (1500 °F) for steel and 550 °C (1000 °F) for aluminium. At these temperatures the metal and the glass combine, producing a product with the surface hardness of glass and the strength of metal. Thicker layers of vitreous enamel, usually white, are used on steel and cast iron for baths, and occasionally washbasins. The thicker layers are necessary for abrasion resistance, but they are more easily chipped by a hard blow because of the brittleness of the enamel.

vitrified pipes or tiles Clay pipes or tiles, which have been baked hard and then glazed to make them impervious to water.

vitrine A glass display case or cabinet, as used in museums.

vitriol *(a) Oil of vitriol*: concentrated sulphuric acid (H_2SO_4). *(b) Blue vitriol*: copper sulphate ($CuSO_4.5H_2O$). *(c) Green vitriol*: ferrous sulphate ($FeSO_4.7H_2O$). *(d) White vitriol*: zinc sulphate ($Zn\ SO_4.7H_2O$).

VLSI *Abbreviation for* Very Large Scale Integration, a CHIP containing a very large number of circuits.

VOC *Abbreviation for* Volatile Organic Compound.

voice recognition Methods for enabling the computer to digitise speech (*see* DIGITAL SOUND) and interpret spoken messages.

voids The spaces between the particles of soil or concrete aggregate, whether occupied by air or water, or both.

voids ratio (v) The ratio of voids to solids in a sample. The *porosity* is $v/(1 + v)$.

volatile *(a)* (of a liquid) Readily evaporating at room temperature. *(b)* (of computing memory) Maintained only by the power supply operating the computer. When the computer is turned off or restarted, data in volatile memory are lost.

volt (V) Unit of electrical potential, or electromotive force *(emf)*, named after the eighteenth-century Italian physicist, A. G. A. A. Volta. It represents the potential difference against which one JOULE of

work is done in the transfer of one COULOMB.

voltage Electromotive force measured in VOLTS.

voltage fluctuation A series of voltage changes or a cyclical variation of the voltage envelope.

voltage imbalance A condition in which the three-phase voltages differ in amplitude or are displaced from their normal 120° phase relationship, or both. Frequently expressed as the ratio of the negative sequence or zero sequence voltage to the positive sequence voltage, in per cent.

voltage regulation The ability of a power conditioner to maintain a stable output voltage when input voltage fluctuates.

voltage regulator A circuit that has a constant output voltage when input voltage fluctuates.

voltage transformer *See* TRANSFORMER.

volt-amps The units of the APPARENT POWER in an alternating current circuit, distinguished from the REAL POWER measured in *watts* and REACTIVE POWER measured in *volt-amps-reactive*.

voltmeter Instrument for measuring the electromotive force (or electric potential) directly, calibrated in volts.

volume (sound) The volume of a sound has several meanings. It is usually used as a non-technical term for LOUDNESS but it can be used for INTENSITY and, more technically, as a measure of the size of the sound.

volute casing A casing around the impeller of a centrifugal compressor, fan or pump that gradually increases in cross-sectional area towards the outlet for the purpose of conversion of velocity pressure to static pressure.

VOM *Abbreviation for* Volt-Ohm-Meter.

vortex A whirl of fluid.

vortex shedding A wind phenomenon in which a tall building, and particularly a tall round chimney, sways from side to side due to the periodic shedding of *vortices*.

voussoir A wedge-shaped stone or brick, used in the construction of an arch. The voussoir at the CROWN is called the *keystone*.

voussoir arch An arch, often circular, built from VOUSSOIRS (*see figure*).

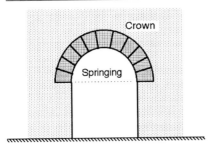

Voussoir arch

VR *Abbreviation for* VIRTUAL REALITY.
VRML *Abbreviation for* Virtual Reality Mark-up Language.
VSD *Abbreviation for* Variable Speed Drive. Used to control the output of some machines such as centrifugal fans and centrifugal pumps.
vulcanisation Treatment of rubber with sulphur to cross-link the elastomer chains.

W

W *(a)* Chemical symbol for *tungsten* (wolframium). *(b)* Symbol for WATT.
waferboard A mat-formed wood structural panel product composed of thin rectangular wood wafers arranged in random layers and bonded with waterproof adhesive. *Also known as flakeboard* or *OSB*.
waffle slab A two-way RIBBED SLAB.
wagon vault *Same as* BARREL VAULT.
wainscot Wood-panelling of the lower part of an interior wall, usually terminating with a DADO.
waiting time The time a passenger waits for a lift (elevator) from the time the call is registered until the lift arrives.
wake The region of turbulent flow downstream from the point of separation, characterised by a reversal of flow.
Waldram diagram A projection method for depicting the sky component of daylighting for a particular reference point. The diagram is a specially scaled grid representing half the hemisphere of sky. The area of visible sky seen through the window from the reference point is plotted onto the grid and this area is proportional to the sky component at the reference point.

walk-up apartment house An apartment house without a lift (elevator), generally four storeys or less.
wall arcade A blind ARCADE used as an ornament to a wall.
wall board BUILDING BOARD suitable for interior walls.
wall column *(a)* A column which is so wide that it might also be considered a short load-bearing wall. *(b)* A column EMBEDDED in the wall.
wall jet The 'jet' induced by a fire when the CEILING JET strikes a wall.
wall paper (or wallpaper) Decorative printed paper usually sold in rolls, for sticking on a plastered wall. The wall requires a sealer, to prevent it from discolouring wall paper.
wall plate A horizontal piece of timber, laid flat along the top of the wall at the level of the ceiling; it carries the RAFTERS.
wall tie *(a)* Tie in a CAVITY WALL (*see figure*). *(b)* Tie that secures the facing material to its backup wall.

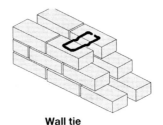

Wall tie

wall tile *See* TILE.
wall, retaining *See* RETAINING WALL.
wall–floor ratio The ratio of wall area to floor area of a particular space. It is one measure of plan efficiency.
wallwasher A ceiling-mounted LUMINAIRE used to light the walls of a room.
WAN *Abbreviation for* WIDE AREA NETWORK.
wane Bark, or the lack of wood, on the corner of a piece of timber.
warble tone A tone where the frequency is continually varying in a regular manner within certain frequency limits.
Ward–Leonard control *See* MOTOR–GENERATOR SET.

warmth In music, a term used to describe the relative level of the bass sound to the mid-frequency sound (see also *bass ratio*).

warp *(a)* Distortion in the shape of a plane timber surface, usually due to MOISTURE MOVEMENT. *(b)* Yarn that is stretched lengthwise in the loom, and runs along the *length* of the fabric or carpet, passing alternately under and over the WEFT.

warping Distortion from a plane surface, particularly in timber; it may be caused by careless seasoning.

Warren truss A STATICALLY DETERMINATE truss consisting of top and bottom chords connected only by diagonals without vertical members (*see figure*), as distinct from a HOWE and a PRATT TRUSS. Some of the diagonals are in tension and some are in compression.

Warren truss

washer *(a)* A ring placed under a nut or a bolt head. *See also* SPRING WASHER *and* TAPERED WASHER. *(b)* A disc or annulus of compressible material, used to seal the valve seat in a water tap.

washing soda Sodium carbonate (Na_2CO_3).

waste heat Heat in a fluid that will be lost to atmosphere unless recovered by an exchange process.

waste pipe The pipe that discharges liquid waste into the SOIL DRAIN.

waste water treatment Treatment of sewage (and some industrial waste water) to allow it to be either returned to the natural drainage system, or re-used. Primary treatment involves screening, grit removal, sedimentation, grease flotation and sludge disposal. Secondary treatment involves also a biological process to remove organic matter. Tertiary treatment involves also filtration and/or disinfection.

water balance The condition achieved in a HYDRONIC system when the maximum quantity of fluid that can be delivered to each point of use is just sufficient to meet its heat transfer requirement at full load.

water blasting Cleaning of a surface by impinging with water at very high pressure (approximately 20–50 MPa). May be used in conjunction with dilute hydrochloric acid for cleaning of mortar stains from brickwork.

water closet (WC) A plumbing fixture used to receive human excrement, and to discharge it through a waste pipe, using water for conveyance. Hence a room containing a water closet.

water gauge A U-tube MANOMETER, filled with water.

water gun A device to discharge water automatically to a fire.

water hammer A sudden, very high pressure in a pipe, often indicated by a loud noise, caused by stopping the flow of water too rapidly.

water heater, instantaneous *See* INSTANTANEOUS WATER HEATER.

water heater, storage A device in which water is heated and stored for later use. A storage heater can therefore cope with a sudden large demand, better than an *instantaneous* heater. *See also* OFF-PEAK WATER HEATER, THERMOSIPHON, *and* SOLAR WATER HEATER.

water level A simple instrument for setting out levels on a building site. It consists of a transparent tube filled with water, with the two ends held up. The level of the water in both is the same, if there are no air locks in the tube. *See also* SPIRIT LEVEL.

water mist A water spray producing very fine water droplets through a *water mist nozzle* for the purpose of suppressing or extinguishing a fire. It may be useful for oil or fat fires, particularly when the presence of personnel restricts the use of more hazardous extinguishants.

water of capillarity Water held in CAPILLARY ACTION in the soil *above* the water table.

water paint Any paint that can be thinned with water. The term includes oil-bound or emulsion paints, whose binder is insoluble in water, but which can be thinned with water.

water seal The seal in the TRAP of a drain, which prevents odours from the sewer from entering the building.

water softener A material that removes

the calcium and magnesium salts from HARD WATER, usually by an ion exchange. *See* SCALE *and* ZEOLITE.

water stain *(a)* Water-soluble dye used for staining timber. *See also* OIL STAIN *and* SPIRIT STAIN. *(b)* Discoloration on converted timber, caused by water.

water supply riser *See* RISER *(c)*.

water table The level below which the ground is saturated with water.

water treatment A process that uses chemicals to alter an undesirable condition of water in a circulating system. May be used to prevent corrosion and deposit of insoluble substances on surfaces or to kill dangerous biological organisms.

water, combined *See* COMBINED WATER.

water–cement ratio The ratio of the amount of water, excluding that absorbed by the concrete aggregate, to the amount of cement in concrete or mortar. It has a determining influence on the strength of concrete and mortar. *See* ABRAMS' LAW *and* MIX PROPORTIONS.

water-cooled chiller A water CHILLER that rejects its waste heat to atmosphere by way of a COOLING TOWER.

water-cooled condenser A *heat sink* for a refrigeration system, in which coils containing the hot refrigerant gas are cooled by spraying with water in an air stream. The evaporation of some of the water adds to the cooling effect of the air.

water-glass A concentrated solution of *sodium* or *potassium silicate*. It is used for waterproofing brick, stone and concrete, and as a surface hardener for concrete floors.

waterproofing *See* SURFACE *and* INTE-GRAL WATERPROOFING.

watt (W) The derived SI UNIT of power. One watt is dissipated by doing 1 joule of work per second, that is 1 W = 1 J/s. In electricity, 1 W = 1 VA. Named after J. Watt, the eighteenth-century inventor of the steam engine.

watt hour (Wh) A unit of electrical energy. It is the energy delivered by 1 watt in 1 hour. It is customary to use kilowatt hours; 1 kWh = 1000 Wh = 3.6×10^6 JOULE = 3.6 MJ.

wattle-and-daub Infilling for the walls of HALF-TIMBERED houses, traditional in some parts of Europe, and widely used in the early colonial period in Australia. It consists of branches or thin laths *(wattles)* plastered with clay *(daub)*.

wavelength The distance between successive maxima or minima in a periodic function (*i.e.* a regular wave).

waves (acoustics) Sound is transmitted by *longitudinal waves* or compression waves in fluids and gases but can be transmitted by a variety of waves in solids such as surface waves, shear waves, flexural and lateral waves. These waves have differing velocities of propagation and attenuation rates. Methods of attenuating one wave type will not necessarily affect the propagation of another wave type.

wax stain A semi-transparent pigment dispersed in BEESWAX, thinned with turpentine.

wayfinding The study of the needs of people to find their way, particularly in unfamiliar surroundings. Wayfinding is facilitated by signage, and also by the planning, lighting and detailing of a building.

WBGT *Abbreviation for* WET-BULB GLOBE THERMOMETER INDEX.

WBT *Abbreviation for* WET-BULB TEMPERATURE.

WC *Abbreviation for* WATER CLOSET.

WCI *Abbreviation for* Wind Chill Index, used in cold climates to indicate the cooling effect of wind

$$WCI = (12.15 + 11.6\sqrt{v} - v) \times (33 - DBT)$$

WCT *Abbreviation for* Wind Chill Temperature, the temperature equivalent of DBT and the wind chill. WCT = 33 − 0.03738 × WCI. *e.g.* if DBT = −10°C and v = 16 m/s then WCI = (12.15 + 11.6 × 4−16) × (33 + 10) = 1829.65. and WCT = 33 − 0.03738 × 1829.65 = −35.4°C.

wear tests *See* ABRASION.

weatherboard A long, thin board graduating in thickness from one edge to the other, used for WOOD SIDING. The thick edge is usually rebated to overlap the thin portion of the next board. Called *clapboard* in the USA.

weatherometer A machine for determining the weather-resisting properties of materials (such as paints and plastics) by cycles imitating as closely as possible natural weathering conditions. Most machines employ ultraviolet light, high or low temperatures and moisture. The result is not as accurate as placing the samples on an exposed site for natural weathering; however, since the cycles are speeded up, the result is obtained very much more quickly. Like ABRASION testing machines, weatherometers are useful for comparing a new material with a similar material of known performance. Their reliability for predicting the performance of a completely new type of material is questionable.

weather-struck joint or weather joint A STRUCK JOINT for exterior work.

web *(a)* The vertical part of a joist. *(b)* The plate connecting the flanges of a PLATE GIRDER. *(c)* The RIB of a concrete T-beam *(d) See* WORLD WIDE WEB.

web browser *See* BROWSER.

web master Someone who builds, manages or administers a WEB SITE.

web page A document created with HTML (Hypertext Markup Language) that is part of a group of HYPERTEXT documents or resources available on the World Wide Web. Collectively, a set of documents and resources form a WEB SITE.

web server A program that serves up web pages upon request. Every computer on the INTERNET that contains a web site must have a WEB SERVER program.

web site A collection of network services, primarily HTML documents, that are linked together and that exist on the Web at a particular SERVER. Exploring a web site usually begins with the HOME PAGE, which may lead to more information about that site. A single server may support multiple web sites.

web stiffener *See* STIFFENER.

Weber's law A person's response to a change in an environmental stimulus, such as sound, is proportional to the magnitude of the original stimulus. This can be expressed as $\Delta S/S$ = constant, which is Weber's law. The law can also be expressed in a logarithmic form. The change in the perceived loudness of a sound, for instance, can be expressed in terms of the $10 \log_{10}$ (ratio of the new to the original intensities) in dB.

wedge theory A theory for the stability of a retaining wall, based on the weight of the wedge of soil which would slide forward if the wall failed. It was originally proposed by C. A. Coulomb in 1776 and revised by C. F. Jenkin in 1931.

weephole A small hole left at the base of a retaining wall, cavity wall, window or curtain wall to allow accumulated condensation or other moisture to escape.

weft Yarn that runs across the *width* of a woven fabric, from edge to edge. It is made to pass over and under the WARP.

weigh batcher A batching plant for concrete in which all materials (except the water) are weighed.

weight The force resulting from the action of gravity upon a mass. In SI UNITS, weight is measured in newtons; in CGS and FPS UNITS, and in common language, weight and MASS are used interchangeably.

weighted sound reduction index *See* SOUND TRANSMISSION CLASS.

weighting curve A prescribed frequency response for use in a system of measurement. The A-weighting curve, which approximately corresponds to the frequency response of the human ear is commonly used as a measure of sound. *See also* C-WEIGHTING.

weighting statistical data Multiplying the data by a factor, or weight, if the data are of unequal reliability, and if the difference between their trustworthiness and importance can be properly assessed.

welded beam A large steel I-section, fabricated by welding from plates instead of *hot rolling*. Essentially the same as *plate girder*.

welding Uniting two pieces of metal by raising the temperature of the metal surfaces to a plastic or molten condition, with or without the addition of extra welding metal, and with or without the application of pressure. SOLDERING and BRAZING are carried out at a lower temperature. *See* ARC WELDING, SHIELDED-ARC WELDING, ACETYLENE, FUSION WELDING *and* RESISTANCE WELDING.

well *See* LIFT WELL.

wellpoint dewatering Draining a volume of soil to be excavated by sinking wellpoints around it, and pumping the water from them. Wellpoints are usually tubes, approximately 50 mm (2 in.) diameter, which are jetted into the soil. The method is particularly suitable for soils that do not contain too much fine material, when it may be much cheaper than SHEET PILING. WPD can be assisted by ELECTRO-OSMOSIS.

Welsbach mantle An INCANDESCENT mantle composed of cotton impregnated with thorium and cerium oxide, invented by Welsbach in 1885 to improve the performance of *gaslight*.

wet construction Conventional construction, which relies for jointing on wet concrete, mortar or plaster, as opposed to DRY CONSTRUCTION.

wet mix A concrete mix containing too much water. To the untrained observer it may look like a better concrete than a correctly proportioned mix, and it is also easier to place and to finish; however, its strength is lower, and it may produce LAITANCE. *See* ABRAMS' LAW.

wet rot A fungus disease in timber caused by excessive and continuous dampness. It results in decomposition of the fibres of the timber.

wet-and-dry bulb thermometer A PSYCHROMETER, consisting of an ordinary thermometer *(dry-bulb thermometer)*, which records air temperature (DRY-BULB TEMPERATURE) in the ordinary way; and another thermometer (WET-BULB THERMOMETER) whose bulb is wrapped in a damp wick dipping into water. The *wet-bulb temperature* is lower because of the cooling effect of the wick due to evaporation. Tables are provided that give the RELATIVE HUMIDITY in terms of the wet-bulb and the dry-bulb temperature. *See also* ASSMAN PSYCHROMETER *and* WHIRLING PSYCHROMETER.

wet-bulb depression The difference between the DRY-BULB and the WET-BULB TEMPERATURES.

wet-bulb globe thermometer index (WBGT) Criterion for determining the COMFORT ZONE evolved by Yaglou and Minard in 1957 for the control of heat casualties at military training centres in the USA. It takes into account the temperature and humidity of the air, and radiation from the sun and the terrain, and it makes some allowance for wind speed. *See* GLOBE THERMOMETER.

wet-bulb temperature (WBT) The temperature recorded by a WET-BULB THERMOMETER. It is lower than the DRY-BULB TEMPERATURE; the difference increases as the RELATIVE HUMIDITY decreases. The relative humidity is determined from a table or from the PSYCHROMETRIC CHART.

wet-bulb thermometer A thermometer whose bulb is wrapped in a damp wick dipping into water.

wetland Low-lying and swampy area of land that is subject to occasional flooding. In combination with water-dwelling plants, wetlands may be useful for improving the condition of drainage water.

wetting agent A substance that lowers the surface tension of liquids, and thus facilitates the wetting of solid surfaces and the penetration of liquids into capillaries.

WF *Abbreviation for* WIDE-FLANGE SECTION.

WG *Abbreviation for* Wire Gauge.

Wheatstone bridge An apparatus for measuring electrical resistance by the zero method, comprising two parallel resistance branches, each branch consisting of two resistances in series. It is employed in conjunction with THERMISTORS and ELECTRIC RESISTANCE STRAIN GAUGES *(see figure)*.

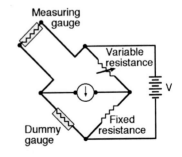

Wheatstone bridge

whip A small hoist or crane.

whirling psychrometer A psychrometer

in which the WET-AND-DRY-BULB THER-
MOMETERS are mounted on a handle, so
that they can be rotated in the air to give
an approximately standardised rate of
ventilation.

whispering gallery A room with curved
surfaces that allows faint sounds, made at
one part of the room, to be heard clearly
at another part without the sound being
audible throughout the room.

white ant *See* TERMITE.

white cast iron CAST IRON in which all the
carbon is in the form of IRON CARBIDE, as
distinct from *grey cast iron*.

white cement A pure white PORTLAND
CEMENT. Since the grey colour of Portland
cement comes from impurities, a white
cement requires raw materials of low
iron content, or firing of the clinker by a
reducing flame. The resulting material
is much more expensive than ordinary
(grey) Portland cement. It is used for
decorative surface finishes, and as the
basis for the lighter COLOURED CEMENTS.
See also OFF-WHITE CEMENT.

white gold Gold alloyed with palladium,
nickel or zinc.

white lead An opaque white pigment,
used extensively as an undercoat for
exterior paint, and for pottery glazes.
Because it is poisonous (*see* LITHOPONE
and TITANIUM WHITE) it is now rarely used
for finishing coats. It consists of basic lead
carbonate ($2PbCO_3 . Pb(OH)_2$).

white metal A general term covering
alloys based on antimony, lead or tin, used
to reduce friction.

white noise Broadband noise, which
randomly varies in phase and intensity
at each frequency and which has equal
energy per *proportional* bandwidth. *See
also* PINK NOISE.

white spirit A THINNER for oil paint,
distilled from petroleum at 150–200°C.
It is frequently used as a substitute for
TURPENTINE.

whitewash A cheap finish for external
walls formed by soaking QUICKLIME in
an excess of water. A binder, such as
casein, is sometimes added. *Also called
limewash.*

whiting Crushed chalk ($CaCO_3$), probably
the cheapest white pigment. *Also called*

Paris white. It is used in distemper, putty
and as an extender for other pigments.

WI *Abbreviation for* WROUGHT IRON.

wide area network (WAN) A NETWORK
that connects computers spread over a
large geographic area. Contrast with
LOCAL AREA NETWORK (LAN).

wide-flange section A structural section
whose cross-section resembles the letter
H rather than the letter I. It is particularly
used for columns, because it has a
relatively high RADIUS OF GYRATION, both
parallel and perpendicular to its web.
Abbreviated WF section.

widespread (faucet) Bathroom tap
(lavatory faucet) in which separate hot
and cold handles and valves are installed
into fixture holes set wider apart than
normal.

Wien's law The law relating the wavelength of the peak intensity of radiation
from a hot body, to the temperature of the
body:

$$\lambda_{max} = \frac{2.88 \times 10^{-3}}{T} \text{ metre}$$

where λ_{max} is the wavelength and T is the
absolute temperature of the body in
Kelvin.

Williot–Mohr diagram A graphical
method for determining the deflection of
pinjointed trusses.

wind baffle A sheet of material positioned
to divert wind into or away from an
opening in a building envelope.

wind bracing Structural members,
usually diagonal, specially designed to
resist the wind forces.

wind chill index A measure of the
apparent reduction of air temperature due
to its contact velocity with skin.

wind deflector *See* WIND BAFFLE.

wind driven ventilation Ventilation by air
flows that are driven through openings in
the building envelope by wind forces.

wind load The (positive or negative) force
of the wind acting on a building (*see
figure*). *See* WIND PRESSURE DISTRIBUTION.
From fluid mechanics and the density of
the air, the horizontal wind pressure (in
Pa) is approximately

$$p = 0.6v^2$$

where v is the wind velocity in m/s. The wind velocity increases with height, and it can be obtained from the empirical formula

$$\frac{v_1}{v_2} = \left(\frac{h_1}{h_2}\right)^{1/7}$$

See also DAMPING OF STRUCTURAL VIBRATIONS.

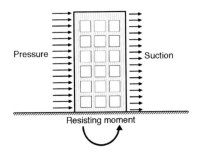

Wind load

wind power plant An array of interconnected wind turbines that generate electricity for delivery to a utility transmission–distribution system.

wind pressure distribution The wind blowing against a building exerts positive pressure on a windward vertical face and negative pressure, or *suction*, on a leeward vertical face. A flat roof is invariably subject to suction, irrespective of the direction of the wind. A sloping roof also is always subject to suction if the wind blows parallel to the ridge. If it blows perpendicular to the ridge, then the windward side is subject to positive wind pressure only if the slope of the roof is more than 30°. There are also local increases in suction around some leading edges (*see figure*). *See also* WIND LOAD.

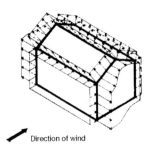

Direction of wind

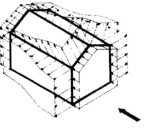

Direction of wind

Wind pressure distribution

wind rose A graphical method of depicting the frequency of monthly prevailing wind direction for a particular location.

wind scoop Ventilation device with large intake openings used to provide a controlled air supply by capturing wind above roof level and channelling air movement into the space.

wind shadow Low pressure area on the leeward side of an object.

wind tunnel An apparatus for AERODYNAMIC investigations on MODELS to study ventilation inside a building; the wind pressure acting on a building; the vibrations produced by wind in a tall, flexible structure; the eddies in circular courtyards, etc. *See also* ANEMOMETER, BOUNDARY LAYER WIND TUNNEL *and* SMOKE TUNNEL.

wind turbine (WT) A device to convert wind energy into mechanical work (rotation); it may have a low solidity (propeller) or high solidity (fan) rotor, and may be either of horizontal axis (HAWT) or vertical axis (VAWT) type.

window *(a) See* CASEMENT WINDOW, SASH WINDOW, DEAD LIGHT, SKYLIGHT *and* LANTERN. *(b)* In computing, an area of a screen defined so as to allow an application to be processed independently of other applications.

window glass *See* SHEET GLASS.

window shutters *See* SHUTTERS.

window wall An outside wall consisting largely of glass.

window weights Balance weights used in SASH WINDOWS.

windowing In computing, creating WINDOWS *(b)*.

windward On the side exposed to the wind; the opposite of *leeward.*

wing Part of a building projecting from one side of the main body.

wing nut A nut with two projections, to enable it to be tightened by the thumb and one other finger. *Also called* a *thumb nut.*

wire rope *See* SUSPENSION CABLE *and* TENDON.

wirecut brick Bricks shaped by extrusion and then cut to length by a set of wires. They are less dense than PRESSED BRICKS, and they have no FROG.

wired glass Safety glass containing thin wire reinforcement.

wireframe In computer graphics, a three-dimensional display consisting of lines, as opposed to SURFACE MODELS and SOLID MODELS.

wireless networking NETWORKS whose connections are implemented through radio frequency or infrared frequency communications.

withdrawal load The resistance of a nail to being pulled out after driving.

withe *Same as* WYTHE.

wood alcohol *Same as* METHANOL.

wood preservative A substance that inhibits decay, infection, or attack by fungi, insects or marine borers in timber.

wood siding Wall cladding for frame building consisting of wooden boards. *Called weatherboard* in the UK and Australia, and *clapboard* in the USA.

wood veneer Thin layer of wood of uniform thickness, used as a facing. The object may be to strengthen the wood by varying the direction of the grain (as in PLYWOOD) or to attach a decorative surface to a less attractive timber. Decorative veneers are made as thin as possible. They may be *sliced*, *i.e.* cut transversely, or *rotary*, *i.e.* cut on a lathe. *See also* MATCHED VENEER.

wooden lath *See* LATH.

woofer Loudspeaker for reproducing low frequency sound (< 500–1000 Hz). A *sub-woofer* is used for reproducing frequencies below 125 Hz.

wool *See* MINERAL WOOL. *See also* CARPET.

word processing program APPLICATIONS SOFTWARE designed for the preparation and editing of textual documents.

work The product of an applied force and the distance moved by that force. The SI unit for work is the JOULE (J). *See also* ENERGY.

work hardening Increasing the strength of metal by COLD WORKING. It is the normal method for producing cables for suspension structures and tendons for prestressed concrete by drawing high-carbon steel wires through a die.

workability of concrete The ability of freshly mixed concrete or mortar to flow, and fill the formwork without voids. *Also called consistency.* It is commonly measured by the SLUMP TEST, the BALL TEST or the COMPACTING FACTOR TEST.

working drawings Drawings containing the information needed for construction. *See also* SHOP DRAWINGS.

working load The normal dead, live, wind and earthquake load that a structure is required to support in service. It is generally specified in building codes, *also called service load.* In *limit design* the working load is multiplied by a load factor to give the ultimate load at which the building is designed to fail.

working load design Design based on the working loads. The stresses in the structure under these loads may not exceed the MAXIMUM PERMISSIBLE STRESSES.

working plane The real or imaginary surface at which work is normally done, and at which, consequently, the illumination is specified and measured. This plane is normally horizontal, and 850 mm or 2 ft 9 in. above the floor.

working stress The MAXIMUM PERMISSIBLE STRESS under the action of the working loads, specified in the building code.

working stress design *See* WORKING LOAD DESIGN.

workplace *(a)* The place of employment. *(b)* The location of a specific task.

workplane *Same as* WORKING PLANE.

workspace A work area occupied by one or more employees, exclusive of support spaces.

workstation *(a)* Usually a desk or more complex furniture arrangement, complete with computers and communications facilities and, sometimes, local lighting and other services. *(b)* A desktop computer, usually connected to a network.

World Wide Web (WWW) A virtual network operating over the *Internet* allowing multimedia interaction.

wow Speed variations of up to a few cycles per second in sound reproduction systems that produce a cyclic pitch variation in sounds

WP *Abbreviation for* Word Processor or Word Processing.

wrap of suspension rope *(a) Single*: a roping arrangement where the suspension ropes joining the lift car and counterweight pass over the drive SHEAVE once. *(b) Double*: a roping arrangement where, in order to increase the traction, the suspension ropes joining the lift car and counterweight pass over the drive SHEAVE twice.

wrecking Demolition of a building or other structure.

wrecking ball *Same as* BALL BREAKER.

write-protection The protection of data so that they cannot be overwritten. Usually refers to the physical protection of a disk or cassette. Software protection of data is achieved by designating the file or device as *read-only*, but the effect is the same.

writing, memory Storing information in computer MEMORY. The write operation is destructive, meaning that it destroys the information currently stored at the memory location. *See also* READING MEMORY.

written-down value The value of an asset after depreciation.

wrot timber *Same as* DRESSED TIMBER.

wrought iron Iron with less than 0.1 per cent of carbon. It is one of the two traditional forms of iron, the other being CAST IRON. Steel is intermediate between the two, but prior to the invention of the BESSEMER PROCESS it could only be produced at great expense. Wrought iron is soft, easily worked and rusts less than steel.

wrought timber *Same as* DRESSED TIMBER.

WWW *Abbreviation for* WORLD WIDE WEB.

wye connection *Same as* STAR CONNECTION, especially in the USA.

WYSIWYG Literally, What You See Is What You Get. The style of interface for a word processor that attempts to display the text document in a format that closely resembles how it will look when printed or displayed on a screen.

wythe *(a)* One leaf of a cavity wall. *(b)* A half-brick wall. *Also spelled withe.*

xenon lamp An ELECTRIC DISCHARGE LAMP employing a short length arc in xenon gas, and replacing the CARBON ARC LAMP in cine projectors and similar applications.

xeriscape Derived from the combination of a Greek word 'Xeros' meaning dry and 'scape' from the word 'landscape,' xeriscape refers to landscape that uses water efficiently and matches appropriate design to the site, soil, topography and intended use. The term is often inaccurately used to describe rock and cactus gardens.

X-rays Electromagnetic RADIATION of very short wavelength, *also called Röntgen rays* after W. J. K. von Röntgen, the German physicist who discovered them in 1895. They have the capacity to penetrate materials opaque to light, and are employed in *radiography* to produce photographic pictures of certain invisible features. Apart from the important medical applications, they can be used for non-destructive testing, *e.g.* to show up defects in WELDING. GAMMA RAYS are similar rays produced by radioactive materials.

xyz space Three-dimensional space defined orthographically by *x*-, *y*- and *z*-axes.

yard A traditional measure of length, equal to 3 ft = 0.9144 m.

Y-connection *Same as* STAR CONNECTION, especially in the USA. *Usually spelled wye.*

yield stress The lowest stress at which STRAIN increases without increase in

STRESS. It shows up as a horizontal line on a STRESS–STRAIN DIAGRAM. Only a few materials (including structural steel) exhibit a marked yield point which delineates the boundary between the elastic and plastic state. For other materials the transition from elastic to plastic behaviour is gradual, and a PROOF STRESS is defined as an artificial boundary. *Also called yield point.*

yield-line theory A theory for the ULTIMATE STRENGTH of reinforced concrete slabs, proposed by the Danish engineer K. W. Johansen in 1943. It is based on the observation that concrete slabs fail following the formation of a number of *large* cracks, just sufficient to turn the statically indeterminate slab into a MECHANISM. Their failing loads can therefore be derived from considerations of LIMIT DESIGN.

YMCK *Abbreviation for* Yellow, Magenta, Cyan, blacK. *See* CMYK.

Young's modulus *Same as* MODULUS OF ELASTICITY.

Z

Z Symbol for the SECTION MODULUS in the UK and Australia. (The symbol S is used in the USA).

zenith The highest point in the sky, immediately overhead at the time of an observation. Its altitude is 90°.

zenith angle The angular distance of a point of the sky (*e.g.* of the sun) from the vertical, from the zenith; it is the supplementary angle of the ALTITUDE angle.

zeolites Alumino-silicates of light metals used in WATER SOFTENERS.

zero energy band The part of the control cycle of some air conditioning systems when neither supplementary heating nor cooling is provided because the indoor temperature falls within a range or band considered acceptable. An energy conservation measure. *Also called dead band.*

zero energy band control Control of the operation of refrigeration and heating plant so that neither operates when the controlled room temperature is within an acceptable band; also known as *dead band control.*

zinc A white metallic element, which is highly resistant to atmospheric corrosion, and is consequently used to protect steel by GALVANISING or SHERARDISING. It is one of the constituents of BRASS. Its chemical symbol is Zn, its atomic number is 30, its valency is 2, its atomic weight is 65.38, its specific gravity is 7.14, and its melting point is 419 °C.

zinc coating *See* GALVANISING.

zinc plating Applying a protective layer of zinc to steel items by electroplating. The zinc layer is thinner (and therefore less effective) than GALVANISING, but the finish is smoother, and it does not interfere with the fit of nuts and bolts as galvanising does.

zinc white Zinc oxide (ZnO), a permanent, non-poisonous white pigment. *Also called Chinese white.*

zinc-rich primer PRIMER consisting of paint rich in colloidal zinc, which provides GALVANIC PROTECTION against corrosion of steel.

Zincalume Trade name for a protective treatment on steel sheet, similar to GALVANISING, but using an alloy of zinc and aluminium instead of zinc alone.

Zn Chemical symbol for *zinc.*

zonal flux The luminous flux emitted through zones of either constant solid angles (Russell angles) or plane angles, used in the calculation of UTILISATION FACTORS for the LUMEN METHOD.

zone *(a)* A number of floors, usually adjacent, in a building served by a GROUP, or groups, of LIFTS. *(b)* A defined separate part of an air conditioned space that is subject to heat gains or losses of different magnitude from those occurring at the same time in other parts of the space, not necessarily defined by physical boundaries. It is usual to arrange the control system to control conditions separately in each zone. *See also* ZONING.

zone of protection In a LIGHTNING PROTECTION SYSTEM, the space considered to be protected from a lightning strike.

zoning The allocation of land use by a statutory authority for planning purposes.

zoom In computer graphics, a facility for increasing or decreasing the size of an image without redefining the parameters of the elements. Carried out by either specifying the zoom factor or by defining the area to occupy the screen.

Z-section A metal section shaped like the letter z.

Z-tie A Z-shaped WALL TIE.

Lightning Source UK Ltd.
Milton Keynes UK
UKOW04f0618110614

233210UK00005B/61/P